# Costume History and Style

Douglas A. Russell
*Stanford University*

D0169188

Prentice-Hall, Inc. Englewood Cliffs, New Jersey 07632

*Library of Congress Cataloging in Publication Data*

RUSSELL, DOUGLAS A.
  Costume history and style.

  Bibliography:  p. 514
  Includes index.
  1. Costume—History.  I. Title
GT511.R87    1983    391'.009    82-9822
ISBN  O-13-181214-9            AACR2

Cover photo: *Empress Eugénie and Her Ladies in Waiting* by Franz Winterhalter.
Used with permission of the French Musées Nationaux.

*Editorial/production supervision
and interior design:
Barbara Kelly Kittle*
*Cover Design: Diane Saxe*

*Page layout: Gail Cocker*
*Art paste up:*
*Charles Pelletreau and Gail Collis*
*Manufacturing Buyer:*
*Ron Chapman*

© 1983 by Prentice-Hall, Inc., Englewood Cliffs, N.J. 07632

Printed in the United States of America

10  9  8  7  6  5  4  3  2  1

ISBN 0-13-181214-9

Prentice-Hall International, Inc., *London*
Prentice-Hall of Australia Pty. Limited, *Sydney*
Editoria Prentice-Hall do Brazil, Ltda, *Rio de Janeiro*
Prentice-Hall Canada Inc., *Toronto*
Prentice-Hall of India Private Limited, *New Delhi*
Prentice-Hall of Japan, Inc., *Tokyo*
Prentice-Hall of Southeast Asia Pte. Ltd., *Singapore*
Whitehall Books Limited, Wellington, *New Zealand*

# Contents

# 4

## Ancient Greece  44

# 5

## Ancient Rome  66

# 6

## Early Christian and Byzantine  88

# 7

## Barbaric, Carolingian, and Romanesque  104

# 8

## Early and High Gothic  124

# 9

## Middle Gothic 139

# 10

## Late Gothic and Early Italian Renaissance 157

# 11

## High Renaissance 176

# 12

## Early Mannerist Renaissance 196

# 13

## Elizabethan-Jacobean (Late Mannerist Renaissance) 213

# 14

## Early Baroque (Cavalier) 232

# 15

## Late Baroque (Restoration) 250

# 16

## Rococo 270

# 17

## Neoclassicism and Revolution 290

# 18

## Directoire and Empire 308

# 19

## Romantic 327

# 20

## Victorian and Second Empire 346

# 21

## Later Victorian: The Gilded Age 365

# 22

## Late Victorian and Edwardian: Art Nouveau 384

# 23

## World War I and the Twenties: Early Art Deco 404

# 24

## The Thirties and World War II: Late Art Deco 423

# 25

## The Cold War 443

# 26

## Contemporary 462

# Preface

When I wrote my first text, *Stage Costume Design,* in 1973, with Prentice-Hall, I included in the last section an "Outline History of Western Costume" with a page of information on each period, accompanied by two typical figures, some recommended sources, and a list of frequently used costume terms for each period. Over the years I have been told by students and colleagues that this format has been very useful to them as a quick review of basic costume history information; and thus, several years ago I decided to expand this format with a combination of prints, photographs, and personal illustrations as visual support. When I presented the idea to the editors at Prentice-Hall, they were interested but said that if a new text on costume history were to be published by the company, it should include not only the basics or essentials but also a fuller treatment in discussion and illustration for each of the twenty-six period chapters that I had outlined. They felt that many teachers *did* need a new costume text but wanted both the essentials and a more in-depth treatment side-by-side in the same single source book. I agreed, therefore, to double the size of the book to include more visual information and to strengthen the background ma-

terial as well as to include a fuller treatment of clothing styles in each of the twenty-six periods. The present textbook has been the result.

Let me now explain the format of the book and why I feel that in its arrangement it is stronger as a text than the other standard works in the field. First of all, it is conceived as a text—a book to be used by students in a course on costume history—not as a source for designers or a coffee-table volume on the story of costume and fashion. Second, believing as I do that students need a running series of chronological figures to go with dates and events, each chapter opens with such a chronology, accompanied by figures based on famous paintings or drawings. Third, since I believe that students need to know something of the visual setting against which each set of fashions would appear, I have included an exterior or interior photograph at the beginning of each chapter that is intended to sum up the essence of architecture, interior decoration, or furnishings for that period. Fourth, as background for each chapter, I have attempted to give essential information about the outlook, cultural values, artistic ideals, and political events of the period that affected directly or indirectly the nature of the fashions of the time. Fifth, I have attempted to retain a discussion of the essentials of the fashions for each period and the reasons for their development in a section following the background, entitled "The Basic Costume Silhouette." It is this section that I feel gives the essential picture of the clothing of the times. It is illustrated by two or three photographs of paintings, fashion designs, or other sources that are intended to capture the essence of the period line of the time, and these photos are surrounded with many line drawings that give details of hats, coats, shoes, wraps, underwear, and other items and fashion variations that might not be suggested by the photos. Again, these are the visual sources for review rather than the full range of illustrations. Sixth, I have included material that fills about one-half of each chapter on the complexities and changes in costume for each period, with an attempt to look at male and female dress separately in the wide range of their development from the beginning to the end of each time frame. This is supported by six to eight more photographs of fashion taken from painting, sculpture, or fashion illustration. A brief mention of military dress is included with reference to a single line drawing as illustration.

Finally, the end of each chapter has information on the fabrics used in each period; the art and artifacts that were used, from the interior decoration and furnishings to the individual costume properties and decorative personal accessories; the best sources for visual information including individual artists, various books and magazines, and the famous institutions that house the art or the costumes from which information can be gained; and a summary of the key points made in the chapter. Again, line drawings (grouped with the essential photos for each period) are included to illustrate items of furniture, interior detail, important per-

sonal accessories, and jewelry. A full glossary of terms is included at the end of the text.

The concept for this book and the need for its publication have developed over a period of thirty years in which time I have taught costume history at least thirty times. Thus the ideas have developed through a trial-and-error process, as well as my working with many different teachers and a variety of classes in many varied institutions. Therefore, I would like to thank all of my students over the years as well as my teachers, Frank Bevan and Virginia Opsvig. From Frank Bevan, in particular, I learned much about the essential line of each period in costume as well as a healthy respect for style and its relation to the larger cultural patterns to which it relates. I would also like to thank Hubert Heffner, head of the Stanford Drama Department when I obtained my M.A. in Drama, who suggested that one day I would have to write just such a book as this; and Norman Philbrick, whose friendship, advice, and encouragement have meant a great deal to me during the writing of my various books. His extensive personal library has also been indispensable on many occasions. I would also like to pay my respects to the American Conservatory Theatre, under its leaders Allen Fletcher and Bill Ball, where I have taught courses for actors in costume history, period style, interior decoration, and furnishings over the past half decade. It was in teaching these actors about fashion and costume that I deepened my sense of what was essential for students of dress to know about each period. Finally, above all I wish to thank my wife Marilyn for her patience, helpful advice, and essential editorial assistance in this book as well as in my other publications over the years, and Ruth Lewis, my typist and friend, for her exacting work and great patience.

# Introduction

Before embarking on a survey of fashion in the western world from primitive man to the present, a few definitions and explanations are in order. First, one must give some rationale for excluding African and oriental dress from such a survey. Probably the standard argument is that, until very recently, information on the development of western dress was more important to students and teachers than Asian and African dress, because the major plays and stories to be costumed in Europe and the Americas were from this western tradition. As with other histories that concentrate on the development of the western world, choices must be made; and since nonwestern dress in the past only occasionally has made major contributions to cultural development in Europe and America, it usually is easier to write the history of clothing in the nonwestern world as a separate story. One minor point is that western dress has followed the dynamics of western civilization in its devotion to experiment and change, and so takes as much space to explain as a book that covers all oriental, African, and Oceanic dress. All nonwestern dress has retained a much more conservative and traditional line and cut down through the ages than has been the case in the west.

A second point that is often little mentioned in costume history surveys is the classification of western dress according to the cut and line of the garments. Primitive man used a basically wraparound or laced-to-the-body approach to clothing with some hanging effects from the shoulder. When weaving and sewing arrived, a kind of semifitted effect was achieved, and with supple weaves and the use of brooches and pins, a draped effect was developed. Finally, a sophisticated ability to improve on nature came with the development of the artificial silhouette, in which man improved on nature with padding, cinching the waist, and stiffening the fabric. Thus, all western garments tend to fall into these categories:

1. Draped costumes like those of the Greeks;
2. Slip-on garments like the Roman *paenula* and other poncholike garments;
3. Sewn, semi-fitted garments like the many T-shaped tunics, coats and gowns that have been used throughout the history of dress;
4. The sheath costume that is close-fitted to the body like tight trousers, the *cotehardie* and other body hugging garments; and finally,
5. The artificial garments in which the body is rebuilt by padding, stiffening, and corsetting to improve upon nature.

Basically, all garments in the history of Man fall under these classifications or an intermingling of them.

Another important point that should be mentioned here is the way in which dress is used by Man. It obviously works on two levels, one very practical in which it gives warmth and protection, the other, far more varied, in which it is a form of expression and communication. In the area of protection, items of clothing are also a kind of extension of the human body. For example, boots with spurs convert the feet into an improved means of transportation, just as glasses are both an extension of the body as well as a means of facilitating interaction with one's surroundings. In the area of communication, clothing acts as a means of identification, often giving such information as: position in society, personal feelings about conformity and rebellion against the social norm, positions within a religion or an army through vestments and uniforms, occupations and craft skills (more in the past than at present), and even identification with transitory states like festive or ceremonial occasions. On a more personal level, clothing also gives information and communicates the wearer's mood, as well as becoming codified to reflect cultural moods such as the use of black for mourning. Dress also demonstrates and communicates the knowledge that people have developed about the world in which they live— awareness of cultural standards, alertness to dress codes for certain social situations, and a sensitivity to fashion changes and what they mean. Related to this is the communication of fashion skills by which certain people demonstrate their ability to wear the latest fashions or even develop new ones, both as a statement of personality and of social leadership. Finally, a person's own beliefs about life can be communicated by clothing, such as in a man's refusal to wear a tie, the wearing of a sweater in place of a jacket, or the refusal to wear a hat.

Thus, dress is not just a passive reflection of self but an active, changing, unspoken means of expression that maintains a daily developing interaction with friends and society. Comfort plays a very small part in all of this. What is important is a sense of personal identity in relation to self and to society at large. Dress, through subtle as well as obvious symbolism, gives daily clues about people and their inner thoughts and attitudes, while on a broader level keeps them interconnected with each other and society. Dress or fashion thus serves the social system by acting both as an agent and as a symbol of changing social attitudes. Fashion becomes a great unspoken language for sustaining a culture and expressing its underlying cultural beliefs. Fashion and its development is a great and ongoing interaction between leaders of fashion who wish to create and invent new styles for others to follow and the great social unconscious that slowly or rapidly accepts or rejects such fashion innovations, depending upon whether they seem to reflect the needs and unconscious yearnings of the moment.

To move away from the level of communication and social psychology in dress to somewhat more concrete factors that influence the form and function of dress, a word should be said about climate, natural resources, trade, technology, economic and political conditions, and a society's artistic expression. It is obvious that climate directly affects dress through both the amount of clothing worn and the weight, thickness, and texture of its fabric. Thus, wraparound and close-to-the-body garments usually develop in cold climates while light draping usually develops in warmer areas. Natural resources, of course, influence dress style tremendously.

If an area raises vegetable fibers to weave into fabric, like the linen used in Egypt, then the garments that result will be very different from those made from woolens in an area that raises sheep. Byzantine costume might have developed quite differently if Justinian had not been able to develop a native silk industry. Trade and cultural contact also make it possible for the fabrics and jewelled accessories from one area to intermingle with and sometimes dominate those of another, and changes of shape in garments are also due to such interaction and trade. Neither can technology be underestimated as an influence on the development of dress, as witness the changes through the late nineteenth century to the present in manufacture and marketing as well as in the increase in career "uniforms." As for social, economic, and political changes and their effect on dress, there have been great influences. Armor frequently influenced civil dress in the late medieval and Renaissance periods; the tricolor of the French Revolution led to a dominant color palette in France for half a decade; after World War II the surplus stores with their military supplies made a marked inroad on certain areas of fashion. The economics of the Great Depression led to escapist, fantasy fashions in the films at the same time that clothes at the lower level of society became simple and practical, as with overalls and Hoover aprons. The need for social change in the early 1960's produced that rebellion in the young that was most strongly expressed in clothing through the use of faded jeans, fringed leathers, primitive beads and girdles, and other items that were meant to be an attack and a challenge to the Establishment.

As for clothing's relationship with the other arts, the interaction has never been simple, but it has always been fascinating. Usually, artistic ideals have developed in one of the other arts and then been reflected in dress, but there are times when a particular body shape and its attendant clothing lines seems to appear first or at the same time. The rounded and circular body and clothing lines of the High Renaissance certainly do not follow the other arts but come at exactly the same time or slightly before. On the other hand, the interest in the poses and flat patterns of Japanese prints that were admired by Art Nouveau artists did not affect clothing until a decade later; and yet when the style came to clothing, it was felt more strongly than in any of the other arts.

In discussing the aesthetics of dress, the question always arises whether fashion is truly an art form. Certainly, one can make the case that since the development of the dress house and the *couturier* designer in the nineteenth century, the creations of individual fashion artists like Dior are works of art; but on a broader scale one can say, as we do about the art of the cave paintings, that dress as a combination of personal and cultural aesthetic impulses is also definitely a form of art. But if we concede that dress is an art form along with painting and sculpture, what is the relationship between a painting and a sculpture that depicts period clothing and the artistic style of the clothing itself? It is a different question, as each work of art has its special function, style, and audience. We can neither assume that all past artistic depictions of dress are distortions of reality, nor completely believable depictions of fashion. We know that Byzantine dress was intended to make the wearer look like a walking mosaic, just as we know that portraits of Queen Elizabeth were deliberately distorted to make her look even more like an unreal manikin than was the case when she sat in full dress for a portrait. Thus, one would assume that sketches from life, engravings that record manners and customs like those of Abraham Bosse, or photos that were meant to record reality, are usually safer sources to believe than royal portraits. On the other hand, fashion portraits from *Vogue* magazine are just as distorted and unreal as mosaics or certain royal portraits. One must look, therefore, at all records of clothing in art in terms of the function of the work and the intention of the artist.

A final word should be said about countermovements in fashion which may gain little if any treatment in a survey of dress and yet may be very instructive as to the underlying social, artistic, and personal tensions within a culture. The aesthetic movement, led by Oscar Wilde and others in the late nineteenth century, indicates a strong minority need for color, texture, and decoration in male dress during a period of utter conservatism and dullness in matters of texture, color, and decoration, just as the women's dress-reform movement of the period gives an even more vivid picture of a minority revolt against the deformities of the hoop, the bustle, and the corset. Later, the minority aesthetic movement led to some of the dash in Edwardian male dress, just as Amelia Bloomer's harem pants came to be used in women's cycling costumes.

Thus, these opening introductory remarks, set down before the survey of western dress begins, suggest that there are many things to consider in the historical study of fashion. One must always ask questions about the surrounding culture, the political and social events, the geographic location in which styles grew up, the functions for which a style was originally intended and how that function became lost as the style continued to evolve, how clothing is to be interpreted when seen within a piece of art, and how it expresses similar or different things from what the art work itself expresses. Thus, the study of historic dress is not a simple process but a complex psychological, sociological, aesthetic interaction of forces.

# Costume History and Style

# chapter 1

# Prehistoric

## Chronology

(600,000–50 B.C.)

**PALEOLITHIC**

| | |
|---|---|
| 600,000 to 160,000 B.C. | Early Paleolithic. Humans as hunters of mammoth and reindeer |
| 160,000 to 40,000 B.C. | Middle Paleolithic. Use of fur garments |
| 40,000 to 8000 B.C. | Late Paleolithic: Aurignacian, Solutrian, Magdalenian |
| 15,000 to 10,000 B.C. | The Venus of Willendorf; cave paintings at Lascaux, Font de Gaume, and elsewhere |

**MESOLITHIC**

| | |
|---|---|
| 8000 to 6000 B.C. | The beginnings of the transition toward the Neolithic Age. Humans as hunters and fishermen; use of hide garments |

| | | |
|---|---|---|
| NEOLITHIC | 5000 to 1000 B.C. | The Neolithic Revolution during which humans became shepherds and farmers; flax cultivation, hide garments refined, early weaving developed |
| Bronze Age | 2100 to 1000 B.C. | Bronze weapons and ornaments developed; humans add sailing and the craft of the artisan to their accomplishments; early use of wool; decorated, woven garments developed |
| Iron Age | 1000 to 50 B.C. | Iron weapons and ornaments developed |
| | 1000 to 500 B.C. | Hallstatt Period centered in Austria; further development of decorated woven fabric |
| | 500 to 50 B.C. | La Tène Period centered in west central Europe; further refinement of craftsmanship |

# BACKGROUND

It has always been remarkable that the naturalism and fidelity to fact found in the cave paintings of southern France and northern Spain are at the earliest and most primitive level of mankind's cultural development. These images made some 20,000 years ago are from a time when the human race had not developed the ability to keep cattle and raise crops, and their survival depended on hunting supplemented by fishing and the gathering of berries, nuts, and roots. They thus spent an inordinate amount of time following and observing animals, particularly various forms of deer and buffalo, waiting for the right time for the big kill. They had to use simple weapons of bone, wood, or stone, since metal was as yet unknown, and had to track and kill on foot since horses had not yet been tamed. Thus it is not a wonder that the images of animals that were to be killed for food and whose skins were to be used for warmth and primitive forms of clothing loomed large in the minds and imaginations of the cave people and became the basis for visual images in painting and sculpture.

But where did the idea of such visual images come from, and why were they first done? No one can be sure, but probably vague raised shapes on the walls of the caves in which early humans lived suggested animal shapes. A hungry cave man may then have outlined such shapes with burnt charcoal as a means of psychologically or magically "capturing" an animal deeply imprinted on his visual imagination after hours of stalking and observing a particular animal herd. Thus early Stone Age art is really a form of sympathetic magic incised on walls so deep within the caves that no one but the artist probably saw the animal images. Humans at this point evidently made no distinction between such images and reality, and the picture became a trap for or a control over a particular animal or group of animals. From constant observation of these animals in the process of preparing for the hunt, the primitive hunter had memorized their movements, shapes, and textures so vividly that the images drawn on the wall were almost mental photographs.

Other visual images of this Paleolithic Period include numerous fertility talismans, and here, too, the desire was to create an image that would increase procreation within the group. The famous Venus of Willendorf pays no attention to the many female attributes of the human figure, but is compiled of busts, hips, and genital area with all other details neglected. The few images of men also concentrate on the genital area as the most important and valuable part of the human body. The human figure is thus quite inhuman or unreal compared to the animal images, but that is not surprising, when one realizes that the hunter spent all day observing the herd, while male and female contacts were primarily sexual and related to childbearing.

About 8000 B.C., with the coming of the Neolithic Revolution, when primitive people turned from hunting to animal husbandry and agriculture, we have the historical moment metaphorically expressed in the Biblical story of the Expulsion from the Garden of Eden. Earlier humans had been children of nature, at one with the universe, dealing with instincts and sensations rather than with facts. With the Neolithic Revolution, humans began to gain self-knowledge and to use their intellect to organize and categorize life. Whereas Old Stone Age people had led an unsettled life at the mercy of nature, humans now settled into communities, had greater control of the food supply, and began to develop a disciplined order in group living. Pottery and weaving were introduced, and primitive forms of architecture were attempted. But the direct naturalism of the Old Stone Age was now absent, replaced by complex, abstract geometric forms. The period of transition from the Old Stone Age to the New is known as the Mesolithic Period and lasted roughly from 8000 to 6000 B.C.

Why this change to the abstract and the geometric? With the transition to agriculture, the rhythms of life changed abruptly. Human beings now saw themselves as separate from the animal and plant world, and thus gradually developed a dualistic concept of a real world and a supernatural one. They believed that everything had both an inner and an outer reality—the human body and the spirit within, the rocks and the trees and the spirits that inhabited them. This world produced complex rituals, architecture, idols, and modes of worship in which humans were forever attempting to influence the spirit world that lay beyond their real everyday world. The visual arts gradually turned away from naturalistic wall paintings to signs, symbols, and visual abbreviations that led to pictographic sign language and finally to hieroglyphs. This use of signs and symbols in abstract geometric form indicated a more tightly organized, disciplined, and stable social order, a more intellectual view of nature, and a dualistic religious outlook.

Within this new social order an entire class of "nonproductive specialists" developed—specialists devoted not only to the augmentation of the myths and rituals that were rapidly growing in numbers, but also to the explanation of the connections between the complex spirit world and the world of everyday reality. Fantastic and varied masks and costumes supported dramatic expression and creative imagination as these primitive people developed stories about the spirits and attempts to win their favor. There were rituals of ancestor worship, fertility, initiation, and medicine, as well as ceremonies to influence crops, the weather, and the outcome of warfare. Eventually, massive stone ceremo-nial sites were erected, such as the famous astronomical observatory and ritual religious site at Stonehenge in England. Although Stonehenge is an awe-inspiring sight even today, due to its size and location, when it was built sometime around 1500 B.C. or earlier it must have had a tremendous impact on the participants gathered to watch the sun rise on the morning of the summer solstice. Even sophisticated and blasé modern observers would probably be struck with a certain primitive awe if they were to watch the great ritual ceremony that probably took place as the sun rose and threw a finger of shadow across the altar at the climax of the rites during the dawn of the summer solstice (Fig. 1-1). Stonehenge, among many other prehistoric ritual sites, reminds us of the complexity of primitive people's beliefs and the importance of religion and religious ceremonies in their everyday lives.

## THE BASIC COSTUME SILHOUETTE

Through many surveys and studies of a variety of primitive cultures, anthropologists have concluded that the natural state of the human form from the period of the cave dwellers onward is not naked but clothed or decorated in some way to make up for the human being's lack of rich animal fur or outer skin of appealing natural markings. Primitive people dressed and covered themselves as much for reasons of decoration and symbol as for warmth and protection. Unlike the standard Christian interpretation of the Adam and Eve story, primitive man and woman did not cover his or her private parts for purposes of modesty. When such areas were covered or decorated, it was to call attention to them or to give them added symbolic significance.

Our knowledge of prehistoric clothing is extremely limited and comes from a number of images that have survived because they were made of bone, metal, or stone; from a few objects or pictures crudely depicting limited items of dress; and from a few later Early Bronze Age burials in the frozen north in which parts of garments still remain intact. From these sources we can deduce that primitive clothing usually consists of the loincloth, the skirt, and the primitive tunic, and that the basic divisions by shape are closely related to the two basic textures used: skins, hides, and furs, or woven vegetable and animal fibers.

## OLD STONE AGE (PALEOLITHIC) DRESS

The dry and penetrating cold of southern Europe during the Old Stone Age left cave dwellers only two or three summer months for hunting; thus, both for warmth and because animal hides were a byproduct of hunting, skins became the logical basis for loin-cloths, wraparound skirts, and shawls. In other climates we are convinced that plaited grasses and leaves were probably the earliest form of clothing, but there is little solid information on this until Neolithic times. Also we must include skin decoration as a form of clothing for

(a)
the cave

(b)
the tent

Stonehenge; Salisbury Plain; Wiltshire, England; ca. 1800–1400 B.C. A circle of stones 97′ in diameter and $13^{1}/_{2}$′ high, used as a religious ceremonial site and as an astronomical calendar. Photo courtesy of the British Tourist Authority, New York.

(c)
the beehive hut: Ireland

(d)
the hut

primitive people, and we have abundant information about painting, tattooing, and reshaping the human form from tribes at the Neolithic level from all over the world. Much of it was associated with puberty rites and usually involved the scarring of the skin in certain patterns, filing the teeth, binding parts of the body, tattooing, or some form of flagellation. All were meant to be permanent records to be carried throughout later life.

But our knowledge of the simple garments of the cave dwellers from Paleolithic times is limited to a few items of skin, fur, and leather.

FIG. 1–3 Two women in procession. Tsisab Ravine in the Southwest African Desert. ca. 8,000–2,000 B.C. These ladies wear high coiffures laced with beads, bead-trimmed brassieres, and beaded loin skirts with a tail-like appendage. They are in every way sophisticated female figures from a warm climate during the Mesolithic or early Neolithic periods. From the collection of the author.

FIG. 1–2 Venus of Lespugne; Haute Garonne, France; ca. 15,000–8000 B.C. A statuette that probably depicts in the striations on the thighs the sort of loincloth made of woven bands and edged with fringe that has been uncovered in the Egtved tomb in Denmark. Photo courtesy of the Musee de l'Homme, Paris. Cliché: Oster.

We know that the tools used for the preparation of the skins included scrapers made of flint, flint knives for cutting the leather, reindeer horn combs for preparing furs, and strands of animal ligaments or twisted hair used as thread to lace pieces of skin together. Holes were punched in the skins, and then needles of bone or ivory carried the thread in a zigzag laced pattern until large areas and varied shapes were connected. Probably the garments of the cave dwellers during the Paleolithic Period were related to the garments that can still be observed among the Eskimos, though in far less developed form, and may even have included the use of bone buttons or toggles. A new representation of an Eskimo-like garment has been discovered at Angles-sur-l' Anglin (Vienne, France) that gives a fairly precise picture of an early fur garment: a fur covering opening in front over a kind of plastron with a headdress decorated with dangling bobbles.

The groups of seal teeth found on female skeletons in Sweden, the summer costumes of certain Eskimos, and descriptions of the German barbarians by Tacitus suggest that skins of various kinds were used both as loincloths and as wraparound coverings for the body. The animal skins were usually kept in their natural shape, often with the tail or even the paws still attached and used as decoration or as a kind of symbolic accent. The statuette known as Venus of Lespugne has a loincloth-like appendage at the back of the figure that may actually represent an animal tail (Fig. 1–2). This effect also appears in a cliff painting of the Tsisab Ravine in the desert of southwest Africa. Here two ladies in procession wear high coiffures, beaded brassieres, and loin skirts with a tail at the rear (Fig. 1–3). Even later, in the cloth articles found in some of the frozen burial sites in the far north, one can tell that the original model was of fur or skin, that the shoulder straps derived from an animal's paws, and that the measurements of the garments corresponded to the dimensions of the animals.

In general, with most garments made of skins, the line of the clothing remained close to the body, except for large skins used as shawls, and the skins were usually laced to the body of the wearer to gain the feeling of a second skin or a tight wraparound effect.

## TRANSITIONAL AGE (MESOLITHIC) DRESS

In more temperate climates than those inhabited by the cave dwellers of southern France and northern Spain, hunting people were clothed more for adornment and decoration than for warmth. Items of clothing often came from plaiting bark or grasses together to gain a primitive fabric effect and from the decorative use of feathers, sparkling stones, and other ornamental accessories. As time passed, human beings began their great transition from the nomadic life of the hunter toward settled communities and agriculture. This period, roughly between 8000 and 6000 B.C., usually known as the Mesolithic Age, is the time during which loom weaving probably developed. Thread became finer, needles slimmer, primitive thimbles for pushing the needle through fabric were invented, and the fibers spun from flax and wool were roughly woven into the first fabrics. With the new domestication of certain animals and the ability to raise certain plants, sheep and goats came to occupy a dominant place among domestic herds, and flax and cotton plants became prized plants amidst items grown primarily for food. During this period primitive cloth pieces were characterized by their small dimensions and by their basically square or rectangular shape. The resultant fabric was not cut, but pieces were sewn together to create shape variations like the T-shaped tunic.

## NEW STONE AGE (NEOLITHIC) DRESS

By the beginning of what we call the New Stone Age (as early as 6000 B.C. in the eastern Mediterranean), the basic lines of dress for all primitive tribes down into the nineteenth century were set: skirts, coats, T-shaped tunics, and wraparound shawls. Neolithic dress was no longer as tightly body-fitting as in Paleolithic times, but tended toward skirts or kilts hung from the waist complemented by T-shaped garments that, in general, gave a semifitted rather than a tightly fitted look. It may be an excessive generalization (and yet has some basis in fact) to say that Paleolithic dress tended to be tight to the body, whereas Neolithic tended to be hung or semidraped.

Dyestuffs also developed in the Neolithic Period and consisted of a wide range of vegetable and mineral colors such as blue from woad, lilac from myrtle, yellow from the artichoke, red from orach, orange from the bedstraw in marshes, and red ochre from chalk. Woven ornaments also appeared at this time along with a great variety of jewelry, head-dresses, and natural ornamental accessories.

Though it is not really possible to speak of "form" in relation to prehistoric dress, there did seem to be a great stress on the skirt or kilt in many areas of the world during Neolithic times. One of the best and earliest depictions of the effect is to be seen in a cave painting from Kogul near Lérida in Catalonia, which shows a dance scene with nine barebreasted women wearing bell skirts attached at the waist, which stop at the knee (Fig. 1-4). These seem remarkably like the earliest form of the *kaunakes,* or fleece kilt, found in the earliest stages of Mesopotamian development in Sumeria at the beginning of the third millenium B.C. (see Fig. 3-3).

Interesting excavations in Denmark have given us actual examples of early Bronze Age costume. The excavators found skirts made of vertical cords about 18 inches deep and almost 5 feet in length attached to a woven fringed girdle. The garment for the upper body is a sleeved jacket or shirt in plain wool, woven in one piece with the cut front and back edges hemmed at the bottom and sewn together at the top (Fig. 1-5). From this and other similar garments found through excavation, it is possible to say that the garments of northern Europe during the Bronze Age consisted of a shirt, skirt, girdle, cap, and shoes for women and a cloak, long tunic, shoes, and cap for men. The shoes from these excavations are similar to Indian moccasins. Several examples of the male long cloak have been found in Denmark, and there is a description of it by Posidonius (first century B.C.) as quoted by Strabo that makes it seem identical with the coarse woolen *sagum* worn by the Celts of the British Isles.

We also have cliff paintings from the Spanish Levant that depict men wearing a sort of leather trouser, possibly the Neolithic development of the earlier effect of skins wrapped about the leg. Certainly in later barbaric German costume (see Chap. 7), the effect of leather leg coverings wrapped or cross-gartered with thongs suggests an outgrowth from both of these primitive clothing ideas.

Women's coiffures during prehistoric times,

FIG. 1-4 Women wearing fur skirts; Reindeer period; cave painting from Kogul; ca. 15,000–8000 B.C. The women shown in this ritual scene are wearing skirts which are very similar to the early skirt kilts, or *kaunakes,* worn in Sumeria during the foundation of Mesopotamian culture (see Fig. 3-3). Photo courtesy of M. Almagro and the Museo Arqueológico, Madrid.

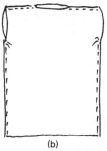

(b)
later development of tunic

(a)
first shirt-tunic

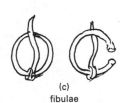

(c)
fibulae

(g)
wraparound skirt

(d)
drawers or bracco

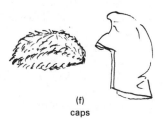

(e)
Iron Age
shoe

Early Bronze Age clothing; Egtved tomb; ca. 2100–1000 B.C. The photo depicts a short-sleeved tunic or shirt to be slipped on over the head, a belt ending in a loop carrying a metal disk, and a string skirt ending in fringe and sewn to a woven waistband. Photo courtesy of the National Museum, Copenhagen.

(f)
caps

FIGURE 1–5

9

depicted in various sculptured representations, show that the head was covered by a cap or net. Even in the earlier years of the Old Stone Age we have a figurine from the Brassempouy Cave in Les Landes, France, that seems to represent a kind of hood, but which probably is plaited hair held by a net. In the Bronze Age excavations from Denmark, there is the body of a woman wearing a horsehair net, and there are other indications of a similar coiffure from other sources at various points during Neolithic development.

From the Iron Age there are a number of caps made of skins. One of particular interest from the Dürnberg saltmines of Austria is made of six pieces of hide with the fur side turned inwards and a tassel of twisted thongs attached to the crown. This type of cap with some kind of dangling pendants is repeated in a Scandinavian cap woven of thick wool with bristling knots of thread all over the outside and in a Cretan cap with a curl of hair and dangling-olive shaped pendants attached on the outside.

It is this basic cap that evolves into the Phrygian cap of Ancient Mesopotamia, Ancient Greece, and in the classic revival at the time of the French Revolution.

Ornaments of various kinds were key items in prehistoric dress and usually consisted of necklaces, girdles, pectorals, bracelets, and headbands. At first these items were most often crafted from animal teeth, paws, and claws, fish vertebrae, shells, and bone. Later they were far more complex combinations of all of these with the addition of ivory, amber, and other precious multicolored stones (Fig. 1-6).

It is probably permissible to conclude from bits of materials found, techniques chronicled, and forms discovered that in Paleolithic and even early Neolithic times human beings dressed much the same in western Europe, the Mediterranean basin, Africa, and even the Orient, with due allowance for the changes in climate and terrain and the differences in materials available.

# chapter II

# Ancient Egypt

## Chronology

### (3100–30 B.C.)

| | | |
|---|---|---|
| **EARLY DYNASTIC PERIOD 3100–2686 B.C.** | ca. 3100 | Upper and Lower Egypt united under Menes, the first pharaoh, who built his capital at Memphis; development of the calendar and hieroglyphic writing |
| | 3100–2890 | I Dynasty: trade with the Levant, expeditions to Sudan, large irrigation and drainage projects undertaken, copper tools |
| | 2890–2686 | II Dynasty: religious and political strife between Upper and Lower Egypt, reunification under Pharaoh Khasekhemy; skillful use of metal, ivory, wood, and faience work |

First Dynasty

---

| | | |
|---|---|---|
| **OLD KINGDOM 2686–2181 B.C.** | 2686–2613 | III Dynasty: large-scale stone building and sculpture, step pyramid at Sakkara |
| | 2613–2494 | IV Dynasty: outstanding pharaohs are Khufu, Khafre, and Menkaure; the Great Pyramid and the Sphinx built at Giza; *kalasiris* skirts for women, kilts for men |

| | | |
|---|---|---|
| | 2494–2345 | V Dynasty: famed pyramid texts, records of funerary customs, rise of importance of the sun god, Re, weakening of pharaoh's absolute power |
| Old Kingdom | 2345–2181 | VI Dynasty: internal strife increases, rise of feudal lords to anarchy |
| INTERMEDIATE PERIOD 2181–2040 B.C. | 2181–2130 | VII, VIII, IX Dynasties: many kings with short reigns, social and political chaos; artistic traditions disrupted, pyramids ransacked, tombs and temples destroyed |
| | 2130–2040 | X Dynasty: rulers of Lower and Middle Egypt battle Theban rulers of Upper Egypt; coffin texts and funerary writings inscribed in tombs of nobles |
| MIDDLE KINGDOM 2133–1786 B.C. | 2133–1991 | XI Dynasty: reunification of Egypt under Pharaoh Mentuhotep II, who established Thebes as his capital; artistic renaissance follows restoration of order; geometry in use; books on astronomy written; calendar perfected |
| | 1991–1786 | XII Dynasty: powerful pharaohs suppress the feudal nobility and undertake irrigation schemes, develop copper mines, and establish outposts as far as third cataract of the Nile; capes, shawls, and tunics added to Egyptian dress; development of portraiture, classical literature, temples, and sculpture on a colossal scale |

| | | |
|---|---|---|
| **INTERMEDIATE PERIOD** 1786–1567 B.C. | 1786–1603 | XIII, XIV Dynasties: decay of central authority, seizure of power by Asian Hyksos kings, disintegration of traditional culture |
| | 1603–1567 | XV, XVI, XVII Dynasties: under the Hyksos, Egypt introduced heavy Asian equipment and horse-drawn chariots; improved weaving, bronze metal widely used, new musical instruments |
| **NEW KINGDOM— EMPIRE PERIOD** 1567–1085 B.C. | 1567–1320 | XVIII Dynasty: Hyksos ousted by Ahmose I; Thutmose III expands empire to Euphrates; key rulers—Hatshepsut, Amenhotep IV (Akhenaten), Tutankhamen; opulent craftsmanship, peak in literature, monotheism fails, elaborate temples in the Valley of the Kings; excessive use of starched pleating and rich ornamentation in dress; use of the robe |
| | 1320–1200 | XIX Dynasty: Ramses II maintains Egyptian power and repels the Hittites; temple of Ramses II at Thebes, hypostyle hall at Karnak, Abu Simbel, "Books of the Dead" on papyrus; exodus of the Hebrews; fall of Troy |
| | 1200–1085 | XX Dynasty: rule of Ramses III–XI, invasions of Libyans and Sea People repelled, loss of Asian provinces, increasing lawlessness, tombs at Thebes looted |

Empire

| | | |
|---|---|---|
| **LATE DYNASTIC PERIOD** 1085–341 B.C. | 1085–730 | XXI, XXII, XXIII Dynasties: Egypt divided, kings of Libyan origin, invasion of Palestine, Solomon's Temple plundered followed by invasion of Nubians; bronze casting perfected, skilled metal and faience work |
| | 730–525 | XXIV, XXV, XXVI Dynasties: rule by Nubian pharaohs. Thebes sacked |

|  |  | by Assyrians, trade with Greece; brief cultural renaissance, new realism in sculpture; Phoenicians circumnavigated Africa |
|  | 525–341 | XXVII, XXVIII, XXIX, XXX Dynasties: Persians conquer Egypt; canal from Red Sea to Nile; Greeks help to expel Persians, but they reconquer Egypt in 341; Darius I codifies Egyptian law; last flowering of Egyptian art |
| PTOLEMAIC PERIOD 332–30 B.C. | 332–30 | Alexander the Great conquers Egypt; on his death one of his generals founds Ptolemaic Dynasty; Temple of Horus at Edfu, Temple of Hathor at Dendera; in 30 B.C., Egypt becomes a Roman province |

# BACKGROUND

Long before the climax of Neolithic cultural development and the erection of ritualistic architecture such as the Great Circle at Stonehenge, "historic cultures" developed in the fertile river basins of the eastern Mediterranean, replacing the prehistoric cultures of the New Stone Age. With the development of written records some 6000 years ago and the development of organized states around a central urban center, the pace of human events increased; with the development of written history, humans came to want to participate in the making of such history. Thus in the fertile river valleys of Egypt and Mesopotamia sometime between 5000 and 3500 B.C., societies developed that were challenged less by nature and natural disasters than by the human forces within their own culture or in neighboring societies. One of the first and most important social developments was the foundation of an urban, or city-dwelling, concentration of population supported by a surrounding rural society. The close contact of different levels of society in this central urban hub then stimulated a strong artistic and intellectual climate that affected the entire national state. This development we refer to as *civilization*.

To look at Egypt from a modern perspective, one would not think that it could represent an increasing pace of cultural change. It appears to be one of the most rigidly conservative civilizations that has ever existed. Yet when its history is placed against prehistoric cultures, it seems crowded with change and incident. There were, however, strong cultural patterns in Egyptian art and institutions during the nearly 3000 years of its ancient history that endured beyond the ebb and flow of political change.

The Egyptians recorded their history through the dynasties of their pharaohs, and this system of recording time underlines the Egyptian worship of continuity and the overwhelming importance of the pharaoh, or god-king. This sense of the absolute divinity of the ruler gave Egyptian art, clothing, and ritual a

(a)
mastaba tomb shapes

(b)
temple of Hathor Dendara

(c)
chair
with leopard-
covered
footstool

Great Sphinx and Pyramid of Khafre; Giza near modern Cairo; ca. 2600 B.C. These images are massive monuments to the Egyptian belief in life after death and the imperishability of the Egyptian god-kings. Photo courtesy of the Hirmer Fotoarchiv, Munich.

(d)
papyrus
capital

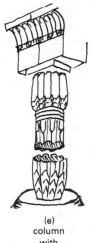

(e)
column
with
bud capital

(f)
palm
capital

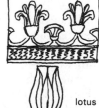

(g)
versions of lotus
flower

lotus
bud
closed

(h)

FIGURE 2-1

15

very strong hierarchical character and formality, while the Egyptian belief in life after death led to the development of complex burial rites and massive tomb construction. To achieve permanence these tombs and their appended statuary were constructed out of imperishable stone, even though normal dwellings were of mud brick. In the timeless, cyclical world of the seasons created by the climate of Egypt and the predictability of the Nile, a civilization developed that was devoted to permanence, severity, regularity, religion, rhythmical repetition, and an ageless sense of order.

Thus there are more artifacts and relics of ancient Egyptian civilization than there are of any western European culture between the Roman and Gothic Periods. No matter from which dynasty one chooses a work of art, the overriding effect is one of precision, exactness of measurement, careful placement, and planned proportion. The Egyptian artist seemed to concentrate on achieving a timeless image of his or her subject—an offering to a social system that believed that every artistic product was a kind of punctuation mark in the unrolling scroll of his cultural development.

Most of us have imbedded in our visual memory the image of the Great Sphinx framed against the Great Pyramid as our idea of ancient Egypt, and no matter how many times we see that picture, it never fails to give a sense of the power of the pharaohs and the unchanging formality of Egyptian art and culture (Fig. 2-1). But it would be wrong to leave this one-sided view to stand alone in the mind. One should also sense in Egyptian art the experimentation, individualism, and dynamics of this great civilization. The dynamic forces on balance were probably greater than the static if one were to compare this first great urban historic culture with any Neolithic one; but today, as we look at the angular figures of Egyptian art going about their formal assigned tasks in an almost ritualistic way, it is the drive for continuity, formality, and absolute control over the forces of nature that strikes our imagination.

## THE BASIC COSTUME SILHOUETTE

When we look at Egyptian art for information about Egyptian dress, one immediately tends to assume that the lines of the clothing are extremely distorted by the formal angularity and symmetry emphasized by the artist. But the more we study the information on clothing, the more we are forced to realize that, as in all cultures, the people will always attempt to look as much like the stylistic elements stressed in their art as possible. Women today may not look exactly like the elongated, hat-rack fashion figures drawn in newspapers and magazines, but they do all in their power to achieve a close approximation. The same was true in ancient Egypt. Look, for example, at a bas-relief of funeral ceremonies from the XIX Dynasty now in the Archaeological Museum in Florence (Fig. 2-2). The figures have a flat, side-view angularity in position and dress that would lead the viewer to think that all the items of clothing as well as the bodies are distorted for effect; but when we realize that these angular clothing lines were actually possible through the use of starched and pleated linen, we begin to understand what effort the human spirit will make to look like the human form created in the arts of a particular culture. The same is true of the suggested transparency in certain tunics, particularly for women. We know that the linen was woven into such a thin, transparent texture that the body was glimpsed as through a pleated veil—a weaving technique unequaled to this day. Such pleated tunics and skirts fell into fine lines which not only emphasized the cut of the garment but also clung to the body in fluid, pleated lines. In Egyptian fashions as in all fashion since, life reflects art more than art reflects life.

The other most important aspect of Egyptian dress was the concentration of the fullness of the drapery from the waist down over the genital area. This obviously was a sophisticated remnant from earlier times in which ritual decoration of the pubic area called attention to that part of the body most involved in the continuity and procreation of the tribe. In

(a)
white crown of
upper Egypt inside
red crown
of lower
Egypt

(b)
vulture
headdress

(c)

Queen's
headdress
worn by
Nefertiti,
wife of
Akhenaten
1375–1358 B.C.

(d)

(e)

selected
hairdressing
and wigs
for women

(f)

Funeral Ceremonies; bas-relief; nineteenth dynasty; Archaeological Museum Florence; 1320–1200 B.C. Illustrates the angular, formal, starched linen garments, symbolic accessories and headdresses, and general air of sophisticated abstraction that one finds in Egyptian dress. Photo courtesy of Alinari, Florence.

(g)
diadem
of Princess
Sathathor-ant 12th
dynasty

(i)
mirror

(h)
fan

(j)
pectoral

(k)
sacred
uraeus

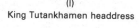

(l)
King Tutankhamen headdress

**FIGURE 2–2**

17

its earliest form the Egyptian loincloth was wrapped about the loins in such a way that the ends hung down in full folds at the front. Later on this loincloth was formalized in cut and starched for angular stiffness until a rigid triangle was created at the front of the body. To this decorative girdles were added with the ends hanging down over and accenting the skirt or loincloth pleating. Eventually tunics, robes, and skirts were also gathered so that the fullness and strength of the pleating was concentrated at the front of the body. Note that this is true in every one of the figures in the bas-relief of funeral ceremonies (Fig. 2-2) and in all other Egyptian clothing that you will see in this chapter. It is also interesting to note, relating clothing to architecture, that the triangular shape at the front of the various figures in this chapter, particularly the high official, Methethy, from the VI Dynasty (Fig. 2-5), are exactly the shape of the Great Pyramid. Just as the circle in the High Renaissance infused architecture, painting, female body forms, and clothing ideals, so stiffness, angularity, formality, and the pyramid shape can be found as an ideal in all Egyptian art and culture.

## EARLY DYNASTIC PERIOD AND OLD KINGDOM COSTUME

**Masculine Dress**   The king who succeeded in uniting Upper and Lower Egypt is supposed to have been the legendary Menes who is probably the ruler Narmer seen in the famous Palette of Narmer, c. 2990 B.C. (Fig. 2-3). As the uniter of the two kingdoms he had the right to wear the crowns of Upper and Lower Egypt (often combined), but in the Palette he wears only the high, white crown of Upper Egypt (the southern part of modern Egypt or northern Sudan). The crown of Lower Egypt (coastal Egypt) was of red wicker, relatively low in front with a high panel at the back. The body garment on Narmer looks as if it were wrapped around the body under the right arm and tied or fastened up over the left shoulder. It must have had folds, but these were left out by the artist. The waist is confined by a belt or girdle with four beaded pendants containing horned cow heads, symbolic of the Goddess Hathor. Down the back hangs a lion's tail, a symbol of power among ancient chieftains of this area. This figure with headdress and loincloth stands at the beginning of the Early Dynastic Period as a symbol of the importance of the headdress, loincloth, and girdle in later Egyptian clothing development.

The first period of real prosperity and artistic development came with the Old Kingdom which began with the III Dynasty about 2686 B.C. The masculine garment during this period was the short, plain loincloth wrapped tightly around the hips with the ends caught together at the waistline in the center front by a girdle or by a belt with a loop. For workmen there was the diaper, put on as a triangle with the base at the waistline and the apex brought between the legs and tied with the other corners at the center front. Loincloths were of varying lengths, and in the figure called Sheik-el-Beled (Fig. 2-4), the loincloth becomes more of a skirt or kilt, reaching to the knees. Note the easy way in which the end of the skirt curls forward when tucked into the waist. The royal dress for this period was also a loinskirt but usually not of linen. It was more frequently woven of gold, often in striped or even plaid design. In a series of statues from the Old Kingdom, one can see many experiments with the development of the triangular projection at the front of the loin skirt or kilt. One very strong costume image of this period is that of a high government official, Methethy (Fig. 2-5) from the late VI Dynasty. Here the pleated striping, the starched triangularity, and the calf length are clearly seen.

One of the most typical images of the Old Kingdom is that of Menkaure and his queen (Fig. 2-6). Here the loin skirt is pleated all the way around, and the front panel hanging down from the inside has horizontal pleats. The ends of the loin skirt are rounded and the overlap in front is slight so that it is very probable that the panel hanging down the front is part of the belt or girdle. But it is the headdress that is the most

**FIG. 2-3** Palette of Narmer; from Hierakonpolis; Egyptian Museum, Cairo; ca. 2990 B.C. Narmer is usually placed as the first king of the first dynasty who succeeded in joining Upper and Lower Egypt into a single kingdom. Here he wears a loin skirt with an end brought up and fastened on the left shoulder, an interesting girdle with four beaded pendants in front, and the high white crown of Upper Egypt. Photo courtesy of the Hirmer Fotoarchiv, Munich.

**FIG. 2-4** Sheik-el-Beled; Sakkara; Egyptian Museum, Cairo; ca. 2600 B.C. This work, which represents a man whose function it was to serve the pharaoh, wears a loin skirt in which the end of the skirt curls forward in an easy natural way after having been tucked into the waist. Photo courtesy of the Hirmer Fotoarchiv, Munich.

**FIG. 2-5** Methethy as a Mature Man; Sixth Dynasty; Brooklyn Museum; ca. 2250 B.C. The loin skirt here is quite long with a starched triangle of fabric at the front that contains horizontal pleating or striping, and whose shape both reminds one of the pyramids and calls attention to the genital area. Photo courtesy of the Brooklyn Museum; Charles Edwin Wilbour Fund.

on the Sphinx (Fig. 2–1). The lines on such a stiffened headcloth represented in rigid abstract form the curls of the wig.

As for other famous headdresses of royalty during the Old Kingdom, the most famous is probably the *pschent,* or the combined crowns of Upper and Lower Egypt, usually with the sacred *uraeus,* or asp, the symbol of the king's power of life over death, at its center front (Fig. 2–2b,c,g,k,l). Other sacred symbols incorporated into a royal headdress include the two upright feathers of the God Amon, the ostrich feathers of Osiris, the ram's horns of Khnum, the sun disc of Re—all on various headdresses that give an air of exotic fantasy to the wearer.

The final interesting accessory in the statue of Menkaure and his queen is the beard, or *postiche,* which is artificial and reserved for the pharaoh's use on ceremonial occasions (Fig. 2–6). Otherwise, with their stress on smooth

**FIG. 2–6**  Menkaure and His Queen; Fourth Dynasty; Museum of Fine Arts, Boston; ca. 2500 B.C. An excellent example of the use of the *klaft,* or stiffened hair covering; *postiche,* or false beard; and *schenti,* or loincloth, worn by a typical pharaoh during the Old Kingdom. The wife wears a wig and the tight, cylindrical, body-fitting sheath, or *kalasiris,* which usually ended just below the bust line. Photo courtesy of the Museum of Fine Arts, Boston; Harvard-MFA Expedition Fund.

interesting in this particular statue, and at the time when the body was wrapped so minimally, such accessories assumed great importance. Because of the heat and a desire for cleanliness, royalty shaved their heads and wore wigs—both to give dignity and to protect the head from the heat of the sun. But here we do not see the surface of the wig, only its cloth covering which followed exactly in its stiff form the lines of the false hair (Fig. 2–21). It is this wig with headcovering known as a *klaft* that we see

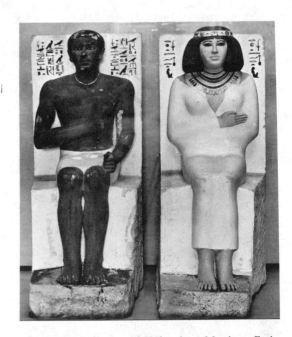

**FIG. 2–7**  Rahotep and Nofret from Meydum; Early Fourth Dynasty; Egyptian Museum, Cairo; ca. 2650–2500 B.C. The Pharaoh wears a simple loin skirt; his wife wears a wig, crown, decorative collar, *kalasiris* sheath, and a lightweight shawl wrapped tightly around the shoulders. Photo courtesy of the Hirmer Fotoarchiv, Munich.

bodies and cleanliness, the Egyptians were all cleanshaven.

Although Menkaure does not wear a decorative collar, collars and necklaces had been a part of Egyptian dress since early predynastic times. These were made of geometrically arranged combinations of shells, faience beads, and precious stones, sometimes as a necklace but more often attached to a circular leather or cloth collar. A simple early necklace may be seen on Prince Rahotep at the end of the IV Dynasty of the Old Kingdom (Fig. 2-7). Neither Menkaure or Rahotep wears sandals, and it is usually assumed that sandals were not widely used until the Empire Period, even though we know that sandals of papyrus, palm fiber, and goatskin were possible.

**Feminine Dress**   The dress for women during the Old Kingdom consisted of a single garment—a long, closefitting skirt, or *kalasiris,* covering the body from just under the breast to the ankles usually held up by thin shoulder straps—that was probably not as form-fitting as shown by the artist. This is the garment worn by Menkaure's queen (Fig. 2-6), and she also wears a very carefully shaped abstract wig. Prince Rahotep's wife, Nofret, wears a wig under which one can see the natural hairline at the center of the forehead. She also wears an example of a lightweight shawl tightly wrapped about her shoulders, as well as a decorative fillet around the head and a typical example of the Egyptian collar with the five rows of circular beading set to a cloth or leather base (Fig. 2-7).

# INTERMEDIATE PERIODS AND THE MIDDLE-KINGDOM COSTUME

**Masculine Dress**   After a period of chaos and unrest, a new period of prosperity came to Egypt after the collapse of the Old Kingdom. Although the period is better remembered for developments in mining and irrigation, there were also some changes and additions to fashion. In general, longer skirts were now worn over the loincloth, and shawls were now seen on men as well as women. With the use of skirts over the loincloth, the starched, pyramidal projection at the front of the loin skirt was seen more and more infrequently. Sometimes there are examples of one skirt tightly draped to the center front of the figure worn over a longer skirt underneath, with a girdle and hanging tabs to finish off the costume at the front (Fig. 2-10).

**Feminine Dress**   Women in the Middle Kingdom continued to wear the sheath dress that fitted tightly under the bust line, with shoulder straps. In the women bearing offer-

**FIG. 2-8**   Women Bearing Offerings; Tomb of Meket-re, Thebes; Eleventh Dynasty; Metropolitan Museum of Art, New York; 2133-1991 B.C. These serving women wear the tight *kalasiris* sheath held over the shoulder by wide shoulder straps. The white fabric is covered with a beaded or multicolored, cut leather netting, examples of which have been found on mummies of the Saite period. Photo courtesy of the Metropolitan Museum of Art, Museum Excavations, 1919-1920, Rogers Fund, supplemented by contributions of Edward S. Harkness.

ings from the Tomb of Meket-re, Thebes, the skirt may look more like a tunic, but it is still a sheath with shoulder straps. What gives us some confusion is the collar, which at first glance appears to be part of the skirt. As for the fascinating geometric pattern of the gown, it is possible that it was a white, body-fitting skirt covered with a multicolored, cut leather net (Fig. 2–8). Also at this period we have illustrations of the vulture headdress as worn by the queens of Egypt (Fig. 2–2b). It fitted the head smoothly with the tips of the wings resting on the shoulders and the sacred uraeus just above the forehead. Another headdress that was part of the jewelry of Princess Sathathor-ant is a diadem of gold, set with jewels, the sacred uraeus, and two gold feathers (Fig. 2–2g). Jeweled accessories, such as necklaces, collars, and girdles, also became richer and more varied during the Middle Kingdom; and the necklace or pendant effect known as the *pectoral* became far more important as a decorative item (Fig. 2–2j).

# EMPIRE PERIOD COSTUME

**Masculine Dress**   After another period of anarchy and unrest caused by foreign invasion, the country settled down to a third period of greatness—the period usually thought of as the high point of ancient Egyptian civilization. Masculine clothing now underwent some radical transformations after the Egyptian conquest of Syria. The seamed tunic now became a part of Egyptian clothing.

The lower classes and servants still wore the loin skirt, and the figures guarding Tutankhamen's tomb still wore the great triangular projections at the front. But the innovative new garment was the robe, which consisted of a length of cloth twice the height of the wearer and of a width that reached from elbow to elbow with an opening for the head. Sometimes it was joined at the sides, but frequently the sides of the back panel were brought forward over the front, and all fullness was gathered at the front of the waist and held by a girdle. This carried on the tradition of having all fabric folds and decorative interest focused at the center front over the genital area. A good example of draping focused to the front of the male figure can be seen in the bas-relief of King Seti I from the XIX Dynasty shown wearing a tunic with the royal girdle and ceremonial apron to the knees (Fig. 2–9). Such a robe or tunic could also be held by a length of fabric wrapped like the old loincloth skirt over the tunic to reveal the shape of the buttocks and to draw all the folds to the front to fall under the tied ends of the loincloth. Still another fashion of the Empire was to have the tunic so sheer as to be almost transparent and then to have an opaque loin skirt wrapped over it. Sheer skirts instead of the fuller tunic were also sometimes worn under opaque loin skirts, and a shirt and skirt combination was introduced in which a kimono-cut shirt was tucked into a loin skirt of varying lengths.

Battle dress of the Empire consisted of wide leather straps that wrapped around the body of the military tunic. The straps were richly decorated, often with metal ornaments that gave the effect of the wings of the sacred vulture. A leather apron, loin skirt, and high battle helmet with sacred uraeus completed the outfit. The seated statue of Ramses II from the Turin Museum, though he is otherwise in fashionable civilian dress, wears the military helmet as a major accessory (Fig. 2–10).

A major decorative accessory that developed out of the older girdle form at this time was the royal apron, already mentioned, which can be seen in the figures of Seti I and Tutankhamen (Figs. 2–9,11). It consisted of a grouping of tapered decorative panels flanked by other hanging pendants. We know from the figure of Tutankhamen that these aprons were richly colored in blue and gold, probably a compound of jewels, inlay work, and beaten gold accents. This symbol of royalty was suspended from a girdle belt of matching design. Other royal accessories (that can be seen held in the hands of the coffin cover image of Tutankhamen) are the crook and the flail, the crook representing power over the shepherds of the realm and the flail representing authority over the growers of flax and grains. This crook can also be seen in the seated figure of Ramses II now at the Turin Museum (Fig. 2-10).

Wigs became even more esoteric during this period as can be seen in the matching blue wigs displayed on Tutankhamen and his wife on the inside back of his throne (Fig. 2-11). The com-

FIG. 2-10 Ramses II; Turin Museum; Nineteenth Dynasty; 1292–1225 B.C. The Pharaoh wears a kimono-cut, tightly pleated, starched linen tunic with the blue military helmet restricted to royalty with its sacred *uraeus* symbol at the front. In his hand he holds the crook, a symbol of royal power. Photo courtesy of Alinari, Florence.

FIG. 2-9 King Seti I with the Goddess Hathor; Nineteenth Dynasty; Archaeological Museum, Florence; 1313–1292 B.C. Illustrates a kimono-cut tunic with side edges brought to the front by a decorative girdle around the hips with tabs in front, known as the royal apron. The symbolic sun disk appears on the headdress of the goddess, Hathor, and the sacred *uraeus*, or hooded cobra, appears on Seti's wig. Photo courtesy of Alinari, Florence.

plexity and exotic fantasy of ceremonial headdresses reached a peak during this time. The symbolic motifs included in these headdresses included the ever-present solar disc, symbol of eternity; the sacred uraeus, or hooded cobra; the wings of the sacred hawk or vulture, for protection; and the feather plumes of royalty. Such headdresses were the very essence of Egyptian preoccupation with religion and eternity.

Sandals came into more common use during this period, especially for the nobility. A good example of the male sandal can be seen on the seated figure of Ramses II (Fig. 2-10), while a

**FIG. 2-11** Back panel of the Golden Throne depicting Tutankhamen and his wife Ankhesenamen; Eighteenth Dynasty; Metropolitan Museum of Art, New York; ca. 1360 B.C. Illustrates the beauty, sophistication, and ceremonial fantasy—with blue wigs, complex headdresses, jeweled collars, decorative girdles, and pleated tunics and skirts—that mark dress at the height of the New Kingdom, or Empire period. Photo courtesy of the Metropolitan Museum of Art; photo by Harry Burton.

often of so fine a texture that the naked body was revealed as through a veil. The stylized folds of the pleated fabric created patterns of fine lines which followed the shape of the drapery and the body with the emphasis as always to the front. Some of the complexities of draping (which remind one of the Indian sari) have never been adequately deciphered, but they seem based on the concept of wrapping the fabric first around the body and then up over the shoulder and down across the front to tie or fasten to the original corner of the fabric at the center front of the figure.

Women's wigs reached their greatest size during the Empire Period, often coming well below the shoulders and frequently richly decorated with gold bands or rings, colored glass, and jewels, or with a wig covering of inlaid carnelian and colored glass such as the lovely one in the Metropolitan Museum from the reign of Thutmose III (Fig. 2-2d, e, f). As for the headdresses, there was the simple fillet with the sacred uraeus in front with two prongs representing the feathers of Isis; the vulture headdress (Fig. 2-2b); a cone four or five inches high worn on top of the head containing perfumed ointment; the crowns of Upper and Lower Egypt, like the ones worn by the pharaohs (Fig. 2-2a); and the unique and best known headdress of all, that worn by the beautiful Nefertiti, wife of Akhenaten (Fig. 2-2c). This stiff blue miter is banded with a polychromed ribbon and highlighted in gold. The angularity of this headdress reflects once again the Egyptian love of beautifully proportioned, angular shapes.

Necklaces and collars continued their same general lines, decorative patterns, and richness of color, but with more elaboration. The final sophisticated touch to female adornment among the upper classes came from the adept use of cosmetics. Perfumes and ointments were widely used, and the eyes and eyebrows were heavily made up with kohl. We also have an Egyptian cartoon depicting the application of lipstick, and as early as the statue of Rahotep and Nofret (Fig. 2-7), the Lady Nofret's face shows the use of a white cream. This cream was used to give a desired pallor as well as to act as a protective agent against the drying of the skin in the hot Egyptian climate.

slightly more oriental line can be seen in those worn by Seti (Fig. 2-9).

**_Feminine Dress_** Although the simple sheath dress, either plain or patterned, still continued to be worn, the wives of the pharaohs and the nobility developed a taste for a variety of draped garments of hand-pleated bleached linen that must have taken hours of starching and preparation on the part of the servants. The tunic was the major new garment, just as it was for the men, but instead of using a wide girdle or royal apron, the fullness of folds gathered to the front were held by a narrow girdle with long flowing ends to the ankles, as can be seen on the wife of Tutankhamen (Fig. 2-11). This tunic was also often coupled with a shawl or shoulder cape, and this cape was worn with just a skirt and girdle which left the breast semiexposed, as had been the case with the older sheath skirt with shoulder straps. In these elaborately pleated and draped costumes, the linen was

# LATE DYNASTIC AND PTOLEMAIC PERIOD COSTUME

As Egyptian civilization declined after the close of the Empire Period, there was little innovation in dress and frequent revivals of rigidly archaic styles from the earliest dynasties. As Greek influence developed and spread throughout the eastern Mediterranean, we can see the gradual mixing and integration of Greek draping styles with the stiffer pleating of the ancient Egyptian mode. In a woman's torso from this later Saite Period, one can see a tunic with a draped skirt over it that reflects early classic Grecian lines (Fig. 2–12). Here the shawl is knotted on the chest and attached to the front of the draped skirt. Note that even at this late date the Egyptian love of frontal focus from the bust or hips down is still paramount.

**FIG. 2–12** Woman's Torso; Saite statue; The Louvre, Paris; ca. 600–341 B.C. Example of a light-linen garment, somewhat transparent, that is finely pleated and wrapped several times around the body in the Greek style with the shawl knot on the chest. Photo courtesy of the Réunion des Musées Nationaux, the Louvre, Paris.

# FABRICS

It is important to remember that early Egyptian clothing was exclusively fabricated from linen and supplemented by leather and reed matting and that the wool from sheep arrived only with the Empire Period. Linen was woven in very wide pieces and could be exceedingly fine and sheer. Although it could be colored in red, yellow, blue, and blue-green, white was preferred with color used in accessories and accents. The interest came in the pleating. In the Cairo Museum and the Boston Museum of Fine Arts there are examples of elaborate and meticulously pleated pieces of linen in which the pleats range from 1/8 to 3/16 of an inch. Some looped-pile effects in weaving were used during the Empire Period, and from the tomb of Tutankhamen there are examples of embroidered fabrics, tapestry weaving, and gold beading used in a fashion similar to the effect of modern sequins.

# ARTS AND ARTIFACTS

Egyptian architecture was heavy, horizontal, and solidly durable in character, with a stress on size and grandeur. Abstract floral effects such as the lotus and the papyrus were incorporated into rigid decorative motifs on the column capitals, and the great columns of the portals were frequently brightly painted. The lotus and papyrus flowers were used as sacred flowers by the Egyptians in all kinds of ornamentation; and in their temples, where the ceilings were the heavens, the columns were thought of as abstract plants rising from the earth to the heavens and flowering just before they reached the sky. The interiors of the palaces and temples were also decorated with carved and painted columns and wall paintings incorporating many of the sacred motifs found in costume (Fig. 2–1a, b, d, e, f, g, h).

The furniture was heavy but simple in line, though frequently richly carved, painted, and embellished with inlaid effects in gold and other precious metals (Fig. 2–1c). The materials for furniture were ivory, wood, and metal. There were chairs with great animal legs and feet and animal heads at the ends of the arms, small sturdy chairs with straight legs and rush seats, stools that remind one of the modern camp chair, inlaid chests, and narrow beds structured like a modern folding cot. Beds had rich tapestry or animal skin coverings without a mattress or pillow. Evidently the head rested on a dishlike headrest of wood or ivory that is reminiscent of the Japanese bolster. Items that might be labeled costume properties included glazed urns, small faience jars for cosmetics, ivory combs, palm fans, various items of makeup, bronze or silver mirrors, papyrus scrolls, reed brushes and inkpots for writing, dolls of terra cotta or wood, clay animals, ivory dice, various games such as knucklebones and draughts, and walking sticks of wood, metal, or ivory that were frequently topped by a lotus flower.

## VISUAL SOURCES

Visual sources from which one can gain information about clothing include all the sources in this chapter and many others. Sculpture, wall paintings, bas-reliefs, and a few actual items that have come down to us from ancient Egypt are the primary sources. The primary institutional repositories are the Cairo Museum, the British Museum, the Louvre, the Metropolitan Museum of Art, the Archaelogical Museum of Florence, and the Brooklyn Museum. Good written sources include Mary Houston's *Ancient Egyptian, Mesopotamian and Persian Costume,* and Lionel Casson's *Daily Life in Ancient Egypt.*

## SUMMARY

Egyptian clothing, as with all its other arts, was calculated to demonstrate man's triumph over nature, and it was this need to reaffirm human beings' dominance over the natural and animal world and to secure a continuity of culture and civilization that produced the angularity, severity, and often-unnatural textures, lines, and forms of Egyptian fashion. Nothing was more symbolic of this attitude than the removable beard of the pharaoh. Normally all Egyptian men were totally cleanshaven as a statement of their rise to civilization out of a lower, natural, animal existence, but the pharaoh (shown with an animal's powerful body in the Great Sphinx) had the power to add and remove the beard, as a symbol of animal power, at any time that he ceremonially chose to do so. The same was true with the heavy use of cosmetics by women; through this means the noble woman was able to demonstrate her civilized rise above and beyond that of a human tribal animal. Even the bleached linen worn on the body represented the ability of humans to remove fabric woven from flax from its natural color and to make it even more abstract by the use of starching and pleating.

But the Egyptian's deep-seated connection with the natural world out of which their civilization had risen was never forgotten. Scores of symbolic birds, animals, and vegetable images attest to this fact as does the continual focus through folds, pleating, draping, and girdle placement on the genital area of the body. The Egyptians were the first great civilization to place abstractions from nature as a symbol of their culture's dominance over nature.

# chapter **III**

# Mesopotamia

### Chronology
(3500–333 B.C.)

| | | |
|---|---|---|
| **PRE–SUMERIAN**<br>5000–3500 B.C. | ca. 5000 | Semitic nomads from Syria and the Arabian Peninsula invade southern Mesopotamian territory and mingle with the local farming population |
| | ca. 4000 | Irrigation, fine pottery, and permanent dwellings introduced; division of labor appears; villages and temples of mud brick |
| **SUMERIAN**<br>3500–1900 B.C. | ca. 3500 | Sumerians settle on the banks of the Euphrates after migrating from central Asia; cylinder seals are used to identify ownership of documents; a temple at Eridu, an early prototype of the ziggurat, is built on a mud terrace |
| | ca. 3200 | Democratic assemblages give way to kingships of limited authority; Sumerians introduce pictographs to keep administrative records; sculptors begin making three-dimensional statues |
| | ca. 3000 | Traditional design of the ziggurat appears in the White Temple which includes approach stairway; colored mosaics begin to be used for building decoration; Kish becomes the leading Sumerian city; foundation of the city of Troy |

Sumerian

| | | |
|---|---|---|
| | ca. 2750 | First formal land sales contracts in cuneiform; first use of copper helmets; origins of story of the Deluge |
| | ca. 2600 | Gilgamesh, hero of Sumerian legend, king of Erech; the "Standard of Ur," an inlaid plaque commemorating peace and war buried with other gold and silver artifacts at Ur; Abraham goes to Canaan from Ur |
| | ca. 2500 | Sumerian city-states united by King Lugalannemundu of Adab, who unites the states which then vie for domination over the next 200 years |
| | 2400–2300 | First Lagash and later Akkad dominate the area; Naram-Sin, grandson of Sargon the Great of Akkad, spreads Akkadian dominance to Armenia and Iran |
| | 2200–2150 | Gudea, Prince of Lagash, becomes a patron of art and literature, and magnificent statues are created in his honor |
| | ca. 2000 | Sumerian power declines, Elamites attack and destroy Ur; architecture and art decline |

| | | |
|---|---|---|
| **BABYLONIAN** 1900–1150 B.C. | ca. 1900 | The Amorite Sheikh Sumuabum founds first dynasty of Babylon; horses introduced; schools founded |
| | 1800–1750 | Hammurabi ascends the throne of Babylon and brings most of Mesopotamia under his control; he introduces his law code; Semiramis is queen of Babylon |
| | ca. 1600 | End of Hammurabi Dynasty marked by Hittite invasions from Turkey; slightly later the Kassites from the Zagros Mountains assume control of Babylon for the next four centuries |

Babylonian

| | ca. 1500 | Bas-relief of baked brick appears as a dominant art form in the Karaindash Temple in Erech |
| | ca. 1350 | In northern Mesopotamia, Assyrian independence is reestablished after the decline of Hurrian power |
| | ca. 1300 | King Kurigalzu of Babylon builds the fortified city of Dur-Kurigalzu dominated by a lofty ziggurat |
| | 1250–1200 | Moses flourishes, leads his people from Egypt |

---

| | | |
|---|---|---|
| **ASSYRIAN**<br>1150–612 B.C. | ca. 1150 | Nebuchadnezzar I expels the Elamites from Babylonia; Babylonians invade Assyria but are routed before reaching Assur; iron is introduced and is used extensively in Assyria for tools and weapons |
| | ca. 1100 | King Tiglath-Pileser I leads Assyria to a new era of power; tribute exacted from Mediterranean coastal cities |
| | 1025–922 | United Kingdom of Israel; Saul reigns |
| | 1000–968 | David reigns in Israel, followed by Solomon the Great (968–937) |
| | ca. 950 | Adadnirari II leads Assyria out of a century and a half of decline to a position of renewed power |
| Assyrian | 922–783 | Two kingdoms in Palestine, Israel and Judah |
| | 884–859 | Assyria's Assurnasirpal II, grandson of Adadnirari, builds a new capital (present-day Nimrud) to replace the old capital of Assur; Assyrian bas-reliefs glorify war and kings |
| | 722–705 | Sargon II enthroned and subdues an empire in revolt and begins the task of building a new capital at Dur-Sharrukin |

| | | |
|---|---|---|
| | 669–627 | Assurbanipal assumes rule of Assyria, governing an empire that extends from the Nile to the Caucasus; period of rich artistry centered at Nineveh |
| **NEO–BABYLONIAN** 612–539 B.C. | 612 | Chaldeans and Iranian Medes overrun Assyria, destroying Nineveh and Assur and establishing the Neo-Babylonian Empire; city of Babylon rebuilt |
| | 605 | Nebuchadnezzar II rules the Neo-Babylonian Empire, builds the "Tower of Babel" and a temple to Marduk; razes Jerusalem and takes Jews into captivity in Babylon |
| | 575 | Ishtar Gate to Babylon completed |
| **PERSIAN** 539–333 B.C. | 539 | Cyrus the Great, Persia's great warrior and statesman, conquers Babylon; takes Egypt in 525 |
| | 499–478 | Persian wars with Greece; rules of Darius and Xerxes; rebuilding of the Temple in Jerusalem; building of the Palace of Persepolis |
| | 333 | Conquest of the Near East by Alexander the Great, complete defeat of the Persian Empire |

Persian

# BACKGROUND

In the extremely fertile valley of the Tigris and Euphrates Rivers, another historic, urban culture developed at about the same time that Egyptian civilization was established. But unlike the valley of the Nile, protected by deserts and the sea, this area was very exposed, and thus the chronicle of history that we call Mesopotamian is filled with rivalries, foreign invasions, and the rapid rise and collapse of political and military power. By virtue of its geography and a very different religious and societal outlook, the art, costume, and customs of this area appear quite different from the Egyptian.

Since stone was very difficult to obtain in the delta area of the Tigris and Euphrates, the early Sumerian culture that developed there built and sculpted in brick and clay rather than stone. Since life after death and the sense of continuity of life in death was not as important here, there was less stress on preserving aspects of the culture in furniture and tomb decoration. This, coupled with the perishability of brick and sculpted clay art and architecture, has led to many fewer artifacts preserved from the ancient past than was the case in Egypt. Also, the geography of the area left it more open to foreign invasion than was Egypt. Thus the history of ancient times is a chaotic and tumultuous record of invasions, wars, changes in political control, and lack of a stable cultural continuity.

Early in the history of Sumeria, the first civilization to rise in the Tigris and Euphrates delta, the major occupation shifted away from sheepherding and agriculture to business and finance. As a result of this shift, very early in the development of written communication the people of the area had devised a complex system of hieroglyphic writing to record financial business transactions. By the time of the promulgation of the Code of Hammurabi (about 1800 B.C.), the development of trade, crafts, bookkeeping, and the granting of credit had been developed to such a high degree that one could label the Babylonians the business experts of the ancient world.

The geography of the area and the materials available to the artists who helped civilization develop in this area influenced the images and shapes of this culture. These basic images and shapes remained, to some extent, throughout all the changes in Mesopotamian cultural development. For example, an early Sumerian statue has the same rounded, cylindrical lines and interest in fringe and fleece that can be found in a more refined and sophisticated manner in an Assyrian figure (Figs. 3-3,6). Even though later art was of stone, not clay, the sense of the rounded forms created by the potter remained, and this made the statuary of Mesopotamia seem in sharp contrast to the angularity of Egyptian forms. The early involvement of this area with sheep and sheepherding also seems to have given the culture a strong identification with fleece as a symbol of virility and fertility. Although the idea was later abstracted into complicated fringe effects, stylized beard and hair curls, and various kinds of shredded ornament and decoration, the basic, underlying textural interest remained, even in the period of the Persian Empire.

Another symbolic image that occurs repeatedly in the cultures that followed one another in the area is the winged bull, sometimes with a human head as on the Sphinx in Egypt (Fig. 3-1). For example, the colossal winged figures which flanked the gateway at the Palace of Khorsabad are still frightening images of power, strength, and virility—metaphors for the power in nature that was worshipped by the Assyrians. The head is the image of an Assyrian king, while the powerful body displays the Mesopotamian interest in rounded and cylindrical shapes that set the art of this region apart from the angularity admired by the Egyptians. The strongly conventionalized beard, hair, and fur are major ornamental accents that had been evident from the beginning of civilization in this area, and one might well say that this image stands for Mesopotamian civilization in the same way that the Sphinx stands for the Egyptian civilization.

portal
in
Khorsabad

(a)

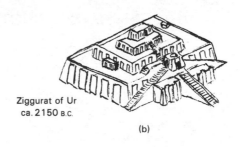

Ziggurat of Ur
ca. 2150 B.C.

(b)

Winged Bull; a guardian of the gate from the Palace of Assurnasirpal II at Khorsabad, modern Nimrud; Metropolitan Museum of Art; ca. 885–860 B.C. Illustrates the Assyrian worship of a bull's strength combined with the intelligence of man. Photo courtesy of the Metropolitan Museum of Art, New York; gift of John D. Rockefeller, Jr., 1932.

(c)
Assyrian stool
and throne

Persian
double-bull
capital

(d)

**FIGURE 3–1**

# THE BASIC COSTUME SILHOUETTE

As might be surmised from the brief preceding discussion about Mesopotamian artistic images, the qualities found in the dress of this area, though they certainly change markedly from Sumerian to Persian times, do have a few constants. There is a heavy emphasis on the spiral draping of great shawls, the cylindrical shape of the long tunics, the heavy use of fringe as ornamentation, and the striking emphasis on carefully curled beards, hair, and mustaches. As might be expected, this is strongly related to the materials and fibers available and admired in clothing and decoration. Where the Egyptians placed great emphasis on the variety of textural effects that could be obtained from linen, the fabric used in the Tigris Euphrates Valley was wool; and because there had been an early emphasis on fleece textures, this rich tactile effect continued to play an ornamental role in the clothing of this area through the use of fringe and the way hair and beards were curled. It was gradually put aside by the Persians, except in their beard and hair effects, in favor of decorative draping taken from the Greeks.

The Bas Relief of Assurbanipal and his Queen, Ashur-Sharrat celebrating the king's victories in the Palace at Nineveh, may be taken as both representative of the major aspects of Assyrian dress and as an image of the major attributes of Mesopotamian clothing (Fig. 3–2). The most striking ornamental element is the curled hair of both the king and queen, with the added strength of the beard on the king. The second point that strikes the viewer is the tight cylindrical line of the tunics and the spiral drape of the shawl on the queen, with its edge accented with fringe. Here it is the tight wraparound effect created in applying fabric to the body that is paramount, with none of the interest in loose draping later admired by the Greeks. All of the ornament seems to be based on a tight circular repeat inside tight borders, and it is quite apparent that there is no difference between the dress of the male and the female except that the woman is without a beard. Even the fans held by the slaves partake of a tight, tufted, woven look that seems related to the early Mesopotamian love of rough weaving and tufted fleece.

# SUMERIAN COSTUME

**Masculine Dress**    The earliest human images from Sumeria, dated around 3000 B.C., show men wearing a wraparound skirt that reaches from the waist to the ankles and hair that already displays a fascination with its decorative possibilities. It is also known that weaving was well developed by this time and that both woolen and linen fabrics were available. A few fragments of linen preserved from this early time are as fine as linens produced today, and needles have also been found that indicate that the sewing of garments was fully developed.

Thus the standard male costume of the early Sumerian period was probably a wraparound skirt reaching to the mid-calf or below, overlapping at the left side toward the back and fastened with three or four ties or toggles and loops. Such skirts were finished off at the bottom edge with fringe or tabs of material which could either be a mere band of decoration or cover over half the length of the skirt. It is assumed that this band of fringe was a separate piece sewn to the skirt. Sometimes the fringe took over the whole skirt and resembled a hula skirt, while at other times there were a series of overlapping triangular petals around the waist with fringe below. Almost all of these skirts were cinched into the waist by a tubular girdle fastened at the back with ends hanging down. The men's hair in this early period was somewhat of a problem since they sometimes were bald and sometimes had long hair, carefully parted and coming forward over the shoulders. Possibly the head was shaved for certain religious rites, and wigs were worn for others. Artwork shows both bearded and beardless men, and it has usually been assumed that the bearded men are the older ones.

Somewhat later than the smooth wrap-

(a)

(b)

designs

(c)

(d)

(e)

various
Hebrew
headdresses

(f)

(g)

(h)
Neo-
Babylonian

(i)
Persian

Assurbanipal Feasting with His Queen in the Royal Garden after the
Defeat of Teumman; British Museum; 660 B.C. Illustrates the interest in
heavily curled beards and hair as well as the interest in fringed trim that
typifies Assyrian dress. Also note the high furniture with symbolic ornament. Photo courtesy of the Hirmer Fotoarchiv, Munich.

(j)
fan

(k)
helmet of
Meskalamidug
ca. 2400 B.C.

(l)
umbrella

(m)
Hebrew
high
priest

(n)

(o)
variations
in high priest
mitres

(p)
levite

(q)
Hebrew
maiden

(r)

FIGURE 3-2

35

**FIG. 3-3** Urnina, King of Lagash, and family; Ur Dynasty I; The Louvre, Paris; ca. 2450 B.C. An example of the tufted or fringed *kaunakes,* which may have started as a fleece skirt but by Sumerian times was a skirt set with rows or tiers of fringe or tufting attached. Photo courtesy of the Department of Antiquités, The Louvre, Paris.

around skirt trimmed in fringe, the controversial *kaunakes* arrived on the scene, probably about 2500 B.C. Originally it was thought that this garment when represented in sculpture indicated a sheepskin wrapped about the body, and that the tiered effect was the sculptor's way of indicating fleece. This now seems most unlikely since sewing, fringing, and weaving were already highly developed by this time. It is much more possible that this tufted, decorative, wraparound skirt was a smoothly woven garment with rows of fringe attached or with tufting set into the base as in shag rugs (Fig. 3-3). In the stele depicting Urnina, King of Lagash, and his family, we also have some of the figures with fringed drapes up over the chest and shoulder. It is impossible to know if this is a separate fringed shawl or some kind of end attached to the skirt. Whatever it is, it already indicates the interest in spiral draping. In all depictions of Sumerian dress, men's feet are without covering.

Several stele from this period also give us images of soldiers who wear the fringed kaunakes, carry shields that cover the body from neck to ankle, and wear closefitting helmets with chin straps. It is assumed that both helmets and shields were of leather. The helmets look as if they had a wig or hair texture built into the actual shape of the helmet (Fig. 3-2k).

**Feminine Dress** The early Sumerian woman's costume seems to have consisted of a shawl which had an end thrown back over the left shoulder while the body was drawn across the front under the right arm, across the back and over the left shoulder, covering the left arm but keeping the right arm completely free. It was usually finished with a simple band and later with a band of fringe. Sometimes there was an allover geometric pattern, of triangles or circles. The hairdressing that went with this simple garment was very complex, with four to six coils or braids worked around the head into a coronet in a variety of ways with gold, ribbons, loops, wires, leaves, and rosettes often added. Wrapped turbans were also used to cover the hair.

After about 2500 B.C., as with the men, we get a much more complicated tiered costume for women; and again we assume that this was a carefully cut and shaped garment with tiers of fringe added. It is thought that the tunic itself had four or five deep layers of fringe, either worked into the original weaving process or added afterward, and that a short shoulder cape was then added. However, in the case of a female suppliant figure from Mari (Fig. 3-4), we appear to have a full-length, tiered cape of fringe. The headdress in this figure appears to be of stiffened fabric, possibly leather, and it

**FIG. 3-4** Figure of a Female Suppliant, Mari; The Louvre, Paris; ca. 2600 B.C. Illustrates female use of a tufted, tiered cape over a tiered *kaunakes*. Note the high, mitrelike hat that later became a standard headdress for the priesthood in ancient Israel. Photo courtesy of the Department of Antiquités, the Louvre, Paris.

represents the beginning of mitrelike head-dresses in this area used for religious services. They culminated in the mitres of the Jewish priests in Israel. As with the men, no footwear was ever shown for women.

Many excellent examples of female jewelry from this period have been discovered. They were made of alabaster, rock crystal, lapis lazuli, carnelian, and gold. These items include earrings, varied hair ornaments, ball necklaces of gold and precious stones, animal pendants, and even remnants of a shoulder cape composed of strands of beads.

## BABYLONIAN COSTUMES

***Masculine Dress*** Around 2399 B.C. the Sumerian Period actually came to a close to be replaced by the cultural dominance of two city-states—first Lagash, then Akkad. One famous and outstanding figure of whom we have several statues is Gudea of Lagash, whose costume invariably consists of a tight-fitting tubular tunic and a fringed shawl draped in a spiraling line under the right arm and over the left shoulder. His distinctive headdress, a short cylindrical crown, appears to have been made of sheepskin set tightly with small gold rings or disks (Fig. 3-2r).

After a further period of decline in the power of the city-states of the Tigris-Euphrates Basin, a new dynastic development took place around 1900 B.C. at the city of Babylon. Its first great ruler was the great Hammurabi, and his dress is the same as that seen earlier on statues of Gudea. In a bas-relief from the top of the column on which the famed Code of Hammurabi is inscribed, we see Hammurabi before the Sun God Shamash (Fig. 3-5). He has a plain helmet cap or headdress and faces an image of the god dressed in a tiered garment of many spiral folds, elaborately curled, with a square beard halfway down the chest. His headdress already has the truncated funnel shape and spiraling grooves that will later be used by the Assyrians in their great winged human-headed bulls at Khorsabad (Fig. 3-1).

FIG. 3-5 Hammurabi before the Sun God Shamash; The Louvre, Paris; 1790–1750 B.C. Here the god wears a tiered garment of fringe that appears to cover from ankle to shoulder in a spiral. It is probably a skirt and shawl combination. Note that the headdress or tiara is also tiered upward in a spiral and that Hammurabi is draped in a shawl and wears a half-spherical bronze helmet. Photo courtesy of the Department of Antiquités, The Louvre, Paris.

**Feminine Dress** The information on women's dress of this period is limited to that available in depictions of various goddesses. Some wear the tiered, spiral decoration seen on the male gods, with many colored yarns evidently used in the weaving; others wear kimono-cut bodices with short sleeves, fitted about the torso and merging into a slim sheath skirt. Hair is abundant and carefully curled, and various exotic religious headdresses similar to those worn by the male gods are shown.

## ASSYRIAN COSTUME

By the middle of the fourteenth century B.C. a power rose in the rocky north of Mesopotamia which was to dominate the Near East from Persia to the Mediterranean and from Turkey to Egypt by the seventh century B.C. These were the Assyrians—fierce, warlike, ostentatious, and cruel. If the Babylonians had been the civilizing, cultural power in the area, the Assyrians were the fighting, military presence. They had a heavy-handed masculine mystique, and female figures were only very occasionally represented in the vast architectural and artistic remains that they left at great centers like Nimrud, Khorsabad, and Nineveh.

**Masculine Dress** Though the basic shape of the cylindrical, fringed tunic wrapped with the great spirals of a fringed shawl seem similar to the late Sumerian and Babylonian dress, the amount of ostentatious decoration is quite different. Tunics have allover woven geometric patterns of embroidery, the fringe is thicker and richer than ever before, and there is great stress on metal and jeweled armlets, earrings, gold collars and rings, while beards and hair are curled and cultivated as never before as a symbol of physical animal power. In the statue of Assurnasirpal II (883–859 B.C.) in the British Museum (Fig. 3-6), the king is dressed for a religious ceremony. He wears a tight-fitting tubular tunic fringed at the bottom, and over it a fringed shawl, one end of which is caught by a strap or cord to the belt or girdle at the right side of the waist. The remainder of the shawl is

FIG. 3-6 King Ashurbanipal (Assurnasirpal) II, from Nimrud; British Museum; ca. 883-859 B.C. This warlike figure with heavily curled hair and fringed shawl is an excellent image of the hairdressing and clothing worn by the Assyrians during the height of their power. Reproduced by courtesy of the Trustees of the British Museum.

FIG. 3-7 Relief from the First Assyrian Empire; from Nimrud; British Museum; ca. 885-856 B.C. To the left there is a priest who wears the priest's apron fastened by knotted cords, the fringed scarf or shawl, and ankle-length fringed skirt. The enthroned king has a spiked tiara, fringed cloak, fringed tunic, and sandals. Reproduced by courtesy of the Trustees of the British Museum.

folded so that there are two unequal tiers of fringe. It is then drawn across the back, over the left arm, across the front, under the right arm across the back of the waist, and then tucked into the belt or girdle on the left side.

In an Assyrian Empire bas-relief from Nimrud, now in the British Museum (Fig. 3-7), there is another depiction of Assurnasirpal with attendants and a priest. The king wears the same heavily fringed tunic and shawl with the famous truncated cone with spike on top—a kind of trademark of Assyrian royalty. His beard, like the priest's, is heavy and richly curled, and the priest is dressed with the wings

of the gods. He is carrying a pail and pine cone and is about to anoint the king with the juice of Enurta in a fertility ritual. The priest has a headdress with bullock's horns in front, and he wears the priestly apron over a short fringed shirt as well as the fringed scarf or small shawl that belongs to his position. The unbearded attendants with fly whisks may be eunuchs who are also dressed in fringed tunics. All the figures wear simple leather sandals strapped over the feet.

In a number of warlike scenes from various bas-reliefs we can see that the dress of the Assyrian warrior consisted of a knee-length fringed tunic, a decorative baldric, laced leather boots or leggings to the knee, and a peaked metal helmet with earflaps (Fig. 3-8, bottom). A coat of mail made of overlapping metal discs or scales was also often used over the tunic.

**Feminine Dress** There are few depictions of women, since their status was very low in the society and they were the property first of their fathers and then of their husbands. One rare image is that of Ashur-Sharrat, wife of Assur-

banipal in a bas-relief from the British Museum (Fig. 3–2). She wears a fringed tunic similar to the one worn by her husband, except that it has longer sleeves. She is draped in a fringed shawl that leaves the right arm free and wears a kind of carved gold dog collar, bulky earrings and bracelets, and a jeweled coronet over her carefully curled hair. Her low shoes are more like Indian moccasins than like the sandals worn by the men.

## HEBREW COSTUME

It is during the brief period of the resurgence of power in the rebuilt city of Babylon, following the fall of the Assyrian Empire, that we come upon references to and depictions of the Hebrews at the time that Nebuchadnezzar II razed the temple in Jerusalem and took the Jews into captivity. We do not have many original visual sources on which to base clothing information; but in the late nineteenth century, James Tissot, an artist living in the Holy Land studying Babylonian and other foreign artistic representations and Biblical references, composed an illustrated Bible that is still an invaluable source of information.

**Masculine Dress**  The major difference from the costume lines already seen as basic to the various civilizations of the Tigris-Euphrates Valley is that Hebrew costume has the large, enveloping draperies still found among the desert peoples of Arabia, Morocco, and Algeria. This use of full, flowing garments protects the head and body from the fierce heat of the sun and the penetration of blowing sands.

In early periods the loincloth was frequently the sole garment; later it was merely an undergarment. After the Hebrews' return from Babylonian captivity, there were references to breeches of fine linen, possibly similar to the trousers worn by the Persians. Fringed tunics were also worn, sometimes a wide, open-sleeved wool tunic over a longer and tighter-sleeved linen one. An even more distinctive garment was the wide-sleeved tunic, open down the front like a coat, known as a *caftan*. A good example of this can be seen in a bas-relief from Astartu of Hebrew-dressed prisoners (Fig. 3–8, top). When this garment had wider bell-shaped sleeves and was cut on fuller lines, it was known as the *aba* and can still be seen in the Near East today. The standard, Mesopotamian fringed shawl was also often used in Palestine (Fig. 3–2). This fringed shawl was gradually made into a ritual garment by the Hebrews and remains the basis of the Jewish prayer shawl to this day.

Ecclesiastical garments for the under priests, or Levites, consisted of the linen breeches similar to those worn by the Persians and a soft linen tunic with wrist-length sleeves and an ankle-length skirt. It was wrapped with an embroidered ribbon in the ritual colors of blue, purple, and scarlet and was started like a stole across the back of the neck, then brought across the front to form a V, and finally wrapped four times about the waist, the final ends hanging to the ankle at the front (Fig. 3–2p). About eight yards of ribbon, three inches wide, were needed. The Levites also wore white linen caps that rose to a slight peak similar to those worn by the prisoners in the Assyrian bas-relief (Fig. 3–8, top).

The high priest wore over his soft linen tunic a knee-length narrow robe in a deep blue or violet. It was embroidered all the way around the hem in blue, purple, and scarlet with little gold bells added in a set pattern. Over the robe went the *ephod,* a kind of scapular or sandwich board made of two rectangles of about 30 inches by 10 inches and fastened by straps on the shoulders. Over it, around the waist, was wrapped the same ribboned girding worn by the Levites. On the chest was worn the purse or breastplate of judgment—a nine-inch double rectangle made like a purse and decorated with

rows of jewels representing the twelve tribes of Israel. It was fastened to the ephod and the girdle by gold chains (Fig. 3–2m). As for the head, it was crowned with a mitre that was basically the same shape as the Levite cap but much exaggerated. On its front was a gold plate engraved in Hebrew that said, ''Holiness to the Lord.'' There were variations to this mitre, but it established a general character that is still seen in Catholic bishops' mitres to this day (Fig. 3–2m,n,o).

**Feminine Dress** Women always wore headcoverings of some sort over their carefully braided hair, and these varied from pointed to flat caps and earcoverings variously trimmed in sequins. Large shawls were often further draped over the headcoverings as a protection from wind and sun. The body was usually covered by a slim, almost sleeveless tunic, and over this was a wide open gown with bell sleeves like the male aba that was worn for outdoors (Fig. 3–2q). This tendency toward swathing the body in voluminous flowing garments increased as Hebrew history merged into New Testament times.

# PERSIAN COSTUME

After the short-lived Neo-Babylonian resurgence of culture and power, the next great empire was the Persian, led by the fiery Cyrus the Great who conquered Babylonia, Media, and Lydia in 539 B.C. The later rulers of this new Achaemenid Dynasty, Xerxes and Darius, are well known to us primarily through their conflict with the Greeks at Marathon and Salamis and through the ruins of their great palace at Persepolis.

**Masculine Dress** It is from the great royal processions carved on the stairway of the palace at Persepolis that we gain most of our information about Persian dress. In depictions of the rulers, we see that the Persians adopted the flowing robe in a kimono cut that is similar to the Egyptian robe and the one that we know was worn by the Medians (Fig. 3–9). This robe is made of two rectangles of cloth closed only from

waist to hem with the centered fullness held by a sash. The ruler on the north side of the Apadana Stairway at Persepolis wears a fluted helmet, or *toque,* that is striking only in that it flares in an opposite direction from those of the Assyrians. Also (and this is an important point in distinguishing Persians from Assyrians), the beards in this group are all pointed rather than square, as had been the case with Assyrians and Babylonians.

But the major new contribution of the Persians came in the return to almost fitted garments from the draped, pleated, and wraparound effects that had dominated in Egypt and Mesopotamia until this time. The Persians, coming from the rugged and mountainous northeast, probably originally devised clothing of skins that hugged the legs and body. This finally evolved into a kind of closefitting tailoring that produced tight-fitting tunics, trousers, and

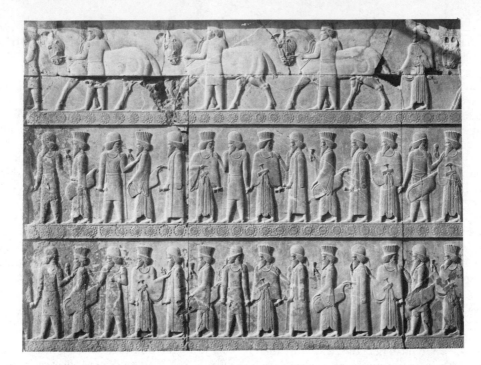

**FIG. 3-9** Detail of a Royal Procession; from the stairway to the Royal Audience Hall, Persepolis; ca. 500 B.C. Illustrates both the Persian use of Greek-influenced draping in the loose robe, or *candys,* and the close-fitting, sleeved coats and long trousers brought by the Persians from the East. Photo courtesy of the Oriental Institute, University of Chicago.

coats. In the figures on the left and right of the Apadana Stairway we can see the tubular nature of the trousers, the fitted character of the tunic, and the nature of a coat worn draped over the shoulders.

The Persians had a variety of headdresses, but the stiff domed caps, sometimes with a point, are the most typical (Fig. 3-2i). Even their helmets had this domical shape, with the addition of ear and cheek plates and a panel at the back to protect the neck. Shoes were like soft, form-fitting boots to the ankle.

**Feminine Dress** There is even less information on women's dress than was the case with the Assyrians, but from one or two statues and reliefs we get a very modern silhouette that is slightly like that of the Minoan Greek (see Fig. 4-3). There was evidently a fitted bodice and skirt trimmed in deep fringe and sometimes sequins, or a slim tunic and shawl trimmed in fringe. Whichever line was worn, the emphasis was on a slim figure with a fitted look, with only the shawl giving a drapery accent. The hair could be either in short curls held by a fillet or elaborately dressed with a chignon at the back of the neck and a fillet to hold in the coiffure. Feet were either completely uncovered or sheathed in soft, moccasinlike shoes.

# FABRICS

Woolens, linens, and dressed leathers were the major fabrics, with great emphasis placed on the use of wool fringe. There was also some use of luxuriant silks for the court dress of rulers, particularly during the famed Neo-Babylonian period that marked the famous Babylonian captivity of the Hebrews.

# ARTS AND ARTIFACTS

The architecture of this area was as heavy and monolithic as the Egyptian, but it utilized the arch as a major element of structure (Fig. 3-1a). Glazed brick, along with stone, was an important building material, and the motifs worked into columns and arches included the lotus, the palm, the rosette, and particularly winged lions and bulls. (Fig. 3-1d and 3-2a,b,c). Furniture was heavy but simple in line with great use of inlaid metals, ivory trim, and painted and carved decoration. Thrones were high and invariably accompanied by a footstool (Fig. 3-1c), and the seated figure could eat from or lay things on several accompanying small tables.

Military accessories included large swords worn on a diagonal shoulder baldric, daggers thrust into the belt, bows and quivers of arrows, javelins, and shields that could be flat and round, long and rectangular, or convex and round, scooped out at the sides. Personal accessories included the mace with its ornamental knob, the umbrella, or parasol, carried by servants for royal ladies, mirrors, handsomely carved ivory combs, walking sticks for Persian royalty, and the fly whisks shown being manipulated by many servants to keep insects away from seated royalty (Fig. 3-2j,l). Household accessories included tablets and stylus, jugs and basins, and musical instruments like the harp.

Hebrew accessories included the *phylacteries,* or narrow bands of parchment containing sacred writings bound to forehead and wrist; the famous religious scrolls; and the famous ram's horn. Other musical instruments included cymbals, the taboret or small drum, the tambourine, and the harp.

## VISUAL SOURCES

Once again the primary visual sources are from statues, bas-reliefs, and architectural decoration, and these come from the great centers of Nineveh, Khorsabad, Babylon, Persepolis, Susa, Lagash, and Tello. The major repositories for these remains today are the British Museum, the Louvre, Persepolis, the Berlin Museum, and the Oriental Museum of Chicago. For Hebrew costume the best source is a copy of the Bible with carefully researched illustrations by James Tissot. Another written source that is useful is Mary Houston's *Ancient Egyptian, Mesopotamian and Persian Costume.*

## SUMMARY

The major image that we retain after a survey of the clothing of this area through many changes of culture is that of heavily draped figures, richly accented with fringe and fleecelike decoration with the addition by the Persians of fitted coats and trousers. In every way it is heavier, less sophisticated and subtly ordered than that of the Egyptian, and it uses rounded and cylindrical forms rather than angular, blocklike shapes. Never does Mesopotamian dress reach the fascinating level of symbolic abstraction achieved by the Egyptians, and the colors of this area are far more earthy and lack the clarity and subtlety of the colors found in the tombs of the pharaohs. Always there is a dusty feeling to the coloration that never appears in the absolutely distilled clarity of Egyptian hues.

Whereas the Egyptians seem to have risen above the animal and human level of existence in their art and clothing, the cultures of Mesopotamia seem to build upon the earthy and animal characteristics of human beings to achieve triumphant images of strength and power. Nothing could make this clearer than comparing the clean-shaven face of the Egyptian adorned occasionally by an abstract, symbolic beard with the heavily curled and cultivated animal fleece beards and hair of the Mesopotamians.

# chapter *IV*

# Ancient Greece

## Chronology
### (2800–146 B.C.)

| | | |
|---|---|---|
| **MINOAN CIVILIZATION** ca. 2800–1400 B.C. | ca. 2800 | Date usually set for the beginning of civilization in the Aegean |
| | ca. 2000 | Start of the Palace at Knossos |
| | ca. 1700–1500 | Flowering of Minoan civilization; introduction of the tunic (*chiton*) from Babylonia |
| | ca. 1600 | Various statues of snake goddesses |
| | ca. 1450 | Destruction of the palaces by earthquake |

Minoan

| | | |
|---|---|---|
| **MYCENAEAN CIVILIZATION** ca. 1700–1100 B.C. | ca. 1700 | Shaft graves at Mycenae |
| | ca. 1500 | The Vaphio cups; gradual domination of Crete |
| | ca. 1300 | The treasury of Atreus and Lion Gate of Mycenae |
| | ca. 1200 | The Warrior Vase; the Dorians invade Greece and begin destruction of Mycenaean civilization |

| | | |
|---|---|---|
| Mycenaean | ca. 1130 | Iron comes into general use for weapons and tools |
| DARK AGES ca. 1200–800 B.C. | ca. 1100 | Greeks begin the colonization of the Ionian coast of Asia Minor |
| HELLENIC–ARCHAIC PERIOD ca. 800–480 B.C. | ca. 776 | First Olympic Games are held |
| | ca. 750 | Greek colonies are begun in Italy |
| | ca. 750–700 | Homer's epics, the *Iliad* and the *Odyssey*, are set down; Amos and Isaiah, prophets in Israel |
| | ca. 705 | Greek architects begin building in stone |
| | ca. 700 | Athens combines with the towns of Attica to form a single political unit |
| | ca. 683 | An aristocratic republic is established in Athens, ruled by archons elected for one-year terms |
| | ca. 650 | Large free-standing sculpture is developed |
| | ca. 600 | The use of coined money spreads on the Greek mainland; Attic black-figure pottery is developed; lyric poetry reaches its height under Sappho on the island of Lesbos |
| | 594 | Solon initiates social and constitutional reforms in Athens |

| | | |
|---|---|---|
| Archaic | ca. 580 | Philosophy and science begin with the teachings of Thales and Anaximander |
| | 561 | The tyrant Peisistratus seizes power in Athens |
| | ca. 550 | Doric architecture is standardized, and Ionic influences appear in mainland Greece and the West |
| | 539 | Cyrus the Persian conquers Babylonia |
| | ca. 534 | Thespis, the first actor and reputed founder of Greek tragedy, wins first place in Athens' drama festival |
| | 520 | Persia completes its domination of Ionia |
| | ca. 525 | Attic red-figured pottery is developed |
| | 507 | Athenian democracy is restored and broadened by Cleisthenes |
| | 499 | Ionian Greeks rebel against Persian rule |
| | 490 | Darius of Persia launches an attack on the Greek mainland, starting the Persian Wars, but is repelled at the Battle of Marathon |
| | 484 | Aeschylus achieves his first victory at the Athens' drama festival |
| | 480 | The Greeks are crushed at Thermopylae, the Acropolis is destroyed by the Persians, but they, in turn, are defeated at Salamis |

| | | |
|---|---|---|
| HELLENIC-CLASSICAL PERIOD 480–400 B.C. | ca. 480–445 | The sculptor Myron is at work in Athens |
| | 478–447 | Athens leads in the formation of the Delian League of Greek states |
| | 468 | The dramatist Sophocles introduces the use of the third actor in Greek tragedy, and the first contest between Sophocles and Aeschylus is won by Sophocles |

| | | |
|---|---|---|
| | 462–461 | Pericles brings democratic reforms to Athens, while the rivalry between Athens and Sparta increases |
| | 458 | *The Oresteia* is produced |
| | 455 | Temple of Zeus at Olympia is completed; Euripides' first tragedy is performed |
| Classical | 454–453 | Treasury of the Delian League is moved to Athens, demonstrating Athenian dominance |
| | 447 | Parthenon begun under Ictinus and Callicrates; Athenian defeat at Coronea begins the decline of the Athenian Empire |
| | ca. 435–405 | Cotton used in clothing along with wool and linen |
| | 431 | The Peloponnesian War begins; Euripides' *Medea* is produced |
| | ca. 430 | *Oedipus Rex* is produced |
| | 413 | The naval battle at Syracuse ends in the defeat of Athens; Euripides' *Electra* is produced |
| | 404 | Athens surrenders to Sparta |

| | | |
|---|---|---|
| HELLENIC–POST OR LATE-CLASSICAL PERIOD 400–323 B.C. | 399 | Socrates is tried and condemned to death, commits suicide by drinking the hemlock |
| | ca. 385 | Plato starts teaching at Athens |
| | 371 | Sparta is defeated by its former ally, Thebes |
| | 359 | Philip II takes the throne of Macedonia and begins the expansion of his realm |
| | ca. 350 | The sculptor Praxiteles at the height of his power; Mausoleum at Halicarnassus built with frieze by Scopas. |
| | 338 | Philip of Macedonia defeats Athens and becomes the supreme power in Greece |

| | | |
|---|---|---|
| | 336 | Philip is assassinated and succeeded by his son, Alexander; Aristotle teaches at his newly founded school in Athens |
| | 334 | Alexander launches a great expedition against the Persians |
| | 330 | Alexander enters Persepolis and, with the total defeat of the Persians, moves into Asia; statues of Aeschylus, Sophocles, and Euripides are erected in the new Theater of Dionysus in Athens; silk fabric introduced to the Mediterranean world |
| | 323 | Alexander dies in Babylon, and his successors carve up his massive empire |
| HELLENISTIC PERIOD 323–146 B.C. | 241–197 | Attalus I ruled as King of Pergamon; defeated the Gauls in Galatia; erected a monument to this victory; patron of first school of Pergamene sculpture |
| | 197–159 | Eumenes II, King of Pergamon, brought kingdom to its zenith; founded the famous Library of Pergamon and commissioned the Altar of Zeus |
| | ca. 150–100 | *Aphrodite of Melos; Old Market Woman* |
| | 146 | Corinth burned and its treasures carried off to Rome |
| | ca. 100 | *The Laocoön* |

# BACKGROUND

When Homer wrote about the power and grandeur of the Greek hosts deployed against the Trojans, he listed soldiers from a great list of places like Athens, Argos, Tiryns, Corinth, Knossos in Crete, and many other places until the entire geography of the western side of the Aegean Sea had been listed. For centuries some of these places were thought to be figments of his mythical imagination. In the late nineteenth century, however, Heinrich Schliemann began excavations on the site of what he thought must have been Troy and found exact remains of the city of legend. Later he launched excavations at Tiryns and Mycenae on the Greek mainland,

and there his discoveries were even more startling. Fortress-palaces, tombs, jewelry, weapons, and sculpture proved convincingly that there had been a flourishing Bronze Age civilization in and around Mycenae from which the Trojan Wars of legend had indeed been launched. Somewhat later Sir Arthur Evans uncovered the Palace of Knossos on the island of Crete that documented the famous legend of King Minos and the Minotaur and uncovered an earlier, highly developed civilization in the unfortified palaces of the sea kings of ancient Crete.

From these excavations it became clear that the Mycenaeans on the mainland of Greece conquered and dominated the earlier Minoan civilization on the island of Crete, only to be overwhelmed in turn by invading Dorians from Macedonia and the Balkans sometime around 1100 B.C. These new invaders learned much from the inhabitants whom they conquered as well as from the Egyptians and the nations of Asia Minor, and gradually they built a civilization unlike any that had existed to date.

Many of the Greeks of the mainland were driven by the Dorians to the coast of Asia Minor, and there thus developed two strands of Greek Archaic culture—Dorian and Ionian. Between 776 and 480 B.C.—that is, between the first Olympic Games and the close of the Persian Wars—Archaic Greek culture developed along lines that were to produce a totally new kind of civilization during the later fifth century B.C. In Egyptian and Mesopotamian culture the arts were official or religious, with little place for individual initiative, whereas in Greek culture, organized around a series of small city-states, both religion and government officialdom were mere extensions of individual human attitudes and ideas. Individual achievements were at the center of Greek life, organized around the good of the individual in the community. This Greek sense of individualism is most apparent in the arts. For example, when a Greek artist or architect began something, he or she would see it to its conclusion as his or her individual, creative contribution to the community culture. Moreover, the work of art was always complete within itself; any changes or additions would alter its basic character. This is certainly the case with the famous Parthenon, as with the other famous buildings on the Acropolis in Athens (Fig. 4–1). This concept is totally different from that followed in Egypt and Mesopotamia where temples, palaces, and sculptural friezes were done by anonymous artisans over many decades.

This individual character in art led to great unity in the design of temples, statuary, paintings, and literature, but it also led to variety since unity to the Greeks meant avoidance of monotony and dull repetition. In the Parthenon there are subtle differences in different parts of the structure, so that it has the alive sense of the human body. Force and counterforce are so carefully proportioned that an effect of perfect equilibrium is achieved. And this is accomplished by enlarging corner columns, making the distance between columns subtly change, and by actually bending the base platform. The Parthenon is both a balanced harmony of shapes of varying size and an integration of harmoniously balanced forces (Fig. 4–1).

This sense of balance was at the heart of all aspects of Greek culture including religion, philosophy, and drama, and the Greeks had a deep-seated belief that a failure to do honor to any part of nature could lead to destruction. The two great areas of life—the emotional, irrational, instinctive, physical, procreative on the one side, and the intellectual, organizational, rational on the other—were symbolized by the gods, Dionysus and Apollo; and thus fifth-century art, literature, and drama were devoted to maintaining an integrated balance between the two. Even in fifth-century politics and social development, there was always a drive to balance aristocratic organization with democratic individualism, as illustrated in the central argument of Sophocles' *Antigone* in which the organization and power of the state are pitted against the need for individual human freedom. When individualism and particularism began to take precedence over balance in the fourth century, classical balance began to falter. The end result was an excess of Hellenistic art and culture in which theatricality, melodrama, excess realistic detail, and decorative display overwhelmed the simplicity and balance of the Golden Age.

(a)
chair

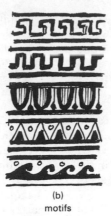

(b)
motifs

Doric       Ionian

Corinthian
(c)

View of the Acropolis, Athens. Illustrates how ancient Athens grew up around the fortified hill, or *acra,* that became the site of its most sacred temples. It had as its centerpiece the Parthenon, whose subtle classical architecture balances highly sophisticated proportions with simple natural forms. Photo courtesy of the Hirmer Fotoarchiv, Munich.

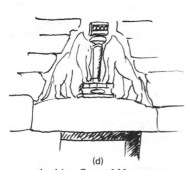

(d)
the Lion Gate of Mycenae

(e)
the
Parthenon

the Mausoleum of Halicarnassus
(f)

FIGURE 4–1

50

# THE BASIC COSTUME SILHOUETTE

There were basically four distinct costume silhouettes in the development of Greek clothing from Minoan times to the Hellenistic: Cretan-Minoan, Mycenaean, Archaic, and Classical-Hellenistic. Minoan costume made itself felt primarily through the images of the snake goddesses with their artificial silhouette, fitted lines, and exaggerated presentation of the female form (Fig. 4–3). The costume seems only vaguely related to certain Mesopotamian female images and hardly at all to the Egyptian, particularly since the effect was playful, sophisticated, and artificial with none of the dignity, grandeur, and strength found in human images from Mesopotamia and Egypt. The Minoans appeared to have had no interest in the folds of draped fabric, and the pinched waistline, exposed breasts, tiered skirts, and serpentine hair curls have an almost modern look, as if late Victorian dress were being parodied in a whimsical comedy. Even the early nude images of males have the same pinched waist and serpentine curled hair, and the overall image that remains of this culture is that of a sophisticated, playful, fun-loving people more interested in enjoying life than in expanding power over others or in documenting their strength as a culture.

Mycenaean dress, though much of it was borrowed from the Minoan, had a character that is summed up by the figures on the famous Warrior Vase from Mycenae (Fig. 4–4). The image is very barbaric with a great use of leather, thongs, fringe, horns, and heavy metal—all attributes of modern motorcycle garb. Despite more sophisticated female images that show great borrowings from female Minoan costume, the barbaric image seems to be the correct one when we look at the cavelike tunnels of the Palace of Tiryns and the heavy stone construction of the Lion Gate of Mycenae.

Archaic Greek clothing, because of the spread of Greek culture to Ionia in Asia Minor, reflected the tunic and shawl usage of Mesopotamian dress and its oriental-geometric border ornamentation. But it differed, as in the case of Archaic Greek art, in the symmetrical, geometric, structured control of the costume line. The stress on the square nature of the overfold on the *Doric chiton,* on the long rectangular line of the chiton proper, and the tight geometric nature of the border decorations —all of these emphasized the fact the clothing was meant to frame and shape the human body in a very simple but controlled manner (Fig. 4–5).

At the opening of the Classical Period, the change in clothing ideals was striking. Instead

FIG. 4–2 Priest-King from Knossus; Late Minoan; Palace of Minos, Knossus; ca. 1500–1450 B.C. This priest-king wears an iris crown with three feathers, a red and white rolled girdle that cinches the waist, and a short loin skirt probably of leather. Taken from Evans, *The Palace of Minos,* Vol. II, Part II.

(a)
Petsofa figurine
ca. 2000–1850 B.C.

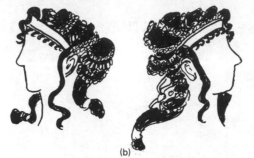

(b)
hairdos from Ladies in Blue
fresco, Palace of Minos 1700–1500 B.C.

(c)
drawn
from Procession
fresco, Palace of Minos
ca. 1450–1375 B.C.

(e)
Minoan
motifs

(f)
Minoan
male slipper
shoe

Snake Goddess; fertility symbol from the Archaeological Museum, Heraklion; ca. 1600 B.C. Illustrates the tight-fitting bodice with breast exposed, narrow waist, sacred apron, and tiered cylindrical skirt that typified upper-class female dress on the island of Crete during the height of Minoan culture. Photo courtesy of the Hirmer Fotoarchiv, Munich.

(d)
figure from a sarcophagus,
Hagia Triada, Crete, ca. 1400 B.C.

FIGURE 4–3

52

**FIG. 4-4** The Warrior Vase; from Mycenae; National Museum, Athens; ca. 1200 B.C. An image of what the Mycenaean soldiers, who went to reclaim Helen of Troy, may have looked like in their skins, furs, and studded helmets. Photo courtesy of the Hirmer Fotoarchiv, Munich.

of structured formality, a great stress was placed on soft fabric draping in beautiful, natural folds over the human body. Cutting and sewing were simplified or eliminated in favor of complete draping from points of accent created by simple pins or wrapped cording. Since the sewing of fabric tends to stiffen it and limit its easy natural flow, the ultimate ideal during the Classical Period (not always fully practiced) was to forego all sewing and to stress the grace and controlled beauty of natural body movement, which was supported and enhanced by the soft flow of finely woven linens and woolens over the body. The ultimate in this ideal was the so-called wet drapery effect found on figures taken from the Parthenon. Whether garments were ever actually wetted down or not, this soft flow of nearly transparent fabric that shows the natural beauty of the body as completely as possible without inhibition or constriction was a cultural ideal (Figs. 4-8, 10). Even in the short tunics, or *chitons,* worn by the men, there was this same stress on the beauty of the draped line enhancing and underlining

grace and freedom in movement. Even the draped shawl, or *himation,* derived from the Near East was draped for easy, relaxed movement rather than being tightly wrapped as in Mesopotamia. The Greeks created a stylization of fabric on the human body so subtle that the real and the ideal seem identical.

But this ideal of beauty in draping joined to beauty in movement could not last. With the decline of classical balance in all the arts in the fourth century and after, bodies were swathed in rumpled draperies that hid the lines of the body in thick, twisted folds of fabric (Fig. 4-11). With the coming of the Hellenistic Age after the death of Alexander the Great, renewed contact was established with the East, and simplicity and natural beauty in dress gave way to oriental embroidery, rich metallic decoration, and great variety in cut and ornament. Individuality and richness were the ideal, and garments were once again cut and sewn, and these T-shaped tunics, though easier to wear, hid the movement of the human body. Greek classical dress emphasized every movement

(a)
drape of
the chlamys

basic
wearing
diagram
for
the Doric
chiton

(b)

(c)
hairdressings

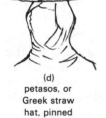

(d)
petasos, or
Greek straw
hat, pinned
over a wrapped
himation

Scene from the Francois Vase; Archaeological Museum, Florence; ca. 575 B.C. Depicts the Archaic version of the Doric *peplos* with its overfold to above the waist and the pinning of back over front at the shoulder. From Fürtwangler and Reichhold, *Griechische Vasenmalerei.*

(h)
sandal

(e)
drape of the Ionic chiton

(f)
Phrygian
bonnet

(g)
one form
of draping the
himation

**FIGURE 4-5**

54

and gesture through constantly shifting folds of soft fabric, and in its simplicity, lucidity, and beauty underlined the difference between movement and repose. Hellenistic dress em-phasized individuality, position, and personal display and appropriately complemented the mercantile capitalist culture of the time that was soon to be dominated by Rome.

# MINOAN COSTUME

**Masculine Dress**  The earliest images of the male figure date from the middle Minoan Period (around 2000 B.C.) and show a simple, stiff apron-cloth with a pinched-in waist secured by a tight girdle that could also support a scabbard and sword. One of the best preserved male images is that of a priest-king from the late Minoan Period, 1500–1450 B.C. (Fig. 4–2). His fairly elaborate headdress consists of an iris crown sporting three feathers of rose, purple, and blue. He has two necklaces, one with a lily motif, and a blue loincloth with a tight, rolled, blue girdle at the waist, worn in conjunction with a white apron lined in red, which has been reduced to a flap at the rear. Ridged lines on the right thigh suggest that this figure wears a kind of sash in conjunction with the costume.

Another garment that developed in the middle Minoan Period was the loin skirt or decorated, bordered fabric worn with a wide, cinched-in belt, probably of metal. By the late Minoan Period (c. 1550–1450 B.C.), this had lengthened so that it reached to the mid-thighs on the sides while dipping down in front where it was weighted with a heavy, beaded tassel, all somewhat reminiscent of the Egyptian focus on the genital area. These skirts were usually brightly decorated in tight geometric patterns (Fig. 4–3c.).

Usually the men's hair, by the late Minoan Period, was worn in long, wavy strands held by a fillet, or occasionally caught into a beretlike cap. Footwear seems to have consisted of soft patterned moccasin-socks, sometimes worn under thonged sandals (Fig. 4–3f).

**Feminine Dress**  The female figure was dressed in the typical bell-shaped skirt as early as 2000 B.C., and there is strong reason to believe that this shape developed from a stiff shawl that was originally wrapped around the body and girdled at the waist. The stiffness of this garment would have made it frame the head like a collar, while it covered the arms and left the busts open to view. There is a figurine from Petsofa dated anywhere from 2000 to 1850 B.C. that combines these characteristics with a peaked headdress that is as sophisticated as a *hennin* of the late medieval period (Fig. 4–3a).

By the late middle Minoan Period (c. 1700–1550 B.C.), the distinctive female form, that everyone remembers from seeing reproductions of snake goddess figurines, was fully developed. The very tight-fitting bodice had sleeves that reached almost to the elbow, and the front opening was tightly laced together below the breasts in such a way as to frame and project them. The waist was very tightly cinched in to what seems almost inhuman narrowness by various girdle styles, usually with a rolled or twisted effect at top and bottom. The stiff, conical, gored skirts were sometimes composed of a series of tiers; at other times they were merely tightly patterned in colorful geometric decoration, and usually were surmounted by a stiff apron that fell both to the front and back of the figure (Fig. 4–3).

Somewhat less shaped garments that gave further variety are illustrated in a ritual procession painted on a sarcophagus from Hagia Triada that is dated about 1400 B.C. The lady pouring a libation has the tight, fashionable bodice but is wearing a skirt of fur with a curved bottom edge, front and back. The two figures following her wear the usual tight bodice with flared skirt that carries a wide, vertical band down the front, making the figures appear quite different from the female forms seen in the snake goddess figurines (Fig. 4–3d).

In addition to interesting mitre, dish, and conical headdresses, the hairdressing of Minoan ladies was evidently also very sophisticated—curled in long wavy strands and then bunched into fascinating shapes with ropes of pearls and other gems and held by gold filigree fillets or coronets (Fig. 4–3b). Female feet, when seen, seem to be bare.

# MYCENAEAN COSTUME

***Masculine Dress*** Although Mycenaean dress was much influenced by the Minoan, since the Island of Crete appears to have been under Mycenaean domination after 1450 B.C., it did have some major differences, particularly in the male dress. Because of rougher terrain and a slightly colder climate, the use of the tunic was preferred to the loin skirt, and the legs were often protected in some way to the knees. However, there are examples of men hunting in almost exactly the same girdle and loincloth garments seen in Crete.

The best image of male costume from Mycenae happens to be that of warriors who appear in procession on the famous Warrior Vase in the National Museum at Athens, dated about 1200 B.C. They wear fringed tunics with long sleeves, probably made of leather. They seem to have tight leather hose or leggings gartered above the knee and tightly wrapped sandals to the ankle. The colander-shaped helmets are studded with metal nails, or bosses, and have boars' tusks and animal tails, while the spears also carry a pendant animal tail or leather pouch. Unlike the Minoan male, the men are all bearded, and the entire image is quite barbaric compared to that of the sophisticated Minoan male figure (Fig. 4–4). This is probably the image presented by the Mycenaean Greeks when they traveled to Troy to rescue Helen.

***Feminine Dress*** The few images of women that we have from Tiryns and Mycenae reveal that the female figure was in almost every way dressed like its Minoan counterpart. Some scholars have interpreted the dividing line seen down the front of some of the skirts as an indication that they may have been divided into pants, but it is more likely that it represents a seam or a fold. It is probably quite correct to assume that Helen of Troy would have worn a sophisticated, pinched-waisted costume on Minoan lines with breasts fully exposed.

# ARCHAIC GREEK

***Masculine Dress*** There is little to show what was worn by males in the early years of the Archaic Greek development since the few early figurines show the men nude. But by the end of the seventh century, vase paintings began to show the male figures wearing a short, tight-fitting tunic known as the *chiton*. It was made from two rectangles of cloth sewn together at the shoulders and down the sides and decorated top and bottom with a band of simple geometric decoration (Fig. 4–8j). In addition to this short chiton, there were also longer versions that were ankle length and frequently had an allover pattern. Both the long and the short chiton worn by the men during this period were known as Ionic since they lacked an overfold at the top that distinguished the Doric chiton, a garment worn almost exclusively by women.

In a scene from the early sixth century François Vase in Florence, three men in the chariot are wearing the long chiton with the tight geometric borders, and one even has a large geometric pattern covering the entire chiton (Fig. 4–5). The outer wrap depicted is the himation, a rectangular shawl, that in this early period was modest in size and usually draped over the left shoulder, under the right arm, and back over the left arm. Here, however, the figure on the outside has his himation worn over both shoulders like a shawl. It is also important to make the point here that the basic chiton and himation of the Archaic period were of tighter proportions than was the case with the flowing versions of Classical Greek times. Since Greek garments were woven in square or rectangular shapes and to the proportions of the wearer, the change in proportions from archaic to classical times is significant of a major change in outlook toward the human form.

The other outer male wrap that developed early in archaic times was the *chlamys,* which was usually square, weighted on the corners and worn over the left shoulder with the top corners pinned together with a pin, or *fibula,* on the right shoulder. If both arms had to be free, it was then pinned in front. It could be decorated with a mere border or with intricate, geometric designs over its entire surface.

Men's hair was usually long and curly with a narrow band, or *fillet,* to hold it in. Sometimes the hair was braided, twisted into a club bound with ribbons, wound in a roll about the head or rolled over the fillet and tucked under its edge. Beards were very prevalent during the Archaic Period, with the younger men favoring a short, rounded shape, while the older men preferred longer, pointed ones (Fig. 4–8b).

There were two male styles in hats: the simple cap, narrow-brimmed or brimless, known as the *pilos;* and the broad-brimmed, low-crowned *petasos,* usually worn by travelers as a sun hat. The pilos was usually molded of felted wool fibers, whereas the petasos was woven of straw (Fig. 4–5d). Occasionally the Phrygian cap from Asia Minor was also seen (Fig. 4–5f).

Most archaic male figures were barefoot, but we do have references to sandals which were made with a simple leather sole with a leather thong between the second and third toes, and then connected with another thong going around the heel. Late in the period sandals became more complex, with an interweaving of thongs up to the ankle, or above, and boots were added that were like soft leather stockings open in the front and laced to the leg (Fig. 4–8e, i).

Male jewelry in this period is limited to the simple or ornamental pin or brooch called the *fibula* and seal rings used for sealing letters and documents (Fig. 4–8g). At first these were of iron but later of gold and carved with an insignia of rich and intricate design.

### Feminine Dress

The most typical female Greek garment during the Archaic Period was the *peplos.* It was a tubular tunic woven in one piece or seamed up one side with a generous overfold called the *apotygma* at the top and reaching to the ankles at the bottom. The fold at the top, which usually reached to just above the waist, was held on the shoulders by pinning the back over the front. An apotygma like this can be seen on the female figure from the Vase of Volci (Fig. 4–6). This chiton was bordered top and bottom as well as along the bottom edge of the overfold, and sometimes there was a vertical band of decoration up the center front. Often the peplos also had an allover pattern of some kind.

The hair styles shown in the François Vase consist either of wavy ringlets down the back or looped-up buns at the back of the head, and the coiffure is almost invariably held in place by a head band, or *fillet.* For an outer garment the women also wore the himation draped as a

**FIG. 4–6** Section of the Vase from Volci by Exekias; Etruscan-Gregorian Museum, Vatican City; sixth century B.C. Illustrates the rectangular, geometric form of Archaic Greek clothing before the use of soft, supple draping began to dominate dress at the beginning of the fifth century. Photo courtesy of the Vatican Museum.

shawl or worn as the men did, draped over the left shoulder, under the right arm, and again over the left arm or shoulder.

It is interesting to note that toward the end of the Archaic Period when soft folds and draping began to supplant the tighter rectangular forms, we get a number of complexly draped female figures in which fascination with draping takes precedence over the beauty and simplicity in draped garments that were to mark the following Classical Age. First of all, this new and complex draping was done not over the historic female peplos, but over the Ionic chiton that became popular in late Archaic times as Ionia and Asia Minor became more important to Greek culture. A number of lovely Archaic Greek *kores* (smiling female statues) from the late sixth century B.C. show a light, crinkled chiton without an overfold and cut much wider, probably twice the distance from fingertip to fingertip with arms outstretched. The fabric was no longer wool but a very lightweight linen, and the garment was held together along the shoulders and arms by many small brooches, or *fibulae*. This chiton was also cut much longer than the height of the body, with the excess length draped over a girdle at the waist to create a blousing-up on the hips known as the *kolpos*. Sometimes with the crinkled folds in the top and the smooth look of the skirt, this garment looks as if it were in two parts, but the answer here is in the skill with which the upper area could be subtly pleated, while the lower area remained almost smooth. In the Archaic kores from the Acropolis the neckline of the chiton often looks as if the pleating had been sewn into a band, but this may well have been a convention of the sculptor for depicting tight draping (Fig. 4–7). These same kores also have an interesting draping for the narrow himation, which differs markedly in size from the more voluminous standard himation worn by men and women. This narrow, folded shawl runs from the right shoulder across the chest and under the left arm, then up over the back to the right shoulder again, with the loose ends hanging down in a fluted triangular pattern. It sometimes looks as if this effect were created by pleating and sewing in place, but this again may be a convention of the sculptor attempting to show only a slight rolled effect at the

FIG. 4–7 Archaic Kore; Acropolis Museum; ca. 520 B.C. An example of the intricate pleating that began to appear, particularly in female dress, late in the sixth century B.C. Note the so-called narrow *himation* which has also been pleated before it drapes over the one shoulder and under the other arm. Photo courtesy of the Hirmer Fotoarchiv, Munich.

top fold edge of this narrow himation. The hair ringlets of these maidens are as tightly set as the pleating.

Both the peplos and the Ionic chiton were made of uncut lengths of fabric draped over the body with the use of brooches, and the only sewing that took place was to join selvages. What may look like sleeves are really formed by pinning down the arm and girding at the waist. By the close of the Archaic Period all Greek garments were based on fullness in pleating and draping, and tight-fitting garments with sleeves were always of foreign origin.

# CLASSICAL GREEK

**Masculine Dress** In the Classical Period male clothing moved toward even greater simplification with great stress on the natural movement of the human body through softly draped natural folds. The first part of this period is labeled Severe Classical in art, and certainly softness in folds is not yet complete. In the famed Charioteer of Delphi from about 475 B.C., we see the long Ionic chiton that was the correct wear for charioteers, girded at the waist, around the neck, and under the arms to give complete fabric control when in action, while the shoulders were seamed, rather than caught with pins (Fig. 4–8). The standard wear for philosophers and intellectual leaders was usually the himation and sandals without the need for a chiton; a man involved in active work fastened his short chiton on only the left shoulder, leaving his right arm totally free for work. The short male chiton was often bloused at the waist with a cording or belt above, as may be seen in a copy of a relief showing Orpheus, Eurydice, and Hermes; the chlamys was still the standard short cloak for younger men (Figs. 4–5a, 4–9).

Footwear still ranged from the simple sandal to a sturdier style—with cork or wooden sole and leather side pieces to give greater protection. Soft boots, which could rise as high as the upper calf, were laced tightly to the leg up the front (Fig. 4–8f, i). The petasos and pilos were still the only male headgear, and the hair was usually cut short with soft curls that clustered closely about the head like a cap. Beards were now seen only on philosophers and old men (Fig. 4–8b).

Military wear usually consisted of a short, stiff, pleated chiton with a *cuirass,* or breast-plate, of cast bronze or leather plated with overlapping bronze scales. Shin guards or *greaves* of metal protected the lower leg, and the head was covered by a metal helmet, usually topped by an immense curved crest of metal set with horsehair or feathers (Fig. 4–8e). Shields at first were oval and convex but then became circular; swords were short and thick and worn diagonally over the cuirass on the left side. Other weapons included the spear, javelin, sling slot, and bow and arrow.

**Feminine Dress** With the arrival of the Classical Period after the close of the Persian Wars, the old-fashioned peplos, which had given way to the complex draping effects achieved with the Ionic chiton plus the narrow himation, gained a new popularity as the Doric chiton (Fig. 4–5b). It was viewed as a return to the simpler lines of the distant past but was cut much fuller so that it fell in graceful folds. It was woven with borders, but not an allover pattern as in the past, and it was not seamed at all but left completely open on the right side except for the closure created by girding at the waist. Often the overfold was long enough that the girding at the waist went over it, creating the effect of a short skirt, or peplum, below the waist. Many variations in the *kolpos,* or blousing at the waist, can also be seen during the Classical Period. A very clear example of the classical Doric chiton may be seen in one of the Dancing Maidens from Herculaneum, which are bronze copies of Greek originals (Fig. 4–10).

It is important to realize that the Ionic chiton was woven of linen, sometimes almost transparent, and gave a much lighter look than the heavier folds and lines of the woolen Doric chiton. A lovely example of the softness and transparency in Greek weaving may be seen in the Grave Stele of Hegeso, dated about 410–400 B.C. (Fig. 4–11). This demonstrates the ideal of liquid fluidity in draping without constriction that shows off the natural lines of the human body. It is interesting to note that the serving girl has a seamed, sleeved tunic, based on those used in Asia Minor, which is more practical than the draped chiton worn by her mistress. It is also interesting to note how the graceful lines of the chair support and enhance the draping and body lines of the sitter.

After the close of the Persian Wars the long, carefully set ringlets of the Archaic Period disappeared in favor of hair that was pulled up and to the back in a number of ways, the most prevalent of which was a knot at the back of the head to balance the profile of the nose. Although hair was often uncovered and unornamented, it was frequently confined by a number of bags, kerchiefs, or nets. The simplest effect was a fillet wound one to three times

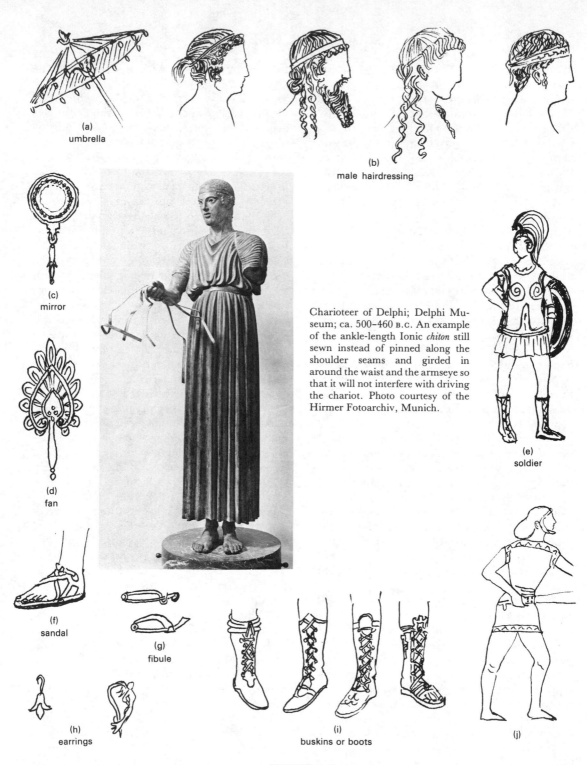

(a)
umbrella

(b)
male hairdressing

(c)
mirror

(d)
fan

Charioteer of Delphi; Delphi Museum; ca. 500–460 B.C. An example of the ankle-length Ionic *chiton* still sewn instead of pinned along the shoulder seams and girded in around the waist and the armseye so that it will not interfere with driving the chariot. Photo courtesy of the Hirmer Fotoarchiv, Munich.

(e)
soldier

(f)
sandal

(g)
fibule

(h)
earrings

(i)
buskins or boots

(j)

FIGURE 4-8

FIG. 4-9 Orpheus, Eurydice, and Hermes; copy of the last original of the School of Phidias; National Museum, Naples; ca. 420 B.C. From left to right, note Orpheus in the Ionic *chiton* with bloused *kolpos* at the waist covered by the short *chlamys;* then Eurydice in a graceful Doric *chiton* with long overfold; and finally Hermes in a spiked helmet, leg greaves, Ionic *chiton,* and *chlamys.* Photo courtesy of the Department of Antiquités, The Louvre, Paris.

FIG. 4-10 Dancing Maiden of Herculaneum; Roman copy of a Greek bronze statue; National Museum, Naples; ca. 450 B.C. Illustrates the revived popularity of the Doric *peplos* during the Golden Age of Greece. It is now known as the Doric *chiton* and is worn pinned at the shoulders without seams. Photo courtesy of Alinari, Florence.

FIG. 4-11 Grave Stele of Hegeso from the Dipylon Cemetery, Athens; National Museum, Athens; ca. 410–400 B.C. Illustrates the liquid softness in the draping of the Greek *chiton* at the close of the fifth century. Note the graceful furniture lines that complement the grace in clothing. Photo courtesy of the Hirmer Fotoarchiv, Munich.

about the hair. Scarfs were also used, wound twice about the head—covering the knot in back and binding in the top of the head in front. Also worn was a fairly tight-fitting cap known as the *saccus,* sometimes with a tassel at the back and nets or snoods of various sorts which enclosed and supported the hair at the back. The most well-known headdress or tiara was the *stephanie,* which gave a very regal look to the female head (Fig. 4–5c). Women also wore the petasos, or sun hat, used by men (Fig. 4–13) as well as the Phrygian cap which was worn almost exclusively in Asia Minor and which became the basis for the Medieval-Renaissance caps of the doges of Venice and the liberty cap of the French Revolution (Fig. 4–5f).

Greek women were moderate in their use of jewelry, but brooches or *fibulae* were absolutely necessary in the draping of the classical chiton, and a number of beautiful pieces have survived (Fig. 4–8g). Originally just large stickpins, by classical times fibulae had evolved into safety pins which became more intricate and elaborate in decoration as one moves toward Hellenistic times. The heads were carved like cameos or inset with gems, and pins were often handed down and became collectors' items. Other jewelry items included bracelets, earrings, rings, hairpins, and necklaces (Fig. 4–8h).

Though we are often aware through the costume patterns shown in vase paintings that color was much used in the clothing of archaic times, there sometimes is the mistaken impression that Greek classical dress was off-white, beige, or grey, with color used only on borders. This is far from the case as we can tell by remnants of color that cling to the folds in statue draperies and prove that statues were once polychromed. Colors were evidently clear and unmuddied and included olive green, violet, dark red, dark purple, henna, rust, and, of course, white, and black.

## HELLENISTIC GREEK

*Masculine Dress*  As the Classical Period waned and individuality and particularism increased, the distinctions between different garments and their mode of wearing gradually disappeared. With the campaign of Alexander the Great to India, Greece was brought into a new contact with the East. Cotton and silk were added to the repertory of fabrics available, and Eastern influences, such as embroidery with gold and silver threads, were introduced. Draping now became a matter of personal pleasure and was usually done for practical comfort or to project an image of power rather than for an ideal beauty. An excellent example of both of these can be seen in a portrait statue from the Mausoleum of Halicarnassus, ca. 350 B.C. (Fig. 4–12).

*Feminine Dress*  Again, as with the men, the female dress after the close of the Classical Age lost many of its distinctions. It shows a great mixture of effects, combining Doric chitons over Ionic ones, as well as individual varieties in girdling—bands crossing around the shoulder between the breasts, or high above the waist to create the silhouette that was later revived as the Empire waistline at the time of Napoleon. Also in Hellenistic times, with the renewed influences of the East, the long-sleeved tunic reappeared, and decoration became richer and more oriental.

The outer garment for women was usually still the himation, which was now draped in many individual ways other than according to the classical precepts of the Golden Age. An excellent example of individualized practical draping may be seen in the lovely figurines from Tanagra, dating from the fourth to third century B.C. (Fig. 4–13). The young woman wears the straw sun hat, or petasos, over a himation that swathes both head and body in an attractive, protective manner. The women are also depicted wearing a shorter cloak like the male chlamys, which was fastened on the right shoulder, known as the *diplax.*

**FIG. 4-12** *Mausolus;* from the Mausoleum of Halicarnassus; British Museum; ca. 351–339 B.C. A postclassical image of individualism, theatricality, and grandeur in which the draping gives strength and weight but without the ideal beauty of fifth-century Greek sculpture. Photo courtesy of the Hirmer Fotoarchiv, Munich.

**FIG. 4-13** Statuette of a Young Woman; Tanagra terra cotta; Metropolitan Museum of Art; fourth to third century B.C. Over a fine linen *chiton,* women in the later Hellenistic period draped themselves in a variety of ways with a linen *himation*. The pointed straw hat held by pins is the *petasos*. Photo courtesy of The Metropolitan Museum of Art, Gift of Mrs. Sadie Adler, May, 1930.

# FABRICS

The Greeks wore primarily woolens and linens with silk added in Hellenistic times. Woolens were the original fabric, woven in many weights from thin, loose, and supple to coarser and heavier weights—more like that in modern blankets. Linen was also woven in both coarse and fine textures, with near-transparency in some lightweight specimens. Silk imported from China was seldom worn until the time of Alexander, and it was like raw silk or shantung. Great variety in silk usage came in the years following the death of Alexander when some was woven with metallic threads. Throughout Greek development, wool felt was available for shaped hats and caps.

# ARTS AND ARTIFACTS

There are always questions as to how the Ionic and Doric column capitals from Greek architecture are related to the Ionic and Doric chitons (Fig. 4-1). The Doric column with its wide flutings had no base and rested directly on the temple platform with a top that supported a circular cushion, which merged into a simple square block. In somewhat the same way, the female Doric chiton gave the feminine form a solid, heavy look, and the overfold acted as a strong square accent at the top of the figure. The Ionic capital and column were light and slender, and the fluting was much narrower. The column rested on a circular base, and the capital had an intricate spiral, or *volute*, framing the top. In a similar way the Ionic chiton was lighter and more delicate in its draping, since it was made of linen rather than wool. The false sleeves created by its great width gave a delicate spreading accent to the top of the figure—much like the volutes of the Ionic capital. In fact, all Classical Greek clothing mirrored in the folds of the draping the fluting of Greek columns. By proportioning the garment to an ideal body, the clothing reflected the careful proportioning that went into the base, cornice, columns, capitals, and pediments of Greek architecture. As with clothing, Greek classical architecture was not pure white but contained strong accents of clear, rich color.

Private houses looked inward to a court with rooms grouped about this airy, open-air living room. Walls were covered with simple wall paintings that must have reflected the designs on Greek vases; and in Hellenistic times mosaics were used. Furniture was made of bronze or wood and shaped in beautiful straight or curving lines to give ample opportunity for the designer to underline Greek ideals of beauty (Fig. 4-1a). A lovely example of a chair may be seen in the Grave Stele of Hegeso (Fig. 4-11). Tables were small and low and were used with low, narrow couches equipped with mattresses and used for banqueting. Beds were also narrow and had decorated heads and footboards.

In the many artifacts and ornamental effects used by the Greeks, patterns were usually geometric and included the rosette, key, dentil, guilloche, egg and dart, wave, and meander. Abstracted vegetable patterns included the acanthus, laurel, waterleaf, anthemion, and ivy (Fig. 4-1b).

Women's artifacts included fans, tiny parasols, mirrors, and the contents of a carved box used for the female toilet (Fig. 4-8a, c, d). Inside one would find a hand mirror, jewelry, and small bottles of ivory, metal, or alabaster for perfumes or ointments. The most pervasive artifact in the Greek household was probably the vase, and the shapes of these vases are a full study in themselves. Lamps were shaped somewhat like a modern gravy boat and held a wick which floated in oil. Musical instruments included the cithara, flute, shepherd's pipes, bagpipe, cymbals, and drum. Books were inscribed on papyrus rolls, and wax tablets and a stylus were used for everyday writing.

# VISUAL SOURCES

The visual sources for costume in ancient Greece include primarily the beautiful statues of Archaic, Classical, and Hellenistic times, with some information derived from vase paintings. The richest locations for statuary are the Louvre, the British Museum, Roman copies of Greek originals in the Vatican and the National Museum in Naples, and the various museums in Greece: particularly the Acropolis Museum, the National Museum of Athens, the Museum at Delphi, and the Archaeological Museum of Heraklion, Crete. The same sources also have strong pottery collections. Good written sources are Mary Houston's *Ancient Greek, Roman and Byzantine Costume and Decoration* and C. M. Bowra's *Classical Greece*.

# SUMMARY

It is a fascinating study to move from the tight, artificial lines of Minoan costume through the barbaric effects in Mycenaean clothing to the structured geometric garments of the Archaic Greeks, and then to see the whole process blossom into the beautifully draped, idealized yet natural clothing of the Classical Greeks. Greek clothing at the height of the Classical Period is a great lesson in limitation, simplicity, balance, and proportion, using an idealized natural body (not its cloth covering) as the measure by which soft, subtle draping effects are achieved to enhance and extend the natural grace of that human body. Never in the history of man has such strong limitation in cutting and sewing achieved such beauty of effect.

# chapter V

# Ancient Rome

## Chronology

### (753 B.C.–A.D. 476)

| | | |
|---|---|---|
| **ETRUSCAN MONARCHY 753–509** B.C. | 753 | Legendary founding of Rome by Romulus |
| | 753–509 | Horatius, Tarquin, and Lucrece celebrated in poetry |
| | ca. 612–509 | Rome is ruled by Etruscan kings |
| | ca. 600–500 | High period of development in Etruscan bronze and ironware |
| | 509 | Expulsion of the last Etruscan king and establishment of a Republic; Temple of Jupiter on the Capitol is established; struggle of plebeians for equal rights |

Etruscan

| | | |
|---|---|---|
| **THE REPUBLIC 508–27** B.C. | 494 | The office of tribune created to protect the rights of the plebeians |
| | 493 | The Romans join the Latin League formed by its neighbors for mutual defense |
| | 486–466 | Wars with Aequians, Volscians (Coriolanus) |
| | 449 | Publication is begun on the Law of the Twelve Tribes, which codified Roman law |

| | |
|---|---|
| 396 | Rome violates the agreements of the Latin League by annexing new territory |
| 390 | The Gauls sack Rome, but then withdraw |
| 367 | Licinian Law provides that one consul should be a plebeian |
| 340–338 | Latin League is defeated and dissolved by Rome |
| 312 | Rome's first highway, the Appian Way, is built, as well as the first aqueduct |
| 287 | The Hortensian Law shifts power to plebeians |
| 278–270 | The Septuagint (translation of the Old Testament into Greek) |
| 275 | Rome becomes master of all southern Italy |
| 264 | Earliest record of gladiatorial fights; Roman silver coins are distributed |
| 264–241 | First Punic War with Carthage; Romans are victorious |
| 240 | Latin tragedy and comedy inaugurated by Livius Andronicus |
| 221–220 | Circus Flaminius and Via Flaminia constructed |
| 218–201 | Second Punic War; Hannibal crosses the Alps; Rome victorious over Hannibal |
| ca. 205 | Plautus' comedy *The Braggart Warrior* is performed |
| 197 | Rome defeats Philip V of Macedon at Cynoscephalae |
| 185 | Major work begins on urban planning |
| 166 | Terence's comedy *Andria* is produced |

Republican

| | |
|---|---|
| 149–146 | The Third Punic War; Carthage and Corinth destroyed; Africa and Macedonia become Roman provinces, Archimedes announces the principle of the lever |
| 133–122 | Land reforms of the Gracchi; distribution of free grain; vellum (calfskin) and parchment (sheep and goat skin) used for writing; first library in Rome |
| 131 | Satires by Lucilius are published |
| 121 | Rome conquers southern Gaul |
| 119–66 | Marius, Drusus, Lucullus; Sulla becomes dictator and restores the power of the Senate; judicial system improved |
| 81 | Cicero delivers his first oration |
| 73–71 | Spartacus leads a slave revolt that ends with bloody reprisals against the rebellious slaves |
| 63–62 | Cicero becomes Consul; the lyric poet Catullus arrives in Rome |
| 60 | The first triumvirate is formed; Pompey, Caesar, and Crassus |
| 58–51 | Caesar conducts a series of brilliant campaigns in Gaul; first stone theater in Rome, Pompey's Theater, is built; death of the philosopher-poet Lucretius; murals at the Villa of Mysteries of Pompeii are begun |
| 49–48 | Civil Wars begin; Caesar defeats Pompey; Library of Alexandria is destroyed by fire; Caesar meets Cleopatra in Egypt |
| 46 | Caesar appointed dictator for ten years; Caesar's Forum Julian is dedicated |
| 44 | Caesar is assassinated; Mark Antony commands Rome; Cicero's *Philippics,* attacking Mark Antony, are delivered |

| | 43–42 | Octavian, Caesar's heir, is elected consul; second triumvirate with Antony and Lepidus; second triumvirate defeats Brutus and Cassius at Philippi |
|---|---|---|
| | 37–30 | Vergil's *Georgic's* are written; Horace's *Satires* appear; Antony and Cleopatra are defeated at Actium |
| | 27 | Octavian becomes emperor and assumes the name of Augustus; The Pantheon is built by Agrippa |

---

| | | |
|---|---|---|
| EARLY EMPIRE 27 B.C.–A.D. 305 | 19–13 | Vergil dies; *The Aeneid* is published posthumously; Theater of Marcellus is dedicated |
| | 4–2 | Christ is born; Augustus dedicates the Forum of Augustus |
| | 8 A.D. | Ovid exiled from Rome; *The Metamorphoses* |
| | 14–37 | Augustus dies; Tiberius becomes emperor; crucifixion of Christ; death of the historian Livy, author of a 142-volume history of Rome |
| | 37–41 | Caligula as emperor |
| | 41–54 | Claudius as emperor; Claudian aqueducts built; southern Britain conquered; St. Peter and St. Paul in Rome; Basilica of Porta Maggiore built |
| | 54–68 | Nero as emperor; Rome burns, giving Nero excuse for the persecution of Christians; Nero orders the murders of his mother, Agrippina; his wives, Octavia and Poppaea; his brother, Britannicus; Seneca, his tutor; and Petronius, Lucan, and others; Boadicea in revolt in England |
| Empire | 70–79 | Vespasian as emperor; destruction of Jerusalem; Forum of Peace dedicated; Pliny the Elder's *Natural History* appears; the Colosseum dedicated; Mount Vesuvius erupts, burying Herculaneum and Pompeii |

| | | |
|---|---|---|
| | 79–81 | Emperor Titus completes conquest of the Jews; arch commemorating this victory is dedicated |
| | 81–96 | Domitian as emperor; Britain conquered by Agricola; Roman wall in the north of England is built; first book of Martial's *Epigrams;* Tacitus' *Germania* |
| | 98–117 | Trajan as emperor; his Forum established; Trajan's Column; Pliny the Younger describes Christian persecutions |
| | 117–138 | Hadrian as emperor; Jewish revolt supressed; Great Wall in Britain; Pantheon rebuilt; Suetonius' *Lives;* Hadrian's villa at Tivoli |
| | 161–192 | Marcus Aurelius as emperor; column of Marcus Aurelius built |
| | 212–216 | Roman citizenship given in all provinces; Baths of Caracalla |
| | 252 | Roman provinces in Europe are invaded by Goths and others |
| | 284–305 | Diocletian as emperor; continued persecution of Christians; Baths of Diocletian |
| LATE EMPIRE<br>A.D. 305–476 | 312–337 | Constantine the Great as emperor; Christianity the new religion of the Empire; seat of imperial government moved to Byzantium; Constantinople founded; Arch of Constantine and St. Paul's outside the Walls are built |
| | 361–363 | Julian the Apostate tries to revive paganism |
| | 395 | Roman Empire permanently divided into East and West |
| | 410 | Alaric, king of the Visigoths, captures and sacks Rome |
| | 413–426 | St. Augustine composes his treatise, *The City of God* |
| | 452 | Attila the Hun threatens Rome |

Late Empire

476       Odoacer, Germanic chieftain,
becomes king of Rome

# BACKGROUND

Although the cultures of both the Etruscans and the Romans were strongly influenced by outside contacts, particularly by eastern Mediterranean cultures, each had strong characteristics of its own. Their cultures were a synthesis of strong native characteristics and an aptitude for the assimilation of outside influences, particularly from the Archaic, Classical, and Hellenistic Greeks. By the end of the second century B.C., the great city on the banks of the Tiber and its subsidiary provinces had merged the practical, individualized theatrical qualities of Hellenistic Greek art with their own cultural inheritance. After Rome threw off the dominance of the Etruscan monarchy and established an oligarchic republic, which stressed stoic discipline and military valor, Rome expanded rapidly into the greatest power the Mediterranean basin had ever seen. As it grew, the administrative methods of the original Roman city-state proved unsuited for imperial ambitions. After a bitter civil war, Julius Caesar became dictator; after his assassination his great-nephew, Octavian, assumed the title of Augustus and became the first Roman emperor.

During the first century of the Christian era, Rome was indeed an awesome power stretching from the Tigris-Euphrates Valley in present-day Iraq to the borders of Scotland, with an energetic, efficient, but ruthless, central administration. The Romans ruled over many races, creeds, traditions, cultures, and languages; and although they borrowed many of their intellectual and artistic ideals from the Greeks, the particular nature of Roman genius showed itself in law, government, and practical architecture based on engineering skills. For maximum efficiency such a vast administration spread over an immense empire required the construction of bridges, roads, sewers, aqueducts, and grand public monuments that would appropriately express the dignity and power of the state.

Roman culture after the Republic took its character largely from the imperial role that Rome played in Europe and the Mediterranean basin. But the seed of Roman character developed during the Republican period in a succession of wars of expansion and internal conflict between leaders within the fledgling state. During these wars—the most violent and dangerous of which were the three Punic Wars against the great maritime power of Carthage in North Africa—the Romans developed their very special qualities of character: iron discipline, stoic courage, tenacity, obedience to authority, absolute realism, and staunch conservatism. All of these qualities infused their culture and art and gave a distinctive Roman character to all the arts borrowed from Greece.

The Romans had a very ambivalent attitude toward the Greeks, admiring their sense of beauty, grace, and idealism, but having nothing but contempt for their lack of realism, practicality, virility, and stoic courage. It is the uneasy balance between realism and idealism that makes Greco-Roman art difficult to define, whereas true Roman art of the Empire is almost always characterized by its strength, realism, and power.

To clarify the differences between Roman and Greek artistic attitudes, compare the Athenian Parthenon with the Roman Colosseum (see Figs. 4-1, 5-1). In the Parthenon there is refinement in the horizontal and vertical forces to achieve unity, simplicity, balance, and beauty. Everything has an austere, graceful balance, and if one measures its parts with the eye, one will find subtle variations in the proportions and the horizontal-vertical interplay of forces that increase the sense of beauty and perfection. The Roman Colosseum, on the other hand, created over 500 years later as an amphitheater for gladiatorial games, was created for practical purposes and to express power, strength, and grandeur. The imperial Romans placed far more emphasis on entertainment and high living than on religion and abstract beauty, and Roman imperial public buildings underline this fact. The Colosseum is also a monument to Roman prowess in engineering, and the great arena is as much a feat of engineering as it is a display of architecture. With their practical pragmatism the Romans perfected the use of concrete, tunnel vaulting, and round arches, enabling them to build bridges, amphitheaters, law courts, baths, and viaducts of great size, utility, richness, and flexibility. The Colosseum used piled tiers of arches covering rings of vaulted tunnels that gave a spatial variety and flexibility unknown to the Greeks; all that remained Greek were the architectural orders (Doric, Ionic, and Corinthian) applied as outside decoration. The Colosseum may stand as a metaphor for Roman culture: a realistic-practical base on a grand scale adorned with some of the refinements of Greek art.

## THE BASIC COSTUME SILHOUETTE

At first glance Romans often look very like the Greeks, and as has been noted, Greek ideals did have a strong influence on Roman culture. But as with architecture and sculpture, the Romans in their dress were more interested in images of grandeur and power as well as comfort and variety than in the Greek ideals of grace and beauty. Thus Roman clothing had the draped lines of the Greeks without their simplicity, subtlety, and beauty. The women's clothing was closest to the Greek with the *chiton* transformed into the *stola* and the *himation* into the *palla*. Although sometimes the sleeves of the stola were still pinned rather than sewn, the Roman ladies were much more apt to have the lines of the stola cut in a T-shape for comfort and practicality. Fabrics were still primarily linen or wool, but by the Empire Period, wealthy ladies were dressed in costly silk imported overland from China. The most characteristic quality of Roman female dress was the size, variety, and complexity of the Roman matron's coiffure. Here decoration, display, individual ingenuity, and the vagaries of personal taste created coiffure confections that sometimes defy analysis. We know that Roman women were adept with curling irons, hairnets, dyes, switches, hairpins, and even blonde wigs made from the tresses of captured German women. Imperial female hair styles epitomized the Roman sense of display (Fig. 5-12).

But the one garment that dominates all our thinking about Roman dress is the male *toga*—a masterpiece of draped grandeur that became the symbol of Roman authority and power, and remained so, long after that power had died. Neither before nor since has such a magnificently imposing garment been created out of a single piece of cloth without complex cutting, pinning, or stitching. Usually of off-white

(a)
temple of Fortuna
virilis

(b)
furniture

(c)
motif

(c)
motif

The Colosseum; Rome; A.D. 72–80. Illustrates the great size of imperial
Roman architecture and the complex technical skill of Roman architects
in their use of the round arch, barrel vault, and concrete construction
faced in stone. Photo courtesy of Alinari, Florence.

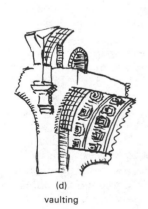

(d)
vaulting

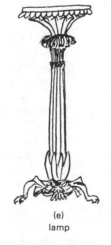

(e)
lamp

(f)
Roman capital

**FIGURE 5-1**

or bleached wool with darker colors for funerals, it was bordered in Tyrian purple for senators and aristocrats. It was worn over a T-shaped tunic and was usually a folded semi-circle placed on the left shoulder with the point reaching to the floor. The remainder of the fabric was passed across the back, under the right arm, and back over the left shoulder and arm in the manner of the Greek himation. The overfold across the back could be pulled up over the head for ceremonies or protection, and the fabric down the left side could be pulled through that across the front to form a pocket in which the right hand could be rested (Fig. 5-2). Imperial togas were often of an elliptical shape, and even larger—four or five yards long and three yards wide—and sometimes made of rich silk embroidered in gold and worn over a wide-sleeved embroidered tunic known as a *dal-matic*—a ceremonial garb that remained in various forms as an Imperial coronation costume until the sixteenth century.

The toga was a Roman symbol of citizenship, and it was worn on all public occasions. The smaller *pallium* (Greek himation) was worn over the male *tunica* for everyday occasions. As with the other arts, Roman dress developed from Republican simplicity, soberness, and dignity to oriental richness and luxury under the later Empire. In general, Roman costume was more layered, heavier, and often more complicated than the Greek and in the Imperial times involved far more fabric, especially in the toga. More decoration was involved, and the draped line borrowed from the Greeks was developed more for grandeur and display than for simplicity, grace, beauty, and projection of natural body movement.

## ETRUSCAN COSTUME

The Etruscans came over the Alps into Italy shortly after the Dorian Greeks moved from the Balkans into Greece (about the ninth century B.C.), and were probably originally from Asia Minor. They brought with them inheritances from Egypt, Mesopotamia, and Crete, and the later Romans were deeply indebted to them in matters of daily living. By the sixth century B.C., the Etruscans ruled from the River Po in the north to the Greek colonies south of Rome; they were expelled from Rome in 509, their power and influence then waned until they were finally engulfed by the Romans in the third century B.C. The Etruscans were brilliant workers in bronze and left behind richly colored, vigorous frescoes in underground tombs, displaying the great love of music, dancing, feasting, and the enjoyment of life that were characteristic of the Etruscan temperament.

**Masculine Dress** Depictions of males in the seventh century B.C. show them in loin skirts and T-shaped short tunics. By the sixth century B.C., the typical Etruscan tunic was sometimes ankle length, often with an allover geometric pattern. Male dancers usually appeared nude except for the semi-circular *tebenna*, which was worn centered in the front with ends over the shoulders and brought back under the arms for security during active movement. The rectangular shawl or mantle, roughly analogous to the Greek himation, was also often worn by men of dignity as a standard outer wrap and frequently carried a plaid pattern. The flat bands on these shawls demonstrate the origins of the purple borders on the later Roman toga, just as the vertical lines on tunics developed into the *clavi*, which were a mark of position on the tunics of Roman aristocrats (Fig. 5-2d).

The famed Apollo of Veii, often represented as the high point in Etruscan sculpture (Fig. 5-3), wears a knee-length tunic, and his tebenna, probably semicircular, is draped under the right shoulder and over the left. The marvelous symmetry of the folds at the top of the chest and on the left side are probably the artist's idealization and not a factual representation. The hair falls in long, twisted curls from the back of the head and is remarkably like hair effects on Archaic Greek statues. This is not surprising since the Etruscan border pushed directly against the Greek colonies of southern Italy in the sixth century B.C.

The shorter cloak for active men, analogous to the Greek *chlamys*, is also seen on Etruscan

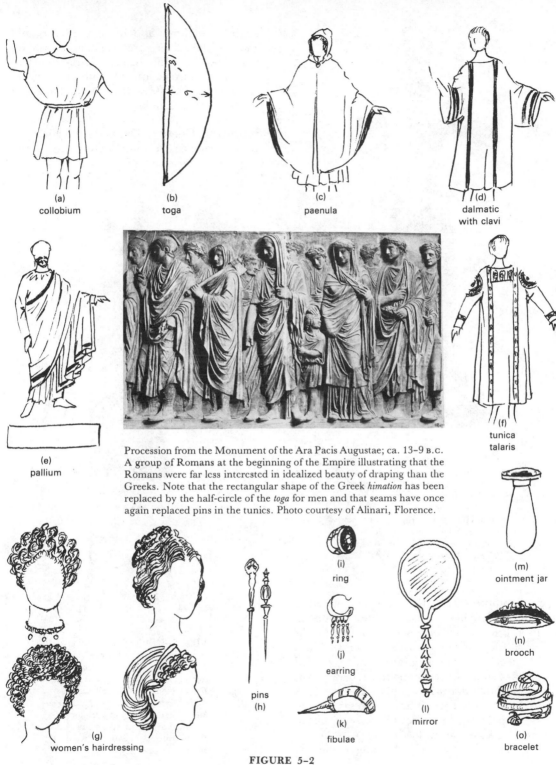

(a) collobium

(b) toga

(c) paenula

(d) dalmatic with clavi

(e) pallium

(f) tunica talaris

Procession from the Monument of the Ara Pacis Augustae; ca. 13–9 B.C. A group of Romans at the beginning of the Empire illustrating that the Romans were far less interested in idealized beauty of draping than the Greeks. Note that the rectangular shape of the Greek *himation* has been replaced by the half-circle of the *toga* for men and that seams have once again replaced pins in the tunics. Photo courtesy of Alinari, Florence.

(g) women's hairdressing

(h) pins

(i) ring

(j) earring

(k) fibulae

(l) mirror

(m) ointment jar

(n) brooch

(o) bracelet

FIGURE 5-2

75

height sometimes also binding in the ankle (Fig. 5–10e). There are also examples of low boots and the standard sandal, ranging from very open construction with minimum protection to complex cuts and strapping that almost totally covered the foot.

**Feminine Dress**   The earliest figurines of women from the seventh century B.C. show a

**FIG. 5–3**   Apollo of Veii; Villa Guilia, Rome; ca. 500 B.C. The god here wears a knee-length tunic that clung to the body and draped in the *tebenna,* forerunner of the *toga.* The organized, geometric character of the drapery and the drapery edges show a direct relationship to that of the Archaic Greeks. Photo courtesy of Alinari, Florence.

representations as is the Greek *petasos.* Other headgear were like berets, sometimes quite flat and at other times of a very imposing height (Fig. 5–10e). Armor consisted of round helmets with neck and cheek guards and a plaited cuirass of small, overlapping metal plates sewn to tight leather doublets or tunics. Feet were left bare in the early period, but later on they were shod in pointed, soft shoes that rose to a peak at the back to the middle of the calf. Sometimes decorative straps held a tongue of equal

**FIG. 5–4**   Woman with Offerings; bronze statuette from Monteguragazza; Museo Civico Bologna; ca. 480 B.C. Illustrates the female clothing of the Etruscans under Greek influence with crinkle-pleated Ionic chiton under a *tebenna* that is worn like a shawl. Photo courtesy of Museo Civico, Bologna.

tunic, or *chiton,* that has short sleeves, reaches to the ankle, and is girdled twice about the body. The hair is pulled smoothly to the back and then braided into a length that reaches to the ankles. Often the tunic has an allover geometric pattern plus a banded or embroidered border. Shawls, if worn, are usually over the head (Fig. 5-10f).

But the sources which give the most information about the Etruscan spirit and life style for both men and women are the wall paintings from the fifth-century B.C. tombs depicting a gay, robust, colorful way of life with great emphasis on food, drink, dancing, and music. A typical female figure in these paintings wears a long, sheer tunic under a heavier tunic with elbow-length sleeves and decorated with a border at the neck, ends of sleeves, and hem, sometimes with a band down the center front. If an outer shawl is worn, it is draped like the himation under the right arm and over the left or worn with the ends over both shoulders and the center over the head like a shawl. Dancing girls often wear a kind of sweater blouse over their chiton-tunic with straps of bells passing under the arms and across the shoulders. Heads are usually swathed in leaf or floral wreaths, and the tunic is usually covered in an allover pattern of dots, zigzags, or geometric design.

Colors are gay and are dominated by light yellow, brick red, and occasional blue accents in the bordering.

The Etruscan interest in dots and zigzags is also illustrated in a bronze statue of a woman making offerings from Monteguragazza (Fig. 5-4). She has a tunic decorated in large zigzags accompanied by dots, a short over-blouse or jumper with zigzag folds, that may relate to the overfold of the Greek peplos; she wears a shawl that repeats the delicate design of zigzags.

Hairdressing varied from the hair parted in the middle with braids or curls down the back to frizzed curls over the forehead and ears with the remainder of the hair bound into a braid or held inside of a snood at the back of the head. The head was also adorned with coronets of metal, jewels, or leaves. The one distinctly Etruscan hat was the *tutulus,* a stiff, pointed headdress with a tiaralike brim in front (Fig. 5-10k). Spiral bracelets, disc earrings, lockets, pendants, fibulae, and jeweled necklaces in delicately carved and repoussé designs were also important to the Etruscan lady of fashion. Shoes varied from red, blue, or black soft moccasin shoes to the standard sandals.

## ROMAN COSTUME OF THE REPUBLIC

Though Rome was as great a contributor to law, government, and administration as it was to practical engineering, its arts and clothing were mostly adaptations from the Etruscans and the Greeks. Even the famous Roman toga was basically an enlargement of the Etruscan tebenna. Therefore, it is sometimes difficult to differentiate Roman from Etruscan or Greek dress.

**Masculine Dress**  The early Roman tunic was relatively narrow, and sleeves were almost nonexistent, as shown in the famous statute of the Orator (Fig. 5-5). The toga in this early portrait statute is semicircular, with a border, or *praetexta,* three or four inches wide around the semicircular edge (Fig. 5-2b). The draping, as

with the Greek himation, starts with one point at the left ankle, the straight edge facing to the center; the mass of material is then carried over the left shoulder, under the right arm, across the chest, and then over the left shoulder a second time to hang down the back to the tunic hem or ankle. Toward the Empire Period, the width of the tunic, the length of the sleeves (to just above the elbow), and the size of the toga all increased.

An important mark of rank during the Republic (that later became mere decoration under the Empire) was the *clavi*—vertical, Tyrian purple bands down the front and back of the tunic. The *augusta clavi* were two bands about an inch-and-a-half wide that went over each shoulder and down the front and back.

**FIG. 5-5** The Orator; Archaeological Museum, Florence; ca. 200 B.C. Illustrates the narrowness of Republican tunics, this one actually qualifying as a *collobium* since it has no sleeves. The toga is here a very limited, half-circular garment probably only half the size of the imperial toga (Fig. 5-8). Photo courtesy of Alinari, Florence.

The *latus clavus* was a three- to four-inch band that went either over both shoulders or down the center front and back of the tunic. The former marked all men of rank; the latter, a senator (Fig. 5-2d). The color of these *clavi* was Tyrian purple.

Most male tunics during the Republic were girded to end just below the knee with a slight blousing below the waist. When cut without sleeves, it was known as a *collobium* (Fig. 5-2a). A shorter tunic was worn by the military; a longer one, by old men. Neatness in girding was always considered a mark of good breeding.

Other outer wraps worn in the Republican and Empire Periods were as follows:

(1) The *lacerna* was a small, semicircular wrap that fastened on the right shoulder with a fibula. This protective wrap was made of woolen fabric in a variety of colors, and varied from hip to calf length. It was worn over a toga for added warmth.

(2) The *sagum* was a sort of blanket adopted by Roman soldiers during the Republic from the mantles worn by the Gauls. It was usually in dark colors or red and was usually reserved for the common soldier, although it was sometimes used by ordinary citizenry during wartime because of its practicality.

(3) The *pallium,* the Roman version of the Greek himation, was rectangular rather than semicircular like the toga. It was adopted by the Romans during the height of the influence of Hellenistic Greek culture, and it remained a garment favored by intellectuals and those who admired things Greek (Fig. 5-2e). It was to have a long history since it was the favored outer garment of the early Christians and was much used in Byzantine costume and later ecclesiastical dress.

(4) The *paludamentum,* a larger version of the Greek chlamys, was worn by generals. It was fastened with a fibula on the right shoulder and became even more important under the Empire. Cut in ever greater size, it became the imperial mantle of the Byzantines.

(5) The *laena* was semicircular and either folded in two or lined to create a warm wrap that fastened on the right shoulder. It was worn by all classes and varied from hip to mid-calf in length.

(6) The *paenula,* probably more often worn than any other wrap, was a cape, open down the center front, often with a peaked hood and collar (*cucullus*) attached. It was usually made of sturdy wool in natural colors like grey, brown, or black and was basic wear, particularly for peasants, as a rain cape (Fig. 5-2c).

(7) The *casula,* a poncholike outer wrap, slipped over the head and usually carried the peaked hood, or *cucullus,* with its own shoulder cape. The whole ensemble became very important during the later Romanesque and early Gothic periods.

Although outer wraps were similar and thus difficult to distinguish, male underclothing was very simple. Roman men wore an undertunic, or *subucula,* that was shorter and narrower than the outer one. Under this garment was worn a loincloth, or *subigaculum,* as a statement of propriety rather than as a necessity.

In addition there was a leg covering or short, tight, knee-length pair of breeches, or *feminalia,* that was worn primarily by the military (Fig. 5–10d). The dedicated Roman citizen despised such a garment as a symbol of barbarism since the garment was connected with the Gauls during Julius Caesar's famous campaigns in France. But the cold northern climates where so many Roman campaigns took place made such a garment important for the common soldier, and even generals are depicted wearing it. It is also thought that Roman citizens of rank wore the feminalia while hunting and riding.

Men's hair was fairly close clipped, with younger men having short locks on the forehead and the nape of the neck. From the second century B.C. to the reign of Hadrian, men were clean shaven. The barbershop was thus a very popular place; equipment consisted of razors, scissors, combs, tweezers, curling irons, mirrors, towels, and the barber's gown. Philosophers and farmers were bearded, and occasionally a clipped beard and mustache were worn by someone of higher rank. Headgear was seldom used, except for the hooded casula or the toga pulled up over the head to form the *sinus.* Lower-class Romans did wear a version of the Greek pilos and a brimmed hat like the Greek petasos.

As for footwear, the Roman male had many varieties of sandals and boots to choose from. The *solea* was the simple walking sandal similar to those of the Greeks. The *calcaeus* was really a shoe that tied over the instep with straps that wrapped around the ankle. The *crepida* was half low-cut shoe and half laced sandal, while the high-calf boot, the *cothurnus* or *caligula,* was a soft leather boot that laced up the front, usually with a heavy turnover at the top (Fig. 5–10h, i, j). Generals often wore these boots, ornamented at the front with lions' heads or other raised and heavily tooled designs.

Jewelry was limited in Republican Roman men's wear to fibulae and rings usually made of iron (Fig. 5–2i, k). Government officials, however, wore gold rings used for sealing letters.

***Feminine Dress*** The Roman woman's dress, essentially the same as that worn by the Greeks, consisted of the tunic, now called the *stola,* usually in Ionic form without an overfold. It was cut very full so that the garment was caught together all down the shoulder and upper arm with fibulae or buttons to produce a sleeve. One may sometimes see a statue with an Ionic style stola under one with a Doric overfold, but this is uncommon. The stola was usually girded fairly high so that the figure is short waisted, often with fullness that falls on the floor.

For an outer wrap the woman wore a feminine version of the Greek himation known as the *palla.* The woman was never allowed to wear the toga, and the palla was usually worn over the left shoulder and under the right arm. It was frequently brought up over the head to form a kind of hood, as may be seen in the second-century B.C. statue of a mother and her sons from the Gallery Borghese in Rome (Fig. 5–6).

Underwear consisted of the interior tunic, or *camisa,* which fitted closely to the body and the *strophium* which was a foundation garment that supported the breasts.

Hairdressing during the Republic was based on Greek styles with the hair parted in the middle, softly waved, and then drawn back into a knot or chignon at the back of the neck. Toward the end of the Republic, a fuller coronet of hair was made around the face by lifting the hair and making a roll at the front or by braiding the hair about the head to create a crown. The great explosion in varieties of hair styling came later during the Empire Period. The only covering for the hair was the veil, or *flammeum,* and very occasionally some form of Greek petasos.

Footwear for women in the earlier period was usually limited to the simple sandal, or *solea,* although occasionally one sees the *calcaeus,* or shoe.

Under the Republic jewelry was again very simple, usually limited to the fibulae that caught up the stola down the upper arm to form a sleeve and the wedding ring (first made of iron and later of gold). Really rich jewelry came only under the Empire.

FIG. 5–6 Mother and Sons; Borghese Gallery, Rome, second century B.C. The sons wear full togas, probably the bleached *toga pura* that represented the arrival at manhood, while the mother wears a simple *stola* or tunic draped with the *palla,* the Roman version of the *himation.* Photo courtesy of Alinari, Florence.

## ROMAN COSTUME OF THE EMPIRE

***Masculine Dress*** During the Empire the male tunica became fuller, and even the sleeveless collobium reached from forearm to forearm (Fig. 5–7). The *tunica talaris,* a tunic with tight sleeves to the wrists and skirts to the ankle, appeared for the first time. The clavi which had been marks of rank gradually became mere ornamentation, and other forms of allover embroidery and ornamentation were added to the tunics of the wealthy and powerful. From the time of the Emperor Nero, the *tunica palmata,* a long-sleeved purple tunic of floor length, embroidered all over with palm leaves in gold metallic thread, was worn with the ornamental, embroidered purple silk *toga picta* by Roman emperors for ceremonial occasions. Other late ornamental devices, which became even more important in later Byzantine dress, included the *segmentae,* or embroidered circles and squares placed on the shoulders and at the top front of the tunic.

The most important new tunic to be added during the Empire Period was the *tunica dalmatica* (or dalmatic), a wide-cut tunic with wide sleeves usually worn over the *tunica talaris.* Heliogabalus, who ruled from A.D. 218 to 222, is thought to have introduced the wide-sleeved tunic from Dalmatia, probably because its loose, flowing lines reminded him of his native Syrian dress.

The distinctive Roman citizen's outer garment, the toga, also underwent changes under the Empire, particularly in size and ornamentation. The toga worn by the Emperor Tiberius on the statue now in the Louvre is the full *imperial toga* of the early Empire (Fig. 5–8). The length, carefully measured to the size of the wearer, was 15 to 20 feet and the width 5 or 6 feet. It was now folded in the middle, and the border was moved from the bottom lower edge to the top edge that was folded over. Shaping often moved from the semicircle to a kind of

FIG. 5-7  Camillus; bronze statue of the Early Empire; Capitoline Museum, Rome. Illustrates the influence of Greek draping on the *collobium* (tunic without sleeves), and if one looks closely there are narrow *clavii* bands on each side from shoulder to waist. Photo courtesy of Alinari, Florence.

toga of the ordinary Roman citizen; the *toga praetexta* was the purple-bordered toga of office worn by all officials of the state; the *toga candida* was the bleached white toga worn by those seeking office; the *toga pulla* was the dark grey or black toga worn for funerals; the *toga trabea* was a striped ceremonial toga with various color combinations, such as the striped purple and scarlet toga worn by augurers; and, of course, there was the *toga picta* for the emperor.

By the second century A.D. impressiveness of size seems to have lost importance, and there were experiments in wearing the garment—especially attempts to control the slipping of the unpinned fabric of the toga. In the statue of an *aedile,* or official, from the third century A.D., the toga appears to be cut longer and narrower

FIG. 5-8  The Emperor Tiberius; first century A.D.; The Louvre, Paris. Illustrates the size, suppleness, and draping line of the Roman toga as it was worn over a simple tunic during the early Empire. Photo courtesy of the French Musées Nationaux.

trapezoidal shape in which sections of the circular shape were cut away (Fig. 5–10g). The overfold could be drawn up over the head to form the *sinus,* or hood, an effect used for religious ceremonies or for protection against the weather. The little pouch of fabric from the left side drawn out over the fabric crossing the chest, as in the statue of Tiberius, was known as the *umbo,* and the right hand, when not gesturing, frequently rested in this pouch.

By the early Empire the nature and use of the various togas had been codified as follows: The *toga pura* or *virilis* was the cream-white woolen

and is wrapped about the body twice to hold it all firmly in place before the end is brought across the front and draped over the left arm (Fig. 5 9). Other variations occurred in the late Empire, but the trend was always toward a flatter, narrower, rectangular shape, rather than semicircular or trapezoidal.

Other outer garments developed under the Republic remained essentially the same under the Empire except that richer ornamentation frequently prevailed.

Hairdressing and faces remained the same until after the time of the Emperor Hadrian, when longer hair and various trimmed beards frequently appeared. Jewelry increased in richness with rings of gold, enamel, and

FIG. 5–9 Aedile; Museo dei Conservatori, Rome; third century A.D. The dimensions of the toga are smaller in the late Empire, and it is wrapped in varying ways. Note that a wide-sleeved *tunica dalmatica* is worn over a long-sleeved *tunica talaris*. Photo courtesy of Alinari, Florence.

precious stones frequently worn on every finger. By the time of Heliogabalus, there is a record of the emperor wearing a necklace of pearls, bracelets covering both arms, and heavy rings covering his hands. The imperial crown was a wreath of laurels in solid gold, although Nero adopted a crown of radiating sun rays. It was not until Diocletian that the eastern-style crown—a broad band of gold set with jewels—became the model for most later medieval crowns.

Finally, a word should be said about military wear. The basic garment of the Roman soldier was the rust red, short tunic under some form of cuirass known as a *lorica*. Of these, there were four kinds: (1) the cast metal variety that repeated the form of the body in exaggerated form and was richly decorated; (2) a leather base covered with overlapping metal scales; (3) chain shirts made of iron links; and (4) articulated horizontal metal plates around the torso with articulated vertical links over the shoulders (Fig. 5–10b, c, d). It is usually the cast metal *lorica* that one sees on military leaders and emperors, such as the second-century A.D. statue of the Emperor Trajan (Fig. 5–10). The breeches (*feminalia* or *bracchae*) mentioned earlier as an item borrowed by the Romans from the barbarians were usually worn under all this, and the boot with a cuff that was then laced up the front, the *caligula*, was worn on the feet (Fig. 5–10i). The metal helmet usually had a permanent visor at the front and a brush instead of a plume for a crest (Fig. 5–10a). The soldier's cloak was the *sagum;* the general's was the *paludamentum*. Shields were of metal or leather, stretched on an oblong, convex metal frame with metal decorations. Swords were short and thick and kept in an ornamental scabbard with the sword belt hung diagonally over the shoulder. Roman military standards displayed the crest of each company; legion standards were topped by the Roman eagle with a thunderbolt in its claws.

**Feminine Dress**  Feminine apparel did not make the same changes from the Republic to the Empire that occurred in men's dress, except in the realm of hairdressing. What does occur is much more variety in wearing under and outer

(a)
helmet

(b) (c)
corselets

(d)

feminalia

(e)
Etruscan man

(g)
toga

(h)
crepida

(j)
solea

(f)
Etruscan woman

(i)
caligula

(k)

The Emperor Trajan; The Louvre, Paris; second century
A.D. The emperor wears a molded metal cuirass, or *lorica,*
with leather straps trimmed with metal at his shoulders and
abdomen. His drape is probably the general's cloak, or
*paludamentum,* here carried rather than worn as a cloak.
Photo courtesy of the French Musées Nationaux.

**FIGURE 5–10**

stolas and in the draping of the palla. A statue of Agrippina, wife of Germanicus, from the first century A.D. wears a stola that fastens with many fibulae on the shoulders and upper arm, but also includes a Doric overfold. It demonstrates the great fullness of fabric used in Roman imperial times and is finished off with a small palla or possibly a shawl known as a *sapparum.* Her feet are shod in the simple *solea,* or sandal (Fig. 5–11).

But it is in the feminine coiffure that the richness and elaboration seen in imperial art and architecture makes its major contribution to feminine beauty. One of the most elaborate examples is that worn by a Flavian lady, possibly Julia, the wife of the Emperor Titus (Fig. 5–12a). Her hair is piled in a tiara of massed curls high on the head in front, while the back is braided into a huge knot at the back of the head. Another style was to wrap the hair in a great coil about the head to create a coronet of hair, or the braid might be coiled in an elongated knot on the crown of the head (Fig. 5–12b). Softer variations included a

number of styles in which the hair was softly waved away from the front of the head or from a central part and then caught into a soft roll or knot at the back (Fig. 5–12c). The most exaggerated rolls of coiled hair are on the statues of the vestal virgins. The veil, or *flammeum,* was often worked into these rich coiffures; hats were relatively unknown except for the country straw, shaped like the Greek petasos.

Female jewelry was the other item of clothing that became more elaborate under the Empire. For example, Pliny tells of Paulina, wife of the Emperor Caligula, appearing at a feast with neck, arms, hair, and girdle all covered with emeralds and pearls, while Sabina, wife of the Emperor Hadrian, wore a jeweled tiara that was estimated to have cost nearly a million dollars by current standards. Rings, fibulae, bracelets, necklaces, earrings, and jeweled girdles made up the wealthy woman's jewel collection, and these items were fashioned into intricate and complex patterns and shapes by mixing gems, gold, enamel inlay, and tiny chains (Fig. 5–2h, i, j, k, n, o).

FIG. 5–11 Agrippina; Museo del Campidoglio; first century A.D. The empress is dressed in the Greek style with a *chiton* overfold at the top of her *stola, fibulae* fastenings on her arms, and the *palla* draped loosely over her body. Note the distinctly Roman hairdressing. Photo courtesy of Alinari, Florence.

**FIG. 5–12** (*a*) Giulia (or Julia), wife of the Emperor Titus; Capitoline Museum, Rome; ca. A.D. 90. (*b*) Plotina; Museo Nazionale, Naples; second century A.D. (*c*) Annia Faustina; Capitoline Museum, Rome; third century A.D. (*d*) Antonia, wife of Drusus; Museo Nazionale, Naples; first to second century A.D. Examples of female hairdressing in Rome during the Empire. Photos courtesy of Alinari, Florence.

# FABRICS

Woolen and linen fabrics were the staples in Republican and early Imperial times, with silk imported from China added in the later Empire. Cotton was occasionally used in various parts of the Empire.

# ARTS AND ARTIFACTS

Roman arts reflected the great Roman admiration, appreciation, and borrowings from Greek art. The architectural methods were very similar except for the great use by the Romans of the vault and arch and the greater mixture and elaboration of the Greek Doric, Ionic, and Corinthian orders (Fig. 5-1f). Roman houses, like the Greek, were built around a central open court with elaborate mosaic floors and rich wall frescoes that ranged from flat geometric, decorative arrangements to rich and complex illusionistic scenes in perspective. Colors used were Tuscan or tile red, black, greenish gold, and various shades of greyed purplish red. Furniture was basically similar to the Greek but without its gracefulness, and the furniture ornamentation was rich, even florid. Couches for conversation and eating were more prevalent than chairs, and the latter were usually quite high and required the use of a footstool (Fig. 5-1b). Although most decoration was based on natural sources, the Romans of Republican times usually abstracted and geometricized these sources. Under the Empire, patterns and motifs tended toward rich illusionism (Fig. 5-1c).

Standard accessories included many items that demonstrated official authority, such as the *fasces,* or bundle of rods enclosing an axe, that lictors carried before consuls and other officials, or the scepter, carried by a consul as a symbol of his office. Another accessory carried by emperors and consuls and waved for the beginnings of gladiatorial contests or royal games was the *mappa,* or handkerchief, which was worn over the right wrist or held folded in the right hand (see Fig. 6-2).

Personal accessories included the contents of the women's makeup table with its mirror, hairpins, curling iron, salves, creams, jewel boxes, fan, and a lamp that was very like the Greek one with its wick floating in oil (Figs. 5-1e, 5-2k, l). A table or shelf might carry the scroll-books of the time; a lyre, pipes, or a cithara might be seen; a few toys such as dolls, a spinning top, or a small child's wagon or pushcart might be placed in a corner. Basically, the upper-class enjoyed quite comfortable, richly domestic lives, while the lower-middle and lower-class urban dwellers were crammed into small apartments in buildings with four or five floors.

# VISUAL SOURCES

The sources for information on Roman dress are legion. For Etruscan items the best museums are the Metropolitan in New York, the Archaeological Museum in Florence, and the Etruscan-Gregorian Museum in the Vatican. For Roman costume the best repositories are the Terme, Capitoline, Vatican, and Conservatori Museums in Rome; the Louvre; the Museo Nazionale in Naples; and various monuments, such as the Arch of Titus and Arch of Constantine, as well as certain wall paintings at Pompeii. Good written source books are Herbert Norris's *Costume and Fashion: The Evolution of European Dress through the Earlier Ages,* and Mary Houston's *Ancient Greek, Roman and Byzantine Costume and Decoration.*

# SUMMARY

Rome was the great cultural bridge between Greek civilization and that which was to develop in northern and western Europe. It was through Rome that most information about the Greeks was filtered in medieval and Renaissance times. In the archaeological revivals of the eighteenth and nineteenth centuries, it was Roman, rather than Greek classicism that was the major source of inspiration in clothing, furniture, and interior design. Even in the twentieth century when we have moved beyond the beaux-arts tradition with its eclectic use of Roman columns, capitals, pediments, and domes, we are still surrounded by Roman eagles, Roman mottoes, Roman practicality in building and engineering, and Roman ideals of business, finance, administration, and government.

Roman dress, though similar to the Greek, was based on symbolism combined with a certain pragmatic practicality and lacked the beauty and fluid grace of Greek clothing at its best. Under the Republic it remained austere, simple, and symbolic. Under the Empire, however, it added richness and the symbols of grandeur and power until late imperial dress took on an almost Eastern magnificence in color, texture, and ornament. Roman dress took the beauty of draping that was the ideal of the Greeks and placed it at the service of symbolism and power imagery.

# chapter VI

# Early Christian and Byzantine

## Chronology

(A.D. 324–1453)

| | | |
|---|---|---|
| **EARLY CHRISTIAN AND EARLY BYZANTINE** <br> A.D. 324–527 | 324 | Constantine becomes sole emperor of the entire Roman Empire |
| | 330 | Constantine moves his capital to Byzantium |
| | 337 | Constantine the Great dies |
| | 374 | St. Ambrose becomes Bishop of Milan |
| | 379 | Theodosius I begins 16-year reign and establishes the Theodosian Dynasty |
| | 395 | Arcadius becomes emperor; Empire divided into East and West |
| | 410 | Rome is sacked by Alaric the Visigoth |
| | ca. 425 | Tomb of Galla Placidia is begun in Ravenna |
| | 455 | Rome is sacked by the Vandals |
| | 476 | The last Roman emperor, Romulus Augustulus, is deposed by Odoacer the Ostrogoth, and the imperial domain in the west comes to an end |

| FIRST GOLDEN AGE<br>A.D. 527–726 | 527 | Justinian the Great becomes emperor and reigns for 38 years with his wife Theodora; Constantinople reaches its cultural peak; Church of Sts. Sergius and Bacchus is built |
| | 529 | Code of Justinian adopted as Byzantine law |
| | 532 | Hagia Sophia is begun |
| | 547 | Ravenna is captured by Justinian's general, Belisarius, and becomes the capital of Byzantine Italy |
| | ca. 550 | Silkworms brought from China to Justinian by Nestorian monks |
| | 565 | Justinian dies and Justin II becomes emperor |
| | 590 | Gregory the Great becomes pope in Rome |
| | 614 | Jerusalem is captured by the Persians |
| | 635 | Arab conquest of Persia begins |
| | 638 | Jerusalem falls to the Arabs under Caliph Omar I |
| | 673 | Arabs begin their first attack on Constantinople |
| | 697 | Carthage, last Byzantine stronghold in Africa, falls to the Arabs |
| | 717 | Arabs begin another siege of Constantinople, but are defeated by the Emperor-General Leo III |
| PERIOD OF THE ICONOCLASTIC CONTROVERSY<br>A.D. 726–843 | 726 | The iconoclastic controversy begins, and the human figure in art is suppressed in favor of symbolic images |
| | 732 | Charles Martel is victorious over the Arabs at Poitiers |
| | 751 | Ravenna is captured by the Lombards, and the Byzantine exarchate in Italy comes to an end |

ca. A.D. 550

| | | |
|---|---|---|
| | 762 | Baghdad is founded by Caliph el Mansur |
| | 797 | The politically ambitious Irene, mother of Constantine VI, blinds her own son to become sole ruler and is sought in marriage by Charlemagne |
| **SECOND GOLDEN AGE** <br> A.D. 843–1100 | 867 | Basil I founds the Macedonian Dynasty |
| | 878 | Sicily lost to the Arabs |
| | 904 | The Arabs seize Thessalonica, the second city of the Byzantine Empire |
| | 948 | Romanus I, one of Byzantium's greatest rulers, dies in exile as a monk |
| | 975 | Damascus retaken from the Arabs |
| | 1017 | Basil II, last great ruler in the Macedonian Dynasty, conquers the Bulgarian kingdom and annexes its lands |
| ca. A.D. 1000 | 1054 | The Byzantine Church makes a final and permanent break with Rome |
| | 1063 | St. Mark's Cathedral begun in Venice |
| | 1096 | The First Crusade is launched |
| | 1099 | The Kingdom of Jerusalem is established |
| **FINAL DECLINE** <br> A.D. 1100–1453 | 1147 | The Second Crusade begins |
| | 1187 | Jerusalem is captured by Saladin |
| | 1189 | The Third Crusade is launched |
| | 1201 | The Fourth Crusade begins |
| | 1204 | Constantinople is captured by Christian troops of the Fourth Crusade |

## BACKGROUND

Rome, with all its influence on culture, law, art, and administration, took a long time to die. Even as late as the fifth and sixth centuries Roman methods of organization, institutions, and artistic ideals remained in the cultural life of many centers around the Mediterranean. But it was the acceptance by the Emperor Constantine of Christianity as the state religion of the Empire and his decision to move his capital to Byzantium early in the fourth century that were the events that marked the beginning of the change from a classical to a medieval view of life. By A.D. 395 the Roman Empire had been officially divided into East and West with one capital in Rome and the other in Constantinople. From then on the decline of power, influence, and classical ideals in the West was

rapid. Western Catholic Christianity began to separate from Eastern Orthodox Christianity, and the philosophy and cultural outlook of the Roman Church was in sharp contrast to the religious and cultural ideals of the Eastern Church with its center in Byzantium.

Rome also fell prey to renewed invasions by the Germanic tribes from north of the Alps, while the Eastern, or Byzantine, part of the Empire grew in strength and power. In 476 Romulus, the last of the Roman emperors, was deposed by the Ostrogothic leader Odoacer, and for all official purposes the Roman Empire came to an end. Meanwhile the Byzantine Empire reached its peak of power between 527 and 565 during the reign of the Emperor Justinian. After his famous general, Belisarius, reconquered parts of Italy, Byzantine rule in that area centered in the city of Ravenna for the next 200 years. The First Golden Age of Byzantium, under Justinian and his wife Theodora, was marked by a fusion of Eastern and Western artistic ideals—Mesopotamian and Egyptian artistic inheritances merged into the classical inheritance from Greece and Rome. The architectural masterpiece of this age, Hagia Sophia, clearly shows this fusion of artistic ideals. Planned by Justinian and begun in 532, the church remains one of the great architectural triumphs of all time and a perfect symbol of the cultural and artistic outlook of the leaders of the Byzantine Empire (Fig. 6-1). The central feature is a square nave set between two half-circles that changes to a circle at the top through the support of four spherical triangles, or *pendentives,* at the corners. Above this circular rim "floats" a dome seemingly supported by a glowing ring of light created by the many small windows that ring the base. This light, falling on the mosaics that originally adorned most of the walls, must have given a mysterious, celestial glow to the entire interior. Looking

down into the subtle glitter of this world of unreality from one of the galleries, one can still gain some of that sense of awesome mystery and ritual that was so important to this Eastern Empire.

Once the Eastern Empire separated from the remains of the Roman Empire, it reverted to the Greek language, used more and more oriental rituals, customs and artistic ideals, and developed a very oriental conservatism, reminiscent of the ancient Near East. The Eastern Orthodox faith was based on a complete fusion of church and state in the person of the Byzantine emperor, and thus this potentate was regarded as a god as well as a man as were ancient Egyptian pharaohs. The Byzantine Empire, in struggling to preserve the forms of its origin against militant Islam, remained isolated from new ideals and developments, weak in power but strong in its determination to preserve the past. When it finally succumbed to the Ottoman Turks in 1453, it was a quaint relic of an age that had reached its peak almost a thousand years ealier.

## THE BASIC COSTUME SILHOUETTE

The garments worn by the early leaders of the Christian Church were quite naturally based on the standard dress of the Roman lower classes of the late Empire with ornamental borrowings from the aristocrats. These garments were the basis for the liturgical vestments used in the Catholic Church today. Basic tunics like the *tunica talaris* and the *tunica dalmatica* were used with *clavi* bands as the basis for the under vestments, while the *paenula* and *casula* used by the Roman lower classes for protection against the elements were developed into the outer vestments of *cope* and *chasuble.* Because the early Christian concept was that the body was sinful and should not be exposed, all adaptations of Roman garments stressed long sleeves and a full ankle length. Because draping was believed to call attention to the graceful, physical movement of the body under clothing, a trend developed toward semifitted garments, which still recalled Roman lines, but gave a more muffled, flat figure that called less attention to

the body beneath the garments. One can readily see this by comparing the semifitted effects in the famed Justinian mosaic with the statue of Tiberius Caesar (see Figs. 5-8 and 6-3).

The shift from Roman to early Christian to Byzantine ideals in dress was a subtle process influenced first by the ideals of the new Christian faith and then by the oriental influences affecting Roman dress after the capital of the Empire was moved to Constantinople by the Emperor Constantine in 330. By the time that the famed Justinian and Theodora mosaics were created in the Church of San Vitale in Ravenna about 547, the basic precepts of Byzantine dress had already been established.

In the scene depicting the Empress Theodora and her retinue, the rich, bejeweled effects had already begun to dominate parts of the costume and begun that process by which Byzantine rulers came to resemble walking mosaics (Fig. 6-2). The silks, the major form of aristocratic fabric after Justinian introduced

(a)
Santa Sophia  N.E. elevation

(b)
motifs

(c)
Byzantine
throne

Interior of Santa Sophia, Istanbul; A.D. 532–537. Note the
monumental size created by Justinian and his architects by
employing a circular plan between two halves of a square,
with the dome supported by triangular pendentives resting
on great piers. The lighting is awesome and mysterious as
it falls from porthole openings onto what were originally
rich, mosaic wall surfaces. Photo courtesy of the Hirmer
Fotoarchiv, Munich.

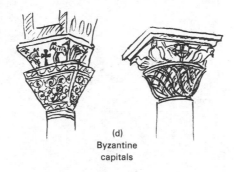

(d)
Byzantine
capitals

**FIGURE 6-1**

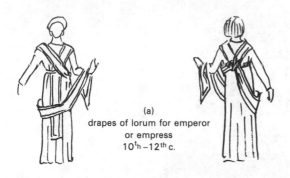

(a)
drapes of lorum for emperor
or empress
10th – 12th c.

(b)
metallic and silk
fabric designs

(c)
ecclesiastical vestments

(d)
fitted jeweled
tunic

*The Empress Theodora and Her Retinue;* a mosaic from the Church of San Vitale, Ravenna; ca. A.D. 547. The empress carries a golden chalice for the celebration of the Eucharist and is dressed in a tunic and mantle of silk interwoven with metallic threads and set with precious stones. Her hairdressing and crown of pearls, along with her jeweled collar, give her the look of a walking mosaic. Photo courtesy of Alinari, Florence.

(e)
empress crown 10th c.

(f)
earring

(g)
bracelet

(h)
pectoral
cross

(i)
headdress
10th – 12th c.

**FIGURE 6-2**

94

silkworm culture from China, were already becoming stiff with jewels and metallic thread embroidery, and the headdress and collar of the empress already suggest the otherworldly power that one remembers from images of the pharoah and his wife (see Fig. 2–11).

## EARLY CHRISTIAN AND EARLY BYZANTINE DRESS

In the early Byzantine Period both the rendering of sacred figures and the development of ecclesiastical dress remained close to their Roman origins and to the ideal of Roman draping, even though the body was almost completely covered by the garments. The key garments for sacred figures were always the dalmatic and the draped pallium, or for the women the Roman stola draped with the palla and finished with the *flammeum,* or veil. Ornamentation was usually limited to derivations from the *clavi* or *praetexta* borders. Although Byzantine civil dress moved almost completely away from soft draping, this draped effect remained into Gothic times for the depiction of sacred characters.

**Ecclesiastical Dress** Probably one of the first and most important early items of ecclesiastical dress was the *pallium,* or pall, the Roman version of the Greek himation and symbolically related to the Roman toga. It later became merely a long narrow strip of cloth decorated with crosses and draped around the shoulders and down the front of the body. Today it is a mere circle dropped over the shoulders with a tab hanging down the front and marked with four crosses (Fig. 6–2c). The *stole,* another long narrow strip of material marked with three crosses and fringed at the ends, was worn over the shoulders under the chasuble with ends hanging down the front on either side during the actual celebration of the mass. It may have derived from the fringed *orarion,* a long handkerchief waved by the Roman emperor at official games, although it is also sometimes linked to the *clavi* on aristocratic tunics or to the fringed ends of the Jewish prayer shawl. This item is still part of the vestments for the mass (Fig. 6–2c). The garment which became the most important item in the celebration of the mass was the *chasuble,* the poncholike garment derived from the Roman peasants' paenula and casula, which can be seen on Bishop Maximianus in the Justinian mosaic (Fig. 6–3). With very little modification, it is still worn by all priests and bishops officiating at mass (Fig. 6–2c). Somewhat related to this vestment item is the bishop's cape, or *cope,* which is also thought to derive from the Roman paenula and still has a symbolic remainder of a hood at the back of the neck. It is a processional garment that is never worn during the celebration of the mass.

The standard undergarment, based on the bleached *tunica alba* of the Romans, was the snow white, long-sleeved *alb* which is seen in many early paintings, statues, and mosaics, and which remains the basic under tunic for vestments today. Over this was worn the dalmatic, the wide-sleeved tunic based on the Roman tunica dalmatica that seems to be the most prominent ecclesiastical garment in depictions of early church figures. In the Justinian mosaic, Bishop Maximianus wears an especially wide-sleeved version of the dalmatic (as do his supporting clerics) which also displays the clavi bands from Roman times (Fig. 6–3). The *cassock* was another tunic derived from the Roman-Barbaric *caracalla.* It was later lengthened and developed into a basic coat-tunic for everyday ecclesiastical use.

Other modern Catholic Church vestment items from these times are the bishop's mitre, probably derived from the great domical headdress of the Hebrew high priest, and the decorative *orphreys* and *apparels* (embroidered squares and bands) seen on the alb, dalmatic, and chasuble, probably developed from the decorative *tablion* and *segmentae* of Byzantine aristocrats. Thus as with the establishment of any formal institution, the forms, customs, and uniform vestments established at the beginning of the institution tend to remain with only minimal modification throughout its development.

**FIG. 6-3** *Justinian and Attendants;* a mosaic from the Church of San Vitale, Ravenna; ca. A.D. 547. The emperor is seen as a god-king with a halo and carrying the paten for celebration of the Eucharist. The clothing, though vaguely Roman, now covers the entire body, and the draping, done primarily in silks interwoven with metallics, is stiff, formal, and hierarchical. Photo courtesy of Alinari, Florence.

***Masculine Dress*** During the 200 years from the time of Constantine to the reign of Justinian, clothing changed only minimally but always in the direction of covering all but the hands and face of the human body. Coptic Christian tunics remain from this period, and their major distinction is the rich embroidery on their borders marking neck and wrists as well as the clavi bands over the shoulder and down each side of the tunic. Embroidered segmentae on shoulders and sleeves were also popular. These Coptic tunics were usually of colored wool in green, yellow, red, or purple, but the richest examples are embroidered over silk. The legs were covered with fitted trousers that soon developed into the smooth-fitting leg coverings, often with feet sewn in, that became the *hosa* of later Byzantine times. In the famous *Diptych of Stilicho and Serena,* it is difficult to tell whether Stilicho's legs have a covering (Fig. 6-4). His tunic is long-sleeved, has an allover pattern, and probably is of silk. His mantle also

has an allover pattern, and his feet are clad, not in sandals, but in slipperlike shoes strapped over the instep.

A much more ceremonial garment worn by consuls of the empire may be seen in the *Diptych of Flavius Anastasius* (Fig. 6-5). He wears a *tunica talaris* with rich embroidered wristbands and embroidered clavi that show just above his feet. Over this is worn a richly embroidered dalmatic in an allover pattern that fits closely around the neck. His official robe of office is still a version of the toga, now usually referred to as a *pallium.* It is wrapped about the body quite differently than in Roman times, beginning in the center front of the figure, traveling up over the right shoulder, under the right arm, across the chest, over the left shoulder, and then around the lower left part of the body, widening out into a much wider piece of fabric as it is draped over the left arm. It, too, is heavily embroidered, probably in metallic threads; all of the garments are probably of silk. In his right hand he carries

FIG. 6-4 *Diptych of Stilicho and Serena;* Monza Cathedral, Italy; A.D. 395. The Vandal Stilicho, commander-in-chief of the Roman army and briefly virtual ruler of the Eastern Empire, wears a long-sleeved, knee-length tunic of patterned silk girded at the waist under a *paludamentum* fastened by a *fibula* on the right shoulder. His wife wears a wide-sleeved tunic (*dalmatic*) over a long-sleeved *stola,* the draped *palla,* a turban headdress, and pointed slippers. Photo courtesy of Alinari, Florence.

FIG. 6-5 *Consular Diptych of Anastasius;* Bibliothèque Nationale, Paris; A.D. 517. Illustrates how the *pallium,* successor to the toga as a symbol of imperial power, had narrowed and changed in draping since Roman imperial times. He also wears a *dalmatic* over a long-sleeved tunic and holds in his right hand the *mappa,* or imperial kerchief, that formerly was carried by the Roman emperor to signal the beginning of games. Photo courtesy of the Bibliothèque Nationale, Paris.

the *scepter,* or baton of office; in his left, the *mappa* or *orarium,* a rolled napkin that had originally been waved to mark the beginning of imperial games. His shoes are really soft slippers that have cross-straps over the instep and fasten twice about the ankle.

The military wear of this early period is very similar to that of the earlier Roman Empire. An excellent record of this is in a porphyry group, dated shortly after Constantine moved his capital to Byzantium (Fig. 6-6). The figures wear smooth breastplates with double rows of leather straps below the hips and triple ones on the shoulders. A tight, long-sleeved tunic covers the arms, legs may or may not be covered with hosa, and feet are not shod in sandals but in slipper shoes with cross-straps. The helmet is not the typical Roman style but more Near Eastern, like the helmet of Gudea from early Babylonian times (see Fig. 3-2r). The military cloak is the standard Roman paluda-mentum, or military *chlamys,* worn by generals during the Empire.

**Feminine Dress**  The change for women from Roman to Byzantine was also gradual with the stress on more ornamentation, the use of the tunica dalmatica over the stola, and a desire to cover all of the body except for the hands and feet. The figure of Serena from the *Diptych of Stilicho and Serena* is a good example of the very early Byzantine development (Fig. 6-4). She is wearing the stola with long sleeves under what appears to be an early form of the dalmatic with the palla loosely draped over all. She wears large earrings and necklace, a turban or very artificial wig, and pointed shoes rather than sandals. Although the draped line of the Romans is still maintained in the muffled look, ornamentation and artificiality of the Byzantine are beginning to appear.

## FIRST BYZANTINE GOLDEN AGE

Probably the most important event of the Emperor Justinian's reign, as far as the history of dress is concerned, was the introduction of the silkworm into the Byzantine realm. Instead of having to import silks overland from China, they were now manufactured at home in centers like Thebes and Corinth. The art of weaving complicated patterns with colored and metallic threads came from two sources—the Sassanian Persians and the Christian Copts of Egypt. As time passed, silks became thicker, stiffer, and heavier. A silk known as *samite,* which was quite strong, became the basic weave and was embroidered with metallic threads and set with precious stones and metals. Lightweight tissue silks were used for veils; linen, woolen, and cotton were available for more mundane clothing.

**Masculine Dress**  Stiffness in clothing was already apparent in the garments of the men in the famed Justinian and Theodora mosaics (Figs. 6-2, 3). The tunics were now all long-sleeved and varied from just below the knee to ankle length. They were usually decorated with embroidered segmentae on the shoulders and the skirt. Legs were clad in tight-fitting *hosa,* or trousers, and one can distinguish the soldiers' legs in the Justinian mosaic from the aristocrats' primarily by the trouser look to the leg covering on the former versus the sense of tights worn by the nobility. Shoes were soft slippers with straps, and the overgarment was the mantle, or *paludamentum,* that fastened on the right shoulder. This garment had replaced the Roman toga or its more common rectangular derivative, the *pallium,* as a state garment during the period of Justinian, even though the pallium in its civil dress form (as opposed to ecclesiastical usage) was to take on new importance as the *lorum* during the Second Golden Age of Byzantium. The paludamentum changed very little through the centuries except for the *tablions,* richly ornamented square or rectangular plaques, placed along the front and back open sides of the mantle and for the added jewelry and embroidery that came during the Second Golden Age. The one garment that increased in importance as time passed was the dalmatic, based on the long, wide-sleeved tunica dalmatica of the Romans. It and the mantle became heavier and more richly en-

(a)
Byzantine
armor
at the
opening
of
the
5<sup>th</sup> c.

(b)
helmet

(c)
Emperor's
armor

(d)
common
man

(e)
ordinary
woman

*The Tetrarchs;* St. Marks, Venice; early fourth century A.D. These tetrarchs are in molded *loricas* decorated with multiple tiers of leather straps, the draped cloak or *paludamentum,* elaborate sandals, and short, cylindrical helmet crowns. Photo courtesy of Alinari, Florence.

**FIGURE 6–6**

99

crusted with jewels and metallic embroidery as the centuries passed.

As for headcoverings, there were practically none used except for the imperial crown. By Justinian's time this had become rigid and imposing and consisted of a flaring gold band edged with pearls and encircled with precious stones (Fig. 6–3). A series of pear-shaped pearls hang like a set of long earrings over each ear. For common people the Greek petasos was still worn; hoods were used for protection against the weather, and the eastern Phrygian bonnet was sometimes mentioned.

Soldiers during this period continued to wear basically Roman armor. The only change was the common military helmet which now had a brim, only a tiny crest, and no longer framed the face. (Fig. 6–6a, b).

**Feminine Dress**   The growing amount of richness in jewelry and embroidery for female costume in the First Golden Age is quite apparent in the mosaic of Theodora and her retinue (Fig. 6–2). Theodora wears a long-sleeved white stola embroidered in gold under a purple paludamentum that is symbolically embroidered with the three Magi bearing gifts. Next to her stands Antonina, wife of Justinian's great general Belisarius, who was a close friend and confidante of the empress. Her purple stola has strong embroidered clavi in red, white, and green down each side and a white palla with an allover pattern and embroidered on the corners with rich segmentae. Other ladies wear various patterned stolas and pallas, including a white stola patterned in blue under a rich gold palla marked with red and green motifs, and a green stola under an orange-red palla.

Shoes are little red slippers that peep out from under the hem of the stolas; jewelry runs to very rich jeweled collars and necklaces and discreet earrings, as well as bracelet effects which are actually rings of precious stones or pearls sewn to the wrist of the stolas. The headdress of the Empress Theodora is especially grand and is the central focus of the whole scene. It consists of a donut-shaped turban surmounted by a soft rounded crown that completely hides the hair to which is added a rich coronet of gold, also completely set with bands of precious stones. Down the side of the head in hanging pendular strands are more jewels that would shimmer and undulate with each slight movement of the head, and this profusion of jewels then mingles with a collar again comprised of ring after ring of precious stones (Fig. 6–2). It is an imposing image, made more striking by the rather modest turbans or hairdressing of the ladies-in-waiting. It is clear that even when a turban was not worn, the lady's hair was rolled to look like a turban.

## SECOND BYZANTINE GOLDEN AGE

**Masculine Dress**   After the close of the Iconoclastic Controversy which produced a period of art in which few human images were depicted, we have a period of new richness in dress, one that is even heavier and more body-encompassing than anything seen during the reign of Justinian. For example, let us look at the manuscript depicting the Emperor Nicephoras Botaniates (Fig. 6–7). The emperor wears a very heavy dalmatic with wide sleeves that now reach well down the forearm over a very tight-sleeved tunic. The dalmatic has a tight allover pattern, a very heavy, embroidered band on the sleeves, and a border at the bottom. It looks as if it were very stiff and heavy. Over this is draped, or rather laid, the *lorum,* which is the imperial counterpart of the ecclesiastical pallium and the item that links the Byzantine emperor's dress directly to the imperial toga picta of Roman times. This long, richly embroidered heavy strip starts at the center front of the figure, goes over the right shoulder and probably under the right arm, then up across the front, over the left shoulder, across the back, under the left arm, and back across the front. What holds the final end in front is unclear; possibly it was hooked to the dalmatic in some way, although it is usually thought that it was draped over or held by the right hand (Fig. 6–2a).

Theodora in the mosaic at Ravenna (Fig. 6-2), and in its richness and bejeweled weight represents the later Byzantine emphasis on further rigidity, formality, and abstraction from reality that dominated all phases of late Byzantine culture. By the twelfth century the Byzantine imperial crown had become dome-shaped; and in the last century of Byzantine power, it spread into a bejeweled bulbous shape that is still reflected in the great headdress of the pope (Fig. 6-2i).

**FIG. 6-7** *Nicephoras Botaniates with St. John Chrysostom and the Archangel Gabriel;* Bibliothèque Nationale, Paris; A.D. 1078-1081. The Emperor wears a formal *dalmatic* of rich purple silk emblazoned with gold and jewels, a crown with pendant pearls and a collar of gold leaf on leather. From Coislin MS 79. Photo courtesy of the Bibliothèque Nationale, Paris.

**FIG. 6-8** *Christ Crowning the Emperor Romanus IV and the Empress Eudoxia;* cover of the gospel of Saint John of Besancon; Bibliothèque Nationale, Paris; eleventh century A.D. The emperor and the empress are depicted in mosaics through the use of silk, metallic embroidery, and precious jewels. The sandwich-board covering worn by the emperor, with a trailing end brought around and draped over the left arm, is a memory of the *toga* and is known as the *lorum*. Photo courtesy of the Bibliothèque Nationale, Paris.

A different wearing of this heavy lorum may be seen in the ivory book cover from the eleventh century depicting Christ crowning the Emperor Romanus and his wife Eudoxia (Fig. 6-8). Here the embroidered panel is of greater width and somewhat shorter length; instead of being draped about the body, it has an opening for the head and is worn like a clerical scapular, with the long trailing end behind brought around the left side of the body and draped over the right arm. Variations of this derivation from the Roman pallium or toga were seen in coronation costume until the opening of the six teenth century.

The headdress of the Emperor Romanus (Fig. 6-8) is similar to that worn by the Empress

In the Second Golden Age of Byzantium, hosa remained the common leg covering, but the emperor and his courtiers frequently wore soft leather or cloth boots (most frequently in red) that were richly sewn with pearls or other jewels. Armor for the military retained its Roman character until the period of the Crusades and then gradually changed to incorporate the shirts of chain mail and helmets with cheek, nose, or face protection that were worn by western European warriors (Fig. 6-6c).

**Feminine Dress** During the Second Golden Age of Byzantium, the stola and palla combination retained from Roman imperial times all but disappeared in favor of a long-sleeved undertunic, a wide-sleeved dalmatic, and an embroidered and bejeweled paludamentum (Fig. 6-8), or a feminine version of the masculine pallium or lorum (Fig. 6-7). This latter was frequently just a richly embroidered strip that hung down the front and back of the body from under a broad, high collar. The back panel, which was wider at the end and longer than the body, was brought around to the front under the right arm and spread across the front of the figure as if in mock remembrance of the draping of the imperial Roman toga or palla.

One Byzantine style often seen in western Europe during the period of the Crusades was the fitted or laced tunic to the hips worn over a full-length undertunic. It was often richly decorated with jewels and embroidery and gave the female torso the look of being encased in a jeweled breastplate (Fig. 6-2d). Sometimes these tight overtunics had tight sleeves; at other times they appeared to have no sleeves at all.

Women of the middle and lower class were probably even more conservative in their dress, retaining the basic *stola*, or tunic, from Roman times draped with a shawl, or *palla* (Fig. 6-6e). The stola was often girdled in a high-waisted manner that gave a kind of Empire line to the female figure, and the palla was draped in a variety of ways that covered the upper part of the body and even the head.

Headdresses were primarily reserved for ladies of the court; other ladies merely wore the palla draped up over their hair. These headdresses had many shapes but were usually composed of a series of jeweled rings or circlets sometimes holding an inner turban or mitre effect (Fig. 6-2e, i). Pendant jewels over each ear were common. Hairdressing was most commonly based on a center part, with coils of hair twisted about the head and then finished in a knot or coil at the top of the head. Sometimes in the eleventh and twelfth centuries, single coils of hair were allowed to fall to the shoulder on either side of the head.

Footwear consisted of soft slippers, sometimes with pointed toes that gave an Eastern look. For ladies of the court these slippers were usually in red, although in some mosaics one can see black slippers with orange hose. Though most jewelry was overpowered by the embroidery and jewels of the costume itself, there are beautiful extant examples of gold bracelets, jeweled earrings, and enamel inlay rings (Fig. 6-2f, g, h).

## FABRICS

Fabrics for the court were overwhelmingly rich, with an emphasis on gold and silver threads woven in with silk. Since Justinian the Great introduced silkworm culture into the Byzantine domain, all manner of silks were now woven locally without importation from China, and the result was great richness of experimentation in colors and pattern combinations (Fig. 6-2b).

There were simple dots, stars, and circles as well as more complex, geometricized vegetable and animal motifs and a great emphasis on embroidery application and jeweled surfaces. The silk from this period, known as *samite*, was strong, thick, and stiff. Tissue silks were used for scarfs and veils, while more basic clothes were woven of linen, cotton, or wool.

# ARTS AND ARTIFACTS

The round arch and the dome were inherited from the Romans, but the Byzantines added many ingenious refinements to the use of the dome, starting with the use of *pendentives,* or triangular sections of a sphere to support a dome on four great piers, as is the case with Santa Sophia (Fig. 6–1a). Their major contribution to interior decoration lay in the perfection of the wall mosaic as a subtly mysterious, gently glowing adornment for church and palace interiors. The mosaic was the quintessential Byzantine artifact, and Byzantine clothing came to resemble this art form as the centuries passed. Other interior artifacts included rich wall hangings embroidered in metallic threads and furnishings embellished with carved ivory. The finest chairs, tables, and even book covers were all inlaid or covered with carved ivory (Fig. 6–1c). Another richly ornamental method of decoration for jewelry, furnishings, book covers, and personal accessories was colored enamel inlay set inside tiny gold *cloisons,* or fences that outline the design. Favored decorative motifs were the many Christian symbols such as the vine, peacock, cross, dove, lamb, pelican, and fish. Other motifs include the gryphon, horse, imperial eagle, and various floral shapes (Fig. 6–1b).

Accessories included the *codex,* or book, often with richly inlaid covers, that took precedence over the scroll at the beginning of the First Byzantine Golden Age. The pages of these books were in parchment and rich vellum, the latter often dyed purple to set off the written inscriptions in gold and silver. Royal appurtenances were the gold orb topped with a cross held in the right hand of the emperor and the scepter or holy lance held in the left hand.

# VISUAL SOURCES

One excellent source for Byzantine manuscripts, book covers, and illustrations is the Bibliothèque Nationale in Paris. The best mosaics are those in Ravenna at San Vitale and San Apollinare Nuovo, and Santa Sophia in Istanbul. Another excellent source of information is the City Museum in Istanbul. Good written sources are Herbert Norris's *Costume and Fashion: The Evolution of European Dress through the Earlier Ages* and Mary G. Houston's *Ancient Greek, Roman and Byzantine Costume and Decoration.*

# SUMMARY

Byzantine culture and fashion is a fascinating mixture of Greek, Roman, and Near Eastern elements—a mysterious amalgamation of abstract and realistic decorative elements brought together to create a world of motifs, forms, and conventions that tied the world of Christian otherworldliness to Roman imperial power. It created a distinctive kind of dress by mixing silk fabric with metallic thread and jeweled appliqué; light then reflected a rich mysterious glow of unreality from the stiff-clad human form. Folds of soft, plain fabric were replaced by stiff garments that made the most lavish costumes seem like wall mosaics brought to life. The splendor of a conventional unreality took the place of plastic, moving, fabric effects on the natural human form.

# chapter VII

# Barbaric, Carolingian, and Romanesque

## Chronology
### (ca. A.D. 400–1150)

| | | |
|---|---|---|
| BARBARIC<br>ca. 400–750 | 409 | Alaric, king of the Visigoths, lays siege to Rome and exacts tribute; Vandals arrive in Spain |
| | ca. 410 | Rome withdraws its troops from Britain; Rome is captured and sacked by the Visigoths under Alaric; Alaric dies and leadership passes to Ataulf |
| | ca. 420 | St. Augustine of Hippo is engaged in writing *The City of God* |
| | 429 | Vandals from Spain spread across the Straits of Gilbraltar and begin the conquest of North Africa |
| | 443 | Burgundian tribes settle near the Rhone where they create the Burgundian kingdom |
| | ca. 450 | Angles, Saxons, and Jutes invade Britain |
| | 451–453 | Attila the Hun invades Gaul but then retreats across the Rhine and invades northern Italy; he dies suddenly in 453 |
| | 476 | Odoacer chosen king of the barbarians in Italy and deposes the Emperor Romulus, bringing the fall of the Western Roman Empire |

| | |
|---|---|
| 481 | Clovis becomes King of the Franks |
| 489 | Theodoric, king of the Ostrogoths, invades Italy with the backing of the Emperor Zeno in Constantinople |
| 493 | Odoacer is slain by Theodoric, who assumes supreme power in Italy; Clovis married the Burgundian Princess Clothilde, a Catholic |
| 496–511 | Clovis is baptized a Catholic; the Visigoths are defeated by Clovis near Poitiers and driven back to Spain; Clovis dies and the Frankish kingdom is divided among his four sons; quills are used as pens |
| 527 | Justinian comes to the throne of the Eastern Roman Empire |
| 529–536 | Western monasticism is born with St. Benedict founding the monastery of Mt. Cassino in Italy; Belisarius, general to Justinian, campaigns in Africa against the Vandals and invades Italy, taking Naples and Rome |
| 563 | Justinian's armies crush the last of the Ostrogoths and bring all Italy under Eastern rule |
| 572 | The Lombard conquest of north Italy concludes the Germanic invasions of the west |
| 577 | Britons make a last stand against the Angles and Saxons and are defeated |
| ca. 590 | Irish monks begin to establish monasteries in Europe; Gregory the Great is raised to the papacy; Gregory of Tours writes *History of the Franks;* block printing in China |
| ca. 598 | Ethelbert, king of Kent, is baptized into the Catholic faith; the Bishopric of Canterbury is founded; Isadore of Seville writes of the Visigoths |
| 622 | The Hegira, or flight of Mohammed |

Barbaric

| | | |
|---|---|---|
| | 627 | King Edwin of Northumbria and his Anglo-Saxon followers are converted to Christianity |
| | ca. 635 | Islam begins its military expansion |
| | 663 | The Conference of Whitby is called, and Church jurisdiction in England passes to the Church of Rome, ending Irish influence |
| | 711 | The conquest of Spain is begun by Muslims from North Africa |
| | 714 | Charles Martel inherits the Frankish post of mayor of the palace under a weak Merovingian king |
| | 732 | The Muslims are defeated near Poitiers by Charles Martel, and he becomes the hero of the west; St. Boniface is created an archbishop |
| | 741–751 | Charles Martel dies and is succeeded by his son Pepin; St. Boniface is invited to reform the Frankish Church; Pepin deposes the last Merovingian king and becomes the first of the Carolingian monarchs |
| CAROLINGIAN ca. 750–1000 | 768 | Pepin dies, and the Frankish crown passes to Charles the Great, or Charlemagne |
| | 773 | Charlemagne invades Italy |
| | 779 | Charlemagne campaigns in Spain; during his return Count Roland is killed at the Pass of Roncesvalles |
| | 782 | Alcuin of York joins Charlemagne's court and founds the Palace School of Art and Literature at Aachen |
| | 797 | Irene becomes Byzantine empress after usurping the throne from her son; there are doubts about the legality of a woman ruling the Byzantine Empire |

| | |
|---|---|
| 800 | Charlemagne completes his submission of the Saxons in northeast Germany; the Carolingian miniscule style of handwriting is adopted throughout the Frankish Empire; the famed Chapel of Aachen is begun; Pope Leo III crowns Charlemagne emperor of the Holy Roman Empire on Christmas Day |
| 810 | The Danish Vikings begin their attack on the edges of the Frankish Empire |
| 814 | Charlemagne dies and is succeeded by his son, Louis the Pious |
| ca. 840 | Viking attacks on England and the continent increase in size and frequency; Norwegian Vikings found Dublin in Ireland; candle clock devised |
| 843 | The Treaty of Verdun divides the Carolingian Empire among Charlemagne's three grandsons: Lothar, Charles the Bald, and Louis the German |
| 871 | Alfred the Great becomes king of Wessex |
| 884 | The Carolingian Empire is reunited for the last time under Charles the Fat |
| ca. 890 | The Magyar hordes from Asia start invading central Europe; the feudal system begins |
| 910 | The great Burgundian monastery of Cluny is founded |
| 911 | Rollo the Northman settles in France and founds the duchy of Normandy |
| 925 | *Quem Quaeritis Trope,* the first mystery play |
| 955 | The Magyars are defeated by the German King Otto in the Battle of Lechfeld |

Carolingian

| | | |
|---|---|---|
| | 972 | Saracens continue raids on the French Riviera and kidnap the Abbot of Cluny; their Riviera base is destroyed by French nobles |
| | 978 | London Bridge is built |
| | 987 | The last Carolingian on the French throne is succeeded by Hugh Capet, first of the Capetian dynasty |

| | | |
|---|---|---|
| **ROMANESQUE** ca. 1000–1150 | ca. 1000 | Norwegian Vikings reach the North American coast; Venice, already a great commercial center, begins to spread its influence along the Yugoslavian coast; Christianity takes a new lease on life after the world does not come to an end after the millennium |
| | 1035 | William, descendant of Rollo the Viking, becomes duke of Normandy |
| | 1066 | Edward, king of England, dies; the Norman invasion of England is launched by William the Conqueror |
| | 1091 | The Normans complete the conquest of Muslim Sicily |
| | 1095 | Pope Urban II exhorts Christians to liberate the Holy Land, and the First Crusade begins |
| **Norman** | 1099 | Capture of Jerusalem |
| | 1078–1142 | Peter Abelard, French philosopher writes *Sic et non,* hymns, letters to Heloise, and other works |
| | ca. 1120 | Founding of military orders of Templars and Hospitalers |
| | 1122 | Concordat of Worms reconciled the Empire and the papacy |
| | 1135–1154 | Turbulent civil war in England |
| | 1144 | Dedication of the choir at St. Denis outside Paris |
| **Later Romanesque** | 1146–1149 | St. Bernard of Clairvaux preaches Second Crusade; it fails to capture Edessa from the Turks |
| | ca. 1150 | Importation of silk culture to Sicily |

# BACKGROUND

During the decline and fall of the Roman Empire while the new Eastern Empire was developing in Constantinople, the nomadic tribes of barbarians who had been moving into northern and western Europe for centuries from the Asiatic east came into continuous conflict and contact with the remains of Roman culture. They gradually became Christians and absorbed many of the artistic ideals of late Roman and early Christian times, but they also brought with them an art and culture that had a tense, abstract, almost nightmarish preoccupation with animal motifs in conflict. This entangled, geometric art echoed the Iron Age art of the Scythians and the Sarmatic ornaments of central Asia and was in every way in conflict with the classical ideals of the Mediterranean basin. Except for a brief resurgence of late Roman-early Byzantine values in Italy under Justinian, who reconquered Italy for a brief time during the sixth century, a period known as the Dark Ages developed and lasted until the founding of the Holy Roman Empire under Charlemagne at the close of the eighth century. The art and culture of this period was basically tribal and rural with a few memories of classical times added to art and architecture. Cities declined in size and importance. Art and the preservation of culture became the domain of monks in rural monasteries. These monks were not oriented toward Rome and prepared manuscripts, book covers, and other artifacts reflecting the pagan, barbaric, zoomorphic artistic ideals of an earlier tribal culture. The famed Hiberno-Saxon artist-monks created an art that wed Christian symbolism to the barbaric animal interlace method and carried this tense, animal-based art into the Roman revival of the Holy Roman Empire under Charlemagne and his successors.

Throughout this period of the Dark Ages, from the reign of Justinian until the crowning of Charlemagne on Christmas Day 800, European society was at a standstill, marked by the continuous shifting and warring of the large tribal groupings that gradually became the basis for the modern kingdoms of western Europe. Although the old urban Roman life died slowly, it was gradually replaced by a rural culture of small villages, provincial loyalties, and the beginnings of feudalism with its complex duties, rights, and political and social fragmentation. The only cities in Europe that actually expanded during this period were the centers of art and culture in Spain under the rule of the Islamic Moors.

Under the rule of Emperor Charles the Great (Charlemagne), there was a deliberate attempt to return to classical tradition through a kind of Carolingian Renaissance, which lasted until a new Dark Age set in with the Viking and Magyar invasions in the late ninth century. Charlemagne, by gathering at his court city of Aachen (Aix-la-Chapelle) the most civilized artists and intellects, hoped to revive the ideals, institutions, and traditions of imperial Rome.

One of his most significant contributions to the art of this era and the succeeding Romanesque Period was his palace chapel at Aachen (Fig. 7-1). Dedicated in 805, it has a central plan similar to San Vitale in Ravenna, but otherwise does not reflect the early Byzantine style. The interior is strong, heavy, masculine, and stark, with an emphasis on massive simplicity and strong, angular, geometric decoration. The strength and geometric simplicity found here was to dominate western European art until the arrival of the Gothic, and the striping on its arches was to be reflected in architecture, costume, artifacts, and accessories for the next three centuries.

Charlemagne's empire survived him by less than 30 years before it was swamped by Viking and Magyar invasions, but in the mid-tenth century the German part of his empire came to new prestige and power under the leadership of a series of Saxon kings known as the Ottonian emperors. Their centers of culture were primarily in the Rhine Valley, and their influence spread through northern Italy to Rome. Because one of the emperors married a Byzantine princess, however, the art and culture of the times reflected a mixture of Carolingian and Byzantine ideals.

As the tenth century drew to a close, Christians throughout Europe prepared for the Last Judgment that was to occur at the close of the

(a)
Romanesque
capital

(b)
Romanesque
tympanum

(c)
Anglo-
Saxon
church

Interior of the Palatine Chapel of Charlemagne, Aachen;
A.D. 792–805. Although based superficially on the interior of San Vitale in Ravenna, the character here is simpler,
less sophisticated, more massive, with striped arches that emphasize the barbaric background of the structure. Photo
courtesy of Ann Münchow, Aachen.

(e)
Romanesque
borders

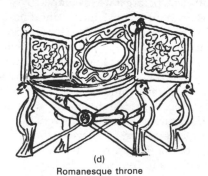

(d)
Romanesque throne

**FIGURE 7–1**

110

first millennium. When the year 1000 passed and this did not occur, there was a great feeling of relief—a sense of a new lease on life—and throughout Europe there was a surge of artistic activity that culminated in the great sculptural and architectural programs of the Romanesque style. The monasteries were the leaders in this movement, particularly the powerful and wealthy Cluniac order centered at Cluny in Burgundy. Despite the unifying artistic ideals spread by the Cluniac monks, the cultural and political divisions of feudalism caused Romanesque art and culture to be as varied as the provinces that made up the kingdoms of western Europe. After 1095, when the First Crusade began and trade routes began to open up again to the Mediterranean and the East, the static, rural, localized nature of Western culture began to change. Cities developed, commerce expanded, travel increased, and by the middle of the twelfth century the provincial spirit was gradually replaced by a much more international Christian outlook in religion and politics with a much greater stress on intellect, education, and the revival of a high civilization.

## THE BASIC COSTUME SILHOUETTE

During the period from the fall of the Roman Empire until the rise of Gothic art in western Europe, the most striking difference between the older classical clothing and the garments worn by the new barbaric people (who eventually created the kingdoms of western Europe) was the difference in draping. During the Graeco-Roman periods, clothing was based on simple tunics and the overdraping of square and semicircular outer garments, whereas the new order of clothing was based on closer-fitting tunics and some form of trousers or leggings—a development (as had been the case with the Persians) brought by migrating tribes from the mountains of central Asia who settled northern and western Europe. Although knee-length trousers (*feminalia*) had been introduced to the Roman soldiers by the Gauls and were used for protection and comfort by the military on their northern campaigns, they were always viewed as an uncivilized garment by the true Roman. Even the sophisticated legcovering adopted by the Byzantines, the tight, form-fitting *hosa,* were related to Persian trousers and barbaric legcoverings.

In Germany and France prior to the reign of Charlemagne, trousers, or *bracchae,* were usually cross-laced with thongs and often covered with knee-high leggings, obviously an inheritance from early barbaric love of leathercraft work with thongs and the tense interwoven art of the animal interlace. The body was usually covered by a coarsely woven T-shaped tunic, often in a plaid or stripe, and the outer garment was a mantle of skins or coarse wool fastened on the right shoulder with a large metal brooch. Hair was usually long, faces bearded, and metal helmets set with horns or wings often covered the head. Women also wore long hair that was braided and long semifitted tunics with a mantle again pinned over the shoulders. The emphasis in both cases was on a semifitted, semidraped silhouette rather than on the draped lines of the Greeks or Romans.

With the arrival of the Carolingian Empire under Charlemagne, dress became more sophisticated. Clothing fit more carefully, was of finer-woven fabrics, and there was more attempt at draping, in honor of Charlemagne's attempt to revive the Roman Empire. The standard male dress was an undershirt and drawers, a long-sleeved, knee-length or floor-length tunic bloused over a girdle, and close-fitting legcoverings. The outer garment was the half-circular mantle fastened on the right shoulder with a brooch; the moderately long hair was held by a metal circlet, and the feet were shod in soft leather slippers. The Byzantine *dalmatic* was worn only on very ceremonial occasions. Women wore a chemise, or *camisa,* which was the undertunic next to the body. On top of this was worn another undertunic and over this a wider-sleeved tunic somewhat like a dalmatic. A semicircular mantle was fastened over the shoulders, and the hair was covered by a large kerchief.

This basic style did not change with the coming of the Romanesque Period; it was merely refined. Tunics were now laced to the body to give a tense play of stretched folds on various parts of the figure, reflecting the animal interlace style in art. This new laced tunic was known as a *bliaut* and was worn by both men and women, although the female version was floor length or longer and laced to fit the body to the hips without complex darting or cutting. The older, looser, floor-length tunic was worn by older men and women. Women's heads, except for young unmarried women, were covered with a kerchief that swathed both the head and the neck. Mantles for both men and women were usually half-circles fastened with a brooch on the right shoulder. The only new outergarment, which was similar to the Roman peasant outergarment, was the hood and collar worn for travel and adopted as a part of a

monk's habit. With a long tail and scalloped edges to the collar, it was even adopted for court wear.

In *The Coronation of St. Edmund,* one can obtain some sense of this Romanesque interest in the lacing and blousing of tunics into tense, abstract, linear decorative effects that first appeared in early barbaric art, while the body is treated as a totally covered and undefined physical mass, as befits the Christian concept that the body is sinful (Fig. 7–2). The clothing, with a few exceptions, looked as muffled, closed, and defensive as the architecture of the time. The decorative patterns continued the early barbaric interest in tense, interlocking geometric shapes; the colors were muted and earthy in tone.

# BARBARIC DRESS

Representations of Teutonic people in northern and western Europe in the years just after the fall of Rome are infrequent, but there are items of actual clothing from this period and even earlier from Germany, Denmark, and Holland that were preserved in peat or frozen mud. Although the information is fragmented, the basic line and character of Teutonic costume from about 400 to 750 is not in doubt.

**Masculine Dress**   Even before the fall of Rome, the character of Germanic costume was clearly described by the Roman historian Tacitus, who mentioned a mantle, or *sagum,* fastened with a large, metal brooch. Under this, he described a very form-fitting vest of skins, leather (often with metal studs), or roughly woven woolen with a heavy texture. He commented particularly on the manner in which skins and leather were sewn together to make simple, bold patterns in stripes and plaids, and he mentioned that men wore their hair long and often tied it in a knot at the back of the head in order to appear taller.

But the best clues about Teutonic tribal dress are from a man's costume found in the Thorsberg bog in Germany which is now in the Schleswig-Holstein Museum. It consists of a diaper-weave shirt and trousers—the shirt with

set-in sleeves and the trousers with feet set onto the leg. The garments have a semifitted cut that suggests that all such woven garments originally were based on animal skins laced and sewn to fit closely to the body.

From the time of the Roman invasions, Julius Caesar described the Britons as wearing skins, painting their bodies with blue woad, and wearing very long hair while shaving the rest of their bodies. With the arrival of the Angles and Saxons, about 450, there was probably little change since we have descriptions of loose tunics to the knee or ankle, covered by a mantle fastened by a brooch on the chest. Tunics were evidently put on over the head and were ornamented with bands of rough decoration at the neck, sleeve ends, and skirt bottom. Legs were covered with leggings or bandaged to the knee under cross-strapping, and sometimes boots to above the knee were worn. Feet were clad in leather slipper-shoes. Hair was long and loose, and the head was often covered with a pointed, leather cap or a metal helmet adorned with horns, wings, or feathers (Fig. 7–4c). Some of the heavy, metal jewelry used has been found in southeastern England.

A gold statuette of a man, found near Le Mans, France, gives some indication of the nature of French male dress about the time of

(a)
bliaut
ca. 1130

(b)
helmets

ca. 600–700

mid–11 c.

12th c.

(c)
chain hauberk
ca. 1060–1150

Norman
hairstyles
(d)

ca. 1066

*The Coronation of St. Edmund;* from The Life of St. Edmund; Pierpont Morgan Library; twelfth century A.D. An excellent example of the tense, bold, decorative patterns to be found in Romanesque dress as well as the constancy of the tunic and mantle shapes. Photo courtesy of the Pierpont Morgan Library.

ca. 1100

(e)
breeches or
drawers of worker
12th c.

ca. 1125

(f)
English
hairstyles

(g)
Romanesque
shoes

(h)
brooches

(i)
buckle

(j)
rings

(k)
shirt-tunic
tucked up over
braies or drawers
10th c.

FIGURE 7–2

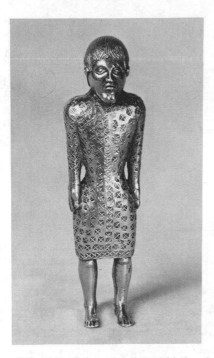

FIG. 7-3 Statue of a man, gold, found near Le Mans; Dumbarton Oaks Collection, Washington; ca. A.D. 400. Illustrates the simple, tight-fitting tunic decorated with circular ornaments worn by a Merovingian aristocrat at the beginning of the fifth century. Photo courtesy of the Dumbarton Oaks Collection, Washington.

the establishment of the Merovingian Dynasty (Fig. 7-3). He wears a sewn, fitted, knee-length tunic that follows the body lines the way skins might once have been laced to the body. It is decorated with an overall pattern of crosses inside irregular circles, and the figure is bearded with fairly long hair. The decoration is particularly interesting as it relates directly to the tense, allover geometric or interlace patterns found in barbaric art and jewelry. The *Breviary of Alaric* also shows breeches tied at the ankle with crossed thongs, short-skirted tunics with rich border decoration, pleated overtunics, and short cloaks (Fig. 7-4).

### Feminine Dress
As early as Tacitus' writing in imperial Roman times, we have the comment that the barbaric women looked much like

the men, except that they more frequently wore linen stained purple than the rough woolens of the men; and their tunics had no sleeves, but exposed the whole arm and part of the breast (Fig. 7-4b). A second-century female costume found at Huldremose in Denmark, now exhibited in the Danish National Museum in Copenhagen, consists of a full skirt made of wool plaid and a skin cape. A length of wool plaid was also found with these garments that may have been used as a shawl. Another costume in the Museum was made like a Greek chiton with a narrow overfold that was caught on the shoulders with brooches and girdled at the waist. Once again, one is struck by the barbaric interest in plaids, inherited from Celtic times, that is still reflected in the kilts and plaids of Scotland. This plaid motif also appears on the nose of the famous animal-head Viking ship prow from the Oseberg ship burial, c. 825, that is now in the University Museum of Oslo, Norway.

In Briton the famed Celtic-Barbaric British Queen Boadicea was described about A.D. 61 by the Roman historian Cassius Dio. He says that she was very large, had yellow hair below her waist, and wore a large golden necklace, a tunic of many colors (probably a plaid), and over it a thick mantle fastened with a brooch. When the Angles and the Saxons invaded, the clothing evidently changed very little. Women are described as wearing long, loose tunics with wide sleeves ornamented with wide borders of different colors at all the open edges. Their heads were covered with a large draped scarf or veil, and their feet were shod in soft slipper-shoes.

Except for the few items of actual clothing found in burial sites, we have little information about female dress until Carolingian times, since there were few images of women until the eighth century. Most of the limited commentary says that women's wear was similar to men's except that women usually did not use legcoverings. But from the fragments of cloth that remain from the tomb of the Merovingian queen, Arnegonde, buried about 570, we can see that she was buried in a chemise of fine woolen fabric under a tunic of knee length, which was of ribbed, indigo violet satin. Her legs were covered in woolen cloth hose with

(a)
Franks
4<sup>th</sup>–5<sup>th</sup> c.

(b)
Teutonic
woman ca. 5<sup>th</sup> c.

(c)
Teutonic
chieftain
6<sup>th</sup>–7<sup>th</sup> c.

(d)
Frankish
chieftain
5 –8<sup>th</sup> c.

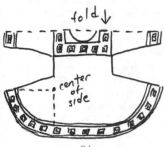

(h)
diagram of half a
male tunic ca. 1000

(g)
diagram
of gown or
cote 9<sup>th</sup>–10<sup>th</sup> c.

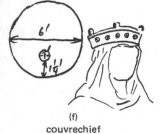

(e)
mantle
diagram
ca. 1000
(- - - stitch marks)

(f)
couvrechief
or veil with
diagram of cut
ca. 1000

*Breviary of Alaric;* Bibliothèque Nationale, Paris, ms lat. 4404 f. 197 v.; fifth century A.D. An illustration of undertunics, overtunics, mantles, *braies* or *bracchae* laced to the knees, and border ornamentation of disks sewn to narrow bands. Photo courtesy of the Bibliothèque Nationale, Paris.

**FIGURE 7–4**

115

crossed thongs just like the men of the period, and over all of this she wore a long, loose tunic of red silk lined with linen that reached to the floor. It was open in front with wide, long sleeves and was fastened by a gold brooch and a girdle that went twice around the waist and was knotted in front. On her feet were black, laced, leather boots.

# CAROLINGIAN DRESS

In the latter part of the eighth century, attempts were made to revive certain Roman ideals of dress. Charlemagne was determined to recreate the grandeur of Rome, and although the basic garments were a continuation of the barbaric silhouette, there was a much greater refinement in draping, fabric, and fit, coupled with a borrowing of certain Roman imperial clothing symbols for ceremonial occasions.

**Masculine Dress**  One very important development during this period was the codification of the legcoverings by rank. The term *drawers* was used to indicate underwear which usually consisted of a kind of diaper. Trousers (also called breeches, *braies, bracchae,* or *bracco*) were pulled on over the feet and were fastened around the waist (Fig. 7–2e). Hose, socks, or *pedules* and leg bands wrapped upward from the feet were put on over trousers or without them, but they were always thought of as lower legcoverings. Trousers or breeches were made of fine wool or linen for the upper classes, of rough wool for the common man. The smoothness of fit always depended on one's station or rank. Hose also were both smooth or wrinkled, depending on the wearer's station, but even when they disappeared under the tunic, they only reached to the top of the leg and were never fastened together from the crotch to the waist, although they were often secured to the waist with straps or thongs. Some shorter hose reached only to the knee; socks came only to the ankle. Sometimes breeches, hose, and socks were worn all at once. Legs were still wrapped to the knee in bands of varying widths, and persons of royal rank used a light crisscrossing of thongs over this (Fig. 7–6).

A bronze statuette of Charlemagne shows him on horseback clad in a tunic to just above the knees, a mantle of about calf length fastened on the right shoulder, and breeches covered by leggings or short hose to the knee. His high slipper-shoes are laced up the front, and he wears a simple crown on his head (Fig. 7–5). His biographer, Einhard, has also left us a vivid picture of his master's clothing:

> He used to wear the national, that is to say, the Frank dress: next his skin a linen shirt and linen breeches and above these a tunic fringed with silk, while hose fastened by bands covered his lower limbs, shoes and feet, and he protected his shoulders and chest in winter by a close-fitting coat of otter or marten skins. Over all he flung a blue cloak, and he always had a sword girt about him, usually one with a gold or silver hilt and belt. He sometimes carried a jewelled sword, but only on great feast days, or at the reception of ambassadors from foreign nations. He despised foreign costumes however handsome, and never allowed himself to be robed in them except twice in Rome when he donned the Roman tunic, chlamys and shoes. On great feast days he made use of embroidered clothes and shoes bedecked with precious stones; his cloak was fastened by a golden buckle, and he appeared crowned with a diadem of gold and gems; but on other days his dress varied little from the common dress of the people.[1]

One of the best pieces of information about the clothing at the time comes from the illumination depicting his grandson, Charles the Bald, enthroned (Fig. 7–6). The king's tunic is probably knee-length like those of his courtiers, and he wears a mantle of ankle length fastened with a brooch on the right shoulder. He and his courtiers wear trousers or long hose (one cannot tell whether the legs are covered separately or by a pair of breeches unified at the waist) that are covered with carefully wrapped bands; their feet are covered with soft slipper-boots or shoes.

[1]Einhard, *Life of Charlemagne,* Harper's School Classics (New York: American Book Co., 1880), pp. 58–59.

FIG. 7-5 Bronze statue of Charlemagne; The Louvre, Paris; ninth century A.D. Illustrates the simple helmet-crown, tunic, mantle fastened on the right shoulder, close-fitting breeches or *bracchae,* hose cross-gartered to the knee, and laced slipper-shoes. Photo courtesy of the French Musées Nationaux.

Their hair is moderately long but not flowing or of shoulder length and is confined with metal or leather bands or circlets. Their faces are both bearded and clean shaven. The only garment decoration seems to be the embroidery around the edges of tunics and mantles and on the shoulder of the tunics—like the *segmentae* of Byzantine origin.

The manuscript illumination also gives an example of ecclesiastical garments of the time,

with the clerics in the foreground clad in albs, dalmatics, and the over-the-head chasuble with orphreys on the dalmatics derived from the clavi of Roman times.

There are also two guards in military garb in the illumination, in military wear derived from the Byzantines (Fig. 7-4d). Over the tunic the guards wear a cuirass, or *broigne,* a leather waistcoat covered with metal plates and with tabs at shoulder and waist, also embossed in metal. One cannot see the legs, but they are probably wrapped in leather as were the courtiers'. The cloaks are the same as the civilian mantle and directly related to the military sagum of Roman times. The helmet, or *heaume,*

FIG. 7-6 *Bible of Charles the Bald;* Bibliothèque Nationale, Paris, ms lat. 1, f. 423; ninth century A.D. Illustrates tunics, mantles, *bracchae,* and gartered hose in which tense folds and wrinkles are created by lacing and pulling fabric through belts. Note helmets and armor that are derived from Byzantium and Rome as well as the *dalmatics* and *chasubles.* Photo courtesy of the Bibliothèque Nationale, Paris.

barbaric, carolingian, and romanesque 117

is very close to the Byzantine style with a central ridge to the crown with a crest on it and a small brim that rises to a point in front and back (Fig. 7-6).

During the tenth century, garments began to be fitted more carefully by the use of lacing and pulling fabric through belts and girdles to gain flat areas versus tense areas of tight wrinkles. In Germany, with the rise of the Ottonian emperors as leaders of the Holy Roman Empire, the influence of Byzantium on dress was pronounced, since Otto II, emperor from 980 to 983, had married Theophano, daughter of Romanus II, emperor of Byzantium. An illumination of Otto II enthroned from the famed manuscript of the *Registrum Gregorii*

**FIG. 7-7** *Otto II Receiving the Homage of the Nations;* from the *Registrum Gregorii;* Musée Condé, Chantilly; ca. A.D. 983. A formal ceremonial image in which the emperor wears a long-sleeved tunic, square crown, large semi-Byzantine mantle, and ornamentation in the Byzantine style. Note that the fabric in the tunics of the women paying homage is laid out in flat areas surrounded by tense, closely packed folds. Photo courtesy of the Bibliothèque Nationale, Paris.

shows the amount of Byzantine influence incorporated into royal clothing at this time (Fig. 7-7). The deep embroidery on the neckline, sleeve edges, hemline, and down the front of his silk tunic is richer than was usual in the west at this time. His mantle has an allover design that may incorporate three-dimensional jewels, and he has a bejeweled, square crown with the corners front, back, and over the ears. His soft ankle-high shoes are also jeweled down the center front, and he carries the imperial orb in one hand and the staff of power in the other. Although this imperial costume was retained for coronations for centuries, it was not typical of civil dress in northern and western Europe during this or the succeeding Romanesque Period.

***Feminine Dress*** Although we do not have a great many visual images of women during the Carolingian Period, the typical woman's costume appears to have consisted of an ankle-length undergown or tunic with tight sleeves, over which was worn a second tunic or gown with shorter open sleeves (Fig. 7-4g). Necklines came to the base of the neck and all edges, as with the male figure, were usually bordered in embroidered bands. The outer figure was usually covered by a mantle (or a large shawl that also covered the head), and the head was always covered by a veil, or *couvrechief* (Fig. 7-4f). Sometimes mantles for women were not fastened on the shoulder, as was the case with men, but were circular with an opening for the head that allowed them to be worn much like the ecclesiastical chasuble (Fig. 7-7). As with male clothing, there was a love of color—blue, rust, purple, red, ochre, and yellow—but all color, no matter how bright, always had a slightly muted, earthy tonality.

The tenth-century women's costume, unlike the men's, seems to have become fuller and looser with more stress on full folds swathing the body. One new style had the wide, open sleeves of the outer tunic longer than the arm so that when the arms were at the sides, the sleeves fell down well over the hand. They could be fastened back by bracelets or merely by pushing the sleeves up the arm and holding the arms above the waist (Fig. 7-8). The chasuble-

**FIG. 7–8** *Procession;* from Claudius MS. B IV, Folio 66b; British Museum; tenth century A.D. The men here wear the usual loose, knee-length tunics with flat areas played against draped areas, while the central woman wears a loose ankle-length gown with knee-length sleeves and a swathed *couvrechief.* The sleeves sometimes were anchored at the wrists with bracelets. Photo courtesy of the British Library.

shaped mantle with a hole for the head became more and more popular at this time also, with the opening off-center to allow more fullness in the back and less in the front (Fig. 7–4f). Sometimes this mantle was girdled into the waist by a cord passed through slits in the mantle. The under- and outertunics changed little during this period, as did head- and footwear.

In the illumination of Otto II enthroned, a number of women are depicted giving homage to the emperor, and they give an excellent idea of the fashions of the late tenth century (Fig. 7–7). An undertunic extends to the floor and is covered by an outertunic or gown with rich embroidery bands about the neck, part way down the front, and at the edges of the sleeves. The outer gown is girdled low and then bloused, and the fabric is pulled through the girdle to give us a sense of alternation between flat fabric areas versus tight, wrinkled effects. The hair is covered with a couvrechief which in this case hangs down the back almost to the floor, while on top of the veil are square crowns that look like limited versions of the one worn by the emperor.

## ROMANESQUE DRESS

No great break or change in fashion occurred with the development of the Romanesque style in art and architecture, but there was more variety in cut and in the way garments were worn.

***Masculine Dress*** The main trend in male dress during this century and a half of development was toward a closer-cut line with more lacing to fit the figure. The major garment was now the *bliaut,* a tight-fitting tunic laced at each

wearing under the arms, girdled at the waist, with a fairly full skirt that could be anywhere from just above the knee to the ankle in length (Fig. 7–4h). Sometimes the semicircular skirts were cut separately and sewn to the waist (Fig. 7–2a). The sleeves could be tight-fitting to the wrist, wider and reaching to the mid-forearm, or long and opening very wide below the forearm so that it created a kind of open hanging sleeve around the wrist (Fig. 7–9). In some cases, when the bliaut was very long, it was split on the sides all the way up to the top of the thigh, revealing the hosed leg almost to that point where it met the drawers. Sometimes these hose were richly patterned in circles, rosettes, or other geometricized motifs; even tunics, bliauts, and mantles frequently carried such allover, sprinkled geometric patterns. The love

FIG. 7–9  *St. George and the Dragon;* from Moralia in Job, a Cistercian manuscript, ms 168, f. 4 v.; Dijon Library; early twelfth century A.D. Illustrates the sophisticated, close-fitted long *bliaut* slit to the groin with open, full sleeves beyond the elbow. Again it is laced and pulled through a hip girdle to give maximum flat versus draped effects. Photo courtesy of the Dijon Library.

of wrinkled effects versus flat areas of fabric continued to increase, and one also sees images in which smooth hose were contrasted with knee-length hose that were wrinkled down the lower leg (Fig. 7–2).

For the lower-class males of this period we usually see just a loose smock or shirt pulled over diaper-like drawers (Fig. 7–2k). Legs might have trousers with loose, knee-high hose cross-gartered to the leg, but more often loosely woven rough hose to the knee were put on the bare leg and allowed to slip down, or were gartered or bandaged to the leg (Fig. 7–10).

Hair was somewhat longer in this period, and beards were trimmer or nonexistent (Fig. 7–9). Many younger men were now completely clean shaven (Fig. 7–2d, f). Hats or headcoverings were still almost unknown, but the *fillet,* or circlet, was still popular and the Phrygian cap was now frequently seen, as in the famous enamel plaque depicting Geoffrey of Anjou as a lawgiver. Outer garments were still limited to the rectangular or half-circular cloak or the chasuble-like circular cape now often coupled with a hood for very inclement weather. Cloaks were still usually fastened on the right shoulder, but some examples show them fastened at the center front of the neck (Fig. 7–4e).

Military wear began to change sharply during this period, and the last remnants of the Roman and Byzantine style disappeared. On the soldiers of William the Conqueror, depicted in the Bayeux Tapestry, helmets were conical with a heavy metal noseguard and rested on a tight hood of linked chain (Fig. 7–2b,c). A shirt, or *hauberk,* of mail covered the body to the knees with the chain sleeves reaching to the elbow or wrist. Sometimes the legs were clad in chain-mail trousers, or they were covered to the knee in boots or heavy, leather-gartered hose. A loose outertunic, or *surcote,* was sometimes worn over all. The short Roman sword had now given way to the huge, double-handed, two-edged broad sword with a cruciform hilt that was hung in a scabbard from a belt or a baldric over the shoulder. Ordinary foot soldiers usually did not wear chain mail but leather jackets (sometimes studded with metal) over a heavy, rough tunic, heavily wrapped legs, and a head covered with a thick cap rather than a helmet.

(a)
peasant
ca. 1100

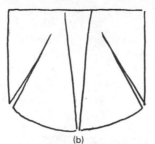

(b)
oriental surcote
for women after First Crusade

(c)
middle-
class
woman
ca. 1100

(f)
knotted bell sleeves

(e)
hanging sleeve
ca. 1100–1150

(d)
crimped or pleated
bliaut under sleeveless
quilted corsage

Column-statues from the West Portal of Chartres Cathedral; ca. A.D. 1150. The pleated, goffered *bliaut* worn by the
queen represents the new luxury of silk materials introduced from the East by the coming of the Crusades.
Around her waist and hips she wears a *corsage* held by a double girdle of plaited thongs. The long sleeves were frequently knotted to prevent them trailing on the ground.
Photo courtesy of Jean Roubier, Paris.

**FIGURE 7–10**

**Feminine Dress** The bliaut as worn by women also fitted the body by being laced under the arms or up the back from the neck to the hips. Below the hips the skirts spread out into a semicircular shape that gave a large amount of fullness to the hem (Fig. 7–10c). Sleeves now assumed great importance and often spread out into a wide bell shape from the elbow or from the armseye or hung down to the calf with a hole halfway down for the arm (Fig. 7–10d, e). Often the figure was ungirdled, or if a girdle was worn, it was placed very low on the hips (Fig. 7–10f). This garment was usually worn over a close-fitting chemise or undertunic that showed at the wrists as they emerged from inside the wide sleeves of the bliaut. A more sophisticated version of this style that came to full development about 1150 was the court bliaut in which the skirt was cut separately and sewn on at the hips. The top was often creped or honeycombed in texture, possibly through a smocking technique; the bottom of very soft fabric was sewn on with a multitude of fine pleats at the hips (Fig. 7–10d). The garment had very wide, open sleeves and was richly girdled with knotted silk cord, cut leather, or linked chain at the hips. Sometimes when sleeves were excessively wide, the ends were knotted to keep them from touching the floor (Fig. 7–10f). An example of this style may be seen in the statue of the Queen of Juda from Chartres Cathedral (Fig. 7–10).

The less elaborate style was the outertunic, or *cote,* cut in one with moderately wide sleeves and worn over an undertunic or chemise with tight sleeves. An exotic style brought back from the Crusades was the oriental *surcote* (Fig. 7–10b). The outer garment was still the mantle fastened on the shoulder or cut like the chasuble and put on over the head (Fig. 7–4e). Braided, uncovered hair held by a fillet was still the style for young women, but all other women covered the head with the couvrechief. Sometimes a kind of wrapped turban effect was used to cover the head, possibly an oriental influence produced by the Crusades.

Decoration for women was usually confined to bands of embroidery on the edges of outer garments and mantles, but there were also examples of sprinkled allover patterns of simple geometric form and some use of allover zigzag patterns like that seen on the ecclesiastic in the *Coronation of St. Edmund* (Fig. 7–2). Colors centered around blue, orange and rust reds, yellow, and purple.

## FABRICS

The chief fabric used in Carolingian and Romanesque times was wool that was manufactured domestically in France as far back as Roman times. In the beginnings of western civilization, there was great use of stripes and plaids in weaving and the texture was coarse, but by Romanesque times there were beautifully subtle, highly drapable, soft textures. Linen was used for undergarments and couvrechiefs and was also manufactured domestically, although until the twelfth century cotton was imported from Egypt. A heavy, all-purpose, canvaslike cotton was *fustian.* Silk was imported from Byzantium in all its varieties; after the beginning of the Crusades, it was imported directly from the Orient.

## ARTS AND ARTIFACTS

The architecture of this period, of which we have examples from the seventh century onward, was heavy, fortresslike, and earthy and made of blocks, cut stone, or smaller, bricklike stones. At first the structures were small and contained, having a cavelike sense of refuge from the outer world (Fig. 7–1c), but as the millenium passed, the structures, particularly the churches, became larger until some of the pilgrimage churches equaled Roman basilicas in their dimensions. The basic shapes were the round arch supported by thick piers or columns with very small, arched openings as windows (Fig. 7–1b). Interiors were always dark and defensive. Decoration was limited to geometric vegetable or animal motifs carved into stone plus some human scenes heavily abstracted and compacted into the basket area of column capitals. (Fig. 7–1a). Churches were much more heavily carved than were castles or domestic interiors, but the latter were made somewhat less cold and spare by the use of wall hangings and fresco murals. In the great hall of a castle, the master's chair and his dining table were placed on a raised dais or platform at the end of the chamber (Fig. 7–1d). The fireplace, originally in the center of the hall, was by the twelfth century placed against the wall with a great hood over a high opening leading to a flue built into the wall. Furniture was simple and heavy, usually made of thick oak and consisting of benches, long refectory-style tables, couches with crossed-rope bottoms covered in furs, and a few large carved chairs.

Motifs that were particularly admired and used in many ways included abstract eagles and other birds, usually made up of small geometric parts; lions and mythical beasts, such as gryphons and dragons, also made in abstracted geometric patterns; the complex interlace of animal tails or thongs, such as one finds on the borders of many Irish manuscripts; and the usual simple shapes like circles, squares, and zigzags (Fig. 7–1e). The major artifacts were richly ornamented purses, often done in gold and enamel inlay, daggers with richly carved hilts, the orb and scepter of royalty, crowns, and the richly carved and ornamented metal jewelry, particularly clasps, brooches, and buckles (Fig. 7–2h,i,j). This jewelry from Celtic through Romanesque development is some of the most interesting ever to be conceived and is still admired and copied today.

## VISUAL SOURCES

The best sources of information are manuscript illuminations and statuary. Two great repositories for manuscripts of this period are the Bibliothèque Nationale in Paris and the Morgan Library in New York, while the Musée Condé in Chantilly, France, has a few very important manuscript items. The best sources of statuary—besides the actual churches of the Romanesque Period spread throughout England, France, Germany, and Italy—are the

Louvre and the Victoria and Albert Museum. Exquisite examples of Barbaric and Romanesque jewelry are found in the Musée Cluny in Paris, the Church of St. Denis in the outskirts of Paris, the Stockholm Historical Museum, and the National Museum in Dublin. Useful written sources are Mary Houston's *Medieval Costume in England and France* and Herbert Norris's *Costume and Fashion,* Volumes 1 and 2.

## SUMMARY

The period stretching from the decline of the Roman Empire to the rise of Gothic art in western Europe was a fascinating saga of tense, geometric, abstract, animal interlace imagery slowly merging with memories of late Roman art. In clothing this manifested itself in bodies that were at first heavily muffled in tight-fitting garments and skins often laced to the body with thongs, through a period where some elements of Roman draping were added so that one gains a sense of semifitted, semidraped garments that muffled the ''sinful'' body in accordance with

early Christian principles. Finally during the culmination of this clothing style, in the Romanesque Period, there was much greater sophistication and complexity in the way semi-draped garments were cut and fitted to gain a maximum contrast between flat areas of tight fit and areas of tense, complex wrinkles and stretched draping. The Romanesque sense of texture and design with fabric was the end result of merging the early animal interlace style and the tight animal skins thonged to the body with the uses of Roman drapery.

## chapter VIII

# Early and High Gothic

## Chronology
(ca. 1150–1325)

| | | |
|---|---|---|
| **EARLY GOTHIC**<br>**1144–1194** | 1144 | Dedication of the Choir of St. Denis near Paris |
| | 1146 | St. Bernard of Clairvaux preaches the Second Crusade |
| | 1163 | Cathedral of Notre Dame, Paris, is begun |
| | 1164 | Constitution of Clarendon extends jurisdiction of English civil courts at expense of Church courts |
| | 1167 | Venice forms the Lombard League of northern Italian cities |
| | 1170 | Thomas à Becket, Archbishop of Canterbury, is murdered by knights of Henry II; Chrétien de Troyes is the first great poet of the Arthurian legend |
| ca. 1180 | 1189–1192 | The Third Crusade fails to capture Jerusalem; siege of Acre |
| | 1190 | The first windmills in Europe; original composition of the *Nibelungenlied* |
| **HIGH GOTHIC** | 1194 | A great fire consumes the town and Cathedral of Chartres, and a new cathedral is begun |

| | | |
|---|---|---|
| | 1198–1216 | The Pontificate of Innocent III marks the height of the medieval papacy |
| | 1202–1204 | The Fourth Crusade established the Latin Empire; plundering of Constantinople |
| | 1207–1208 | The order of St. Francis is established; Percivale poems later develop into Parsifal and the Grail legends |
| | 1209 | Cambridge University is established |
| | 1208–1229 | Albigensian Crusades strengthen the power of the French kings and ruin the nobles of southern France |
| | 1215 | King John signs the Magna Carta; fourth Lateran Council establishes the rules for the clergy |
| | 1217–1221 | The Fifth Crusade to Egypt fails to destroy Moslem centers of power |
| | 1228–1229 | The Sixth Crusade recovers Jerusalem, Nazareth, and Bethlehem by treaty |
| | 1233 | Gregory IX begins Inquisition for trial of the Albigensian heretics in southern France |
| | 1233–1248 | Gothic architecture reaches its zenith |
| | ca. 1235 | Le Roman de la Rose begun by Guillaume de Lorris |
| ca. 1250 | 1248–1254 | Louix IX leads the Seventh Crusade to Egypt |

| | | |
|---|---|---|
| LATER HIGH GOTHIC 1248–1325 | 1248 | St. Chapelle in Paris is completed |
| | 1250 | Robert Grosseteste, Bishop of Lincoln, protests the papal appointment of Italians to English posts |
| | 1260 | Completed Cathedral of Chartres is consecrated |
| | 1264 | Founding of Merton College begins the collegiate system at Oxford |

| | |
|---|---|
| ca. 1265 | Marco Polo travels to the Far East; Inquisition established |
| 1267–1273 | St. Thomas Aquinas writes *Summa Theologica* |
| 1270 | St. Louis dies in Tunis on the Eighth Crusade; oldest paper manufacturer in Europe at Fabriano |
| 1273 | Rudolph of Hapsburg elected emperor |
| 1274–1281 | Brief reunion of Roman and Greek churches |
| ca. 1277 | Jean de Meun completes *Le Roman de la Rose* |
| 1282 | Sicilians revolt against Charles of Anjou, and Peter of Aragon becomes their king |
| ca. 1285 | Eyeglasses first made in northern Italy |
| 1291 | Genoese vessels attempt to circumnavigate Africa; Forest Cantons of the Alps form the Swiss Confederation |
| 1302 | Boniface VIII's Bull *Unam Sanctam* asserts papal supremacy in temporal affairs; Philip IV convenes the first Estates-General in France at which all three Estates are represented |
| 1305 | Clement V becomes pope and moves papacy to Avignon, starting the Babylonian Captivity |
| 1305–1306 | Giotto paints *The Lamentation* at Padua |
| 1307–1312 | Trial and abolishment of the Knights Templars |
| ca. 1310 | Perfection of the mechanical clock |
| ca. 1320 | Use of firearms developed with the small cannon |
| ca. 1321 | Dante completes *Divina Commedia* |

ca. 1310

# BACKGROUND

No particular date signaled the change from the Romanesque attitude toward life to the Gothic outlook in religion, culture, and life, although there is a very specific date in June 1144 when the embryonic ideals of Gothic architecture were unveiled at the dedication of the new choir to the Church of St. Denis in the outskirts of Paris. During the twelfth century after the First Crusade, a gradual change occurred from a narrow provincialism to a new awareness about humanity in relation to the Church and nature. Pagan philosophers like Plato and Aristotle were adapted to Christian doctrine, universities were founded, towns and trade grew on renewed trade routes throughout Europe, and scientific attitudes and new material goods were accepted from the infidel world of Islam. Stimulated by the experience of the Crusades, the center of life and culture shifted from the rural monasteries and feudal castles to the cathedrals and merchant townhouses of the new and revived urban centers. Western capitalists emerged, as well as the rise of the middle class, as another small group interposed between lord and peasant. Money, not barter, now became the means of exchange, and banks began to develop that gave loans and credit—even to kings and emperors. Such expansion caused a gradual breakdown in the temporal power of the individual duke and feudal lord as well as the spiritual power of the pope and the great centralized power of the Church. Nationalism based on geography, language, and ethnic inheritance increased, giving rise to powerful royal families and modern nation-states. For example, at the end of the twelfth century the royal domain in France extended only about a hundred miles from Paris; at the close of the fifteenth century, it included almost all of what is now modern France.

Another important change in art, society, and cultural symbolism was the change from a masculine to a feminine imagery. Henry Adams in his *Mt. St. Michel and Chartres* used these two structures and their attendant architectural and sculptural decoration to demonstrate the heavy masculine outlook of the Romanesque as compared to the new feminine mystique of the Gothic. Minstrels now sang less of warfare and heroic deeds and more of love, beauty, and the inspiration to be received from women. Within the Church, cathedrals were no longer named after warrior saints like Michael, Andrew, Stephen, and George, but were almost exclusively dedicated to Our Lady, the Virgin Mary. Eleanor of Aquitaine, wife first of Louis VII of France and then of Henry II of England, ruled over "a court of love" from which developed the elaborate code of chivalry of the later medieval period. Sensual pleasure—formerly depicted as a woman with serpents at the breasts—was now depicted as a pretty girl looking in a mirror. The cult of the Virgin was the religious outgrowth of this new attitude, and the "Mother of God" was now worshipped as an intercessor with God the Father, a compassionate voice raised in behalf of all God's children. Mary became the spiritual queen of chivalry and the court of love, and gradually became transformed from a matronly mother-figure to a charming, youthful princess presiding over the festivities of love.

The period from 1150 to 1250 also saw the highest development in Church philosophy and scholarship since its foundation. With the founding of universities in western Europe, theologians indulged in debates on questions hitherto unknown, and great compendiums of Church knowledge were developed, such as St. Thomas Aquinas' *Summa Theologica,* which was the first great systematic compilation of Church theology. This scholastic mode of thought was reflected in the great Gothic cathedrals, in all other religious art, and in the framework of the Church for the next three centuries. The thirteenth century represents the summit of achievement for a unified Christendom—a synthesis of religion, philosophy, life, and art. The center of this development was the city, and the center of the city was the Gothic cathedral—an open book of history and theology for all to read.

Abbot Suger, when planning the choir at St. Denis, wanted more spiritual values than in past architecture. With his innovative use of ribbed vaulting and skeletal construction, large windows with stained-glass panes became the great glory of Gothic architecture. Structure and light were the twin drives in Gothic architecture until ornament came to crowd out spiritual principles. All around Paris during the last half of the twelfth century, bishops and architects vied with one another in developing the new style, but the Cathedral of Notre Dame, begun in 1163, includes examples of all the various developments in early and high Gothic art (Fig. 8-1). Compared to the separate, accumulated look of Romanesque churches, it is extraordinarily unified and compact. Walls disappeared in favor of skeletal ribbing and buttressing, and clerestory windows greatly increased in size. There was both a feeling of lightness and spirituality as well as a disciplined sense of unity and order. Only in the late-thirteenth-century additions to the cathedral did virtuoso ornamentation begin to obscure structure and undermine spirituality.

## THE BASIC COSTUME SILHOUETTE

The costume of the High Gothic Period demonstrated a new sense of sophistication in draping as well as a new appreciation for the human body under draped fabric, although there was little study of the anatomy of the body in art or medicine. Just as the art of the period stressed structure, simplicity, and a graceful spirituality, so the clothing stressed proportion, graceful draping, simplicity, and a lack of the tensions and zigzag edges that had been so much admired in Romanesque clothing.

There were also changes brought about by refinements in weaving and fabric. Fine-woven woolens, domestically manufactured, allowed for a new softness of line, and the greater use of silk also created softer, more elegant effects. Since ornament in dress was kept to a minimum, the line of the costume now attracted attention, not pattern or decorative detail.

The Crusades did, however, introduce a symbolic decorative scheme in military wear to distinguish a person's family through certain emblems; this eventually led to the complex decorative development of heraldry that influenced decoration in many kinds of clothing.

But during the High Gothic Period, the simple crosses, lions, eagles, and dragons used to emboss the *surcotes* worn over armor were kept for strictly military purposes and were not allowed to dominate civil dress, as in later medieval times. Even the use of family colors to achieve a particolored effect behind the family crest was not allowed to dominate the beauties of the almost classically draped lines of civil dress garments. Such particoloring remained primarily an aspect of military wear until well into the fourteenth century.

The two basic garments of this period were the *cote* and the *surcote* for both men and women. It is usually assumed that the particular lines of the cote came from the long Byzantine tunic, which had been reserved for royalty and special occasions. It must be remembered that the Fourth Crusade actually conquered Constantinople and turned the Byzantine Empire into the Latin Empire for a short period. Although many Byzantine ideas reached western Europe, the richness of Byzantine dress did not find its way into High Gothic costume because of the strong emphasis on simplicity, unity, and

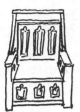

(a)
carved
oak
chair
ca. 1240

(b)
candle holder
ca. 1240

(c)
13<sup>th</sup> c.
foliated
puff ball
capitals

(d)
fireplace
with stone
hood ca. 12<sup>th</sup> c.

Southeastern view of Notre Dame Cathedral, Paris; ca. 1163–1250. Illustrates the growing complexity and delicacy of Gothic architectural decoration around the middle of the thirteenth century. Particularly in the rose window and surrounding areas of the south transept, structural unity and simplicity give way to rich decoration. Photo courtesy of the French Government Tourist Office.

(e)
rib and
panel
vault 13<sup>th</sup> c.

(f)
Gothic
piscina
or
toilet

(g)
motifs and borders

**FIGURE 8–1**

balance in scholasticism and early Gothic art. The outertunic was also known as the *cyclas,* and it had developed originally as an overgarment to protect armor during the Crusades. Even in civil dress the cyclas was often sleeveless, although there were versions with open, hanging sleeves known as the *gardcorp* or the *ganache* and a fur-lined version known as a *peliçon.* When worn as a military garment, the surcote covered a shirt and leggings of chain mail, topped with a bucket or crested helmet. Outerwear during this period was the hooded cloak, and the hood with a caped collar was considered fashionable even for interior court wear. The female costume usually consisted of a *camisa,* or undertunic; a long-sleeved *cote;* an overtunic or *surcote;* with the *wimple,* or kerchief, draped over the head and the *gorget* draped tightly under the chin. Sometimes the hair was placed in a pillbox, or *toque,* with a chin strap, sometimes coiled over the ears into a jeweled net, or (for young women) loosely confined by a gold fillet.

A good example of this style, which reached its culmination in the first half of the thirteenth century, may be seen in the polychromed statues of Ekkehard and Uta, life-sized statues from the west choir of Naumberg Cathedral (Fig. 8-2). Their garments are in the draped tradition found on so many religious statues of the period; the basic fashion is sober, balanced, simple, and unfrivolous. The most striking characteristics are the great heraldic shield and sword of Ekkehard and the muffling cloak and chic *toque* headdress of Uta. She is already an excellent symbol of the new High Gothic interest in the female figure, linked to the worship of the Virgin and presented as the spiritual queen of chivalry. These statues represent the style of art and clothing from 1200 to 1250 sometimes referred to as *Classic Gothic.*

## EARLY GOTHIC DRESS

Although not a major break, a new element in dress gradually began to appear during the twelfth century—a fullness and sobriety in dress not characteristic of the Romanesque. There was a gradual lessening of the profuse decoration and tense draping that characterized late Romanesque dress, but Romanesque clothing ideals continued until the beginning of the thirteenth century.

**Masculine Dress**  The major new item of dress in the latter half of the twelfth century was the *cyclas* or *surcote.* Originally it was a long panel, widening slightly toward the two ends from the hole in the center that went over the head (Fig. 8-2g, r). Thus, it hung in front and back about to the knee and was usually open, although it could be caught together or even sewn together on the sides. If this was the case, it was usually split up the center in front and back to the crotch. Related to this overgarment was the *tabard,* which was cut in much the same way but was emblazoned with the coat of arms of the wearer or his sovereign. This garment soon became, and still is, the traditional ceremonial covering for heralds.

The basic lines of the tunic, or *cote,* under this new *cyclas* or *surcote* differed only slightly from the tightly laced *bliaut;* the skirt was full but always cut in one with the top, and sleeves were wider at the armseye than at the wrist (Fig. 8-3). This cote, which varied in length from just below the knees to the ankle, always had much fullness directly under the arm (Fig. 8-2f). Trim was usually confined to a wide border of embroidered decoration at the neck, hem, and wrists.

Aside from being worn under the cyclas, this undertunic, or *cote,* (which was always tight at the wrists) could also be worn under a wider-sleeved outertunic that derived from the ancient *dalmatic.* As this garment began to have more variety in cut, the wide-sleeved overtunic was also frequently called a *surcote* or *cyclas.*

The ultimate outergarment was still the great half-circular mantle, now more often fastened at the front of the throat than on the right shoulder. Even at this early date we have the beginnings of embroidered symbols or family crests on the outside back of some of these mantles. Although this decorative form became much more prevalent in later Gothic

(a)
lacing
of
gown up
the back
late 12<sup>th</sup> c.

(b)
fur-lined peliçon
ca. 1200

(c)
male headgear 1200

(d)
barbette

(e)
crispinette

(f)
tunic or cote
period of Richard I
of England

(g)
diagram of cyclas

(h)
diagram of
a hood

(i)
diagram of gardcorp

*Ekkehard and Uta;* Cathedral of Naumberg; ca. 1250–1260. Illustrates the heavy, muffled clothing of the early Gothic period, which consisted primarily of tunics and mantles trimmed with fur and simple jewelry. Photo courtesy of Bildarchiv Foto Marburg.

(j)
pouch

(k)
coronation mantle
of the Holy Roman
Emperor 12<sup>th</sup> c.

(l)
13<sup>th</sup> c. glove

(m)
pleated
linen toque
with chinband
or barbette
ca. 1250

(n)
shoe
late 12<sup>th</sup> c.

(o)
the gorget

(p)
late 13<sup>th</sup> c. shoe

(q)
ganache

(r)
surcote

(s)
fermail or
brooch

(t)
pendant

**FIGURE 8-2**

**FIG. 8-3** *Birth and Christening of St. John the Baptist;* wall painting from St. Gabriel's Chapel, Canterbury Cathedral; ca. 1180-1190. A grouping of tunics and mantles with decorated hose and studded shoes. The woman wears a *couvrechief* on her head; the king, an acorn-shaped hat. Tunic decoration remains in broad bands at hem, wrists, and collar. Photo courtesy of Canterbury Cathedral.

times, the Coronation Mantle of the Holy Roman Emperor from the late twelfth century (now in the Schatzkammer in Vienna) already displayed a great abstract design that combined images of lions and camels done in gold thread on crimson silk with pearls outlining designs and borders (Fig. 8-2k). Another outergarment, that had been known since Roman times but came in for a great revival during the late twelfth century, was the hood and collar, known as a *capuchon*. It had been used by peasants for centuries, but now made its appearance among the upper classes with a peaked point to the back of the hood and a circular cape falling loosely over the shoulders (Fig. 8-2h).

Another decorative form used on the hood and cape and later even on the hem of the cyclas was a scalloped effect (related to the castellations on a castle wall) produced by cutting into the edges of the garment an inch or two to make petals called *dagges*. This slight decorative innovation was to blossom into a rampant profusion of cut-edged decoration in the period of the Middle Gothic.

There are few examples of headcoverings during this period except for the broad-brimmed straw hat of the farmer and the bell-shaped version of the Phrygian-style bonnet often seen on professional men like doctors and merchants (Figs. 8-3, 5). One new headcovering was the *coif,* a small white hood or cap that tied under the chin and looked like a baby's bonnet. It became associated with older men and lawyers, and in the thirteenth century it was worn under various small caps (Fig. 8-4).

During this period footwear gradually moved away from the lacing and thonging of the lower leg that had been so prevalent from early barbaric times through the Romanesque (Fig. 8-3). Gradually the soft slipper-shoe or boot, usually at least ankle high, was worn directly over hose without further gartering—a further disappearance of the interlace tension effect of the Romanesque (Fig. 8-2n, p).

Military wear remained much the same as it had in the late Romanesque style—that is, a shirt and leggings of chain mail under a cyclas or surcote with a bucket helmet with noseguard and a great shield and sword.

**Feminine Dress**    During the second part of the twelfth century the complex smocking and tensions of the royal *bliauts* seen on the female

**FIG. 8-4** *Abraham and Isaac, Rebecca and the Beasts;* from the *Psalter of St. Louis,* Latin MS 10525, Folio 11; Bibliothèque Nationale, Paris; 1252-1270. Note that Abraham wears a straw sun hat and a fur-lined mantle while Isaac wears a *coif* and the surcote with hanging sleeves known as the *gardcorp.* Also note the proliferation of delicate, peripheral, serpentine decoration. Photo courtesy of the Bibliothèque Nationale, Paris.

statues on the west front of Chartres Cathedral (see Fig. 7-10) were gradually replaced by a simpler gown that was more like the male cote—straight to the hips and then spreading out into a full skirt. This gown, or cote, was usually laced up the back (Fig. 8-2a). A representation at Fontevrault Abbey of Eleanor of Aquitaine, from about 1170, shows that her gown lacks the tensions of the older Romanesque bliaut and falls loosely over the bust to a jeweled belt just below the waist. It then falls in expanding soft folds to the floor with a train in the back and is covered by a circular mantle fastened on either shoulder by a cord that passes across the lower neck area. The gown is white and covered with embroidered gold trellis work and crescents, finished at the neck and wrists by bands of embroidery. The sleeves are fairly close on the upper arm and tight at the wrist, and the head is covered with a silk or gauze *wimple,* or veil, under a rich crown. Under the veil a piece of fine linen, known as a *barbette,* acts as a chin strap to secure the hair and veil (Fig. 8-2d).

Even when the tighter-fitting form of the gown was worn, laced up the back like the bliaut, it was allowed to fit the figure to the hips without wrinkled tension and to flow gracefully into a full skirt that trained on the floor. Such a gown often had sleeves that widened from the elbow to the wrist and were turned back over the undertunic, or *camise;* it was sometimes lined in fur and called a *peliçon* (Fig. 8-2a, b).

The wimple is the new headcovering of the late twelfth century, and at first it seems the same as the former *couvrechief.* But after closer analysis it becomes clear that the wimple was a shaped piece of linen usually draped under the chin over the band of linen known as a *gorget,* or *barbette* (Fig. 8-2d, o). Sometimes this closer-fitting, but shaped and draped, kerchief was still worn under a free-flowing veil held to the head by a *fillet,* or circlet.

Jewelry took the form of brooches to hold on mantels, rich girdles, and some rings (Fig. 8-2s, t). Necklaces were seldom seen, since the neckline of the cote was too high. Hooded cloaks were used for travel.

## HIGH GOTHIC DRESS

With the thirteenth century, a period of religious fervor began, symbolized by the king of France, Louis IX, who ruled from 1226 to 1270 and became a saint. Dress, which had seen so many exotic experiments in the middle of the twelfth century after the start of the Crusades, became much simpler and more dignified—almost classic in its draped lines and a fitting companion to the architecture of the High Gothic Period.

**Masculine Dress** The basic line of the costume was similar to that of the late twelfth century—that is, an undertunic, often with wide dolman sleeves at the shoulders, under a surcote, either having no sleeves like the cyclas or wide sleeves of various kinds that did not reach the wrist and allowed the undertunic to show.

Two of the most interesting and common variations are the *ganache* and the *gardcorp*. When the shoulder line of the surcote was extended to create a cap sleeve, the garment was known as a *ganache* (Fig. 8-2q). It gave a relaxed and soft draped line to the upper arm to match the full draped line of the skirt, and it was frequently worn with a hood that was thrown back on the shoulders. As a garment for merchants and older men, this garment continued until the latter part of the fourteenth century. When long, full sleeves were set into the armseye and shirred at the top to control the fullness, the *gardcorp* was created. It usually had a long slit in the front of the sleeve through which the arm could come; thus the sleeve itself hung down behind. This garment (from which the modern academic master's gown derives) was used primarily for travel and inclement weather in the thirteenth century (Fig. 8-2i). A slightly different version of this can be seen in the *Psalter of St. Louis* in which the sleeve is not sewn up the front seam at all; the arm of the undertunic is thus seen all the way to the armseye with the sleeve hanging behind (Fig. 8-4).

In other elements male clothing did not make any major changes. Footwear remained constant. Outerwraps remained the cloak and the caped hood; headcoverings still included the coif, the Phrygian cap, and the fillet to hold the hair. The only significant changes in headgear were the addition of a small acorn-cup cap that was frequently used over a coif; a cap often with a fur brim in four sections, any part of which could be turned down to protect the side or back of the head; and the peaked hat used for hunting (Fig. 8-2c).

A word should be said about the working classes of this time, as more of them were depicted in art than in the past. They usually wore the short *cotte* split in front so that its ends could be tucked into the girdle about the waist.

This usually allowed the diaperlike drawers to show, as can be seen in a scene of threshers from the Maciejowski Bible from the mid-thirteenth century (Fig. 8-5). Sometimes these diaper-drawers were as long and full as pants, as seen in the figure of the thresher to the right. They seem to be cut much like Siamese pants from southeast Asia and are rolled at the waist over a cord. The thresher on the left has hose on each leg drawn up over his drawers and fastened to a waist string, showing how all male hose, or *chausses,* were worn at this time—like hip boots drawn tightly up the leg to the drawers and fastened to a belt or vest with thongs or cords. Note that all the threshers wear the coif, which acted like a sweat cap, and one wears the straw sun hat that has a lineage back to Greece and Rome.

**FIG. 8-5** *Ruth and Naomi, The Threshers;* from the Maciejowski Bible; The Pierpont Morgan Library; mid-thirteenth century. Note the use of the shaped *wimple* over the draped neck *gorget* on the two seated women, as well as the fullness of the *cotes* or tunics and the sleeveless nature of the *surcote,* top left. The threshers wear shirts and *coifs,* and one wears breeches of oriental derivation. Photo courtesy of The Pierpont Morgan Library.

We also have a lovely example of shepherd's dress from the Royal Portal of Chartres Cathedral which shows the use of the cotte with a cape on one shepherd and a caped hood, or *capuchon,* on the other (Fig. 8–6). One appears to be bare-legged with ankle boots, the other has loose wrinkled chausses that were probably loosely attached to the belt that held his drawers.

As for military wear, we have an ideal example in the famed statue of St. Theodore from the South Portal of Chartres Cathedral (Fig. 8–7). He wears a shirt of chain mail that has mittened handcoverings in one with the sleeves and a built-in hood that is thrown back on the shoulders. His legs are protected by chain-mail chausses with built-in feet that are laced to a

FIG. 8–7  Jamb statues from the south transept portal of Chartres Cathedral; ca. 1215–1220. The folds and the drape of these clothes are much more relaxed and natural than in the late Romanesque period. The figure to the left, the Christian knight St. Theodore, wears a shirt and leggings of chain mail covered with a sleeveless *surcote* of heavy silk. Photo courtesy of Jean Roubier, Paris.

FIG. 8–6  *Shepherds in the Fields;* from the Royal Portal of Chartres Cathedral; early thirteenth century. Illustrates the simple clothing with stress on decorative wrinkles and folds and the importance of the hood found in depictions of the lower class at the beginning of the early Gothic. Photo courtesy of Jean Roubier, Paris.

leather sole. He has a long surcote or *cyclas,* probably of silk, encircled low on the waist by a great sword belt that supports his large, cruciform-hilted sword. He carries a lance with a spirally furrowed handgrip and a rounded triangular shield embossed with the arms of France. Helmets were usually conical or rounded and fitted over the chain-mail hood. Sometimes a visor fitted down over the face; as the century passed, plumes and crest began to appear at the top of the helmet.

**Feminine Dress**  The thirteenth century for women, as for men, was a quiet interlude between the elaboration of mid-twelfth-century fashions and the fantasies in dress that were to develop in the mid-fourteenth century. For example, the costume worn by the Lady, usually known as the Queen of Sheba (ca. 1230), from the North Portal of Chartres Cathedral seems classically simple as compared to the gown worn by the Queen of Juda (ca. 1150) from the West, or Royal, Portal (see Figs. 8–8, 7–10). The latter's cote has very modest embroidery at the neck, a modest brooch closing her chemise at the throat, and a beautifully draped circular mantle caught across the chest by a cord. The turnover collar of the cote looks as if it may have been of fur, and the head is covered with a *toque,* or pillbox headdress, fastened under the chin by a barbette (Fig. 8–2m). Sometimes a cyclas or sleeveless surcote was worn over this cote, as can be seen in the second figure from the left in the scene of Ruth and Naomi (Fig. 8–5). Sometimes these garments were somewhat open under the armseye and unbelted, more often they were girdled low on the waist.

The scene of Ruth and Naomi (Fig. 8–5) also gives good examples of hairdressing, particularly in the central figure's use of the wimple and the gorget. The wimple was somewhat shaped to the head, and the gorget, folded on the bias, was softly draped under the chin and fastened at the back of the head. The hair, braided into a bun at the nape of the neck, was usually confined by a net known as a *crispine,* or *crispinette,* as seen in the two figures at the left. Later in the century this net changed its shape as the hair was coiled more prominently over the ears (Fig. 8–2e).

Hooded cloaks were worn for travel. Shoes were usually soft slippers but seldom seen under the long gowns, although striped hose and low dark hose are glimpsed under the figure second from the left in the Ruth and Naomi scene (Fig. 8–5).

**FIG. 8–8** *The Queen of Sheba;* from the North Portal of Chartres Cathedral; ca. 1215–1220. Illustrates the simplicity of High Gothic clothing. The pillbox hat is a *toque;* the chin band, a *barbe* or *barbette.* The body is swathed in the folds of the *cote* surmounted by a half-circular mantle. Photo courtesy of Jean Roubier, Paris.

## FABRICS

Linen weaves included sheer lawn and fine batiste for wimples and veils as well as a linen canvas for certain lower-class garments. Cottons in various weights were used primarily for undergarments. Woolen in a variety of weights and weaves was the basic fabric, with camel's hair imported from Cyprus or Syria and jersey imported from southern Italy. The finest grade of wool was *camelot* which was eventually woven domestically in France. There were also serge, flannel, wool crepe, a double-faced woolen, and dyed-in-the-yarn *scarlet.* Silk was also woven domestically and came in many lush finishes, particularly *cendal,* a heavy, supple satin. Furs were also essential for trim and winter linings.

# ARTS AND ARTIFACTS

The great innovation to come in architecture during this period was the use of the pointed vault and arch coupled with flexibility in skeletal ribbed construction and the use of flying buttresses. The most beautiful and innovative examples of this new style of architecture were cathedrals and churches, but castles and townhouses also made practical use of many Gothic design elements (Fig. 8-1e,f). Doorways were deeply set in a series of decorative receding arches, fireplaces projected from walls under slanting hoods decorated with Gothic tracery, windows were set with lead mullions inside stone ribbing, and stone walls were decorated with frescoes and hung with tapestries and embroidered wall hangings filled with Gothic tales of war and romance (Fig. 8-1d,e,f). Heavy oak furniture was richly decorated in Gothic tracery and adorned with cushions and draperies of silk decorated with heraldic designs (Fig. 8-1a,g). Heraldry was also apparent in banners, shields, and plaques set with coats of arms that adorned the walls and ceilings of the great halls of the nobility. In these halls the long, narrow, refectory-style oak table was placed on a raised dais at one end of the hall, covered with a richly embroidered covering, and set with heavy gold or silver plate. The lord's great chair with high back and massive arms was placed at the center of the table, with benches or stools for the other guests. Bedrooms usually contained a great oak bed raised on a platform with a canopy suspended above and a great carved chest for clothing nearby.

More personal accessories included certain musical instruments such as the harp or psaltery, the rebeck or four-stringed fiddle, and the flute. Royal accessories continued to be the crown, orb, and scepter, although from about 1200, French kings held a "hand of justice" (a staff topped by a hand with forefinger raised) when they meted out royal judgment. As for personal body accouterments, the purse or pouch was the most universal, hanging from a belt or concealed by an unbelted cyclas or surcote (Fig. 8-2j). Peasants and travelers frequently wore knapsack-sized pouches on a bandolier over the shoulder, while royal messengers carried dispatch boxes that were about the size of a medium-sized purse. The ever-present dagger was sometimes worn thrust through the belt; at other times, thrust through a strap in the purse or even hung about the neck on a chain or cord. Other items that might be appended to the belt were scissors, keys, and sewing kits. Gloves, another common accessory, ranged from peasants' rough mittens to smooth gauntlet gloves used by aristocrats in the practice of falconry (Fig. 8-2 l).

Jewelry consisted primarily of the brooches worked in gold and set with unfaceted gems used to fasten mantles; belts and girdles of leather, knotted cords, and worked silk set with elaborate buckles; and circlets or headbands of gold and silver set with jewels and inlaid enamel (Fig. 8-2s,t). Bracelets and earrings were seldom used. Gems and inlaid enamel work were also seen in sword and dagger hilts and on book covers.

The major decorative motifs were the family crests and coats of arms developed from animal and geometric forms, which were first seen only on banners and military surcotes, but by the fourteenth century also on the surcotes of civil dress.

# VISUAL SOURCES

For this period there is a great proliferation of sources, the best being manuscript illuminations and sculpture. The finest sculptural sources are on the North and South Portals at Chartres Cathedral; the best illuminations— like the *Psalter of St. Louis* and the Maciejowski Bible—are in the Bibliothèque Nationale in Paris and the Morgan Library in New York. There are other helpful supplementary manuscripts in the British Museum, and the frescoes of Giotto in Padua and Florence are useful for assessing Italian costume at the close of this period. Good written sources are the Cunningtons' *Handbook of English Medieval Costume* and Dorothy Hartley and Margaret Elliot's *Life and Work of the People of England from the Eleventh to the Thirteenth Century*.

# SUMMARY

This exciting period saw the foundations of modern western Europe established through the rise of cities, national states, and capitalism. It also marked the high point of development in the Catholic faith with spiritual values that spread from architecture to clothing. The beauty, balance, and simplicity found in High Gothic art and fashion caused it to be labeled *classic*. In clothing the soft, draped lines marked the first time since the Greek that so much attention was placed on the ideal beauties of the draped body. It was a period that restrained the rampant decoration that was later released on the medieval world by late Gothic art and fashion.

# chapter IX

# Middle Gothic

## Chronology

(ca. 1325–1425)

| REIGN OF EDWARD III IN ENGLAND 1327–1377 | | |
|---|---|---|
| | 1328–1350 | Ambrogio and Pietro Lorenzetti active in Italy as painters |
| | 1325–1348 | Philip VI, king of France |
| | 1325–1374 | Petrarch active as a poet |
| | ca. 1334 | Andrea Pisano and Giotto collaborated on sculpture for the Campanile of Florence Cathedral |
| | 1337 | Outbreak of the Hundred Year's War between England and France |
| | 1338 | German Diet declares independence of papal approval in the election of the Holy Roman Emperor |
| | 1341 | Petrarch crowned in Rome with the poet's laurel |
| | 1346 | Famed Battle of Crécy won by Edward III; first military use of cannon |
| | 1347–1354 | Cola di Rienzi, dreaming of Rome's past greatness, leads a revolt against the Roman nobility |
| | ca. 1348 | Order of the Garter instituted in England by Edward III. |

ca. 1335

| | | |
|---|---|---|
| | 1348–1350 | The Black Plague is at its peak throughout Europe, especially in Italy |
| | 1348–1353 | Boccaccio writes *The Decameron* |
| | 1356–1358 | Constitutional crisis in France; the Estates-General led by the Parisian merchant Etienne Marcel attempts reforms |
| | 1358 | Revolt of the peasants or Jacquerie in northern France |
| | 1353–1363 | Cardinal Albornoz restores the pope's power over the papal states |
| | ca. 1362 | William Langland writes *Piers Plowman* |
| | 1370 | Hanseatic League at the height of its power |
| | 1377 | Death of Edward III and the end of the Avignon Captivity for the papacy |

---

REIGNS OF
RICHARD II,
HENRY IV, AND
HENRY V IN
ENGLAND
ca. 1380

| | | |
|---|---|---|
| | 1378 | Great Schism in the papacy begins as two elected popes contend for power |
| | ca. 1380 | The first translation of the Bible into English done by the followers of John Wycliffe |
| | 1381 | The peasants revolt in England, led by Wat Tyler and John Ball |
| | 1386 | The Swiss Confederation defeats the Austrians at Sempach; University of Heidelberg founded |
| | 1388 | First urban sanitary act passed by English Parliament |
| | ca. 1387 | Chaucer begins *The Canterbury Tales* |
| | 1396 | Twenty-eight-year truce begins between England and France; Richard II marries Isabella of France |

| | |
|---|---|
| 1399 | Richard II betrayed and forced to abdicate |
| 1400 | Manuel II Palaeologus, emperor of Byzantium, visits Paris and London to solicit aid against the Turkish sultan |
| 1401 | The competition instituted for the completion of the north doors of the Baptistry in Florence |
| 1403–1424 | Ghiberti wins the competition and works on the north doors of the Baptistry |
| 1406 | Pisa under Florentine rule |
| 1409 | Council of Pisa ends with a threefold schism in the papacy |
| 1414–1418 | The Council of Constance ends the Great Schism |
| 1416 | Sigismund, Holy Roman emperor and king of Hungary, visits London to help make peace between England and France |
| 1420 | Brunelleschi begins to build the dome for the Cathedral of Florence; Treaty of Troyes which disinherited the French dauphin and bestowed the crown of France on Henry V of England at the death of Charles VI of France |
| 1421 | Giovanni de Medici elected magistrate in Florence |
| 1422 | Death of Henry V of England after a long illness; Henry VI accedes to the throne under the regency of his uncle, the Duke of Gloucester |
| 1425 | Ghiberti begins work on the east doors of the Baptistry of Florence |

ca. 1415

# BACKGROUND

The brilliant and exciting attempt to accommodate both reason and faith in the same scholastic synthesis of all art and knowledge began to disintegrate by the close of the thirteenth century. That impossible balance between the world of nature and the world of the spirit that lead to Gothic vaults that leaped upward to the sky, Gothic flying buttresses that spang out into space, and airy openwork that gave a laciness to ornament and translucent openness to interior space finally lead to strain, instability, and dangerous impracticality in construction. In 1284 the vaults that had just been completed in the choir of the Cathedral of Beauvais collapsed after the stone piers had risen to a height of 157 feet, the highest interior in Gothic architecture. The collapse of the vaults at Beauvais symbolically brought an end to the period of High Gothic balance, and analogously the followers of Thomas Aquinas and his colleagues also came to sense that balance and integration of faith and reason were impossible. From the beginning of the fourteenth century until Late Gothic times, each was to go its own way, and this process led to the destruction of the unity that had made Christendom under the High Gothic the greatest moment in Church history.

By the early fourteenth century, the High Gothic style was replaced by the courtly, charming late Gothic style which continued until the stirrings of the Renaissance. Delicate, lacy, ornamental effects in art began to erode the disciplined, structural unity that had characterized the High Gothic. Spiritual values throughout Europe were gradually replaced by far more secular concerns, and the religious ceremonies and the church art reflected the richness and sophistication that now dominated the courts of Europe. The growth in middle-class power and wealth and the tremendous expansion of business and trade made materialism a dominant goal in life. Chivalry, knighthood, feudal vows, and belief in the absolute power of the Church were slowly transformed into ornamental accessories to life. The nobility, supported by the wealth of the upper middle class, continued the make-believe world of knightly tournaments, courtly love, and religious ceremonies supported by a fantastic art of lacy arabesques and edges that dematerialized every solid form to which it was applied. It is this period, from about the second quarter of the fourteenth century until the rise of the early Renaissance in Italy in the second quarter of the fifteenth century, that we think of as the age of fairy tales, of princesses and princes, of knights acting out deeds of great valor.

To see the change in religious outlook, one need only compare a statue of the Virgin from the fourteenth century to one from the thirteenth. During the High Gothic period, the Virgin was viewed as a humble, unassuming mother who projected warmth, goodness, and simplicity; the Later Gothic Virgin was viewed as a sweet, elegant princess who often holds the Christchild as a mere appendage on one arm, while her true concentration is placed upon her own elegant person. This new image in lovely clothing and wearing a rich crown embodied the ideals of courtly love—the unattainable, beautiful, idealized woman of medieval love poetry. The concentration in all depictions of this youthful princess was on elegance, decorative sophistication, and a fairy-tale unreality.

An even more striking image may be the interior of the great hall of a noble castle in the late fourteenth century. The fireplace in the Great Hall of the Counts of Poitou dating from about 1384 to 1386 demonstrates fully that the heroic age of the Gothic had given way to a refinement of detail and open arabesques of spiny elegance that removed structural strength in favor of flamboyant decoration (Fig. 9-1). Even the great chimney of the fireplace has been replaced by a number of cyclindrical stone stacks behind the great window, so that the elegance of the indoor effect is not broken by the size and monumental weight of a great chimney. Thus decorative elegance was to remain the major force in art and culture until the triumph of the Renaissance in the fifteenth century.

(a)
middle-Gothic
(decorated Gothic)

(b)
decorated Gothic
window

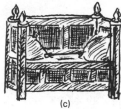

(c)
bench chair

decorated capital

(d)

decorated Gothic
piscina

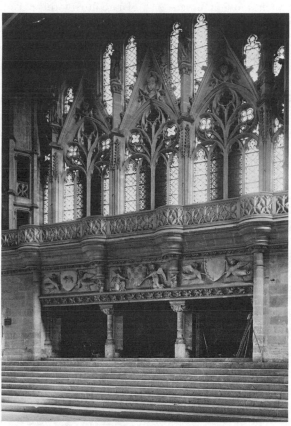

(e)
motifs

Fireplace in the Palace of the Counts of Poitou, Poitiers, France; 1384–1386. Illustrates the sophistication, fantasy, and elegance to be found in interior decoration in the later Gothic period. Note particularly the openwork serpentine line in the flamelike tracery and the scalloped effect created by the puff balls along the gables—elements to be found in the edges of clothing. Photo courtesy of the Caisse Nationale des Monuments Historiques et des Sites, Martin-Sabon, © Arch. Phot. Paris.

**FIGURE 9-1.**

143

# THE BASIC COSTUME SILHOUETTE

The spare, draped lines of clothing of the High Gothic Period were transformed into slim, closefitting garments by the second quarter of the fourteenth century, with much stress on ornamentation, especially in the lacy effects placed along the edges of garments. Elegant, graceful movement based on an S-curved line (created by the pregnant stance admired by women as a symbolic compliment to the pregnant Virgin) dominated the movement of both men and women, and such movement enhanced the artificial elegance of clothing.

The basic male garment now shifted from the loose-fitting *cote* and *surcote* to the close-fitting tunic to the hips known as the *cotehardie,* which was often coupled with a hood and collar with richly scalloped edges. This effect, known as *dagging* or *foliation,* became dominant during this period and is sharply reminiscent of the *crocket* effects in Gothic architectural decoration. Often the male cotehardie had elbow cuffs known as *tippets* that also often flared into foliations, as did the bottom of the cotehardie at the top of the thigh. During the reign of Richard II, a voluminous robe known as the *houppelande* was added to this ensemble. It had great trailing bell sleeves and a high collar, with rich foliated effects on the edges of the great sleeves and along the slits at the sides that accommodated the great strides of wearer movement necessary to make these robes look effective. A fantastic headdress, or *chaperon,* was also worn—the hood had the face opening placed around the head, the dagged edges of the collar fell down one side, and the long tail, or *liripipe,* of the hood was wrapped around the head and then draped over one shoulder. This exotic, almost Eastern look fully supported the fairy-tale imagery prevalent in the arts of this period. Hose and shoes changed little except that the toes of the soft, slipper-shoes grew long points which, though making walking difficult, added to the spiky elegance of the entire male ensemble.

The woman's version of the cotehardie was a close-fitting princess gown with a low neckline and a full skirt. It was now darted, cut to fit to the hips, and revealed all the grace and beauty of the youthful female form. Over these cotehardies the old surcote was now cut away to the hips and was known as a *sideless gown.* It was often emblazoned with heraldic symbols and in time was so fully cut away that only a narrow fur *plastron* seemed to hold the garment up to the shoulders at the front and back of the figure. Toward the end of the century, women also adopted the great houppelande, similar to the male version but belted high under the bustline. Headdresses for women also became more ornate during this period, such as the *reticulated* headdress which consisted of metal cages to hold the braids of hair curled over the ears and

**FIG. 9–2** *The Exchange of the Rings* from *Très Riches Heures du Duc de Berry;* Musée Condé, Chantilly; ca. 1415. Illustrates the elegant fantasy fashions at the beginning of the fifteenth century with their dagged and foliated edges, turbans, flowing lines, and sprinkled ornamentation. Photo courtesy of the Bibliothèque Nationale, Paris.

was usually coupled with a crown or coronet to unify the whole effect. Other headdresses included heart-shaped rolls that finished in a veil, small, conical horns on either side of the head to support a flowing veil, and turbans of various kinds.

One of the most richly appealing visual sources for this period is the famous *Très Riches Heures,* probably the work of the Limbourg brothers, containing beautiful manuscript illuminations that illustrate the various months of the year. The scene for April shows a lavishly dressed couple exchanging rings in front of their parents as a sign of betrothal (Fig. 9–2)—a

depiction of the escapist fantasy apparently sought by the aristocrats during this period. The robes are sprinkled in crests embroidered in gold, and the sleeves are cut fancifully into foliated and scalloped edges echoing the puffball decorative edges found in Gothic architecture. The serpentine line of garments and body poses reflect the swaying figures in manuscript illuminations, stained-glass windows, and statuary. Once again one is struck by the fact that the fashions of a period tend to imitate the art of the period, not the facts of daily living or the history of current events.

## DECORATED GOTHIC (THE COTEHARDIE)

The reign of Edward III as king of England marked the point at which proliferation of decoration and fanciful ornamentation began to overwhelm structure, composition, and simplicity in dress. This period has sometimes been called the *Decorated Gothic Period,* an apt description for what occurred in dress between 1327 and 1377.

**Masculine Dress** One of the first decorative effects of this time that must be noted was the proliferation of heraldic devices on clothing. Originally developed during the feudal age of the late Romanesque to identify family members or servants, *heraldry,* or coats of arms, had been quite simple. But with the intermarriage of families, the colors and crests from one family were frequently combined with those of the family with which it had merged, resulting in a brilliant, complex, and decorative effect. When these heraldic effects were adapted for use on clothing, the results were startling. Surcotes were often half one color and half another; one hose might be a single color and the other several different colors; and the coat of arms itself might cover the entire back of a mantle or the full width of a skirt. The traditional court-jester's costume, reflecting this usage, has been incorporated into modern clown costumes. Even the horses ridden in tournaments and into battle were bedecked in heraldic trappings.

The most remarkable change in male dress came about the beginning of the second quarter of the fifteenth century with the introduction of the hip-length, body-fitting garment known as the *cotehardie* (Fig. 9–3a). It probably developed from the tight-fitting, padded undergarment known as the *jupon* or *pourpoint* that was introduced into military wear at the beginning of the century to protect the body from the sharp edges of the new plate armor that was gradually replacing the chain-mail *hauberk* of the thirteenth century. This padded pourpoint, designed to fit very tightly, had a remarkably sophisticated cut that appears to have marked the beginning of a new era in tailoring and dressmaking. Pieces were now cut and shaped to fit the body; darts and seams developed and were refined to give the body what amounted to a second skin of padded cloth. This development in western European dress marked an entirely new departure in the history of clothing which had not made use of fitted garments since primitive skins had been laced to the body. Pourpoints may originally have been made out of coarse fabric, but very quickly they were fashioned from silks and brocades quilted over cotton wadding to a refined linen canvas (Fig. 9–3e). Pourpoints also represented the first major use of buttons and buttonholes to close the front of a garment.

A good example of a cotehardie may be seen

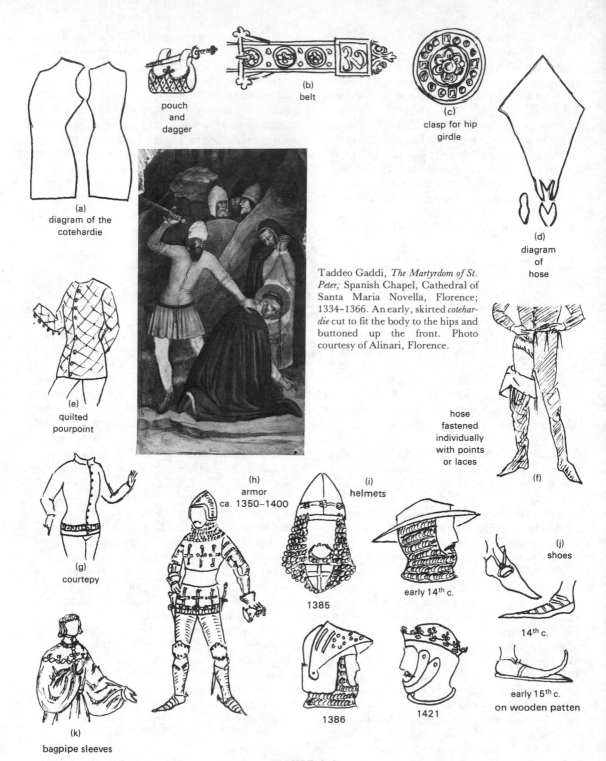

(a)
diagram of the
cotehardie

pouch
and
dagger

(b)
belt

(c)
clasp for hip
girdle

(d)
diagram
of
hose

Taddeo Gaddi, *The Martyrdom of St. Peter;* Spanish Chapel, Cathedral of Santa Maria Novella, Florence; 1334–1366. An early, skirted *cotehardie* cut to fit the body to the hips and buttoned up the front. Photo courtesy of Alinari, Florence.

(e)
quilted
pourpoint

hose
fastened
individually
with points
or laces

(f)

(g)
courtepy

(h)
armor
ca. 1350–1400

(i)
helmets

1385

early 14th c.

1386

1421

(j)
shoes

14th c.

early 15th c.
on wooden patten

(k)
bagpipe sleeves

**FIGURE 9–3**

146

in a detail from the *Martyrdom of St. Peter* by Taddeo Gaddi dated before the middle of the century (Fig. 9–3). Very short versions were known as the *courtepy* (Fig. 9–3g). The cotehardie frequently carried elbow length sleeves that ended in tippets, or streamers, that reached to the knee. As the new style for scalloping or *dagging* proliferated after the middle of the century, the tippets bloomed into foliated, leaf-shaped edges that hung like a leafy vine from the elbow. Such edges also were used at the bottom edge of the cotehardie, and if a hood was worn, the edge of the shoulder cape was cut in scallops, foliations, or castellations (cut like the top of a castle wall). Invariably the cotehardie, whether hip length or much longer, was worn with a hip girdle or belt that was frequently set with jewels, making it one of the most costly items in the wardrobe (Fig. 9–3b, c).

As for looser garments still favored by older men, the variations of the surcote continued. There was still the gardcorp with its hanging sleeves, the ganache with its cape sleeves at the top of each arm, the peliçon, with its wide sleeves and fur lining (very popular for winter), and many other variations of that loose, gown-like overgarment. Examples of the surcote with three-quarter-length sleeves may be seen on the horsemen in the *The Triumph of Death* attributed to Andrea Orcogna, painted as a memorial to the terrors of the Black Death that decimated the population of Italy between 1348 and 1350 (Fig. 9–4).

From 1325 to 1377 mantles were usually fastened on the right shoulder either by buttons or with a clasp or brooch, and they were often sprinkled with the family crest or completely covered with the family coat of arms. Sometimes they were lined in fur, and frequently the edges were embellished with dagging. The furs used during this period included ermine, miniver, sable, and lamb.

The hose worn during this period, now much more exposed by the short pourpoint and

**FIG. 9-4** Andrea Orcagna (?), *The Triumph of Death;* Camposanto, Pisa; ca. 1360–1375. Illustrates equestrian aristocrats escaping the terrors of the Black Plague. Note the variety of open-sleeved *surcotes,* the use of caped hoods, the variety of high-crowned, peak-brimmed hunting hats, the donut *roundlet* on the man to the left, and the continuing use of the draped *wimple* under the hats of the women. Photo courtesy of Alinari, Florence.

cotehardie, were given more attention in cut and fit than in the past. Bias cut provided the stretch needed to hug the leg and give a smooth line, and the length now reached almost to the waist where the top was fastened with *points* to the pourpoint or jupon or to a belt (Fig. 9-3d, f). Subtle cutting and shaping were done to make the hose fit smoothly over the foot, and sometimes in lieu of a shoe a leather sole was sewn into the bottom of the hose.

Shoes still had a soft sole, were low cut, and were laced or fastened with a button on the inside of the foot. The toes were exceedingly elongated, often up to ten inches; six-inch pointed toes were common. These elongated shoes were called *poulaines,* or *crackowes,* indicating that the style was thought to have come from Poland (Fig. 9-3j). Although there are stories about the toes becoming so long that they had to be fastened to the knee, there is no pictorial evidence to that effect. However, they were difficult to walk in and demanded that the toes be pointed out at all times.

Hair styles ranged from just below the ear to shoulder length with moderate fullness, and beards were about as common as the clean-shaven look. Major headcoverings were the ornamental band, or *fillet,* around the hair or the caped hood, most usually worn with the hood thrown back on the shoulders. The hood itself had an exceedingly long tail, or *liripipe,* and this hung decoratively down the back. Hats included the peaked riding hat with high crown and upturned brim projecting into a point at the front that is prominent on the horsemen in the *Triumph of Death* (Fig. 9-4), small bag caps with a rolled edge, small pillboxes edged in fur, and some of the old acorn-shaped caps with a turned-up brim on all sides (Fig. 9-5a).

In military dress the use of suits of plate armor had almost completely replaced the chainmail hauberk by the early fourteenth century. A shirt of mail was still worn under the *brigandine,* which was the padded metal breastplate that was hinged and buckled into position under the closefitting sleeveless surcote of fabric that was usually covered with armorial bearings (Fig. 9-3h). The neck was protected by a metal *gorget;* the arms and legs, by articulated metal plates over chain mail; and the head, by a slightly pointed helmet with an articulated visor (Fig. 9-3i).

The foot soldier usually had only a metal helmet, and his torso was protected by a heavy canvas or leather *gambeson* interlined, quilted, and studded with nail heads that might or might not be worn over a shirt of mail. His legs and feet were seldom given more protection than a very heavy set of hose. Spears, crossbows, and sometimes the long bows were the major weapons, and bowmen occasionally carried a shield.

**Feminine Dress**   The two new garments for women that developed about the beginning of the second quarter of the fourteenth century were the cotehardie and the sideless gown (Fig. 9-5c, d). The cotehardie was based on the same form-fitting lines to the hips as was the male fashion and then spread out from the hips in a floor-length skirt. It usually had long, tight sleeves that buttoned at the wrist, although the sleeves sometimes ended just above the elbow in the dangling cuffs known as *tippets* (Fig. 9-5c). The neckline was wide, rounded, and lower than at any time since classical dress, and the gown usually fastened up the back (although sometimes buttoning up the front). As with the male version, the woman's cotehardie frequently had an ornamental girdle at the hips. Under the cotehardie the thin, tight-fitting *camise* was the basic undergarment.

The cotehardie had vertical slits in the top front of the skirt in order for the lady to keep her hands covered or to reach the purse which hung from an inside belt. Some rough dresses from this period found frozen in a burial site in Greenland demonstrate the complex gored cut of these garments. With its inset *godets,* darts, and many seams, the cotehardie was a masterpiece of the seamstress's art and a far cry from the simple lines of the earlier cotes and surcotes. Occasionally, as shown in some Italian paintings, the skirt to the cotehardie was set on separately at the waist.

Over the cotehardie the major outergown that developed from the old cyclas or surcote was the sideless gown. Its name describes exactly the nature of the gown since it was a gown with the sides cut away from shoulder to hip so

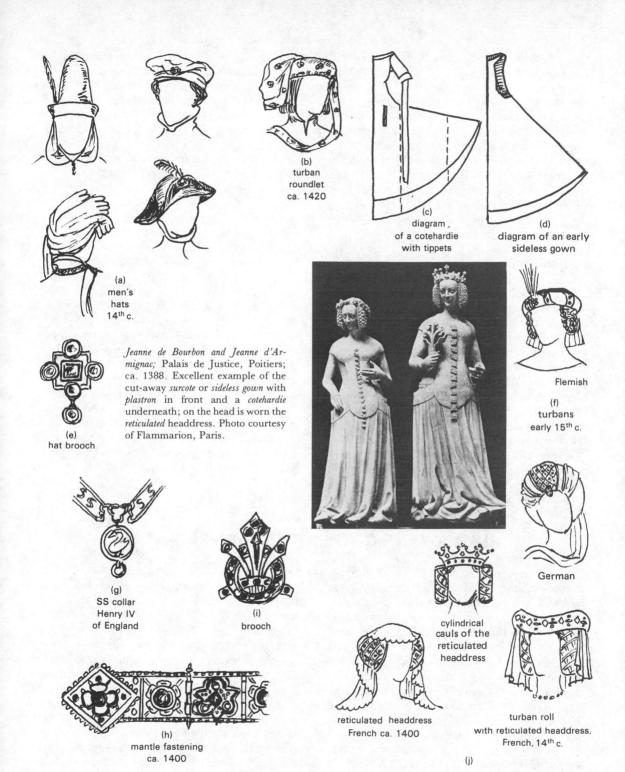

(a)
men's
hats
14th c.

(b)
turban
roundlet
ca. 1420

(c)
diagram
of a cotehardie
with tippets

(d)
diagram of an early
sideless gown

(e)
hat brooch

*Jeanne de Bourbon and Jeanne d'Armignac;* Palais de Justice, Poitiers; ca. 1388. Excellent example of the cut-away *surcote* or *sideless gown* with *plastron* in front and a *cotehardie* underneath; on the head is worn the *reticulated* headdress. Photo courtesy of Flammarion, Paris.

Flemish

(f)
turbans
early 15th c.

(g)
SS collar
Henry IV
of England

(i)
brooch

German

cylindrical
cauls of the
reticulated
headdress

(h)
mantle fastening
ca. 1400

reticulated headdress
French ca. 1400

turban roll
with reticulated headdress,
French, 14th c.

(j)

FIGURE 9–5

149

that one could see the sleek body lines of the cotehardie in a kind of oval window. Priests vividly referred to the effect as the "windows of hell" (Fig. 9–5). As the century progressed, the top-front section of the sideless gown was covered with an extra piece of fabric covered in fur or brocade that was known as a *plastron,* and the skirt more frequently was emblazoned in a heraldic coat of arms. By the early fifteenth century, when other styles superseded it, the sideless gown remained the traditional official dress worn on conservative ceremonial occasions to display the family or royal arms.

In headdresses and hairdressing the styles of the later fourteenth century show a great sense of fantasy and imagination, with an emphasis on width rather than height. This, however, was reversed by the middle of the fifteenth century. The hair was usually heavily braided and then coiled at the back of the neck, across the front of the head, or much more frequently over the ears. The coils were often placed inside of a *caul,* or net, and the head was covered by a wimple. These cauls later often became solid metal cages studded in jewels that developed into the reticulated headdress often seen on women by the third quarter of the fourteenth century. These metal cages were usually held in place by a coronet or crown that made the entire headdress very broad, ornamental, and somewhat unnatural (Fig. 9–5j).

Older ladies still wore the gorget and wimple combination, and sometimes the gorget was worn alone, covering the neck and chin up to the base of the heavy coils of braided hair placed over each ear. In Germany, Flanders, and Italy various turban effects were very popular (Fig. 9–5f).

Outerwraps changed very little from those of the thirteenth century, except that the circular and half-circular mantle more frequently displayed the entire family coat of arms blazoned across its outer surface. Mantles were frequently lined in fur, and some mantles had slits for the arms and hands at a convenient height on the front sides. Mantles now usually fastened at the center front with a cord or brooch, and some closed with buttons down the entire front of the figure. A few mantles had hoods, but more frequently women wore the female version of the gardcorp with hood attached as a practical outdoor garment.

One can seldom see a lady's feet in paintings, illuminations, or statues of the period, but when one does glimpse them, they are pointed, soft-soled slippers like the men's. As for accessories aside from headdresses, gloves were worn, and jewelry usually consisted of elaborate hip girdles, belts, jeweled buttons, and neck pendants (Fig. 9–5e,g,h,i).

## FLAMBOYANT GOTHIC (THE HOUPPELANDE)

With the arrival of Richard II on the English throne—a king very interested in all the latest fads and fashions—Gothic clothing burst into a new phase of decorative excess, marked primarily by the introduction of the houppelande and more variations in the use of dagged and foliated edges. It was also a period in which the flamelike motifs in Gothic tracery created an ornamental architectural style known as *Flamboyant Gothic*—an apt description, as well, for the costume fashions from 1377 to approximately 1425.

***Masculine Dress***   In the third quarter of the fourteenth century the houppelande, a new

and very dramatic outer robe, was added to the male wardrobe. It probably originated in Spain but was adopted throughout western Europe by the last quarter of the fourteenth century. Originally it was a full, floor-length robe with a very high collar and open bell sleeves of floor length. The collar pushed up against the ears and the back of the head, the skirts trailed on the floor, and the sleeves, most frequently richly dagged or foliated, spread out like great wings below the outstretched arm. It was usually richly girdled at the waist, was frequently worn with a great *bandolier,* or baldric, draped diagonally across the body, and the sides were sometimes slit and foliated to show off the leg and to ease the problem of walking. In its most exuberant form, it was sometimes equipped with tiny bells on the baldric, at the base of the collar, or hanging in long tails down the back of the gown. Beautiful examples of the theatrical flamboyance achieved by this new fashion may be seen in the lovely illuminations in the famous *Très Riches Heures* (Figs. 9–2, 6). The garment was made more impressive when sprinkled with an embroidered crest and when the foliated or dagged sleeves were turned back to show the rich silk lining in contrasting color. So-called *bastard houppelandes* were much shorter, some ankle length, some just below the

knee, but all had the wide sleeves and the high collar (Fig. 9–7a,b). The houppelande was usually worn over a cotehardie or a pourpoint whose sleeves show beyond the plain or foliated edges of the houppelande's bell sleeves. Sometimes the houppelande was unbelted, but much more commonly it was richly belted at the waist or on the hips.

With the houppelande there usually was no need for a mantle, so these circular and half-circular outer garments were usually reserved for wear with the older cotehardie or shorter gowns with narrower sleeves than those found on the houppelande. One such gown that was very popular in the opening years of the fifteenth century had bagpipe or bellows sleeves in which a great width of material was gathered into a cuff to create a great expansion and contraction of width from elbow to wrist (Fig. 9–3k). Sometimes such a sleeve had a slit up the center front so that the arm could come through to create a hanging sleeve, or it could be worn normally with the hand coming through the wrist opening.

There were also a number of older, looser surcotes that were less fashionable that retained the lines found in the thirteenth-century ganache and gardcorp. Shoes were generally as pointed, if not more so, than in the years before 1377, and fur was an even more admired trim for all garments as well as being a preferred lining in winter.

As with the women of this period, the great center for display was the head, and a variety of new headdresses made their appearance in the years between 1377 and 1415. Certainly the most exotic and exuberant was the chaperon, which some clever wit may have invented at a party by wearing his hood with the face opening around the circumference of his head, allowing the shoulder cape to fall to one side while he wrapped the liripipe once around the head and draped it over the shoulder (Figs. 9–6,7a,b, 8). Soon this usage became set by making a kind of turban roll around what used to be the face opening; other variations developed in which twin peaks were added to the hood, the hood became an elongated bag, two peaks were created over each ear within the bag shape, and the stuffed roll at the edge of the headdress be-

**FIG. 9–6** *Falconry Scene;* from *Très Riches Heures du Duc de Berry;* Musée Condé, Chantilly; ca. 1415. Illustrates the unworldly elegance and fantasy in aristocratic fashions early in the fifteenth century. Note particularly the soft, curved lines of the clothing, the fanciful headdresses, and the tracery edges to the garments. Photo courtesy of the Bibliothèque Nationale, Paris.

**FIG. 9-7** Four statuettes from the Dam Chimney-piece, Amsterdam; early fifteenth century. (*a*) The Flemish count here wears a long *houppelande* with organpipe folds, wide bell sleeves, dagged edges, and a donut *roundlet*. (*b*) A Dutch count is in a *bastard* (short) *houppelande* with open bell sleeves with scalloped edges; his headdress is the new *chaperon* or open hood with its point or *liripipe* draped over the shoulder. (*c*) The woman is in a *houppelande* with open hanging sleeves and a rolled turban *chaperon* headdress and veil. (*d*) A Dutch countess is in a *surcote* with short sleeves over an undergown with hanging sleeves from the elbow and a split-loaf, heart-shaped headdress fastened to an embroidered *caul*. Photos courtesy of Giraudon, Paris.

**FIG. 9–8** Pol de Limbourg, *The Duc de Berry Setting Out on a Journey;* from the *Grandes Heures du Duc de Berry;* Bibliothèque Nationale, Paris; 1415. The Duke wears a black *gardcorp* that is fur-lined and embroidered in gold, while his herald wears a pink *houppelande* lined in white with scalloped edges. His headdress is the turbanlike *chaperon.* Photo courtesy of the Bibliothèque Nationale, Paris.

lars in gold and jewels down through the period of Richard II, Henry IV, and Henry V (Fig. 9–5g). The most famous continental order established by Philip the Good of Burgundy was the Order of the Golden Fleece, instituted in 1429.

Finally a word should be said about the common man of the period. From the *Très Riches Heures* for the month of June, we see several men using the scythe on the grain in the fields (Fig. 9–9). They all wear simple tunics or shirts with their legs bare, although we have other figures from this same series in which the men wear hose to the knee and rough leather slipper-shoes. On their heads they wear straw sun hats

**FIG. 9–9** *The Labours of the Months: June;* from the *Très Riches Heures du Duc de Berry;* Musée Condé, Chantilly; ca. 1415. Illustrates the peasant women wearing the *kirtle* girdled up over the *camise* at the hips with a *couvrechief* on the head, and the men wearing *jupes* or *cottes* (a peasant shirt) and either a sweat cloth or a straw hat. Photo courtesy of Giraudon, Paris.

came so large that it dominated the entire effect (Figs. 9–5a,b, 7a, 8). At first these effects were achieved at each wearing by wrapping and setting the various chaperon shapes in place, but gradually they were sewn into a permanent headdress, known as a *roundel,* that kept its shape and look when removed from the head. There were also simpler bag caps, small spherical caps with turned-up fur brims, and the older Robin Hood hat for riding and hunting; but the most distinctive headdress was the chaperon.

As for accessories, the most distinctive were the various orders developed to be worn about the neck during this period. The famed Order of the Garter was developed by Edward III of England in 1348, and there were many other minor orders that allowed for richly worked color a cloth wrapped like a turban, and the shirts or tunics are tucked up into the belt to facilitate movement. Under these simple garments these men would still have worn the diaperlike underdrawers that had been worn for many centuries. As one would expect, these basic garments had not changed since Romanesque times; in the history of dress, the common people were frequently as much as two centuries behind the upper classes in dress.

Enough has already been said about armor during the period prior to 1377 to indicate that the trend in the later period was toward more refinement in the articulation of the various metal pieces that made up a full suit of armor, as well as to cover more and more parts of the body in full plate. Finally by the period of Joan of Arc (around 1430), the complete suit of plate armor had been fully developed.

*Feminine Dress* The new garment for women as for men during the period between 1377 and 1425 was the houppelande, which for women was usually belted high under the bustline with a collar that lay down on the shoulder rather than rising up to enclose the neck as with the men. It was often sprinkled with the em-

broidered crest of the family, and the sleeves were lined either in fur or contrasting silk material with the favored dagged or foliated edges very much in evidence. In the lovely Exchange of the Rings from the *Très Riches Heures,* the betrothed wears a gown that has the sleeves of the houppelande with a fitted body like the cotehardie (Fig. 9–2), but the lady directly behind her wears the houppelande in the traditional cut. The maid-in-waiting, further back in the illumination, wears the cotehardie with tippets at the elbow, and all the ladies have interesting hairdos or headdresses primarily based on versions of the padded roll or turban effect derived from the male chaperon (Fig. 9–5f). In the Falconry scene, also from the *Très Riches Heures,* there are wonderful variations in the foliated bell sleeves, sprinkled decorative crests, and fitted or belted gowns, but probably only the sixth figure from the right is wearing a true female houppelande (Fig. 9–6). Necklines varied during this period from the houppelande neck with its collar that laid back from the base of the throat to the low cut of the fitted cotehardie, sideless gown, or combination of cotehardie with the foliated bell sleeves of the houppelande. In both the scenes from the *Très Riches*

**FIG. 9–10** *The Valiant Ladies,* fresco in the castle of Mantua in Piedmont; ca. 1386. Note the variety of turbanlike headdresses, the female version of the bell-shaped *houppelande* in the first and third figures from the left; the dagged and foliated edges on sleeves and mantles; the sideless gown on the second figure from the right; and the powdered decoration. Photo courtesy of Alinari, Florence.

*Heures* the image projected is one of charm, fantasy, and exotic escape from reality.

As with men, headdresses for women during this period became more exotic. First the coils of hair were moved forward into horn-shaped protrusions on either side of the head. These were then covered with cauls, and the entire effect was loosely covered with a veil. Then various turbanlike rolls were added that gave a further touch of the exotic, and finally a number of heart-shaped rolls were placed on top of the horns of hair covered with the caul. All in all, these inventive fantasies created more concentration on the head than had ever existed in women's fashions to date. An excellent confirmation of this comes from looking at the *Valiant Ladies* (Fig. 9–10). There seems no end to the variations in horns, flared rolls, turbans set with leaves, and rolled twists of hair, yet in the 50 years following 1415, headdresses were to reach even greater heights and achieve even more exotic shapes.

As for shoes, hose, and mantles, these changed little from the earlier fourteenth century, and jewelry continued also in the direction that had begun before 1377.

But a word should again be said about lower-class women who, like the men, are shown in the *Très Riches Heures* as working in the fields in very simple and basic garments (Fig. 9–9). They are barefoot and wear simple kirtles that are shaped and fitted like a short version of the cotehardie. Under this they wear a simple white chemise. The outer dress is frequently bloused somewhat over a belt or hip girdle to lift the kirtle away from the feet, and at times the skirt is tucked into the waist to make a container for carrying produce back from the fields. On their heads these women of the fields wear a simple cloth like a wimple that is sometimes knotted and twisted about the head to make a kind of turban.

## FABRICS

The increase in the variety of silks available during this century was remarkable. European textile workers were growing ever more skillful and were now able to imitate oriental and Near Eastern refinements in silks. In addition to the range of linens, woolens, and cottons that had been staples in western Europe for several centuries, there were many new silk velvets, taffetas, brocades, and *samite,* a most sumptuous silk fabric. One might say that with the opening of the fifteenth century Europe entered into an age of velvet and brocade.

## ARTS AND ARTIFACTS

We have already noted in looking at the Great Hall of the Counts of Poitou that the use of flamelike tracery and feathery stone decoration was the norm of this period, with ornament dominant over structure (Fig. 9–1). Domestic interiors included oak-paneled walls, tapestried wall hangings, ornate trefoiled and quatrefoiled Gothic arches, and heavy oak furniture richly carved with architectural tracery motifs. Dining tables were of the long refectory style, covered with embroidered cloths, and dining chairs were either carved benches or carved stools with or without backs (Fig. 9–1a,b,c,d,e).

Musical instruments that might be found in a noble household included the viol or rebeck, the harp, the recorder or English flute, a portable organ, a bagpipe, and early versions of the guitar and lute. Personal accessories that were prominently used were the purse fastened to the belt; the pomander that hung from the waist and was filled with a perfumed sponge to be used to ward off the evil smells of the streets or of the Plague; the baldric or bandolier slung diagonally over the shoulder to suspend a sword, dagger, or purse; and the soft gloves for indoor wear or the heavier variety with the stiff cuff for hunting and falconry. The baldric was probably the most lavish accessory. It was made of leather, silk, or metallic cloth studded with jewels and often cut with foliated edges and fringed with small bells.

Jewelry included the rich crowns and coronets that often mirrored Late Gothic tracery in their ornate, foliated arabesque effects; the collar that represented various chivalric orders like that of the Golden Fleece; various jeweled pendants and chains; various pins and brooches used to fasten capes and close the slits in hanging sleeves; large rings set with cut or faceted gems; belts, often of linked gold and silver disks set with jewels, as well as those of jewel-studded leather; and the very rich accessory effects created by jeweled swords, daggers, and scabbards (Fig. 9–5e,g,h,i).

## VISUAL SOURCES

Once again one has a profusion of sources that may be consulted for fashion information. Sculpture and manuscript illuminations are very important, but painting also is a major source. The major centers for illuminations are the Bibliothèque Nationale in Paris and the British Museum of London; the most brilliant set of illuminations for the later part of this period, the *Très Riches Heures du Duc de Berry,* are in the Musée Condé at Chantilly. Helpful Italian painters are Taddeo Gaddi, Pietro and Ambrogio Lorenzetti, and Simone Martini. Useful books are Mary Houston's *Medieval Costume in England and France,* the Cunningtons' *Handbook of English Medieval Costume,* and Herbert Norris's *Costume and Fashion, Volume II.*

## SUMMARY

This period saw the flowering into architectural decoration, manuscript ornamentation, and fashion display of all those elements of creative fantasy released when the spiritual, otherworldly values of the High Gothic began to wane. Fashion truly moved, as did architecture, from decorative to flamboyant, and the costume mirrored the profusion of tracery, crockets, and finials found in the architecture and repeated in fanciful headdresses and foliated and dagged edges of garments. It was an age of daring, dash, and flare in costume in which the large gesture, the sweeping movement, the serpentine curve of the body carried a message of self-conscious artificiality and escape from the restraints of earthly reality. To look at the fashions of the time, one would never guess the nature of the great events of this period: the Hundred Years' War, the Great Plague, and the miserable living conditions surrounding the great noble castles.

# chapter X

# Late Gothic and
# Early Italian Renaissance

## Chronology
### (ca. 1425–1485)

| | | |
|---|---|---|
| REIGN OF HENRY V IN ENGLAND 1422–1461 | 1422–1461 | Charles VII, king of France |
| | 1428 | The painter Masaccio dies in Italy |
| | 1429 | Siege of Orléans |
| | 1431 | Joan of Arc burned at Rouen |
| | 1432 | Jan van Eyck completes the altarpiece in Ghent, the first really major work in Flemish painting |
| | 1434 | Cosimo de Medici begins 30-year domination of Florence |
| Burgundian ca. 1435–1440 | 1436 | Leon Battista Alberti writes first treatise on theory of painting |
| | 1438 | Charles VII of France issues *Pragmatic Sanction of Bourges,* establishing the liberty of the Gallican Church |
| | 1442 | Naples and Sicily come under the rule of the Spanish House of Aragon |
| | ca.1440–1442 | Donatello casts *David,* the first free-standing nude figure since antiquity |

Italian
ca. 1450–1460

| | | |
|---|---|---|
| ca. 1440–1450 | Fra Angelico paints the *Annunciation* |
| 1447 | Pope Nicholas V founds the Vatican library |
| ca. 1450 | Invention of printing with movable type |
| 1450 | Francesco Sforza, mercenary soldier and son-in-law of Duke Filippo Maria, conquers Milan and becomes duke |
| ca. 1452 | Alberti writes the first modern work on architecture, *De re aedificatoria* |
| 1453 | Constantinople falls to the Turks; many scholarly refugees come to Italy and bring Greek manuscripts; the Hundred Years' War ends between France and England |
| 1454 | Peace of Lodi ushers in 40 years of relative peace among the Italian states |
| 1455 | The Wars of the Roses begin in England between the rival houses of Lancaster and York |
| 1458 | Pius II (Aeneas Silvius Piccolomini), a humanist, becomes pope |

---

REIGNS OF
EDWARD IV,
EDWARD V AND
RICHARD III
IN ENGLAND
1461–1485

| | | |
|---|---|---|
| 1462 | Platonic Academy, headed by Marsilio Ficino, is founded in Florence |
| 1463 | Venice begins a 16-year war with the Turks |

| | |
|---|---|
| 1465 | The first Italian printing press is set up at Subiaco, near Rome |
| 1469 | Lorenzo de Medici heads the Florentine state; Ferdinand and Isabella unite Spain; Ivan III founds the first united Russian monarchy at Moscow |
| 1471 | Sixtus IV becomes pope and turns the Papal States into a strong dominion; Edward IV of England gains decisive victories at Barnet and Tewkesbury, and Queen Margaret is captured and sent to the Tower; death of Henry VI in the Tower |
| 1475 | Edward IV invades France with the aid of Charles the Bold of Burgundy |
| 1477 | Charles the Bold of Burgundy killed by the Swiss at Nancy; his daughter, Mary, married Maximilian of Austria |
| 1478 | Pazzi conspiracy against the Medici fails; birth of Sir Thomas More |
| 1479 | Venice is defeated by the Turks and forced to pay for trading privileges; Lodovico Sforza seizes control of Milan from his nephew Gian Galeazzo, which marks the opening of the Golden Age of the Renaissance in Milan |
| ca. 1480 | Botticelli paints *The Birth of Venus* |
| ca. 1482 | Leonardo da Vinci goes to work at the Court of Milan |
| 1483 | Death of Edward IV in England, accession and murder of Edward V in the Tower, accession of Richard III |
| 1484 | Innocent VIII becomes pope |
| 1485 | Battle of Bosworth and the death of Richard III |

Franco-Burgundian
1460–1470

Italian
ca. 1480

# BACKGROUND

At the very height of Flamboyant Gothic development, the city of Florence experienced a new classical style that caused scholars and artists to compare it to Athens of the fifth century B.C. The Florentines, like the Athenians after their defeat of the Persians, felt a similar flush of national pride after they repulsed the forces of the Duke of Milan in the late fourteenth century. There followed an explosion of artistic and cultural activity that came to be seen as a *Renaissance* of classical ideals. The new Florentine cultural explosion was based on many artistic experiments of the early fourteenth century that were abandoned when the Black Plague swept all Europe at the middle of the fourteenth century. Italian cultural development was curtailed for almost a half century. Only at the opening of the fifteenth century, when the city had once again become a center of trade and wealth and when certain patrician families became interested in being patrons of the arts, did Florence become the center of a great new artistic Golden Age.

On March 25, 1436, the dedication of Florence's newly completed cathedral marked a high point in this new artistic development. It brought together city dignitaries, influential churchmen, diplomats, artists and men of letters in a ceremony presided over by Pope Eugene IV and seven cardinals and many bishops and archbishops. The cathedral, begun in the thirteenth century, had remained incomplete for over a century because no architect had possessed the creative ingenuity to complete the dome over the crossing. Finally Filippo Brunelleschi, the artist who was to be the greatest architect of the fifteenth century in Italy, completed the cupola with an ingenuous use of ribs combined with an inner and outer shell.

Opposite the facade of the cathedral were a new set of bronze doors set into the old Romanesque Baptistry by Lorenzo Ghiberti, who was already at work on an east set of doors that Michelangelo would later call the "Gates of Paradise." The painters Uccello, Gozzoli, and Masaccio were also adding to the glories of the new artistic style throughout Florence at

this time, and the sculptural genius of Donatello was already making itself felt in the statues that he was preparing for exterior niches in the cathedral and its campanile.

In the pope's entourage were leading humanist artist-scholars such as Leon Battista Alberti, who had just completed his book *On Painting* and was at work on a treatise entitled *On Architecture,* and Guillaume Dufay, the famed musician who had composed the commemorative motet for the papal choir on this illustrious occasion. The streets were lined with members of Florence's leading mercantile families, whose rich trappings equaled those of royal households. They, in turn, were surrounded by members of the many trade guilds that made Florentine industry one of the wealthiest in all Europe. The most renowned family present was presided over by Cosimo de Mediei, who dominated the politics of the city without holding a title. These Medicis were fast becoming the bankers to all the royal families of Europe, had offices in Lyons, Antwerp, and London, and made the Florentine *florin* the soundest currency in Europe.

But it was Cosimo's son, Lorenzo the Magnificent, who was to become one of the greatest patrons of arts and letters of all time. He extended the Medici Library, revitalized the academy for instruction in the arts, established the Platonic Academy of Philosophy, and lavished personal and city funds on buildings, festivals, and other forms of public art. Symbolically as well as practically, the Medici sponsored, subsidized, and endowed the Florentine Renaissance.

The artistic and cultural outlook of this Florentine style broke sharply with the older Gothic style. It was an age of experiment, particularly in the use of mathematical perspective. Human beings were now set in a real space and were the focus in paintings. It was also an age of mathematical naturalism in which the curving lines and flat patterns of the international Gothic style were replaced by tactile forms, mathematical precision, and simple human dignity.

To show the difference in terms of architecture, let us look at the Pazzi Chapel designed by the great Filippo Brunelleschi between 1430 and 1433 and compare it to St. Maclou, a late French Gothic Church begun in Rouen at this same time (Figs. 10-1, 2). The facade of the Pazzi Chapel is delicate and flat, consisting of an entablature supported by slender columns broken in the middle by a large central arch, with flat decoration created from circles, squares, and rectangles. It is a cool, mathematical, intellectual design with each larger section a multiple of the smaller ones and the whole a series of separate space compartments, very different from the ever-changing, skeletal openness and complex emotional decoration of the Gothic structures being erected in France at this time.

Florence was not, however, the only center of money and power in the fifteenth century; the other center of trade and mercantile affluence was in Flanders. Although the artistic tenets in this area remained primarily Gothic until the close of the fifteenth century, the new, detailed realism found in the Flemish painting of this period has led some historians to speak of the artistic and cultural explosion in this second center of trade and banking as the Flemish Renaissance. The most important cities for art and trade in the north were Antwerp, Bruges, and Ghent; one of the great Medici banking offices outside Italy was in Antwerp.

Politically this area of Flanders (modern-day Belgium and Holland) was governed by the Duke of Burgundy, who nominally ruled a province of France with its capital in Dijon; however, through intermarriage in the fourteenth century, the dukedom had gained control over the wealthy lowland areas and had become almost totally independent of the French king. Bruges, Ghent, and Antwerp became three of the busiest ports in Europe with wool brought in from England and then carried

FIG. 10-1 Filippo Brunelleschi and others, Pazzi Chapel, Church of Santa Croce, Florence; ca. 1430-1433. Note the slender classical arcading, simple geometric forms, and delicate decoration in the colonnaded loggia and dome. Photo courtesy of Alinari, Florence. (Line art on p. 162.)

(1a)
Italian
renaissance
candelabrum
ca. 1480

(1b)
a first-floor window
in an early Renaissance palace

(1c)
a ground-floor window

Church of St. Maclou, Rouen; begun in 1434. A Late Gothic church in which refinement of detail and open arabesques of spiny, elegant tracery have replaced unity, simplicity, and monumentality of structure. Photo courtesy of the Caisse Nationale des Monuments Historiques et des Sites.

(2a)
linenfold
paneled armchair
ca. 1475
English

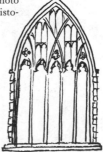

(1d)
Italian
chair
ca. 1485

(2b)
flamboyant
Gothic
window
French

(2c)
perpendicular
Gothic
window
English

**FIGURE 10-2**

162

away again as the finest manufactured cloth in Europe. The wool trade brought with it bankers and money, and Bruges in particular became the financial clearinghouse for all northern Europe. The Duke of Burgundy soon set up his court in Flanders instead of Dijon, and during the fifteenth century until the death of Charles the Bold in 1477, the court of Burgundy was one of the most gorgeous in Europe, carrying to flamboyant excess the dying fall of Gothic art and decoration. All the countries of the north took their fashions from the court of Burgundy, whereas few copied the new Italian fashions until the end of the fifteenth century.

Thus in Europe between 1425 and 1485 there were two foci of fashion and artistic development, one located in Italy with its center in Florence, the other located at the Burgundian court of Flanders with its three centers—Antwerp, Bruges, and Ghent.

## THE BASIC COSTUME SILHOUETTE

As one would guess from the brief discussion of the differences between the court of Burgundy and the city of Florence between 1425 and 1485, the basic costume silhouette in each setting was quite distinct, even though there are areas in which they did resemble each other. The Renaissance clothing of Italy, like the art of the time, stressed simplicity, balance, and an emphasis on the natural form. While Gothic costume was reaching a final climax of development at the court of Burgundy, the Renaissance in Florence brought a revival of many classical concepts to the dress of Italy. By the middle of the fifteenth century the Florentines were integrating certain classical ideals with motifs and silhouettes inherited from the north. The early Renaissance style stressed the horizontal over the vertical, the simple and geometric over the complex and decorative, earth tonalities over bright heraldic color, and a natural silhouette over exaggerated and artificial lines. The new Italian Renaissance view of dress underlined the concept that beauty lay in a rational and harmonious relationship of all parts of the costume rather than in decoration for its own sake.

In masculine dress by the middle of the fifteenth century in Italy, the undergarment was usually a sleeveless doublet to which long hose could be fashioned with ties, or *points*. The hose of cloth or leather were sometimes sewn together at the top to form a single garment since the outertunic, or doublet, was often slightly shorter than the crotch line. If the hose remained separate, they were drawn up over diaperlike drawers which were hidden by the skirt of the outer doublet. A collarless shirt was worn under the doublet, and the latter fitted smoothly over the body or was pleated softly to it. Loose or belted robes were also often worn, sometimes with hanging sleeves that fell to the hips or even the ankles. Heads were usually covered with soft caps, large fur hats, or a simple version of the northern *roundlet*. Hair was usually full to the base of the neck. The general effect when compared with the heavier, more decorative northern style was looser, followed the natural lines of the body to a greater extent, and projected a conscious simplicity and balance.

In feminine fashion the same precepts prevailed. Gowns fitted smoothly to the body with top and bottom cut in one, or the bodice was separate from the skirt and carried a slightly higher than normal waistline. Sometimes the outergown was sleeveless to display a rich, natural sleeve from the undergown, and occasionally the seam of this undersleeve was left open at the elbow to allow the chemise sleeve to show through. Necklines were usually relatively low and rounded, or the outergown made a laced V-opening over the material of the undergown. Hair either flowed loosely onto the shoulders or was braided in interesting ways about the head. As in the north, a very high brow was prized, and the hairline often plucked to create this effect. Headdresses were much less used in Italy than in the north, although rounded *escoffions* (a padded horn shape rising from the head) were sometimes seen, as were some exotic-looking turbans.

A painting illustrating the general qualities

of this new Renaissance style is *The Bridal Pair,* painted by an anonymous Swabian artist about 1470 who seems to have been very conscious of the new Italian Renaissance style (Fig. 10-3). The young man is in a simple, striped tunic in which the stripes are a form of simple geometric decoration rather than part of heraldic particoloring, and the girl is in a simple, soft gown that shows her youthful figure to perfection. The couple perfectly exemplifies the youth of the new Renaissance through their clothing as well as through their age.

Meanwhile in the Flemish court of the Duke of Burgundy, another style projecting the final phase of the richness and splendor of the Gothic style was reaching its climax. This Burgundian style is represented by an illuminated manuscript depicting the betrothal of the daughter of King Yon of Gascoigne (Fig. 10-4). Here we see that the shoes are elegantly pointed; broad-shouldered, pleated doublets have replaced the cotehardie and houppelande; and hats are now very tall bag or sugar-loaf shapes with an occasional roundlet with its draped liripipe. Hose, sometimes still particolored, are frequently connected at the top due to the shortness of many doublets, and mantles or long gowns with hanging sleeves are used as outergarments or worn by older men.

Women's gowns, worn over a rich under-gown, at the Burgundian court usually had a slightly lifted waistline, a train that was quite full, a deep V-shaped neck often outlined in ermine or other fur, and sleeves that were usually long, narrow, and finished with a fur cuff. Heads were usually covered with towering, pointed hennins with trailing veils. These head-dresses could be most complex—some with three horns instead of one, some with starched and wired veils in butterfly formation, some with high, rich, padded escoffions pinned over the hair. Though the heraldic mantle and cotehardie were still worn for ceremonial occasions, the new style projected its primary decorative accent through the flamboyant headdresses. Decorative richness, as in Flamboyant Gothic art, was the key to the Burgundian style as was distortion of the human body for decorative effect. Only in Italy was simplicity and naturalness of costume line a virtue.

## THE EARLY ITALIAN RENAISSANCE

Italy about 1425 was composed of many rival city states; therefore, fashion was anything but uniform during the succeeding 60 years. In general, Venice, Verona, and Milan were more influenced by fashion from over the Alps; Florence and Rome attempted to do more with pleating and draping in the classical manner; and southern Italy was still under many of the cultural influences of Islam and Byzantium. But throughout Italy—with its wealth of trade with the Orient and the lowlands—rich fabrics, fine jeweled craftsmanship, and exotic imagination were the key elements in clothing.

***Masculine Dress*** Before the middle of the century the smooth-shouldered, wide-sleeved Italian version of the bastard houppelande was still widely seen, often with bagpipe sleeves rather than the more common bell-shaped vari-ety. Dagged edges were still used, but not in as much profusion as in the north, and were usually cut in a kind of mathematical-geometric scallop along the edge of the garment (Fig. 10-3). Collars were of the moderate, standing variety; hair was of a full, moderate length (usually to the base of the neck); and hats came in wide varieties from turbans to moderately broad-brimmed hats with brims turned up on one side for variations of the coif.

Gradually as the new stress on balance and geometric symmetry developed, the knee-length gown, with open bell or hanging sleeves, displayed very carefully arranged organ pleating below the waist and in the sleeves. The fabric was stiffer and often woven in a rich brocaded pattern rather than embroidered, and the pleating below the waist and in the sleeves was massed and held in place by the lin-

(a)
Italian gown
ca. 1445

(b)
Italian female
hairdressing
ca. 1450–1480

(c)
Italian
men's
caps
ca. 1450–1480

(d)
Italian fur-trimmed
cyclas tabard
with cartridge pleats
ca. 1460

(e)
older man's gown
ca. 1450

Swabian School, *The Bridal Pair;* The Cleveland Museum of Art; ca. 1470. These costumes illustrate the new, body-hugging line that began to be adopted in youthful fashion by the third quarter of the fifteenth century. This couple wears simple, particolored clothing based on the styles of northern Italy. Photo courtesy of the Cleveland Museum of Art, Delia E. and L. E. Holden Fund.

hose tied to
doublet over
shirt and drawers

hose over
drawers tied
to doublet

hose and boots
fastened to doublet

(f)

**FIGURE 10–3**

(a)
sleeves: English, French
1425-1450

(b)
bagpipe sleeves

French gown
ca. 1460
(c)

(d)
English-French gown
1425-1485

1460

1435

(e)
hats

1450

1480

1485

*The Betrothal of Rénaud de Montaubon and Clarisse, Daughter of King Yon of Gascoigne;* from the *Roman de la Violette;* Bibliothèque Nationale; ca. 1460. Illustrates the taller figures, padded clothing, and exaggerated headdresses, shoes, and shoulders of the Franco-Burgundian style of the fifteenth century. Photo courtesy of the Bibliothèque Nationale, Paris.

1460

1480
(f)
Burgundian
hennins

Italian fabric motifs

Burgundian
motif
(i)

(g)
common
soldier

(h)
shoes

(j)
woman of
the people

Italian
headdress
1460

(k)
Burgundian
escoffion
1440

**FIGURE 10-4**

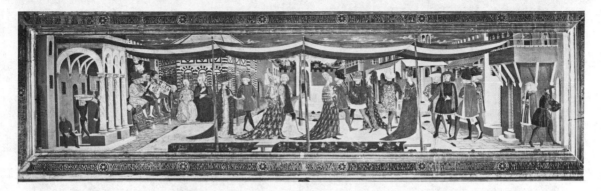

**FIG. 10–5**  *The Adimari Wedding,* from a fifteenth-century cassone. Illustrates the elegant life style of the Florentine aristocracy in the mid-fifteenth century. Note the mixture of exotic Gothic fantasy and the new solidity and three-dimensionality of form ushered in by the Early Renaissance. Photo courtesy of Alinari, Florence.

ing in such a way as to give each pleat a perfect conical shape (Fig. 10–3a). Such a gown was usually worn with a moderately wide-brimmed hat turned up at the sides or with a padded turban.

But by the middle of the century most of the excess fullness of this gown with open or bagpipe sleeves had given way to a shorter and less bulky fashion shown on the younger men in the famous Adimari-Ricasoli Wedding Procession painted by an anonymous Florentine artist on a great *cassone,* or storage chest, about 1450 (Fig. 10–5). The majority of the men in this painting wear *surcotes,* or short gowns, to above the knee wtih open, capelike, hanging sleeves over a rich, tight-fitting undertunic that was the successor to the abbreviated cotehardie. Three of the young gentlemen wear the roundlet with liripipe. Others wear full bag caps with or without a turned-up brim, and some of the hose are still particolored. The hose have feet of leather with slightly pointed toes.

To gain a sense of what the hose looked like without the covering of the surcote, let us look at a figure drawn wearing just the under pourpoint, or doublet, which held up the hose by points (Fig. 10–3f). Note that the hose was still separate, not sewn together at the crotch, and the points on the inside of the waist of the pourpoint are then tied to the points on the hose.

A famous fresco in the chapel of the Medici-Riccardi Palace shows an imagined *Journey of the Magi* in which all of the members of the procession are members or supporters of the Medici family (Fig. 10–6). One is struck by the richness of the fabrics, the simple, square body lines of the pleated garments, and the great care that was taken in presenting the mathematical pleating. Collars are of the simple, straight-line mandarin variety, rising only about an inch above the outer doublet and sloping down in the back. Under the pleated line of the hanging sleeves are extremely rich undersleeves in brocaded patterns, but the overall effect of costume line is very simple. Headgear, except for the crown on the mounted Magi, are of the simple molded bag-cap variety.

Thus until almost the end of the fifteenth century, the basic male costume in Italy was usually a doublet carefully pleated in tubular folds over a lining, with moderately full or short, open bell sleeves (Fig. 10–3a), or a carefully pleated surcote with hanging sleeves that might be either looped through the belt or over one another at the back. A favorite variation of this surcote was a sleeveless, pleated garment belted at the waist in the front and free-hanging in the back (Fig. 10–4a). Hats were usually of the soft-cap variety, with an occasional turban or roundlet, and footwear usually consisted of

**FIG. 10–6** Benozzo Gozzoli, *Journey of the Magi* (detail); Chapel of the Medici-Riccardi Palace, Florence; 1459–1462. Note the small bag hats, the pleated doublets with simple mandarin collars, hanging sleeves, and brocaded rather than sprinkled or powdered decorative patterns. Photo courtesy of Alinari, Florence.

leather soles in hose or short, form-fitting soft boots (Figs. 10–3c, 4h). Gowns were used by older men; cloaks were the standard outergarment (Fig. 10–3e).

***Feminine Dress*** During the second quarter of the fifteenth century the most common garment worn by women was a soft, flowing version of the northern houppelande often with a decorated, donut-shaped turban as headgear, and this style remained in northern Italy until about 1460. In the *Adimari Wedding* painting, the style had shifted slightly to a somewhat high-waisted gown, apparently sleeveless, but with pendant hanging sleeves at the back of the armseye thus making the rich sleeves of the underdress very prominent (Fig. 10–5). The

headdresses worn by women—escoffions of the padded sugar-loaf variety—were much more northern and owed little to the Italian style, which preferred the hair uncovered or braided into coils around or to the back of the head (Fig. 10–3b). Generally the Early Renaissance style of haircoverings for women changed from the high and unnatural headdresses of the northern Gothic style in favor of natural hair, veils, beads, and nets.

In Piero della Francesca's famous fresco *The Arrival of the Queen of Sheba,* the queen and her attendants wear high-waisted gowns that fall in generous fullness to the floor (Fig. 10–7). One has the pendant hanging sleeve found on one of the gowns in the *Adimari Wedding;* another has a surcote that is girdled over the gown in front

FIG. 10-7 Piero della Francesca, *Arrival of the Queen of Sheba,* fresco from the Church of San Francesco, Arezzo; 1452–1466. Illustrates the low, braided hairdressing and small *hennins* compared to the Burgundian fashion and the simple, naturally draped lines and classic pleating preferred by Italian fifteenth-century artists when depicting current fashion. Photo courtesy of Alinari, Florence.

By 1467 when Fra Carnevale painted *The Birth of the Virgin,* Italian female fashions had moved almost entirely away from northern late Gothic fashions (Fig. 10–8). The garments were fuller, there was more stress on a draped line, fabrics were simpler, and colors were used against one another in bold contrasts of blond tonality. The basic garments were a high-waisted, sleeveless overgown worn over a contrasting undergown with, in several cases, a very loose cyclas, cut away to the knees at the sides, over the whole. A few hanging sleeves were seen, and skirts trailed voluminously on the floor. Headdresses varied from a simple veil

FIG. 10-8 Master of the Barberini Panels (Fra Carnevale), *The Birth of the Virgin;* Metropolitan Museum of Art; ca. 1447–1475. Illustrates the full line, simple fabric textures, and importance of draping in Italian female fashion in the third quarter of the fifteenth century. Note the use of hairdressing without headdresses, sleeveless outer gowns, and unadorned necks. Photo courtesy of the Metropolitan Museum of Art, Rogers and Gwynne M. Andrews Funds, 1935.

and then falls free in the back with the edges done in the old-fashioned dagged manner. Two of the headdresses show the hair wrapped and coiled with cloth; two others wear low, padded escoffions with veils. All demonstrate the fifteenth-century interest in a high plucked hairline. But more important than the garments themselves in this fresco is the attitude of the artist, Piero della Francesca, that typifies the new outlook of the early Italian Renaissance. There is a solid, dignified, undecorated balance and mass to this grouping that typifies the Italian move away from the exaggeration, decoration, and flamboyance of the northern Gothic international style. It was this quality, rather than the actual garments, that made the Italian outlook on people and fashion so different from that found in the northern courts of Europe at this same time.

to simple braiding and coiling with nets and fabric (Fig. 10–3b). Although we seldom see shoes in such paintings, they were of the simple slipper variety with moderately pointed toes.

Jewelry was kept to a minimum except for the beads worked into the hair and an occasional necklace.

# THE BURGUNDIAN STYLE

In the late fourteenth century the duke of Burgundy in France, Philip the Good, became regent for the king of France, Charles VI, during his minority; Philip also, by his marriage to Margaret of Flanders, became Count of Flanders. Thus by the end of the reign of Duke John the Fearless in 1419, Burgundy was almost a fully independent nation that had turned against France and sided with England against the dauphin who was to be the future Charles VII of France. Under Philip the Good (1419–1467), Burgundy sided with the English in their attempt to seat the young son of Henry V on the French throne, and it was the Burgundians who captured Joan of Arc and sold her to the British for execution. During this same period the Burgundians through their holdings in Flanders became one of the wealthiest courts of Europe, and their fashions demanded attention everywhere through their richness, splendor, and ceremonial sense of display.

***Masculine Dress*** First let us look at the costume worn by a wealthy banker and merchant about 1434. Giovanni Arnolfini, painted by Jan van Eyck on his marriage, was an Italian banker, long resident of Flanders, whose clothing represents the elegance of the Burgundian-Flemish tradition, even though it lacks the flamboyant imagination found in the court dress of the time (Fig. 10–9). He wears a fur-lined cyclas with front and back panels open from shoulder to hem, and he has a huge, high-crowned beaver hat with a large brim that lacks the elegance of court headgear but stresses through its rich surface the affluence of the wearer. His footwear reaches to the ankle with moderately pointed toes; the wooden pattens beside him would have been worn outdoors.

To contrast that with court fashions we might look at the famous Rose tapestries in the Metropolitan Museum of Art, designed

and made in Flanders between 1435 and 1440, even though the subject matter was French (Fig. 10–10). The short gowns with full, padded sleeves represent the transition from the full gowns and houppelandes of the first quarter of the fifteenth century to the slimmer, taller look of the middle of the century. There is much stress on organ-pipe pleats, rich brocaded patterns, and fur trim. Some of the gowns have their short skirts open on the sides to an inch or two below the waist, the sleeves in one case are slit from wrist to shoulder to show an even richer pourpoint undersleeve, and shoulders are full and broad due to the deep sleeve folds set into the armseye. Necklines have a narrow standing collar of fur (fur trim for all garment edges was very popular at this time). These short, pleated gowns were often left unfastened from neck to waist and held in place only by the tight waist girdle and the inner lining of the rich pleating. The headdress is the excessively large, donut roundlet with dagged edges, cockades, and liripipe that drape on the shoulder or fall to the hem of the gown. Hose are very form-fitting, and footgear consists of smooth-fitting, pointed shoes or ankle boots (Fig. 10–4h).

Around 1460 the Burgundian style began to stress a very vertical, elongated look for men. In the manuscript illumination that depicts the betrothal of the daughter of King Yon of Gascoigne, we have an excellent example of this new Burgundian style that was prominent in the north between 1460 and 1480 (Fig. 10–4). The younger men's doublets now had very short skirts that frequently show that the hose have now been joined at the crotch. Shoulders were very broad and padded, sleeves tapered somewhat to the wrist and were sometimes open to display the undersleeve. Necklines had a straight mandarin collar or a V-shape with the pourpoint showing above. Sometimes the doublet had no waist at all but

FIG. 10-9 Jan van Eyck, *Giovanni and Giovanna Arnolfini;* National Gallery of Art, London; 1432. Arnolfini wears a sable-edged tabard-cloak over tunic and hose with a flaring, crowned, broad-brimmed hat of beaver. At the left of the painting are his wooden *pattens.* His wife wears a trailing velvet gown edged in fur with hanging bag sleeves and a small horned headdress under a kerchief edged with layers of fluting. Photo courtesy of the National Gallery of Art, London.

hung in folds straight down from the shoulder to the crotch. Such a garment was known as a *journade.* Hair was fuller and longer, and tall, sugar-loaf caps had replaced the roundlet for the most part. Another style that alternated with the sugar-loaf hat was the rounded crown with a small brim turned up higher in the back than in the front. One can see this style of hat being worn by the three men at the far right (Fig. 10-4). Sometimes the brim was actually a small donut roll, and sometimes this hat still had a liripipe by which the hat could be slung over the shoulder when not worn (Fig. 10-4e). Longer gowns were also popular, as may be seen on the figure at the far right (Fig. 10-4), and these also had broad shoulders, a long, tapered line to the floor, and a stress on pleating, particularly at the center front and center back (Fig. 10-4c). Only older middle-class men still wore the ankle-length houppelande with bell sleeves (Fig. 10-4d). Hose were very form-fitting with soft slipper-shoes that had extremely long, pointed toes. Until the decline of the Burgundian style after the defeat and death of Duke Charles the Bold at the Battle of Nancy in 1477, the sugar-loaf hats were the tallest, the shoulders of the gowns and doublets the highest and broadest, waists the slimmest, toes the most pointed, and hose the most fitting of any in northern Europe. The Burgundian style was also the most elegant and the most admired fashion in northern and western Europe from about 1440 to 1480.

By 1425 armor was completely of plate and covered every exposed area of the body. It was worn over a quilted pourpoint of cloth or

**FIG. 10–10** *Courtiers With Roses;* from the Franco-Flemish Rose Tapestries; Metropolitan Museum of Art; ca. 1435–1440. The overabundance of fabric in the *houppelande* has been replaced for men by the organ-fold pleats of a thigh-length *surcote* with moderate sleeves and large donut-shaped *roundels* or *roundlets*. The ladies wear large butterfly *hennins* or padded *escoffions* and trailing gowns belted at the waist with smooth sleeves and a V-shaped neck. Photo courtesy of the Metropolitan Museum of Art, Rogers Fund, 1909.

leather, and the body and arms were still covered by a shirt of chain mail. On its exterior the *brigandine,* or breastplate assemblage, was usually covered with a tight-fitting sleeveless jupon or later by a short, T-shaped, stiffened tabard emblazoned with a heraldic coat of arms, although by the middle of the fifteenth century, complete suits of armor without any exterior covering were sometimes seen. The foot soldier usually wore only a steel helmet over a chain hood, a shirt of chain over a tight-fitting jupon, and an outer gambeson of quilted canvas or leather (Fig. 10–4g). His legs and feet

were usually unprotected except by heavy hose and soft leather boots. Equipment for the knight was sword, shield, and lance; for the soldier, the longbow, crossbow, shield, and short sword.

**Feminine Dress** Flemish or Burgundian feminine fashion had two components during the fifteenth century—the fashions worn by the wealthy merchant class and the extravagant styles worn at the court of Burgundy. The famous van Eyck painting of Arnolfini and his bride is a typical example of the sober richness of bourgeois dress in the years before 1450 (Fig. 10–9). The bride wears an early version of the double-horned hennin, which here appears as two small horns over each temple under a kerchief or veil edged in tiny, delicate ruffles. Her gown is a late version of the houppelande with magnificent sleeves richly but unostentatiously decorated in a complex, quilted pattern. The houppelande no longer has a high collar as it did for both men and women in the first quarter of the fifteenth century, and the new interest in carefully controlled pleating is apparent above and below the waist. There is a massive amount of rich velvet fabric in the gown that is held just below the waist in the pregnant stance so typical of the late Gothic Period, and there is rich fur in edges and lining. All in all, it is a rich and sober costume for a lady of wealth who does not partake of the manners and mores of the court.

At the court of Burgundy the female fashions were definitely the most extravagant in Europe, particularly in the realm of the headdress. Other key cities, such as Paris, London, and the cities of the Rhine, looked to Brussels, Ghent, and Bruges for signals on what to wear for the next court ball or ceremonial function. One of the most dramatic headdress styles was that of the high, rounded escoffion, elaborately jeweled and slanting backward from a very high hairline (Fig. 10–4k). The dome-shaped escoffion was then covered by a richly patterned and bejeweled *fall,* or heavy kerchief. Other headdresses consisted of larger variations on the horned headdress worn by Arnolfini's bride—the true hennin which developed around the middle of the century as a great cone slanting back from a raised hairline and a velvet cuff to end in a floating veil, the truncated cone that was similar but not as tall, and the great butterfly hennin that had one, two, or three horns under a wired veil that suggested butterfly wings (Fig. 10–4f,k).

Both the butterfly hennin and the escoffion styles may be seen in the romantic Rose tapestries in the Metropolitan Museum of Art dated about 1440 (Fig. 10–10). In fact, it is the headdress that dominates the entire costume in these fantasy figures and seems to fulfill all our expectations of the princess figure of the typical medieval fairy tale. The gowns are a fitted, V-necked style that was the standard by the middle of the century in the north, with closely fitted sleeves, fur trim, a very tight waist, and voluminous skirts spreading out in pools of fabric around the feet of the wearer.

Much the same style is in evidence in Fig. 10–4. Here the unadorned conical hennin is used since it was preferred by the French to the truncated version so often seen in later Burgundian court portraits. The cone again begins far back on the plucked brow with only a loop of velvet to break the whiteness of the forehead. The gowns are cut somewhat wide on the shoulder and in the standard V-line to the waist, with a modesty front filling in the deep *décolleté*. The waist is a little higher than normal, very slim, and the figure still protrudes below in the pregnant pose that compliments the Virgin. The skirt spreads out in pools of fabric on the floor, is fur-trimmed, and the underskirt is of floor length and in a contrasting fabric and color. Sleeves are slim to the wrist, flaring over the knuckles, and often end in a small fur cuff. Shoes are still moderately pointed and of the soft slipper variety. Mantles and open robes, often furlined, were worn for outdoors or for travel.

Lower-class women usually wore a much more voluminous *kirtle,* or gown, of ankle length with a skirt tucked up at the waist, often over a rough, red woolen petticoat, while the white chemise showed under lacings at the bosom and sometimes under rolled-up sleeves of the outergown. Kerchiefs or linen caps usually covered the head; wooden or leather shoes, the feet (Fig. 10–4j).

## FABRICS

During this period the Flemish weaving industry surpassed itself in developing some of the most elaborate brocades ever woven (Fig. 10–4i), rivaling the rich patterned fabrics of the Orient and Byzantium in their richness and complexity. It should be remembered that Byzantium fell to the Turks in 1453, removing it as a center of weaving for the West. Samite was an especially sumptuous and heavy silk and taffeta became very popular, but it was velvet—figured, cut, and brocaded—that swept northern court tastes with its richness and variety. Various thin silks such as chiffons and crepes were developed for scarfs, kerchiefs, and veils, and in Italy metallic and silk nets were developed for hairdressing. Woolen was still the staple fabric for the lower classes, and linen was used for many basic undergarments. One of the most-used trims of the period was fur, especially ermine, but there were also marten, grey squirrel, lamb, fox, muskrat, and rabbit.

## ARTS AND ARTIFACTS

In Italy the Gothic style in interior decoration had all but disappeared by this time. Walls were of plaster and often decorated with frescoes and tapestries; ceilings were usually beamed and heavily carved and painted; columns, pilasters, and staircases were usually of inlaid marble or decorated tile and antique-style statuary; and rich rugs were used in abundance. Door and window frames were based on classical arches. Columns, pediments, and furniture, although still of heavy oak in square massive silhouettes, were now carved with classical rather than Gothic motifs (Fig. 10–1 and 2a,b,c,g).

In the north, Gothic lines still predominated in furniture, interiors, decoration, and especially in the tracery carving in wall paneling, beams, around windows and door frames, and on the doors of cabinets (Fig. 10–2d,e,f). Enormous fireplaces with great sloping hoods, often embossed with coats of arms, still dominated most chambers, and rich Flemish tapestries were the major decorative wall accent in a room.

A major personal accessory was the purse, which was envelope-shaped and usually carried by a loop over a belt. Some were very rich, others of simple leather, and they could be quite small or as large as a handbag. Sometimes men carried a walking stick, and gloves were sometimes worn, but more often carried, by both men and women. Men wore daggers at the waist (dress swords did not arrive until about 1550), and both men and women often carried a filigreed *pomander,* a hollow ball of metal, hinged on one side to hold a religious relic, a sponge containing perfume to ward off street smells, or medicine to ward off the Plague.

Musical instruments in a household might be a viol or rebeck, a harp, a recorder or English flute, a portable organ, a bagpipe, and a lute or guitar. Decorative motifs included the standard components of heraldry, the decorative floral effects of Gothic architectural design, and in Italy all the re-found shapes and patterns from antiquity (Fig. 10–4i). Particoloring was still a standard method for decorating clothing, but in Italy it was done for mathematical-geometric pattern effects rather than as a reflection of heraldry.

Jewelry, especially pearls, seemed to be on everything by the middle of the century. Jewelry was used in allover designs on fabric, on edges of headdresses and garments, and even on hats and shoes. Men wore jeweled brooches on hats and sleeves, rings, sometimes earrings, and they prized jeweled orders like that of the Golden Fleece. Girdles were also often set with gold and jeweled trim, as were the dagger hilts and sheaths. Women occasionally wore earrings and frequently wore rich jeweled necklaces, pendants, or medallions. Brooches were worn on sleeves; girdles were especially bejeweled and were used as well for supporting silver or gold keys, needle cases, scissors, rosaries, or pomanders.

## VISUAL SOURCES

The major source for visual information on this period is painting, especially the artists of Italy such as Gozzoli, Masolino, Uccello, Piero della Francesca, Domenico di Bartolo, Domenico Veneziano, Antonio Pisanello, Fra Filippo Lippi, Fra Angelico, Andrea Mantegna, Fra Carnevale, Cosimo Tura, Francesco Cossa, Ercole Roberti, and Sandro Botticelli. The best repository for Italian painting is the Uffizi in Florence along with the Louvre, the Metropolitan Museum in New York, and the National Gallery in London. For the minor artists, museums in their local towns are usually the best repository.

Illuminated manuscripts are still a source for information on French and Flemish costume, and the major repository is the Bibliothèque Nationale in Paris. Another good source for the Burgundian style are the figures in tapestries such as the Franco-Flemish ones in the Metropolitan Museum of New York. The northern painters that are the most useful are Roger van der Weyden, Jan van Eyck, Jean Fouquet, and Hans Memling. Some of the best examples are in the Metropolitan and in the National Galleries, London and Washington. Useful written sources are Herbert Norris's *Costume and Fashion, Volume II,* for northern Europe, and for Italy, John Hale's *The Renaissance,* and Charles Mee, Jr.'s *Daily Life in Renaissance Italy.*

# SUMMARY

This 60-year period saw fascinating changes—from the Gothic to the Renaissance in Italy and from the Gothic to its final extravagant climax and demise in the courts of Burgundy, France, and England. By 1485 the Renaissance ideal had triumphed, and in the next half-century this ideal was to spread to all of Europe. In Italy it was a time of discovery and experiment in all the arts with a firm connection to classical antiquity. In fashion it was a move away from the fantasies of the Gothic to geometric and mathematical balance and proportion—away from richness in decoration toward richness in texture and solid grandeur in silhouette. In the north a final flamboyant explosion of the Gothic, with all of its decorative tendencies and exaggerations, climaxed in a fantasy of headdresses and jewelry that still could not hide the inexorable move toward more solidity in silhouette and form.

# chapter XI

# High Renaissance

## Chronology

(c. 1485–1520)

| | | |
|---|---|---|
| RENAISSANCE 1485–1500 | 1484 | Innocent VIII becomes pope |
| | 1485 | Henry VII founds the Tudor dynasty, ending the civil war in England |
| | 1486 | Pico della Mirandola, humanist, writes his *Oration on the Dignity of Man* |
| | 1488 | Bartolomeu Dias rounds the Cape of Good Hope |
| | 1490 | Verrocchio's statue of *Condottiere Colleoni* is cast; Aldine Press of Venice is established by Aldus Manutius |
| | 1492 | Alexander VI (Rodrigo Borgia) becomes pope; Columbus discovers America; the Spanish monarchs Ferdinand and Isabella conquer Granada and expel the Moors and Jews; Lorenzo de Medici dies; silk factory established at Lyons; Jesus Christ made king of Florence |
| | 1493 | Columbus sights Puerto Rico and Jamaica on his second voyage |

ca. 1495 Italian

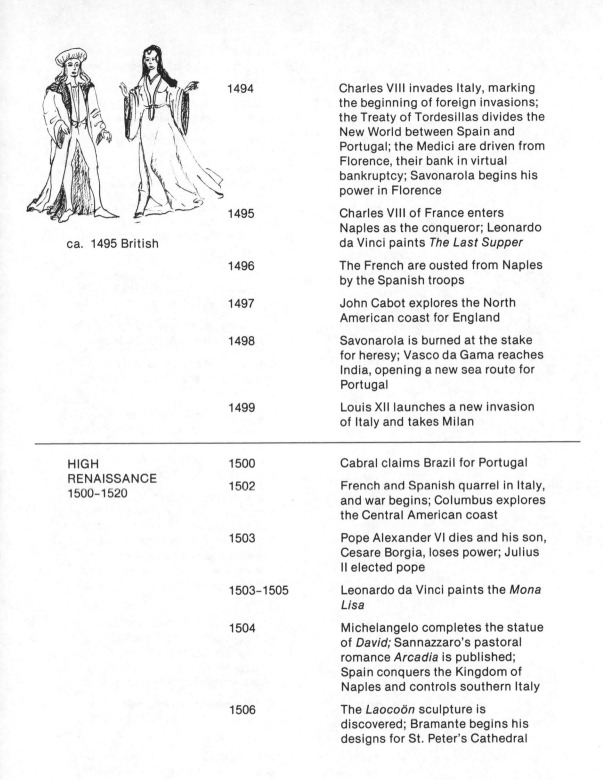

ca. 1495 British

| | |
|---|---|
| 1494 | Charles VIII invades Italy, marking the beginning of foreign invasions; the Treaty of Tordesillas divides the New World between Spain and Portugal; the Medici are driven from Florence, their bank in virtual bankruptcy; Savonarola begins his power in Florence |
| 1495 | Charles VIII of France enters Naples as the conqueror; Leonardo da Vinci paints *The Last Supper* |
| 1496 | The French are ousted from Naples by the Spanish troops |
| 1497 | John Cabot explores the North American coast for England |
| 1498 | Savonarola is burned at the stake for heresy; Vasco da Gama reaches India, opening a new sea route for Portugal |
| 1499 | Louis XII launches a new invasion of Italy and takes Milan |

| HIGH RENAISSANCE 1500-1520 | | |
|---|---|---|
| | 1500 | Cabral claims Brazil for Portugal |
| | 1502 | French and Spanish quarrel in Italy, and war begins; Columbus explores the Central American coast |
| | 1503 | Pope Alexander VI dies and his son, Cesare Borgia, loses power; Julius II elected pope |
| | 1503-1505 | Leonardo da Vinci paints the *Mona Lisa* |
| | 1504 | Michelangelo completes the statue of *David;* Sannazzaro's pastoral romance *Arcadia* is published; Spain conquers the Kingdom of Naples and controls southern Italy |
| | 1506 | The *Laocoön* sculpture is discovered; Bramante begins his designs for St. Peter's Cathedral |

| | |
|---|---|
| 1507 | Martin Waldseemüller's world map labels the new southern continent *America* |
| 1508 | Michelangelo begins to paint the Sistine Chapel ceiling |
| 1509 | Erasmus publishes *In Praise of Folly;* the Portuguese overwhelm Moslem sea power at the Battle of Diu; Henry VIII king of England |
| ca. 1510 | Venetian sea power begins to decline along with its trade following the discovery of the new sea route to India |
| 1510 | Albuquerque takes the Indian city of Goa for Portugal; Martin Luther on a mission to Rome |
| ca. 1510–1511 | Raphael paints his masterpiece *The School of Athens* for the Vatican |
| 1511 | Albuquerque occupies Malacca, giving Portugal a firm base in the Indian Ocean |
| 1512 | The French defeat the Spanish and papal forces at Ravenna; Medici power is restored in Florence; the Swiss conquer Milan and install Maximilian Sforza as duke |
| 1513 | Leo X, son of Lorenzo de Medici, becomes pope; Portuguese ships reach China and the Moluccas; Balboa crosses the Isthmus of Panama and sights the Pacific Ocean; Machiavelli publishes *The Prince;* Raphael paints *The Sistine Madonna* |
| 1515 | Francis I of France invades Italy and begins to bring Italian artists to work at his court; the French recover Milan after defeating the Swiss at the Battle of Marignano |
| 1516 | Ariosto's epic *Orlando Furioso* is published; Thomas More publishes *Utopia* |
| 1517 | Luther posts his 95 theses on the door of Wittenberg Castle Church |

1515 Italian

| | | |
|---|---|---|
| 1515 French | 1519 | Charles I of Spain is elected Holy Roman emperor and becomes Charles V; Luther debates John Eck in Leipzig; Ulrich Zwingli begins the Reformation in Switzerland |
| | 1520 | Henry VIII and Francis I meet near Calais on the Field of the Cloth of Gold to arrange an alliance; Luther burns the papal bull condemning him; Suleiman the Magnificent takes over the Ottoman Empire; death of Raphael |

# BACKGROUND

The year 1485 may be considered the close of the Gothic Period, since in that year the Wars of the Roses had ended in England, and a new Tudor era was ushered in with the reign of Henry VII; the Burgundian court with its elegant, late Gothic flamboyance had already dissolved with the death of Charles the Bold in 1477; and a new High Renaissance style was beginning in Milan. The age of experimentation and discovery in the arts, now known as the *early Renaissance* style, was ending, and a new era of unification and consolidation in artistic achievement was at hand. The new High Renaissance, lasting roughly twenty years from 1500 until the death of Raphael and the rise of the Reformation, was both a climax to the early

Renaissance as well as a departure into a subtler, more complicated, and grander view of the natural world.

By April 18, 1506, when the cornerstone of St. Peter's Basilica was laid in Rome, this city had replaced Florence as the center for the arts in Italy and was soon to become the artistic and intellectual center of the western world. Pope Julius II was gathering in the Eternal City some of the greatest artistic geniuses in the history of the west, and Rome began to be transformed from a medieval city into the resplendent metropolis of the seventeenth and eighteenth centuries. Bramante had come from Milan to design the monumental new Basilica of St. Peter's; Michelangelo had been drawn from

Florence first to design a tomb for Pope Julius II and later to paint the Sistine Chapel ceiling; Pinturicchio came from the north to cover the choir vaults of Santa Maria del Popolo with frescos; the singer-composer Josquin des Prés from Flanders was already papal choir master; and Raphael was soon to begin painting his famous Vatican frescoes after coming from his native Umbria to Florence and then to Rome. The flight of the Medici from Florence in 1494 and the burning of Savonarola three years later signaled the close of Florentine dominance in the arts; with the arrival on the papal throne of two great patrons of art—Julius II and later Leo X, son of Lorenzo the Magnificent—the Eternal City became for a brief period of time the fountainhead for some of the most magnificent, grand, and noble artistic projects since classical times.

Meanwhile important events were also happening outside Italy that were to spell the death of the Gothic style and the medieval mind. Spain had become united with the marriage of Ferdinand of Aragon and Isabella of Castille, and in 1492 these monarchs sponsored the voyage of Columbus that discovered America and also drove the final remnants of Moorish power from Spain. The discovery of the New World gave rise to greed, curiosity, and visions of adventure and power throughout Europe. A new age of exploration and discovery opened that led to increasing wealth and power for the countries that sponsored such adventures, particularly the court of Spain. By the time Charles I of Spain was elected Holy Roman emperor in 1519, Spain, with its overseas land and wealth coupled with its new control in Flanders and southern Italy, was established as the foremost political power of the sixteenth century.

In France the invasions of Italy by Charles VIII, Louis XII, and Francis I had awakened the French court to the glories of the Italian Renaissance. In particular, Francis I, a great lover and patron of the arts, imported many artists and artifacts from the Italian peninsula, including one of the greatest creators of the High Renaissance style—Leonardo da Vinci. By 1519 a great flood of Italian art and artistic ideals was beginning to pour into France and into England as well. Although Henry VII was more involved in consolidating Tudor power than in patronizing the arts, his son Henry VIII was a true prince in the Renaissance mold. He was a composer, a poet, a brilliant horseman, a lover of music, dance, and the new Italian arts, and a benevolent patron of the arts. When he and Francis I met on the Field of the Cloth of Gold on the north coast of France in 1520, their richness and grandeur projected the complete fascination of royalty with the new Renaissance styles that had made Gothic styles passé within a generation.

To illustrate the nature of High Renaissance achievement, particularly in the way people were grouped against the new architecture, let us look at one of the great representative works of the period, *The School of Athens,* by Raphael (Fig. 11-1). In this Vatican fresco a vast perspective space has been created in which many human figures have been orchestrated and choreographed in an expansive, easy, undulating manner. Each character blends both into the great groupings on the stairs as well as signaling his or her own mood and temperament, and all are made to support the central figures of Plato and Aristotle. The architecture is of a grandeur and size not seen since Roman imperial times—grand, rounded, strong, symmetrical, and projecting a monumental harmony. It is well to remember that Leonardo some years earlier had clearly established the circle as the perfect, most pervasive form in all nature, and this work draws extensively from that form.

## THE BASIC COSTUME SILHOUETTE

It is one of those peculiar coincidences of history that one of the major fashion attributes of the Renaissance was born out of the death of the famous northern fashion center—the court of Burgundy. In 1477 when the forces of Charles the Bold (the last of the rulers of the dukedom of Burgundy) were overwhelmed by Swiss forces in Nancy, their camp was pillaged

(a)
English fireplace
ca. 1505

(b)
Italian
fireplace
ca. 1500

(c)
Italian table
ca. 1500

Raphael, *The School of Athens;* fresco from the Stanza della Segnatura, Vatican Palace; 1510–1511. The balanced and organized grandeur and the swaying, rounded gestures and movement are typical of the High Renaissance. Note the size and classic orientation of the architecture. Photo courtesy of Alinari, Florence.

(d)
Italian-style chair
also used in England and France
ca. 1515

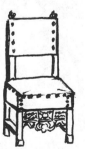

(e)
French-English
chair
ca. 1520

(f)
English
window
ca. 1515

(g)
Roman
window
ca. 1515

**FIGURE 11–1**

by the conquering Swiss who cut up the tents, the gorgeous banners, and the sumptuous costumes that they found and thrust them through the rents and tears in their own clothing. Out of this bizarre effect grew a new style known as *slashing* in which seams were left open and colored linings thrust through, or cuts were made in an entire costume and contrasting material puffed out of the cuts. This style became one of the most characteristic fashion motifs of the later Renaissance and a key way of identifying clothing dated after 1485. But it was the *landsknechtes,* or mercenaries, of the emperor whose clothing style grew to the most bizarre and wildly exaggerated expression, making them among the most colorful and fanciful fashion figures in the history of Western dress (Fig. 11-2).

Another element that characterized Renaissance costume after 1485 was the use of *points,* or laces, to hold a costume together. On both men and women, points, which for years had been used to secure male hose to a belt or pourpoint, were now used to lace parts of a sleeve together over a shirt or chemise and to secure that sleeve to a doublet or bodice. Thus the typical male costume from about 1485 to 1500 was dominated by a loose, low-necked shirt under a doublet laced over it with sleeves laced together to show the shirt at the elbow, the back of the arms, the shoulder, and the waist. The hose, now sewn together except in the front where a triangle known as a *codpiece* tied over the opening, were laced with points to this doublet. The general effect, suitable to the new Renaissance admiration and acceptance of the body with all its physical sensuality, was loose and casual, as if when the lacings were untied, the outer costume would casually fall off, an effect clearly seen in Dürer's *Self-Portrait* (Fig. 11-3). Overgowns were also loose, casual, and either quite short, calf-length, or ankle-length, with wide lapels and cuffs and a square look. The headgear alternated between the various caps

**FIG. 11-2** Albrecht Dürer, *Triumphal Procession of Maximilian I* (detail); 1514–1516. In this print of five *landsknechtes* (mercenaries) there is hardly an unslashed or unbroken surface above the knees. An underset of hose is worn beneath those that are slashed, just as the shirt shows beneath slashed sleeves. Slashing thus became an "attack" on fabric and clothing that remained in varying forms for a century. Photo courtesy of the Metropolitan Museum of Art, Harris Brisbane Dick Fund, 1932.

(a)
Italian
upper stocks
ca. 1505

(b)
shirt

(c)
paltock

(d)
Italian
sleeve

(e)
simarre
ca. 1490–1500

(f)
Italian
upper stocks
ca. 1502

(g)
pouch

1490

1510

(h)
shoes

Albrecht Dürer, *Self-Portrait;* Prado, Madrid: ca. 1495. Illustrates the youthful, loose, sensual dress of the Italian Renaissance at the time of Dürer's visit to Venice in 1494 to 1495. Photo courtesy of The Prado, Madrid.

(i)
German-style
slashing
ca. 1515

(j)
codpiece
ca. 1495

(k)
caps

inside

outside

(l)
bases

(m)
codpiece ca. 1520

**FIGURE 11–3**

183

sleeve of the Queen of Portugal 1518

(a)

Spanish ca. 1505

(b)

blow-up of sleeve

Empress Eleanor of Portugal 1503

(c)

(d)
French headdresses 1500–1520

Domenico Ghirlandaio, *The Birth of the Virgin;* fresco, Church of Santa Maria Novella, Florence; ca. 1485–1490. Illustrates the opening of sleeves at the shoulder and then tying them together or into the bodice with laces, or *points.* Note the youthful simplicity in hairdressing, necklines, and dress silhouette. Photo courtesy of Alinari, Florence.

(k)
patterns

(e)
English gable hood ca. 1500

German ca. 1510

(f)

(g)
Italian 1505–1515

Spanish ca. 1505

(h)

(i)
pendant

(j)
ring

(l)
pendant

**FIGURE 11-4**

of the earlier Renaissance, some with turned-up brims like a sailor hat, and wide-brimmed hats turned up on one side and decorated with plumes, the latter frequently worn over a coif. The young men's hair was usually worn quite long (Fig. 11–3), whereas that of older men was somewhat shorter. Shoes were still like the slipper-shoes of the late Gothic Period, without the exaggerated toes, and sometimes with slashing.

In female costume many of the same ideals pertained. The lacing seen on the male costume was also used on the bodice of the female gown and on the various pieces of sleeve laced to the shoulder over the chemise. The gown was frequently divided into bodice and skirt and worn under a sleeveless outergown slit below the waist on each side or in the front. Sometimes the outergown was loose and flowing, but more frequently it was fitted smoothly to a slightly raised waistline and cut in a V-shape to show the lacing of the undergown. Older women, servants, and ladies-in-waiting frequently still wore kerchiefs, but younger women preferred their hair unadorned except for the jewels set in the complex knots and braids of the hairdressing. Domenico Ghirlandaio's *The Birth of the Virgin* illustrates well the qualities of Renaissance female dress during the last decade of the fifteenth century (Fig. 11–4).

In the first decade of the sixteenth century with the arrival of the High Renaissance in art, clothing styles began to change, particularly in Italy, to reflect the change to nobility, gravity and grandeur that one finds in the works of Bramante, Michelangelo, and Raphael, especially in the latter's *School of Athens* (Fig. 11–1). Fabrics became thicker, sleeves and doublet skirts fuller, beards rounded and more prominent, and berets rounded and full. The ideal, as in art, was to base clothing on the expansive, rounded lines of the circle, and men and women, in general, came to look 20 pounds heavier than they had at the close of the fifteenth century. One need only compare Raphael's portrait of Count Baldassare Castiglione, painted in 1515, with the *Self-Portrait* of Dürer, to see the difference (Figs. 11–5, 3). In Raphael's painting we have a full, rounded, solid clothing silhouette in fur and velvet that

**FIG. 11–5** Raphael, *Portrait of Baldassare Castiglione;* The Louvre, Paris; 1515. Illustrates the expanding, rounded forms and thick, solid textures of clothing in the High Renaissance. Photo courtesy of Alinari, Florence.

high renaissance     185

gives the Count an aloof, but humane, self-assurance and gravity—a true representative of the ideals of the High Renaissance.

The same was true for female dress in the early years of the sixteenth century. By 1515 when Raphael painted *La Donna Velata,* we also

have circular forms, full sleeves, rich, soft, expansive fabrics, and sculptural roundedness in rich textures that exemplified the cultural and artistic ideals of the High Renaissance (Fig. 11-6).

FIG. 11-6 Raphael, *La Donna Velata;* Pitti Pallace, Florence; ca. 1515. Illustrates the full, rounded lines and rich, natural fabrics admired in fashion during the High Renaissance. Photo courtesy of Alinari, Florence.

## THE RENAISSANCE

Probably the most striking change in Italian fashion from the late 1470s to the early 1490s was the realistic acceptance of the beauty of the human body with a minimum of illusion and idealism. For a brief period during the 1490s a casualness in dress allowed the sensuous characteristics of the human body to be expressed fully.

**Masculine Dress**   Younger men in Italy carried this latest style to fruition and allowed their hair to grow until a full glory of loose waves or curls fell on the shoulders (Fig. 11-3). Various loose caps or small berets topped off this glory of hair, and an occasional large-brimmed hat with plumes was then pinned to a tight cap, or *coif*. But the true character of the

style came in the doublet which was tight and very skimpy, defining the low-necked softness of the shirt in the front and through the many openings in the laced sleeve. Vittore Carpaccio, a great Venetian artist, beautifully recorded this new young man's style in *The Arrival of the Ambassadors* (Fig. 11-7). In the two men leaning on the metal railing to the left, we see the scanty doublet laced across the front of the soft shirt and the slashed sleeves laced up the back, over the open elbow, and into the shoulder of the doublet (Fig. 11-3a,b,c,d). One wears a very loose, wide-lapeled gown to just above the knees that lacks any feeling of formality; rather it has the casual looseness of a bathrobe. The hose are smooth-fitting and rise all the way to the waist, presumably with a cod-

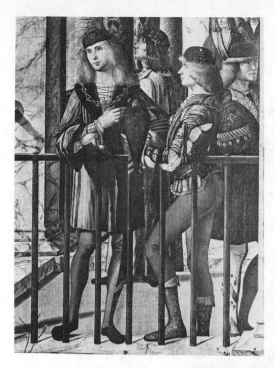

FIG. 11-7 Vittore Carpaccio, *The Arrival of the English Ambassadors;* from *The Legend of St. Ursula;* The Accademia, Venice; 1490-1495. Illustrates the looser, natural, draped lines of Italian Renaissance garments during the last decade of the fifteenth century as opposed to the exaggerated, artificial fashion lines of late Gothic clothing. Photos courtesy of Alinari, Florence.

piece tied in at the front. One wears soft shoes; the other, stocking boots. In *The Ordeal by Fire of Moses* by Giorgione, another somewhat younger Venetian artist (Fig. 11-8), we have two young gentlemen in the height of fashion displaying slashing as used on male hose. One of the shortened doublets laces down the front;

the other fastens asymmetrically across the body with one side over the other. Vertical slashes appear on the upper left leg of the man at the left in a manner that suggests the upper hose slashing that will proliferate in the first three decades of the sixteenth century. Decorative garters are tied below the knee, and the at-

**FIG. 11–8** Giorgione, *The Ordeal by Fire of Moses;* ca. 1500. Illustrates the early use of the *codpiece* after hose were sewn together at the crotch as well as asymmetrical effects in slashing, ribbon decoration, and doublet cut at the close of the early Renaissance. Photo courtesy of Alinari, Florence.

tached codpiece is prominently displayed (Fig. 11–3j). On the man to the right, decorative points are attached over the thighs to call attention to that area of the body, and his hose are not attached to the doublet, thus allowing the shirt to blouse without inhibition out of the doublet and hose. Shoes are soft and resemble modern ballet or dancing slippers (Fig. 11–3h).

The gowns worn by older men or by those less concerned with fashion may also be seen in Carpaccio's *The Arrival of the Ambassadors,* and the effect again is of casual bathrobes. Sleeves are long, widening below the elbow, and turned back into cuffs, and the fabric is either rich brocade or soft, flowing velour velvet. Note that the wide lapels of the gowns lack a collar at the back, and this makes the lapels very soft and loose, adding to the casual look of the robes. With hanging sleeves, this loose gown is often known as a *simarre* (Fig. 11–3e).

In the north these styles were not widely accepted; yet it is surprising how much of this casualness crept into male styles in England,

France, and Germany in the last decade of the fifteenth century. Look at the illuminated Flemish manuscript *La Roman de la Rose* in a scene depicting a dance in a garden (Fig. 11–9). The two men in the foreground display many of the characteristics found in the two paintings just studied. The young man in the left foreground has a scanty doublet with a V-opening, even though the sleeves are puffed at the top and tapered into a tight forearm instead of slashed and held over the shirt sleeve with points. The hose are even more exuberantly striped and gartered at the top than those the young men wear in the Giorgione painting (Fig. 11–8). The gentleman in the right foreground has the loose gown seen on the gentleman to the far right in the Carpaccio painting (Fig. 11–7), although he has long hanging sleeves rather than full sleeves with cuffs. His broad-brimmed hat set with plumes sits on a tight cap, or *coif,* and his hair falls in unrestrained fullness to his shoulders (Fig. 11–3k). Only his shoes have a broadness sug-

**FIG. 11-9** *Dance of Mirth in a Garden;* from the Flemish manuscript *La Roman de la Rose* (Romance of the Rose); MS. 4425, Folio 14b, British Museum; late fifteenth century. Illustrates intervention of Italian Renaissance styles into late Gothic clothing. Some of the background figures still have dagged-edged sleeves and gowns, while the foreground figure with the plumed hat has a loose gown with hanging sleeves and an expansive hat that is very Italianate. Photo courtesy of the British Library.

gesting styles to come, rather than the slim slipper-look of the Italian. Other figures in the background, however, still wear the dagged-edged and bagpipe sleeves of the past late Gothic style.

***Feminine Dress*** In the last decades of the fifteenth century, Italy produced some outstanding women of great learning and political influence who were also very concerned with fashion. The most famous were undoubtedly Isabella and Beatrice d'Este but there were also Caterina Sforza, Elisabetta Gonzaga and Lucretia Tornabuoni. In fact, Ghirlandaio, one of the best recorders of Florentine costumes and manners during this period, probably used Lucretia Tornabuoni and her women as models for *The Birth of the Virgin,* since the Tornabuoni family were the donors of the fresco series (Fig. 11-4). Lucretia wears a richly patterned gown with a slightly raised waist; the bodice is cut away in a V-shape and filled in with a rich

stomacher or modesty piece. But the unique new contribution, as in male dress at this time, was the sleeves, open at the shoulder, elbow, and along the back seam toward the wrist to reveal the soft white linen of the chemise (Fig. 11-3d). The sleeves are held together and to the bodice by points, and the neckline of the dress is low and softly rounded without decoration. The hair is also unadorned and creates interest only through the coils and braids of the hairdressing. Thus except for the very rich, brocaded pattern of the gown, the entire ensemble is very soft, simple, and natural—in sharp contrast to the excesses of the dying Gothic style in the north with its high headdresses and massed skirt material swirling around the feet. As with the male styles of the end of the fifteenth century in Italy, the stress was on the natural body clothed in simple lines with the new concept of slashing and open seams caught together with points as the major garment accent. The other women in the fresco are dressed in the older costume lines with more fullness and length in their gowns and use the kerchief and wimple remaining from the Gothic past. However, the woman immediately behind Lucretia has outersleeves attached only with points at the shoulder and a V-shaped front to her overgown loosely laced over the chemise.

In the north at this same time many of these tendencies were gradually being assimilated into fashion without completely losing the last vestiges of the late Gothic style. In *La Roman de la Rose,* dated about 1490, we see the transition in the Franco-Flemish style from the exaggerations and excesses of the late Gothic or Burgundian to the simpler body lines of the new Renaissance ideals (Fig. 11-9). The lady in the foreground no longer wears the hennin, only the black cuff that used to edge it with a black velvet hood down the back, a style that would persist in various forms for the next 60 to 70 years (Fig. 11-4e,h). The dress is even simpler than the Italian ones of this period with no rich brocaded surface but with a long train fastened up out of the way in the back. The neckline is relatively high with a turned-down collar edged in velvet, and the sleeve already has an open-seam effect along the back below the elbow, which is caught together over the chemise to make puffs. The woman to the left

has a turban, definitely of Italian derivation (Fig. 11-4g), a simple gown with full sleeves, a *plastron,* or stomacher, in the front laced to the waist, and a pomander hanging in front. Both ladies still prominently display the pregnant stance so admired for ladies throughout the late Gothic Period. The ladies to the far right each expose the lining of the gown by once again having the train lifted at the back and fastened at the waist, almost in a bustle effect. One wears the standard hood and fall, the other a complex jeweled cap over flowing hair. The impression, as with all the women in the scene, is that of the sober *hausfrau* reinforced by some rigid Spanish lines, rather than the open, natural lines worn by Italian women, which the northern ladies could not accept.

Although shoes are difficult to see under Italian or northern gowns of this period, they were usually of the soft slipper variety without exaggerated pointed toes. Sometimes, especially among courtesans in Venice, *chopines,* or raised platform shoes, were worn over the slipper-shoe to give height to the wearer. This style persisted throughout the sixteenth century. Outergarments for travel and night outings continued to be the hooded circular cape, and the heraldic court mantle was still worn on formal ceremonial occasions.

## HIGH RENAISSANCE

As travel, communication, and the passion for the new Renaissance artistic ideals increased throughout Europe after the turn of the century, the distinction in fashion between north and south and between countries almost disappeared, even though it was to appear again later in the sixteenth century. For example, the enthusiasm of Charles VIII and Louis XII of France for things Italian swept the French court like a disease, and by the time Francis I came to the throne, everyone wanted everything, including fashion, to be in the new Italian style. These styles often changed during their passage over the Alps, but they were assimilated very rapidly as was also the case in southern Germany and in England. Only conservative Spain accepted the new Italian ideals reluctantly.

**Masculine Dress**   In Italy slashing was used sparingly and always as a loosening effect and accent within a very harmonious and unified whole, while in Germany, where it was invented, the style quickly proliferated and became so exaggerated that it became ridiculous and absurd. In a detail from *The Procession of Maximilian I,* the variety of ways in which slashing was used is quite overpowering (Fig. 11-2). By 1515 when this engraving was done, hardly an unbroken surface was left on the male figure above the knees. The outer hose, often of suede or leather, were so heavily slashed that a second pair of cloth hose were usually worn underneath, and the doublets usually displayed the rich fullness of the shirt beneath (Fig. 11-3i). Italian hose of the first decade of the century made very sparing use of some of these ideals, but always subordinated the slashing to the overall unity of the costume. The concept of slashing hose above the knees more than below gradually led to a separation between *upper stocks* and lower hose (Fig. 11–3f) that eventually led to trunks with hose beneath. In doublets the Italians also avoided the excesses and asymmetry of the Germans and favored sleeves that were puffed and paned from the shoulder to the elbow with a fitted sleeve from elbow to wrist; the body of the doublet often replaced slashing with geometric color striping or contrasting colors from one side to another. But the tight-fitting, youthful lines of hose and doublets did not last in Italy because the new High Renaissance ideals demanded a fuller, grander, and more dignified male silhouette. By the time that Raphael painted his fresco, *The Mass of Bolsena,* the male silhouette had expanded considerably and spread out in full folds and thick fabrics to give a very grand and dignified costume line (Fig. 11–10). The major changes were in the new fullness of the sleeve and in the organ-pleated skirt—sometimes attached to the doublet, sometimes worn separately—called *bases* (Fig. 11–3l) which became a major part of male dress in Italy and in the north until almost the middle of the sixteenth century. In the detail from *The Mass of Bolsena* (Fig. 11–10), we can see that the pleating often included alternate color striping and gave great width and stability to the male form. Shirts were still gathered low on the neck and prominently displayed above the doublet, and hair was still full, although not quite as long as in the 1490s. One man wears a turban and his hair does not show; the one shoe that is displayed shows the new wide-toe effect with cross-strap over the instep that became standard by the second decade of the sixteenth century (Fig. 11–3h).

Another fine pictorial image of the new solidity and sobriety in male dress during the High Renaissance is in the portrait of Castiglione painted by Raphael (Fig. 11–5). Here the beard has become full and rounded, the hat is a slashed beret that creates a full and expansive circle around the head, the doublet has become much heavier with a collar that frames the shirt, and the upper sleeves are of full pleated fur merging into a tight sleeve on the forearm. Although we do not see below the waist, it is probably correct to assume that he wears some form of the pleated bases seen on the younger men in *The Mass of Bolsena* (Fig. 11–10) and that his shoes are of the round-toed variety also seen in the earlier Raphael painting. Thus the ideal of the High Renaissance—fullness, dignity,

FIG. 11–10 Raphael, *The Mass of Bolsena* (detail); fresco from the Stanza di Eliodoro, Vatican Palace; ca. 1512. Illustrates the new maturity, weight, and grandeur in dress that arrived in fashion in Italy with the High Renaissance after 1505. Note particularly the great organ-pleated *bases* that give such formality and width from waist to knee. Photo courtesy of Alinari, Florence.

and grandeur based on the expanding lines of the circle—was fulfilled in dress as well as in the other arts.

In Germany, which was soon to become the source of most new elements of fashion, there was little participation in the ideals of the Italian High Renaissance. Although a new weight and bulk appeared in the costume, the general obsession was still with the decorative excesses of slashing and puffing (Figs. 11–2 and 3i). Loose gowns with full sleeves were often worn over the slashed doublet and hose; broad-brimmed hats or berets, related to that worn by Castiglione (Fig. 10–5), but much more excessive, were the norm; trim and ornamentation were usually created by more small slashed effects (Fig. 11–3k). Codpieces, far less discreet than the Italian ones, were also slashed and ribboned, and the sleeves of doublets were usually slashed and paned all down the arm—or at least well below the elbow (Fig. 11–3m). It was these German excesses in slashing and puffing that were to become the basis of most male European styles after 1520 rather than the more controlled and unified effects of Italian male fashion.

Military wear for the nobleman now consisted of full plate armor heavily engraved and without a *tabard,* or cloth covering. Swords were of the heavy cruciform variety, and the tilting lance was still used for tournaments. The foot soldier was protected by a quilted or padded leather gambeson with a rounded helmet over a chain-mail hood. Weapons were the crossbow, the arquebus, the halberd, or the lance; shields were limited to the small, round buckler and the larger shield carried by crossbowmen.

**Feminine Dress** Once the armies of Charles VIII had returned from the first invasion of Italy, Italian styles spread rapidly into France, just as Albrecht Dürer's trips to Venice at about the same time popularized Italian styles in southern Germany. By the time these new Italian feminine styles became integrated into fashion in the north, the Italian High Renaissance emphasis on full, rounded lines had come to dominate almost all feminine styles. One difference was that the Italians

preferred a rounded or oval neckline, whereas northern women preferred a low, square neckline. As in the earlier Renaissance, Italian women preferred various braided and coiled coiffures or turbans based on the circle, whereas northern women preferred the so-called French hood, which consisted of a crescent-shaped tiara over a linen cap with a velvet fall at the back (Fig. 11–4b,d,e,h). In the north and in Italy waists were a little above the normal waistline, skirts were full, and sleeves were large and bell-shaped with cuffs turned back to show a fur or velvet lining and a rich undersleeve (Fig. 11–4a,b,c,).

A very typical portrait of an Italian lady about 1515 is that of *La Donna Velata* by Raphael (Fig. 11–6). The hair is parted in the middle and drawn in coils of soft hair around the head to emphasize the circular lines of the face; only a soft veil covers the head and flows down over the body. The rounded lines of neck and neckline are emphasized by the amber necklace and the soft ruffle of the chemise which disappears inside a very low-cut bodice split at the center front and following the same rounded neckline as the chemise. The sleeves are soft, rounded, and full at the top, gathered into a narrower oversleeve on the forearm with slashes that show the chemise beneath. The chemise also shows at the lower forearm and wrist. The entire ensemble—full, rounded, soft, sensuous, feminine, and very appealing—is representative of the High Renaissance emphasis on full, rounded forms in all of its arts.

A Venetian gown from this period is shown in the famed Titian painting *Sacred and Profane Love* (Fig. 11–11). The very figure of the woman herself has become full and rounded in order to complement the rounded, full lines of the gown; other Italian portraits of this period, show that the ideal among all women of the High Renaissance was the full, rounded body with full hips and breasts, indicating an acceptance of the natural body in all its richness of flesh and fullness of form. In the Titian painting, the dressed lady has full hair, a rounded neckline, and very full upper sleeves softly and casually turned back over puffed undersleeves that gather into a narrower, lower, forearm sleeve. The neckline is low cut to show ample

**FIG. 11-11** Titian, *Sacred and Profane Love;* Borghese Gallery, Rome; ca. 1515. Fully illustrates the fuller female proportions that were the ideal at this time as well as the rounded expansive clothing that was admired. Photo courtesy of Alinari, Florence.

breasts, the waist is relatively high, and the skirt very soft and full as it spreads out in great folds around the hips and legs. At this point there is no stiffness of any kind, and the ornamentation is minimal so that the rich fabrics and form may speak for themselves. Shoes were like heavy slippers, often with slashed, rounded toes.

In the north, however, this High Renaissance ideal was never fully accepted; many earlier stylistic elements remained, as may be seen in portraits of Juana of Castille (Fig. 11-4b,h) and Anne of Brittany. In the north the crescent-shaped French hood, the square neckline, a more conical than billowing skirt, and bell-shaped oversleeves gave more angularity to the female form, with only limited emphasis on High Renaissance circularity and roundness of line and form.

Working women of the lower classes throughout this rich Renaissance Period continued to wear the simple *kirtle,* or dress, with sleeves turned back for work and the skirt tucked up at the waist to show the heavy woolen petticoat. The kirtle was usually laced over a V-shaped stomacher set between the chemise and the lacing, or it was laced directly over the chemise itself. Aprons were often worn, and a straw hat was used outdoors. The feet were shod in heavy slippers indoors and wooden clogs or shoes outdoors. Heads, both indoors and out, were usually wrapped in a kerchief that was a descendant of the old wimple.

## FABRICS

The weaving of rich fabrics became much more varied, subtle, and complex during this period, and metallic cloths, satins, taffetas, and particularly cut velvets appeared in a variety of patterns (Fig. 11-4k). In general, the richness of the fabric was allowed to speak for itself without being covered by braids, beads, or embroidery. Thin silks, chiffons, crepes, and gauzes were used for veils and scarfs; silk and metallic nets were popular for the hair. Woolens were still a staple with the middle and lower classes and ranged from very supple weaves to coarse homespun. Linen and, less often, cotton were also used, but with little innovation or change from the past.

# ARTS AND ARTIFACTS

During this period Italian Renaissance architectural design and interior decoration began to sweep over Europe as a new classical style to be integrated with or to replace the last of the old Gothic motifs. In Italy architecture was heavier, grander, and more sculpturally three-dimensional than in the past, while in France, Germany, and England, Italian pediments, arches, cornices, and decorative motifs were worked into buildings that in basic design still retained much medieval form (Fig. 11–1b,f,g). Furniture was square and massive, but began to take on the balanced geometric lines of the classical Renaissance and to replace Gothic tracery with motifs from antiquity. Chairs were now often upholstered on back and seats, beds were canopied and placed on raised platforms, and all furniture had a more sophisticated, civilized look than in Gothic times (Fig. 11–1c,d,e).

Major personal accessories were the dagger for men and, after about 1510, the dress sword. The latter was lighter than a fighting weapon and had either a cruciform hilt or a curved handguard from hilt to pommel. Purses were still carried at the waist on a girdle, and walking sticks were occasionally used (Fig. 11–3g). Gloves were worn or carried by both men and women, and outdoor styles usually had decorated gauntlets. Musical instruments remained as in the past, although the pipe and tabor greatly increased in popularity at this time.

Jewels were used as an accent in coiffures and occasionally on garments, particularly pearls, but the major use was in accessories such as hat brooches, sleeve brooches, earrings, finger rings, and in neck chains and orders (Fig. 11–4,i,j,l). The latter ornamentation in which complex jeweled collars representing membership in an elite order such as that of the Fleece, the Rose, or the George was a particularly prominent male fashion accent. Women's jewelry concentrated on earrings, necklaces, pendants, crucifixes, jeweled girdles, and the chain from the center waist that held the pomander, keys, needle cases, or a rosary.

# VISUAL SOURCES

Once again this period is rich with famous painters and paintings that are excellent costume sources. Major Italian artists that should be consulted are Titian, Raphael, Giorgione, Signorelli, Pinturicchio, Carpaccio, Andrea del Sarto, and Leonardo da Vinci. Lesser artists who are very useful are Bartolommeo Veneto, Tommaso Fiorentino, Baldassare Peruzzi, Giovanni di Benvenuto, Bernardino Luini, Bernardo di Conti, and Sebastiano del Piombo. In the north there are a number of anonymous portraits and illuminated manuscripts as well as artists like Albrecht Dürer, Gerard David, Lucas Cranach, Hans Baldung, Mathias Grünewald, Lucas van Leyden, Bernard Strigel, Quentin Matsys, and Claus Berg. The major source for illuminations is always the Bibliothèque Nationale, Paris. The best painting collections are the Civic Museum of Venice, the Borghese Gallery in Rome, the Metropolitan Museum in New York, the Church of Santa Maria Novella in Florence, the Cathedral of Orvieto, the National Gallery of Washington, the Louvre, the Dresden Picture Gallery, the Alte Pinakothek in Munich, and the Cologne Museum. Useful written sources are Charles Mee, Jr.'s *Daily Life in Renaissance Italy,* Herbert Norris's *Costume and Fashion,* Volume III, Book 1, and John Hale's *Renaissance.*

# SUMMARY

This period of the High Renaissance marked the rapid assimilation of Italian styles into northern fashion after the first French invasions of Italy and the change in Italian fashion from the loose, youthful look of the last decade of the fifteenth century to the full, rounded, relaxed fullness and maturity of the first two decades of the sixteenth century. In Italy it was one of the great golden ages in the history of the west, comparable in its balance and idealism with the Golden Age in fifth-century Athens. All of its arts, including costume, were dominated by the artistic ideals projected by Bramante, Raphael, Michelangelo, and Leonardo da Vinci—the great geniuses of the time. That artistic ideal was to use circularity, unity, balance, and dignity to achieve a noble grandeur and maturity; clothing styles also reflected this ideal. In the north this rounded fullness and mature dignity was less apparent as Italian ideals and motifs were integrated with late medieval silhouettes and forms.

# chapter XII

# Early Mannerist Renaissance

## Chronology

(ca. 1520–1560)

| | | |
|---|---|---|
| EARLY REFORMATION 1520–1545 | 1520 | Henry VIII and Francis I meet near Calais on the Field of the Cloth of Gold to arrange an alliance; Martin Luther burns the papal bull condemning him |
| | 1521 | At the Diet of Worms the emperor Charles V issues an edict declaring Luther an outlaw; Cortez conquers Mexico; war between Francis I and Charles V |
| | 1522 | Franz von Sickingen and Ulrich von Hutten lead the Knights' War against the ecclesiastical principalities; Sickingen is killed, and Hutten flees Germany; Luther's New Testament appears with woodcuts by Lucas Cranach; Ignatius Loyola publishes his *Spiritual Exercises;* Magellan completes his circumnavigation of the globe |
| | 1523 | Lefèvre d'Etaples publishes the New Testament in French |
| | 1524 | Verrazano explores the mouth of the Hudson River for France; the Peasants' War begins to ravage Germany; soap manufactured in London |

ca. 1528
French

| 1525 | Francis I is defeated by the forces of Charles V at Pavia; William Tyndale begins to publish the New Testament in English |
|---|---|
| 1526 | Mogul dynasty is established in India |
| 1527 | Second war begins between Francis I and Charles V; Rome is sacked by the troops of Charles V, and Pope Clement VII is imprisoned; Paracelsus lectures on his "new medicine" at the University of Basel |
| 1528 | Castiglione publishes his book *The Courtier;* Simon Fish publishes the *Supplication of Beggars,* an attack on the English clergy |
| 1529 | The princes supporting Luther protest the Edict of Worms at the Diet of Speyer and become known as *Protestants;* the Turks unsuccessfully besiege Vienna |
| 1530 | The Lutheran doctrine is set forth by Melanchthon at the Diet of Augsburg; Francis I establishes the Collège de France as a center for humanism; first portable clock |
| 1531 | Zwingli is killed in Zurich by the army of the Catholic League |
| 1532 | Rabelais begins publishing his comic masterpiece *Gargantua and Pantagruel;* Pizarro conquers the Inca Empire |
| 1533 | Henry VIII marries Anne Boleyn and is excommunicated by the pope |
| 1534 | Henry VIII breaks with the pope and founds the Anglican Church; first complete edition of Luther's Bible appears; suppression of the monasteries in England |
| 1535 | Sir Thomas More is beheaded for opposing Henry VIII's break with Rome; Hans Holbein the Younger paints *The Ambassadors;* Cartier explores the St. Lawrence River; the Spanish establish the city of Lima, Peru |

| | | |
|---|---|---|
| | 1536 | Henry VIII beheads Anne Boleyn and suppresses English monasteries; John Calvin publishes *Institutes of the Christian Religion* |
| | 1538 | Lucas Cranach paints his *Crucifixion* |
| | 1539 | De Soto explores what is now the southeastern United States; the *Great Bible* by Miles Coverdale is issued in the name of Henry VIII |
| | 1540 | The Society of Jesus (the Jesuits), is founded, revitalizing Catholicism; the Inquisition is in full force in Spain, Italy, and the Netherlands |
| | 1541 | Calvin rules Geneva as a theocracy; Coronado explores the territory west of the Mississippi |
| | 1543 | Copernicus' *Revolutions of the Celestial Orbs* is published; Vesalius publishes his *Structure of the Human Body* |
| ca. 1540 English | 1545 | The Council of Trent undertakes the reform of the Church under Jesuit guidance |

---

| | | |
|---|---|---|
| LATER REFORMATION ca. 1545–1560 | 1546 | Architect Pierre Lescot is commissioned by Francis I to build the new Louvre |
| | 1547 | Edward VI becomes king of England; Henry II becomes king of France; Ivan IV adopts the title of czar of Russia |
| | 1549 | The Portuguese reach Kagoshima in Japan |
| | 1552 | War breaks out between the emperor Charles V and Henry II of France; Ronsard, lyric poet of France, completes his *Amours* |
| | 1553 | Sir Hugh Willoughby perishes while seeking a northeast passage to China; Lady Jane Grey is queen of England for nine days |

| 1554 | Queen Mary I of England, a Catholic, marries Philip II of Spain; Protestant clergyman John Foxe publishes *The Book of Martyrs* |
|---|---|

ca. 1555
English-French

| 1555 | Restoration of Catholicism in England leads to Protestant persecution; the Peace of Augsburg divides Germany between Catholic and Lutheran princes |
|---|---|
| 1556 | Emperor Charles V abdicates and the Hapsburg realms are divided; Agricola writes *De re metallica* on metallurgy and mining; Philip II becomes king of Spain; Ferdinand I becomes the ruler of the Hapsburg lands |
| 1557 | Genevan ministers in Brazil hold the first Protestant service in the New World |
| 1558 | Elizabeth I becomes queen of England and restores Protestantism |
| 1559 | Pope Paul IV publishes the Index of Forbidden Books naming 48 heretical editions of the Bible |

# BACKGROUND

The period dating from the meeting on the Field of the Cloth of Gold, the accession of Charles V, and the death of Raphael to the accession of Elizabeth I of England used to be called the *later Renaissance,* but today, particularly in art circles, it is known as the *early Mannerist Renaissance.* The term *mannerism* was derived from the Italian *maniera* which referred to the personal, virtuoso manner of the artists who came to prominence in Italy during the early years of the Reformation. But by the beginning of the seventeenth century, *mannerism* was used as a depreciatory term for the

post-classical Renaissance art that was thought to be arbitrary, shallow, and inferior to the great works of the High Renaissance. The art and culture of this Mannerist Renaissance extended from 1520 until about 1620, and its whimsical, inward, personalized, ambiguous sense of design, composition, and mood (known in Italy as *desegno interno*) was a direct result of the dislocations and confusions in western European society caused by the Reformation and the inflation created by the influx of gold from the New World. The early mannerist phase of artistic and cultural development included the work of Bronzino, Pontormo, and Parmigianino in Italy and Cranach in Germany. The period is sometimes referred to as the German style, especially in dress, since the broad German costume silhouette tended to dominate the fashions of the time.

Sociologically and politically the period from 1520 to 1560 was one of political realism. It was a period in which the rivalry of great nation-states such as England, France, and Spain and the cynicism that governed their political moves led to violent acts such as the sack of Rome in 1527 in which the mercenary troops of the Holy Roman emperor Charles I unleashed their fury on the capital of Christendom. The Reformation and its attendant events divided Europe psychologically in a way that it had not been divided, even in the darkest periods of the early Middle Ages. Without knowing it, Luther and his fellow reformers unleashed a wave of fear, distrust, and inwardness that caused the culture of the time to be reflected through artificiality and contrivance in art rather than through art derived from nature.

While the Reformation was reshaping Europe's religious values, economic revolution was reshaping the daily lives of citizens from Italy to the Baltic. Old concepts of barter and land-based wealth were replaced by a monetary economy in which money could be used to create more money and anything could be had for a price. The gold and silver which poured in from the New World had become, as Sir Thomas More said, "the blood of the whole body social." The increasing supply of precious metals raised prices and caused terrible inflation. To increase profits, merchants and bankers pooled resources, creating great trading firms similar to modern corporations. Some of the larger firms, through complex and diversified operations involving loan interest, trade profits, mining, and real estate, became so powerful that even kings were at their mercy.

As an example of the new style of interior decoration, let us look at the Gallery of Francis I, designed by Rosso Fiorentino (Fig. 12-1). This richly ornamented tunnellike interior became a model for picture galleries and interior promenades throughout northern Europe after the middle of the sixteenth century; its unique form was based on the spatial arrangements of Michelangelo's Laurentian Library reading room. Its extreme length and tight decoration create an oppressive atmosphere of great tension that was typical of mannerist interiors. Sculpture, painting, and architecture overlap one another and are a complement to the distorted, artificial clothing styles of the period.

## THE BASIC COSTUME SILHOUETTE

Reformation fashion is divided into two periods—from 1520 to about 1560 when German influences and ideals predominated, and from 1560 to about 1620 when Spanish styles were in the ascendancy. Both periods stressed an artificial distortion of the human body into a grotesque, ornamental encasement. Fantastically varied use of puffed linings forced through small slits in the outergarment, like the interpenetration of plot lines in Elizabethan plays and the interpenetrating scrollwork in interior decoration, achieved a rich, ornamental tension in dress.

From 1520 to 1560 the emphasis was on a broad, horizontal, square silhouette for men and a conical, angular silhouette for women.

The major elements in the silhouette were distortion and a padding of the body; the major decorative accent that created a sense of tension was the slashing—outergarments literally attacked with a knife so that lining fabric could be forced through the slits. To see the changes in European culture that occurred in only 25 years, compare the portrait of Castiglione by Raphael, painted about 1516 (see Fig. 11-5), with the portrait of Henry VIII by Holbein, painted about 1540 (Fig. 12-2). The former exists in a real world of beautiful, rounded forms, natural fabrics, and a relaxed dignity. The latter portrays an immobile, ruthless, commanding personality surrounded by excessive richness which both fascinates and repels.

(a)
English buffet

The Gallery of Francis I from the Palace of Fontainebleau; ca. 1530–1540. Illustrates the tunnellike proportions, oppressiveness of decoration, tension in ornamentation, and ambiguity as to where sculpture, painting, and architecture meet that was the hallmark of the new European international mannerist style of the sixteenth century. Photo courtesy of the French Government Tourist Office.

(b)
Italian fireplace

(c)
German window

(d)
Spanish chair

**FIGURE 12-1**

(a)
wearing of the
chamarre with diagram
of cut

collar added

(b)
vest and skirt 1530

lapel

armhole

(c)
cut of surcote
or gown with
hanging sleeve

ca. 1530

shoes    (j)
1545

(k)
section
of a collar

(d)
English

(e)
French

(f)
old man

(g)
French

(h)
German

(i)
a merchant

helmets
(m)

(l)
soldier
(archer)
ca. 1550

Hans Holbein the Younger, *Henry VIII;*
Galleria Nazionale, Rome; 1540. Creates
through distorted body lines, excess ornamentation, and linings tightly pushed
through slits in the outergarments, an artificial, immobile, almost grotesque
authority figure that is both fascinating and
repellent. Photo courtesy of the Galleria Nazionale, Rome.

**FIGURE 12-2**

202

(a) Spanish farthingale (boned linen or canvas petticoat)

turned-back sleeve

side

back

(b)

(c) French ca. 1524

hinge and pin

hinge and pin

(d) half corset

(e) German ca. 1530

(f) French ca. 1535

(g) French ca. 1550

(h) Spanish ca. 1525

(i) German style

Agnolo Bronzino, *Eleanor of Toledo and Her Son Giovanni de Medici;* The Uffizi, Florence; ca. 1550. Illustrates the unnatural, grotesque, artificial fashions worn by the upper classes by the middle of the sixteenth century. The decorative pattern is excessive; fabric is forced through slits in the outer garment; shoulders are distorted; the bust line has been removed; and the lines of the costume have been rigidified with braid and pearls. Photo courtesy of Alinari, Florence.

(j) bodice

(k) false sleeve

(l) organ pleats

(m) jewelled sleeve clasps

(n) skirts

(o) Flemish ca. 1540

(p) English ca. 1545

**FIGURE 12-3**

203

The same contrast can be seen in two portraits of women: one High Renaissance, the other Mannerist. Raphael's portrait of *La Donna Velata,* painted about 1514, has simple, full, rounded lines and rich, natural fabrics (see Fig. 11–6). It is true that she is a lady of the upper class, not a queen or princess; yet if we compare her with Bronzino's portrait of Eleanor of Toledo, wife of the duke of Florence, painted about 1550, we can see a shocking difference in cultural outlook that cannot be explained by difference in station (Fig. 12–3). The duchess is not an individual personality, but an exemplification of position. Her body is rendered unnatural and grotesque by the alarming scale of the dress pattern, the tight puffs of lining forced through slits in the sleeve and choked off by braid and jewels, the shoulder netting nailed down with pearls, the hair confined by a tight net of pearls, and the breasts absolutely removed by the rigidities of the corseting. In every way it indicates that by mid-century the ideals of mannerism had triumphed in dress as in all the other arts throughout Europe.

The female silhouette was heavier in the north than in Italy, and the fabric was thicker and more frequently trimmed with fur. Skirts were pleated to the bodice over a V-shaped front panel that was richly patterned; fur-lined, bell-shaped sleeves were folded back over a slashed and puffed undersleeve; and headdresses were usually gable- or crescent-shaped hoods that framed the face. Italian ladies were loath to accept the added rigidities of the *farthingale,* but northern ladies wore a funnel-shaped, boned petticoat (originally from Spain) that gave a rigid, triangular line to the lower part of the female figure.

## THE EARLY MANNERIST RENAISSANCE

As always happens when a culture reaches a climax and then is plunged into dislocation and confusion by a rending of the unity that shaped that culture, the period after 1520 saw many of the balanced and physically beautifying attributes of High Renaissance clothing exaggerated and distorted by personal whimsy and social insecurity. Two items vividly illustrated the change. One was the codpiece of the late fifteenth and early sixteenth century which had been a practical, pleasing, sensuous covering of the opening at the front of the hose; after 1520 it developed into a grotesque, stuffed, beribboned appendage on the front of a man's costume. The other change was in slashing and puffing which had originated as a loosening of tight seams by lacing sleeves and jackets together over puffed linings or undergarments; in the later sixteenth century it became tight slits made in the outer fabric through which linings were forced in a tortuous, tense, uncomfortable manner. In these cases, and in many others, the move was from a relaxed, opulent balance of costume and body to a tense distortion of the human figure.

***Masculine Dress*** To begin a study of the shifts in male costume after the first stirrings of the Reformation, let us look at the portrait of Francis I by Jean Clouet (Fig. 12–4). The hair is shorter and curled under in a roll that slopes back from the forehead to a point at the back of the neck opposite to the jaw line. The hat has a tighter and stiffer brim than that worn in Italy ten years earlier by Castiglione (see Fig. 11–5), and the very low crown does not even show above the plumed edge. Jewels tightly accent the brim and indicate the arrival of a period in which the number of gems set on garments will be greater than at any time since the Byzantine Empire (Fig. 12–2d,e,g).

The neckline is still relatively low at this point, but the tiny ruffle at its edge already looks tight and tense, as does the embroidery, the striping, and the slashing on the front of the doublet. The jerkin, which is cut away in the front to display the doublet, looks stiff in the extreme (Fig. 12–2b), and the sleeves that come from under the *chamarre,* or outer garment, at first seem softly slashed or paned until one notices that tight clips or brooches have re-

FIG. 12-4 Jean Clouet, *Francis I;* The Louvre, Paris; ca. 1525. The doublet with a wide-cut neck is worn over a shirt that is pushed through slashings; the outergarment is probably the *chamarre* folded back and fastened at the shoulder to look like sleeves; the headgear is a flat-brimmed beret trimmed with a white feather and studded with gems. The breadth of the entire costume is typical of the European male silhouette from 1520 to 1545. Photo courtesy of the Réunion des Musées Nationaux, the Louvre.

placed lacing, and the panes themselves have been stiffened by tight gold embroidery. The chamarre, which looks a bit like a wide-sleeved robe with cuffs turned back, is actually a rectangular mantle with a hole for the head in the center, an opening up the front, and a deep lapel closely resembling those on regular gowns. In the portrait, the straight edges to the sides of the chamarre, which would normally fall to the hand or below, have been folded upward under the lapels to the shoulder, revealing the sleeve of the doublet and the rich lining (Fig. 12-2a). Although we cannot see these in this portrait, we know from others that Francis is wearing bases related to those seen on the

gentlemen in Raphael's *Mass of Bolsena* (see Fig. 11-10); however, these are now much stiffer and more rigid. In an anonymous equestrian portrait of Francis, in which he wears almost the same garments as in the Clouet portrait, one can see under the edge of the bases the further development of upper stocks as separate bloused breeches with panes set over them.

Another version of these upper stocks may be seen in the famous Titian portrait of Emperor Charles V (Fig. 12-5). Here the

FIG. 12-5 Titian, *Charles V;* The Prado, Madrid; ca. 1530. The emperor wears a stiffened doublet under a padded outergown with large fur collar and puffed sleeves. The undersleeves make a series of tight slashed rings down the forearm that give great tension as do the slashed upper hose with stuffed *codpiece*. The lower legs are covered with *nether stocks* rolled above the knee. Photo courtesy of the Prado, Madrid.

emperor does not wear bases and, therefore, the upper hose are clearly seen from the crotch to just above the knee. They are similar to those seen in Giorgione's painting *The Ordeal By Fire of Moses* (see Fig. 11–8), but here the slashing has turned into very rigid, stiff panes held in by tight bands of braid around the leg from crotch to knee. In every way the effect is rigid and uncomfortable looking. Also the emperor's jerkin has a heavily padded lining that gives it a very rigid shape to the waist, and the codpiece is no longer a simple covering for an opening in the upper stocks but a stiff, padded horn shape that is repulsive in the extreme. The sleeves of the underdoublet are again tightly banded between tight slashed puffs and tiered down the arm from under the huge puffed sleeves of the knee-length overgown. This overgown has an excessively wide fur collar that spreads far out over the puffed sleeves to give the emperor an extremely horizontal and distorted shoulder width. By 1530 the costume had become an encasement of the body rather than a suit of clothing.

A magnificent example of a northern gown (gowns were certainly more common in the north than in Italy) may be seen in the famous Holbein painting *The French Ambassadors* (Fig. 12–6). The ambassador to the left wears a gown of great weight with huge puffed sleeves lined and trimmed with fur and with a massive fur collar. The fabric of the gown is probably heavy velour, although many were also made of rich brocade. He wears a skirted tunic rather than bases and an order about the neck, and the doublet of rich satin now rises to the base of the neck in contrast to the earlier portrait of Francis I (Fig. 12–4). The sleeves of the doublet are so padded that they make the arm look completely distorted in thickness. In fact, only the fullness of the beard and the flatness of the hat keep the ambassador's head from looking far too small for his body. His legs, though, do tend to look too thin for his torso.

The best-known images from this period are the various portraits of Henry VIII done by his court painter, Hans Holbein. The three-quarter-length portrait painted in 1540 shows

**FIG. 12–6** Hans Holbein the Younger, *The French Ambassadors;* National Gallery, London; 1533. Illustrates the bulk and weight of the so-called German style at the height of its popularity. Note the thickness of the fabric in the outergown to the left, the amount of fur trim, the width of the puff on the hanging sleeves, and the width of the toes on the shoes. Photo courtesy of the National Gallery, London.

that the hat has flattened out extremely to complement the width of the shoulders (Fig. 12-2). The hair is cut very short, and the jewels on the hat brim look nailed into place. The doublet, worn without a jerkin, is close to the neck with a small collar above and is covered with tight gold embroidery. Bits of lining are forced through tight cuts or slashed in the doublet and sleeves, and the wide panes of the sleeves and the front opening of the doublet are pinched together with great, dark brooches. It is indeed a forbidding costume image. One interesting effect on the huge, puffed sleeves of the overgown are the hanging sleeve projections that fall behind the arm (Fig. 12-2c). These were also used on a great range of longer gowns and are the basis of the academic master's gowns to this day. Here the upper part is puffed, but on many gowns there was merely a vertical and horizontal opening through which the arm could be thrust, and the remainder hung to the bottom of the gown behind (Fig. 12-2i).

By the middle of the century, bases had disappeared, and the paned upper stocks and codpiece were fully exposed below the doublet peplum on the now sharply pointed waist. The upper stocks were sometimes tightly fitted over the cheeks of the buttocks in back and down to the groin in front, with puffing and paning used only below this low hip line. The codpiece, now rigidly stuffed, was also used to carry extra pins and even small accessories such as spectacles, coins, and even a dagger. The bottom of the doublet was frequently padded in the front to create the famous *peascod belly* (see Chapter 13), and the doublet now rose into a standing collar that was finished with a pleated ruffle. The Titian portrait of Philip II, dated 1550, gives these mid-century essentials (Fig. 12-7).

These portraits show that the footwear now harmonizes with the spreading width of the costume by having a breadth to the toe that mirrors that in the shoulders (Fig. 12-2j). Some German shoes were so broad in the toes and with such marked slashing and so shallow at the back of the uppers that it is amazing the wearer was ever able to keep the shoes on. Some did have ankle straps, and certainly these seemed much more practical.

**FIG. 12-7** Titian, *Philip II of Spain;* Pitti Palace, Florence; 1550. This portrait illustrates the transition from the German to the Spanish silhouette about the middle of the century. Note the higher collar, the padded *peascod* doublet, and the new *melon* or *trunk hose* that have now become the *upper stocks.* The silhouette remains stiff, padded, and distorted. Photo courtesy of Alinari, Florence.

In general, the hair after 1520 was shortened to chin level, and after about 1530 it was very much like moderate modern cuts. Beards and mustaches were much in favor throughout the period, although they were fuller and broader in the beginning and later became more shaped to the contours of the face. The headgear between 1520 and 1560 was based on the flat beret with a stiff, flat brim, sometimes turned quite sharply up, but more often only slightly slanted upwards or worn quite flat. The brim was narrower by mid-century than earlier, and in Italy such hats were frequently worn over a head-hugging cap, or *caul* (Fig. 12–2d,e,f,g,h). The Germans wore the widest brims with much slashing, and more aristocratic caps and hats were trimmed with plumes and jewelry.

Long gowns with wide fur collars were worn by most older men, and variations on such robes were used for indoor undress by younger men over shirt and hose. For travel and outdoor wear, cloaks were still the standard accessory.

For the lower-class man, the basic wear was a tunic or jerkin over a shirt with roughly cut hose to the thigh, covered at the top by the skirt of the tunic or jerkin. Protective gaiters or outerhose were often pulled on over these to protect the lower leg, and shoes were of very rudely formed leather or wood. Hooded capes, caps, or brimmed flat hats or straws usually completed the ensemble. Sometimes a simple form of upper stock was also included.

Military armor of the second quarter of the sixteenth century was beautifully and intricately decorated—the period was considered the high watermark of the armorer-goldsmith. It was entirely of plate, shaped to cover the bodily distortions produced by the new clothing, with a visored and crested helmet that might contain gold dragons, carved eagles, shiny salamanders, or any number of other fantastic birds or beasts. Swords for men in full armor were still heavy with a cruciform hilt, and the armor was frequently made to accommodate the lowered tilting lance at the shoulder.

Foot soldiers usually wore helmets; quilted and padded jerkins, sometimes still worn over shirts of mail; and unprotected legs covered only by hose. The crossbow was the important weapon, and the two kinds of shields were the large, rectangular one of the bowman and the small, round buckler used by the swordsman or halberd-bearer (Fig. 12–2l,m).

**Feminine Dress**   Although there was not an abrupt change in clothing until the year 1520, the general movement in fashion was toward heavier garments, stiffer interlinings, and a more covered-up look. The most striking new item introduced in most countries outside Italy and southern Germany was the Spanish *farthingale*—a petticoat stiffened into a conical shape by rings of boning (Fig. 12–3a). The smooth, rigid, conical form that was created below the waist when the heavy skirt was placed over this farthingale gave the female figure a very angular form that was reinforced by large, triangular bell sleeves folded back to the elbow and an exaggerated rectangular or trapezoidal neckline.

An excellent example of the new Spanish style may be seen in Titian's portrait of Isabella of Portugal, painted in 1535 (Fig. 12–8). The rectangular neckline is now filled in with a shirred, transparent *partlet* set with jewels and ending in a ruffle at the neck. Her gown is of a heavy, brocaded fabric with open triangular sleeves caught to the puffed undersleeve with

**FIG. 12–8**   Titian, *Isabella of Portugal, Wife of Charles V;* The Prado, Madrid; ca. 1535. Note the corseted bodice with shoulders and neck covered by a soft *partlet,* and skirt held out by a boned petticoat or *farthingale.* Unlike in France and England, there is no headdress, only a complex, braided hairdressing. Photo courtesy of the Prado, Madrid.

brooches intermittently placed from shoulder to elbow. The skirt is cut to open in an inverted V-shape over the underskirt and the farthingale, and the bodice is fitted over a corset to remove all hint of the bulging breast. The corset, or *basquine,* that created this effect was either of heavily boned canvas or sometimes a metal cage operated with bolts and hinges (Fig. 12-3d). Although the dress is in the new heavy, angular, stiff tradition, the hair is more in the Italian style, with many braids wrapped tightly about the head instead of a crescent- or gable-shaped hood which was the standard headdress in England and France by this time. In these countries the hair was seldom completely uncovered as it was in Italy.

An example of the English style in the 1540s may be seen in the stiff, formal portrait of Lady Jane Grey, painted by a follower of Hans Holbein (Fig. 12-9). The bodice has a very angular neckline, is tightly fitted without a wrinkle or a bulge of the breast over a rigid corset, and now reaches downward at the front of the waist in a marked point (Fig. 12-3j). The bell-shaped outersleeves are lined in fur and turned back to the elbow over great padded undersleeves with the lining rigidly puffed through openings in the back seam (Fig. 12-3b,k). The brocaded fabric of the dress is extremely stiff and ornate, and the outer and underskirts are rigidly flattened without a wrinkle over the stiff, triangular line of the farthingale (Fig. 12-3a). Note the number of heavy finger rings, the focus given to the pomander down the front panel of the underskirt, and the tension created by the necklaces. Even the crescent-shaped hood has a beaded stiffness, and the entire image is that of a stiff, angular doll or mannequin. All of this was reinforced by the portrait style based on Holbein, which in its stiff formality was quite unlike the more realistic styles used in earlier European court portraits.

To contrast this English costume with that of an Italian duchess of about 1550, let us look at Bronzino's portrait of Eleanor of Toledo (Fig. 12-3). Here the neckline is partially filled in with heavy gold net, the headdress has been replaced with a *caul,* or net, and the farthingale is missing; however, the same stiffness and

**FIG. 12-9** Master John (?), *Lady Jane Dudley* (Grey); National Portrait Gallery, London; ca. 1545. Illustrates the full angular style that we associate with the later court of Henry VIII. Note the rectangular neckline, pointed and rigidly corsetted bodice, the conical line of the skirt over a *farthingale* and the large triangular cuffs created by the turned back fur at the elbows. The headdress is the French crescent hood. Photo courtesy of the National Portrait Gallery, London.

angularity are evident, and the brocaded pattern has been so enlarged that it seems to be growing in size as one looks at the portrait. Although the sleeves lack the excessive size created by the open bell-shaped line turned back over exaggerated puffs, the slashing on the arm is still very tensely treated with braid and jeweled pins. The look of the whole portrait is coldly formal in much the same way as that of *Lady Jane Dudley.*

German ladies of the same period, though similar in some ways, had a style of their own that included a series of heavy chains over a pleated partlet ending in a ruffle, a tightly puffed sleeve down the arm, a stiff, pleated skirt that lacked the exaggerated width created by the farthingale, and a broad-brimmed hat set with plumes that held over from the great Landsknechte hats of the early years of the century (Fig. 12-3i).

Antonio Moro's portrait *Mary, Queen of England,* painted in 1554, shows a major change in the neckline which now closes in around the neck and removes the strong rectangular line of the earlier style (Fig. 12-10). The crescent-shaped hood is worn further back on the head, and the hair is beginning to roll up slightly at the temples. The sleeves of the outergown still turn back to the elbow, and the brocaded pattern of the undersleeves and underskirt dominate the composition and focus the eye as they did in the portrait of Eleanor of Toledo (Fig. 12-3). The costume suggests the transitions that were about to take place in female costume at the time of the accession of Queen Elizabeth.

Feet were seldom seen during this period, but if they were, the shoe was a soft slipper-shoe, slightly pointed and without high heels. Hair was usually parted in the middle and close to the head when drawn back into a net, caul, or French hood; when uncovered (as usually in Italy), it was frequently braided about the head (Fig. 12-3f,g,h). The two types of headgear that were most prominent during this period were the crescent-shaped hood and the gable headdress, although large-brimmed, slashed hats appeared in Germany and occasionally donut-shaped turbans were seen in Italy (Fig. 12-3c,e,f,g,h,o,p). The gable headdress seems to have been used almost exclusively in England and consisted of a gable form that was heavily jeweled in front with a two-part hood or bag effect in the back, with one side frequently pinned up. The crescent headdress was less overpowering and usually showed some hair in the front, but it also ended with a hood at the back.

Middle-class women usually wore a gown,

**FIG. 12-10** Antonio Moro, *Mary Queen of England;* Isabella Steward Gardner Museum, Boston; ca. 1554. Illustrates the heavy oversleeves, crescent headdress, and conical *farthingale* fashionable in northern Europe in the second third of the sixteenth century. Note that the neckline is now much higher for women than during the period of Henry VIII. Photo courtesy of the Isabella Stewart Gardner Museum, Boston.

or *kirtle,* with a fitted bodice to the waist with the skirt draped up over the petticoat or underskirt; sleeves were often fairly short with the sleeves of the chemise showing below. Caps were of starched linen, with longer fronts that were turned back and pinned in a kind of cuff that framed the face. There were many variations of this basic housewives' cap.

Outergarments for women, like the men, usually consisted of a hooded cloak—sometimes with armholes to give freer action for the arms while wearing this enveloping garment. Long, fur-trimmed gowns were also used for indoor undress over the underbodice and underskirt when in the privacy of one's own chambers.

# FABRICS

In general, fabrics increased in weight and stiffness during this period, with great stress placed on complex brocades, cut velvets, metallic cloths, and heavy satins and taffetas. Nets of metallic thread or twisted silk were used for cauls and necklines, and soft gauzes were used for partlets and veils. Woolens were used by the middle classes, and country people still made do with very roughly woven homespuns. Linen and sometimes cotton were used for undergarments; the former was woven into interesting laces that were to increase in cost, complexity, and importance in the later part of the century.

# ARTS AND ARTIFACTS

The interiors of the period more frequently had elaborately carved wooden paneled walls, and the new strapwork ceilings of intricately worked plaster created a tight, intricate, decorative canopy above, which gradually replaced the painted beams of late Gothic times. Although the depressed Tudor arch, based on a late Gothic ideal, remained in England during this period, in most areas of Europe the motifs of the Italian Renaissance dominated interiors, even though these were now frosted one on top of the other to create a rich tension of ornamentation rather than a sense of relaxed beauty and harmony (Fig. 12–1b,c). Furniture was usually of heavy oak, cut into blocky forms that were then carved with the new arches, pediments, and brackets. With the help of the hand lathe, woodworkers carved tables with legs having great melon bulbs in between areas of slimmer, circular carving. Canopied beds also displayed these melon bulb effects. (Fig. 12–1a,d). Tapestries were still very important as decorative wall coverings and as door, arch, and bed hangings. These usually had a heavier tension in their ornamental patterns than in the past (Fig. 12–1).

Accessories for men included swords, daggers, purses, and especially orders worn about the neck (Fig. 12–2k). Swords were usually still of the cruciform-hilt variety, although they now frequently had a guard to protect the hand. Purses were still of the drawstring or pouch-with-flap variety; gloves, often slashed on the fingers and the back of the hand, were still worn or carried; walking sticks were occasionally used; and various orders, laid across the shoulders like a rich, ornamental chain, were very much in evidence at court.

Women's accessories included rings, necklaces, pendants, pomanders, brooches, medallions, and occasional earrings. This period marked the beginning of a new bejeweled age in which all court garments were heavily accented or encrusted with various gems, and the combination of rich, stiffened, metallic fabrics encrusted with such gems made costumes almost as inflexible, rigid, and heavy as they had been in Byzantine times (Fig. 12–3m).

The major motifs in patterns, orders, and jewelry were abstracted either from the animal or vegetable world with the pineapple, rose, pomegranate, bay leaf, and swirl as the most prominent of the latter; the salamander, lion, eagle, dragon, and various mythological beasts, the most prominent of the former.

# VISUAL SOURCES

Certainly the most prominent artist in depicting the styles of this period was Hans Holbein, the German artist who eventually became court painter to Henry VIII. Even though he left us primarily a record of English dress, his body of portraits gives us the essence of the horizontal, heavy, stiff German style that we think of as the fashion from 1520 to about 1550. Other excellent source artists in Italy are Pontormo, Bronzino, and Titian. Jean and François

Clouet are the best sources for French costume, along with the anonymous artists of the School of Fontainebleau; Spanish and Flemish styles are best seen in the works of Antonio Moro and Joos van Cleve.

The best collections for this period are the Metropolitan Museum of Art, the Louvre, the Prado, the National Gallery of London, the Uffizi, the Kunsthistorisches in Vienna, and the Royal Collection at Windsor. Useful written sources include Norris's *Costume and Fashion,* Volume III, Book 1; Laver's *Costume of the Western World;* and the Cunningtons' *Handbook of English Costume in the Sixteenth Century.*

## SUMMARY

This period marked the shift from the balanced, relaxed, expansive beauty of the High Renaissance to the inward tensions and grotesque dislocations of the Mannerist Renaissance. It was one of the strongest periods in the history of clothing for antinatural, artificial silhouettes and surfaces; everything took on a twisted, layered, interpenetrated, tense look. This first phase of the Mannerist Renaissance was marked by the bulk and angularity of the so-called German style, with great weight placed on the horizontal spread of clothing. Such antinatural clothing clearly marked a withdrawal from interest in the outer natural world to the imaginative, personal world within.

# chapter XIII

# Elizabethan-Jacobean
# (Late Mannerist Renaissance)

### Chronology

(c. 1560–1620)

| | | |
|---|---|---|
| **ELIZABETHAN**<br>**1558–1603** | 1558 | Elizabeth is crowned queen of England and restores the Church of England |
| | 1559 | Under the Treaty of Cateau-Cambrésis, France abandons her claims in Italy; John Knox leads religious reforms in Scotland |
| | 1561 | Mary Stuart becomes queen of Scotland |
| | 1562 | France enters 30 years of religious wars and civil strife as the Huguenots take up arms |
| | 1563 | Philip II begins the building of the Palace of Escorial |
| | 1564 | John Knox completes his *History of the Reformation in Scotland* |
| | 1567 | The Spanish army under the Duke of Alva moves into the Netherlands to suppress a revolt |
| ca. 1568 French | 1568 | Pieter Brueghel the Elder paints *The Blind Leading the Blind* |

| | |
|---|---|
| 1569 | Gerhardus Mercator publishes a world map, using his famous projection; coaches first used in England |
| 1571 | Spanish and Venetian navies defeat the Turks at Lepanto; the Spanish found Manila in the Philippines |
| 1572 | The Portuguese poet Luís de Camões publishes his epic work *The Lusiads;* a large part of the Protestant Huguenot population of France is massacred on St. Bartholomew's Day |
| 1573 | Tycho Brahe publishes *On the New Star;* Lope de Vega writes his first play, *El Verdadero Amante,* at the age of 12; tobacco introduced into England from America by Sir Walter Raleigh |
| 1574 | The Italian poet Torquato Tasso finishes *Jerusalem Delivered* |
| 1576 | French political philosopher Jean Bodín writes *The Republic;* the Netherlands provinces unite under the Pacification of Ghent to drive out the Spaniards |
| 1580 | Sir Francis Drake completes his circumnavigation of the globe and in the process lands near San Francisco; Montaigne publishes his *Essays* on various forms of government; Portugal is incorporated into the Spanish Empire |
| 1581 | The northern Netherlands provinces declare their independence from Spain; Dutch Republic is founded |
| 1582 | Pope Gregory XIII commissions a reform of the calendar |
| 1586 | El Greco paints *The Burial of Count Orgaz* |
| 1587 | Mary Queen of Scots is executed for conspiracy against Queen Elizabeth I of England |

ca. 1580 Spanish

| | | |
|---|---|---|
| | 1588 | The Spanish Armada is routed by the English and dispersed by storms in the North Sea |
| | 1589 | Henry IV founds the Bourbon dynasty in France, ending the religious wars; Hakluyt publishes *The Principal Navigations of the English Nation;* forks are introduced into table service |
| | 1596 | First six books of Edmund Spenser's *The Faerie Queene* are published |
| | 1597 | The Irish Rebellion against England is lead by Hugh O'Neill, earl of Tyrone; the Japanese expel Western missionaries |
| | 1598 | The Edict of Nantes gives the Huguenots legal recognition in France |
| ca. 1590 England | 1599 | Shakespeare becomes a partner in the building of London's new Globe Theater |
| | 1600 | English East India Company is chartered; Sully reforms the administration of the French government |
| | 1602 | The Dutch East India Company is chartered; *Hamlet* is registered with the Lord Chamberlain's Office |
| | 1603 | Queen Elizabeth I dies after a reign of 45 years |
| JACOBEAN 1603–1625 | 1603 | James I of the House of Stuart is crowned king of England |
| | 1604 | Guy Fawkes is executed for the "Gunpowder Plot" to blow up Parliament |
| | 1605 | Cervantes begins the publication of *Don Quixote* |
| | 1606 | Queiros discovers the northern New Hebrides Islands; Janszoon sights the coast of Australia; Torres sails south around New Guinea |

| | |
|---|---|
| 1607 | The English settle in Jamestown and prosper by raising tobacco; Claudio Monteverdi's first opera, *Orfeo,* is produced |
| 1608 | Champlain founds a French colony at Quebec |
| 1609 | Johannes Kepler publishes *Astronomia Nova;* Galileo builds his telescope |
| 1610 | Henry Hudson explores Hudson Bay; Henry IV of France is assassinated, and his son, Louis XIII, becomes king |
| 1611 | John Donne writes *An Anatomie of the World;* the King James version of the Bible is printed; Shakespeare's *The Tempest* is performed |
| 1613 | The Romanov dynasty increases the power of Russia |
| 1615 | The Dutch settle Manhattan Island as a fur-trading post |
| 1618 | A group of Protestant German princes and the Catholic Hapsburgs begin the Thirty Years' War; Brandenburg and Prussia unite under one ruler |
| 1619 | Kepler publishes *De Harmonica Mundi* explaining "celestial harmonics"; Protestant Bohemians elect Frederick V, a Calvinist, as their king, and the deposed King Ferdinand is elected Holy Roman emperor |
| 1620 | The army of the Catholic League routes the forces of Frederick V in the Battle of White Mountain; Francis Bacon publishes *Novum Organum,* expounding a new method of learning; English Pilgrims land at Plymouth Bay |

ca. 1610–1615 English

# BACKGROUND

The late sixteenth and early seventeenth centuries in European art and culture were not so much tied to the ideals of later mannerism as to the remarkable literary contribution that flowed from England during this time. Thus the period is better known as the *Elizabethan-Jacobean,* for the two contemporary rulers of England (*Jacobean* was the Latinized name for James I), than by the artistic title *Late Mannerist Renaissance.* Certainly Queen Elizabeth I of England was one of the outstanding royal personalities of all time, outshining even her father, Henry VIII, in the many events and contributions of her reign. The reign of James I is best remembered for the brilliant drama of Shakespeare and his contemporaries that flourished in England during this time.

Under Queen Elizabeth, England defeated the greatest nation on earth in 1588 when the English fleet under Sir Francis Drake completely destroyed the Spanish Armada. Sir Francis Drake also circumnavigated the globe and by constantly harassing Spanish galleons began that gradual shift of overseas authority from Spain to England that in the next 150 years made England master of the maritime world. Elizabeth also became patroness to a great golden age in English literature beginning with the early work of William Shakespeare. This great upsurge in the literary arts was due to the national pride that followed the defeat of the Armada and the cessation of religious conflicts that had all but destroyed the arts in many other centers of European culture during the late sixteenth century. Because England had remained devoted to many medieval ideals longer than in many other areas of Europe, the years after the defeat of the Armada saw the full experience of the Renaissance from the medieval past to the Baroque future embraced by writers, musicians, architects, and painters.

In Italy, which had been the fountainhead of the Renaissance, there was much doubt and confusion in the late sixteenth century that was only slowly resolved by the Catholic church's counterattack on Protestantism, known as the Counter-Reformation. By the close of the century, art had begun to be used as a weapon of propaganda to sell the populace on the greatness and grandeur of the Catholic faith; out of these experiments came the new baroque style that was fully developed in Italy by 1620 and accepted throughout Europe shortly thereafter. The center of artistic strength and political stability in Italy during this time was Venice, and it produced a number of magnificent artists such as Palladio, Veronese, and Tintoretto and the finest examples of mannerist music in the works of Gabrieli.

Germany was caught up in a continuous debate over religion that divided north from south, the emperor from his subject princes, and family from family. It was finally to be resolved in the terrible bloodletting of the Thirty Years' War that did not begin until 1618. France also saw 30 years of religious and political strife that did not end until the accession of Henry IV in 1589. Some of the most bizarre late mannerist cultural and artistic effects are to be found in France during the reign of Henry III, particularly in the area of dress. Spain was outwardly the greatest nation on earth at this time, wealthy with imported New World treasure and surfeited with power in Europe and abroad. Yet it was wasted from within by the fanaticism of the Inquisition and from abroad by the cruelty and naked greed of its explorer-conquerors. Its unsuccessful attempt to crush a revolt against its power in the Netherlands, one of the wealthiest areas of Europe, and its eventual loss of much of that area coupled with the destruction of the Armada dealt fatal blows to Spain's greatness and power.

During this age America also began to figure directly in western history; European history and cultural development from this time forward was influenced by the New World.

Art during the late sixteenth and early seventeenth century remained relentlessly antinatural—lost in the intricacies and tensions of mannerism. Plates were covered with snakes, frogs, and salamanders; glasses had stems fabricated from twisted serpents; portraits were made from elements of crawling marine life;

and architecture continued to include variations on that carved, glittering interior, the Gallery of Francis I, that we saw as the admired prototype for northern European mannerist rooms (see Fig. 12–1). Its tunnellike plan was adopted throughout Europe for walking galleries. For example, the Gallery of Hatfield House, (Fig. 13–1), in its extreme length, tight decoration, and oppressive atmosphere, is typical of Elizabethan as well as other northern European interiors. The elegant, artificial, almost grotesque human figures drawn by the artist in their rich, stiff, tortured fabrics and exaggerated costume lines demonstrate how clothing added its own mannerist embellishment to that of the architecture.

## THE BASIC COSTUME SILHOUETTE

During the Elizabethan-Jacobean Period the modes in male and female dress were loosely characterized as the *Spanish style* because in color and somewhat less in line and silhouette, their major inspiration came from the fashions of the formal Spanish court. The body was still artificially distorted and treated in a variety of unnatural ways, but the stress had changed from the great width and triangular angularity of the earlier *German style* to a taller, vertical line with many rounded, exaggerated extensions down the body. Tight slashing and puffing were still a major accent, although tight paning often replaced slashing on sleeves, bodices, and doublets. Heavy metallic embroidery accented with sprinkled gems and jewelry was standard for aristocratic decoration, and all fabrics were stiffened with linings, metallic threads, or complex braided accents. Padding became tighter and more compact as did all the distortions and extensions from the normal line of the human body. Even color was much more sharply limited than in the past since the admired colors at the Spanish court were gold, black, silver, and white, and these soon came to be the most fashionable color combinations throughout the courts of Europe. There was even a conscious return to late Gothic exaggerations in combination with Renaissance distortions. In general, in the Spanish style the wearer was encased in an armor of ornamentation like an idol covered with gold, pearls, and precious stones, while the dark-colored silk and velvet fabrics reflected and absorbed light like the lining of a jewel case. Dress represented the decorative equivalent to the use of words in the literary conceits of prose and poetry.

In masculine dress a high-crowned, narrow-brimmed bag hat was now used more frequently than the flat-brimmed beret; the wide, short gown was now more frequently replaced by a stiff, circular, collared cape. The small neck ruffle on the shirt was now replaced by a starched, white, circular *ruff,* pleated with hot irons into a series of figure-eight patterns around the neck; such an arrangement placed on a high, standing doublet collar presented the head as if on a platter (a metaphor to be seen in many paintings of the period about Salome with the head of John the Baptist and Judith with the head of Holofernes). The doublet became even stiffer and more long-waisted and was often padded to a curving ridge at the waist front in what was known as a *peascod belly.* On each shoulder stuffed crescent rolls or stiffened wings were added to obtain width; sleeves were padded into a bladder shape, which seemed to separate the arms from the body, or puffed and padded in a series of rounded extensions and contractions down the entire arm. A sleeveless jerkin was sometimes worn over the doublet, and it could have sleeves tied into it with points (laces) under shoulder wings. Waists were deeply pointed, and the legs were enclosed in *melon hose* over tight hose of soft cloth (though knitted hose became more popular by the close of the century). During the fourth quarter of the century thighs were more frequently covered with tight breeches, or *canions,* worn under the melon hose or a padded half-roll, known as a *pansid slop.* In this case the lower leg was covered by *nether stocks,* or stockings, which were often gartered over the canions either above or below the knee. Wider breeches to the

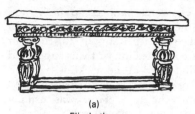

(a)
Elizabethan
table

(b)
Elizabethan
doorway

(c)
Elizabethan
bed

Drawing of the Gallery of Hatfield
House, an English Elizabethan
manor house; 1607–1611. Illustrates
the continuation of the tunnellike arrangement, tight decoration, and
oppressive atmosphere found in the
Gallery of Francis I at Fontainebleau and in most long galleries
throughout Europe from 1520 to
1620. From Nash, *The Mansions of
England in Olden Times*, 1849.

(d)
Elizabethan
chair

(e)
Spanish door

(f)
English
chair

**FIGURE 13–1**

knee with some fullness at the hips were known as *Venetians*. Shoes were narrow slipper-shoes with soft soles and heels until the very last years of the century when firm soles with moderately high heels were introduced.

After the turn of the century, certain modifications took place in male dress before the transition to the new baroque style was accepted in the 1620s. Although stiffness remained, the peascod belly disappeared, the ruff was more frequently replaced by a stiffened and wired lace collar known as a *whisk* (*golilla* in Spain), doublet sleeves became tight and straight, and *slops*, or trunk hose, became longer and fuller at the bottom, usually finishing just above the knee. Cuffs were finished in stiff lace rather than stiff, pleated ruffles, and shoes with heels were decorated prominently with *shoe roses*. In short, the costume took on straighter, more angular lines, and these were also reflected in hats which now had stiffened sloping crowns and wider brims.

Feminine costume also stressed padded sleeves and hips and a very long and pointed waist, stiffened by the use of a rigid decorated stomacher that plunged from the neckline to the crotch or below. Iron corsets or absolutely rigid boning were part of the bodice of every gown. The farthingale that earlier had created a conical distention of the skirt was modified to give more fullness at the hips. In the last quarter of the century, it was often put aside in favor of a great donut-shaped roll, or *bolster,* placed on the hips under the skirt or by a cartwheel farthingale that distended the female figure ever further. Shoulders were finished in rolls or wings, sleeves were padded, puffed, and slashed, and the ruff was used at the neck. In Spain the bodice rose up to support the ruff, but in most other countries the ruff was supported by a partlet that filled in the neckline between dress and ruff or was treated as an open, pleated collar to frame the face. Hair was usually brought up in a heart-shaped roll to a small jeweled cap. Shoes were similar to those of the men.

Fewer changes took place in female dress with the turn of the century, but in general the cartwheel verdingale, or farthingale, almost completely replaced the bolster or conical farthingale, and the pointed waist was frequently accented by a large cartwheel ruff out of the same material as the gown. The stiff lace cuff replaced the cuff ruff, and neck ruffs were replaced by a pleated, stiff fan collar edged in lace.

For representative images of the Elizabethan period, let us look at the portraits of Charles IX of France and Queen Elizabeth (Figs. 13–2, 3). Each is artificial, padded, and grotesque—a complete perversion of the natural lines of the human body. Both Clouet and the anonymous artist who painted Queen Elizabeth presented their subjects as fashion mannequins rather than as individuals.

# ELIZABETHAN

**Masculine Dress**   With the ascendancy of Spanish style in dress, by 1560 whatever ease or softness there was in fabric or posture began to disappear totally. The major new addition to all costumes was the starched, white ruff at the neck. The doublet now had a collar that rose to the very base of the ear; set inside was a starched ruffle that soon spread out into a pleated platter for the head. Let us look at the *Portrait of a Man* by Antonio Moro for an example of the transitional effect in neckwear (Fig. 13–4). Here the doublet collar is still open in front, even though it rises to the ear lobes and halfway up the head in back. Into it is set (separate from the shirt) a collar with a stiff figure-eight pleated edge that lies on the doublet collar to frame the entire face. It gave great dignity and formality to the wearer and marked the beginning of a fashion accent that did not disappear entirely until the second quarter of the seventeenth century. The remainder of the costume is very simple by fashion standards of the day but stresses the slightly bulging waist with a central ridge that will turn into the peascod belly and the rounded and firmly padded melon hose or upper stocks covered in panes and edged in braid. Between these panes one glimpses the crinkled, light-reflective silk that gave such a mysterious and

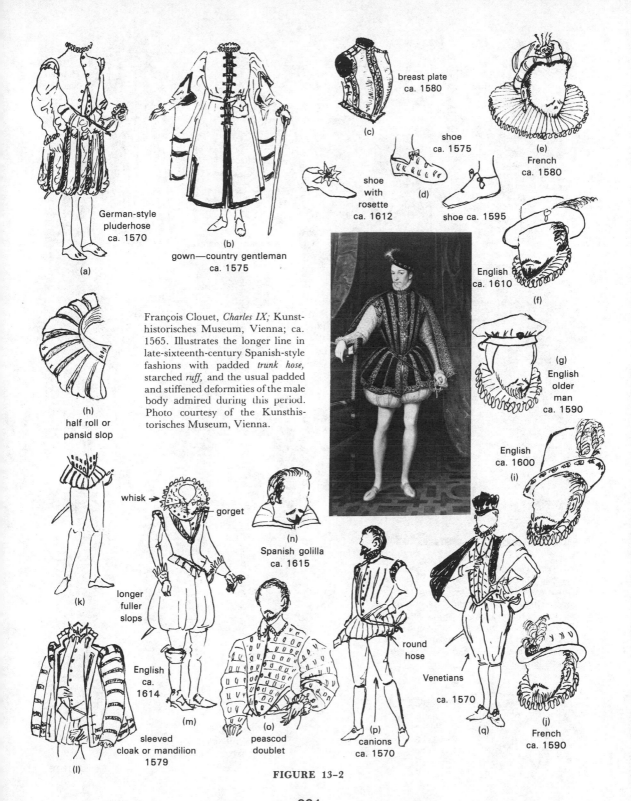

German-style
pluderhose
ca. 1570

(a)

(b)

gown—country gentleman
ca. 1575

(c)

breast plate
ca. 1580

shoe
ca. 1575

(d)

shoe
with
rosette
ca. 1612

shoe ca. 1595

(e)

French
ca. 1580

(f)

English
ca. 1610

(g)

English
older
man
ca. 1590

English
ca. 1600

(i)

(h)

half roll or
pansid slop

François Clouet, *Charles IX;* Kunsthistorisches Museum, Vienna; ca. 1565. Illustrates the longer line in late-sixteenth-century Spanish-style fashions with padded *trunk hose,* starched *ruff,* and the usual padded and stiffened deformities of the male body admired during this period. Photo courtesy of the Kunsthistorisches Museum, Vienna.

(k)

whisk

gorget

(n)

Spanish golilla
ca. 1615

longer
fuller
slops

English
ca.
1614

round
hose

Venetians

ca. 1570

(m)

(o)

peascod
doublet

(p)

canions
ca. 1570

(q)

(j)

French
ca. 1590

(l)

sleeved
cloak or mandilion
1579

**FIGURE 13–2**

221

(a) bolotor

(d) iron corset

French 1527

(b) cartwheel farthingale

(c) Roman overgown ca. 1580

(e) Spanish 1585

(f) French 1615

(j) motif

(g) country girl

motif

(m) English 1575

(i) aiglet

(k) English fur-trimmed overgown 1585

(l) necklace

(n) English 1615

Anonymous, *Queen Elizabeth I;* National Portrait Gallery, London; ca. 1592. Illustrates the grotesque perversion of the natural lines of the human body through padding, stiffness, excess decoration, and the use of white makeup and a wig—all fashion effects admired by England's Virgin Queen. Photo courtesy of the National Portrait Gallery, London.

(h) poking stick to set a ruff

**FIGURE 13-3**

**FIG. 13–4** Antonio Moro, *Portrait of a Gentleman;* National Gallery of Art, Washington; 1569. An exceptionally high-collared *jerkin* over a doublet of violet silk, with melon hose stuffed with *bombast*. The neckband has been left open in the Flemish style. Photo courtesy of the National Gallery of Art, Washington.

agitated accent to even the most sober dress of the times. The simple, straight, satin sleeves also have a slight shirring along the seams so that they will reflect light in a slightly agitated way, and the long cuts in the doublet also allow us to glimpse the light-reflective lining beneath. This sober, dignified, formal image was to be copied in much more ornate interpretations throughout Europe until the end of the century.

For example, the habit of Charles IX in the portrait by Clouet was directly derived from the Spanish style (Fig. 13–2). Once again the basic color is black, but instead of two simple loops of gold chain, the entire suit is heavily embroidered in metallic gold—vibrating tensely within rigidly controlled vertical stripes. The doublet collar is now tightly closed, and thus the embryonic ruff is already beginning to support

the head as if it were on a white saucer. The hat is still the flat beret with a narrow brim of the mid-century but is stiffer and is placed at a sharp angle on the head to give added height. The sleeveless jerkin allows the stiff, white and gold sleeves of the doublet, decorated with small cuts, to show, and the whole is framed by a very stiff, half-circular cape. The jerkin has a long, peplum skirt spread out over the very rounded padding of the melon hose or upper stocks, and a padded codpiece peeps out from the opening in the peplum skirt. The pointed waist is padded into the peascod; the sword belt is contoured to fit the pointed waist and hold the sword low on the hip. The legs, clad in fitted hose, seem too slim for the figure they support, and the slipper-shoes do not seem to give a firm base to the figure. The inner padding of the very distinctive upper stocks was now usually made from horsehair, rags, or tow (an inferior flax fiber) and was known as *bombast*.

Germany was almost the only country to prefer the loose *pluderhose*—that were the successors to the landsknechte hose of the early sixteenth century—to the melon hose worn in the rest of Europe. These were usually loose breeches of extravagant silk yardage that bloused through four or five panes down to the knee and also puffed around the hips (Fig. 13–2a). They were considered barbaric and most unfashionable throughout the rest of Europe.

In the fourth quarter of the century, a number of variations in the male upper hose appeared. From Venice came knee breeches, known as *Venetians,* that were frequently padded at the hips and tapered to just below the knee. They became the basis for the major male breeches of the seventeenth century (Fig. 13–2q). Another variation was abbreviated melon hose, known as *pansid slops,* that were really just a padded roll below the waist and worn over very tight-fitting knee breeches, known as *canions* (Fig. 13–2h,k,p). Frequently the roll worn with these canions was so small that one must look closely at a portrait to distinguish between Venetians and canions. Another less-fashionable style was *galligaskins,* straight leg breeches loose at the knee (like long Bermuda shorts) that originated in Gascony. Also in the last decade of the century the melon hose changed their lines from globular to angular—slanting outward and down from the waist and then turning sharply inward to the leg at the bottom to form a more square-based version of padded hose (Fig. 13–2m).

Let us look at a scene from the court of Henry III of France during the 1580s to see how French fashion ideals differed from the Spanish and note the variations in upper hose (Fig. 13–5). First of all, a word should be said about the platter ruff that had developed by this time and is fully displayed in the painting. This starched, pleated fabric framing the face could not stay in place by itself; therefore, methods of support had to be devised (Fig. 13–2e). At first when it was still an enlarged ruffle, it was usually supported by a series of stiffened tabs known as *piccadils,* also often seen at the shoulder and waist (see Fig. 12–7). Later these were deepened to as much as two inches and stiffened with cardboard. The next step was to devise an ornamental frame of wire, sometimes gilded or wrapped in gold or silk thread. This frame, known as an *underproper, supportasse,* or *rebato,* was then attached to the collar of the bodice or doublet to hold the ruff at the correct angle.

In the painting *Ball for the Wedding of the Duc de Joyeuse,* most of the men wear these wide platter ruffs supported by wire frames that cannot be seen (Fig. 13–5). The doublets are heavily padded, especially in the sleeves and on the stomachs, the latter creating the famous peascod belly look (Fig. 13–2o). The sleeves are also sewn down with bands of braid that circle the arm, creating a scalelike effect. This same effect is used on the padded canions with pleats and tiny slashes that cover the upper leg under pansid slops. The whole effect is arbitrary, unnatural, uncomfortable looking, and gives the viewer an unpleasant feeling—all images that were much admired in late-sixteenth-century dress.

One costume that looks rather different is that worn by the man on the far right in this painting (Fig. 13–5). He wears no ruff but a falling band or collar, an effect that was far more comfortable and usually worn by those who placed less importance on following the

**FIG. 13–5** French School of the sixteenth century, *Ball for the Wedding of the Duc de Joyeuse;* The Louvre, Paris; ca. 1581–1582. Illustrates the use of great platter *ruffs,* large hip rolls for the ladies, and the tight *canions* for the upper leg on men not wearing *trunk hose.* Also note how the body leads with the hips in a processional walk, thus creating a slow, rolling, curved movement. Photo courtesy of the French Musées Nationaux.

latest fashions in neckwear (Fig. 13–2p). This gentleman also has hanging sleeves in his jerkin that frame the soft, unpadded, full sleeves of his doublet which ends in a narrow peplum rather than a half-roll. His upper stocks or hose are probably technically Venetians since they are not worn under a roll at the waist but appear to fit the leg as tightly as canions, and his *nether stocks,* or hose, are gartered over them at the knee.

The male headgear in this painting shows the many variations on the higher crowned hats that were worn at this period (Fig. 13–5). Most are sloping crowns with pleated or smooth coverings and brims that vary from narrow to wide and from flat to a soft, padded roll (Fig. 13–2e,f,g,i,j). From other paintings of the French court, we know that Henry III and those closest to him preferred a soft roll around a tiny beret crown, all set far back on the head with the hair plucked back so that the brow disappears inside the hat (Fig. 13–2e).

Finally, let us look at the painting *Queen Elizabeth at Blackfriars* by Marcus Gheeraerts (Fig. 13–6). Here, at the close of Queen Elizabeth's reign, we have still the platter ruffs for men but much less use of the padded peascod belly. The men still wear full upper stocks or trunk hose, but they are no longer pumpkin- or melon-shaped, tending to spread downward over the hips and then to come in sharply to the leg from wide, full bottoms. These are worn over tight canions to the knee or just above, and the hose or nether stocks are all worn gartered over the knee. Sometimes these garters were wrapped twice about the leg as decoration above and below the knee. Shoes are beginning to show bowlike lacings that will soon turn into rosettes (Fig. 13–2d). In some cases the men wear only doublets, in others they wear sleeveless jerkins over the doublet, and many still have the stiff, circular or half-circular cloak balanced on the shoulders. Sometimes this cloak had sleeves in it and became a kind of coat

**FIG. 13–6** Marcus Gheeraerts, *Queen Elizabeth at Blackfriars;* Collection of Simon Wingfield Digby, Sherbourne Castle; ca. 1596. Illustrates the use of the wheel *farthingale,* the open *ruff* behind a lowcut neckline, and the disproportion in line to be found in late Elizabethan women's dress as well as the use of melon hose over *canions* in men's clothing of this time. Photo courtesy of Simon Winfield Digby.

that was thrown over the shoulders, known as a *mandilion* (Fig. 13–2l). Sometimes the sleeves were open all the way to the wrist, and at other times the cloak was worn so far over one shoulder that the right sleeve hung down the center front. Older men, of course, wore great fur-collared gowns with hanging sleeves and much gold-braided trim (Fig. 13–2b). Hooded cloaks were used for travel.

**Feminine Dress**   As the Spanish style in fashion gradually replaced the German style after the middle of the century, a more vertical fashion line began to replace the angular line with horizontal accents that had been prevalent in most of Europe since the late 1520s. A good example of the conservative Spanish-style silhouette may be seen in Sanchez Coello's portrait of Anne of Austria, Queen of Spain (Fig. 13–7). The Queen retains the bell farthingale that began to disappear in France and England at this time (Italian ladies seldom wore a farthingale at all) (Fig. 13–3c), and the neckline of the gown now climbs to the base of the ears and is finished in a small, starched ruff, giving an extremely dignified and formal image. The hair is done in a tight, heart-shaped roll back into a small cap (a style that was to remain the most common female hairdressing style throughout Europe until the close of the century). The stiff, black material of the princess-line gown is heavily ornamented in gold. The hanging sleeves remain open bell sleeves caught together on the lower forearm with brooches over tight, ornamentally braided undersleeves. The front of the gown is decorated with *aiglets*—metal casing tips or ends added to a ribbon or cord to create a tie closing (Fig. 13–3i)—and the only other accent is the knotted strand of pearls looped twice around the neck.

To contrast this with a much less formal and more comfortable Italian style from about the same date, let us look at Moroni's portrait *Pace Rivola Spini,* (Fig. 13–8). The subject wears a basically upper-middle-class or lower aristocratic dress that uses an open, soft ruff, an undergown that is probably not boned and is worn only over a small bolster or hip roll, an outergown that fastens only at the waist and has

**FIG. 13–7**   Sanchez Coello, *Anne of Austria;* Kunsthistorisches Museum, Vienna; 1571. Illustrates the full effect of the Spanish style with its continuation of the conical *farthingale,* the stress on a very high neckline, the open bell sleeves caught to the forearm, and the stiffness and tension in the braid and trim. The metal-tipped ribbons are points finished in metal *aiglets.* Photo courtesy of the Kunsthistorisches Museum, Vienna.

moderate, hanging sleeves, and a simple hairdo drawn back into a net. It is a pleasing antidote to the unpleasant, uncomfortable fashions usually seen for women in the Elizabethan Period. This style may have been a model for those individuals in the later sixteenth century who refused to accept the suffering and deformities of late mannerist high style.

**FIG. 13-8** Gianbattista Moroni, *Portrait of Pace Rivola Spini;* Accademia Carrara, Bergamo; ca. 1570. Illustrates an upper-middle-class lady with less distortion, stiffness, and tension in dress than that found in aristocrats. Note the open collar-ruff, the shoulder rolls, and the modest hip roll. Photo courtesy of Flammarian Publishers, Paris.

But by the 1580s the high style for aristocratic women in general had become even more severely distorted from the natural lines of the body, as shown in *Ball for the Wedding of the Duc de Joyeuse* (Fig. 13-5). The Spanish farthingale had been replaced by a great padded *bolster,* or roll with pointed ends tied around the hips under the skirt (Fig. 13-3a). It is said to have been introduced by Marguerite de Valois, wife of Henry IV and daughter of Catherine de Medici, to disguise her very wide hips. Some-

times when quite wide, this roll actually had a frame of wire or boning in it to create a true cartwheel farthingale (Fig. 13-3b), and it was this latter extended form that was much admired by Queen Elizabeth (Figs. 13-3, 6). Sometimes this wheel effect had a cartwheel ruff set on top of it to further emphasize the width of the hips and to balance the width of the ruff at the neck.

The ladies in *Ball for the Wedding of the Duc de Joyeuse* wear the new-style bolster without a waist ruff, and the neck ruffs are either of the open fan variety, framing the neckline in front, or of the platter variety. The forming and maintaining of such ruffs was a magnificent art. Starch, which had been developed in Flanders, was used to gain the appropriate stiffness, then metal poking sticks were used to set the desired figure-eight line (Fig. 13-3h). Sometimes the ruffs were made in layers, and all of the large ones were supported with metal frames, as has been described for men. The padded sleeves worn by the French women were enormous, and one can understand why Shakespeare referred to such as "demi-cannons" in *The Taming of the Shrew*. It must have been almost impossible to bend the arm freely. The corsets under these gowns were iron cages with sharp, pointed fronts that made possible the rigid, long line of the stomacher that reached from the neckline to well below the crotch (Fig. 13-3d). The hairdos, again with the hairline plucked high on the forehead, were primarily heart-shaped rolls that rose up on either side of the central part into spreading protrusions over the temple and finished in back either in braids or under a small cap (Fig. 13-3e,m). Shoes, although they are not really seen in this painting, were slipper-shoes with relatively soft soles and heels. Raised platform *chopines* were worn in Italy as well as in other countries (Fig. 13-3).

Now let us look at the two images of Queen Elizabeth which may well show the same gown (Figs. 13-3, 6). Elizabeth, after having had smallpox that left her face pockmarked and her head with little hair, wore heavy, white makeup and a red wig in which the fashionable heart shape had been drawn much higher to make a corona of hair high on the head. The stomacher, padded sleeves, wheel farthingale, and open fan ruff all make the queen look like an unreal mannequin rather than a person. Supposedly the open neck with the fan collar worn by the queen and certain of her ladies marked them as unmarried women, while the closed Spanish neck was worn by married women (the lady in black directly behind the queen's litter), but there is no proof of this. Probably the most distinctive English element in female fashions was the excessive width of the farthingale and its low setting on the hips.

Thus by the end of the century, English female costume was probably the stiffest and the most distorted in Europe, while the Italian, without a bolster or only a very small one and having small open ruffs and many variations of soft, hanging sleeves, was probably the least distorted.

Outerwraps for women also included fur-trimmed, loose gowns, traveling coats, hooded mantles, and in Germany short fur-lined boxy jackets (Fig. 13-3k).

# JACOBEAN

In the first two decades of the seventeenth century, as the mannerist style began to decay and be diluted by artistic ideals that were to lead to the new baroque style, clothing changed only slightly, either in the direction of less padding and distortion or into ever-more complex and subtle games of decoration. After almost a century of devotion to an unnatural treatment of fabric, decoration, and the human body, a return to more comfortable, simple, relaxed styles took several decades to occur.

**Masculine Dress**  By 1610 the ruff had been replaced among men of fashion by the new, flat collar edged in lace, known as the *whisk* in England and the *golilla* in Spain (Figs. 13-2m,n,9). Doublets remained pointed but not as deeply so as in the past, and the peascod belly all but disappeared. Sleeves tended to be tight rather than puffed or padded, and cuffs were of stiff lace rather than ending in a figure-eight, starched ruff. But most important for the male movement was the addition of hard-soled shoes with a heel of an inch or more (Fig. 13-9).

An excellent English portrait that shows these changes is Isaac Oliver's *Richard Sackville, Earl of Dorset* (Fig. 13-9). Sackville, a Jacobean dandy, displays the new line of the upper hose in which the broad angular line is maintained by the lining and stiff fabric rather than with *bombast* padding. Shoulder wings are smaller, the sleeves are tight, the starched whisk is worn on a decorative metal *gorget* (a piece of ornamental armor), and the hose, or *nether stocks,*

FIG. 13-9  Isaac Oliver, *Richard Sackville, Earl of Dorset;* Victoria and Albert Museum; 1616. This costume illustrates the changes in English male dress during the Jacobean Period. Note the starched *whisk* instead of the *ruff,* the slim sleeves and cuffs, the longer *trunk hose,* and the addition of heeled shoes with *shoe roses.* Photo courtesy of the Victoria and Albert Museum, London.

are elaborately clocked with embroidery. Most important of all, the heeled shoes are finished in rosettes—the new form of shoe decoration of the Jacobean Period. Note also that slashing and paning have all but disappeared. Although Sackville does not wear one, hats in general had higher crowns and wider brims and were larger than those of the late sixteenth century (Fig. 13-2f,i). A good example of continental male styles at this same time may be seen in Francken and Pourbus' *Ball at the Court of Albert of Austria and His Wife Isabelle Clara Eugenia* (Fig. 13-10).

As for military dress during the Elizabethan-Jacobean Period, complete suits of engraved tilting armor were still used for ceremonial occasions, but the practical armor of the time usually consisted of the boat-brimmed *morion* helmet and a breastplate (Fig. 13-2c), the latter sometimes accompanied by a neck gorget (Fig. 13-9), shoulder *pauldrons,* and hip *taces.* Foot soldiers usually wore buff jerkins reinforced with steel plates, heavily quilted canvas or padded leather, and a *burgonet* or morion helmet. Weapons and equipment included the sword, halberd, small shield or buckler, dagger, pistol, or arquebus.

The urban working man wore crude approximations of the styles at court—trunk hose without panes, unstiffened doublets with moderate waist and sleeves, small neck ruffle or collar, and a flat cap. The peasant wore a tunic or smock over a shirt, and rough hose with or without knee pants or upper stocks.

**Feminine Dress**   Few changes occurred in female costume during the first years of the seventeenth century except for somewhat less bulk and padding for the figure, a somewhat taller look—especially in coiffures—and a greater variety of stiffened lace collars that came to rival the ruff in importance (Fig. 13-10). Gradually the great cartwheel farthingale or extremely wide bolster was replaced once again by a smaller hip roll, while the stiff stomacher often bent forward at the waist so that the absolute rigidity of its line from neck to crotch was finally broken. One finds this bent look especially in a number of Dutch portraits of this second decade of the century (Fig. 13-10). Collars tended to fall into four categories: the open ruff that framed the face in a stiff fan of lace, the smaller *whisk,* or stiffened

**FIG. 13-10**   Frans Francken the Younger, *Ball at the Court of Albert of Austria and His Wife Isabella Clara Eugenia;* Mauritshuis, The Hague; 1611. This painting of the governors of the Netherlands and their court represents fashion just before the transition to the new baroque-cavalier style. Note the squarer trunk hose, the use of both platter *ruffs* and flat *whisks,* the continued use of the *hip roll,* and the new straight-legged knee breeches on some of the men. Photo courtesy of the Mauritshuis, The Hague.

lace collar, that closed in front and spread out under the chin and base of the head, the standard pleated platter ruff, and the open standing collar that framed the head in a flat fan of lace without pleating. Hairdressing was high and often built up over padding (Figs. 13–3f,n,10).

During the entire Elizabethan-Jacobean age, the merchant's wife and townswomen wore imitations of court costumes without the extreme boning, padding, and exaggerations in waistlines, ruffs, and bolsters. Coat-dresses were very popular with small ruffs or ruffles at the neck, a modest hip roll, and a complexly folded, starched cap. A country woman usually wore a simple, loose gown, sometimes laced over the chemise in front, with an apron, plain collar, and a soft cap or broadbrimmed hat to complete the ensemble (Fig. 13–3g).

# FABRICS

Fabrics in this period were usually woven in dark colors with a stiff body in silk, satin, taffeta, brocaded damask, metallic cloth, and plain or cut velvet. The stress was always on stiffness, thickness, and body, even if there had to be much interlining. Brocades were very important, and patterns were always tightly limited and squeezed into restrictive framing devices (Fig. 13–3j). Wool was the standard fabric for the more practical, sober garments, and *fustian* (a heavy, cotton canvas) was in demand for linings and some outergarments. Ruffs and collars were of lace and lawn—some with metallic threads—and veils were of silk gauze.

# ARTS AND ARTIFACTS

Interiors of the time stressed tightly carved, wooden paneling, intricate strapwork ceilings of interpenetrating forms of tightly worked plaster, small-paned, mullioned windows, and furniture that was heavy and dark, with much use of the heavy, turned, melon-bulb accents on the legs (Fig. 13–1a,b,c,d,e,f). Tapestries were still used on walls and as coverings for doorways, although they were not as dominant a wall accent as in the past. Canopied beds were still massive and even more oppressive in their ceiling height and proportions than in the early part of the sixteenth century (Fig. 13–1c). Furniture contained a minimum of fabric accessories such as cushions or upholstery, and the feeling of all interiors was dark, tense, and oppressive. Motifs were now universally of the Italian Renaissance variety but intertwined and interwoven in bizarre and often complex ways.

Musical instruments still included the lute, pipe and tabor, viol, and recorder, the latter an exclusively English form of a flute. At the end of the sixteenth century the virginal, an embryonic form of the piano, was a portable addition to the standard musical instruments.

Accessories for men included the many jeweled collars or orders that accented court costume; the ever-present sword and dagger, usually worn low on the hip on a belt that fit the point of the waistline; gloves, often slashed, that could be worn or carried; decorative garters, baldrics, or sashes, often tied in large bows on the right shoulder; and occasionally the use of a single earring along with other finger rings. Women sometimes wore decorative aprons, jeweled pomanders, gloves, rich necklaces (Fig. 13–3l), finger rings, occasionally earrings, embroidered purses, solid, shield-shaped fans, and occasionally the platform shoes, or *chopines,* that were primarily popular in Italy.

This was an age in which jeweled accents and accessories twinkled and winked throughout a candle- or torchlit ballroom to give the feeling that dark interiors were only alive when peopled by figures whose clothing and accessories threw back sparks of reflection with every slight movement.

# VISUAL SOURCES

This is an age overflowing with source material. The best artists for information are the Flemish-Spanish portraitist Antonio Moro; the French court artist, François Clouet and a series of anonymous court artists who surrounded him; the Spanish court artist Sanchez Coello; the northern Italian realist, Gianbattista Moroni; the late work of the Italian portraitist Agnolo Bronzino; the English miniaturists Nicholas Hilliard and Isaac Oliver; and the Jacobean Flemish artists Marcus Gheeraerts, Paul van Somer, and Frans Pourbus. There are also any number of anonymous portraits that give considerable information about clothing, but are not very good portraits. Sometimes one can gain valuable information from the master artists of this period, like Tintoretto and El Greco, who usually devoted their attention to religious themes, and from the many engravings of the time done by such men as Hendrik Goltzius, Théodore de Bry, and Abraham de Bruyn. Pieter Brueghel is excellent as a source for peasant costume in Flanders during the early part of the period.

It is difficult to pinpoint the best collections of paintings and engravings since they are in museums all over Europe and America, but the royal collections of the queen of England, the National Portrait Gallery in London, the Kunsthistorisches in Vienna, the Louvre, the Prado, the Uffizi in Florence, the Victoria and Albert in London, the Metropolitan Museum of Art in New York, and the National Gallery in Washington are the most important public repositories. The Victoria and Albert also has a very fine collection of actual garments from the period, as does the Metropolitan in New York on a more limited scale. Useful books are Herbert Norris's *Costume and Fashion,* Volume III, Book 2; James Laver's *Costume of the Western World;* and Harriet Morse's *Elizabethan Pageantry.*

# SUMMARY

This was a very rich, complex age with a great variety in clothing line, even though the period was dominated by the rigidities and deformities of the so-called Spanish style. Never in the history of dress has there been a period that so consistently and singlemindedly worked against comfort and the natural lines and movements of the human body. Every step and movement in such tortuous clothing demanded great effort and absolute control, and every appearance in public was a performance to be applauded. It was an age that was both frigid and exotic—artificial, intellectual, aristocratic, and exclusive. The most outstanding characteristics were undoubtedly the ruff and the farthingale or bolster, but all the intricacies of padding, boning, corseting, slashing, and puffing were complex and unique. If ever there was an age of tension and torture in all aspects of art and dress, the Elizabethan-Jacobean Period was that age.

# chapter *XIV*

# *Early Baroque (Cavalier)*

| THIRTY YEARS' WAR 1618–1648 | 1621 | The English House of Commons enters a protest in its journal against James I, which he rips out |
| | 1622 | Jean Baptiste Poquelin, later known as Molière the playwright, is born in Paris |
| | 1623 | Velásquez is made court painter to Philip IV of Spain; Gianlorenzo Bernini at age 25 creates his Baroque statue of David |
| | 1624 | Richelieu is made Louis XIII's first minister |
| | 1625 | Charles I ascends the throne of England; King Christian IV of Denmark enters the Thirty Years' War on the Protestant side, and Wallenstein creates an army for the emperor Ferdinand; Hugo Grotius writes *On the Law of War and Peace,* a pioneering text in international law |
| | 1626 | Army of the Catholic League defeats Christian IV in the Battle of Lutter |

French 1625

| | |
|---|---|
| 1628 | William Harvey publishes his treatise on the circulation of blood; Parliament in England adopts the Petition of Right, asking the king to suspend his use of the royal prerogative |
| 1629 | Emperor Ferdinand issues the Edict of Restitution, returning all lands seized from the Catholic Church since 1555; Bernini is appointed official architect in charge of St. Peter's |
| 1630 | Gustavus Adolphus enters the Thirty Years' War to aid the German Protestants |
| 1631 | Adolphus defeats the army of the Catholic League at the Battle of Breitenfeld in the first significant Protestant victory of the war |
| 1632 | Galileo publishes the *Dialogue on the Two Chief Systems of the World;* the Swedish army defeats Wallenstein's army in the Battle of Lützen, but the Swedish king is killed; Anthony Van Dyck becomes court painter to Charles I |
| 1633 | Galileo is forced by the Inquisition to recant his heretical ideas |
| 1635 | The Peace of Prague ends the third phase of the Thirty Years' War; France declares war on the Hapsburgs; the French Academy is founded by Cardinal Richelieu to purify language and literature |
| 1636 | Harvard University is founded |
| 1637 | Ferdinand dies and is succeeded as Holy Roman emperor by his son; René Descartes publishes his *Discourse on Method,* setting forth his universe based on reason |
| 1638 | *Dialogues Concerning Two New Sciences* by Galileo appears; Louis XIV is born to Anne of Austria and Louis XIII |

French 1635

| 1639 | Jean Racine, classical French dramatist, is born |
|------|------|
| 1640 | Frederick William, the Great Elector, begins his 48-year rule in Brandenburg-Prussia; Wenceslaus Hollar publishes *Habits of English Women* |
| 1641 | Descartes' *Meditations* appear, arguing the superiority of the mind over the senses |
| 1642 | England's Long Parliament presents its nineteen propositions designed to transfer sovereignty from the king to Parliament; Charles I rejects them, and the English civil war begins; Rembrandt paints *The Night Watch,* a group portrait of a Dutch shooting company; Cardinal Richelieu dies, and Cardinal Mazarin succeeds him as chief minister of France; Sir Isaac Newton is born; theaters in England are closed |
| 1643 | Louix XIII dies and is succeeded by five-year-old Louis XIV under the regency of his mother; Evangelista Torricelli, Italian physicist, invents the barometer |
| 1644 | Oliver Cromwell's army defeats the Royalists in the Battle of Marston Moor, winning his first decisive victory for Parliamentarians; Milton writes his *Areopagitica,* Descartes his *Principles of Philosophy* |
| 1645 | Cromwell's victory at Naseby ends England's first civil war; Pascal perfects his *pascaline,* the world's first calculating machine |
| 1646 | Charles I surrenders to the Scots; Gottfried Wilhelm Leibnitz, German mathematician and philosopher, is born |
| 1647 | Johannes Helveius publishes *Selenographia,* an illustrated study of the moon |

| | 1648 | England's second civil war begins with the Scots, now allies of Charles I; the Peace of Westphalia ends the Thirty Years' War; Academy of Painting and Sculpture is founded in France |
|---|---|---|
| **RECONSTRUCTION IN GERMANY, THE FRONDE IN FRANCE, THE COMMONWEALTH IN ENGLAND** c. 1648–1660 | 1649 | The Wars of the Fronde begin in France; Charles I is tried and beheaded as a tyrant, traitor, murderer and public enemy |
| | 1650 | René Descartes dies in Stockholm |
| | 1651 | Thomas Hobbes publishes *The Leviathan,* his political treatise on the nature of the state |
| | 1652 | England and Holland begin the first of three wars for control of overseas commerce; the Italian composer Jean Baptiste Lully enters the service of Louis XIV |
| | 1653 | England's first and only written constitution makes Cromwell Lord Protector of the English Commonwealth; the Long Parliament is dissolved |
| | 1654 | Queen Christina of Sweden abdicates and is succeeded by Charles X; Pascal has a vision of God and turns from mathematics to religion |
| | 1655 | Charles X attacks Poland to make the Baltic a Swedish lake |
| | 1656 | James Harrington completes *Oceana,* his concept of a utopian commonwealth |
| | 1659 | *Les Préscieuses Ridicules,* Molière's first comedy of manners, is produced in Paris |
| | 1660 | Charles II is asked to restore the monarchy in England; Von Guericke invents the first rotating electrical generator |

French 1650

# BACKGROUND

By the close of the sixteenth century the dis-unity and dissension caused by the Reformation had still not been resolved, and it took the terrible bloodletting of the Thirty Years' War, a struggle which lasted from 1618 to 1648 and involved all of Europe, to finally expiate the tensions between Protestants and Catholics. Meanwhile a new cultural style, called *Baroque,* had begun to develop in Italy around 1600 as a result of the Council of Trent's attempt to renew the Catholic faith by using the arts as propaganda, working directly on the senses to convince the viewer of the richness, grandeur, and glory of the Catholic faith. This upsurge in the arts and renewal of faith came to be known as the *Counter-Reformation,* and Rome once again became the center for this reintegration of art and culture with the power of the Church.

The term *Baroque* (which may have come from the Portuguese term for irregular pearl) was first used in a disparaging way to describe the asymmetry and excess of early-seven-teenth-century Italian art, but today it has become a generic term for describing the art and culture of the period between 1600 and 1750. There are many artistic tendencies within this style—the most important of which are the flamboyant, classical, and realistic. The *flamboyant,* or operatic Baroque, occurred in Italy and Flanders in the first half of the seventeenth century and is closely related to the invention of opera. The *classical Baroque* is connected with the court of Louis XIV, the theater of Molière and Racine, and the painting of Poussin. The *realistic Baroque* developed as a minor artistic outlook under the painter Caravaggio in Italy and spread to Spain in the art of Velásquez and to Holland in the art of Rembrandt and his contemporaries.

The new era was passionate, colorful, extravagant, and theatrical. Explorations of the sixteenth century had opened up an expanded world, and Baroque expansiveness led to a new concept of human beings and their universe. The study by Galileo, Kepler, and Copernicus of heavenly bodies and celestial light reinforced interest in theatrical lighting in painting, sculpture, and theater and in move-ment outward and upward in all the arts. Descartes made space and what occupies it the sole basis for reality; Pascal spoke of the infinite spaces of the universe; and Milton coined the phrase "the vast and boundless deep." *Light* became a metaphor for *truth* in an age devoted to rational thought, and from this concept developed the term *enlightenment.*

The Baroque Period was an age of theater in which opera was invented as an art form to combine spectacle, music, cloud machines, choreographed action, dance, and human passion, thus involving the viewer in the delights of sensuous experience after a century of inward-ness and repression. Even the literary arts acquired a richly expressive language involving the description, presentation, conflict, and resolution of powerful human emotions. Magnificence and splendor framed the life at the Catholic courts of Europe, and even in Protestant countries such as Holland, there was a sober expansiveness and conservative richness.

In politics, Britain, was embroiled in a civil war that was partly religious but more specifically a contest between the old medieval ideal of kingship and a new, enlightened view of monarchy in which the king listened to the people's representatives. It ended with the closing of all the theaters, the beheading of the king, and a period of repressed Puritanism that was not released until Charles II came back to England in 1660. In central Europe the ruin of the Thirty Years' War caused Germany to be removed from the cultural-artistic scene until the eighteenth century and fostered a rampant nationalism among all the participants that came to replace religion as the key to war and politics. Spain, weakened both by the loss of Holland and by overextension abroad, declined as a major participant in European politics, even though it still had great financial and land assets abroad. Its court remained very conservative, looking to the past instead of the future, as can be seen from the court portraits by Velásquez. Protestant Holland, having established its independence, entered a golden age of commerce and art, while the Catholic Netherlands to the south also entered upon a golden age of art and culture—richly represented by great artists such as Rubens and Van Dyck. In France the weakness of Louis XIII led his chief minister, Cardinal Richelieu, to consolidate all power in the central government, preparing the way for the personal power and dictatorial authority of Louis XIV. After one last uprising of the nobles in the Wars of the Fronde, France became one of the most tightly organized and centralized governments in Europe. Italy, although once again established as the home of the Catholic Church with Rome as one of the great Baroque cities of Europe, was still disunited and powerfully influenced by Spanish culture which still ruled the southern half of the peninsula. Finally the colonies in the New World began to grow and prosper and became a source of money, a place for excess population, a markct for goods, and a secondary battlefield for European dynastic politics.

As an example of the compositional patterns that were at work in the new Baroque style, let us look at an aerial view of St. Peter's in Rome (Fig. 14-1). The facade, designed by Maderna, used colossal columns, similar to the pilasters Michelangelo had used at the sides and the rear of the church, and created a crescendo of movement to the center by beginning on the outside with flat pilasters and then working to round columns toward the center—creating an increased spatial movement and projection outward from the facade. But this sense of movement was not fully realized until Bernini added the great piazza based on an expanding ellipse connected to a diverging square. The effect is of a great embracing, expansive gesture that reaches out to enclose space in a dynamic thrust of movement. This was the basis of all flamboyant Baroque design—expansion and contraction of space to give movement and climax—a pattern used in architecture, sculpture, painting, clothing, and in the blocking of opera choruses and corps de ballet.

## THE BASIC COSTUME SILHOUETTE

After a century of rigidity and repression, the clothing of the early Baroque, mirroring the new philosophical and artistic outlook, used relaxed fabrics that flowed and expanded outward from the body. Compare, for example, the qualities of dress in the *Evening Ball for the Wedding of the Duc de Joyeuse,* dated about 1581 (see Fig. 13-5), with those in the famous *The Garden of Love* by Rubens, dated about 1632 (Fig. 14-2). It is as if the ruffs had suddenly melted into soft lace collars and the boning, padding, and forcing of the body had relaxed into an easy expansion of the clothing away from the contours of the body. The tortured, excessively decorated fabric surfaces have been replaced by an interest in the natural character of the fabric itself. Like architecture, sculpture, and painting in the Baroque era, the costumes moved, expanded, and spread out into space to create a sense of size and grandeur. The men's hats, in particular, had bigger brims than ever before and were worn casually on one side of the head. Women's skirts blossomed out from the body without the inhibiting control of braid and jewelry, and the natural fabric surfaces shimmered and moved with a new sense of freedom.

Rubens' *The Garden of Love,* an imaginative painting rathcr than an exact rendering of fashion, gives us the mood and feeling of the new style, but not the facts and details. However, a look at Abraham Bosse's print *The Costume Ball* gives an excellent example of the overall fashion silhouettes of this early Baroque dress as well as information on individual variations (Fig. 14-3).

The male doublet was usually unstiffened with a slightly raised waist, and skirts could be cut in one with the top or added as peplum tabs at the waist. The waist was frequently decorated with *points,* or metal-tagged ribbon bows, which had originally been drawn through eyelets in the waist to hold up the knee breeches. The latter had now lost their padding and could be either loose or baggy to the knee or long and tapering, often with buttons, bows, or braid on the outside seam. They usually fin-

(a)
design for choir screen for Winchester
Cathedral by Inigo Jones, ca. 1638

(b)
Baroque
cartouche—Fountain
of Trevi, Rome

Aerial view of St. Peter's; facade designed by Maderna in 1607, colonnade and piazza designed by Bernini in A.D. 1656. The facade moves toward the center, while the colonnade expands into an ellipse, contracts sharply, and then expands again into an expanding square or trapezoid—all to give dynamic movement and expansion to the space enclosed. Photo courtesy of Alinari, Florence.

(c)
English chair
1630

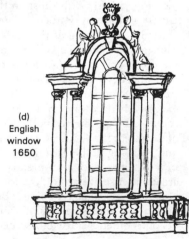

(d)
English
window
1650

FIGURE 14-1

238

(a) shirt with drawstring at waist ca. 1650

(b) basic cut of the rabat collar ca. 1650

(c) falling band or lace collar ca. 1635

(d) narrow breeches

(e) linen underdrawers

(f) full breeches

(g) cassock slung over shoulder

(h) wide breeches

(n) embroidered linen boot hose to protect silk stockings

Peter Paul Rubens, *The Garden of Love;* The Prado, Madrid; ca. 1632–1634. Illustrates the expanding costume forms on full earthy bodies that mark the height of the early Baroque style. The tensions of mannerism have been released into soft collars and boots, rich natural textures that speak for themselves without jewelry and braid coverings, and hats that expand out into space and away from the head. Photo courtesy of the Prado, Madrid.

(o) leather boot with extra sole

(i) cassock made into a cape by buttoning sleeves to body at the front and back sides

hats

(j)

(k)

(l) shoe with shoe rose

(m) lobster-tail helmet—English

(p) motif

**FIGURE 14–2**

239

(a)
dutch boned jacket

(b)
laced
stomacher
under
lace collar 1640

hat for upper-
middle-class
woman 1640s
(c)

(d)
English lady's riding
hat 1635

(e)
sleeve

(f)
basic
hairdo
1630s

(g)
sleeve

Abraham Bosse, *The Costume Ball;* engraving; ca. 1635. Illustrates the looser, softer, more relaxed fashions that replaced the tense, artificial, grotesque dress of late mannerism. Note the growing attention placed on the feet through the use of boots, heeled shoes, large *shoe roses,* and the new ballet positions for poses. Photo courtesy of the Bibliothèque Nationale, Paris.

(i)
boned
corset,
mid–17th c.

(h)
Spanish 1635

(j)
lady's
shoe
inside a
velvet covered
overshoe

(k)
housewife

(l)
wealthy
middle-class
woman ca. 1640s

**FIGURE 14–3**

240

ished in loose ribbon garters tied below the knee. Sometimes the bottom of the trousers was loose and finished with a row or two of ribbon loops, a style that was to gain great importance about the middle of the century. High, soft leather boots were worn indoors, as well as out, over silk boot hose with lace tops that fell over the cuffs of the boots. When boots were not worn, silk stockings covered the lower legs, and shoes with moderate heels and rosettes for decoration shod the feet. Collars were of the finest lace and fell widely over the shoulders. Sleeves were full, usually with one or more openings up the arm to expose the rich material of the shirt beneath, and such openings were frequently set with buttons and holes down the length of the arm. Circular, half-length cloaks were worn over one shoulder and under the other arm, falling diagonally across the back. Hats were soft felt or beaver, wide-brimmed, trimmed with ostrich plumes, and worn at a jaunty angle.

In feminine dress the corset and farthingale were put aside, the waistline rose and was no longer pointed, and several full skirts, the top one often draped up over the ones beneath, gave the female form a full, healthy, sensuous silhouette (Figs. 14–2,3). The bodice was usually low-cut with a rich lace collar to cover or frame the bosom and finished in a waistline of square tabs. The sleeves, which like the male costume ended in wide lace cuffs, were full and large, sometimes open down the entire length to show a lining or undersleeve and caught at the elbow with silk ribbon bows. Sometimes the waistline was also finished with a silk ribbon sash or with ribbon points like the male doublet. The hair was worn with a fringe of bangs on the forehead and two puffs of shoulder-length ringlets falling forward over the ears. Hats similar to those of the men were worn for riding, while the hooded cloak was the standard wrap for evening and travel.

## THE EARLY BAROQUE (CAVALIER)

**Masculine Dress**  As the stiffened and wired collars of the early 1620s gradually relaxed and softened into flat collars or limp, unstarched ruffs, men's hair also began to grow longer and to fall in a casual flow of soft curls on the shoulder, as if released from the inhibitions against length and fullness created by the high neckwear of the Elizabethan-Jacobean Period.

Daniel Mytens' portrait of Charles I of England, painted in 1629 (Fig. 14–4), gives an excellent view of the new collar and hair styles along with changing developments in footwear, doublet, and breeches. The limp ruff looks a little formal but much more comfortable than the wired and starched ruff of preceding years. The hair, too, seems to fall easily and naturally on the shoulders. The doublet has vertical openings down the front and in the sleeves that allow the shirt to show, giving a renewed sense of ease to the figure beneath. It also gives the illusion that the inner body garment, the shirt, is expanding outward through the outergarment with ease and without constriction. The waist is still pointed but not as stiff as in the past, and

the waist itself is higher than normal and set with points or ribbon bows that connect both breeches and hose to the doublet. The peplum is divided into a series of wide tabs. The knee-length breeches are quite slim and taper to the knee, finishing in a row of ribbon points, while the boot hose are drawn up over the knee. The soft, tight-fitting, deerskin boots fall loosely about the ankles and are equipped with large quatre-foil spur leathers over the instep with spurs at the heel, giving a manly, outdoor, sporting touch to this basically indoor court costume.

Compare this portrait of Charles I with another done by the famous Flemish court painter Anthony Van Dyck, painted about six years later in 1635 (Fig. 14–5). The king has chosen to be painted outdoors after dismounting from his horse. His kingliness lies not in his accouterments or robes of state, and he therefore has none of the heavy look of authority that one finds in the portraits of Henry VIII (see Fig. 12–2) or Queen Elizabeth (see Fig. 13–3). Charles seems to dominate with the force of his

FIG. 14-4 Daniel Mytens, *Charles I of England;* Metropolitan Museum of Art; 1629. This is a transition costume from late mannerism to early Baroque. Note the continuance of the *ruff,* the disappearance of the *peascod* stomach, the less rigid line now followed by the doublet, the slim unstiffened knee breeches, and the soft boots. Photo courtesy of the Metropolitan Museum of Art.

FIG. 14-5 Anthony Van Dyck, *Charles I Hunting;* The Louvre, Paris; ca. 1635. Illustrates by contrast with the preceding portrait the rich simplicity without decoration that prevailed in the best of male fashions by the middle of the thirties. Note the angle of the beaver hat, the simple richness and relaxation of the satin doublet and suede breeches, and the perfect fit of the deerskin boots. Photo courtesy of the French Musées Nationaux.

inner personality and aristocratic manner and is dressed in the simplest of fashions, with no trim or decoration of any kind. The richness comes from the fabrics themselves—beaver hat, lace collar, satin doublet, suede breeches, and deerskin boots. The beaver hat with a single white plume is cocked jauntily to one side, framing the face, and his hair falls freely onto the shoulders and down the back; the lace collar is restrained and unostentatious; the satin doublet is apparently cut-in-one without a defined waistline; the breeches have no trim whatsoever; the boot hose are conservatively but casually gartered just below the knee; and the slim boots have a moderate cuff, spur

leathers, and spurs. The sword is slung casually over the shoulder on a bandolier, and one hand is gloved and loosely holds the other. It is a portrait that beautifully sums up the casual elegance of the early Baroque style and fulfills the descriptive, rather than political, use of the term *cavalier.*

Abraham Bosse in his engraving *The Costume Ball* gives us an excellent picture of the basics of the new early Baroque style as well as its many variations (Fig. 14-3). One is struck by the central figure with a large-brimmed, soft hat set with plumes that lead up and out into space (Fig. 14-2j,k), as well as by the varied, loose-flowing hair styles worn by the other men in the scene. Note the *love-lock* worn by the man seated at left. This hair style in which a curl or strand of hair was tied with a ribbon was meant to be a love token to a particular lady admirer. The style is usually attributed to Louis XIII who had beautiful, flowing hair and loved to call attention to it with the use of the bow tied to the love-lock.

Note, also, that most of the doublets in the scene have either no pointed waist or very moderate ones, and the waistline is slightly raised. By this time most of the rosette bows or points about the waist are just decorative, as it had been discovered that hooks on pants and hose fastened to eyelets on the inside belt of the doublet gave the best form of support. Notice that most of the doublet skirts are moderately long and cut in fewer sections, while sleeves seem shorter and are frequently open to reveal the shirt. The most striking accents on the doublet are the extremely rich, Flemish lace collars and cuffs (Fig. 14-2c). The breeches are usually loose at the hips and taper to the knee, although there are also examples of blousy bloomers to the knee. Some breeches fasten to the knee with ribbon garters; others are somewhat looser and finished with ribbon loops (Fig. 14-2d,f,h).

Shirts became very important at this time and were cut with much fullness in sleeves and body, usually from a very fine grade of linen embroidered with openwork trim (Fig. 14-2a). The major decorative accents to the male costume, aside from collars and cuffs, were the ribbon bows, braid, and buttons used on the sides of trousers and along sleeve openings, and the lace tops to boot hose that were worn over the regular hose to protect them from boot leather (Fig. 14-2n). In fact, boots were another unique characteristic of male dress at this time. Even though moderately heeled shoes with rosettes were the chief indoor footwear, soft boots with folded-down cuffs that slid down around the ankle and gave a casual, swinging gait to the wearer were used for both indoor and outdoor wear (Fig. 14-2o). Notice, also, that the sword belt has been replaced with a baldric slung over the shoulder to support the sword in a much looser manner than in the past. When cloaks were worn, they were slung over one shoulder only, although some gentlemen still

wore the Spanish-style cape that fit more formally over both shoulders.

Another form of outerwrap, often seen in the illustrations for *The Three Musketeers,* was a kind of cape-coat in which the sections covering the arms could be unbuttoned from the back and front panels and rebuttoned to form a sleeved outercoat (Fig. 14-2i). Also related to this, usually as part of military wear, was the *cassock,* which was an extended-sleeved jerkin that usually reached to just above the knees and was frequently made of suede or leather (Fig. 14-2g).

By mid-century, changes began to take place in male dress, marked by a shortening of the doublet and a widening of the bottom of the pants (Fig. 14-2b). In a portrait of William II of Orange and his wife painted by Honthorst or one of his followers about 1650, we can see that the collar is a little stiffer and with less frilliness in the lace edges; the doublet is shorter, open below the neck and revealing much more of the shirt; and the breeches are so wide at the knee as to create the effect of a divided skirt (Fig. 14-6). Ribbon loops act as bands of decorative accents at the waist and knee, and the boots ride even lower about the ankle with more of the boot hose showing than ever before (Fig. 14-2h). A variation in the new breeches, a style that was to be important after 1660, was a shorter skirt with many rows of ribbon loops worn over blousy bloomer breeches gartered below the knee. But from 1650 to 1660 most commonly worn were the wide breeches open at the knee, similar to modern culottes, which were known as *Rhinegrave breeches,* since they seem to have originated in the counties along the Rhine River.

Military garb during this period was still very personalized with no set uniforms (even though the French musketeers did wear a version of the cape-coat with the emblem of their corps on front and back) (Fig. 14-2i). Gentlemen soldiers still wore armor—sometimes a full suit to the knees with leather boots, but more frequently a breastplate, gorget, arm and waistpieces, and a richly decorated helmet. The leather cassock was frequently worn with or without the breastplate, although a metal

**FIG. 14-6** Gerrit van Honthorst(?), *William II of Orange and His Wife Mary Stuart;* Gemeentemuseum, The Hague; ca. 1650. Illustrates the changes in dress that began to develop in the middle of the seventeenth century. Note the *rabat* collar on William, the short doublet with much of the shirt showing, and the new petticoat or *Rhinegrave breeches* that are like a modern divided skirt. His wife has returned to the corset and has no collar surrounding her neckline. Photo courtesy of the Gemeentemuseum, The Hague.

gorget was usually worn at all times with a helmet. The most distinctive new style in helmets was that known as the lobster-tail that we now associate with the English Civil War of this period (Fig. 14-2m). Weapons included heavy swords with hand-protecting hilts; muskets; pistols; halberds; and the light dress sword that was similar to modern fencing weapons.

Sober middle-class dress for men usually consisted of a plain, wool jacket or doublet and knee pants with a simple, flat linen collar and cuffs. Stockings were of rough ribbed wool, and shoes were of a heavy leather with the side pieces fastening over the tongue with leather latchets (Fig. 14-2l). Hats were fairly broad-brimmed and often had a high, sloping crown. Peasants still wore a loose jacket or smock over a shirt with nondescript breeches and wooden shoes.

**Feminine Dress** Beginning about 1620 rapid changes occurred in female dress in France, Flanders, and England; in Italy and Spain, however, the last vestiges of mannerist dress ideas continued until almost 1660. As an example of what an aristocratic lady of northern Italy was wearing in 1625, look at Anthony Van Dyck's portrait of Marchesa Balbi, painted while Van Dyck was a resident of Genoa (Fig. 14-7). Here the marchesa still wears a large, platter ruff of semitransparent fabric pleated into very large, open convolutions on top of a very rigidly corseted bodice with a deep stomacher and wide peplum. Hanging sleeves open to show a rich, stiff lining framing stiff, padded undersleeves that also end in pleated ruffs at the cuff. The heavy skirt with strong braided trim down the front and around the bottom appears to be worn over a small bolster or hip roll, while the hair is simply drawn back into a jeweled cap. In every way this costume is a continuation of the Spanish mannerist style and gives no hint of the changes taking place at this time in France and in Flanders.

Eight years later when Van Dyck had returned from Italy to his native Flanders and subsequently became court painter to Charles I of England, his portrait of the English queen Henrietta Maria shows all the elements of the new early Baroque style (Fig. 14-8). The emphasis is now on the soft, full, rounded curves of the female body, with an expansive fullness to the silhouette. Her hair is in loose, full curls at the side of the head with one long curl trailing on the left shoulder. She wears a large-brimmed, tilted hat with a single plume (in imitation of the male styles of the period), and the

FIG. 14-7 Anthony Van Dyck, *Marchesa Balbi;* National Gallery, Washington; 1622-1626. The Antwerp-born marchesa wears a gold-brocaded, dark green gown with a silver *ruff* embroidered in gold, and the effect is still darkly mannerist even though it is much more relaxed in fit and line than the Spanish style of the late sixteenth century. Photo courtesy of the National Gallery, Washington.

FIG. 14-8 Anthony Van Dyck, *Queen Henrietta Maria of England;* National Gallery, Washington; 1633. Note the contrast between female fashion in Italy and England in only five years. This portrait fully illustrates the new normal waistline, expansive silhouette, short sleeves to just below the elbow, the large-brimmed riding hat, and the soft lace collar and cuffs that were the admired female style by the mid-thirties. Photo courtesy of the National Gallery, Washington.

neck is softly covered with an expansive collar of very rich lace (Fig. 14-3d). The bodice still has a slightly stiffened, although very short, stomacher at the center front, a fairly normal waistline, and a series of large peplums that spread out over the skirt all around the waist. The soft, bloused sleeves are quite short, ending in fluffy, lace cuffs just below the elbow (Fig. 14-3g), and the skirt probably has no underpinnings other than several fairly stiff petticoats. Here the costume fabric, except for the soft braid on the edges of the bodice and down the front of the skirt, is allowed to reflect

its natural richness without the mannerist interference from braid, slashing, or jewelry.

Similar silhouette effects are to be seen in Abraham Bosse's *The Costume Ball* from France (Fig. 14-3). The woman in the center has a collar that is still slightly starched and may be wired to stand away from the dress as a frame for the fairly low décolletage. Other women wear the full, lace collar that comes up to the base of the neck like the man's collar or the soft, but deep, lace edging that falls away from the wide, open neckline (sometimes there were several layers in these lace collars). Most of the bodices show a slightly raised waistline, and some have peplum tabs (Fig. 14–3b). The skirts either have a line or two of trim down the center front or are open up the center front over an underskirt or a contrasting panel. Sleeves are much shorter than in the past, ending on the forearm in a deep lace cuff. The sleeves are usually open in one or more places to show the lining or undersleeve, and the whole is puffed out once or twice and caught in with ribbons (Fig. 14–3e,g). The coiffures throughout the Bosse engraving are all quite similar. They involve a fringe of bangs at the front with a part from the temples to the nape of the neck from which the side hair falls in puffs of tight curls over the ears (Fig. 14–3f). The rest of the hair at the back was braided or rolled into a bun, placed high on the back of the head, and then sometimes covered with a jeweled cap or a tiny velvet beret. Hats were worn primarily for riding or travel.

Female accessories during the 1620s and 1630s included muffs of fur for winter; folding fans, as well as some plumed ones and the older rigid variety; masks worn for protection against the cold or as a disguise; and scarfs, used either around the neck or over the head. Shoes had moderately high heels and usually had richly embroidered uppers and leather soles (Fig. 14–3j).

In the latter part of the 1640s, the female bodice once again became quite stiff with a pointed waist and a back opening and was frequently worn over a corset (Fig. 14–3i). Sometimes the bodice opened center front and was caught together with brooches, allowing puffs of the chemise to show, as is the case in the portrait of William of Orange and Mary Stuart (Fig. 14–6). Mary's gown in this portrait also displays the soft sleeves with a little of the chemise showing through one long opening that had replaced the slightly stiffer double puffs that were popular in the previous decade. The center front of the pointed bodice at this time was usually stiffened by a removable ornamental *busk* which was a broad metal,

wooden, or ivory stay that fitted into the lining of the corset or the bodice; the neckline was a soft oval and often without any trim. The center front of the bodice might also be covered by a series of ribbon bows that diminished in size as they approached the point of the bodice (*bows à la échelle*). The skirt lacked the fullness just below the waist that had characterized those of the 1630s and tended to be longer behind than in front giving a slight train. Hair was treated much as in the preceding decade except that it was much fuller and somewhat longer on the sides.

**FIG. 14–9** Diego Velásquez, *Infanta Margarita;* the Prado Museum; ca. 1660. Illustrates the retrogressive female fashions in Spain as late as 1600. Although the neckline and bodice follow the new early Baroque line, the expanding peplum and skirt spread over an elliptical *farthingale* recall the deformities of mannerism. Photo courtesy of The Prado, Madrid.

Because of the conservative reluctance in Spain to forget its great past and to accept the new artistic styles of the seventeenth century (Fig. 14–3h), there remained a strong adherence to the stiff farthingale under the skirt and a rigidity in fabric treatment as shown in the famous portrait *Infanta Margarita* painted by Velásquez in 1659 (Fig. 14–9). The gown is a combination of shimmering silver and light coral silk, and every attempt is made to stiffen it into an enormous horizontal width. The hair is dressed with a great horizontal thrust of hair to the left to be balanced by plumes to the right. The neckline, although reflective of those in France, is very broad and accented by black trim; the sleeves are puffed and padded, ending in an almost sixteenth-century manner, even though deep-layered cuffs were seventeenth; and the ellipse of the peplum and skirt over the supporting farthingale are a fantastic continuance and final perversion of the original farthingales of the sixteenth century. Although sharply out of step with the rest of continental fashion, this unique combination of sixteenth- and seventeenth-century style elements is fascinating, dramatic, and magnificent in its own peculiar way.

Middle- and lower-class women from 1620 to 1660 usually wore severely limited and simplified versions of the upper-class wear. Various lace and linen caps were usually worn on the head, with a broad-brimmed hat with sloping crown worn over it for marketing and travel. The neck was usually covered in a flat, linen collar—sometimes edged with a little simple lace; the bodice was often laced up the front over the chemise; the sleeves were moderately full to the forearm ending in linen cuffs; and the skirt of hard wool was frequently looped up in front over a colored petticoat (Fig. 14–3a, e,k,l). Aprons were also very popular for the middle-class housewife. Lower-class women wore much the same but usually without any collars, cuffs, or trim.

## FABRICS

Satin was one of the mainstay fabrics of the time with soft velvets a close second. What was very different in the fabrics of this period was the softness of the fabric in most of the weaving. Whereas the sixteenth and very early seventeenth centuries had demanded stiff fabrics, the early Baroque usage demanded soft, crisp, flowing fabrics that were neither limp nor stiff. There was also much less use of tightly brocaded materials, allowing the natural surfaces of fabric to speak for themselves, and a great appreciation for the highlights of silken folds and natural, crinkled surfaces. Woolens and linens were also popular—the former for the middle class and common people, the latter for collars, cuffs, and shirts. The newest fabric used as a major costume accent was lace, both Venetian point and bobbin laces from Flanders.

## ARTS AND ARTIFACTS

The interior decorating of the early seventeenth century used many of the design and decoration motifs of the later Mannerist Renaissance but with a new openness and relaxation. There was still oak paneling on the walls, plaster strapwork on the ceilings, floral garlands and mythological gods and animals in the decoration, and heavy carved oak pieces as furniture (Fig. 14–1a,b,c,d). The latter usually followed the architectural usage of arcaded columned backs and legs, although there were still examples of the melon-bulb accent on bed posts and table legs. Tables were set with elaborate silver and gold plate, but the less wealthy set their tables with pewter, horn, and wood. Musical instruments changed little, and the emphasis was on lutes, fiddles, recorders, and occasional virginals.

Accessories included the sash and baldric-bandolier, each used frequently to support the dress sword that accompanied all men of fashion. This was worn instead of the dagger and consisted of a thin blade with a hand-protecting hilt inside a very slim scabbard. Walking sticks became more popular and usually consisted of a simple shaft of wood finished with a metal or carved wooden knob. The walking stick of the period was usually of hip height (as opposed to the chest-high sticks of the later seventeenth century). Gloves were still an important item of male dress and usually had gauntlet cuffs. Pouch purses were still often worn, but sometimes did not show when worn under the peplum of the doublet or jerkin. One interesting new accessory was the velvet patches used as a facial accent to cover a scar or pock from smallpox worn by both men and women. Another accessory that became prominent was the mask, used by ladies to protect their delicate faces or their reputations when they went to taverns or assignations (as well as by hired killers and highwaymen).

Muffs, seen occasionally in the sixteenth century, became a major craze in the seventeenth for court dandies and particularly for women, who during the winter months were seldom seen outdoors without them. Women also wore or carried gloves when outdoors; aprons were used for decoration as well as for practical purposes; and a ribbon or small waist sash was still frequently used for hanging keys, scissors, mirrors, and fans about the waist. Fans were becoming much more popular since the new, folding variety had come to replace the awkward, rigid shapes of the past. Most fans were still of a fairly large size and without the delicacy that would be achieved in the eighteenth century.

Jewelry for men usually consisted of brooches on hats, buttons, various pins, rings, orders for the neck, and sword hilts. The order was still the most rich and striking jeweled accessory for men, representing famous aristocratic honor societies like the Garter in England, the Fleece in Spain and the Netherlands, the Knights of Malta in Spain and southern Italy, and the Order of St. Esprit in France. Women's jewelry consisted of the occasional use of pearl earrings, much use of chokers and necklaces, neck chains, and brooches and clasps for collars, cuffs, and sleeve openings. The shorter sleeves on the gowns made bracelets more popular than at any time in the past, and the braids and buns at the back of the popular coiffures made jeweled combs a subtle accent at the back of the head.

Decorative motifs of the period continued to be formalized floral patterns geometrically arranged, but without the crowding and tension that had marked the use of such motifs in the sixteenth century (Fig. 14–2p).

## VISUAL SOURCES

Probably the outstanding artist to consult for fashions of this period is Anthony Van Dyck, who between 1630 and his death in 1640 recorded all the best-known attributes of the new style as it moved from Flanders and France to England. Other important sources are the engravings of Abraham Bosse, Wenceslaus Hollar, and Jacques Callot and the portraits by Peter Paul Rubens, Frans Hals, Daniel Mytens, Michiel Mierevelt, and Gerrit van Honthorst. The single greatest source for Spanish dress is the portraiture of Velásquez.

The best repositories for these sources are the National Gallery of Art in Washington, the National Gallery in London, the Louvre, the Metropolitan Museum in New York, various private collections in England, the royal collection at Windsor, and the Prado in Madrid. Useful written references are Charles Blitzer's *Age of Kings,* Michael Kitson's *The Age of Baroque,* and the Cunningtons' *Handbook of English Costume in the Seventeenth Century.*

# SUMMARY

This was a period of loosening tension and a return to an admiration of the natural human form expanding outward through clothing into surrounding space. It was a period of theatricality, richness, and grandeur without the inhibitions and restraints applied during the Mannerist Renaissance. The ideal for women during the height of this period was a fullness and ripeness in form and clothing that underlined the ideal of expansion into space. For men the ideal was a swaggering, cavalier manner in clothes that were relatively full and loose, worn with a casual asymmetry in boot tops, hat angles, and cloak drapings.

# chapter XV

# Late Baroque (Restoration)

## Chronology

(ca. 1660–1715)

REIGN OF
CHARLES II
IN ENGLAND
1660–1685

French 1665

| | |
|---|---|
| 1660 | Restoration of the monarchy under Charles II in England |
| 1661 | Mazarin dies and Louis XIV begins his personal rule; Robert Boyle publishes *The Sceptical Chymist* and formulates his famous theory of gases |
| 1664 | New Amsterdam becomes New York; witchcraft at Salem |
| 1665 | Philip IV of Spain dies and is succeeded by his son Charles II, a sickly monarch who becomes the last of the Spanish Hapsburgs; Bernini visits Paris and sculpts a bust of Louis XIV; the Great Plague of London kills more than 60,000 people; English physicist Robert Hooke publishes *Micrographia,* describing cells in plant tissues |
| 1666 | London's Great Fire destroys two-thirds of the city; Jean Baptiste Colbert, Louis XIV's first minister, founds the French Academy of Science |
| 1667 | Louis XIV begins the War of |

Devolution against the Spanish Netherlands to seize them for France; John Milton publishes *Paradise Lost;* Racine writes *Andromaque,* the play that establishes him as a major neoclassical writer of tragedy in the tradition of Corneille

1668      The Triple Alliance is formed by the Dutch, Swedes, and English against Louis XIV's aggression in the Spanish Netherlands; Jean de la Fontaine publishes the first of his sophisticated *Fables*

1670      The Treaty of Dover secretly allies Louis XIV with Charles II; Pascal's *Pensées,* attacking Cartesian thought, are published posthumously

1672      Charles II and Louis XIV join in a war on the Dutch; Jean Baptiste Lully, court composer to Louis XIV, founds the Royal Academy of Music

1674      England withdraws from the Dutch War; Nicolas Boileau publishes *The Art of Poetry,* codifying French literary style; the Dutch scientist Anton van Leeuwenhoek gives the first accurate description of red corpuscles in the blood

1678      Peace of Nijmegen brings the Dutch War to a close; France acquires Franche-Comté; Samuel Butler completes *Hudibras,* his epic mocking Puritanism

1679      Act of Habeas Corpus enacted in England

1682      Louis XIV moves with his court into his newly expanded and remodeled Palace of Versailles; John Dryden's political satire *Absalom and Achitophel* is completed; Edmund Halley observes the comet now bearing his name; William Penn founds Pennsylvania

French 1675

| | 1683 | The Turks invade the Hapsburg lands of eastern Europe and lay siege to Vienna |
| | 1685 | Edict of Nantes, granting French Huguenots religious freedom, is revoked by Louis XIV; Charles II dies and is succeeded by his brother, James II; Johann Sebastian Bach is born in Eisenach; George Frederick Handel is born at Halle |

---

| | 1687 | Newton publishes *Philosophiae Naturalis Principia Mathematica* in which he announced the Law of Universal Gravitation |
| REIGNS OF JAMES II, WILLIAM AND MARY, AND QUEEN ANNE IN ENGLAND 1685–1714 | 1688 | Parliamentary enemies of James II force the king to flee and invite William of Orange to invade England |
| | 1689 | Declaration of Rights establishes England's constitutional government; William and Mary are declared the rulers of England; John Locke's *Letters on Toleration* are published, defending religious liberty |
| | 1690 | Locke's *Two Treatises on Civil Government* appears and is used as a defense of the Glorious Revolution of 1688 |
| | 1693 | College of William and Mary founded |
| | 1694 | Queen Mary of England dies of smallpox; the French Academy issues the first edition of its dictionary; the Bank of England is founded to lend money to the government; François Marie Arouet, later known as Voltaire, is born in Paris |
| | 1699 | Treaty of Karlowitz ends the Holy League's war with the Turks |

English 1688

| | |
|---|---|
| 1700 | The Great Northern War breaks out between Sweden and an alliance of Poland, Denmark, and Russia; the Swedes overwhelm the Russians at the Battle of Narva; William Congreve writes *The Way of the World,* the greatest of the Restoration comedies |
| 1701 | The Grand Alliance unites England, Holland, and Austria against the policies of Louis XIV; the War of Spanish Succession begins, pitting France against the Grand Alliance |
| 1704 | The French forces are routed by an Anglo-Dutch army under Marlborough at the famous Battle of Blenheim |
| 1707 | Union of England and Scotland |
| 1709 | The Russian army crushes the Swedes at the Battle of Poltava; the first critical edition of Shakespeare published by Nicholas Rowe |
| 1711 | Sir Christopher Wren's St. Paul's Cathedral is officially completed |
| 1713 | The Peace of Utrecht ends the War of Spanish Succession and establishes a new order in Europe; Gibraltar ceded to England |
| 1714 | Leibnitz publishes *Monadology,* expounding his famous theory that the universe is made up of particles called *monads;* Queen Anne dies and George of Hanover becomes George I of England |
| 1715 | Louis XIV dies after a 72-year reign as king of France; uprising in behalf of James Stuart, the Old Pretender |

French 1705

# BACKGROUND

When Charles II returned to England in 1660 to restore the monarchy, and Louis XIV on the death of Cardinal Mazarin in 1661 began his personal rule in France, the center of culture began to shift from Rome to Paris, and Baroque art began to move into a phase now known as *classic Baroque*.

Classic Baroque art, developed in Italy by artists such as Guercino, Domenichino, and the Carracci family, was more restrained in character than that of flamboyant Baroque and followed the precepts of the High Renaissance. It was this style that appealed to the dictatorial tastes of Louis XIV, who wished to use the arts to project his vision of centralized government, national unity, and royal control of all aspects of French life. The independent, exuberant noblemen of the past now became tame courtiers living with the king at Versailles, and all the arts were harnessed to propagandize for the disciplined, ordered, tightly controlled life of power and grandeur that was the ideal of the Sun King.

An excellent example of how Louis XIV used interior decoration to propagandize for his artistic ideals may be seen in the work of Charles Le Brun, Louis XIV's dictator of the arts, who designed the Salle des Gardes de la Reine at Versailles (Fig. 15-1). Here the richness that characterized the Roman flamboyant Baroque style has been tightly structured and controlled within the strong and rigid geometric regularity imposed on the rich ornamentation of this chamber.

If one attempted to condense the rules governing literature and the arts of this period, one might list the following five ideas:

1. Every aspect of a painting or a scene in a play should be appropriate to the situation and correctly used in relation to every other scene in a play or aspect in a composition.
2. All art should be composed on a high plane in an elevated style.
3. The subject matter for all serious art should be mythological or based on scenes from Roman, Greek, or Biblical history.
4. The individual aspects of nature or personality should be subordinated to the generalized, universal, and regular as opposed to the abnormal and irregular.
5. All artistic techniques should be based on the rules of the ancients as exemplified in the best classical models in art and literature from Greece, Rome, and the High Renaissance.

As one might expect at the court of a king who ruled for 72 years and believed in tight artistic rules and a closed view of French society, the culture of the French court by the late 1680s became rigid, heavy, tired, and exceedingly oppressive. The clothes, art, architecture, interiors, and furniture of the later years of Louis XIV's reign were, therefore, some of the most heavy, pompous, and formal examples in the history of art and culture.

Meanwhile Charles II of England, who had spent much of his exile in France, established a court that superficially copied much of its taste from the French and yet remained essentially English in its pragmatic and casual mixture of styles. There was no attempt at the single-minded precision, order, and structural unity that so occupied artists and writers in France, and it lacked the excessive grandeur and ceremonial formality that prevailed at the court of the Sun King. Despite many French influences, Restoration culture was more pragmatic, eclectic, comfortable, and even domestic. Like the plays of Shakespeare as compared to those of Corneille, Racine, and Molière, the English combined many influences from the past and present to achieve a Baroque style that was a comfortable pastiche of borrowed and native sources.

At the opening of the Restoration in England, the life of the aristocrats who returned from abroad with Charles II was in sharp contrast to the middle-class cultural life that had been developing in England since before the Commonwealth. The former were devoted to pleasure and the game of sexual pursuit, all of which were brilliantly expressed in the comedies of the Restoration. But after the death of

(a)
dormer window
Hotel des Invalides
ca. 1700

(b)
entry to Vaux le Vicomte
ca. 1660

Charles Le Brun, Salle des Gardes de la Reine, Versailles; ca. 1671–1681. Illustrates the restrained sense of grandeur in which ceiling paintings and wall decorations are locked into rigid geometric frames. Unlike Italian Baroque rooms, this chamber does not open out through illusionistic ceiling painting to another world but is circumscribed, measured, and closed. Photo courtesy of the French Musées Nationaux.

(c)
French
armchair
ca. 1670

(d)
English
chair
ca. 1665

**FIGURE 15–1**

255

Charles II and the expulsion of his brother James II, the reigns of William and Mary and Queen Anne were marked by a sharp turn to middle-class attitudes and bourgeois morality. Thus the arts and clothing between 1690 and 1710 became far more restrained, heavily bourgeois, and formal.

Politics in Europe at this time was mostly involved in containing the ambitious imperialism of Louis XIV. The French king at first tried to wrest the Spanish Netherlands away from Spain when he realized the political weakness of the sickly Charles II, the Spanish king. Later when Charles II died, Louis XIV attempted to set one of his own family on the throne of Spain—thus setting off the European conflagration of the War of Spanish Succession, in which he lost the war and yet gained a Bourbon king for the Spanish throne. In the north the Swedish king Charles XII attempted a great expansion against Russia, Poland and Denmark, but this ended in defeat. The Turks in the southeast also attempted an expansion into the Holy Roman Empire and even laid siege to Vienna, but were eventually driven back by Eugene of Savoy, one of the great generals of the age (along with England's duke of Marlborough). It was after this defeat that Austria and Vienna moved forward into a golden age of Baroque development.

In the New World, England consolidated its control of the eastern seaboard of what is now the United States, France dominated eastern Canada, and Spain held most of south and central America and Florida. Dissension among the countries at home led to the many small colonial wars in the New World.

In this age also major contributions were made to the world of science and the philosophy of government in the work of Isaac Newton and John Locke.

## THE BASIC COSTUME SILHOUETTE

As the center of Baroque artistic development shifted from Rome to Paris after the middle of the seventeenth century, the ideal changed from the passionate, theatrical, flamboyant Baroque of Rubens and Bernini to the logical, structured, classical Baroque of Cardinal Richelieu, Cardinal Mazarin, and Louis XIV. Frequently when one looks at the French clothing styles of the late seventeenth century, one sees only the rich use of bows, ribbons, and embroidered decoration and misses the careful structure that lies beneath.

To better understand this underlying structure, look at Gerard Terborch's *Portrait of an Unknown Man,* depicting an aristocratic Dutch gentleman about 1660 (Fig. 15–2). Since this simple black costume lacks the frivolous ribbons and ornamentation often seen on Louis XIV and his courtiers at this same time, it allows one to concentrate on the structure rather than the decorative accessories. Although the short line harmonies give the costume an undignified, almost humorous look to the modern eye, the basic shapes are very carefully structured from interlocking triangular shapes. Although the lace collar, full skirt, bolero jacket, steeple hat, and high-heeled shoes are often described in books on the early Restoration, rarely described is the carefully planned layering of the parts of the costume from top to bottom within the diamond-shaped silhouette of the whole. Like the interior decoration all richness and decoration were channeled into a controlled and structured silhouette. In women's clothing, the rounded oval neckline, triangular-shaped bodice, and contour-draped skirt—as seen in the anonymous portrait of Hortense Mancini, niece of Cardinal Mazarin—were also structured and controlled although to a lesser extent (Fig. 15–3). The lines of the costume expand up and down from the waist in a controlled manner, and the movement of the overskirt as it is draped over the underskirt to fall in a moderate train at the back is carefully calculated to give elegance and richness within a disciplined control.

The fashions in England at this time, although based on the same costume lines, were far less controlled in structure and silhouette

(a)
German
petticoat
breeches
ca. 1655–1660

(b)
rabat or
falling band
Dutch ca. 1665

(c)
cravat
of
venetian
lace
ca. 1680

(d)
English
hat and
rabat
ca. 1660

(i)
French
ca. 1670

(e)
man's shoe
with red
tongue and
heel
ca. 1670

(f)
shoe
with lace
windmill
wings and red
heels ca. 1675

(h)
cassock
with fringed-embroidered
sword baldric ca. 1670

(g)
Flemish petticoat
breeches ca. 1670

Gerard Terborch, *Portrait of an Unknown Man;* National
Gallery, London; ca. 1665–1670. Illustrates the emphasis
on geometric structure and carefully related short lines of
harmony in male dress of this period. Photo courtesy of the
National Gallery, London.

**FIGURE 15–2**

257

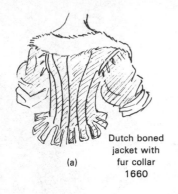

(a)

Dutch boned
jacket with
fur collar
1660

(b)

German
boned
satin
bodice
1680

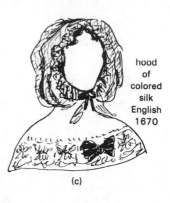

hood
of
colored
silk
English
1670

(c)

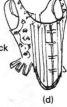

corset
boned in
front and
laced in back
English
1670

(d)

(i)

coiffure with loops
of ribbons
French ca. 1680

(h)

lady's shoe—
white kid
with silk
embroidery
1660–1680

Anonymous, *Hortense Mancini, Duchess of Mazarin;* the Metropolitan Museum of Art; ca. 1660–1675. Illustrates the carefully
controlled, very rich costume silhouette of female fashions during
the third quarter of the seventeenth century. Photo courtesy of the
Metropolitan Museum of Art.

(e)

quilted
corset
laced in
back, hooked
in front
English 1670

(f)

widow's black
coif over wired
heartbreaker curls
French 1660

(g)

lady's silk mask
late 17th c.

**FIGURE 15–3**

(a) curls dressed over wire frame in commode style 1685–1700

(b) powdered wig, tricorne hat trimmed in ostrich, lace cravat 1695

(c) full-bottomed wig with high points, steinkirk cravat ca. 1700

(d) Fontanges open in back with lace and ribbons

(e) officer ca. 1700

(f) silk parasol

Nicolas de Largillière, *Louis XIV and His Family;* Wallace Collection, London; 1711. Illustrates the pretentious dignity and encumbered body stance that marked the end of Baroque fashion. Note the heavy wigs and headdresses and the way the king overlaps his chair with his feet in the third ballet position. Photo courtesy of the Trustees of the Wallace Collection.

(g) Fontanges headdress and bows "a la échelle" on the stomacher 1695

(h) snug-fitting vest with sleeves, steinkirk cravat 1690s

(i) negligee robe corselet of silk, and petticoat 1690

FIGURE 15-4

259

and had a softness and casual sensuality, as shown in the portraits by Peter Lely (Fig. 15–6). This difference can be explained by the difference in English and French taste and by the English Restoration aristocrat's concentration on elegant sensuality as a major cultural attribute.

The costume fashions after about 1685 in all the countries of Europe were much heavier than those in the 1660s and 1670s and often remind one of a great upholstered chair. In the painting *Louis XIV and His Family* by Nicolas de Largillière, we can see the heavy-handed, oppressive clothing that marked the close of the reign of the Sun King (Fig. 15–4). The heavy, fitted coat with rich braid and grand cuffs is surmounted by a monstrously large, full-bottomed wig. A vest now reaches all the way to the knees, and the well-turned legs end in even larger high-heeled shoes (with red heels and large tongues) than had been the case at the opening of his reign. When accompanied by a chest-high walking stick, dress sword, muff, ostrich-trimmed hat, and other accessories, the male figure was grand and imposing indeed. When the three-cornered hat was worn over the great *periwig,* each slight movement of the head seemed grand and portentous, while the neck, swathed in a great *cravat* accented with a bow, gave great dignity to the neck and shoulders. The great cuffs of the coat, with lace ruffles below, made every gesture seem significant, and the upholstered torso, with its long waistcoat and full-skirted coat, gave one the weight found in Louis XIV wall hangings and upholstered furniture.

The clothing for women was equally imposing. The hair was built up to support a many-tiered *Fontanges* or series of fan effects that nodded from the top of the head. The neck was set off with a jeweled choker and framed in a square neckline on top of a triangle of bows that diminished in size to the pointed waist. The arms, sometimes cuffed high on the upper arm, gestured imposingly through tiers of puffed lace that cascaded down to the lace ruffle on the forearm, and the lower torso, covered by the expanding weight of the underskirt, ended in heavy, layered trim that gave a firm base to the silhouette. The overskirt was looped back into an impressive mass of fabric that then spread out into an extended train, much like the bustle of two centuries ago.

Certainly such figures created an imposing couple on any entrance to a chamber, and the ideal of grandeur that Louis XIV espoused above all else was appropriately expressed by such fashions.

## EARLY LOUIS XIV AND THE REIGN OF CHARLES II

***Masculine Dress*** Certainly two elements seemed to dominate male fashion at the opening of the reign of Louis XIV: the use of the exaggerated skirt-breeches, known as *petticoat* or *Rhinegrave* breeches, and the adoption of wigs to replace the shoulder-length hair worn since the late 1620s. It has never been exactly determined whether any of the petticoat breeches were truly skirts or kilts or whether they were merely very wide, divided skirts worn over bloused or fitted breeches. Sometimes they were so long that they reached mid-calf; at other times, so short that they ended in several rows of ribbons above the knee and were worn over a very blousy pair of breeches that were gathered into the leg just below the knee and finished with ribbon garters on the outside (Fig. 15–2a,g). Sometimes there were so many layers of ribbons on the petticoat breeches that they obscured the basic fabric under a series of undulating ribbon loops. Some idea of the variations in these breeches may be seen in the tapestry of the *Interview of Louis XIV and Philip IV of Spain at the Isle of Pheasants,* designed by Charles Le Brun (Fig. 15–5). The amount of ribbon loops, known as *canons,* applied to men's clothing during the 1660s is unbelievable, with critics commenting that it amounted to hundreds of yards. Usually the ribbon loops were massed at the front and sides of the waist and at the bottom and sides of the petticoat breeches with clumps also used on the shoulders and on the hat. Still another complement to the loops were the lace tops of the old boot hose, now used

**FIG. 15-5** Charles Le Brun, *History of the King: Interview of Louis XIV and Philip IV of Spain at the Isle of Pheasants;* from a Gobelin tapestry; The National Museum of Versailles, 1660. Illustrates the contrast between the outdated styles of Spanish royalty and aristocracy and the new fashionable lines of the French nobility, consisting of petticoat breeches, carefully layered short lines of harmony, and massed ribbon trim. Photo courtesy of the French Musécs Nationaux.

to create a decorative cuff from the knee halfway down the leg. A good example of this style can be seen in Terborch's *Portrait of an Unknown Man* (Fig. 15-2).

The shirt was very important with this style, creating a blousy, casual effect in rich silk or soft linen under a very curtailed doublet that had no more body than a modern bolero jacket (Fig. 15-2b). It was very short-waisted, often open up the front, and had cuffed, open, or ribbon-trimmed sleeves that seldom reached below the elbow. Thus the whole forearm was given over to the loose blouse of the ruffled shirt sleeve (Fig. 15-5).

Another variation from the short bolero jacket, one that would develop into the coat worn in the later seventeenth and eighteenth centuries, was the *cassock,* a long doublet similar to leather military cassocks of the early seventeenth century (Fig. 15-2h). One of these may be seen on the left foreground courtier in the tapestry depicting Louis XIV's meeting with

Philip IV (Fig. 15-5). There has always been speculation that this straight, coatlike garment derived from the Persian coat, since there was much interest in Persia at this time (the diarist, John Evelyn, who wrote in 1666 about his visit to Persia, was very admiring of the Persian coat); but the style probably derived from the older military doublet which became more fashionable after the rise of interest in Persian dress. At first this cassock was unfitted, with the same short sleeves as the bolero jacket, but by 1670 it became slighty more fitted with more prominent cuffed sleeves.

The collar of the Cavalier Period was now concentrated toward the front of the neck and was known as a *rabat* (Fig. 15-2b). This attention to the front of the neck was occasioned by the adoption of wigs instead of long hair, and these wigs became fuller in size and longer in length than were the natural curls of the past (Fig. 15-2c,d). One can readily see the difference by comparing Philip IV and his cour-

**FIG. 15-6** Peter Lely, *Portrait of the Duke of York;* National Gallery of Scotland; ca. 1660–1675. Illustrates the sensuous, loose, silky clothing, based on French styles imported by the exiled aristocrats on their return to England but lightened and domesticated to suit English taste. Photo courtesy of the National Gallery of Scotland, Edinburgh.

continued to fall in a great ruffle from below the knee to mid-calf or lower.

In England where the courtiers were all recently returned from exile in France, the styles were similar to those in France but with a great stress on sensuality, as expressed in the work of Peter Lely, court painter. In his *Portrait of the Duke of York,* the brother to the king and later the ill-fated James II, we see this emphasis on casual elegance in the soft, "slithery," satin texture, the reflectivity to light, and the loose fit of the clothing (Fig. 15-6). The garments do not contain the framing accents or punctuation with ribbon loops admired by the French, and one can sense that Restoration court life was less pompous and formal than in France.

The transition from bolero jacket to coat was complete by about 1670, and the *rabat,* or collar, was now replaced by the *cravat,* which was a linen strip ending in lace that went one and half times about the neck and was held in place by a stiff bow at the throat. This new style in neckwear was to remain, with only minor variations, until the early nineteenth century (Fig. 15-2c). Historians say that this form of neckwear was adopted from a regiment of Croatian soldiers in the pay of the French crown; and the native men's neckwear in villages in Croatia before World War I tend to bear this out.

Two other variations also took place in the 1670s. Under the new coat the old doublet (now usually sleeveless) was lengthened into a knee-length vest or waistcoat (Fig. 15-4), and the petticoat breeches were frequently replaced by blousy, balloon trousers to just below the knee. However, there were still many men who wore petticoat breeches trimmed with many ribbon loops under the coat, sometimes with a waistcoat or vest.

A good example of male fashion in the middle of the 1670s may be seen in the anonymous painting *Louis XIV Visiting the Grotto of Thetis* (Fig. 15-7). Coat sleeves are now cuffed well below the elbow, the coat is much more fitted and set with pockets, and the cravat with its large bow at the throat has completely replaced the rabat. Some of the gentlemen are probably wearing waistcoats or vests and full breeches, although the gentleman in the center fore-

tiers with Louis XIV and his in the tapestry by Le Brun (Fig. 15-5). The entourage of Philip IV looks forty years out of date.

The hats of the early years of Louis XIV's reign had a high, sloping crown and a moderate brim, but these soon gave way to lower-crowned hats with a wider brim that was edged with plumes and decorated with clumps of ribbons (Fig. 15-2d,i). Shoes had higher heels and squarer toes than in the past, with red heels for the shoes of all noblemen; the shoe rosettes of the Cavalier Period had now been replaced by wide, stiff bows (Fig. 15-2e,f). Boots were now reserved for riding and hunting, although the lace tops to what formerly had been boot hose

**FIG. 15-7** Anonymous, *Louis XIV Visiting the Grotto of Thetis;* The National Museum of Versailles; ca. 1675. Illustrates the transition from the *petticoat breeches* style to the coat, vest, and breeches fashion. Note that the man in the foreground has a more fitted coat but is still wearing divided skirt breeches over full underbreeches. The lady with her back to us has a skirt looped up to the thighs by a cord. Photo courtesy of the French Musées Nationaux.

**FIG. 15-8** Jean de St. Jean, *Engraving of a Court Gentleman;* ca. 1678. Note the increasing size of the brim of the hat but the loss of the steeple crown, the use of heavy braiding on the coat, the continuance of petticoat breeches over blousy underbreeches, and the use of ribbons as punctuation in the costume from foot to hat. From a contemporary engraving in the collection of the author.

ground is without a vest and still wears moderate, divided petticoat breeches trimmed in lace and ribbons over a blousy pair of breeches to below the knees. An even stronger image of the new styles of the later 1670s may be seen in Jean de St. Jean's drawing of a nobleman wearing a broad-brimmed hat, heavily braided and fitted coat, and beribboned petticoat breeches worn over full, bloused trousers gartered at the knee (Fig. 15-8). One can readily see that the trend by this date was toward more weight in form and fabric and a more fitted line in silhouette.

**Feminine Dress** The women's costume during the 1660s showed few major changes in line (Fig. 15-3). The bodice fitted smoothly without a wrinkle over a corset, or stiffened

*stomacher,* that once again had a moderate point dipping down over the skirt in front (Fig. 15-3b,d,e). Sometimes this stomacher (often reinforced by a removable busk of metal or wood) carried a series of bows *à la échelle* that diminished in size as they approached the waist (Figs. 15-3,4g). The neckline was usually oval-shaped (Fig. 15-3b,c,f) and low cut with an edging of lace or a fold of sheer fabric coming from the chemise under the bodice. The sleeves of the bodice were either short or nonexistent, and the major accent on the upper arm came from a series of lace or sheer fabric puffs that ended in a ruffle just below the elbow. The skirts, worn without any stiffening but over full petticoats, broke on the floor in front and trained slightly at the back. Often the skirt was open in front to show a petticoat panel of contrasting fabric, and it was always set into the waist in carefully set pleating that gave a decorative interest below the waist (Fig. 15-3). Sometimes the outerskirt was looped gently back from the petticoat panels with ribbon bows that matched those on the bodice.

The hairdressing in general became fuller, with more stress on formal curls than in the past, and bangs gradually disappeared. Sometimes to get the frizzed and curled richness at the sides of the head, the hair was actually wired out to the sides. Some of the back hair was often brought forward into a curl on the shoulder, while the remainder was usually formed into a bun at the back of the head (Fig. 15-3b,c,f,i). Broad-brimmed steeple hats like those of the men were worn for riding; when men's hats lost this high crown, the women's riding and travel hats followed suit. Loose hoods and kerchiefs were also worn at night and in inclement weather, and closefitting caps, similar to those worn by the Dutch early in the century, were used at home.

For outerwraps the hooded cloak was preferred, although for indoor winter wear a wrist-length–hip-length jacket trimmed in fur was popular, a style that had been common in Holland for many years (Fig. 15-3a). Shoes were richly embroidered or made of elegant brocade with tapered toes and a slim, high heel (Fig. 15-3h). Patches to cover pockmarks became increasingly popular, and accessories such as fans, parasols, gloves, muffs, and masks added weight and complication to female fashions by the mid-1670s.

Let us look at several examples of female dress during the period from 1660 to 1685 to gain a better sense of the modesty of female dress compared to the rich flamboyance of the male. The anonymous portrait of Hortense Mancini indicates by the plumes in her hair that she is fancifully dressed for a party (Fig. 15-3). She wears pearl earrings and necklace as well as several jeweled brooches and a kind of jeweled chain at the breast. There is a sheer puff of fabric around the neckline of her bodice and its short, petallike sleeves lead to a series of chemise sleeve puffs held in place by a brooch. Her brocaded bodice is tighty fitted over a corset without any decorative ribbon bows, and her matching skirt is not open in the front but undoubtedly trains out in moderate fullness at the back. The figure seems a combination of relaxed youthfulness and formal dignity.

The woman coming down the steps in *Louis XIV Visiting the Grotto of Thetis* wears much the same costume, but here the skirt is open in front over a brocaded underskirt or petticoat (Fig. 15-7). The neckline is covered by a very wide band of lace, and there are many puffs in the lace sleeves that emerge from the short cap sleeve of the bodice. The hair seems much more tightly curled into ringlets than in the portrait of Hortense Mancini, and the bun at the back of the head is more formal. Another lady in the painting with her back to us shows the growing interest in looping up the overskirt at the back to create almost a bustle effect, while both she and the lady to the far right with the fan are wearing the fashionable head kerchiefs of the time. As with the men in the late 1670s, the women are beginning to have a slightly larger silhouette with more formality in cut and draping.

# LATE LOUIS XIV AND THE REIGNS OF
# JAMES II, WILLIAM AND MARY, AND QUEEN ANNE

**Masculine Dress**  By the middle of the 1680s, men's clothing began to assume a fitted look with the coat now cut quite snugly to the body over the hips and then moderately flared into skirts that reached the knee. The front was usually graced with close-set buttons and buttonholes from neck to knee, although the coat was most often left open or only partially buttoned in order to frame the rich fabric of the knee-length vest or waistcoat. By about 1690 pleats were introduced into the side back of the coat, and the skirts were usually slit at the sides and at the center back for ease in riding, so that the sword (usually still worn on a shoulder bandolier) could pass under the left back skirt of the coat. These slits were often set with practical buttons and buttonholes, but the effect was primarily decorative.

Pockets were usually set into these coats quite near the bottom front hem; at first they were just slits and sometimes they were diagonal rather than horizontal, but the straight pockets finally were the most popular. In the 1690s the placement varied from the hip to just above the knee, but the slit was always covered by a flap that could be buttoned down. The size of these flaps increased as fashions moved into the first decade of the eighteenth century.

Coats were made of all kinds of fabric from rich brocade to hard-surfaced, plain silks set with braid and embroidery; but by the late 1680s and the early 1690s there was a great craze for using many layers of complex braid to outline the coat and call attention to the cuffs and the center front. By this time the arms of the coat were quite fitted (down to the lower forearm), and the large cuffs were turned back to just below the elbow, thus leaving a puff of the rich shirt above the full lace ruffles over the wrist (the buttons that were originally set on the cuff to button it closed at the bottom remain to this day as a forgotten decorative accent at the bottom of a man's coat sleeve). By the late 1680s most coat cuffs were made to stay permanently flared and open over the puff of the lower shirt sleeve (Fig. 15-10).

The long, knee-length vest was sleeveless or had very tight sleeves that fitted smoothly under the coat sleeve either without cuffs or with ones that folded back over those of the coat (Fig. 15-4h). Sometimes the tight undersleeve of the vest fit under the outercoat all the way to the wrist allowing only a little ruffle below it.

The neckwear by the 1680s had been standardized into the cravat, a long strip of lawn with lace ends that was wrapped around the neck like a scarf with the lace ends hanging down the front of the chest under a stiffened bow or series of bows (Fig. 15-4b). An event in 1692 introduced another interesting arrangement of the cravat. At the Battle of Steinkirk, French soldiers, caught by surprise in an early dawn attack, twisted their cravats hurriedly around their necks and stuck the ends through a buttonhole of the coat. Since the French were finally victorious, a new style was born that was to last until the death of Louis XIV (Fig. 15-4c). Even the ladies adopted the style for use when riding.

By the late 1680s men's wigs began to reach huge proportions, and the so-called full-bottomed wigs often reached to the waist in front and back as well as rising to great peaks on the top of the head. By the close of the 1690s the fashion of powdering the wig began to develop; despite complaints about untidiness, these white wigs gradually became the standard new style in hairdressing. An example of these full-bottomed wigs may be seen in Louis Silvestre's painting *Louis XIV Receiving Frederick Augustus of Saxony* (Fig. 15-9). By the death of Louix XIV the standard color for the hair was white.

Breeches finally lost their fullness by the 1690s and fitted the leg smoothly, with the hose frequently gartered up over the breeches. Thus the breeches were totally unseen, since the waistcoat came to the knees and the hose came up over the knee. Sometimes boot hose were still worn as a protection for very delicate silk hose, giving a fuller cuff up over the knee; but boots themselves were seen only in military or riding portraits. Shoes remained high-heeled and heavy with great square toes and large tongues (Fig. 15-4), and by the 1690s they usually finished in a buckle rather than a bow. Boots also were very heavy and stiff with great cuffs that came up over the knees. Sometimes these cuffs were cut away behind the knee.

The broad-brimmed hat trimmed in feathers gradually became cocked up on the sides by the 1690s to form the *tricorne,* or three-cornered hat, which was to be popular in Europe for the next century (Fig. 15-4b). For outerwraps there were still cloaks; however, the *Brandenburg greatcoat,* adopted from the coats worn by Prussian soldiers, became the forerunner of the male overcoat of the next three centuries.

An excellent example of the full court cos-

**FIG. 15–9** Louis Silvestre, *Louis XIV Receiving Frederick Augustus of Saxony;* The National Museum of Versailles; ca. 1695. Illustrates the fashions at the close of the reign of Louis XIV. Note the high peaks on the wigs, the buckles replacing bows on men's shoes, and the posing in ballet positions. The ladies wear the *Fontanges* and gowns looped to the back into long trains. Photo courtesy of the French Musées Nationaux.

tume of the 1690s may be seen in Largillière's portrait *Prince James Francis Edward Stuart and His Sister* (Fig. 15–10). The young boy is clad completely in red with a blue shoulder sash across his coat, and he carries a large, three-cornered hat trimmed in ostrich feathers. Another famous Largillière painting of Louis XIV and his family, from 1710, demonstrates how these styles carried on well into the new century (Fig. 15–4). Note particularly that the man leaning on the king's chair has a white powdered wig and that the younger man to the right is wearing a twisted Steinkirk cravat.

The military wear of this late Baroque period relied primarily on heavily braided coats and heavy jackboots, with a military sash worn around the waist and a heavy bandolier slung over the shoulder to carry the sword. By the close of the seventeenth century, however, the sword was usually worn on a hanger attached to a belt underneath the military coat which had

slits side and back for the hilt and sheath to protrude. Although armor was little worn for practical warfare, full-dress military portraits frequently show the use of a steel gorget or full breastplate for ceremonial occasions. Even helmets were little used anymore, and most soldiers fought in wigs and tricorne hats. The legs were clad in thick, leather jackboots with heavy cuffs over the knee, although foot soldiers usually wore cloth or leather leggings buttoned over the knee and fastened under the shoe (Fig. 15–4e).

Middle- and lower-class men usually wore garments like those of the upper classes but in a less fashionable cut, sober colors, and woolen fabrics. The hair might be long instead of covered by a wig; the cravat plain without lace ends; the coat only moderately fitted and cut from durable woolens; the vest plain or embroidered; the breeches full and blousing over cotton or woolen stockings; and the shoes usu-

**FIG. 15-10** Nicolas de Largillière, *Prince James Francis Edward Stuart and His Sister;* National Portrait Gallery, London; 1695. Illustrates the more formal fashions of the close of the seventeenth century. Note the fitted, flared, large-cuffed coat on the prince and the *Fontanges* headdress and long-trained skirt on the girl. Photo courtesy of the National Portrait Gallery, London.

outerskirt actually met at the center back, producing a cascade of fabric down the back into a sizable train. Finally, the overskirt did not come to the front at all, but was appended in great, looped puffs only at the sides and back of the figure. As the exposed underskirt, or petticoat, gained importance, it began to take on decoration—especially at the bottom and usually in horizontal lines of ornamentation known as *pretintailles* (Fig. 15-4i). Tiered petticoats set with a series of horizontal ruffles also became popular.

The bodice also began to change from the oval, rounded lines that it had held since the middle of the century to a square neckline that ended in the strong lines of a V-shaped stomacher (Fig. 15-4g). Thus, the front lines of the bodice now continued on over the shoulders, creating a more matronly and formal effect than at any time since the Jacobean Period. The sleeves also changed from a series of lace or lawn puffs cascading from a cap sleeve to a formal sleeve and cuff that now reached to just above the elbow, with several layers of lace ruffles falling over the upper forearm (Fig. 15-4).

But one of the greatest changes of all came in the hairdressing, which now became high, formal, and heavy without the soft, loose curls formerly used. This Fontanges headdress supposedly derived from Mme. de Fontanges, one of Louis XIV's mistresses, who, when her hair fell while riding, fastened it up with a garter (Fig. 15-4d,g,i). From the bows and ruffles of this garter, fashion soon developed a lace cap fronted with elaborate, tiered ruffles that extended up over a wire frame to give six or eight inches of height to the head. Sometimes the hair was piled up in tiers of curls over a wire frame without the Fontanges, and in such cases the hairdressing was known as the *commode* style (Fig. 15-4a).

In Largillière's painting *Prince James Francis Edward Stuart and His Sister,* the little girl wears one of these Fontanges headdresses as well as the new stomacher bodice and the skirt with fullness at the back, although in this case there is no underskirt (Fig. 15-10). She also wears a lace apron, since at this time a lace or embroidered apron became a distinctive part of female court dress. Other popular accessories

ally as large as those of the aristocrats but with only a moderately high heel. Lower-class men often wore no coat at all, but a jacket or vest over the rough cotton or woolen shirt and a broad-brimmed hat of felt or leather.

**Feminine Dress** By the opening of the 1680s a new look for women began to develop that involved overmanipulation of fabric and decoration and the looping up of the overskirt over a stiff back ruffle that created a bustle effect. This effect had begun modestly when the outer edges of the overskirt had been draped back with ribbon bows or brooches to accent fullness toward the back of the female figure. By the 1680s the reversed lower front edges of the

were the fur muff, hung from about the waist; a scarf or loose hood knotted under the chin and covering the Fontanges; cape-stoles, hooded cloaks for outdoor walking and travel; elbow-length gloves; parasols; masks; fans; and the male Steinkirk for riding.

Although we seldom see the shoes of the time peeping out from beneath the ladies' gowns, they too had become very sophisticated and fashionable, with slender, pointed toes; high, slim, curving heels; high tongues; and narrow straps with small buckles. Most uppers were of a rich, brocaded fabric (Fig. 15-3h).

In Largillière's formal portrait of Louis XIV and his family, painted about 1710, we see Mme. de Maintenon, the last mistress and secret second wife of Louis XIV, in a sober ver-

sion of the style of the last twenty years of the Sun King's reign (Fig. 15-4). Her black Fontanges is covered by a veil, her bodice is set with bows in a diminishing size, her overskirt is draped back to form a bustle effect at the back, and her sleeves are a series of lace puffs emerging from the cap sleeves of the bodice. In every way it is a formidable and stately image. Much the same image of Mme. de Maintenon may be seen in Louis Silvestre's *Louis XIV Receiving Frederick Augustus of Saxony* (Fig. 15-9). Note the draped-up back of the overskirt on the woman at the far right of this painting, as well as the layers of lace ruffles that cascade down from the cuff of the bodice sleeve. Middle-class and lower-class women wore simple modifications of these styles.

# FABRICS

The fabrics of this period were much the same as in the earlier Baroque Period until about 1685 to 1690 when a great array of gold and silver metallic brocades began to make their appearance. These brocades were then set off against costly satins and velvets, and rich laces used in greater profusion than ever before were included as the major accent.

Printed calicoes were introduced during this period for lighter garments and summer wear, and by the turn of the century the block printing of cottons and linens was standard in England and France for the upper middle class. The block printed effects often used Persian and oriental motifs—designed patterns that were just beginning to be popular in western Europe.

# ARTS AND ARTIFACTS

Very palatial interiors of this period were usually decorated with richly patterned inlaid marble, but more intimate chambers were done in carved and gilded wood. Huge tapestries covered the walls, and heavily framed paintings adorned ceilings. At the court of Louis XIV mythology involving the king as Apollo or some other deity was the key subject of such paintings and tapestries. Furniture was heavy, ornately carved, gilded, and upholstered in rich damask. In England and Holland natural wood was more prevalent for wall paneling and furniture, and there was much less use of gilded trim (Fig. 15-1a,b,c,d).

Room accessories included warming pans, kettles, candlesticks, ceramic chamber pots, lutes, spinets, harpsichords, chests, elaborate bed hangings, and statuary.

Personal accessories for men increased enormously by the end of this period and included wig combs, snuff boxes, pocket purses, dress swords, gloves, and the large three-cornered hat. In many ways the dandy of the 1690s must have looked like a walking antique store. The only item that disappeared was the pouch or waist "pocket" since there were now an ample number of deep pockets in both waistcoat and coat.

For the women the most important new accessory was the folding fan, although occasionally the fan was still made of plumes or feathers. Also important were gloves, lace handkerchiefs, muffs, kerchiefs or hoods, parasols, masks, and beauty patches to cover facial blemishes (Figs. 15-3g,4f).

# VISUAL SOURCES

Excellent visual sources of this period are the Gobelin tapestries devoted to the life of Louis XIV; the paintings of Dutch artist Gerard Terborch; and the work of the French artists Hyacinthe Rigaud, Nicolas de Largellière, J. D. de St. Jean, Pierre Mignard, A. Trouvain, Nicolas Arnoult, N. Bonnart, and Louis Silvestre. The best English sources are to be found in the works of Sir Peter Lely, J. M. Wright, and Sir Godfrey Kneller. A useful German-Bohemian artist is Jodokus Verbeeck.

The best repositories for prints, paintings, and actual costumes are the Metropolitan Museum of Art, the Victoria and Albert Museum, the Pierpont Morgan Library, the Versailles National Museum, the royal collections at Hampton Court and Windsor, the London National Gallery, and the Louvre. Useful books are Charles Blitzer's *The Age of Kings;* the Cunningtons' *Handbook of Seventeenth Century English Costume;* and Victor Tapie's *The Age of Grandeur.*

# SUMMARY

The long personal reign of Louis XIV opened with men dressed as beribboned birds of plumage and closed with them having the look of heavily upholstered furniture, whereas women started the reign as youthful maidens and ended it as forbidding matrons. It was a fascinating period of fashion in which all art and clothing basically stemmed from the personal tastes of the Sun King, even in countries far removed from the French court. The natural, easy, outdoor look in manners and dress that was symbolized at the opening of the Baroque style by the Van Dyck portrait of Charles I (see Fig. 14–5) was no longer apparent. By the turn of the century, it had been replaced by a heavy, oppressive, indoor richness (Fig. 15–4).

# chapter *XVI*

# Rococo

## Chronology

### (1715–1775)

| | | |
|---|---|---|
| **EARLY LOUIS XV OF FRANCE AND GEORGE I AND GEORGE II OF ENGLAND 1715–1760** | 1714 | George I of the House of Hanover succeeds to the throne of England |
| | 1715 | Louis XV begins his reign with Philip, duke of Orléans, as regent |
| | 1720 | Financial collapse of the South Sea Bubble in France |
| | 1721 | Robert Walpole begins his 21-year tenure as prime minister of England; inoculation against smallpox introduced |
| | 1723 | Philip, the regent of France, dies, and Louis XV becomes full ruler; Bach becomes musical director in Leipzig |
| | 1724 | Pragmatic Sanction obtained by Charles VI to secure Hapsburg succession for Maria Theresa |
| | 1726 | Fleury becomes chief adviser to Louis XV and principal minister for 17 years; Jonathan Swift completes *Gulliver's Travels* |
| | 1727 | George II is crowned king of England |
| **1725 English** | 1728 | First performance of John Gay's *Beggar's Opera* |

| | |
|---|---|
| 1731 | Prévost's romantic novel *Manon Lescaut* appears |
| 1733 | John Kay patents the flying shuttle, initiating modern mechanical weaving; colony of Georgia is founded; Voltaire completes his *Philosophical Letters on the English* |
| 1735 | The first War of Polish Succession ends with the Treaty of Vienna; William Hogarth's *The Rake's Progress* and Carl Linnaeus' *System of Nature* published |
| 1739 | England and Spain fight the War of Jenkins' Ear over New World trade; Methodist John Wesley starts his preaching mission; David Hume writes *Treatise of Human Nature* |
| 1740 | Frederick the Great assumes the throne in Prussia; Maria Theresa becomes head of the Hapsburg domains; Prussia and France, allied against Austria and England, begin the War of Austrian Succession; Samuel Richardson publishes *Pamela,* or *Virtue Rewarded* |
| 1741 | Debut of David Garrick at Goodman's Fields Theatre |
| 1744 | England and France fight King George's War in Nova Scotia and India |
| 1745 | Madame de Pompadour becomes mistress to Louis XV; uprising of Charles Stuart, The Young Pretender, in Scotland |
| 1746 | College of New Jersey (Princeton) founded |
| 1748 | Treaty of Aix-la-Chapelle ends the War of Austrian Succession and awards Silesia to Prussia |
| 1749 | Fielding's *Tom Jones* is published |
| 1750 | Rousseau wins fame for his *Discourse on the Arts and Sciences* |

1745 French

| | | |
|---|---|---|
| | 1751 | Voltaire at the court of Frederick the Great publishes the *Age of Louis XIV,* and Diderot's *Encyclopédie* begins to appear in installments |
| | 1752 | Gregorian calendar is adopted; Benjamin Franklin does experiments with electricity |
| | 1754 | French and Indian War continues French and English rivalry in the New World; Condillac writes *Treatise on the Sensations* |
| | 1755 | The expulsion of the Acadians from Nova Scotia; Lisbon earthquake lays city in ruins and kills 30,000; Samuel Johnson publishes his *English Dictionary* |
| | 1756 | Diplomatic Revolution leads to Seven Years' War, with Austria and France allied against Prussia and England; Indian uprising leads to "black hole" incident in Calcutta |
| | 1757 | Clive's victory at Plassey in India; ministry of William Pitt the Elder begins; Robert Damiens attempts to assassinate Louis XV |
| | 1758 | Voltaire moves to Ferney and completes *Candide* |
| | 1759 | English capture Quebec from the French, and Wolf and Montcalm both die; British Museum is opened |
| 1760 French | 1760 | King George III begins his 60-year reign |

---

| | | |
|---|---|---|
| LATE LOUIS XV OF FRANCE AND GEORGE III OF ENGLAND 1760–1775 | 1761 | Franz Joseph Hayden begins his 30 years of service with the Esterházys, and Rousseau writes *La Nouvelle Héloïse;* potatoes planted in France |

|  |  |
|---|---|
| 1762 | The Jesuits are condemned and then suppressed in France; Rousseau's masterpieces, *The Social Contract* and *Emile* are published; Gluck's *Orfeo et Euridice* is performed in Vienna; Catherine the Great begins her 34-year rule of Russia, and Jean Calas is unjustly executed and later declared innocent through Voltaire's efforts |
| 1763 | Treaties of Paris and Hubertusburg end the Seven Years' War; Prussia becomes a leading power, and France loses overseas colonies |
| 1764 | Sterne's *Tristram Shandy,* Wincklemann's *Ancient Art,* Beccaria's *On Crimes and Punishment,* Voltaire's *Philosophical Dictionary* appear; Hargreaves invents the spinning jenny |
| 1765 | Joseph II becomes emperor and co-regent of the Hapsburg domains with his mother Maria Theresa; the Stamp Act brings resistance in the American colonies |
| 1767 | Lessing publishes *Minna von Barnhelm,* and Herder becomes a leader of the *Sturm und Drang* movement with his writings |
| 1768 | Captain James Cook sails aboard the *Endeavor* on his voyage around the world |
| 1769 | Madame du Barry becomes mistress to Louis XV; James Watt patents the improved steam engine |
| 1770 | Holbach, materialist philosopher, publishes *System of Nature* |
| 1771 | First edition of the *Encyclopedia Britannica* |
| 1772 | The first partition of Poland by Russia, Prussia, and Austria |

1773 French

| | |
|---|---|
| 1773 | The Jesuit order abolished by the papacy; Boston Tea Party in America |
| 1774 | Louis XVI and Marie Antoinette become king and queen of France; Goethe's *Sorrows of Young Werther* appears |

# BACKGROUND

The reign of Louis XV in France was a period of relaxation after the heavy autocratic rule of Louis XIV from the 1660s to the early 1700s. Louis XIV's exercise of supreme power had become unbearable by the opening of the new century, and the aristocratic court looked forward to the king's death and the duke of Orléans' regency during the minority of Louis XV. The years from the death of Louis XIV to the death of the duke of Orléans, known as the *Regency Period,* marked a transition from the heaviness of the late Baroque to the lightness of the new Rococo style that was fully established by 1730. The new king, dominated by his mistresses and their feminine tastes, presided over a new, elegant, feminine sensibility that, in turn, dominated all art and fashion. The aristocrats, secretly aware of their waning power, turned to frivolous pastimes and entertainments and increasingly left the administrative and executive functions of the state to ambitious members of the middle class. Royalty and nobility were still the major patrons of the arts, however, and the age brilliantly expressed their boredom, escapism, and love of pure pleasure. Art during these years was luxurious, frivolous, sensual, clever, elegant, and self-conciously yet casually artificial. The historical and religious themes of Baroque art were replaced by refined, elegant, intimately charming views of the pursuit and game of love.

Rococo art was the *denouement,* or dying fall, of the aristocratic way of life, and gradually during the eighteenth century the nobility accepted more middle-class patterns of thought, although clothing them in the trappings of aristocracy. Throughout the courts of Europe—which were all modeled on Versailles—there was a slackening of personal discipline, a withdrawal from responsibility, a growing skepticism and atheism, and a movement from a heavy, masculine view to an elegantly feminine sensibility in social attitudes and outlook. In some ways the delicacy, elegance, and charm of the curvilinear lines in Rococo decoration are reminiscent of the feminine imagery in later Gothic art. Certainly the succession of mistresses of Louis XV had more influence on social and artistic matters than did anyone else at the famous court of Versailles. Painters like Watteau, Boucher, and Fragonard—masters of the charming *fête galante,* with its shimmering aristocrats in pastel colors amorously amusing themselves amid the delicacy of feathery forest glades—were completely at the service of this new taste. Sculptors such as Pigalle and Clodion created creamy, rounded figures in pink terra cotta. Architects scaled down the size and weight of their structures and lavished their design talents on the delicate, gay, playfully extravagant interiors and curving gold furniture that had become synonymous with the label *Louis Quinze* or *Rococo.* Rococo decoration also made great use of asymmetrical S-shaped and C-shaped ornamental forms that included shell motifs, bat wings, and palm branches. Straight lines and right angles were systematically avoided in favor of a world of softly undulating curves. Also, with the opening of trade with the Far East, the enthusiasm for oriental ornamental effects created a complete design style known as

(a)
English pediment
ornament ca. 1720

Germain Boffrand, Salon de la Princesse, Hôtel de Soubise, Paris; begun in
1732. Illustrates the elegant, intimate, curving architecture with delicate foliage
ornamentation that characterized aristocratic interiors during the early eighteenth century in France. Photo courtesy of the French Cultural Services, New
York.

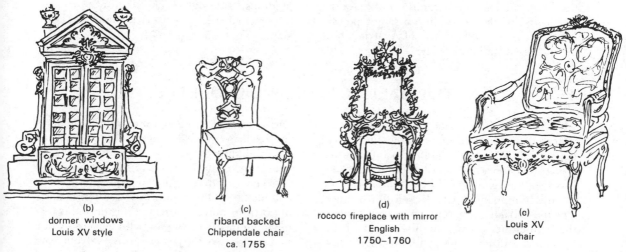

(b)
dormer windows
Louis XV style

(c)
riband backed
Chippendale chair
ca. 1755

(d)
rococo fireplace with mirror
English
1750–1760

(c)
Louis XV
chair

FIGURE 16–1

275

*chinoiserie,* and this style as well as the attributes of the Rococo spread throughout all the courts of Europe by the middle of the century. An excellent example of this elegant style of interior decoration may be seen in the Salon de la Princesse from the Hôtel de Soubise, decorated by Germain Boffrand from 1737 to 1740 (Fig. 16–1).

Politically the period between the death of Louis XIV and the outbreak of the American Revolution was a time of relative relaxation after the exhausting European and colonial conflict known as the War of Spanish Succession. However, the gentlemanly wars of strategy that *were* pursued in this period now always involved the colonial holdings of the major powers.

Russia, a semi-oriental empire until the accession of Peter the Great, was forcibly turned toward Paris and the West during this period and looked to France for all artistic and cultural inspiration. Somewhat the same happened to Prussia where Frederick the Great launched a small German kingdom into a major European power. Frederick built his own French-style Versailles called *Sans Souci* at Potsdam and even invited France's most distinguished philosopher and intellectual, Voltaire, to live in residence at his court. In an age in which culture and art were strongly influenced by feminine taste, it is not surprising that two of Europe's key rulers were women. Catherine the Great carried on the traditions of Peter the Great and made Russia into a major power. Maria Theresa, archduchess of Austria, combined great administrative abilities with unimpeachable moral standards, and several of her 16 children became rulers of Europe, including the doomed Marie Antoinette. In England the royal family switched from Stuart to Hanoverian. George I, the first king in the new line, could not even speak English; George II still spoke with a strong German accent; and not until the time of George III did the English royal family become assimilated into the English cultural scene. There were a number of revolts led by the Stuart pretenders to the throne, the most famous led by Bonnie Prince Charlie in 1745. All of these were unsuccessful, although they left a residue of legend and romantic song, particularly in Scotland. In Spain the new royal family was Bourbon and related to the French royal family, but Spain by this time, despite its overseas colonies, was not a major power on the European scene.

In the New World there was much rivalry among the three great colonial powers—England, Spain, and France. Spain dominated from the bottom of South America all the way up to Florida and California; France held Canada and Louisiana, and England controlled the eastern seaboard of what is now the United States. The greatest rivalry of all—between England and France—finally climaxed in the French and Indian Wars in which the colonists and British regulars were pitted against the French and Indians. The outcome was the loss by France of all her North American holdings, although French cultural heritage lives on to this day in eastern Canada and Louisiana.

## THE BASIC COSTUME SILHOUETTE

The fashions of this period were the perfect accent to the elegant interiors and furnishings of the period. The weight, grandeur, and formal structure bequeathed to fashion by Louis XIV was swept away after 1720 by a smaller, more natural human figure with looser, flaring lines. The most striking difference, however, came in the whitening of the man's wig and the woman's coiffure. The gentlemen's full-bottomed periwig gave way to a white powdered wig with a few curls over the ears and a queue at the back tied with a black ribbon, while the ladies' lightly powdered, tight hairdos were transformed by the close of the period to excessively powdered hair styles of the greatest complexity. One's impression after looking at portraits and paintings of this period is that of gentlemen and ladies with elegant white hair supported by pastel satins, velvets, and brocades.

(a) robe volante or flying gown

(b) bag wig or crapaud

(c) paniers

(d) waistcoat

(e) corset

(f) ladies' shoe 1730

(g) English soldier 1742

(h) jabot

(h) solitaire

(i) house coat with cap French 1730

(j) laced back of an embroidered silk vest 1720

(k) man's cuff 1720

(l) Watteau pleats

(m) grey powdered tie wig

(n) man's cuff 1745

François de Troy, *The Declaration of Love;* Staatliche Schlösser und Gärten, Berlin; 1731. Illustrates the flowered, loose-fitting, Watteau-pleated gowns worn by ladies and the short white wigs, flared coats, long vests, and low-heeled buckled shoes worn by men in the second quarter of the eighteenth century. Photo courtesy of Jorg Anders, Berlin.

**FIGURE 16-2**

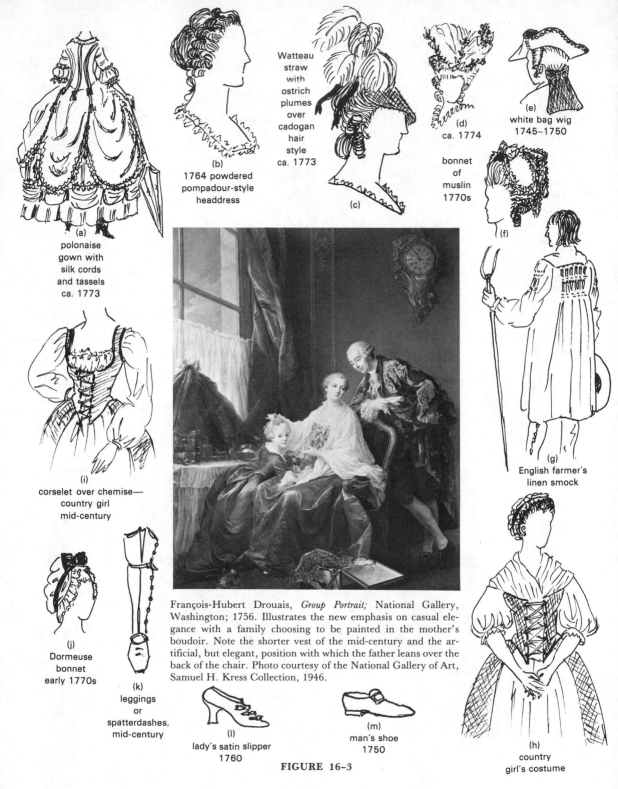

(a)
polonaise
gown with
silk cords
and tassels
ca. 1773

(b)
1764 powdered
pompadour-style
headdress

Watteau
straw
with
ostrich
plumes
over
cadogan
hair
style
ca. 1773

(c)

(d)
ca. 1774

bonnet
of
muslin
1770s

(e)
white bag wig
1745–1750

(f)

(g)
English farmer's
linen smock

(i)
corselet over chemise—
country girl
mid-century

(j)
Dormeuse
bonnet
early 1770s

(k)
leggings
or
spatterdashes,
mid-century

(l)
lady's satin slipper
1760

(m)
man's shoe
1750

(h)
country
girl's costume

François-Hubert Drouais, *Group Portrait;* National Gallery, Washington; 1756. Illustrates the new emphasis on casual elegance with a family choosing to be painted in the mother's boudoir. Note the shorter vest of the mid-century and the artificial, but elegant, position with which the father leans over the back of the chair. Photo courtesy of the National Gallery of Art, Samuel H. Kress Collection, 1946.

**FIGURE 16–3**

278

In the painting *The Declaration of Love* by François de Troy, we have a brilliant evocation of this period and its fashions just as Rococo ideals were reaching their climax (Fig. 16–2). The setting, as was frequently the case in the early eighteenth century, is not an interior but an elegant park or garden behind the palace or chateau, and the whole is carefully calculated to give a mood of artful and self-conscious informality. The ladies are wearing the loose-fitted morning gowns with Watteau pleats at the back that seem sharply opposed to formal court presentation gowns. The kneeling gentleman has a delicately powdered wig curled close to the head, a flaring skirted coat and waistcoat, tight breeches buttoned over his silk stockings, and low-heeled, buckled shoes. Although the ensemble of costumes is rich, nothing is heavy-handed or excessive. The major visual interest comes from the delicately sensuous textures of the satin, velvet, and flowered brocade, and one is particularly aware of how the floral motifs complement the park or garden setting in which they are displayed.

Now let us look at the gentleman in a famous Drouais painting of about 25 years later and note the changes that had taken place in masculine dress (Fig. 16–3). The differences, actually quite small, were mainly in the use of less material and less flare. The coat, although the skirts were somewhat stiffened, did not extend out from the body, and the skirts were cut away so that the front sides of the garment sloped toward the back below the waist. The vest, which had been as long as the coat, was also shortened after the mid-century, while the sleeves and cuffs of the coat were also somewhat less bulky in size and shape. The stockings which had frequently been rolled up over the knees of the tight breeches in the early part of the century were now always worn under them. Shoes still had a low heel and modest buckle. The neckcloth or cravat, which in the de Troy painting often had a black bow at the throat

**FIG. 16–4** François Boucher, *The Marquise de Pompadour;* Wallace Collection, London; 1759. Illustrates the use of crisp, light-reflective, silk fabrics, modest *paniers,* and the trimming with ruffles, bows, and flowers that was the hallmark of Rococo court dress for women in the middle of the eighteenth century. Photo courtesy of the Wallace Collection.

made from the ribbon ends of the bag that held the queue of the wig, now was wrapped simply about the throat, while the ruffle was now part of the shirt. Throughout the period the standard male headgear was the three-cornered hat with or without lace, braid, or ostrich trim, while the trim on coats and vests usually consisted of rich gold or silver braid or embroidery.

The women's gowns in the de Troy painting are all loose, at-home gowns with Watteau pleated backs that give an aristocratic, but domestic, look; however, the standard court presentation gown until about 1770 may be summed up by looking at Boucher's *The Marquise de Pompadour* (Fig. 16–4). The hair is not powdered and is waved back from the face in the simple fashion known as the *pompadour,* while the neck is delicately encircled in a small, lace ruffle. The gown, or *robe à la française,* has a square neckline, the bodice is tightly fitted over a corset, and the front is covered by a ladderlike line of bows *à la échelle.* The sleeves are narrow, reach to the elbow, and are finished in bows above ruffles of lace that spread over the forearm. The skirt opens out over an underskirt which in this case is of the same fabric, and both are richly decorated with ruffles and lacy floral effects. A collapsible, boned basket, or *panier,* probably supported this dress at the sides under the petticoat. These paniers soon became quite wide and gave a distorted, ungraceful, and exaggeratedly artificial look to the figure. By 1770 the hair was piled high on the head over great frames, powdered, and decorated by ribbons, flowers, and even miniature scenes. The major look for women during the Rococo Period was delicate charm and sentimentality; but as it came to an end, this image was lost in a desperate exaggeration of all the long-accepted fashion attributes of the style. This exaggeration of the 1770s was soon to disappear into the image of the natural man and woman promulgated by Jean Jacques Rousseau and the democratic ideals created by the American Revolution.

## ROCOCO AGE OF LOUIS XV

**Masculine Dress**   In the early years of the Regency, the man's coat and waistcoat were rather narrow at the shoulders, the coat was somewhat longer than during the last years of Louis XIV, and the vest was now definitely above the knees. The coat was usually left open, while the waistcoat was buttoned only at the waist. The wig was powdered white and was not as full as in the past; younger men were already placing the back of the wig in a bag with a black tie at the top or twisting it into a queue tied with a black ribbon. The silhouette at this point was rather conical or funnel-shaped as it expanded from the tip of the head to the area of the knees. Knee breeches were very tight, and stockings were frequently rolled over the breeches at the knee.

A very distinctive example of Regency dress in France may be seen in the famous painting *Gersaint's Signboard* by Antoine Watteau (Fig. 16–5). The men are still wearing the same silhouette as that worn in the later years of Louis XIV, but the fabrics seem softer, there is less braid and trim, the silhouette is less heavy and formal, and the colors are lighter. Also, the wigs do not appear to be as heavy and are now powdered grey or white. The male pose has also taken on a less formal and more elegant look (Fig. 16–2j,k).

About 1730 the silhouette changed to a dome shape as the skirts of the slightly shorter coat, as well as the skirts of the above-the-knee-length vest, were flared with horsehair and canvas interlinings (Fig. 16–2d). Many waistcoats were sleeved to the forearm, but without cuffs; the coat sleeve ended in full, turned-back cuffs that allowed the blouse of the shirt sleeve with its lace ruffle to show beneath (Fig. 16–2k,n). Breeches remained tight, with stockings gartered beneath or rolled up over the knee. Shoes, which were much less heavy than under Louis XIV, had a lower heel, invariably finished with a buckle, and had a much shorter tongue (Fig. 16–3m). Fashion decreed that the head appear small despite the wig; the powdered hair, after some soft curls or deep waves over the forehead

**FIG. 16–5** Antoine Watteau; *Gersaint's Signboard;* Palace of Charlottenburg, Berlin; 1720. Illustrates the softly falling pastel silks, Watteau pleats, and close-to-the-head hairdressing that superseded the formal Louis XIV style for ladies after the death of the monarch. Note also the grey color of the men's wigs and the limpness of vests and coats that had replaced Baroque formality. Photo courtesy of Jorg Anders, Berlin.

and ear, was usually drawn into a bag, or *crapaud,* with a black silk band tied in a bow at the back of the neck (Fig. 16–2b). When this ribbon was also brought around to the front to tie over the cravat, it was known as the *solitaire* (Fig. 16–2h). The cravat could be tied with lace ends, but more frequently the ends were merely wrapped to the back and fastened, allowing the ruffle, or *jabot,* on the shirt to show through the opening in the vest or waistcoat (Fig. 16–2h). Hats, though somewhat smaller than in the past, were still three-cornered and often trimmed in ostrich or embroidered in gold (Fig. 16–3e). Suits were heavily embroidered with gold, silver or silk thread, and the color harmonies throughout the period were primarily pastel with some darker tones as accent. Fabrics for men were primarily silks, velvets, and brocades, with woolens used for the middle class and for sporting costumes.

One of the best sources for costume between 1730 and 1750 is the work of William Hogarth in England. In his painting *The Marriage Con-tract,* we can note that the men's stockings are still gartered over their tight breeches, the vests are somewhat wide and flared in the skirts and reach to just above the knee, the cravats are tied loosely in a number of ways, and the young husband-to-be on the left wears the solitaire bow from his wig bag over his cravat (Fig. 16–6). The wigs range from shoulder length for the older men to very small queue wigs with waved fronts for the young groom. The father of the bride at the center still wears the Steinkirk cravat style that had been out of date for at least 20 years. The lawyer speaking with the wife-to-be wears the standard loose, black coat-gown with the starched white bands at the throat that was the standard uniform for attorneys at this time. The groom's father at the right typically has overindulged and has a ripe case of the gout with his foot heavily bandaged and raised on a footstool.

After 1750 only men with more conservative tastes wore the full-skirted coat, while the newer styles began to be cut back below the

**FIG. 16–6**  William Hogarth, *The Marriage Contract;* National Gallery, London; 1745. Note the white *full-bottomed wigs* still worn by the older men, in contrast to the trim white *bag wig* of the groom; the bride's father in the center still wears the twisted *Steinkirk* at the throat, while the groom wears the black *solitaire* over his *cravat.* Photo courtesy of the National Gallery of Art, London.

waist, had less fullness in the skirts, and displayed narrower sleeves and smaller cuffs. The waistcoat also began to rise and by 1760 only came to the crotch line. Pockets in both coat and waistcoat were smaller and were placed much higher on the coat, while shirt ruffles at the wrist now barely showed below the slim coat cuff. By the middle of the 1770s the coat was remarkably slim and fitted when compared to the 1740s.

The seated gentlemen in L. M. Vanloo's *The Cup of Chocolate* display the more abbreviated male costume lines of the period after 1750 (Fig. 16–7). The coats have slimmer-fitting, longer sleeves with slightly smaller cuffs; the fronts are now markedly sloped and cut back toward the back of the figure; the breeches are quite snug and fit down over the stockings; and the shoes are very unobtrusive and low-heeled, with a very modest buckle. Trim tends to be somewhat tighter than in the past, and there are fewer examples at this time of allover brocade vests.

Another similar male image may be seen in Drouais's *Group Portrait,* also painted in 1756 (Fig. 16–3). Here the gold trim is much richer, and the husband's pose over the back of the wife's chair is very typical. It demonstrates the contrived, casual elegance that was so much admired in posing against mantles, doors, and furniture throughout the period of the Rococo.

For outerwear men wore collared capes and mantles throughout the period, but overcoats became increasingly popular—first with the middle class and then with the aristocrats. For indoor undress men wore frogged housecoats and caps in place of the wig (Fig. 16–2i). In military wear this was the era when colors and

**FIG. 16-7** L. M. Vanloo (Charpentier), *The Cup of Chocolate;* The National Museum of Versailles; ca. 1755. Illustrates the elegant artificiality in the domestic manners the aristocracy borrowed from the bourgeois during the middle of the eighteenth century. Note the tight breeches, hip-length vests, and slightly cut-back coats in vogue after 1750. Photo courtesy of the French Musées Nationaux.

coat lines were codified, and the standardized uniform was developed. The cut was not unlike civilian dress except for the braided, turned-back coat facings, colored to distinguish regiments and national allegiance. Coat skirts also were buttoned back by mid-century for freedom in movement and riding, and this again displayed the facings of the coat (Fig. 16–2g). Legs were sheathed in boots if the wearer was an officer, in high-buttoned leggings if an enlisted man (Fig. 16–3k).

In general, the lines of middle-class costume were similar to the nobility, but with little ornamentation and the use of more practical fabrics like cotton and wool. Middle-class clothing usually contained less material and less subtlety of cut than did aristocratic dress. Children were still dressed like little adults, although by the close of this period a revolution in children's dress was in progress, influenced by Rousseau's belief in the innocence and uncorrupted charm of young children.

Jean-Baptiste Siméon Chardin's painting *Card Tricks,* painted about 1744, demonstrates the loose, not too well-tailored, woolen garments without decoration that were the standard wear for the middle class (Fig. 16–8). Note that there is no wig, the hair is tied back in a queue, and the tricorne hat is very modest in size. The shoes look very much like a modern buckled shoe.

Lower-class countrymen usually wore rough textured wool stockings and knee breeches, a loose collarless shirt and scarflike neckcloth, and a straight-cut coat or jacket of about finger-tip length. Sometimes a vest was worn with this ensemble, rough leather aprons were used over it in various trades, and the farmer usually wore a smock instead of a coat or vest. A slouch hat usually was pulled down over hair that might hang free or be twisted into a queue at the back of the neck. Wooden shoes were worn in the fields (Fig. 16–3g).

**Feminine Dress**   During the early Regency Period, a loose-fitting house gown became popular, laced loosely over an underdress or chemise in front and set with Watteau box pleats in back (Fig. 16-2l). These loose gowns were often held out at the sides by wicker-basket *paniers,* or hoops of boning (Fig. 16-2c), thus creating names for them like *robes volantes* (flying gowns) (Fig. 16-2a) or *robes batantes* (ringing gowns) because of the bell shape. If the gown was loose and pleated in front and back, it was known as a *sacque.* If it was not loose in front, but fitted tightly to a corset with the loose box pleats only in the back, it was known as the *robe à la française.*

The women's gowns in Watteau's painting *Gersaint's Signboard* epitomize the delicate, soft, relaxed styles of 1720 (Fig. 16-5). The lady on the left is wearing an early example of Watteau box pleating falling down the back of the gown from neck to floor; it was this style, when the bodice fitted closely to the body in front, that became the famous *robe à la française* (as opposed to the *robe à l'anglaise* in which these pleats at the back were stitched down to the underbody of the gown). The gown appears to be made of a very soft, shimmering silk and is done in a pastel color, while the delicate little lace cap

rests upon a lightly powdered hairdressing drawn tightly to the head. The whole effect is that of a dressing gown worn in the intimacy of private chambers, and that is exactly where this particular gown originated. Under the gown a modified bell hoop is worn, introduced about 1710 in England and about 1720 in France.

The lady seated to the right in the Watteau painting wears a delicately striped bodice and a skirt in shimmering, soft silk with a V-shaped corset showing at the front. A simple jacket open in front is worn over the bodice, and the sleeves of the jacket end in soft cuffs trimmed in ribbons. The ruffles set to the sleeves of the bodice cascade down over the forearm from under the sleeves of the jacket. In this case the tight hairdo is not powdered and is topped by a delicate lace cap.

In each case these ladies look completely different from those at the court of Louis XIV. Formality and excess has given way to soft domesticity. Much the same image is true of the female gowns in de Troy's *The Declaration of Love* (Fig. 16-2), although here the gowns are more richly ornamented. The Watteau-pleated backs still prevail, and delicate, serpentine, floral decoration is lightly sprinkled along edges or all over the gowns. Even the young bride in

Hogarth's *The Marriage Contract,* dating from 1745, retains the basic qualities of ruffly domesticity (Fig. 16-6).

By the middle of the 1740s the bell shape of many skirts held out by modest hoops changed to an elliptical form through the use of a basket arrangement of collapsible boning that held the skirts much further out on the sides than in the back or front. A quite exaggerated example of this change in silhouette may be seen in Arthur Devis' *Alicia Maria Carpenter, Countess of Egremont* (Fig. 16-9). The top of the skirt front and back is actually gathered together along the top line of the panier on each side in order to gain appropriate fullness on top of each panier side.

**FIG. 16-9** Arthur Devis, *Alicia Maria Carpenter, Countess of Egremont;* The Fine Arts Museums of San Francisco; 1745. Illustrates the exaggerated width of the *paniers* used to carry skirts laterally away from the body from 1750 to 1775. Note the rigid corseting and the loosely gathered silk panels held down by braid on the wide skirt. Photo courtesy of the Fine Arts Museums of San Francisco, The Mildred Anna Williams Collection.

During the 1740s there were rounded as well as square necklines on bodices, and closings could be either down the front or down the back. The smooth, V-shaped line of the boned bodice was almost always decorated in some way, either with lace, flowers, ribbons, brooches, or jewels. Sleeves could either be straight to the elbow, ending in ribbon bows and cascades of lace, or consisting of a series of lace puffs ending in ruffles (Fig. 16-4). Sometimes V-shaped bodice fronts were edged in flat folds of fabric which framed the *stomacher,* or corset, which might be of a different fabric or be elaborately embroidered. This is basically the effect seen on the lady seated on the right in Watteau's painting *Gersaint's Signboard* (Fig. 16-5). Sometimes this V-shaped bodice front was laced over the corset that it framed.

After 1750 the lateral paniers became standard wear and often stretched gowns to as much as four yards at the hem. Thus the standard presentation gown of mid-century had a square neckline, often trimmed in lace, with the bodice tightly fitted over a corset tapering to a modest point below the waist. Sleeves were narrow, reached to just above the elbows, and ended in a series of flaring, lace ruffles usually accented with a soft pastel bow or a bunch of imitation flowers. The neck usually carried a small lace ruffle or a ribbon, a small circlet of flowers, or a ribbon and bow, while the fabric that covered the low-cut corset (known as the *modestie*) was usually finished down the center with a series of bows decreasing in size *à la échelle.* The spreading lines of the open skirt revealed a richly decorated underskirt, or *jupe,* often with garlands of fabric, flowers, or lace hung in scallops about the skirt and known as *festoons.* Such gowns were a sea of ruffles, those gathered on one side known as *frills,* those gathered down the center known as *furbelows* or *falbalas.*

These basically are the gowns that appear in Boucher's *The Marquise de Pompadour* (Fig. 16-4) and Vanloo's *The Cup of Chocolate* (Fig. 16-7). They represent the growing complication in women's dress that was to reach an exaggerated excess in the early 1770s.

During the 1760s the great robes of the true Rococo style began to give way to more practical gowns for afternoon promenades, the most popular of which was the *polonaise* with a fitted back and front and an overskirt loosely draped up over an underskirt held out at the hips with starched ruffles and a *petticoat* (Fig. 16-3a). This overskirt was often drawn into a series of looped tiers by cords set into casing in the seams of the bodice. With this costume the heeled walking shoes showed beneath the ankle-length walking skirt, and with this a soft, silken jacket, or *caraco,* was sometimes worn. During these last years of the reign of Louis XV, outdoor promenade costumes were frequently topped by expansive linen and tulle dust caps, precariously placed atop the high coiffures (Fig. 16-3f,j).

Moreau, a marvelous printmaker during the last years of the reign of Louis XV and the early years of Louis XVI, gives us a great insight into the life, manners, and costume excesses of the close of the Rococo style. In *Le Rendez-vous pour Marly,* he captures the exuberance and ruffled fullness that was the standard just before the *style anglaise* was imported from England (Fig. 16-10).

From 1720 until about 1760 the female coiffure was set close to the head and consisted of a series of tight curls and waves, powdered white, silver, or grey, and often set with a small bunch of ribbons or flowers. Then in the last years before the death of Louis XV and the accession of Marie Antoinette and Louis XVI, there was an explosion in coiffure size; hair structures rose to such an incredible size that it is difficult to understand how women supported them (Fig. 16-3b,c). The early 1770s belonged to the hairdresser in women's fashion as no woman could do her own hair, even with the aid of a ser-

vant. The hair was combed up the sides over a horsehair pad and attached with pins and pomade, a looped-up plait and rolls of curls completing the coiffure at the back. Into this the hairdresser worked ribbons, flowers, and sometimes on top a frigate in full sail or miniature scenes. Since it took hours to construct such a coiffure, it was a luxury that could be indulged in only infrequently, and thus some women had their hair taken down and reset only once a month. Therefore it is not surprising, when one realizes that such coiffures were powdered with a form of flour, that they collected vermin and made a scratching stick essential. Also carriages often had to have tops that opened, and doorways sometimes had to be cut higher. Such headdresses were a short-lived fad that died in the late 1770s along with the great, lateral paniers (Fig. 16-3d).

Although nothing has been said of Italy during the Rococo Period, it was the vacation center for Europe, particularly Venice during Carnival. Pietro Longhi in his *Masked Conversation* (Fig. 16-11) captured the essence of this carefree life tinged with the secretiveness and mystery that came with the masks and disguises used by wealthy tourists and locals alike in the six months preceding Mardi Gras.

The clothing of the middle- and lower-class woman was generally a sleeveless bodice laced over a blouse or chemise with a rough outerskirt looped up over the petticoat. Caps were usually of the gathered dust-cap style, aprons were common, and shoes were of rough leather. Wooden shoes were usually worn by peasant women (Fig. 16-3h,i).

## FABRICS

Brocaded fabrics of great magnificence continued in this period in lighter colors and looser floral patterns, all against shimmering taffeta and satin backgrounds. There were also the standard velvets and cut velvets in light pastel colors. But the remarkable new craze was for plain, striped, and printed cottons. Cottons were very expensive and sharply limited by importation quotas, and thus they were con-

sidered a luxury. The craze for cotton also stimulated the local French cotton industry which made great strides in imitation Persian, Indian, and Chinese fabric patterns. Chinoiserie in interior decoration, upholstery, and clothing was the great new fashion throughout the first three quarters of the century, and all decorators borrowed heavily from Chinese sources. After the middle of the century, im-

**FIG. 16-10** Moreau (le jeune), *Le Rendez-vous pour Marly;* 1777. Illustrates the expanding height and complexity of the hairdressing in the 1770s as well as the famous new walking costume known as the *polonaise* with the skirt looped up into three sections by cords in the back seams. Photo courtesy of the Metropolitan Museum of Art, Harris Brisbane Dick Fund, 1933.

**FIG. 16-11** Pietro Longhi, *Masked Conversation;* Musèo Correr, Venice; c. 1760. Illustrates carnival costume in Venice. Note the short cape, the half-white mask with black lace veil, the *tricorne* hat, the ankle-length skirt which is held out by *paniers,* and the lavish use of metallic lace and braid as trim. Photo courtesy of Musèo Correr, Venice.

ported Indian cotton became popular for men's robes, women's house dresses, and certain negligees. White linen and lawn were still used for men's shirts and cravats; woolens were used for middle-class suits and dresses as well as for riding habits, outercloaks, and greatcoats.

## ARTS AND ARTIFACTS

Interior decoration in the second and third quarters of the eighteenth century was dominated by lightness in color and texture and great delicacy in line and form (Fig. 16–1). Woodwork was delicately carved, painted cream or white, and accented with gold leaf. Wall spaces that lacked wooden paneling or mirrors were covered with brocaded silks, hung with tapestries, or decorated with panel paintings. Decorative motifs in carving, upholstery, and wall hangings included loose groupings of baskets of flowers, musical instruments, or leaves and shells (Fig. 16–1a). Furniture was curvilinear in design, light in color and form, and upholstered in light, shimmering satin and taffeta brocades. Chairs now were frequently without arms, and the heavy stretchers between the legs were no longer necessary (Fig. 16–1c,e). Chests, desks, and cabinets were still done in wood marquetry and inlaid with shell or metal. The major new motif, as with fabrics, was the use of chinoiserie, and Chinese screens, lacquer cabinets, and porcelains became the highlight of many an aristocratic chamber (Fig. 16–1b,d).

In England, where Palladian classical influences were more important, decoration included simple Greek and Roman motifs—especially variations on the urn. Furniture was also primarily curvilinear but usually in dark wood rather than painted or gilded. Chinese porcelains also became the craze in table settings and sideboard displays.

Musical instruments included spinets, harpsichords, violins, guitars, and the German flute. Personal accessories for men included the light dress sword, hung from a belt and hanger underneath the coat and waistcoat; a gold or pearl-headed walking stick; inlaid snuff boxes that were carried in the pocket of the coat; the ever-present handkerchief, usually carried inside the cuff of the coat sleeve; the occasional clay pipe that was smoked within private chambers; and such standard items as muffs and gloves. Personal accessories for women included the ever-present folding fan, decorated with delicate paintings and trimmed with pearl and shell inlaid into the ivory that most often was the material for the stretcher sticks; pomanders, back scratchers, combs, scissors, and other such paraphernalia usually hanging from a cord at the waist; long gloves, lace hand mitts with fingers missing, and the ever-popular muff to warm the hands in winter; parasols that were now a must in summer for promenades in the park and were usually carried by a small black servant; and finally, such occasional oddities as the parakeet or pet monkey.

Jewelry for men was reduced to the ring, the badge or order pinned on the coat or worn on a silk baldric across the chest, and the pocket watch. Earrings were not much worn by women of this period, even though the hairdressing left the ears completely exposed. Chokers and necklaces were very popular, some inlaid combs were used in the hair, inlaid brooches often fastened the bodice in front, fingers were loaded with rings, bracelets were used by the more ostentatious ladies, and a small watch was occasionally seen hanging at the waist.

## VISUAL SOURCES

The first painter one should consult with regard to the Rococo is Antoine Watteau, more for his mood, color, and style than for details of civil or court dress. Then there are scores of other artists who developed and popularized this initial Watteau tradition, including Boucher, Lancret, de Troy, Pater, Nattier, Quentin la Tour, Perroneau, Coypel, Drouais, and Fragonard.

In England the key sources are Hogarth, Reynolds, Gainsborough and Zoffany. The middle-class scene in France is dealt with by Chardin and Greuze, and in Italy we have the paintings of Pietro Longhi in Venice. Institutional sources that are outstanding are the New York Public Library Print Collection, the Metropolitan Museum of Art, the Wallace Collection in London, the National Gallery in Washington, the Louvre, the Bibliothèque Nationale, and the Versailles National Museum. Useful books are the Cunningtons' *Handbook of English Costume in the Eighteenth Century,* Peter Gay's *Age of Enlightenment,* and Sidney Fiske Kimball's *The Creation of the Rococo.*

## SUMMARY

In this period the heavy formality of the classic Baroque style of Louis XV was swept away by the light, casual, delicate artificiality of the Rococo—a period usually symbolized by the *fête galantes* of Watteau and Fragonard, in which shimmering aristocrats amorously amused themselves amid the delicate greenery of chateau parks. It was the dying fall of the great Baroque aristocratic style of the past, interspersed with new elements coming from picturesque versions of middle- and lower-class ideals. It was the era of aristocratic game playing and dalliance just before those crucial years that led from the American to the French Revolution.

# chapter XVII

# Neoclassicism and Revolution

## Chronology

### (1775–1795)

| | | |
|---|---|---|
| NEOCLASSIC 1775–1790 | 1774 | Louis XVI and Marie Antoinette become the rulers of France; Geothe publishes *The Sorrows of Young Werther* |
| | 1775 | The battles of Lexington and Concord begin the American Revolution |
| | 1776 | The Americans issue the Declaration of Independence; Bentham publishes *Fragment on Government;* Paine's *Common Sense* appears; the first volume of Gibbon's *Decline and Fall of the Roman Empire* is published; San Francisco is founded; Adam Smith's *Wealth of Nations* is published |
| 1778 French | 1778 | Both Voltaire and Rousseau die; France joins the American colonies in their fight for independence |
| | 1779 | The performance of Gluck's *Iphigénie en Tauride* marks the triumph of the new form of opera; Hume's *Dialogues Concerning Natural Religion* are published; John Paul Jones' first naval victory |

**1782 English**

| 1780 | The first Sunday School is organized by Robert Raikes in England to teach the "3 R's" to working children |
|---|---|
| 1781 | Mozart settles in Vienna; Kant's *Critique of Pure Reason* appears; Joseph II frees the serfs in the Hapsburg domains |
| 1782 | Mozart begins his friendship with Haydn in Vienna |
| 1783 | The Treaty of Paris recognizes the United States as an independent nation; Montgolfier's hot air balloon |
| 1784 | Beaumarchais' play *The Marriage of Figaro* is presented |
| 1785 | The Diamond Necklace Scandal increases the unpopularity of Marie Antoinette; Schiller writes *Ode to Joy* and completes the play *Don Carlos;* the power loom is invented |
| 1786 | Frederick William II succeeds Frederick the Great of Prussia |
| 1787 | The Constitutional Convention is called in the United States; the impeachment of Warren Hastings in England; Mozart's *Don Giovanni* is performed in Prague |
| 1788 | Necker becomes France's Director-General of Finance; Mozart composes his last three symphonies |
| 1789 | The French Revolution begins with the storming of the Bastille; Lavoisier's *Elementary Treatise on Chemistry* is published; Bentham's *Principles of Morals and Legislation* is published; the American Constitution is adopted, and George Washington is inaugurated as the first president; the mutiny of the *H.M.S. Bounty* |

THE FRENCH
REVOLUTION
1790–1795

1788 French

1792 French

1790    Burke writes *Reflections on the Revolution in France;* the Feast of the Federation on the Champs de Mars; Civil Constitution of the Clergy is adopted in France; *Faust,* a fragment, is published by Goethe

1791    Death of Mirabeau; Louis XVI and Marie Antoinette's flight to Varennes; the Massacre of the Champ de Mars; the first French Constitution is formulated; Voltaire's body is taken to the Panthéon in Paris; Mozart dies; Marquis de Sade's *Justine* appears

1792    France declares war on Austria; Eli Whitney invents the cotton gin; the attack on the Palace of the Tuileries; establishment of the First Republic

1793    The second partition of Poland; execution of Louis XVI; The Reign of Terror begins; the fall of the Girondists; the United States establishes a Neutrality Proclamation; Charlotte Corday murders Marat; first daily paper in the U.S.—*The Pennsylvania Evening Post*

1794    The Thermidorean Reaction; *The Progress of the Human Spirit* by Condorcet is published; Robespierre is executed; Lavoisier dies

1795    Hutton's *Theory of the Earth* is published; the Directory is established; Napoleon Bonaparte, a young artillery officer, saves the government by suppressing the mob on October 5; the third partition of Poland

# BACKGROUND

Halfway through the eighteenth century, the rediscovery of Herculaneum and Pompeii caused a widespread passion for art based on details from classical antiquity. In his first history of the fine arts, published in 1775, the German archaeologist Winckelmann spoke with great admiration of the classical style as having "noble simplicity and tranquil grandeur." By the time that Louis XVI came to the throne of France, architecture, furniture, and interior decoration had returned to Greek and Roman sources for much of their inspiration; yet the new Neoclassicism was really an amalgam of many cultural ideals prevalent in the late eighteenth century. The Rococo ideals were now combined with the English Georgian styles, as well as Greek and Roman. Thus it was not a Greek or Roman revival based on the classical principles of composition and structure, but a "dream of the antique"—a charming, delicate, refined use of classical ornament, which after the curvilinear excesses of the Rococo placed great emphasis on horizontal and vertical lines.

At the same time an interest appeared in exotic, or *romantic,* art. This term was first used to describe art and literature based on storytelling romances of medieval times, but it came to include all art that appealed to the emotions. Both Neoclassicism and the new Romantic art included the concept of *associationalism*—that is, enabling the viewer to connect the art with personal or public emotions related to the self, the past, or the deeper realities beyond society, convention, or tradition. Thus the philosophic and cultural concept of "the natural man" developed—a person led by honest and true emotions rather than by convention, tradition, or classical rules of structure and organization. Jean Jacques Rousseau was the father of this concept, and it led to a great admiration for "the noble savage" abroad who had not been corrupted by civilized society.

In architecture and interior decoration, a structure was no longer necessarily admired for its harmony, balance, proportion, or correct details. Rather it was admired for the emotions and associations that could be aroused in the imagination of the viewer. Thus Neoclassic structures called forth feelings about Greek and Roman rationalism, stoicism, and republicanism, whereas exotic oriental and medieval structures (usually reserved for garden pavilions or weekend villas) called forth emotional escapist associations with other past times or faraway places. But the standard urban establishment interior was invariably in the Neoclassic style—a style that symbolized clarity of thinking, logic of organization, coolness of feeling, and an aristocratic status of position. An excellent example of this style of interior decoration may be seen in the Rheem Room, installed in the California Palace of the Legion of Honor in San Francisco (Fig. 17-1). There is the same elegance and sophistication found in a Rococo interior (see Fig. 16-1), but without the feminine curving lines in paneling and decoration. Accurately quoted pilasters frame the mantle mirror, the paneling is strictly rectangular, and the insets over the doors contain exact quotations from Greek sculptural friezes and Roman sarcophagi. The furniture has straight lines and geometric shapes, and the upholstery has a delicate play of symmetrical floral motifs. In every way this is a highly sophisticated, aristocratic interior in the tradition of the Rococo, but without its softness and decadence of relaxed, curved lines.

This was a period of great ferment and transition, both politically and culturally, in which at least three threads of development were at work: a dying Rococo elegance merging into the new Neoclassicism; a great new stress on Reason, the key ideal of the Enlightenment; and a growing interest in the emotional demands of Romanticism. Marie Antoinette, as the leader of fashion and style in France, gave support to all three. In her formal court functions she and her court combined the older Rococo traditions with the Neoclassic ideals in furniture and decoration, while the salons sponsored by intellectuals at her court discussed the latest views of the Enlightenment—freedom of the individual, constitutional government, and justice through law. At the same time in the gardens of the Petit

(a)
Louis
XVI
door

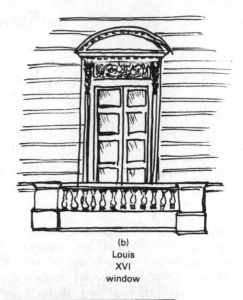

(b)
Louis
XVI
window

(c)
Louis XVI chair

The Rheem Room, from The Palace of the Legion of Honor, San Francisco; ca. 1780. A typical neoclassical interior of the period of Louis XVI that demonstrates the straight lines, elegant restraint, and direct copies of ornamentation from Roman sarcophagi that mark late-eighteenth-century French interiors. Photo courtesy of the Fine Arts Museums of San Francisco.

(d)
English shield
back armchair
ca. 1778

**FIGURE 17–1**

Trianon, the queen built a Rustic Village, or *Hameau,* which contained a Temple of Love, a Dairy, and an Old Mill—romantic settings against which to play out a game of picturesque milkmaids milking scrubbed cows into Sèvres vases. Thus while Marie Antoinette was playing out a dream of romance against theatrical settings of ruins, waterfalls, and make-believe props, intellectual leaders such as Burke, Jefferson, Voltaire, and Lessing were creating a new view of the relationship between a government and its people.

When this period opened, three people dominated European politics—Maria Theresa in Austria, Frederick the Great in Prussia, and Catherine the Great in Russia—but by the time of the French Revolution, all were gone. Younger, aggressive, nonaristocratic opportunists such as Danton and Robespierre in France were waiting in the wings to grab the reigns of power and to sweep away the last vestiges of privilege and tradition. In England it was the intellectual, upper-middle-class members of Parliament, such as William Pitt the Younger, who led thinking and government action, not the king, George III. And in America, men such as Jefferson and Washington, who had led the colonies into self-government under the Constitution of 1789, were admired throughout the Western world as representative of the way of the future.

After the American War of Independence, the balance of power had shifted so that England, France, and Spain all had less influence in North America. In central Europe the duel for power between Prussia and Austria came to a draw with the death of Maria Theresa and Frederick the Great, while Poland was gradually removed from the map of Europe by a series of partitions among Prussia, Austria, and Russia. Although Italy was still the ultimate goal in all grand tours of Europe and the place where artists still went to study, it was very weak politically and divided into many small kingdoms and principalities allied to foreign powers like Spain and Austria. Spain was still in a period of rapid decline with almost no impact on the European scene, either culturally or politically. Thus at the outbreak of the French Revolution, the two greatest powers in western Europe—both politically and culturally—were France and England.

## THE BASIC COSTUME SILHOUETTE

As with all phases of culture, costume and fashion changed greatly in the years just before and during the French Revolution. Before the Revolution women still wore high coiffures, corsets, padding, boning, and several layers of clothing; by the end of the Revolution they were wearing simple chemise dresses of the softest fabrics without boning, corseting, or padding. For men the change was equally great. Since the sixteenth century men had been wearing variations of breeches and hose, and now within about a 15-year period men began to experiment with the long trousers that had been the garb of the lowest peasants for generations. They gave up powdered hair and wigs in favor of natural windblown coiffures and moved to riding pants, boots, and woolen riding coats from the satins, silks, and velvets of the earlier eighteenth century. All of this great ferment and change was a move away from the symbols of aristocracy to the symbols of the lower and middle classes.

The male figure after the American Revolution became slimmer, with the coat cut sharply away in front to round tails at the outside edges of the back. Sleeves were slim, cuffs small or nonexistent, and the waistcoat was snug and waist length or a little below. Breeches were very tight-fitting to the knee and worn over silk stockings, while shoes were small and low-heeled. The materials were still usually delicately colored silks, but stripes were more prevalent, and silver and gold braid and lace on the edges of the coat and waistcoat were less dominant. The hat was still a tricorne edged in braid, wigs were small and powdered with a brushed roll in front, but more often than not, the natural hair was worn in a queue and without powder. At home the wig, if worn, was replaced by a turban or cap and the coat by a silk dressing gown. These styles are evident in the etching *Conversation in the Drawing Room* by François Dequevauviller after a painting by N. Lavreince (Fig. 17-2). Though there are many changes in individual garments, the aristocratic character of the male costume is little changed from the late Rococo.

In the early 1780s, the *style anglaise* made its appearance. Stockings and shoes were replaced by closefitting riding breeches and boots, the tricorne was replaced by a flat-brimmed jockey hat or a *bicorne,* and woolen fabrics replaced silks as the major fabric for the coat. Coats began to have standing, turnover collars, with skirts cut back even more sharply than in the past or stepped back at the waist before receding into tails. These styles continued with additions and embellishments into the Revolution and may be seen in Debucourt's print of *The Public Promenade* (Fig. 17-3). Note that the cravats are very high on the chin and that many of the coats not only have a high collar but also have lapels as do the waistcoats, whose lapels overlap those of the outercoat. Note also that sloping-crowned top hats have made their appearance, the earliest indications of a development that would last in varying form until the present day. A print by R. Kotel of uniforms worn by the National Guard during the Revolution shows the use of the long, straight, striped trousers, or *sans culottes* (Fig. 17-4). Here the men wear military hats, but the headgear for the revolutionary was the *Phrygian cap* of the galley slave, while coats were usually the loose-fitting peasant jackets known as the *carmagnole.*

In feminine fashions the panier and the robe à la française were used only on formal ceremonial occasions and gradually disappeared in the late 1780s in favor of various drapings of an overskirt over padding at the back of the waist. Shoes were of silk with high heels, and ladies *en promenade* had skirts of ankle length and carried walking sticks and parasols. In the late 1770s coiffures were still enormous—built up over frames and pads, held in place by pins and pomade, and culminating in flowers, fruits, or miniature scenes from life. By the 1780s the *costume anglaise,* as with the men, had become the major new fashion. Hoops and paniers disappeared, and the gown fell loosely around the body over many petticoats or a bustle pad at the back of the waist. The hair was arranged in loose curls on top of the head, and the shoulders were usually covered by a soft, transparent scarf, or *fichu.* Sleeves were now usually slim and reached to the wrist, while great straw hats and bonnets often framed the face. These are the basic styles that can be seen in the print *Conversation in the Drawing Room* by Dequevauviller (Fig. 17-2) and even in *The Public Promenade* by Deboucourt (Fig 17-3). In the latter, one is struck by the enormous size of the hats, the large expanse of the fichu, and the strong use of sashes at the waist. One is also very aware that the corset no longer exists, although a laced-bodice effect in a number of dresses sharply controls the waist.

During the height of the Revolution, the only major changes in female dress came in the casual disarray that was displayed in the use of the fichu and muslin gown, plus the addition of tricolor cockades and sashes to identify with the Republic. Also, the first experiments with "antique garb" based on the tunics and draperies of the Greeks and Romans were attempted, but these tunic dresses did not make a firm fashion stand until the years directly following the close of the Revolution.

## NEOCLASSIC AND REVOLUTION

**Masculine Dress** By the late 1770s and early 1780s there were numerous changes in men's fashions, with a variety of ideas tried at the same time. The most noticeable feature was in the tightness and slim lines of the coat, which now had very narrow sleeves, a minimum cuff or no cuff (Fig. 17-3k,m) at all, and a sharply cut-back front line to the coat that made it impossible to button. Collars were also beginning to appear at the coat's neckline (Fig. 17-2c,d,g). The waistcoat was reduced to a very short line that barely reached below the

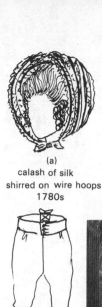

(a)
calash of silk
shirred on wire hoops
1780s

(b)
powdered
wig
covered
by Thérèse 1784

(c)
beaver
hat
and natural
hair
1780s

(d)
flat
beaver
Quaker-style
1780s

(e)
formal
powdered
headdress
1778

(f)
linen
or
flannel drawers—
English late 1780s

(h)
embroidered
French vest
1780s

(g)
black
silk
cravat
over linen
jabot

Francois Dequevauviller, engraving after Lavreince, *Conversation in the Drawing Room,*
1784. Ilustrates the softer feminine clothing lines and the tight sleeves, small cuffs, and
cut-back coats of men's court dress in the decade before the French Revolution, both set
against the delicate, aristocratic, classical interiors of the period of Louis XVI. Photo
courtesy of the Metropolitan Museum of Art, Harris Brisbane Dick Fund, 1935.

(j)
folding paniers
with tapes

military
ca. 1775

caraco gown
French 1785

(i)
fur-trimmed silk pelisse 1778

(k)

(l)

(m)
levite redingote
or great
coat

**FIGURE 17–2**

striped
waistcoat
1795

(a)

(b)
stuffed bolster 1790

English
serving
girl
ca. 1790

(c)

bustle-backed
house costume
ca. 1790

(d)

(e)
felt bicorne
tricolor
cockade

(f)
phrygian
bonnet

(g)
bonnet of tulle
and taffetta

(i)
chemise a l'anglaise

Debucourt, *The Public Promenade;* 1792. Illustrates the mixed styles seen in public gathering places during the Revolution. Note the continued use of cadogan wigs and powdered hair, the high collars and wide lapels, double-breasted, tailed or sharply cut-back coats, and the form-fitting breeches of the men, as well as the soft muslin dresses with large *fichus* and normal waistlines *à la anglaise* on many of the women. Photo courtesy of the Caisse Nationale des Monuments Historiques et des Sites, © Arch. Phot. Paris/S.P.A.D.E.M.

(h)

(j)
sans culotte
tricolor cockade,
red sash

(k)
coat cuff
1780

(l)
bonnet of the
populace—tricolor band

(m)
coat
cuffs
1790—1795

(n)
incroyable 1795

chemise and
tights under
chemise dress
1795

298

**FIG. 17-4** R. Kotel, *Uniforms of Officers and Troops of the National Guard;* 1793–1794. Note the use of striped long trousers, symbols of the proletariat, tight like the old aristocratic riding pants for officers, loose and straight like peasant trousers for the soldiers. Note that coats and hats are copies of the uniforms worn under the old regime. Photo courtesy of the Metropolitan Museum of Art Print Room.

waist (Fig. 17-2h). Wigs were worn less than in the past, since many younger men now wore their own hair in a queue without benefit of powder. When a wig was worn, it was often done in a club-shaped arrangement known as the *cadogan* style with hair rolled under—a style that had originated in the stables. In fact, many of these styles of the 1780s were a result of the English riding habit making itself felt as a major fashion source in the upper-class circles of society.

The standard tricorne that had held sway in male clothing since the last decade of the seventeenth century also began to be replaced by a variety of new hats. First there was the change of the shape of the tricorne to a two-and-a-half-cornered hat called an *androsmane* that was almost a bicorne. This style had been used by army officers for some time but now became fashionable as a civil dress hat (Fig. 17-3e). There was also a low-crowned jockey hat with a moderately narrow brim rolled slightly upward all around, and the beginnings of the low-crowned top hat with sloping sides that made an appearance by the middle of the 1780s (Fig. 17-2c,d).

The male breeches, now fully exposed because of the short waistcoat, fitted so closely that two pairs came with a suit of clothes: one for standing at state occasions; the other for sitting or more active pursuits. The desire for such wrinkle-free breeches led to the use of soft leather as a major material during this period—it had been used in riding and military breeches for some time—since it was one of the few materials that could stand the body strain and that had enough elasticity to give the perfect tight fit. Later in the Empire Period, knitted trousers were used to accomplish the same tight fit (Fig. 17-2f). Boots came in as a major item of male civil dress attire during the late 1780s, once again adopted for riding and military dress. The riding breeches worn with such boots were no longer knee breeches, but were calf-covered breeches that could be worn with regulation riding boots or the new half boots, or *buskins.* The latter were also worn with knee breeches and striped stockings.

The fascination with striping reached a peak during this period as may be seen in the Duhamel engraving of a young man in a striped coat, waistcoat, and stockings (Fig. 17-5). He wears a very large hat that is almost a bicorne, with only a limited point at the front; a stock tied in a bow over a moderately ruffled shirt front; a very tight-fitting, striped coat, with a high, raised collar, buttoned to the waist over a striped vest that shows slightly below the waist. The coat sleeves are very slim and tight-fitting, with the tiniest of cuffs, and the breeches, also form-fitting, are worn over striped hose. This fashionable gentleman wears the new cadogan wig, a watch worn on a striped band or fob at the right side of the waist, and coat skirts that are square cut rather than curved to the back. This so-called *fraque* coat was an adaptation

**FIG. 17-5** Duhamel, engraving of a young man in striped coat, waistcoat, and stockings and *androsmane* hat; 1786–1787. Illustrates the use of stripes, slim lines, high collars, short vests, and very tight breeches that dominated male style in the 1780s. The coat is the frock cut imitated from the English and the forerunner of the nineteenth-century frock coat; the hat is borrowed from the military. Photo courtesy of the Cabinet des Modes, Bibliothèque Nationale, Paris.

from a certain style in English riding coats (Fig. 17–3n). One must remember that this was a street or walking costume, not a formal court or reception dress such as shown in the De-quevauviller etching (Fig. 17–2). In formal afternoon and evening costume, striped fabrics and boots of any kind were still considered out of place.

In J. B. Mallet's painting *An Animated Salon,* dating from about 1790, the male clothing shows a few more changes (Fig. 17–6). One assumes that most of the men are wearing their own hair, not a wig, and that the hair is no longer powdered. The coats fit, if this is possi-ble, with an even greater tightness and slimness of line, and the vests now have wide lapels that overlap the emerging lapels of the coat. The stock around the neck is growing ever higher so that the chin sinks down into this neckcloth that is then framed by an even higher collar on the coat.

For outerwear the long, full, collared cape was still a standard garment, but it was rivaled in its popularity by the triple-collared, double-breasted overcoat, or *redingote,* with large lapels. In fact, on all male coats by 1790 great emphasis was placed on high collars and wide lapels. It is one of the sharpest distinctions between the male coats from 1715 to 1785 and those from 1785 into the following period of the Empire (Fig. 17–2m).

Although one would have thought that wearing fashionable attire during the height of the Reign of Terror would have been extremely dangerous, we have a number of sketches and prints that show the foppish excesses that appeared on the streets of Paris during the most violent years of the French Revolution. In Debucourt's *The Public Promenade* (Fig. 17–3) men with powdered wigs and hair, a symbol of the old aristocracy, jostle with those in the latest styles—tight trousers, boots, striped coats cut sharply away, and large lapels and collars on both coats and waistcoats. By this time a number of men wore the new double-breasted, stepped-back coats with long, *clawhammer* tails that gave more attention to the bottom of the vest and the watch fob at the waist. This became the favorite new male coat style during the succeeding Directoire and Empire Periods. Note also that a number of the male breeches in this print have bunches of loops at the bottom outside of the knee in place of the buttons and buckles that had been prevalent for the past half century, and the buckled shoes have been replaced by low, pointed pumps with bows below the instep (Fig. 17–3).

In contrast to these fashionable people in promenade were the quickly organized, lower-class revolutionaries who made up the National Guard in 1792 (Fig. 17–4). The upper part of their uniform is standard for the last quarter of the eighteenth century: bicorne or leather, hel-metlike hats; the cutaway coat with buttoned-

back lapels over a white, double or single-breasted vest; cartridge boxes carried on white baldric bands over the shoulder; and epaulets, military braid, and gold buttons for trim. The distinctive addition comes in the striped, ankle-length, loose trousers, or sans culottes, of the peasants, which the ghetto revolutionaries adopted as the uniform for the National Guard (Fig. 17-3j). Regular uniforms of the period looked much the same except soldiers wore tight knee breeches that fitted into boots or leggings (Fig. 17-2k). The revolutionary bonnet of the time was the red Phrygian cap with tricolor cockade (Fig. 17-3f).

Finally, let us look at a very famous portrait by Jacques-Louis David that sums up elegant male attire at the close of the French Revolution. In his portrait *Monsieur de Sériziat* dated 1795, David shows the beautifully tailored, double-breasted, high collared riding coat of wool with wide lapels that is standard conservative wear in this period (Fig. 17-7). The cravat, or *stock,* is tied in a moderate bow above the ruffles of the skirt; the trousers are of tight leather buttoned at the knee and also tied together with thongs. The boots do not meet the breeches, and the new sloping, high-crowned hat with rolling brim is in the very latest style and markedly different in shape and feeling from the tricorne of the past ninety years. With this portrait, we are on the brink of a new look for men that would develop into the industrial-capitalist uniform of the nineteenth century and remain with variations to this day.

Throughout this last quarter of the eighteenth century, the middle and lower classes

**FIG. 17-7** Jacques-Louis David, *Monsieur de Sériziat;* The Louvre, Paris; 1795. Note the double-breasted riding coat with wide lapels, high collar, and slim sleeves without cuffs. Also note the short, double-breasted waistcoat with lapels, the *stock,* or *cravat,* above the shirt ruffle, or *jabot,* and the tight doeskin breeches that do not quite reach the riding boots. The hat is the latest style with sloping crown and moderate brim that has replaced the *tricorne.* Photo courtesy of the French Musées Nationaux.

refused to make many changes in their dress. The change was in the upper-class male who now wore unornamented woolen fabrics in beautifully tailored lines that were, although very refined, related to the rough woolens that had been worn by the lower and middle classes for decades.

**Feminine Dress**   Although the full grandeur of the beribboned and ruffled robe à la française was still worn with its ornate coiffure and wide paniers for formal court functions in the late 1770s, promenade costumes were now worn in a variety of draped lines over modified paniers. One example was the *polonaise,* draped

up in three great puffs of skirt over the back and sides of the underskirt (Figs. 17–3, also 16–3a). Sometimes this was accomplished by cords threaded through rings or casings on the inside seams that were then pulled to give the desired draped length. At other times ribbons were used that were fastened at the inside at the waist and looped up over the outerskirt to shape it into desired puffs, while sometimes it was looped up by pleating or shirring the material permanently along the seams. Still another casual way to create a polonaise effect was to place part of the overskirt into a slit or pocket, thus creating a draped-up effect in the back and at the sides.

Since these walking costumes had so much fullness around the waist due to the uses of a collapsible panier under the petticoat (Fig. 17–2j), they were frequently not floor length but ended at the ankle to give freedom in walking. This marked the first time in the history of fashionable female dress that gowns exposed this much of the foot and ankle.

Necklines during the late 1770s and early 1780s were very low and cut in a kind of square with rounded edges outlined in a ruffle (Fig. 17–2). Promenade gowns were also festooned with ribbons, bows, and ruffles as well as with padded, sausage-shaped trimming on overskirts that gave a three-dimensional ornamentation to the skirt and was known as *plastic decoration.*

Still another variation in promenade styles was the caraco gown which had a jacket that flared out over the hips and ended with a double ruffle just below the widest part of the modified panier. It often had a Watteau pleat at the back of the jacket and looked like a polonaise gown cut off at the hips. This style remained in fashion throughout the 1780s (Fig. 17–2l).

But the feature which seemed to be most dominant in the female silhouette of the late 1770s was the huge coiffure that remained until the beginning of the 1780s (Fig. 17–2e). Fabricated from false hair, crinkled crinoline, padding, and flour paste, these hairdos were complex affairs that took hours of patient labor by trained professional hairdressers. Vermin often infested such flour and paste structures and had to be hunted by making a slit in the hard exterior surface of the coiffure to allow the lady to use an ivory scratching stick inside. A poem of the time commented:

> When he views your tresses thin,
> Touched by some French Friseur,
> Horsehair, hemp and wool within
> Garnished with a diamond skiver;
> When he scents the mingled steam
> Which your plastered head is rich in,
> Lard and meal and clotted cream,
> Can he love a walking kitchen?

Why women did not adopt the wigs of the men is unclear. Certainly they would have been more practical as far as time spent at the hairdressers and far more hygienic. In fact, this style (as well as the powder used on men's wigs and hair) so depleted the amount of flour available in France at this time that this fact was used as a major weapon against the aristocrats later during the Revolution when the supply of bread ran low.

Even when the hairdos were not quite as high, stiff, and formal, various voluminous headcoverings were devised to enclose these coiffures. The *thérèse* was a great bag of lightweight material that served as a windbreak for the hair outdoors (Fig. 17-2b). The *calash* was another bonnet that was formed of many ribs or hoops of reed or whalebone under a semitransparent fabric that could be raised and lowered by a ribbon, like the hood of a carriage (Fig. 17-2a). Still another lingerie cap was the *dormeuse,* or sleeping bonnet, which was often worn at night as well as in the morning and in the garden (see Fig. 16-3j). It hugged the head tightly, covering the cheeks, and was threaded with a ribbon tied into a bow on the top of the head, although in the daytime the dormeuse was worn higher on the head with less closeness to the face.

During the 1780s paniers gradually decreased in size and finally disappeared, so that skirts once again fell directly to the floor over ruffles or pads at the rear waist without the draping, looping, and puffing that characterized promenade dresses of the previous decade (Fig. 17-3d). Thus a new silhouette was created that was in many ways analogous to the bustle line of the 1880s–a century later (Fig. 17-3b). The soft, transparent neckcloth, or *fichu,* which surrounded the neck and tucked into the low-cut neckline made the breast area project with great fullness to be balanced by the back projection of the bustle ruffles (Fig. 17-21). Frequently this bustle projection was also accented by having a peplum project from the caraco jacket only at the back of the figure. Sometimes the new line for the caraco jacket contained large lapels in imitation of those emerging in men's wear, and these further framed and accentuated the fullness of the fichu over the breast. The latter was also worn in a variety of ways: crossed at the breast and tucked into a sash; crossed in front and tied at the back of the waistline; and tucked into the jacket under the lapels. Sleeves now were often slim to below the elbow with no bows or cuffs and ending in a ruffle on the forearm, or slim and full length to the wrist with a tiny ruffle over the knuckles.

During this period many styles imported from England for Marie Antoinette and her circle were made by the greatest dressmaker of the day, Rose Bertin. About 1780 she was still designing very ruffly and feminine clothes with many festoons and bows for the queen and her court; but soon after she began to introduce the tailored masculine lines of the redingote gown from England, along with certain sheer muslin gowns tied with a sash at the waist, as seen in the 1780 portraits of Romney, Lawrence, and Gainsborough.

The redingote gown had originally been an English riding habit. The upper part had a collar, collar capes, lapels, and long sleeves. The gown fitted smoothly to the waist, then spread out in a full overskirt usually open in front to show the underskirt (Fig. 17-8). In France this style was often modified into a coat-dress without collar and lapels that came to be known as the *levite gown.* The sheer, white muslin chemise tied with a sash at the waist was the great new style in England in the 1780s. It was based on classical ideals and the imagery of the "natural man (or woman)"—tied to nature, simplicity, and honest sentiment (Fig. 17-3i). In France, where the formalities of the court made such simple, natural styles less acceptable, these *robes en chemise* were reserved for in-this style is in Thomas Gainsborough's *Mrs. Richard Brinsley Sheridan,* painted in 1783 (Fig. 17–9).

As shown in Mrs. Sheridan's portrait, hair in the 1780s was far more loosely coiffured than in the 1770s, and there was also a great stress on millinery to support the new outdoor, natural look. Sometimes hats were soft creations of ruffles and fabric with little shape and a minimal amount of inner framing to give them form; at other times they were great straw hats with high, flaring crowns embellished with flowers and ribbons; and still others were continuations

FIG. 17–8 Duhamel, engraving of a young woman in a *redingote* gown of lemon yellow taffeta; 1786–1787. Illustrates the flat-collared gown buttoned up the front that was inspired by English male riding costume. It is worn over a full underskirt with a *fichu* about the neck and a huge bonnet hat over a loose, wind-swept coiffure. Photo courtesy of the Cabinet des Modes, Bibliothèque Nationale, Paris.

formal walks in the park, picnics, or the Marie Antoinette charade of playing milkmaid with her ladies. Invariably the chemise dress was sheer, white *mousseline,* or muslin, fastened down the back and caught at the waist with a sash. The underskirt and corset, which usually showed through the transparent muslin, were usually of pale blue or pale pink silk. The soft and transparent fichu was usually of linen gauze, and the hairdo that accompanied the style was usually soft and windblown without a trace of formality. One of the best projections of

FIG. 17–9 Thomas Gainsborough, *Mrs. Richard Brinsley Sheridan;* National Gallery of Art, Washington; ca. 1783. Illustrates the new chemise gown introduced into English fashion in the early 1780s and known in France as *la robe à l'anglaise.* This gown, often in layers of transparent muslin, fell loosely about the body over soft petticoats and a bustle pad at the back, while the only accents were the *fichu* at the neck and the sash at the waist. Photo courtesy of the National Gallery of Art, Andrew Mellon Collection, 1937.

of the bonnet effects that had been ushered in with the calash in the 1770s (Fig. 17–3g,l). The 1780s was one of the great highpoints in the art of millinery, when women were crowned with great, loose hairdos framed in the richest inventions of the milliner's art. The hair was now usually very curly, loose and full, with height at the back, fullness on the sides, and frequently loose curls straying onto one or both shoulders. Although to us it certainly does not look like a completely natural look, after the fabrications of the late 1770s, it must have seemed very casual (Fig. 17–2a,b).

Now let us return for a moment to the afternoon formalities in the famous Dequevauviller etching *Conversation in the Drawing Room* (Fig. 17–2). The women here all have the large but loose coiffures, prominent caps and hats, fichus, long sleeves, tight bodices, and full skirts over a bustle that marked the sharp change of silhouette in the 1780s. Let us now compare this etching with J. B. Mallet's painting *An Animated Salon,* from about 1790 (Fig. 17–6). Here many of the same female fashions are still in vogue, with less softness and sentimentality and more exaggeration and excess. Hair seems even fuller, hats larger and more exaggerated, fichus more excessive, and bustles more pronounced than in the earlier work. By 1792, when Debucourt depicted *The Public Promenade,* the styles seem if possible even a trifle more blatant and hysterical (Fig. 17–3). Note the female figure at the far left with the exaggerated bustle, the puffed-out bosom or pouter-pigeon look that is created by the bodice line of the levite gown accentuated by the fichu, while the hair cascades over the shoulders from under a straw hat that has an almost comic jauntiness.

As an example of how these general styles spread rapidly to the rest of Europe, look at the famous Goya portrait *The Marquesa de Pontejos,* usually dated 1790 (Fig. 17–10). Her round-necked, semitransparent dress has flowers and ribbons holding up the overskirt over a pleated underskirt, the sleeves are slim and long, and the halo of full hair supports a very large straw hat. This was the aristocratic look in Spain as the revolution developed in France.

As for outerwraps the fur-trimmed *pelisse,* or

**FIG. 17–10** Francisco Goya, *The Marquesa de Pontejos;* National Gallery of Art, Washington; 1790. Note the lightly powdered hair in a great halo about the face, the gauzy gray costume with touches of pink, the tight sleeves, the outerskirt held up with ribbons, and the round lace collar preferred in Spain in place of the *fichu.* Courtesy of the National Gallery of Art, Andrew Mellon Collection, 1937.

armhole cape, was the most popular along with a fleecy muff, although the simple caped and hooded cloak was also popular (Fig. 17–2). Shoes still had moderate heels and pointed toes with a bow or brooch just below the instep.

Middle- and lower-class women still wore a simple bodice, skirt over a petticoat, three-quarter-length sleeves with a simple ruffle at the bottom, an apron, and some form of a dust cap. The only new item was the fichu or a straw hat for outdoors (Fig. 17–3c).

# FABRICS

The great new fabrics for men in this period were the various woolen broadcloths that began to supersede silks and velvets for men's coats and the sheer muslins that began to be the major dress fabric in many women's styles. In the more masculine female styles like the redingote gown, woolen broadcloth made its appearance as a fabric for women although many levite and caraco styles still used satins and taffetas. Velvets were often used in female fashions for wraps or as an accent in underdresses of muslin or silk gauze.

# ARTS AND ARTIFACTS

The Neoclassic style in interior decoration that became more prominent in the late 1770s and 1780s was based on many exact quotations in paneling, door decoration, upholstery motifs, and furniture treatment from the discoveries at Herculaneum and Pompeii (Fig. 17-1). The Louis XVI style in furniture, in contrast to the Louis XV Rococo treatment, was delicate in line, less ornate in ornament, and stressed straight legs, oval or square backs, and carved inlay in Greek or Roman patterns. Upholstery was in delicate-toned, floral patterns or stripes in satin and grosgrain. There was more use of natural wood, especially satinwood, although there was still much overpainting of paneling and furniture in grey and white. The use of pale, cool colors, especially in imitation Chinese porcelains was widespread.

In England there was an even greater stress on copying from Greece and Rome, particularly in the interiors and furnishings of Robert Adam and in the ceramics of Thomas Wedgewood. The work of the latter in cool rusts, greens, and blues accented in white classical scenes gives us the perfect artifacts for expressing the mood of the period. In fact it is in the ceramics, glass, and porcelains of the last quarter of the eighteenth century that we find our most harmonious and perfected decorative sources for the Late Georgian-Louis XVI Period.

Personal accessories for men included canes—a very large item during this period—as well as snuffboxes, handkerchiefs, and muffs. For women, parasols with long and short handles and varieties of domed shapes were the single most important outdoor accessory, but fans and gloves remained important as did drawstring purses, walking sticks, and muffs.

As for jewelry, the largest new item for men was the watch fob worn at the waist. Often a watch was worn at each side of the man's waist, although men also frequently wore one fob with a watch and one without. The watches themselves were rather cumbersome, with covers of gold and inlaid jewels. Men also wore a ring or two and gold or silver buckles at the knees and on the shoes.

Women used brooches to fasten the fichu and a few wore earrings, but in general the 1780s saw little use of earrings or even necklaces. In a period that stressed the "natural woman," jewelry was considered inappropriate. There were still shoe buckles, rings, and even bracelets, but these were inconspicuous in comparison to their recent usage. One style that was very popular was the cameo brooch, done in cool colors and white and based on classical sources. These could be worn around the throat on a chain or as a pin on the dress.

Middle-class ladies frequently had a hook at the waist from which hung scissors, needle and thimble cases, a watch, and other odd items.

# VISUAL SOURCES

The best visual sources in this period are the many fashion manuals and magazines that developed to demonstrate new clothing styles. The best are *La Galerie des Modes* 1778–1787 and *Cabinet des Modes*. Another excellent source for the early years of this period are the sketches of

Moreau le Jeune, who covered every aspect of French aristocratic life in the late 1770s and early 1780s. Other useful French sources are the engravers Dequevauviller and Debucourt, and the painters Boilly, Vigée-Lebrun, J. L. David, Hubert Robert, and Antoine Vestier. In England the painters Reynolds, Romney, Lawrence, and Gainsborough are very useful, and in Spain the early work of Goya is indispensable. The best institutional sources are the Bibliothèque Nationale in Paris, the National Portrait Gallery in London, the National Galleries in London and Washington, the Louvre, the Metropolitan Museum of Art, the Henry Huntington Art Gallery in San Marino, California, and the Prado in Madrid. Useful books are Stéphane Faniel's *French Art of the Eighteenth Century,* and Peter Gay's *The Enlightenment.*

## SUMMARY

This was a period of transition from the soft, artificial, and somewhat decadent imagery of the Rococo to the excesses of freedom and natural body line exposure that followed the French Revolution. The period was considered Neoclassic because of the craze in interiors and decoration for ornament based on the finds at Herculaneum and Pompeii, but it was also an age of romanticism in which even classical imagery was seen for its emotion-evoking associations rather than for its composition and design. It was also the age of the "natural man (and woman)" in which simplicity, casualness, and natural sentiment were meant to replace artificiality and decadence. In men's clothing fashions shifted from court inspiration to riding costume, from velvets and satins to woolens, from easy artificiality to tight-fitting sleekness. For women formal paniers and ruffles with silks and satins were replaced by windblown coiffures and muslin chemise dresses.

# chapter XVIII

# Directoire and Empire

## Chronology

### (1795–1815)

| | | |
|---|---|---|
| DIRECTOIRE AND CONSULATE 1795–1804 | 1795 | Establishment of the Directory; the third partition of Poland |
| | 1796 | Napoleon's first campaign in Italy for the Directory; Antoine Jean Gros paints the famous portrait *Napoleon at Arcola;* Jenner discovers vaccination serum |
| | 1797 | Mme. Tallien is leader of Parisian society; the waltz is introduced from Germany and becomes the craze of Paris; inauguration of John Adams as President |
| 1798 French | 1798 | Napoleon's campaign in Egypt; the Swiss Confederation becomes the Helvetic Republic; Wordsworth and Coleridge publish *Lyrical Ballads* |
| | 1799 | Napoleon becomes first consul; naval warfare between England, France, and America; Rowland Hill's postal reforms |
| | 1800 | *The Family of Charles IV* is painted by Goya; Napoleon begins the beautification of Paris |
| | 1801 | England and Ireland are united; Beau Brummell begins his reign as fashion arbiter to Regency society in England |

1800 English

| 1802 | West Point is founded; Napoleon made consul for life |
| 1803 | Louisiana purchased by the United States for $15 million; Napoleonic code of laws is issued |

---

EMPIRE
1804–1815

| 1804 | Napoleon is crowned emperor of the French; Aaron Burr kills Alexander Hamilton in a duel; the Lewis and Clark expedition begins the exploration of the sources of the Missouri River; Beethoven finishes the *Eroica* |
| 1805 | The English navy wins the Battle of Trafalgar, and Lord Nelson is killed in the battle; Napoleon wins the Battle of Austerlitz; the column in the Place Vendôme is dedicated in memory of the victory |
| 1806 | The Arc de Triomphe by Chalgrin is planned and begun; the Temple of Glory (later the Church of the Madeleine) is begun by Vignon; the Arc du Carrousel is begun by Percier and Fontaine |
| 1807 | Fulton builds the first practical steamboat, the *Claremont,* which is launched on the Hudson River |

1810 French

1814 French

| 1808 | Canova completes his famous statue of Pauline Bonaparte as Venus; Goethe publishes Part I of *Faust* |
|------|--------|
| 1810 | Napoleon divorces Josephine and marries Marie Louise of Austria; Jacques-Louis David exhibits *The Distribution of the Eagles;* Canova completes his famous nude statue of Napoleon |
| 1811 | The "king of Rome" is born, heir to Napoleon's throne |
| 1812 | War begins between the United States and Great Britain; Napoleon invades Russia |
| 1813 | Napoleon's armies are defeated at the Battle of Leipzig |
| 1814 | Peace talks begin between Great Britain and the United States at Ghent; Paris surrenders to the allies; Napoleon is banished to Elba; Louis XVIII is restored to the throne of France; the Congress of Vienna is called |
| 1815 | The Battle of New Orleans is won by Andrew Jackson after the peace treaty between Great Britain and France had already been signed; Napoleon escapes from Elba and begins his famous reign of a Hundred Days; Wellington leads the allies to a crushing victory over Napoleon at the Battle of Waterloo; Marshal Ney executed, and Louis XVIII returns for a second time; Napoleon is banished to St. Helena |

# BACKGROUND

The use of classical ideals for associational propaganda that had developed during the Revolution did not diminish with the death of Robespierre and the end of the Reign of Terror. Everything that could be associationally and emotionally connected with democratic Greece and republican Rome was exploited to establish the authenticity of the Directoire Period in France as the direct inheritor of the classical republican tradition. Then Napoleon Bonaparte, on behalf of the Directory, began his campaigns in Italy and Egypt and gradually gained total power over the state, not only through his military genius but through a brilliant exploitation of the classical symbols of power. He gradually led the country logically, step by step, from a republican government with Napoleon as first consul to a rebirth of Imperial Rome with Napoleon as emperor. The change in artistic style between 1795 and 1805 is fascinating to watch as the weight, grandeur, and decorative trappings of imperial power gradually replaced the simplicity, lightness, and directness that had marked the character of all arts at the close of the Revolution.

The artistic leader during the Directoire and Empire Periods was Jacques-Louis David who borrowed heavily from the classic art of the past, particularly from the Roman symbols of imperial power, to help create interiors, furnishings, court costumes, and paintings that would surround the new emperor with a modern equivalent of Roman imperial grandeur. The Arc de Triomphe, designed by the architect Chalgrin in 1805, was a case in point. Meant to dominate the entire western end of Paris and based loosely on the Roman triumphal arches of the past, it was so much larger, colder, and more militaristic than its classical sources that it created a new image of vast and overpowering military might that appeals to us as a symbol of military dictatorship, in the same way as do many Nazi and Soviet monuments.

Jacques-Louis David's monumental painting *The Coronation of Napoleon* is also a brilliant example of propaganda for the new imperial regime. The inside of Notre Dame was remodeled to look like a Roman temple; costumes were designed that mixed Renaissance court costumes, seventeenth-century Baroque sources, and contemporary dress; and the entire painting was carried out in such a grand, imperial manner to look like a scene from an opera. It is an excellent example of the new eclecticism in art that was to dominate the nineteenth century (Fig. 18–1).

The same principles were at work in the bedroom at Malmaison of Napoleon's wife Josephine (Fig. 18–2). Unlike the rooms of the Neoclassic Period of Louis XVI and Marie Antoinette, Josephine's bedroom is not delicate and subtle but heavy, ornate, and rather oppressive. There are a few touches of nobility and dignity, but for the most part the delicate poetry of aristocratic design is gone. There is a *nouveau riche, bourgeois* look to the furnishings and a romantic symbolism straining to break through the formalities of the classical style. The bed is meant to suggest a Roman imperial tent, imperial eagles tie Napoleon to the Roman past, the rug relates to wall paintings at Pompeii, and the couch is a heavy-handed copy of those found in Roman homes. In every way the delicacy and elegance of the eighteenth century have been replaced by heavier, thicker, darker effects that have less sophistication and stress an obvious eclecticism.

Politically this was a period of tremendous upheaval and change that remodeled the map of Europe completely for two decades. The Napoleonic Period also produced a new Paris, a city of great monuments, vistas, boulevards, and parks and moved this great city out of its medieval inheritance into the modern world of the nineteenth century. France became the model—in its Napoleonic code of laws, in its divisions into departments, in its organization of the military—of all that was considered modern in the way of national political organization. France in this period of violent upheaval and maximum political change ended forever the feudalism and aristocratic priorities enjoyed by the *ancien régime*.

**FIG. 18-1** Jacques-Louis David, *The Coronation of Napoleon;* The Louvre, Paris; 1805–1807. Illustrates how David rebuilt the interior of Notre Dame as a rich classical setting in which the costumes created the impression of a *nouveau riche* costume ball. This was the beginning of eclecticism in art and culture whereby costume, furniture, and interiors were created from mixed sources in the past or distant places. Photo courtesy of the French Musées Nationaux.

The Napoleonic Wars also gave England new power in Europe, as leader of the allied armies opposed to the French emperor, as well as undisputed ruler of the sea. The opening of the nineteenth century also brought England into the foremost position in industrialization and manufacturing as well as dominance in world commerce through her merchant fleet. It was also a very creative period for England in the arts, particularly in literature and painting. The new school of poetry was dominated by Wordsworth, Byron, Shelley, Keats, and Burns; Sir Walter Scott established the gothic, historical novel as a genre to be copied and admired throughout Europe; Jane Austin became famous for stories about everyday life among the upper classes in rural England; and English portraiture, through the works of Reynolds, Gainsborough, Romney, and Lawrence, came to be admired throughout Europe. In matters of fashion and style the famous Beau Brum-

mell, as adviser in dress to the prince regent, established a new elegance, simplicity, and cleanliness in male dress.

In America this was the famous Federal Period in which the capital city of Washington was planned and laid out, making use of the latest classical planning ideals in the use of monuments, parks, malls, and boulevards. It was a period in which leadership was still in the hands of many of the great political and intellectual leaders of the American Revolution—such as Jefferson, Washington, Adams, and Madison—and it was a period in which a national federal unity was slowly and painfully formed from a group of near-sovereign states. It was also the period that ended in the War of 1812, when the resolve of the new government and the patriotism of the people were put to a great test against the might of England—a test that despite the burning of Washington in 1814 was won by the fledgling country. It was this war

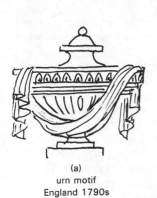

(a)
urn motif
England 1790s

(b)
classical tomb
1805

(c)
English window
1800

Percier and Fontaine, bedroom of the empress Josephine, Malmaison; ca. 1800–1810. A heavy, ornate, rather oppressive environment meant to be associated with imperial military tents used by Napoleon on the battlefields of Europe. Photo courtesy of Giraudon, Paris.

(d)
Regency sabre-legged
chair

(e)
Regency–Empire
library table

(f)
Empire
chair

**FIGURE 18-2**

that produced the hero of New Orleans, Andrew Jackson, and the national anthem, *The Star-Spangled Banner.*

The rest of western culture moved through this period in response to the whims of Napoleon. Italy was first conquered and then given a new sense of nationalism and need for unity that was finally to culminate in independence after the middle of the nineteenth century. In Germany after Napoleon conquered the many separate kingdoms and principalities, a new interest in national freedom also arose. After his defeat of the armies of the Holy Roman emperor, Napoleon abolished this ancient title and eventually, after divorcing Josephine, married the former Holy Roman emperor's daughter. In Spain he set his brother on the throne, only to find himself caught up in a violent revolt that drew the Spaniards together against the hated invader for the first time since the Moors had been driven out in 1494. Even Russia did not escape, but this invasion proved to be one of the greatest military catastrophes of all time and was the downfall of Napoleon. Wherever his armies went, Napoleon carried with him the ideals of the French Revolution as well as the oppressiveness of military dictatorship. Thus he awakened national spirit at the same time that his military government provided many of the concepts of liberty and representation that had caused the French Revolution. Napoleon, therefore, both physically conquered most of Europe and freed its nationalistic spirit.

# THE BASIC COSTUME SILHOUETTE

The period directly after the French Revolution was one of experiment and change in dress for both men and women—a move from clothing based on the hierarchy of aristocracy to clothing that was more revealing of the lines of the physical body and based on the twin ideals of natural and classical symbolism. For men this meant the shift to the simpler, tighter, more physical clothing that had been the basis of the English riding costume; for women this meant the emergence of the classical Greek or Roman tunic or chemise dress without corsets, boning, or underpinning. For a few years the freedom, simplicity, and revealing naturalness in women's clothing was quite breathtaking in its sharp divergence from the fashion ideals for the previous three or four centuries; but this freedom and simplicity began to change, even by the early years of the Empire, as can be seen by looking at the gowns in David's *The Coronation of Napoleon* (Fig. 18–1). The change for men during this period was in many ways even greater. As they adopted sophisticated versions of the peasant's long trousers, knee pants and stockings (part of male dress for two centuries) were relegated to the formal dress of servants and the most ceremonial court occasions. Within 10 to 15 years, men adopted long trousers, cut their hair short or in a loose, wind-blown style, and moved to the use of practical woolens instead of the satins, silks, and velvets that had been the staples for upper-class male attire for centuries. For both men and women the changes were symbolic of the move away from the elegant manners of aristocracy toward a bourgeois image and ideal.

When the Revolution broke out, the first sharp changes in male clothing came in the Phrygian bonnets, carmagnole jackets, tricolor accessories, and sans culotte trousers that were adopted as the uniform of the Revolution by the extremists and the lower-class revolutionaries. From these, directly after the close of the Reign of Terror, came the extreme fashions displayed by the young dandies of the day, known as *Incroyables.* They carried heavy, knotted walking sticks; sported wild and unruly hair; hid their jaws in enormous neckcloths; wore coats with large lapels, collars, and long tails; and displayed skintight breeches over striped stockings. They also wore short boots and a large, beaver, cocked hat, or *bicorne.* It was this fashion madness that marked the emergence from the terrors of the guillotine, and a restrained version of this style may be seen in Boilly's painting *Point de Convention* (Fig. 18–3).

As the Directoire and Consulate merged into the Empire, male clothing firmly adopted

(a) side inset corset 1803

(b) frilled shirt with collar points 1805

(c) bands of elastic webbing 1804

(d) silk turban 1797

(e) bonnet over titus haircut 1797

(f) silk tunic over lingerie skirt 1808

(g) cravat and collar points 1800

(h) English motif

(i) French motif

(j) Napoleonic guard boot

(k) velvet gown lingerie yoke and sleeves 1796

(l) lady's shoe 1805

(m) heavy cloth great coat 1803 Hessian boots

(n) pleated turban 1803

(o) slipper and clocked stockings 1798

(p) French courrobe 1804

Louis Boilly, *Point de Convention;* Collection of Alain de Rothschild; ca. 1800. Illustrates the extreme neckwear, large lapels, windswept hair, and tight boots of the *Incroyables* and the exaggerated transparency and simplicity in the fashions of the female *Merveilleuses*. Photo courtesy of Alain de Rothschild.

**FIGURE 18-3**

315

the long trouser—some long and very snug to the ankle, others looser to the instep. Tightly fitted leather and knitted breeches, ending in knee-high boots, were also popular, while knee breeches with silk stockings and low pumps were reserved for very formal court functions. In England this was the period of the Regency in which male styles were set by the famous Beau Brummell, who prided himself on the spotless linen in his two-point collar that now rose from the carefully wrapped neckcloth and on his midnight blue, woolen, tailed coat that he introduced for evening wear along with knitted, leg-hugging, cream pants that ended at the ankle. Ruffles now decorated shirt fronts and sleeve cuffs; waistcoats were often double-breasted and showed below the buttoned coat front; and coats had a high-rolled collar, sleeves that were slightly gathered into the armseye, and long clawhammer tails. Most male coiffures imitated a windblown, pseudo-Roman, or natural look, and headgear was based on variations of the top hat, either flared or tapering. Caped cloaks or overcoats were used for travel or outdoor dress in winter. A somewhat exaggerated statement of male dress in 1809 may be seen in Debucourt's print *The Dance Mania* (Fig. 18–4).

During the Revolution ladies who wished to be identified with the ideals of the new order adopted a number of symbols such as tricolor sashes and *cockades,* exaggerated striped fichus, and stoles that were meant to be handled in a classical manner to suggest an image of the goddess of liberty. At the close of the Terror the full flush of the new ''antique garb'' swept over the style-setters of the Directory. Nearly transparent muslin chemise or tunic dresses became the rage, with the waistline now located just

below the bustline. All underpinning and corseting completely disappeared, and simple white or pastel frocks in muslin or batiste were worn with no other decoration than a colorful stole and a ribbon under the breast. Flat slippers and even sandals replaced the high-heeled shoes; the large-brimmed straws, popular before the Revolution, were replaced by bonnets with a coal-scuttle scoop over the face; and the hair was done in a series of loose, corkscrew curls arranged in a pseudo-Greek manner. These exaggerated counterparts to the male Incroyables were known as *Merveilleuses* (Fig. 18–3).

Between 1800 and 1803 the upper part of the chemise dress became a small, separate bodice with a square neckline, an overtunic like a Greek peplos was frequently worn over the underskirt, and the hair was done in a more formal Greek coiffure. Heavier fabrics were also introduced for parties, balls, and ceremonial court occasions in the form of the trailing *courrobe* of darkcolored velvet, often embroidered in gold and silver, that was fastened about the waist. Small, puffed sleeves appeared along with long gloves, and a variety of stiff, ruffled lace collars in the Medici tradition were introduced. The short *Spencer jacket* and a longer redingote were worn outdoors, and shawls and stoles were still popular for posing in the classical manner. By 1810 bonnets were closer to the head with only a very moderate frame to the face, long sleeves returned with slashing and heavier trim, and ruffles and braid began to appear in rows at the bottom of the gown. A good, though somewhat exaggerated, sense of female dance dress about 1809 may be seen in Debucourt's *The Dance Mania* (Fig. 18–4).

## DIRECTOIRE AND EMPIRE COSTUME

**Masculine Dress** With the close of the Reign of Terror, youthful fashions exploded in a bombardment of excessive styles that seemed a release from the tensions of Revolution and a needed expression of personal extravagance in order to gain recognition in a world without stability. After a century in which fashionable clothing had been sophisticated and elegant,

the Directoire fashions were consciously inelegant and disheveled. Lapels were too wide, collars too high, coattails too long, boots too loose, and hair too windblown to give a sense of proportioned balance to the *avante-garde* male fashion figure. Look at Horace Vernet's print entitled *Incroyables* (Fig. 18–5). The hair in each case looks like a rat's nest of tangled disarray,

(a) carrick overcoat 1811

(b) gauze bonnet 1814

(c) collar and scarf 1814

(d) veil over frame cherusse or Betsie at neck 1811

(e) corset 1813

(f) cut of man's coat back 1800–1815

(g) Napoleonic officer

Debucourt, *The Dance Mania,* an engraving showing the dancing of the new waltz in 1809. Illustrates the very physical, revealing fashions of the time and the breakdown of aristocratic decorum in the animated, swaying movement demanded by the new dance form. Photo courtesy of the Metropolitan Museum of Art, Harris Brisbane Dick Fund, 1935.

(h) collar and neckcloth 1812

(i) formal court dress 1814

(j) cut of man's overcoat back 1800–1815

(k) redingote 1806

(l) cloth coat and felt bonnet 1814

(m) soldier during Napoleonic wars

**FIGURE 18-4**

the lapels of both coats and waistcoats look as if they were designed by a drunken tailor, and the short boots on the left look like the tops had been cut off. Note also that these particular coats do not have tails but wide, square skirts that place them as the model for the frock coat that will develop in the nineteenth century. Also note the use of stripes, the much-wrapped height of the neckcloth and the two new hat shapes—the flared top hat and the two-sided bicorne. They are wonderful, almost comic inventions like the zoot suits that followed the end of World War II. A slightly more elegant, although still very exaggerated, example of this style may be seen in Boilly's painting *Point de Convention* (Fig. 18–3). Here the lapels are not as large, and the figure in general does not look as disheveled.

With the arrival of greater stability and a new national identity emerging under Napoleon, styles began to develop into the lines and shapes that we think of as "Empire," forming the basis for male dress for the next century. An excellent, although slightly caricatured, image of fashions about 1805 may be seen in Debucourt's print *Les Courses du Matin* (Fig. 18–6). At the left are two delivery men accepting snuff. One has striped trousers, riding boots, and a large bicorne hat and is carrying a magnificent pair of lacquered boots. The other

has a striped neckcloth, earrings, and a very short, cropped hairdo. He seems ahead of his time and could easily be a figure from about 1830 to 1840. The figure giving the snuff still wears a tied wig, a striped tailed coat with striped stockings, short leggings or gaiters, and an apron that marks his trade as a purveyor of cosmetics, chemicals, and costume accessories. Behind him stands a composer, still in a tied wig, with a new high collar and puffed shirt ruffles above the buttons of his waistcoat (Fig. 18–3b,g). His tailed coat sets off his breeches, stockings, and low-cut slipper-shoes while he prominently displays a watch fob at the waist and carries a rolled sheet of music in one hand.

Other figures wear long hair, short hair, wigs, or the new sideburns, while their lower legs are variously clad in breeches and stockings or tight pantaloons that disappear into boots. Hats vary from tricornes to bicornes to top hats, and outerwraps include togalike cloaks and shoulder-caped overcoats (Fig. 18–3m). It was in many ways a world in transition—moving from breeches to pants, from wigs to shorter, natural hair, from the traditional tricorne to the top hat, and from cloaks to overcoats.

Now let us look at a slightly more conservative American gentleman from about 1805 to 1810 (Fig. 18–7). In an unknown artist's *Por-*

**FIG. 18–6** Debucourt, *Les Courses du Matin,* an engraving depicting the styles of 1805. Illustrates chemise tunic dresses worn by the ladies and the boots, tight pants, long trousers,
tailcoats, natural hair, and top hats worn by the men in the early years of the First Empire.
Photo courtesy of the Metropolitan Museum of Art, Harris Brisbane Dick Fund, 1935.

**FIG. 18–7** Anonymous, *Portrait of a Gentleman;*
Philadelphia Museum of Art; ca. 1810. Illustrates the
style that Beau Brummell would have approved of with
its crisp high collar, faultless cravat, freshly pleated shirt
ruffles, high-collared waistcoat, form-fitting breeches,
and a smartly tailored tailed coat with smooth rolling collar and lapels. Photo courtesy of the Philadelphia
Museum of Art.

*trait of a Gentleman,* we can see the complete absence of long or powdered hair and the stress on the short antique cut with the new sideburns. The shirt now has the fashionable high collar in starched linen above a carefully tied cravat with a row of starched and pleated ruffles down the front of the shirt. Note that the neckcloth is once again called a cravat because it ties in the front (Fig. 18-4c). When it went twice around the neck and either buckled or was pinned in the back in the late eighteenth century, it was usually known as a *stock.* The coat here has a high rolled collar and lapel and is sharply cut back into tails at the waist (Fig. 18-4f) to reveal the close fit of the knee breeches that button at the knee. Although the shoes cannot be seen, they undoubtedly are the low-cut slipper-pumps that were now worn with knee breeches and stockings.

In Debucourt's print *The Dance Mania,* all of the above fashion attributes still pertain, but due to the subject of the print, one is struck by two things in the new male styles: the tightness of fit of the clothing and the new sense of physical action that comes with the introduction of the waltz and other fashionable activities (Fig. 18-4). Although this print does not depict any use of the new long trouser, this style continued to develop. At first they were very form-fitting and usually buttoned at the ankle; but by 1810 or 1811 they were much looser, and the slit at the bottom that used to be buttoned was left open to spread over the side of the shoe. By 1815 many of these long trousers began to fasten under the shoe or boot with a strap, and the fullness at the tops of the trousers increased.

With the arrival of darker woolen fabrics for coats and the use of knitted creams and white for breeches and trousers, the one colorful and decorative item in male attire remained the waistcoat. Although many of these were also of white, it was fashionable to have patterned waistcoats in velvet, satin, embroidered silk, or pastel stripes. They could be single- or double-breasted, but there was always a rolled collar or a collar-lapel combination to finish off the top of the waistcoat.

Along with the square skirts of the frock coat (which was less popular than the tailed coat from 1800 to 1812) and the long tails of the stepped-back tailed coat (Fig. 18-4f), court clothing that still used the sloped, cutaway coats of the 1780s; these now had high, standing collars and front sides heavily embroidered in classical patterns in gold and silver metallic thread (Fig. 18-4i). These same coat lines were also used in many Napoleonic uniforms (Fig. 18-4g,m), and this style of braided or embroidered coat remained the model for formal servants' livery well into the early twentieth century.

For outerwear the famous *carrick greatcoat,* an overcoat with several caped collars, now began to replace the cloak as the most practical wear for inclement weather (Fig. 18-4a). A good example of this style may be seen at the far right of Debucourt's print *Les Courses du Matin* (Fig. 18-6). Other overcoats also appeared by 1810 that had a fitted line to the waist with full, ankle-length skirts and fitted sleeves (Fig. 18-4j). Often the collar and lapels were of fur, and sometimes the entire garment was fur-lined.

In footwear boots were more prevalent than at any time since the early seventeenth century. They were most frequently worn with trousers snugly inside, but by the end of the period the looser style of trouser was worn over the boots. The boot styles included the Hessian with a heart-shaped top that sometimes sported a tassel, the Wellington which was somewhat higher and cut away behind the knee, and the jockey boot which had a turned-down top and had been the standard riding boot since the late eighteenth century. Slipper-pumps were standard for indoor formal wear.

Military wear, since European-wide wars dominated the entire period, was dashing and varied in the extreme. Many common soldiers continued to wear uniforms that retained late-eighteeth-century lines, with cutaway coats, button-back lapels, and tight breeches under thigh-high leggings, but there was great innovation and variety in headdresses. The most distinctive (and the one still worn on parade by West Point cadets) was a cylindrical *shako* set with a visor and finished in loops of braid and a brush on the top front (Fig. 18-4m). Cavalry officers frequently wore heavily braided jackets that ended at the waist with form-fitting trousers and boots, and they sometimes wore breastplates and loosely interpreted classical helmets. Many officers had buttoned-back cutaway coats with appliquéd revers and tight pants worn inside high boots that were above the knee in front and cut to the top of the calf in back (Fig. 18-3i). Officers' hats were usually variations on the bicorne, and there was much rich and decorative use of metallic braids, epaulets, plumes, and buttons throughout coats and hats (Fig. 18-4g).

Surprisingly enough, even though the long trouser had originated with the lowest peasant, well-to-do peasants clung to the knee breeches of respectability throughout most of the nineteenth century. In other ways their clothing lines remained what they had been at the close of the eighteenth century—rough full skirts with a neckcloth, waistcoats well below the waist, straight coats to the knees or shorter jackets, flat-brimmed hats, and either the knee breeches and coarse stockings or straight trousers. Always the cut was simple, and the fabric (usually woolens) was coarse.

**Feminine Dress**    The feminine excesses in dress directly after the close of the Revolution seemed to mark a violent break away from centuries of corseting, padding, and layering—a moment of madness after centuries of aristocratic respectability. For a brief moment the more daring women discarded even their underwear and were seen wearing nearly transparent muslins over naked flesh—or at least, over flesh-colored body stockings. Some went barefoot, and even the standard footwear for the time was a simple sandal.

The impulse for these new styles came not just from a symbolic need for freedom from the ways of the past but from a need to demonstrate devotion to the new republican-democratic order by a revival of all things classic. Thus in Boilly's painting *Point de Convention,* dated about 1800, we see a lady in the new, casual, classical hairstyle, the semitransparent chemise dress with a high waist caught under the bust with a ribbon, and the simple Greek sandals (Fig. 18-3). This sleeveless tunic or chemise dress has a flesh-colored body-fitting undergarment that shows on the upper arm; there appears to be a second layer of tunic fabric from

the waist to the upper thigh, but from there down, the lady's legs can be seen fully through the transparent muslin of the dress. In every way the costume shows a shocking difference from the ruffles, bows, drapings, and underpinning of just a few years earlier. This period allowed women a certain ease and freedom in dress and lasted until about 1805 when women were gradually placed back on a pedestal to become the inhibited doll of the later nineteenth century (Fig. 18-3k).

Even as late as 1803 we have a portrait attributed to Jacques-Louis David, the *Portrait of a Young Woman in White* that is shocking in its dishabille (Fig. 18-8). Her hair is cut crudely into a short hairdo that casually frames the face, there are mere shoulder straps to hold up the transparent tunic dress, and the bust is clearly revealed through the outer fabric. Below the very high waistline there appears to be an undergarment, but the entire ensemble looks like a negligee rather than an afternoon visiting dress or an evening party dress.

The shockingly low necklines, semitransparent dresses over limited undergarments, and almost totally bare arms were all justified in the name of classical Greece and natural simplicity; even fairly conservative women accepted the new style (though without the transparency and without quite such revealing décolletage). At first the dress was all cut in one piece, but by 1804 a limited version of the corset returned (Fig. 18-3a,c), and a seam, usually covered by a ribbon, joined the very skimpy bodice to the skirt directly under the bustline. In the earliest dresses the sleeves were made to simulate the draped effects of the Doric chiton; however, by 1804 a small cap sleeve was set into the armseye, and a long sleeve extending to the knuckles from the rounded cap sleeve was introduced (Fig. 18-3f,k). In fact, by 1805 any number of romantic touches borrowed from the sixteenth century were frequently added to women's gowns—transparent lace ruffs or ruffles at the neck, silk or satin puffs coming through slashes in the sleeves, dainty ruffles at the wrist, and the use of soft velvets as a fabric for gowns. An excellent example of these effects may be seen in Jean Dominique Ingres' *Madame de Senonnes* (Fig. 18-9). Court styles

sometimes a kind of sleeveless outergown, sometimes a trained overgown, but in each case it added weight and richness to the earlier classic simplicity (Fig. 18-3p). Thus by 1805 the Greek simplicity of female costume had begun to add the medieval and Renaissance touches that were to carry it into the charming excesses of the following Romantic Period.

One interesting aspect of the dresses of this time was the ingenious way in which the high waist was held in place without being pulled down or out of its stylish line by the weight of the skirt. Most dresses depended on a combination of cords and tapes on the inside of the dress, sometimes set inside of a casing, to pull and tie the outerdraping and line of the gown into its

**FIG. 18-8** Jacques-Louis David, *Portrait of a Young Woman in White;* National Gallery of Art, Washington; ca. 1803. Illustrates the shockingly daring costume styles for women at the close of the Directoire. Note the loose and casual hair style, the transparency of the fabric covering the bust line, the high waist, the minimal sleeve, and the soft, clinging fall of the muslin skirt. The only covering would be the red shawl on the chair. Photo courtesy of the National Gallery, Washington.

also adapted past fashions to add rich touches to the female robes of state that came into being with the coronation of Napoleon and Josephine in 1804. Primarily invented by Jacques-Louis David and his staff to add grandeur to the simple female tunic style, these styles are well presented in David's famous painting of the coronation (Fig. 18-1). Tiaralike crowns have been added; stiff, standing lace collars that look vaguely Elizabethan have been introduced; and most important of all, a long velvet train lined in ermine and embroidered in gold or silver has been fastened around the female waist to become the famous courrobe. It was

**FIG. 18-9** Jean Dominique Ingres, *Madame de Senonnes;* Nantes Museum; 1806. Illustrates the richer fabrics and accessories that arose in feminine styles after the coronation of Napoleon. Note the neck ruffles, the slashed sleeves, the very wide neckline, and the high waistline. The cashmere shawl beside her is a major accessory. Photo courtesy of the Nantes Museum.

fashionable shape. Another interesting point is that bourgeois, middle-class women did not wear the thin, almost transparent muslins and lawns of the court ladies, but chose instead firm white cotton, sometimes with a small pastel stripe.

In Debucourt's *Les Courses du Matin* (Fig. 18–6), we see two typical walking costumes of about 1805 which give an excellent idea of the silhouette and body lines of the Empire style, but the most interesting aspect of the central female costume in this print may be the coiffure. It is a complex, pseudo-Greek affair (possibly a wig) with many small entwined braids wrapped in ribbon to create the conical line well-known from Greek vase paintings. Other coiffures were simple and romantically natural, parted in the center with a few curls about the face or sometimes with a soft chignon at the back top of the head (Fig. 18–4). The simplest hairdressing of all may be seen in the *Portrait of a Young Woman,* attributed to David (Fig. 18–8).

Hats and headdresses varied from those based primarily on classical Greek tiaras to near-eastern turbans and caps to various straw bonnets (Fig. 18–3d,e,n). The turbans and caps were the result of Napoleon's trip to Egypt and Palestine, and the exotic fashion inventions based on this romantic journey dominated Empire fashion until about the middle of the first decade. After that, both the Greek tiara, or *stephanie* (Fig. 18–4d), and the turbans gave way to less exotic, more conservative bonnets of straw and velvet—some with wide brims, others with narrow ones. An excellent example of one of these is in F. Massot's portrait *Isaline Fé* (Fig. 18–10). It is covered in fabric to match the long-sleeved, high-waisted gown and is trimmed in ostrich. Note the rufflike collar on the dress that demonstrates the continuing encroachment of romantic borrowings from the Renaissance and the decreasing classical elements in dress.

In the matter of jackets and outerwraps, the last years of the Directory and the first years of the Empire usually saw outergarments limited to a great stole or drape in imitation of the Greek himation, but by 1805 these were gradually replaced by the short Spencer jacket, the

FIG. 18–10 F. Massot, *Isaline Fé;* Museum of Art and History, Geneva; ca. 1810. Illustrates the growing importance of the closed-brimmed bonnet, long sleeves, and neck ruffles toward the close of the Empire. Only the very high waist gives the costume any relation to the classical look. Photo courtesy of the Museum of Art and History, Geneva.

long, high-waisted redingote, and even versions of the male caped overcoats (Fig. 18–4k,l). Stoles were often large, imported Indian shawls—some hand painted—and usually decorated with rich colorful borders or edged in fringe (Fig. 18–4). Smaller shawls were often of very soft cashmere embroidered in colored silks; less expensive cotton shawls in plain colors either matched or contrasted with the gown. The large shawls were often weighted with tassels to better drape the fabric and to keep it from slipping on the arms. The *Spencer,* or tailless jacket was named for Lord Spencer who, determined to show up the vagaries of fashion, cut the tails off his coat. As he suspected, the new style was quickly adopted, although more by women than by men. It was first seen about 1795 but became the most popular after 1805. It always acted as a rich, dark accent in velvet or wool set against the light muslins of the gowns.

For cold weather the redingote, which had developed from the Englishwoman's riding coat, became the standard wear. It was full length with long sleeves and a cape collar and was smartly tailored to a high waistline with a rolled collar and button tabs or frog fastenings (Fig. 18-4k,l). Similar to the redingote was the pelisse, whose cut and shape was often the same, but it was trimmed or even lined in fur. Occasionally in very inclement weather, a fuller overcoat with larger caped collars was worn by ladies more interested in protection than in fashion.

The footwear of the period changed from tiny laced sandals in direct imitation of the Greek to tiny slippers, some slip-on, others laced (Fig. 18-31,o). They came in a variety of light colors to accent, contrast, or match the dress. They usually had pointed toes, were cut deeply down over the instep, and usually had small bows. By the last years of the Empire, shoes covered more of the foot and became less pointed in the toes.

Middle-class women in general followed these same fashion lines but not with sheer fabrics or low décolleté. They preferred natural colors in soft woolens or cottons and used jackets and coats rather than the draped shawl or stole.

# FABRICS

For men woolens superseded velvets, satins, and other silks during this period, with linen used for collars and cravats and cotton for many shirts and for summer trousers. Nankeen cotton was the summer suiting for areas with very hot climates. The one item that was still made of silk, satin, or velvet with embroidered decoration was the waistcoat, although in summer it, too, was often of cotton. Trousers were elastic woolens or occasionally silk jersey, but tight knee breeches were usually still of satin. Middle-class men's trousers were of cotton twill, rough wool, or ribbed corduroy.

For women the new fabric was cotton, particularly in fine lawns, muslins, and batistes for dresses. For some years silks and satins were not used, but they returned after the institution of the Empire as did lace, sometimes appearing in full lace gowns. Woolens were used for jackets and coats; the muslins and other light cottons of the decade from 1805 to 1815 were often embroidered and printed rather than made semitransparent as in the period of the Directory.

# ARTS AND ARTIFACTS

The delicate aristocratic furniture and interiors that had been produced in France and England during the Neoclassic Period from 1775 to 1790 were replaced by a heavier, more symbolically ornamented style of furniture and interiors after 1800 that was copied quite directly from Greek and Roman sources (Fig. 18-2a,b,c, d,e,f). Animal feet and vulture wings from Egypt, eagles and fasces from Rome, urns and columns from Greece, and an item or two from

the classic Baroque—all mingled to create furniture and interiors that were cold, heavy, and associational. Colors were also often no longer pastel, but symbolically chosen for their associational connection with Empire, Revolution, Democracy, Freedom, and Imperial Power. Chairs were upholstered in striped silks, brocades, velvets, or leather, in black and gold, red and black, blue and silver, or other coldly formal combinations. There was also great use of wall hangings and canopies to suggest the walls and ceilings of military tents, and in more modest interiors such wall hangings often were replaced by striped or printed wallpaper.

Motifs used in clothing and in furnishings included Egyptian elements like palms, lotus flowers, scarabs, and vultures; Graeco-Roman garlands, urns, acanthus leaves, harps, bundled fasces, eagles, and various cornice motifs (Fig. 18–3h,i); as well as some Persian and Eastern elements like turbans and exotic birds.

Following Greek models, the clothing of the Directory was usually trimmed in classic motifs only on the edges and borders of draping and gowns, but after the advent of the Empire, motifs were often sprinkled all over a garment. Also after the advent of the Empire, many eclectic accessories were added to costumes from the Renaissance such as ribbons, slashing, ruffs, and ruffles. Male clothing decoration usually consisted of velvet collars and cuffs with the accent of a rich waistcoat plus carefully chosen buttons and buckles. Only in military uniforms was the love of accessory decoration completely fulfilled.

Specific accessories for men included quizzing glasses, canes, gloves, an occasional snuffbox, cigar and cigarette boxes, and the very important watch fob, usually worn hanging at the front of the waist. For women there were fans (now often of plumes), muffs, above-the-elbow-length gloves, walking sticks, and parasols. Handbags or reticules were a very important part of the lady's ensemble and now took the place of the pockets or pouches that used to hang from the waist or were set into the gown. For middle-class wear the apron was still a major accessory.

Jewelry for men was now limited to imperial orders placed on the coat or on a ribbon about the neck except for an occasional stickpin in the cravat or ruffles of the shirt. Watches, of couse, were frequently richly ornamented with jewels.

Women's jewelry included various jeweled combs and other beaded hair ornaments; small jeweled tiaras, crowns, and gold laurel wreaths; jeweled ornaments for the turban or cap; simple necklaces for the throat, rich bracelets; and the occasional drop earring. It was in this period that a lady could have necklaces, earrings, brooch, tiara, and bracelet all part of a matching set. A good example of the classical symbolism introduced to court wear by David and his assistants may be seen in David's painting of Napoleon's coronation (Fig. 18–1).

## VISUAL SOURCES

The most outstanding style-setter in painting and related arts of Empire decoration was Jacques-Louis David, and his works are an excellent source for the essence of the Napoleonic style. Painter-pupils of David who are very useful as sources are Gérard, Girodet, Gros and Prud'hon, while his contemporary and rival, J. B. Regnault, is also a very useful source. The youthful work of Ingres is an important source, as is the work of Riesener, Danloux, Rouget, F. Massot, and Robert Lefèvre. Non-French artists that are useful are López y Pertana and Goya in Spain, Sulzer and Suhr in Germany and Austria, Borovikovski in Russia, and Lawrence in England. Graphic artists in France that are very useful are Debucourt, La Mésangère, Grasset de Saint-Sauveur, and Desrais and in England, Gillray and Rowlandson. The best fashion journals of the period to consult are *Le Bon Genre, La Belle Assemblée, Journal des Dames et des Modes,* and the *Gallery of Fashion.* The best institutional source for prints, sketches, and plates from magazines and journals is thé Bibliothèque Nationale in Paris; the Louvre, Versailles Museum, the Prado, the Metropolitan Museum of Art, and a number of French and English provincial museums and private collections are the best sources for paintings. Useful books are N. W. Heideloff's *Gallery of Fashion* and Gonzalez-Palacios' *The French Empire Style.*

# SUMMARY

This was a period of transition from the aristocratic court styles of the *ancien régime* to the middle-class styles of the nineteenth century—a period in which women's styles went through a brief period of freedom before moving toward the doll-like decorative modes of the Romantic, and men's clothing moved from velvets and satins to wool and cotton and from knee breeches and stockings to the long trousers that we still wear. Artistically and culturally it was a period in which there was a holding action against the growing ideals of Romanticism, while Napoleon and his imitators developed and propagated an imperial style based on romantic adaptations and interpretations of the classical ideals and symbols of imperial Rome. These imitations and interpretations were found much more in furniture, interiors, and women's clothing than in masculine styles, which were based on riding attire and lower-class symbolism.

# chapter XIX

# Romantic

## Chronology

### (1815-1848)

| | | |
|---|---|---|
| ROMANTIC<br>1815-1848 | 1815 | Wellington crushes Napoleon at the Battle of Waterloo; Napoleon is exiled to St. Helena; the Congress of Vienna meets in the capital of the Austrian Empire; the Battle of New Orleans is won by Andrew Jackson |
| | 1817-1825 | Revolution in Latin America gains independence for Spanish colonies |
| | 1818-1819 | Géricault paints *The Raft of the Medusa* |
| | 1819 | First Atlantic steamship crossing |
| | 1820 | Death of George III, the prince regent is crowned George IV; the passing of the Missouri Compromise |
| | 1821 | Death of Napoleon on the island of St. Helena; Faraday discovers the principle of the electric dynamo |
| 1820 | 1822 | The Greeks declare their independence from Turkey |
| | 1823 | The Monroe Doctrine is proclaimed in the United States |
| | 1824 | Louis XVIII is succeeded by Charles X in France |

| 1825 | The Erie Canal is opened in the United States |
|------|------|
| 1828 | The Baltimore and Ohio horsecar railroad is built |
| 1829 | A systematically organized police force is developed in England by Sir Robert Peel; Catholic emancipation in England through the Catholic Relief Bill |
| 1830 | July Revolution in France overthrows Charles X, and Louis Philippe is installed as a limited monarch; Algiers is conquered by the French; Joseph Smith founds the Mormon Church |
| 1831 | Steam locomotion is developed to replace horse power on a railroad in the United States |
| 1832 | The Great Reform Bill sponsored by Lord Russell is passed; South Carolina threatens nullification over the tariff |
| 1833 | All the Negro slaves in the British West Indies freed by the Act for the Abolition of Slavery |
| 1836 | Texas independence is achieved after the Battle of the Alamo; Louis Napoleon attempts to gain the throne of France but is unsuccessful; *La Marseillaise,* sculpture by Rude, completed; Houses of Parliament begun in England by Barry and Pugin |
| 1837 | Commission for the Preservation of Historical Monuments established by Louis Philippe; Queen Victoria crowned in England |
| 1838 | Chartists in England attempt to gain their six points; Dickens publishes *Oliver Twist* |
| 1839–1840 | The Opium War in China |
| 1839 | Daguerreotype process of photography is introduced |

1830

| | | |
|---|---|---|
| 1841 | 1840 | Guizot, French historian, becomes prime minister; the penny postal system established in England |
| | 1841 | England wins Hong Kong; Carlyle's *On Heroes, Hero Worship, and the Heroic in History* is published |
| | 1842 | The Webster-Ashburton Treaty gains part of Canada for Maine |
| | 1844 | First telegraph line is strung between Baltimore and Washington; in England the Factory Act is passed |
| | 1845 | United States Naval Academy established at Annapolis; annexation of Texas accomplished |
| | 1846 | Potato famine in Ireland resulted in the repeal of the Corn Law in England; the United States' war with Mexico begins; Oregon boundary dispute with Canada |
| | 1847 | Joule formulates first law of thermodynamics |
| 1848 | 1848 | Revolutions in Hungary, Germany, Austria, Italy and France; the government of Louis Philippe is overthrown and Louis Napoleon is elected President of the Second Republic; gold discovered in California |

# BACKGROUND

With the fall of Napoleon all of Europe heaved a sigh of relief, for even though the emperor had replaced the old order with a much more unified and logical system of justice and law, he was still a totalitarian leader whose wars had exhausted all the nations of Europe. Therefore, the Congress of Vienna that met to redraw the map of Europe tended to be very conservative, even reactionary, and in many ways attempted to reestablish the old monarchies and aristocracies that existed before the Revolution. This was not possible after events of the past 25 years, and thus the politics of the next three decades was to be based on liberal, radical, romantic attempts to overthrow these reactionary monarchical systems. Artists, writers, and intellectuals, who were sensitive to the loss of stability in the old aristocratic order but were unwilling to return to the inequities and repressions of the past, found the decades after the fall of Napoleon unsettling and even frightening.

The rationalism that had grown in European society since the Renaissance and had culminated in the ideals of the Enlightenment was set aside, and artists and intellectuals talked of worshipping, feeling, emotion, and the unknown. They saw that industrialization and the end of an agrarian, aristocratic feudalism meant that a whole way of life was coming to an end. With this new self-conscious awareness, coupled with the new scientific impulse to study human beings and their world objectively, there arose among sensitive artists a sense of loss, a sense of removal from the direct inheritance from the classical values of Greece and Rome. Greek and Roman art, literature, and philosophy could still be studied, but as a separate, past, cultural development and not as a direct personal or family inheritance. Out of this sense of loss came a sense of loneliness and alienation from the bustling, capitalist world of industrial development; artists and intellec-

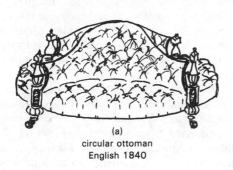

(a)
circular ottoman
English 1840

(b)
doorway, Lonsdale Square, Islington
1838

(c)
dining chair
with button
seat
1845

John Nash, the Dining Room and outside view of the Brighton Pavilion, Brighton, England; 1822. Illustrates the fanciful Indian-Gothic style invented by Nash as an associative decorative frosting to what had been a simple country house in the late Georgian style. This is escapist architecture to fit the mood of seashore fantasy desired by King George IV. Photos courtesy of the British Tourist Authority.

(d)
detail
from Houses
of Parliament
1835–1848

**FIGURE 19-1**

tuals, cut off from the cultivated appreciation of royal and aristocratic patrons, were thrown on the mercies of the marketplace and the gauche tastes of wealthy capitalists. They thus made a determined effort to escape this new world by painting and writing about the tales and events of past times and faraway places. They looked to the exotic, picturesque, and emotional, as well as into the world of private feeling. In opposing the stale formalities and coarse banalities of the new capitalist social order, the Romantics tried to set themselves up as sensitive, individualistic messengers of the truths on which man should act. As the Enlightenment had worshipped reason, so the Romantics worshipped the sublime—any object or effect that awakened awesome emotions and ideals powerful enough to dominate the whole personality. Thus artists identified with nature in all its moods, including ugliness and the grotesque, if it stimulated powerful emotions; and, in general, they attempted to express the inexpressible in art and literature. Thus Romanticism moved from the gentle, sentimental, picturesque beauty of the late eighteenth century to the violent and the sublime in the early nineteenth century.

As an extreme example of the exotic and emotional interiors that were developed as background for human action during this period, let us look at the dining room of the Brighton Pavilion, a romantic indulgence created for George IV of England in 1822 (Fig. 19–1a,b). The exterior of the Brighton Pavilion looks like something out of *Tales From the Arabian Nights,* an Indian-Gothic fantasy as it was described by its architect, John Nash. It evokes images of harem girls, Eastern eroticism, and an excessive escapist associationalism. Inside the dining room the domed ceiling is partly covered by gigantic banana leaves, with a silver dragon at the center holding in his claws the chains of a vast chandelier composed of six small dragons, each supporting in its jaws a crystal cup in the form of a lotus flower. The walls are covered with pseudo-Chinese panels; the doors are crowned with pagodalike forms; the walls are ringed with large lamps of blue Spode porcelain, mounted on dolphins and crowned with flow-

ers; only the chairs look as if they came from the shop of a cabinetmaker of the 1820s. The whole effect is a dreamlike phantasmagoria of forms ranging from China, through India and Arabia, to nineteenth-century England.

Politically Europe after the fall of Napoleon was continuously ruptured by revolutionary uprisings and demands for a constitution or independence from foreign domination. First, there was the Greek demand for independence from the Turks, a struggle that was morally supported by liberals such as the aging Lafayette and conservative romantics such as Chateaubriand, and physically supported by Lord Byron, who lost his life in Greece. Then there was the successful revolt of the Spanish colonies overseas, and most important of all, a major uprising in France in the summer of 1830 in which most of the leading romantic poets, playwrights, and artists played an emotionally supportive role. In England the revolution was industrial, and the economic changes and dislocations caused by this revolution caused great suffering and much violence, with again the Romantics playing an emotionally supportive role on the side of the dislocated lower classes.

Thus the physical world was changing even faster than the political and artistic ones. By 1830 gaslight was the accepted means of illumination in theaters, homes, and on the street; by 1835 the telegraph had become a major new form of communication; by 1837 the *Great Western* steamship had crossed to New York from England in 15 days; by 1840 railroads were being built throughout Europe and the eastern United States; and by the time of the European revolutions of 1848, steam-powered machinery was turning the wheels of industry in factories throughout England and to a lesser degree in western Europe and the United States.

With the failure of the uprisings of 1848, Romanticism became a kind of secondhand world of eclectic artistic borrowings that proved an artist's or a wealthy patron's education and gentility, but did not influence the new realism created by the triumph of the Industrial Revolution.

# THE BASIC COSTUME SILHOUETTE

The fashions of this period, as with furniture, interior decoration, and household accessories, borrowed heavily from the past and the exotic Orient. Particularly Cavalier styles of the early seventeenth century, Rococo elegance of the eighteenth century, and items from the Renaissance and Gothic were used to accent and adorn costumes. This was more easily done in women's dress than in men's, but even within the bourgeois mercantile uniform that began to develop for captains of commerce during this period, there were padded shoulders and chests, pinched waistlines, and padded hips to give the fashionable gentleman the same hourglass line so much admired in female fashion of the time. Also color and trim in both male and female dress were chosen for their emotional, associational values and were changed with the occasion and with the mood of the wearer.

Although it is always difficult to choose a single picture to illustrate the mood and manner of a period, E. L. Lami's illustrations for Jules Janin's *Summer in Paris* projects a languid romantic image that is an excellent place to begin (Fig. 19-2). The ladies wear simple but elegant summer evening gowns and stand or sit in languid poses that point up the rounded lines of the clothing. The visiting lady at the left wears a more ceremonious evening gown, as if she has been to a ball or dinner party, while the lady on the couch is in fashionable ill health which allows her a very romantic pose. The overall effect is of rounded lines, serpentine body curves, a richly textured, heavily furnished interior, and a decorative elegance in all trim and accesories in both costumes and surroundings.

During this period the now full-length masculine trousers usually fastened under the instep so that they would not creep up the ankle when sitting, and they were often padded at the hips to strengthen the admired hourglass line of the male figure. Coats and overcoats fitted snugly with slightly leg-o-mutton sleeves to give height and breadth to the shoulders, while collars rolled high behind the head to accentuate the length of the neck and to frame the

**FIG. 19-2** E. L. Lami, illustration for Jules Janin's *Summer in Paris;* 1843. Illustrates the elegant summer gowns, the languid poses, and the calculated expansive opulence that was the Romantic ideal. Note the nipped-in waists on the men, the low-cut necklines of the women, and the emphasis on expansive curved lines in the dresses. Photo courtesy of the New York Public Library.

removable, white linen top of the shirt with its high pointed collar and tied scarf-cravat. Coats were fitted either with flaring tails or the square skirts of the frock coat, and a girdle or *basque* belt was frequently worn to pinch in the waist under the padded, pigeon-breasted waistcoat and above the padded hips of the trousers. Height was given by the tall, flaring top hat worn on all formal occasions (except with court dress when the cocked bicorne was carried under the arm). Sideburns and clustered curls over the ears gave way to small beards, mustaches, and fuller hair by the end of the period; thus facial hair, which had been considered extremely un-fashionable since the time of Louis XIV, made a major return in fashionable men's wear by the middle of the nineteenth century. Ruffles were still used on shirt fronts and cuffs; mantles and caped overcoats were standard for outdoors and travel; and knee breeches and stockings, which had been part of men's dress for a cen-tury and a half, were relegated to very formal court presentations. Pointed boots were worn under trousers except for riding and sporting events—then they were worn over skintight leather or stretch-knit riding breeches. The fashionable figures depicted in a fashion plate for the winter season of 1837–1838 may be taken as typical romantic male styles of this period (Fig. 19–3).

Female gowns, even in the very last days of the Empire, had added many ruffles and much lacy trim, and by 1820 the high waistline began to drop from just below the bust to just above the waist. The corset now returned; sleeves began to expand in size; skirts began to flare out in many folds over layered petticoats to the ankle; and appliqué, ruching, embroidery, and lace ruffles began to trim all edges of the gown. The bonnet was still popular, but it now flared out into a huge brim decorated with plumes and ribbons framing a hairdo that had great sausage curls at the temple and a complexly curled twist or knot at the back of the head. Flat shoes fastened with cross-lacings up the leg were worn with the ankle-length skirts, and shawls of all sizes and textures were popular. As the width of the gown expanded at the hips and shoulders, the edge of the low-cut boat neckline increased in size until it formed a kind of shelf over the spreading tops of the expansive puffed sleeves, which were now attached to the shoulder well below the shoulder line.

After 1835 the upholsterer, rather than the cabinetmaker, came to dominate interior decoration. As the basic lines of furniture became lost under padded fabric, tassels, and fringe, women's fashions also became weighted down with heavier fabrics and decoration. Skirts lengthened to the floor and were further distended with petticoats; leg-o-mutton puffed sleeves were replaced by tight-fitting slim sleeves; exaggerated coiffures were replaced by a smooth part in the center of the forehead with curls or loops over the ears and a bun at the back; and bonnets now closed in like blinders about the face. The hourglass look gave way to the tea-cozy look as heavier fabrics and trim replaced the ruffles, laces, and flowers of the early 1830s. A costume plate from *Petit Courrier des Dames* of 1829 may be compared with a plate from *Godey's Lady's Book* for April 1842 to see the nature of this transition (Figs. 19–4,5). The most noticeable changes are from the expansive to the tight coiffure and from the expanding puffed sleeves to the tight, sloping-shouldered sleeves of 1843. The change speaks for itself; the ideal for woman had changed in a little over a decade from a gay butterfly to a domesticated doll.

## ROMANTIC COSTUME

**Masculine Dress**   Very few major varia-tions from the late Empire styles made their ap-pearance in male dress until about 1820, and then the silhouette began to change toward the effeminate hourglass line with puffed-out chest, pinched-in waist, and rounded hips analogous to the shape that was developing in female fash-ion during the 1820s. In fact, until the very close of the Romantic Period, men of fashion continued to wear waist cinchers and corsets,

collar and
tie 1820s

(a)
collar and tie
1840s

collar as
part of shirt
1830s

(b)
coat back 1828

(c)
Beau
Brummel
evening
trousers
1820–1840

(d)
man's shirt
1820s

(e)
collar and
waistcoat 1825

(f)
robe
and cap
1839

A display of winter fashions for the *Fashion Journal,* 1837 by Scott and Perkins of New York. Illustrates the romantic, hourglass line in male and female fashions just before styles became more conservative in the 1840s. Photo courtesy of the Library of Congress.

(g)
waistcoat
and
cravat
1830

(h)
waistcoat
and cravat
1840

(i)
countryman's
smock and
leggings

(j)
Count
D'Orsay
black satin
muffler,
pigeon-
breasted
waistcoat
1834

(k)
brocaded
robe
1840s

**FIGURE 19–3**

335

corset
back
1835

(a)

(b)
wicker or wire
mesh rolls
over corset 1840s

evening
headdress
1828

(c)

embroidered
silk bag 1825

(d)

Betsie or
ruffle
at neck—
lingerie
shirtwaist
1829

(e)

(f)
knitted
silk drawers
ca. 1820

(g)
turban 1829

(h)
evening
coiffure
1838

evening
coiffure
1828

(i)

(j)
embroidered
cloak-shawl
1829

(m)
braid and
curls 1844

(k)
taffeta
cape
1841

(n)
lace
negligee
1830

lace and ribbon
coiffure
(l)

A costume plate from *Petit Courrier des Dames;* 1829. Illustrates the beribboned, frivolous, expansive costume and headdress that was the fashion at the height of the Romantic movement. Note the return of excessive ruffles, ribbons, bows and plumes, and the expansiveness of the bonnet brim, sleeves, and skirt. Photo courtesy of the New York Public Library.

**FIGURE 19-4**

**FIG. 19-5** A costume plate from *Godey's Lady's Book;* 1842. Illustrates the change in female fashion from the open expansiveness of the 1830s to the tighter neck and sleeve lines, flattened coiffures, and closed-in bonnets of the 1840s. Photo courtesy of the New York Public Library.

and many had waistcoats padded over the chest. Only the most determined followers of fashion used hip pads; however, the cut of the trousers often made the male look as if he were wearing such padding (Fig. 19-2).

The coat of the 1820s, whether square-coated or tailed, was cut with a high rolled collar that curved down over the waistcoat emphasizing the rounded, pigeon-breasted look that was so much admired. Often this effect was enhanced by wearing two waistcoats, one over another with the bottom one showing over the edge of the top. Many of the cravats were also very full, enhancing through their bulk the fullness of the chest. Usually the shoulder seam on the coat was lengthened to give width to the shoulders, and the sleeves were set into the armseye with fullness at the top to accentuate the outer peak of the shoulder line (Fig. 19-2). Coattails and skirts were also curved subtly outward to make the waist appear smaller and give further accent to the hourglass form (Fig. 19-3b).

At first, the tail coat was definitely the most popular, but by the mid-1820s, it was equaled

in favor by the skirted frock coat. Each style could be double- or single-breasted, and both stressed the peaked shoulders and hourglass waist. Sleeves tapered down beyond the wrist to almost the knuckles, flaring slightly from the wrist over the upper part of the hand.

By this time, as often in the past, there were two distinct levels of fashion—that worn by the fashion-setters of society and that worn by the wealthy, conservative, upper-bourgeois leaders in business and the professions. The latter would not wear the hour-glass fashions like those of the famous Count D'Orsay (who was the supreme arbiter in male styles by 1830 in Paris). They wanted to be practical and relatively comfortable in their dress and usually wore garments that were looser-fitting and with less carefully tailored lines. A good example of a typical bourgeois gentleman of this period may be seen in Carl Begas' painting *The Begas Family* (Fig. 19-6). Note that the father has on a very long, loose coat without much shaping at the waist, chest, and shoulders, the pants are relatively loose, and even the collar and cravat are not fashioned with excessive stiffness or exacting formality. In fact, except for the collar and the length of the coat, the entire ensemble could be from the twentieth century.

This may be compared with a sketch taken from a drawing of Count D'Orsay by an unknown artist (Fig. 19–3j). The harmony of curved lines in his silhouette, the exact placement of his watch chain, the fold of the lapels, and the entire pose are calculated to give a completely dashing, romantic figure.

There were also differences between the conservative and the fashionable in trousers, waistcoats, and neckwear in the 1820s and 1830s. Besides wearing one waistcoat over another, usually in contrasting colors, the neckline of the waistcoat was also lowered, and a deep, rounded collar was added to further emphasize the curve of the padded chest—a style

that lasted until the more tailored lines of the early 1840s appeared (Fig. 19–3e,g,h,j). Trousers had a mass of small pleats at the waist to give a full top and then were tapered sharply to the ankles or to the straps that went under the instep of the boot. The true man of fashion wore the skintight trousers of the late Empire that fitted without a wrinkle from waist to ankle, but most other men wore trousers that were somewhat looser and more comfortable (Figs. 19–3c,6). The neckwear consisted of a stiff, high collar and a layered, wrapped cravat, finished off with a formal flat bow, but later, detachable collars made it possible to attach various collars to the same shirt (Fig. 19–3a). Sometimes the fashionable gentleman wore a black scarf cravat that covered the entire front of the shirt and most of the collar, making a very

**FIG. 19–6** Carl Begas, *The Begas Family;* Wallraf-Richartz Museum, Cologne; 1821. Illustrates the comfortable, bourgeois domesticity idealized in art throughout the nineteenth century, demonstrating the conservative side of Romanticism. Note the special shirts and jackets now created for boys to idealize childhood, as well as the eclectic accessories like ruffs and lace collars from the past to romanticize the women's gowns. Photo courtesy of the Reinisches Painting Archive, Cologne.

dramatic area of focus below the face and hiding the front ruffles of the shirt (Fig. 19-3j). Such a cravat usually had to be kept in place by ingenious folds and many pins. The bow tie that usually acted as the end to the cravat could be striped, plaid, brocaded, or plain, but for evening wear it was usually white.

Hair during the 1820s and 1830s was curled in a halo of fullness, especially toward the front of the head; rich sideburns usually met the edges of the collar; and the face was clean shaven. However, by the end of the 1830s, small mustaches made their appearance. The high, flared silk or beaver hat was the standard wear for men of all stations, although it varied in its shape and size from year to year and from class to class.

A varied group of gentlemen, most of whom were artists, may be seen gathered in the studio of one of their number in Hansen's *Meeting of Danish Artists in Rome* (Fig. 19-7). Note the variety in the brims and crowns of the top hats, and note particularly the exotic note created by the Turkish *fez* worn by the artist seated on the floor. Note that some, but not all, of the trousers fasten under the instep and that all the coats tend to be of the frock coat variety.

Note also that collars and cravats tend to be styled more for comfort than for projecting the latest fashionable line. To contrast these relaxed gentlemen with a true figure of fashion of the same time, look at Bourdet's *Une Promenade* (Fig. 19-8). The primary difference is not in the items of clothing but in the emphasis on the hourglass waistline. Although the peaked shoulders of the earlier part of the decade have given way to a sloped shoulder, there is still the rounded shawl collar on the waistcoat that outlines and accents the chest, the pinched waistline, the rounded, full hips, and the very smooth-fitting trousers fastened under the instep. An excellent example of male winter fashions for 1837–1838 may be seen in a fashion plate for the *Fashion Journal* (Fig. 19-3).

By the 1840s male fashion became less padded and pinched and more subdued in color and texture. The major change in cut came from the much lowered waistline and the dominance of the frock coat for day wear, with tails reserved for night. The vest or waistcoat now had a more tailored collar and lapel like the new sober lines of the coat, and the pants were not as smooth-fitting and often no longer fastened under the instep. Plaid, striped, and

**FIG. 19-7** Carl Hansen, *Meeting of Danish Artists in Rome;* Statens Museum for Kunst, Copenhagen; 1837. Illustrates the dominance of the frock coat, top hat, straight trousers, and bow ties that came to dominate relaxed, informal dress by the late 1830s. Note the exotic and romantic touch of the *fez* as an undress piece of headgear on the man in the foreground. Photo courtesy of the Statens Museum for Kunst.

**FIG. 19-8** Bourdet, *Une Promenade;* a fashion plate of 1838. Note the pinched-in high waist, smoothly curved shoulders, dark, tailed coat against light, skintight pants fastening under the instep: typical wear for the male dandy of the time. The woman is shown as a soft, frilly doll, with the silhouette of a tea cozy. Photo courtesy of the Bibliothèque Nationale, Paris.

checked pants were often seen as an alternative to the smooth, one-color trousers of the 1820s and early 1830s. Collars were much lower; the tie of the cravat was smaller and less flamboyant; larger sideburns, fuller mustaches, and even a few small beards became more important; top hats took on the proverbial stovepipe shape; and top coats lost their narrow waists and flared skirts and became straighter as did the garments worn beneath them. Romantic items like capes almost completely disappeared.

In the very late 1840s, the three-piece business suit arrived in which the short frock or cutaway coat, waistcoat, and trousers were all

cut from the same fabric. (This innovation remains with a few variations as the uniform of the Western capitalist businessman to this day.) By 1848 the flare in male dress had been replaced by the exact tailoring in sober lines and colors that was to characterize male dress until after World War I.

Dress for lower-class men became more like that of the upper classes, but with a poorer cut, rougher fabric, and a stress on practicality and comfort (Fig. 19-3i). Military uniforms retained their richness and variety even as civil male dress became more conservative. Major changes were that the Napoleonic tailed uniform coat was replaced by the short, double-breasted frock coat or tunic; and the tall shakos of the Napoleonic Wars were replaced by lower, hard-crowned, billed hats with sloping crowns. Tight trousers and tall riding boots, sometimes with added breastplate and helmet, were still worn by certain cavalry units, but the more common dress uniforms began to have the long trousers fastened under the instep of the boot, following the standard in civil dress (see Fig. 20-2n). The glory in uniforms came in their bright colors, rich braid and buttons, and dashing accessories.

***Feminine Dress*** By the early 1820s the classical lines in feminine dress introduced just after the French Revolution were all but gone, to be replaced by puffings and swellings in line and ruffles and bows in trim that were to mark the change of the feminine ideal from classical goddess to ornamented doll. The major shifts that came quite quickly were the expansion of the sleeve, the gradual lowering of the waist, and the expanding of the fullness of the skirt. For example, the very middle-class females in *The Begas Family,* 1821, show that the waist is a little lower than during the Empire, the puffed sleeve above the tapered sleeve is becoming more a point of focus, and the ruffles and lace about the collar and neck are definitely borrowed from sixteenth- and seventeenth-century costumes (Fig. 19-6). Compare these ladies with Ingres' sketch *Lady With a Parasol* only two years later in 1823. The skirt is much wider at the bottom with fullness at the back; the puffed sleeves are becoming more prominent; there are more tucks, ruffles, laces, and broken surfaces on the costume in general; and one could sum up the entire effect as soft and "frilly" (Fig. 19-9). One should also note that the simple cutting diagrams of the Empire Period have disappeared in favor of more complex patterning.

Later in the 1820s the sleeves gradually took the focus of attention as they continued to grow in size until they had to be stiffened with special linings. Some were still puffed at the top and then pleated into a slim sleeve below, but the majority were of the tapering, leg-o-mutton variety. Sometimes a sheer outersleeve tapered down over a short puffed sleeve and tight undersleeve or over a short puffed sleeve with the bare arm below. Others were very full to the elbow and then became fitted to the wrist, and some were as full at the wrist as they were at the armseye (Fig. 19-4e).

Necklines spread into a wide oval over the shoulders during the 1820s, and this boat neckline was often edged in a wide, stiffened *bertha* or ruffle. Later the shoulder line of the sleeve was dropped to further enlarge the expansiveness of the neckline and to emphasize the soft, swan neckline that was now so much admired (Fig. 19-4a,b). Sometimes necklines were filled in with ruffles or lace, reminiscent of the sixteenth-century partlet, and sometimes shoulder wings or crescents of lace, ruffles, or ribbon were added just below the shoulder to widen further the shoulders and neckline.

Bodices were usually tight-fitting over a corset (Fig. 19-4a,b), sometimes set with pleating and gathering to give added interest. One interesting effect, toward the end of the 1820s, was to cut a separate piece of fabric and attach it across the bust so that it was pinched in at center and on the sides to give a kind of outside brassiere effect. Other varied effects were achieved by using overlaid sections of ruffled or pleated fabric on the front of the bodice to give further emphasis and definition to the bustline. Virtually all bodices and skirts fastened down the back with buttons, lacings, or hooks and eyes (all concealed).

Skirts became even wider at the bottom during the 1820s, with more ornamentation and definition toward the bottom of the skirt such as

**FIG. 19-9** Jean Dominique Ingres, *Portrait of Countess Antoine Apponyi* or *Lady with a Parasol;* Fogg Art Museum, Cambridge, Mass.; 1823. Illustrates female fashion during the Restoration in France, still with the high waist of the Empire style but without classical associations. Note the ruffles, the puffed and slashed sleeves from the Renaissance, the cashmere shawl, the expanding bonnet, and the parasol. Photo courtesy of the Fogg Museum, Harvard University, Winthrop Bequest.

tucks, pleats, ruffles, appliqué, or loops of silk or fur. Ruffles at the top of the petticoat made the back of the skirt flare much more, and there was much use of bows with long streamers at the back of the waist. The waist of the skirt moved just a tiny bit above a normal waistline (Fig. 19-4e). By 1830 the standard length of the skirt or dress was just slightly longer than ankle length so that the ballet dancing slippers laced over the instep and up the ankle could be plainly seen (Fig. 19-4j). Knitted silk drawers were worn under the petticoats and full skirts (Fig. 19-4f).

Coiffures also grew in size and complexity

during the 1820s. At first hair had a central part with a concentration of curls over the temples, but these soon turned into a pile of sausage curls that massed like horns at the temple, while the simple bun at the back of the head turned into a complex twist or knot decorated with flowers and ribbons. By 1830 some hairdos were so complex that they had to be lacquered to keep them in place. Bonnets also had to change to accommodate the new hair style. The brim gradually lifted as coiffures increased in size, and crowns now perched on top of the head. Bonnets became exaggerated, with very wide brims, high crowns, and excessive amounts of flowers, plumes, ribbons, and bows for trim. The only evening headdress was the exotic turban, once again trimmed with plumes and ribbons (Fig. 19–4c,e,g,i).

Wraps were either the cloak with armholes, the redingote, or the pelisse which was comparable to the male overcoat and cut to fit the line of the gown underneath (Fig. 19–4j,k).

A very good example of the extreme silhouette in women's dress about 1829 may be seen in a fashion plate from the *Petit Courrier des Dames* (Fig. 19–4). A slightly more domesticated and less fashionable version of the same costume line may be seen in a statue by Chaponnière, *Young Woman Seated* (Fig. 19–10). Note the little Elizabethan ruff about the neck, the big sausage rolls at the temple, and the twisted knot at the back of the head. Otherwise her gown is very simple without great ornamentation. As for the boudoir styles, the full lace negligee with soft, rounded sleeves was popular for mornings at home (Fig. 19–4n).

The styles and silhouettes of the late 1820s remained in fashion well into the 1830s with shoulders and sleeves expanding to ever wider and fuller proportions. Some were held out by boning, others by horsehair, and a few by cushions of down. Such costumes were of such a volume that they weighed much more than one would suspect, and they must have been tiring to wear for any length of time. It is at this very moment that we begin to have the image of the sighing, swooning female who often needed smelling salts to revive her. Much of this image may have been based not just on a feminine ideal but on the facts of dress at this time.

FIG. 19–10  Chaponnière, *Young Woman Seated;* Musée des Arts Decoratifs, Paris; ca. 1832. Illustrates the full-blown silhouette of the years 1830 to 1835. Note the sausage curls at the temples, the ruff at the neck, the leg-o-mutton sleeves off the shoulder, the deep décolletage, the slightly raised waist, and the full expansiveness of the skirt. Photo courtesy of Flammarion, Paris.

But by 1837, when Queen Victoria came to the throne of England, the female silhouette was slowly beginning to change. A more moral and less frivolous tone was set at court and in other circles as well. In France the bourgeois king Louis Philippe and wife Adelaide had little dash and flair, and court life took on more of the middle-class ideal that was slowly shouldering flamboyant romanticism off the stage—in fashion as well as in art.

The first major change to take place in female dress was in the coiffure and bonnet. The hair lost its piled-up excess and was once again parted in the middle, ending in soft ringlets or curls at the side of the head or in a loose knot at the back of the neck. In the 1840s groups of ringlets hung down like spaniel's ears and were inseparably connected with the ultra-romantic heroines in prose and poetry of that day (Fig. 19–4h,l,m). With the loss of the great sausage curls at the sides of the head, the bonnet brim once again closed in about the face, and the crown once again moved to the back of the head. Bonnets also lost their excesses of ribbon and floral trim and were more reserved in color—all part of the move from the flamboyant doll figure for women of 1830 to the domesticated, tea-cozy look of the more subdued romanticism of the 1840s.

A French print by Bourdet from the year after the accession of Queen Victoria shows this new image for women (Fig. 19–8). The hair is much more subdued, the bonnet is just beginning to close in about the face, and although the shoulders are covered with a shaped stole, or *mantelette,* one can see that the excessive expansion of the sleeve has been diminished. The upper part of women's sleeves now were narrowed by vertical tucks and pleating above the elbow that allowed some fullness below, but very little at the shoulder. By the 1840s almost all the fullness was gone, and sleeves were slim and long, flowing down from a dropped shoulder line so that the woman still looked as if she lacked an outer shoulder bone. Evening sleeves were now usually short, capped sleeves ending in a ruffle.

During the 1840s the neckline changed from a great lateral expansion to V-shaped, sometimes filled in with a lace *guimpe,* ending in a ruffle at the neck somewhat like an Elizabethan partlet. Day dresses later became very high-necked with no neck showing at all; only evening dresses had a low décolletage. Waistlines were lowered, and the bodice once more became pointed. With this change, many of the pleated overlays of fabric were now added in diagonals to emphasize the line from the shoulder to the center of the pointed waist. The skirt also changed somewhat, once again reaching to the floor without decoration from the knees to the hemline. As heavier, darker fabrics gradually gained in importance, there was also much experimentation with varieties of underskirts and petticoats. Some were quilted, some were stiffened with horsehair, and some were corded around the bottom edge, while a starched and ruffled petticoat was used at the outside just under the outerskirt.

Outer garments during this period molded more closely to the under silhouette than ever before. The redingote was the most popular, but shaped mantelettes or shawls were also worn as well as the collared cape. In footwear, although the square-toed slipper with ribbon laces remained in vogue, a low boot with elastic sides became fashionable for daytime walking; a dainty, short boot laced at the sides was used for afternoon receptions; the slipper-pump became the standard wear for evening.

To gain a sense of the fashions for women in the mid-1840s, look at a fashion plate from *Godey's Lady's Book* from 1842 (Fig. 19–5). Note the flattened hair and central part under the close-to-the-face bonnet, the off-the-shoulder bodice that makes the upper torso look very weak, and the fullness of the skirt that is no longer balanced by expansion in the upper part of the female silhouette. The entire image is wilting and romantic. The same effect is also true of the evening dresses to be seen in Lami's illustration for Janin's *Summer in Paris* (Fig. 19–2).

## FABRICS

For men the standard fabric was a fine grade of woolen broadcloth with trim in velvet, sable, or some less precious fur. Waistcoats were of velvet; brocade; embroidered satin; striped, flowered, or plaid silk; and cottons for summer. Common men of the lower middle class wore homespuns and roughly woven woolens, while in hot climates, men's clothes were made of linen or nankeen cotton imported from China. Pantaloons were of nankeen, cotton twill (known as *drill*), corduroy, a heavy cotton twill (known as *moleskin*), or for the very tight-fitting ones, silk jersey (known as *kerseymere*), or bias-cut wool. Hats were of beaver or felt, caps of leather or cloth.

Lightweight cottons such as chintz, calico,

gauze, and muslin were in vogue with women up through the 1820s, but the older fabrics such as satin, velvet, silk taffetas, and lace also began to return. Woolens became popular for women's daytime wear—especially in winter—while outergarments for cold weather were almost invariably of wool. Furs were also used for linings and trim. Hats were of straw, gauze, crepe, muslin, velvet, satin, and grosgrain, trimmed in taffeta or satin ribbons and artificial flowers.

## ARTS AND ARTIFACTS

After the fall of Napoleon, the interiors and furniture of the Empire remained for a time, but as society moved into the 1820s, romanticism with its interest in decorative effects from many past times and many faraway places caused interiors and furnishings to become excessively decorative and even cluttered with a very eclectic character that gave no sense of unity of style to a room (Fig. 19–1). However, furnishings and interiors, following the bourgeois demands of the period, became more cozy and comfortable than at almost any time in the past. Festooned draperies were heavy, table covers were rich and fringed, chairs were padded and upholstered in velvets and tufted satins, and colors ran to rich, pinkish mauves and faded or greyed reds (Fig. 19–1a,c). The most prominent period of the past from which to borrow ideas was the Gothic, and there was much use of pseudotracery in wall paneling and chair carving (Fig. 19–1b,d). The effect was a bit heavy, cluttered and stiff, but there was a sense of charm and comfort in the rich display of solid, dark wood surfaces.

Motifs now shifted from classical antiquity to the medieval, Renaissance, and Near Eastern decorative ornamentation. Accessories for men included quizzing glasses, gloves, walking sticks, watches—at first on fobs at the waist and later on chains in the waistcoat pocket—a flower in the buttonhole, and occasionally a cigarette, pipe, or snuffbox. For women accessories included gloves—short for daytime, long for evening—the ever-present fan for evening, muffs for winter, parasols, handbags, purses (Fig. 19–4d), and the occasional bandbox in which a lady carried a change of headdress to a party or reception.

As for jewelry men displayed rings, orders on a coat or around the neck on a ribbon, shirt studs for shirt fronts, and occasionally an official seal for stamping wax on letters, worn on a chain in a waistcoat pocket like a watch. Women once again returned to a great use of earrings but used fewer necklaces. Sometimes chains were worn around the neck with a tiny stone or cross at the end, and watches were usually worn pinned at the waist at the end of a chain. Cameos began to be more popular at this time, even for middle-class women, and were most usually seen in brooches used to fasten collars at the throat. Bracelets of every shape and dimension were popular, while other jeweled items included combs, pins, tiaras, and looking glasses.

## VISUAL SOURCES

The best sources for this period are actually the fashion journals of the period, the most useful of which are *Costumes Parisiens, Le Bon Genre, Petit Courrier des Dames, Le Follet Courrier des Salons, La Mode, Court Magazine, Godey's Lady's Book, Journal des Dames et des Modes, La Belle Assemblée, Gazette des Salons* and *Journal des Tailleurs*. Illustrators that are very useful to consult are Paul Gavarni, Honoré Daumier, George Cruikshank, William Heath and Henry Alken. Painters and portrait artists who are of great value include Jean Dominique Ingres, Eugène Delacroix, Ferdinand Waldmüller, A. Devéria, C. Hansen, Théodore Chasseriau, Franz Winterhalter, D. Favas, Horace Vernet, and Gabriel Decamps. The best institutional sources are the Bibliothèque Nationale in Paris, the Versailles Museum, the New York Metropolitan, the New York Public Library, the Österreichische Galerie in Vienna, the Wallraf-Richartz Museum of Col- ogne, the Boston Museum of Fine Arts, and the Museo Romántico of Madrid. Useful books are Pierre Courthion's *Romanticism,* and C. Willet Cunnington's *English Women's Clothing in the Nineteenth Century.*

## SUMMARY

This is a period vivid in our memory from films, book illustrations, and descriptions in romantic novels written at this time. It epitomized a fragile, delicately artificial beauty for women and a dark, somewhat brooding, poetic-romantic image for men, even though it began with a flamboyant early period that closed about the time that Queen Victoria ascended the throne of England and ended with a sober late phase in the 1840s, just before the Revolutions of 1848. It was a period when Romanticism in music, literature, and art reached its greatest peak of tumultuous creative activity about 1830 before tapering off into a long, dying fall of ever-tightening, repressive forms of Romanticism that lasted in varying guises until World War I. The decade of 1830 was in many ways to Romanticism what the first decade of the sixteenth century was to the Renaissance—an exciting peak of development in a style that would remain in tighter, distorted forms for many years.

# chapter XX

# Victorian and Second Empire

## Chronology
### (1848–1870)

VICTORIAN AND
SECOND EMPIRE
1848–1870

| | |
|---|---|
| 1849 | Astor Place riots in New York directed against the English actor Macready; gold rush in California; Lola Montez startled Europe with her escapades |
| 1850 | Clayton-Bulwer treaty on the Panama Canal; Gladstone and Disraeli struggle for parliamentary control; Jenny Lind gives her first concert in New York City |
| 1851 | Louis Napoleon seizes power in France; Crystal Palace Exhibition opens |
| 1852 | France's Second Empire begins after Louis Napoleon is crowned Emperor Napoleon III; Lola Montez dances at a celebration for the American stage in New York |
| 1853 | Commodore Perry opens U.S. trade relations with Japan |
| 1854 | The two-year Crimean War begins; the Roman Catholic Church adopts the doctrine of the Immaculate Conception |
| 1854–1855 | Gold rush in Australia |

1849

| | |
|---|---|
| 1855 | The safety match is invented; first attempt to lay the Atlantic cable |
| 1856 | Henry Bessemer invents his converter to make pig iron into steel |
| 1857 | Louis Pasteur begins his pioneer study of fermentation; Anglo-French War against China ended by the Treaty of Tientsin, which gave economic rights to foreign nations; Gustave Flaubert publishes *Madame Bovary;* John Stuart Mill publishes his essay "On Liberty"; Sepoy Rebellion in India |

1858

| | |
|---|---|
| 1858 | Count Cavour plots with Napoleon III to drive the Austrians from Italy; Rudolph Virchow publishes his work on cellular pathology |
| 1859 | Charles Darwin completes *The Origin of Species;* John Brown's raid; first petroleum wells drilled at Titusville, Pennsylvania |
| 1860 | The Prince of Wales (later Edward VII) visits the United States; South Carolina secedes from the Union; Kingdom of Italy is established; Victor Hugo writes *Les Misérables;* Russia founds the city of Vladivostok. |
| 1861 | Death of Albert, prince consort of England; American Civil War begins with the bombardment of Fort Sumter; Czar Alexander II of Russia emancipates the serfs by imperial decree; Ernest Solvay patents a soda-making process which drastically reduces the cost of making textiles, glass, and soap; Napoleon III begins his six-year campaign to conquer Mexico |

1862

| | |
|---|---|
| 1862 | Count Bismarck becomes prime minister of Prussia; the first annexations by the French take place in Cochin China; Napoleon III made Maximilian of Hapsburg the emperor of Mexico; Abraham Lincoln publishes the Emancipation Proclamation |

victorian and second empire    347

| | |
|---|---|
| 1863 | The Battle of Gettysburg; Edouard Manet paints *Déjeuner sur l'herbe* |
| 1864 | Prussia declares war on Denmark over Schleswig-Holstein; Siemans and Martin introduce the open-hearth process for making steel; a British trading company completes the first Persian telegraph |
| 1865 | Joseph Lister introduces antiseptic surgery; General Lee surrenders at Appomattox; Abraham Lincoln is shot by John Wilkes Booth; the Thirteenth Amendment abolishes slavery |
| 1866 | The Ku Klux Klan is organized; the Seven Weeks' War is won at the Battle of Königgrätz; dynamite is patented by Alfred Nobel; Dostoevsky publishes *Crime and Punishment;* the transatlantic cable is laid |
| 1867 | Werner Siemens introduces his dynamo for generating electricity; Karl Marx completes Volume I of *Das Kapital;* the Second Reform Bill sponsored by Disraeli is passed; Maximilian is executed by Juarez in Mexico; U.S. purchases Alaska from Russia for $7,500,000 |
| 1869 | The Social Democratic Worker's Party is founded in Germany; the Suez Canal is opened; the driving of the golden spike at Ogden, Utah, marks the opening of the transcontinental railroad |
| 1870 | Rome is seized by Victor Emmanuel of Italy, and the pope is a virtual prisoner; the Vatican proclaims the infallibility of the pope; the Franco-Prussian War begins; Napoleon III flees to England |

1868

# BACKGROUND

Although there had been a great upheaval and social change after the French Revolution and during the Napoleonic era, by the middle of the nineteenth century oppressive monarchy and rigid conservatism had returned to most of Europe with the Treaty of Vienna, and little attention was given to written constitutions or human rights. Revolutions had occurred with great regularity and frequency during the Romantic era, but most were a total failure and few reforms were made. After the final defeat of liberal and radical values in the various revolutions that were suppressed in 1848, artists and intellectuals began to develop new modes in art and literature using strong contemporary social themes. Dreams, fantasy, and escapism were gradually put aside by forward-looking artistic leaders in favor of a systematic search into the human personality and society. Observation, clinical analysis, and the scientific study of people and institutions began to replace the shopworn clichés of subjective, Romantic idealism.

Philosophers began to question the entire escapist philosophy on which nineteenth-century artistic eclecticism was based. With factory workers living in urban slums and the general misery of the masses increasing with each expansion of industrialism and urbanization, social reformers and intellectuals demanded a change of outlook. A major contributor to this questioning of the status quo was Auguste Comte, generally regarded as the father of sociology. In his writings between 1830 and the early 1850s, he argued for the study of society according to the new scientific approach, insisting that events in society could be predicted and determined in a cause-and-effect relationship. He called his philosophy *positivism* and called for changes based on careful, factual analysis rather than on ringing slogans and Romantic ideals. This idea was further reinforced by Charles Darwin, whose theory of evolution contributed to current philosophy the concept of survival of the fittest. This theory, coupled with Comte's positivism, made heredity and environment, rather than inspiring ideals, very important to both the new sociologists and the new artists, and human behavior

began to seem beyond the control of the individual. It gradually came to be assumed that only an improvement in society could better the human condition.

Yet these ideas were considered radical and subversive by the mass middle-class public which now dominated the cultural scene. Just as mannerist ideals had twisted and repressed the open and natural ideals of the Renaissance, middle-class society in the late nineteenth century clung to outworn, rigid, and even distorted versions of the subjective Romanticism of the early years of the century. The richness and expansiveness of Romanticism was transformed into an excessive materialism, created from a pastiche of exotic and historical sources, that was supported as art by the wealthy, capitalist nouveau riche who equated this overstuffed and excessively ornamented eclecticism with power, position, and good taste. There was, therefore, a cultural separation between the mass eclectic taste based on the old Romanticism and the avante-garde artistic and intellectual interest in realism and social change.

The greatest nineteenth-century monument to this materialism is undoubtedly the Paris Opera House, planned by Napoleon III and carried out by the architect, Charles Garnier, as the perfect symbol for the wealth, power, and grandeur of the Second Empire (Fig. 20-1). It stands for the two great repressed drives of political leaders and industrialists in the late nineteenth century—the desperate attempt to make nouveau-riche ideals aristocratic and to match the great moments of artistic achievement in France's historic past.

In political developments France had tired of the dull and somewhat inept rule of Louis Philippe, the "citizen king," and set up a new Republic after the Revolution of 1848 which was quickly overturned by its first president, Louis Napoleon, nephew of Napoleon I, in favor of a new or Second Empire. Married to a dazzling beauty from Spain, Eugénie Montijo de Guzmán, who presided with great flair over an opulent and luxurious court, Napoleon III for a time seemed to bring France to a high level of industrial development and a secure sense of

armchair
1865

(a)

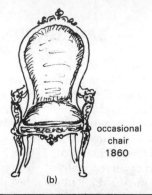

occasional
chair
1860

(b)

London
lamp
1859

(c)

Charles Garnier, the Paris Opera House, 1861–1874. Probably the greatest monument to opulent, excessive, nineteenth-century eclecticism. Planned by Napoleon III as a symbol of the wealth and grandeur of the Second French Empire, it was not opened until the establishment of the Third Republic. Photo courtesy of the French Cultural Services, New York.

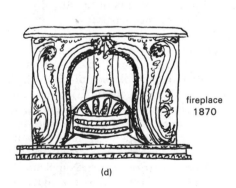

fireplace
1870

(d)

curtained
window
1865

(e)

FIGURE 20-1

350

its own worth and importance on the European scene. If the emperor had not felt compelled to become involved in a series of military adventures in Italy, Turkey, and Mexico that drained the nation as well as giving it a false sense of its own military power, he might have had a much longer reign. But in 1870 he became embroiled in a dispute with Prussia; in the ensuing war France was defeated, the emperor fled to England, and Germany united under the leadership of Prussia.

In Italy with some help from Napoleon III, the Italians were gradually united in a single state under the leadership of Victor Emmanuel of Sardinia. In England under the somewhat unimaginative but steady leadership of the new queen, Victoria, and her prince consort, Albert, the nation moved into a period of steady industrial development and imperialist expansion that was heralded by the great exhibition in Hyde Park in 1851, centered in the famed Crystal Palace. The Crimean War that involved both England and France in support of Turkey against Russian expansionism brought British imperialist tendencies to a new peak

with Prime Minister Disraeli also encouraging British purchase of controlling shares in the Suez Canal.

In the United States the signing of a peace treaty in 1848 to end the infamous war with Mexico brought California under U.S. control at the very moment that it became the center of a feverish gold rush. The westward movement, which had been increasing for several decades, became a great surge. This movement west further aggravated the tensions between those areas that were considered open to slavery and those that were not, and a decade after the California gold rush, events quickly led to the Civil War between North and South. This war was a fierce and terrible bloodletting that split families as well as the nation. When it was over, the reconciliation and reconstruction took many years, and it was to the west once again that Americans looked after the war ended in 1865. In the five years after the war, the continent was spanned by rails, Alaska was purchased from Russia for $7,500,000, and the wave of the future lay west of the Mississippi.

## THE BASIC COSTUME SILHOUETTE

The fashions of this period, like the interiors, were inhibiting and oppressive for the most part, except for a few lighthearted fashions for summer or gala occasions. The many stiffened petticoats that gave the full-skirted, tea-cozy look to women during the 1840s now gave way to the boned cage or crinoline, which held out the skirts in a distended bell shape that was unnatural and frequently grotesque. In many ways, the styles for women during this period were a kind of neomannerist return to the distortions and tensions of the sixteenth century. Even the trim on women's gowns, particularly for evening, was unnatural and disproportionate to the scale of the normal human figure in the same way that the pattern on the gown of Eleanor of Toledo in the middle of the sixteenth century had been excessive (see Fig. 12–3). The fashions in these societies were similar in their repression, tension, and unnatural use of decoration. This similarity tends

to confirm the thesis that the late nineteenth century was an age of repressed Romanticism—a period in which natural romantic sentiments were repressed, codified, and rigidified into unnatural forms.

Male costume after 1848 retained the basic fashion lines of the Romantic era but with straighter lines, darker colors, and little flair. The top hat was obligatory, but was now usually silk, not beaver, and straight, not curved, in its stovepipe contours. The hair was full but not richly curled, and heavy beards and mustaches were standard. By the opening of the American Civil War, the daily outfit of the male tended to be a sober uniform of waistcoat, trousers, and vest—known as a *suit of clothes.* Trousers, although narrow, were no longer tight-fitting or fastened under the shoe but straight and tubular, while tails and frock coats now had a relatively straight line to their cut. Pointed, standing collars and cravats were replaced by straight or turnover, starched collars, and the new four-in-hand or bow ties. Romantic flair had thus been replaced by boxy, sober, formal and somewhat repressive uniform habits of clothing. Also special suits of clothing began to be detailed for special occasions: the frock coat and top hat for formal afternoon wear; the bowler and sack suit for business; short hunting and fishing jackets with leggings for country wear; and a full black outfit of tails with a white vest and tie for formal evening wear. Overcoats superseded the cloak for outdoor wear, and laced shoes and boots began to replace pull-on boots for daily wear. Daytime formal dress can be seen in Frith's painting of *Derby Day,* travel dress in Frith's *The Railway Station,* and evening dress in the engraving *Grand Reception of the Notabilities of the Nation at the White House,* depicting Lincoln's Second Inaugural Ball (Figs. 20–2,3,4).

Feminine dress from 1848 until almost 1870 concentrated on the rise and then the movement to the back of the figure of the great hooped skirt. In the first years of the Second Empire, the weight of the many petticoats that had created the tea-cozy look brought about the introduction of a graduated series of metal or boned hoops suspended from tapes to hold out the fullness of the bell skirts. The width of the skirt increased dramatically from waist to floor. At their greatest width, about 1860–1865, these crinolines were almost grotesque in their width and were often the butt of jokes and cartoons. They became key symbols of the distortion and

repression that had taken place in the original ideals of romanticism. The hair was now parted in the middle, waved over the forehead, caught in a twisted bun or bunch of curls over the ears, or drawn in soft waves from center part to the back of the head and held in a chignon or soft roll. The twist over the ear was preferred by Queen Victoria, the chignon by the Empress Eugénie, who with the help of her couturier, the founder of the House of Worth, was the leader of European female fashion until 1869. She replaced the bonnet with a small brimmed straw with a ribbon at the back, developed the feminine riding habit to a new level of elegance, and introduced the famed Spanish jacket as an exotic accent from her homeland. In the hoop-skirted style, based in many of its decorative details on the Rococo, the skirt often consisted of several layers of varying lengths; a series of overlapping flounces at the hem; graduated panels edged with strong trim that expanded in size as they spread out over the skirt; or flowers, fringe, and garlanded ruching layered over the entire skirt. The trim was repeated in the bertha around the shoulders and in the triangular *pagoda sleeve* with its undersleeve of white tulle that was the most prominent line for daytime wear. For evening short cap sleeves and a low décolletage were the fashion, while daytime wear always dictated long sleeves and a high neckline except for certain summer dresses. Cloth boots were worn by day, slippers by night. Shawls and shaped mantles were worn outdoors.

## VICTORIAN AND SECOND EMPIRE COSTUME

***Masculine Dress*** After the failure of the Revolutions of 1848, men's clothing lost its pleated frills, rich color, dandified tailoring, and smartness and moved into a period of darker colors, restricted tubular lines, and functional "uniforms" for each specific formal and recreational event.

Certainly the most important innovation of the 1850s was the introduction of the business suit, consisting of matching finger-tip-length coat, waistcoat, and trousers. In the early 1850s the coat was often somewhat longer and square

cut like a slightly shortened frock coat, similar to that seen at the left in *Le Lion,* Supplement to *l'Elegance* (Fig. 20–5), but by 1859 the sack coat appeared which was remarkably like a longer version of a modern suit coat (Fig. 20–2f). In general, such coats were boxy in their outlines and with a fuller, tubular sleeve than in the past (Fig. 20–2k). Such suits were often made of striped or checked woolen fabric to call special attention to the fact that all the pieces were from the same bolt of material. Other changes of the late 1850s came in the decreasing size of the coat

attached
turn-down
collar
1862

collar
attached
to shirt
1868

(a)

separate
starched
collar 1862

(f)
1854
sack suit cuts

(i)
back of vest
1850s

(j)
lounge coat
over
waistcoat
1859

waistcoat
outlined in
braid 1850s

(b)

evening
shirt
with
fluted
frills
1860

(c)

linen shirt
and braces
1850s

(g)

Macfarlane
topcoat
1850s

(d)

(e)
natural
straw 1855

black silk
hat 1858

(h)

William Frith, *Derby Day;* Tate Gallery; 1855. Illustrates the muffled, subdued fashions of the third
quarter of the nineteenth century, with particular
emphasis on tightness, tension, and moderate distortion, that have given this period and the bustle
period that follows the title of neomannerist. Photo
courtesy of the Tate Gallery.

(n)
British soldier
1864

summer
suit
French
1857

(k)

(l)
flat neck
cravat and
scarf pin 1857

FIGURE 20–2

(m)
short
topcoat
worn
over
sack
suit
1857

353

(a) "pork pie" straw 1865

(b) frilly front shirt-blouse 1852

feminist bloomer costume 1857

(e) straw bonnet with hairnet at the back 1861

(g) evening coiffure 1867

(h) crinoline or petticoat with steel hoops 1857

(d) red Garibaldi shirt 1862

(f) corset 1850

lady's patent leather boot 1864

(i)

(j) elliptical crinoline 1867

(c)

(k) dress trim 1867

William Frith, *The Railway Station;* Royal Holloway College, University of London; 1862. Illustrates Romanticism within a later Victorian framework. The reserve and restraint of the partings contrast sharply with the Romantic female clothing, which is certainly unrealistic wear for travel. Photo courtesy of Royal Holloway College.

(l) crinoline puffs over hoops 1863

(m) pagoda sleeve 1863

(n) corset 1867

(O) pelisse outergarment 1862

(p) bathing costume 1864

**FIGURE 20–3**

**FIG. 20-4** *Grand Reception of the Notabilities of the Nation at the White House;* engraving in *Leslie's Magazine,* 1865. Illustrates the subdued, restricted sense of Romanticism that prevailed in fashion in the second half of the nineteenth century. Note how the hoops worn by the women give a sense of distortion to the female figure. Photo courtesy of the Library of Congress.

**FIG. 20-5** Men's costumes, from *Le Lion,* Supplement to *l'Elegance,* 1855. Illustrates the new suit of clothes (left) that was the contribution to male fashion in the 1850s in which coat, vest, and trousers are all cut from the same fabric. Also note the low, standing collars and bow ties. Photo from the collection of the author.

collar and lapels, particularly the loss of the high framing line of the collar behind the collar of the shirt. Many coats began to button higher than in the past, and often the fashion was to fasten only the top button on the coat, thus allowing the coat to swing open to show the vest underneath. This effect even carried over to the cutaway coat (usually longer and more sharply cut back than any sack coat), and many of them also now began to cut back slightly above the waist.

The frock coat (or "Prince Albert" as it was called in the U.S.) in the 1850s lost the elegance that it had carried during the Romantic Period with its nipped-in waist and slightly flared skirts and became a sober, dignified, usually double-breasted, coat with straight lines and no flair. It became the habitual mark of respectability in the upper classes and the festive garment for the average man. By the end of the Second Empire, it was considered the formal afternoon coat for all respectable gentlemen. In many ways the frock coat was to the male of the Victorian Age what the toga had been to the Imperial Roman. A good example of a grey frock coat of this period may be seen at the center of Frith's painting *Derby Day* (Fig. 20-2).

From the cut-back coat or sport cutaway of the 1840s, a more formal coat began to develop that by the early 1860s had become the garment that we now know as the *morning coat,* (which is still worn at formal weddings). It came to be considered the formal urban calling costume for the forenoon to be replaced by a frock coat for afternoon formal wear. As for the tailed coat, the daytime version was often buttoned up double-breasted to about the breastline so that the waistcoat showed only at the waist and a tiny bit above the line of the lapels. A single-breasted use of tails for daytime may be seen in *Le Lion,* Supplement to *l'Elegance* (Fig. 20-5). But in general, tails were worn less in the daytime and became the exclusive uniform for formal evening wear. A single-breasted black coat and trousers with a white (or black) waistcoat (sometimes of silk), a starched white shirt, and tie was considered the full male evening dress, and with only minor variations this has remained to this day (Fig. 20-2c). Soft velvet lounge coats were popular for at home

and were the forerunner of the smoking jacket (Fig. 20-2j).

In the 1850s and 1860s waistcoats were often the only accents of richness and color in an otherwise somber suit of clothes. One could still see small, floral-patterned brocades, dotted and cut-velvet patterns, paisley-printed piqués, and an occasional subdued stripe. Waistcoats were either double- or single-breasted, but the sedate gentleman usually wore a single-breasted one. Most buttoned to only a moderate height, although occasionally a waistcoat buttoned almost to the cravat with a small, turn-over collar. All waistcoats had rolled collars, varying in width, some with indented lapels and some without. Although the waistcoat usually matched the trousers or coat or both, the idea of the waistcoat as a rich color and textural accent in a man's habit did not totally die out (Fig. 20-2b,i,j,k).

Just as the sleeves of the coat had become fuller in their tubular line, trousers during this period became easy in cut. They were long enough to reach within an inch of the floor at the back and often slightly graduated upward over the instep. They were worn without any creases, which further accented their tubular line, and they were usually of lighter tones in summer and darker in winter. For daytime wear plaids, checks, and stripes were highly favored with coats that were of a darker solid color. Straps under the foot on trousers were still occasionally seen but were uncommon.

Collars during the 1850s lost the pointed corners and height of the Romantic Period and were now either stiff, straight, and of only moderate height or turnover ones resembling those of the twentieth century (Fig. 20-2a,l). By the close of the 1860s the slightly higher collar with the corners bent over to make wings appeared (and is still worn with formal morning coats and tails). Disposable collars made of linen bonded to paper also made their appearance and were advertised as being more inexpensive than having regular linen collars laundered and starched. The neckwear that went with these new collars was first dominated by small bow ties, but the wide, wrapped cravat with no front tie was still seen, as was the new, knotted tie with ends tucked into the waistcoat, known as the *four-in-hand* after the coachmen who first used them. One other tie that made its appearance was the string tie, which was like a long ribbon tied in a bow with ends hanging loose. Since shirts were all but covered by coat and waistcoat except at the base of the neck and cuffs, they often had separate starched or pleated bosoms and cuffs. Shirts opened either in the back or front, but separate studs were used in the front for effect, even when the opening was in the back (Fig. 20-2c,g).

Although the standard hat was the formal stovepipe top hat, there were other variations, especially for sportswear. There was the low-crowned, wide-brimmed hat in felt for winter, straw for summer; high-crowned caps that looked like those worn by train engineers; the rounded crowned bowler that was often quite high (although there were also low-crowned versions); and the tiny billed hunting caps that were also worn for leisure weekends in the country (Fig. 20-2e,h,k,m).

This interest in special suits for various weekend leisure and sports activities lead to the establishment of a variety of belted, finger-tip-length jackets; knickers or knee trousers; and leggings that protected the leg.

The almost exclusive outergarment for men was the topcoat or overcoat, thus finally placing the mantle almost exclusively in the service of the military. Overcoats were usually cut like the frock coat except with more weight and fullness, and the large collars and several shoulder capes of the past were now gone (Fig. 20-2d,m). Some gentlemen of means still favored the fur-collared or even fur-lined overcoats, as seen in one of the central male figures in Frith's painting *The Railway Station* (Fig. 20-3).

As for the male styling of the hair, the standard look was hair that was relatively full in front and over the ears and then neatly trimmed at the neck above the collar. Some men who considered themselves artists or intellectuals wore it much longer, but the businessman's haircut with a tight trim at the back of the neck was standard. Sideburns now became fuller than in the past and were known as *dundrearies* after a character in the Tom Taylor play *Our American Cousin*. Mustaches were of many varieties including those with waxed, turned-up ends as worn by Napoleon III of France and Victor Emmanuel of Italy. Beards became more popular as the period moved on and ranged from the stilettolike *imperial* of Napoleon III to the very full beards of Darwin and Dickens.

Footwear of the 1850s and 1860s still included the low pumps with bows for evening and half-boots for daytime, but the half-boots were now often fitted with elastic sides for smooth fit without fastenings. Laced, high shoes also came in at this time as did buttoned, high shoes. For sports wear, leggings usually replaced knee-high boots.

An excellent summary example of the male styles of the urban gentleman may be seen in James Tissot's painting *The Rue Royale Circle* (Fig. 20-6). It shows topcoats, sack suits, frock coats, cutaways, waistcoats that match and contrast with coats and trousers, bow ties, full cravats, and various kinds of footwear. Even though the group are artists, there is a subdued, somber, restrained, bourgeois look to all—an image of proper respectability that was the hallmark for men during this period.

Military dress during this period still retained elements of the Napoleonic Period but now diluted by the lines of civil dress. There were tunics like the double-breasted frock coat buttoned to the throat with a standing collar, long trousers with stripes down the side or tight trousers fitted into boots, brimmed caps or higher-crowned shakos in colors that ranged from bright to subdued. A few exotic uniforms based on Algerian costume were seen in the Zouave regiments of France and a similar uniform was used by a Northern volunteer regiment during the American Civil War (Fig. 20-2n).

**Feminine Dress** Although masculine styles began to originate more in London than in Paris during this period, female fashions originated almost exclusively in Paris in the workshops of an Englishman, Charles Worth, who had become couturier to the Empress Eugénie of France. He founded the first great house of female fashion in Europe and for the remainder of the century the mark of having ''arrived'' in society was the ability to have

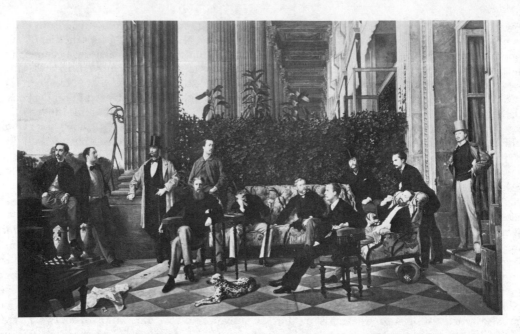

**FIG. 20–6** James Tissot, *The Rue Royale Circle;* Collection of Baron Hottinger; 1867. Illustrates the subdued, conservative, repressed business uniform worn by most men in the late nineteenth century. Note the dominance of the top hat; frock, cutaway, and sack-suit coats; and the stiffness of most collars. Photo courtesy of Baron Hottinger.

one's gowns done exclusively by the House of Worth. The hallmark of such gowns was always the magnificence of the materials used and the complex ingenuity of the dressmaking.

The dominant fashion line of this period was created by the introduction of the hooped skirt, and this rather excessive, sometimes grotesque creation led in turn to a fascinating but abortive attempt to introduce comfort and practicality into female dress. Amelia Jenks Bloomer, the publisher of *The Lily,* a magazine for women in the United States, attempted to introduce a soft jacket, knee-length skirt, and harem pants for women as a healthful and practical antidote to the new hooped fashion (Fig. 20–3c). Although her attempt failed, the idea of *bloomers,* or full harem pants, soon resurfaced in female bathing costume, and somewhat later in cycling and sporting fashions.

As for the introduction of hoops, they were in many ways more practical than layers of starched, padded, or stiffened petticoats. It made the weight of women's skirts lighter,

reduced the petticoat laundering problem, and removed some of the waistband thickness created by many petticoats. Although the hoop was first made of cane or whalebone, it was not long before the American device of circles of spring steel set onto a petticoat, or even better onto tapes of heavy muslin, swept the field of fashion, and the *cage Américaine* became the standard method for creating hoops (Fig. 20–3h,j,l). But the introduction of the hoop also meant that the public would see more of the ruffles of the petticoat and the bottom of a woman's leg, so special care was lavished on shoes, stockings, petticoat ruffles, and the new underwear of ruffled pantalettes that covered the legs to the ankles.

Still another more momentous invention for women during the period was the sewing machine, which gradually brought the demise of hand-stitched garments and slowly but surely introduced the concept of mass production in clothing. Coupled with this was the speeded-up mechanization in weaving mills and the growing ornamental complexities that could be achieved by the Jacquard loom. Railroads and steamships made distribution of fabrics and trim faster so that the latest fabric pattern and weaves could be disseminated quickly throughout Europe and America. In short, the last half of the nineteenth century saw the slow beginnings of mass production, mass distribution, and the triumph of the great centralized fashion houses—elements that were to dominate and dictate fashion until the present day.

Aside from the introduction of the hoop in the early years of the Second Empire, the other innovative fashion shape that made its appearance was the pagoda sleeve, which flared into a quite wide, open sleeve below the elbow and was worn over a full bloused sleeve of soft fabric that was usually gathered into a wrist band (Fig. 20–3m). This widening of the sleeve was intended to balance the widening of the outerskirts.

When skirts were held out by starched and stiffened petticoats, they were given further bouyancy and width by being composed of several flounces or tiers of ruffles sewn one above another. This effect was retained even when hoops were introduced and gave gowns, especially evening gowns, a fluffy charm. With the introduction of the hoop came a return to many court costume ideals of the Rococo Period such as festoons of gauze, garlands of flowers, layers of draped lace, and many ribbons and bows. In fact, in the famous Winterhalter portrait, *Empress Eugénie and her Ladies in Waiting,* the ladies very strongly resemble the fashion images of the third quarter of the eighteenth century (Fig. 20–7). For a typical outdoor daytime dress designed with a skirt of three tiers, look at the central female figure in Frith's *Derby Day* (Fig. 20–2). One cannot be certain that in either of these paintings the ladies are wearing the new hoops, but since they swept into fashion with a vengeance in 1855, it would seem probable.

FIG. 20–7 Franz Winterhalter, *Empress Eugénie and Her Ladies in Waiting;* Palais, Compiegne; 1855. Illustrates the associational connection with the styles of the eighteenth-century Rococo in the use of lace, ribbons, ruffles, and pastel colors. Note the coiffures that are all parted in the middle and then drawn into curls, braids, or full loops over the ears to the back of the head. Photo courtesy of the French Musées Nationaux.

Other influences in the early 1850s came from the fact that the new empress of France was from Spain and that Italy had captured European attention with its bid for independence in 1849. A jacket was introduced through the influence of Empress Eugénie which was reminiscent of the great seventeenth-century peplums seen in the female portraits by Velásquez, and at the close of the 1850s, the Spanish bolero was also added to the world of fashion. Then, inspired by the Algerian Zouave regiments in the French army that helped in the Italian War of Independence, the Zouave jacket was introduced for women, and shortly thereafter the shirt and cap of the Italian patriot Garibaldi were also adapted directly into female fashion (Fig. 20-3d). The introduction of this blouse marked the beginning of the skirt and blouse combination for women that remains a mainstay of female fashion today (Fig. 20-3b). Corsets were very rigid, completely boned, and formed to give the illusion of a very narrow waist (Fig. 20-3f,n).

Thus by the mid-1850s skirts for women were expanding in width, the shoulders of the bodice were smooth, rounded, and dropped slightly at the armseye, the bodice was fitted smoothly over a carefully boned bustline, sleeves were already expanded into the full pagoda shape, the bonnet was worn further back on the head, and hair was seldom seen in bunches of curls over the ears but was almost invariably waved back into a chignon or soft knot at the back of the head.

By 1857 everything had become larger. The pagoda sleeves became quite wide at the elbows; peplums, if worn, were expansive and deep; and skirts spread even further out over the ever-increasing size of the hoop. This expanded width made it more difficult to work all of the fabric into the waist, and thus the concept of gathers or cartridge pleating had to give way to wide box-pleating, often stacked three or four deep. This method took away some of the curved bell line of the skirt, thus giving a somewhat more funnel-shaped silhouette to the skirt. By the early 1860s even the hoop shape had changed; the top rings of the hoop structure were omitted, taking away the expansive rounded line at the top of the skirt. The hoop finally lost its front curves altogether, and the entire affair was engineered to create a great emphasis on fullness to the back from waist to floor (Fig. 20-3j).

An example of middle-class walking fashions that lack the skirt width and elaboration of the fashion plates of the time may be seen in the Danish artist, Hunoeus' painting *Evening Walk, the Evening Before "Prayer Day,"* 1862 (Fig. 20-8). It shows the layered, muffled look that now dominated daytime outdoor dress and demonstrates the sloped shoulder, the fitted curve over the bust, the bonnet placed back on the head, the pagoda sleeve—even in an outdoor jacket—and the move of skirt fullness toward the back of the body.

Now let us compare this with evening dress a few years later. In the print *Grand Reception of the Notables of the Nation at the White House,* 1865, we can see the low décolletage finished in a wide bertha of lace, ruffles, or gauze; the short, capped sleeves (except for one pagoda sleeve); the strong emphasis now placed on the back of the figure by the shape of the hoop; and the complex draped, curved, or geometric trim that expanded down over the skirt from waist to floor (Fig. 20-4). One can certainly understand from looking at these gowns why critics have referred to these female styles as neomannerist—that is, distorted with violent shifts of proportion in shape and trim (Fig. 20-3k).

By 1868 the front of the skirt had become straight and flat, and an abundance of fabric was massed at the back of the figure and flowed out onto the floor in a train. There was even an occasional return to the late-seventeenth-century style of having an overskirt draped to the back and then up to the waist and to the eighteenth-century polonaise in which an outer dress cut without a waist seam with cords in its side and back seams was loosely draped over an underskirt and hoop—a preview of the early bustle of the 1870s. A ball gown of 1868 may be seen in the lovely statuette of the Comtesse Greffühle in the Musée des Arts Decoratifs, Paris (Fig. 20-9). It has great fullness in the back, an overskirt trained over an underskirt, capped sleeves, a low neckline, and gives us the feeling that the draped-up bustle is about to appear.

**FIG. 20-8** A. M. Hunoeus, *Evening Walk, the Evening Before "Prayer Day";* Statens Museum for Kunst, Copenhagen; 1862. Note the muffled, conservative, repressed look that is presented by the fashions in this grouping. For women this is comprised of lightly flounced skirts, metal cages, and small bonnets; for men there are light or dark trousers, dark coats, and top hats. Photo courtesy of Statens Museum for Kunst.

**FIG. 20-9** Statuette of the Comtesse Greffühle; Musée des Arts Decoratifs; ca. 1866. Illustrates the gradual movement of fullness to the back of the female figure in the ball gowns of the late 1860s. Note the shawl bertha collar, the size of the train in the overskirt, and the changing shape of the hoop. Photo courtesy of Flammarion, Paris.

victorian and second empire　　361

There were many outerwraps in a variety of cuts during this period. First, there were shawls—cashmeres from India, paisleys from Scotland, printed silks from China, and Chantilly laces from France. Some of these were cut and shaped to give fullness over the back, less fullness over the arms, and added length to the pieces that hung down the front (Fig. 20-3o). There were also Talma cloaks of circular cut made of silks, velvets, or woolens and other circular mantles with flaring sleeves. Then there was the *mantelette,* a shawllike outergarment with a deep V-shape at the back and tapering ends in front that was held against the body by an inner belt, and directly after the opening of the Crimean War in 1854 the *burnoose*—a very popular Near Eastern hood. A good example of outerwraps for this period may be seen in the Parisian winter modes illustrated in the German fashion journal *Der Bazar* for December 1, 1857 (Fig. 20-10).

In hairdressing the major style was the hair waved softly back from a central part to a bun or low chignon encased in a net at the back of the head (Fig. 20-3a,e,g). The bonnet, with its brim considerably shortened, was moved back onto the head; however, the Empress Eugénie favored a coquettish hat with a curved, tilted brim set with a plume. The bonnet of the 1860s had a high, spoon brim in front, a sharp, jutting crown, and an extension below the crown in back, often set with bows (Fig. 20-3a,e). With shoes exposed under the new hoops, great attention was placed on footwear with the reappearance of heels, the use of very rich fabrics, and the introduction of high buttoned shoes for daywear (Fig. 20-3i).

Special costumes for bathing at the seashore were introduced at this time. Bathing in spas and at the seashore had been practiced since the eighteenth century, but ordinary clothing was worn, usually cotton skirts, blouses, and caps that looked like underwear. In the late 1850s and early 1860s a bathing costume was created,

**FIG. 20-10** Parisian winter modes from *Der Bazar,* December 1, 1857. Illustrates the typical female silhouette when robed for outdoor winter wear during the height of the crinoline or hoop-skirt period. Note the muffled weight and distorted size created by these outerwraps over hoops. Photo from the collection of the author.

consisting of bloomers, a knee-length dress, a dust cap, and a cloak, the whole usually heavily outlined in bands of a contrasting color (Fig. 20–3p). This was just the beginning of a whole series of special garments to be created later in the century for sports and recreation.

# FABRICS

The fabrics for men of this period were primarily a wide variety of woolen weaves with an occasional touch of silk in the vest. For women, however, there was a great variety of choices—dimity, lawn, chambray, chintz, gingham, piqué, nankeen cotton, and Irish poplin for summer, and cashmere, merino, flannel, foulard, challis, grenadine, broadcloth, taffeta, brocade, velvet, moiré, crepe, grosgrain, and satin for winter. Undoubtedly the most-favored fabric was heavy taffeta over full hoops because of the marvelous sound that it made as it moved across a floor. Other important innovations of this period were the introduction of aniline dyes in rather garish colors, and a marked increase in the use of lace, due to Empress Eugénie's love of its soft beauty.

# ARTS AND ARTIFACTS

The interiors of this period were still richly eclectic in the romantic tradition but in somber colors, heavy ornament, and complex inspiration—the major sources were Gothic, Baroque, and Rococo. There were pieces in black walnut, marble-topped tables, heavily upholstered and carved chairs, horsehair sofas, and heavy table scarfs and piano coverings of fringed tapestry and patterned silk. Windows were covered first with lace curtains and then with heavily swagged and fringed brocade or velour draperies, while the walls were covered with paneling, wallpaper, or patterned cloth coverings (Fig. 20–1a,b,c,d,e). The entire effect was unnatural, oppressive, heavy-handed, and dark—yet in a way comfortable. Motifs ranged from the standard borders from Greece and Rome to the quatrefoils and heraldic devices of the Gothic, from the floral motifs of the Rococo to the scrolls of sixteenth-century mannerism.

The standard accessories for men included quizzing glasses and monocles. Pipes, cigars, and occasional cigarettes were generally smoked after dinner out of the presence of the ladies and over a glass of port. Men often carried light canes with richly worked heads, light-colored gloves for daytime, and white gloves for evening. Boutonnieres for the buttonhole were favored as adding a touch of elegance. Men's jewelry consisted of rings, cuff links, shirt studs (often jeweled), scarf or tie pins, and watches worn in a vest pocket on a chain.

Women still carried parasols with relatively short handles and finished in ruffles or fringe. Umbrellas in black silk were also carried as a purely practical accessory. There were still a variety of aprons all the way from the large ones for cooks to the dainty ones for maids, and there were a variety of house caps worn for doing light housework or dusting. For more formal occasions there were the ever-present folding fan, the long white gloves for evening (with short, neutral-colored ones for daytime), and rich necklaces, earrings, and bracelets to go with ball gowns. There were also a variety of brooches for daytime wear, and the cameo on a chain about the neck was still popular. Watches were pinned on the breast or on a chain at the waist. Purses were relatively small, usually of the drawstring variety, and sometimes heavily jeweled. Large bags, known as *carpetbags,* were really satchels made of tapestry fabric or carpet material, and these were sometimes coupled with the leather hatbox which was an enlarged version of the old male bandbox that had once carried male collars and cuffs. For train travel the lady was often accompanied by several small trunks which were carried by servants or porters.

# VISUAL SOURCES

Artists who are very useful for their portraits and ceremonial or family groupings for this period include Franz Winterhalter, J.A.D. Ingres, William Frith, James Tissot, Carmignani, A.M. Hunoeus, A. de Dreux, V. Becquer, Edouard Manet, and Gavarni, who made many sketches of Parisian city life. Periodicals that are useful include *The London Illustrated News, Magasin des Demoiselles, Monthly Belle Assemblée, Petit Courrier des Dames, Il Mondo Elegante, Godey's Lady's Book, Der Bazar, Gazette of Fashion* and *Le Lion,* Supplement to *l'Elegant.* Institutional sources include the New York Public Library, the Bibliothèque Nationale, the Musée des Arts Decoratifs, Archives Photographiques, Culver Picture Service, and the Metropolitan Museum of Art. Useful books are S. C. Burchell's *Age of Progress,* Christopher Hibbert's *Daily Life in Victorian England,* and J. P. Worth's *A Century of Fashion.*

# SUMMARY

This was a period in which the exuberance and emotional excitement of Romanticism became codified, restricted, repressed, and unnatural, and the mood and manner of sixteenth-century mannerism made itself felt in the clothing, public architecture, interiors, and furnishings that were the style of the Second Empire in France and the early to mid-Victorian Period in England. It was a period of excessive complexity and weight in decoration and ornament and of somber colors in all areas of interior decoration and clothing (except for pale pastels in women's ball dresses and summer frocks and in the occasional light-paneled ballroom). In general, life was tightly structured and organized, clothing was layered and formal, and interiors were dark wombs or elegant personal caves of complexly layered, eclectic borrowings from the past or faraway.

# chapter *XXI*

# *Later Victorian:*

# *The Gilded Age*

THE GILDED AGE
1870–1890

French 1873

| 1871 | The Paris Commune seeks to set up a revolutionary government in Paris; the German Empire is established; the Third Republic is founded in France; Charles Darwin publishes his controversial *Descent of Man;* Dmitri Mendeleev discovers gallium to add to the Periodic Table of Elements; Stanley finds Livingstone in Africa; Émile Zola begins *Les Rougon-Macquart;* Giuseppe Verdi composes *Aida;* Great Fire in Chicago |
| --- | --- |
| 1873 | The Three Emperors' League is established by Austria, Russia, and Germany; Clerk Maxwell's study on electricity and magnetism is published; Herbert Spencer completes his *Study of Sociology;* financial panic in United States |
| 1874 | Boss Tweed is jailed; Wilhelm Wundt publishes *Foundations of Physiological Psychology* |

| 1875 | The Suez Canal comes under the control of the English |
|---|---|
| 1876 | The Centennial Exhibition opens in Philadelphia; Nikolaus Otto develops the four-stroke internal combustion engine; Alfonso XII ascends the throne of Spain; Battle of Little Big Horn; Queen Victoria is made empress of India |
| 1877 | The Russo-Turkish War begins; Rodin exhibits his sculpture for the first time in Paris; Parnell is the new leader of the Irish Party |
| 1878 | Congress of Berlin called to prevent a general European war; Africa is partitioned among the European powers; Pasteur lectures on germ theory at the Academy of Medicine in Paris; the International Congo Association is formed by King Leopold of Belgium, H. M. Stanley, and private financiers |

French 1879

| 1879 | Ibsen writes *A Doll's House;* Edison perfects the electric light; the Dual Alliance is formed between Germany and Austria-Hungary |
|---|---|
| 1880 | Dostoevsky publishes *The Brothers Karamazov* |
| 1881 | Emperor Alexander II is assassinated, and Alexander III ascends the throne in Russia; the French occupy Tunis; the American Federation of Labor is organized; President Garfield is assassinated; the Irish Land Act is passed |
| 1882 | Italy joins Germany and Austria-Hungary to create the Triple Alliance; Robert Koch isolates the bacillus of tuberculosis; the British occupy Egypt; Wagner produces *Parsifal* |

French 1885

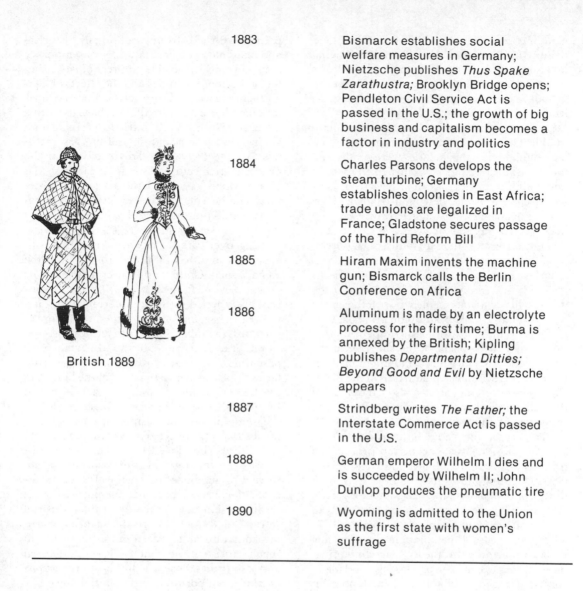

| 1883 | Bismarck establishes social welfare measures in Germany; Nietzsche publishes *Thus Spake Zarathustra;* Brooklyn Bridge opens; Pendleton Civil Service Act is passed in the U.S.; the growth of big business and capitalism becomes a factor in industry and politics |
| 1884 | Charles Parsons develops the steam turbine; Germany establishes colonies in East Africa; trade unions are legalized in France; Gladstone secures passage of the Third Reform Bill |
| 1885 | Hiram Maxim invents the machine gun; Bismarck calls the Berlin Conference on Africa |
| 1886 | Aluminum is made by an electrolyte process for the first time; Burma is annexed by the British; Kipling publishes *Departmental Ditties; Beyond Good and Evil* by Nietzsche appears |
| 1887 | Strindberg writes *The Father;* the Interstate Commerce Act is passed in the U.S. |
| 1888 | German emperor Wilhelm I dies and is succeeded by Wilhelm II; John Dunlop produces the pneumatic tire |
| 1890 | Wyoming is admitted to the Union as the first state with women's suffrage |

British 1889

# BACKGROUND

With the end of the Second Empire in France and the establishment of the Third Republic, the last regime, with some pretense at romantic flair and excitement in its fashionable court ceremonials and public image abroad, disappeared, and Europe settled down to the rather drab but very necessary routine of bureaucratic protocol in government, supported by the ever-increasing tempo of industrial capitalism. By 1870 the shift from an agrarian to an urban industrial economy was nearly complete in the leading nations of the Western World, and the grinding poverty, crowding, insecurity, and dehumanization caused by urban ghetto living had begun to have its effect on the lower levels of society. Social unrest grew, and certain groups in politics began to line up behind those leaders who wanted better conditions for labor. During this period the first tentative attempts to establish labor unions as a means of regulating pay and hours in the factories were made, and many disillusioned idealists turned to socialist and communist ideals as an answer to the suffering caused by the new industrialism. Karl Marx's doctrines were adopted by workers who believed that his goal of a classless society was the only answer for modern industrial laborers.

Another influential writer of this period was Charles Darwin, who published *Origin of Species* in 1859 and *Descent of Man* in 1871. To the devout, his doctrines seemed to spell the end of religious faith; to capitalist industrialists, they seemed to condone a ruthless competition that underlined the concept of the survival of the fittest; and to Christian fundamentalists, it seemed a direct attack on the truths of the Bible. But the concept of evolution also led to a belief that all forward movement in society led to progress and improvement.

As part of the rapid industrialization of Europe and America, this period produced a remarkable number of inventions: domestic electric lighting, introduced by Edison in 1879; the telephone, perfected by Alexander Graham Bell in 1876; the horseless carriage, tested in 1885; and the phonograph, developed in 1877. There were also breakthroughs in medicine with Pasteur on germ theory, Metchnikoff on blood theory, Wundt on psychology, and many contributions in anesthetics and antiseptics. In every direction the application of the new scientific thinking to industrial progress led to discoveries and rapid changes in living in industrial society.

These new scientific principles were also applied to the arts and led to the perfection of an earlier invention, the box camera, that now proceeded to revolutionize the way in which people came to see and record life. Thus in art and literature the new concepts of realism and naturalism were deepened, and writers and painters turned from traditional historical and imaginary subject matter to contemporary scenes of daily living. The impressionists, using the new science of optics and the effects of light on the textures of nature, probed even deeper into the physical nature of visual reality, while novelists like Émile Zola tried to establish an alliance between scientific and literary methods. Architecture was still divided between the practical architecture of modular cast iron and glass—which was considered a branch of structural engineering and reserved for train stations, exhibition halls, and warehouses—and the Beaux Arts architecture that consisted of frosting over rather ordinary structures with ornament and decoration borrowed from the Renaissance, Gothic, and Baroque Periods or other times and faraway places. This latter concept also carried over into interior decorating where there seemed to be a desperate attempt to surround the inhabitants with a thick, layered womb of comfort, memory, and nostalgia for past times, accented with exotic motifs from faraway places. An 1876 photo of the library in the Leland Stanford family residence in San Franciso shows the oppressive, layered effect of the room in which not a single space is left free of decoration, collected memorabilia, or architectural trim (Fig. 21–1). The room epitomizes the romantic idea of associationalism carried to an almost pathological level—a cocoon of collected personal memories that is meant to shut out the reality of the industrial world. Such a room asserts the historical learning and cultural appreciation of the owner in such an insistent way that it demands attention and asserts that those who live here are persons of education, position, and material power.

In England during this period the widowed queen Victoria was quite overshadowed by the dashing prince of Wales and his charming wife, Alexandra, who held court in the salons of London while the prince also carried on a series of discreet affairs with some of the most beautiful and talented ladies of England and the continent. Politically it was a period when the two parliamentary giants of the Tories and the Liberals, Disraeli and Gladstone, still dueled for control of the government; when questions

London
institutional
gateway
1886

(a)

armchair
Schloss
Grafenegg
Austria
1887

(b)

Library of the Leland Stanford family residence in San Francisco; 1876. Illustrates the oppressive, layered, cluttered interiors of the late nineteenth century with great emphasis placed on collected artifacts, memorabilia, and borrowed historical details. Photo courtesy of the Stanford Archives, Stanford University.

(c)
interior wall  London 1882

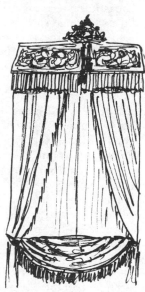

(d)
window France 1880

**FIGURE 21–1**

arose about home rule for Ireland; when the queen was formally made empress of India.

In France this was a period of the final acceptance of parliamentary democracy inside the confines of the Third Republic. It was also a period that ushered in *La Belle Epoque,* an age of sophistication, elegance, and high living that kept Paris the center of art and fashion until the outbreak of World War I.

In Germany this was a period of great national expansion after the unification of the nation into an empire in 1871 under Wilhelm I of Prussia and his Iron Chancellor Bismarck. Bismarck ran the country almost single-handedly, building up the army and the navy, developing the German educational system, supporting the growth of industry, expanding universities, and encouraging patriotic nationalism. At the same time that Germany was increasing in power, its sister state of Austria-Hungary was desperately trying to control its various subject nationalities while living out a strained scenario of pleasure, self-indulgence,

and high culture in its capital city of Vienna where Johann Strauss was the Waltz King.

In Russia this was the period of the great writers, Tolstoy and Dostoevsky, and belated romantic composers like Tchaikowsky, while in Scandinavia the playwright Ibsen altered the course of European drama with the plays that followed his famous *A Doll's House* in 1879.

After the Civil War in the United States and the opening of a cross-country railroad, the drive to expand production and industry and to finish the settlement of the continent became almost an obsession. The United States, with its great natural resources, began its rapid climb toward becoming the greatest industrial nation in the world. While its wealthy went abroad for culture and were thought to be vulgarians by Europeans, its masses at home, with the help of heavy immigration from abroad, completed the removal of the frontier by 1890. This new-rich era came to be known as the *Gilded Age.*

## THE BASIC COSTUME SILHOUETTE

The cultural base for fashion during this period did not change significantly from what it had been during the previous two decades. The male costume was still the basically somber and rather inhibiting uniform of industrial capitalism, while female dress with its distended bustle at the back of the body and heavy boning in the bodice still created a neomannerist effect that was unnatural, if not grotesque. Even the trim on women's gowns was excessive and often disproportionate to the human figure, while the fit of female clothing rigidly distorted the natural lines of the female body.

For men there was little excitement and visual interest in the fashions of the time, which were generally similar to those of the Second Empire, except that the techniques of tailoring continued to improve. The actual changes for men included closer-cropped hair and more carefully trimmed beards, somewhat less variety in the shape and cut of coats and hats, and a greater emphasis on knickerbocker knee pants for sporting and outdoor wear. Since tailoring

rather than rich fabric and colorful accessories made the gentleman stand out in society and since the best men's tailors in the world were in London, this city became the center of the male fashion world and the dictator in men's styles, just as Paris remained the center for female fashion.

Thus masculine dress became, for the most part, rigidly conservative. Formal dress for morning and afternoon became as exact as that for evening. For morning the formal uniform was a stiff-bosomed shirt, wing collar, a carefully folded scarf cravat, a light grey vest, a sloped tail coat, grey striped trousers, pearl grey gloves and spats, and a top hat (a uniform still worn at formal weddings). The formal afternoon wear remained the frock coat, a plain or figured grey vest, medium-light to dark trousers, winged collar and stiff shirt, a formal scarf tie, top hat, and grey spats. During this period the *tuxedo* was introduced for early evening which consisted of a satin-lapelled, black jacket of fingertip length, black trousers and

(a)
double-breasted
waistcoat and
oxford tie
1870s

(b)
Dundreary
whiskers
and
monocle
early
1870s

(c)
sleeveless
Inverness rain
cape or coat 1880s

(d)
separate
collar and silk
cravat 1870s

(e)
starched separate
collar 1885

(f)
bowler
hat 1879

(g)
fore and
aft cap
for travel
and sports
1880s

(h)
dinner
jacket
or
tuxedo
(informal
evening)
1880s

(i)
U.S. cadet
uniform 1880

(j)
James Tissot, *Festivities Aboard Ship;* Tate
Gallery; 1874. Illustrates the shift in distortion for the female figure in the transition
from hoops to bustles. Note the soft,
looped-up fullness at the back of the figure
that marked the first bustle period of the
1870s. Photo courtesy of the Tate Gallery.

(k)
frock coat
for formal daywear
1880s

(l)
evening
formal
dress
—tails
1880

(m)
flat
derby
1870's,
1880s

morning
coat
(formal
daywear)
1880s

(n)
summer
straw
boater
1882

**FIGURE 21-2**

back-lacing
corset
1878
(a)

corset
1880s
(c)

1872
(e)

1878
(g)
1884

(i)
1888

bustle 1870
(j)

laced shoe
1875
(b)

satin evening slipper
1875
(d)

evening slipper
1885
(f)

house slipper
1888
(h)

velvet
handbag
1880s
(k)

(l)
hoop bustle
1873

(n)
ebony
fan
with
feather
1880s

front

back
(o)
fur dolman
1883

(m)
wire mesh
bustles 1880s

Jean Béraud, *Evening Party Given by the Caillebottes:* Collection of Comte Balny d'Avricourt; 1878. A grand gathering including generals, professors, ambassadors, and aristocrats in the salon of a man who had supplied equipment to the armies of Napoleon III. Here female fashion has become more distorted through corseting and the tight, "fish-tail" draping and pleating from the knees down. Photo courtesy of Comte Balny d'Avricourt.

hunting
costume
1880s

yachting
costume 1880s

riding
habit
1880s

(s)
bathing costume
1880s

(p)

(q)

**FIGURE 21-3**

(r)

vest, a stiff shirt with winged collar, and a black tie. Formal evening wear and the business suit remained without much change, and for sports there were a variety of Norfolk jackets, knee-length knickerbockers, straw hats, fore and aft caps, and leggings. Overgarments remained the Inverness caped coat and the Chesterfield overcoat.

In feminine fashion the number and complexity of the fabric pieces comprising a gown greatly increased, and the dressmaker's art, like that of the tailor, became extremely complex. Skirts were now draped up over a bustle, and the complex draping was similar to the draping of windows in interior decoration. Folds were draped across pleats, pleats used over draping, fringe was used over brocade, velvet was placed on top of satin, and all manner of trim was placed over all these layered effects. The first bustle was worn low and was usually a horsehair pad, a boned petticoat, or a small metal-webbed cage worn under the petticoat at the back of the hips. The upper part of the figure was firmly encased in a corset that pushed up the bust and squeezed in the abdomen and waist, while necks were high and sleeves full length except for evening. An excellent illustration of daytime dresses for an outing may be seen in James Tissot's *Festivities Aboard Ship* (Fig. 21–2).

By the late 1870s the bustle began to disappear as the outerskirt was draped more tightly about the lower part of the body with ruffles frequently spreading from under it around the ankles and feet. In this so-called *fish-tailed* style, which reached its peak about 1880, the hips, waist, and bust emerged with a special emphasis due to the careful corseting and the support of some judicious padding. Evening gowns from this moment in fashion may be seen in Jean Béraud's *Evening Party Given by the Caillebottes* (Fig. 21–3). In the early 1880s the bustle returned again but now worn higher at the back of the waist, making the female figure look as if it had four legs like a centaur. A skirt with a bustle was now worn with tailored jackets, skating outfits, and traveling topcoats—all cut to accommodate the exaggerated protrusion at the back of the figure. Hair was piled high toward the back of the head with tight curls coming down the back, and the small hats set with flowers, feathers, ribbons, or little birds perched atop the hairdo and were held in place by a hatpin. Daytime shoes were usually ankle-high, buttoned affairs, while evening shoes were usually the heeled slipper. An excellent view of the everyday female fashions at the end of the 1880s may be seen in Béraud's *Gloppe's Patisserie* (Fig. 21–4). Note the somber, layered look of the inhabitants of the pastry shop and the preponderance of very dark tones in the costumes. A few romantic ideals are still at work in fashion, but they are interpreted in a distorted, heavy, tight, repressed manner.

# LATE VICTORIAN: THE COSTUME OF THE GILDED AGE

**Masculine Dress** These two decades in the history of male clothing brought few innovations but witnessed a marked increase in the factory production of suits of clothes as well as a further refinement among the wealthy in the subtle techniques of tailoring. On the other hand, many authorities have noted that it was also an age of very poor taste in both male and female dress—an age in which more stress was placed on industrial expansion and big business than on fashion.

The daytime coats of this period were either the short sack-suit jacket, the cut-back morning coat, or the square-skirted frock coat (Fig. 21–2j,k). The latter was often double-breasted, and the cutaway was often only slightly longer than the sack-suit coat. The seam line at the waist where the skirt was added to the body of the coat was lower than in the past, lapels in general were larger, and velvet collars were frequently added. The jacket for the sack suit was usually single-breasted and frequently cut away slightly in front so that only the top button was fastened, thus revealing the vest with its prominently displayed pocket watch and chain. A good example of an unbuttoned, long-skirted sack coat may be seen in the drawing *Couple in a Garden* (Fig. 21–5). Double-

**FIG. 21–4** Jean Béraud, *Gloppe's Patisserie:* Musée Carnavalet; 1889. Illustrates the dark, conservative clothing that was still dominant at the end of the nineteenth century. Note the stiffness and formality of the late bustle of the 1880s and the new tailored jacket, shirt, and tie on the woman at the center of the painting. Photo courtesy of Bulloz, Paris.

breasted, boxy sack coats were usually used for seaside costume and were cut looser than the business suit jacket, as may be seen in Tissot's painting *Festivities Aboard Ship* (Fig. 21–2).

The tail coat in black with faultless tailoring remained standard for formal evening wear (Fig. 21-2l). It had very wide lapels partially lined in a constrasting fabric that was usually heavy silk, and the lapels folded back almost to the waist. Good examples of the fit and look of the evening wear for this period may be found in Béraud's painting *Evening Party Given by the Caillebottes* (Fig. 21–3).

Waistcoats were either single- or double-breasted, although single-breasted ones were the most popular (Fig. 21-2a). Some were worn with an underlay or lighter fabric at the top so that one had the illusion that one waistcoat was worn over another, and this was what often

showed above the coat lapels of the business suit when the top button was fastened. Some formal evening habits used black instead of white vests during this period, but the most formal occasions required a white vest, which eventually predominated (except for the black ties and waistcoats worn by servants during formal evening functions) (Fig. 21-2l).

In the 1880s the fashion of fastening only the top button of the business suit gradually waned, and by the end of the decade the suit jacket was usually buttoned from top button to waist. The formal tailed coat on the other hand, was designed with a higher closing that necessitated three decorative buttons on either side instead of the one or two that had been used in the 1870s. The only new coat introduced in this decade was the tuxedo dinner jacket with its silk lapels and slightly longer length than the

FIG. 21-5 *Couple in a Garden,* engraving from 1871. Illustrates fashionable male and female promenade styles of the 1870s. Note the female coiffure with curls raised up to the back of the head and then cascading to the neck, the small flat bonnet, the heavy curve of the corset line, and the looping up of the ruffled overskirt. Note the simple turndown collar and bow tie on the man. Photo courtesy of the Bibliothèque Nationale, Paris.

FIG. 21-6 James Tissot, *Too Early;* London Guildhall Gallery; 1873. Illustrates the fluffy lightness yet fullness of the bustle ball gowns of the 1870s, which were almost exclusively in white or pastels. Photo courtesy of the London Guildhall Library.

daytime suit coat (Fig. 21-2h). It was always worn with a black vest and trousers and usually used a black tie rather than the white bow tie of formal evening costume. It would seem that the gentleman in the center of Tissot's painting *Too Early* is wearing this jacket (Fig. 21-6). In general, waistcoats were single-breasted and seldom showed since the buttoned coat usually covered them.

Trousers showed little change during this 20-year period, although the loud plaids and checks of the previous period were generally much tighter and more subdued. One innovation in shirts and neckwear was the acceptance of figured fabrics for daytime since they soiled less obviously than white. Another was the introduction of the winged collar—a standing collar with the front corners turned back which remained popular for a long time and is still used with formal evening and formal morning attire. The turnover collar that had been favored in the 1850s and 1860s almost disappeared except for sporting wear, only to return in a major way at the opening of the twentieth century (Fig. 21-2d,e). Thus the return to variations of the standing collar brought a new formality to the male clothing of this period.

In cravats the bow tie all but disappeared except for evening and was replaced by the four-in-hand tie with the business suit and the folded scarf cravats for more formal daytime wear (Fig. 21-2a,d,e,f,l,m,n).

Hair was now cut closer to the head, beards were trim and less full, and many men wore only a mustache. Very few, except the very young, however, were clean shaven (Fig. 21-2a,b,f,g,m,n). The top hat and the bowler shared honors as major hat shapes for city wear, although the straw boater was sometimes seen in the summer and was very popular at the seashore (Fig. 21-2f,g,h,j,m,n).

Overcoats now completely dominated the fashion in outdoor traveling or winter wear, and the mantle was worn only by the most ostentatious bohemians. The Chesterfield was the standard overcoat, sometimes trimmed or even lined in fur, while the lighter topcoat, often with a velvet collar, was standard when less warmth was wanted. Shoes followed a conservative line with a polished look, square toes,

and the new rubber heels. They were usually anklelength for daytime and were either laced, buttoned, or inset in the sides with elastic. Low pumps were worn with black silk hose for evening.

A good example of the sporting clothes of the period may be seen in Edith Halyer's *The First of October* (Fig. 21-7). Here the gentlemen still wear the formal wing collars of the time but with bow rather than four-in-hand ties. Jackets are relatively short and are worn with knickerbockers and stockings or knickerbockers and leggings. Two of the caps are the *deerstalker,* or *fore and aft* style, that we associate with Sherlock Holmes and the knitted *tam-o'-shanter* from Scotland. The usual overcoat for sportsmen, also frequently seen in the city since it was rainproof, was the Inverness cape, an overcoat usually in a plaid design and often in a rubberized wool that had a shoulder cape sewn along seams that fell from the back armseye (Fig. 21-2c). Some had a complete cape set on at the collar that reached to the wrist all around the coat.

The military dress tunic of the period was cut like a short or long double-breasted frock coat with a very fitted line and a high, standing military collar. Trousers were usually lighter in tone than the tunic and had a stripe down the outside seam. Cavalry officers wore form-fitting riding pants that disppeared inside of riding boots or the stiff formal boots that rose well above the knee in front but were cut lower behind. Hats varied, but in general were tall or low-crowned shakos with ornamental visors. There were also plumed helmets, and in the United States wide-brimmed Stetsons folded up on one side were worn (Fig. 21-2i).

**Feminine Dress**  For a time the Parisian fashion industry was all but paralyzed by the aftereffects of the Franco-Prussian War and the succeeding Commune, but by 1873, it had once again become the center of focus for fashionable women of the Western world. The styles that now came from Paris may have been some of the most grotesque ever invented for women; yet despite the distortions of the bustle, the House of Worth was able to create some magnificent specimens of the dressmakers' art.

**FIG. 21-7**  Edith Halyer, *The First of October;* Christié's, London; 1888. Illustrates specialized hunting garb for men in the late nineteenth century. Note the *deerstalker* caps (left and right) with the Scottish *tam-o'-shanter,* (center) as well as the leggings used to cover the woolen stockings to the knee. Photo courtesy of Christié's.

At no time during this entire period were women able to move with gracefulness or freedom for they were always heavily boned and corseted. They were either overbalanced by the weight and draping of the bustle, or they were so tightly restricted by narrow skirts that they could hardly move (Fig. 21–3a,c,j,l).

The female silhouette of the 1870s actually went through three phases. First there was the bulky piling up of the full skirts over a padded or boned protrusion at the back of the hips. This was followed by a brief few years when the bodice was extended downward to the hips with the looped-up skirt fabric falling from this lowered line. Finally the lines of the bodice were carried as low as the knees, creating a tubular princess line all the way to the floor, and skirts were so tight that ladies moved with the greatest of difficulty.

Throughout this decade the bodice was tightly fitted over the corset, and for daytime the neckline was either a modest V or a standing band from which the bodice buttoned from throat to waist. The shoulder line was shortened from what it had been in the 1860s, and the armseye moved to its normal position. The *basque,* or peplum extension, below the waist at first was pointed, then extended to hip length. For evening the bodice was very low cut. At first the line of the décolletage was the broad, curving line of the 1860s, but as the whole figure narrowed somewhat after the removal of the hoops, the evening neckline came to have a deep V-line in both front and back. If it was too plunging, it was filled with lace or ruffles. A good example of this neckline may be seen on the evening dresses displayed in Tissot's *Too Early* (Fig. 21–6). Bodice sleeves for daytime were straight and smooth, finished in ruffles at the wrist, and trimmed with braid and passementerie like the rest of the dress. Typical sleeves for 1873 may be seen on the lady in *Cou-*

*ple in a Garden* (Fig. 21–5). In the evening sleeves were usually shorter, either a cap sleeve or one that ended above the elbow.

But it was the skirt that was the showpiece of any dress with its complex interplay of draping, textures, patterns, and trim. Like the interior decoration and furnishing of the time, the skirts displayed a penchant for rich layering, complex draping and pleating, and minute detail. As with furnishings and interiors, swags of material edged in fringe abounded. Although some of the skirts were swamped with this excess, others were truly dignified and noble demonstrations of the complexity of the dressmakers' art.

Let us look at the central gown in Tissot's *Festivities Aboard Ship* (Fig. 21–2). The outerskirt is draped up somewhat like the eighteenth-century polonaise, with ribbons at the sides giving curved, draped lines at the front and layers of piled-up fabric at the rear caught up over the bustle by ribbons. Under this draped and piled-up overskirt is a full underskirt of the same fabric with vertical insets of ribbon to tie in with those on the outerskirt. Another variation may be seen in *Couple in a Garden* (Fig. 21–5). Once again there is an outerskirt edged in braid and ruffles that is pulled softly to the back and draped loosely over a bustle. Under it is an underskirt that is trimmed in a row of ruffles at the knees with a flaring, gathered bottom set on under the ruffle that spreads out to the floor. This gives three lines of accent: the hips accented by the bottom of the bodice, the edge of the outerskirt ending above the knee, and the ruffle set on at the knee line. In the foreground gown in Tissot's *Too Early* (Fig. 21–6), we have the elaborate skirt line for an evening gown of the early to mid-1870s. Here a polonaiselike overgown is pulled high at the sides and trimmed with ruffles and ruching, while the back cascades down into a train on the floor with a sweep of fullness. It is very probable that the back may even be an extra inset of fabric. Under this there is once again an underskirt that ends in slanted ruching at the knee with cascades of ruffles spreading from under it to the floor. Thus with many complex variations the standard line was a draped-up overskirt that created the necessary fullness at the back over a bustle, with a full underskirt trimmed in ruffles beneath.

By the late 1870s the basque of the bodice extended smoothly down over the hips, and the fullness in the skirt disappeared in favor of a much slimmer, sleeker line, with the draped fullness placed below the hip line at the back and the skirt fitted with a certain tightness to below the knees (Fig. 21–8). Daytime dresses often followed a slim princess line so that the lines given the body by the corset were followed without interruption to just above the knees. Then the skirt might be tightly draped toward the back and a pleated bottom to an underskirt allowed to spread out from the knees to the floor. This was the so-called fish-tail look, and it gave a very inhibited, tight line to the knees or below before giving way to pleated fullness. A version of this line in an evening gown may be seen in Béraud's *Evening Party Given by the Caillebottes* (Fig. 21–3). Here the gowns are all cut with an hourglass princess line over the tightly-laced corset, with a series of tightly draped skirt lines from thigh to floor in front and a draped train at the back that expands from the thigh area to the floor.

Although shawls and fitted wraps continued from the 1850–1860 period, the fitted *dolman* of the 1870s had its pseudosleeve cut so that the wearer could move the arm only very slightly from the body (Fig. 21–3o). Dolmans used fabrics ranging from the bougeois woolen and plain silk to brocaded, embroidered, or fringed silks. Often the evening dolman was short and stopped at the waist so as not to interfere with the richness of the draped skirt. Fuller mantles were also worn, and in the late 1870s fitted coats became popular with the middle class.

Coiffures were large and full, piled up toward the back of the head and then hanging in curls, a loose braid, or a confined chignon at the back of the neck to the top of the shoulders (Fig. 21–3e). Toward the end of the decade, hats were small-brimmed with higher crowns. They were trimmed in lace, ribbons, flowers, and feathers, sometimes tied under the chin but most frequently held with hatpins with ribbons cascading down the back.

High-buttoned shoes were still popular, although heeled slippers were sometimes worn

FIG. 21-8  C. Cap, *Souvenir of the National Holiday;* Koninklijk Museum, Antwerp; 1880.
Illustrates the slim outline with minimal bustle and draping activity centered around the
knees that was the female fashion about 1880. Note the tightly wrapped skirts with fullness at
the bottom of the gown; also note the fitted line over the corset to the hips. Photo courtesy of
the Koninklijk Museum, Antwerp, Belgium.

for daytime as well as evening wear (Fig.
21-3b,d). Almost all shoes had a fairly high
French heel, and some daytime shoes buttoned
or laced to well above the ankle. For outdoor
and sporting costumes, oxfords came in, sometimes in two tones of leather. Evening slippers
in satin or soft kid were often elaborately and
richly ornamented.

In the early 1880s the feminine silhouette
began to make another change, although still
using the concept of the bustle. The fullness
once again moved upward at the back of the
figure and the bustle extension returned, this
time directly below the waist at the rear of the
figure. There were boned and laced sections
worked into petticoats, massed ruffles of stiff
fabric at the back of a petticoat all the way to
the floor, and small wire mesh cages shaped to
fit the curve of the back just below the waist
(Fig. 21-3m).

Bodices and skirts for both afternoon and
evening often retained the princess line but
with a great deal more spread to the gores below
the waist, particularly at the back of the figure.
The added skirt fullness was then draped much
more tightly than before over the protruding
line of the bustle. Also in the 1880s women
began to enter the white-collar work force in
limited numbers, so much greater attention
was paid to tailoring skirts over the bustle extension rather than merely piling up fabric.
The women of the eighties even more than
those of the seventies looked like centaurs with
two sets of legs in the front and two behind.
With this new bustle line the *basque,* or fitted
peplum, of the bodice shortened once again,
by the end of the decade there was almost
no extension below the waistline, although all
bodices dipped down in front and evening
bodices were often sharply pointed.

An example of how careful tailoring began to make its appearance in female as well as male dress may be seen by looking at a traveling costume for 1885 that appears in Tissot's painting *Embarcation at Calais* (Fig. 21–9). The coat or jacket is carefully tailored to the lines of the corset beneath, with great fullness over the hips and the bustle at the back. The waistcoat or vest follows the same tailored lines and is exactly fitted to the corset with a low basque that comes well down onto the hips. The overskirt is tightly draped up and cut to fit smoothly over the bustle, while the underskirt of pleated plaid material is floor length. Note the traveling gloves, the small hat with a veil, the fur at the neck, and the pointed laced boots.

Somewhat similar winter costumes with tailored lines may be seen in Béraud's *Gloppe's Patisserie* (Fig. 21–4). Note the fitted jacket, vest, and shirtwaist—all in imitation of the male business suit—on the lady in the center facing left. Also note how all the coats and jackets are tailored to fit over the extended lines of the bustles.

Some interesting variations in the cut of overskirts and visiting coats may be seen in a pair of fashion figures for 1888 (Fig. 21–10). Note how in each case the bodice extends below the waist on each side of the front in richly embroidered panels that frame the underskirt in front and particularly in back where the skirt over its bustle protrudes out from the sides of the rich panels. Many skirts during this period were draped asymmetrically so that emphasis was on the side and back instead of front and back.

During the 1880s the hair was brought in soft waves to the top of the head with frizzed bangs or gently twisted curls on the forehead. Flowers, combs, and ribbons were still used for evening, and hat brims gradually increased in size. Crowns were usually high enough to accommodate the fullness of the coiffure on top of the head and were sometimes tilted rather rakishly. They were trimmed in birds, plumes, and ribbon bows (Fig. 21–3g,i).

Shoes changed very little, although there was somewhat more variety of line and in the

FIG. 21–9 James Tissot, *Embarcation at Calais;* Koninklijk Museum, Antwerp; 1885. Illustrates the tighter bustle line of the second bustle period of the 1880s. Note the fullness of the hips, the fitted corset line, the small bonnet set back on the head, and the high-laced shoes. Photo courtesy of the Koninklijk Museum, Antwerp.

FIG. 21-10 Fashion designs for a housedress and a visiting dress for 1888. Illustrates the tighter hairdressing up and to the back of the head, the high position of the bustle, the increasing brim of hats, and the manner in which coats are cut to fit smoothly over the line of the bustle. Note that arms and neck are covered for daytime wear. From a photo in the collection of the author.

height of the heels (Fig. 21-3f,h). The dolman was still the leading wrap of the period. For dressy occasions they were usually of silk, trimmed in jet, braid fringe, and embroidery, while for daytime they were usually of a simple woolen fabric. Special sporting costumes were also developed for women during this period as they began to participate more in hunting, yachting, riding, and bathing (Fig. 21-3p,q, r,s).

## FABRICS

Fabrics for men differed little from the woolens used today for suits and overcoats. There was much black broadcloth, serge, twill, homespun, and tweeds in checks, plaids, and stripes as well as plain textures. Covert was a very light-colored cloth made into topcoats, while piqué and Marseilles were used for white, washable waistcoats. Some low-keyed silk and brocaded waistcoats were still seen, but these were usually for formal afternoon or evening wear.

Woolens were more popular than ever with women, especially toward the end of the period when tailored suits were worn. A silk warped cashmere was highly regarded as was grenadine, which was a semitransparent, loosely woven silk and wool mixture. There were also serge, merino, wool poplin, and bombazine—a wiry textured silk and wool mix that was often used in black for mourning.

In the silks there was Irish poplin for summer, stiff silk-and-cotton-backed satin, all manner of silk taffetas, various corded silks, watered moiré, crepe de Chine, velvet, silk gauze, and tulle. There was also lavish use of lace, muslin, and piqué cotton for summer and furs of various kinds in winter.

# ARTS AND ARTIFACTS

From a twentieth-century point of view, bad taste in interior decorations and furnishings reached their peak during this period. The swagging of draperies with the addition of fringe, tassels, and cording was an interior decorative touch that reminds one specifically of the same techniques in the handling of women's skirts. This was an age in which every area of a room was layered with carpets, wall coverings, ''throws,'' pictures, and a proliferation of ornamental bric-a-brac—an age in which the inhabitants of a room were literally lost amid a sea of layered decorative detail (Fig. 21-1a,b,c,d). Good examples are the interior of the Leland Stanford Library and the interior in *Souvenir of the National Holiday* (Figs. 21-1,8).

Personal artifacts and accessories for men included watches, canes, and gloves. Gloves were of heavy, stitched leather for riding, soft tan, grey, or black kid for street wear, and white kid for evening wear. Canes were very much in evidence during the period with heavy, carved knob tops, crook handles, and small sticks with polished and engraved silver or gold knobs. Some men wore monocles or the popular pince-nez glasses. Tobacco was smoked in cigarettes, cigars, and pipes and chewed in a plug by those who did not mind being considered vulgar. Handkerchiefs were often carefully displayed in a coat breast pocket and were of cotton, linen, or silk.

Female artifacts and accessories included gloves, muffs, handbags, parasols, umbrellas, fans, and quizzing glasses or lorgnettes (Fig. 21-3k,n). White gloves for evening now often reached well above the elbow and were a very prominent accessory to the gown; street gloves of soft leather and cloth were usually dark in color and could be as short as wrist length or as long as three quarters up the forearm. Most gloves fit very snugly and were buttoned to fit smoothly at the wrist. Muffs were still in evidence, although they were smaller than in the past and were usually worn on chains or ribbons from the waist or neck.

Aprons were used only by housewives and domestics, not by women of fashion. Handbags which had once been considered very unfashionable were carried by almost all ladies out for an afternoon promenade or visit. Often their drawstring reticules were designed to match the dress, but they were not indispensable as they are today since most skirts or petticoats still had hidden inside pockets. Heavy carpet bags and even leather satchels were used for shopping and as overnight bags.

For outdoor promenades the umbrella or parasol was a standard accessory. In the early years of the period, parasols were small, decorated in lace and ribbon, and set with slim, ivory handles. Later the parasols became somewhat larger and not quite as frivolous; it was sometimes impossible to tell the umbrella from the parasol (although the former was usually without ribbons and lace). In the mid-1880s the Japanese parasol made its appearance.

Fans were at first seen only with evening dress, but in the 1880s with the craze for things Japanese, all manner of painted silk and paper fans in the Japanese manner made their appearance.

Men's accessories were limited to scarf pins, shirt studs, cuff links, watches and watch chains, and finger rings. Women's jewelry was dominated by earrings and the evening necklace, but by the late 1880s many younger women gave up using earrings altogether. With the high-necked day dresses, neck chains with a small watch appended were popular as were cameos and lockets on chains. Brooches, large and small and in a great variety of forms, were used at the throat or on the jacket or bodice; jeweled combs were used in the hair; bracelets were frequently worn; and the gold wedding ring was the most important finger ring. Special mourning jewelry was standard for all women for an extended time after a death in the family.

# VISUAL SOURCES

Visual sources for this period are similar to those for the Second Empire. Very helpful artists are Jean Béraud, James Tissot, Giovanni Boldini, Edgar Degas, Edouard Manet, James Lavery, Thomas Eakins, Auguste Renoir, Theodor Alt, Henri Fantin-Latour, John Singer Sargent, Leon Bonnat, and Henri Gervex. The best fashion journals are *Le Moniteur de la Mode, La Mode Artistique, The Gazette of Fashion, Godey's Lady's Book,* and *The World of Fashion.* The best institutional sources are the Metropolitan Museum of Art, the New York Public Library, the Bibliothèque Nationale, the Musée Carnavalet, the Louvre, the Corcoran Gallery of Art, the Archives Photographiques in Paris, and the Photo Collection Sirot. Useful books are H. C. Brown's *New York in the Elegant Eighties,* S. C. Burchell's *The Age of Progress,* Christopher Hibbert's *Daily Life in Victorian England,* and *This Fabulous Century: Prelude, 1870–1900.*

# SUMMARY

This was the period in which neomannerist tension, repression, and bad taste reached a peak in furnishings and female fashion—a period in which expanding capitalism, industrialism, and imperialism placed layered richness above artistry, beauty, and simplicity. It truly was a "gilded age" in which fortunes in Europe and America were made overnight, and the wealthy heiresses of the new world began that search in the old for titled husbands with great estates. It was an age in which the rules of upper-class living and the caste levels in bougeois society became tightly solidified and codified. It was an age of expensive, artificial, upper-class living in which taste was subordinated to a heavy and ostentatious display of position and wealth. For women it was one of the most unnatural and inhibited periods of fashion; for men it was one of the most dull and codified moments in the history of dress.

# chapter XXII

# Late Victorian and Edwardian:

# Art Nouveau

*Chronology*

(1890–1911)

LATE VICTORIAN
1890–1901

1892

| | | |
|---|---|---|
| 1890 | | Bismarck is dismissed in Germany, giving Wilhelm II complete authority; all-steel bridge is completed over the Firth of Forth; Felix Méline, French cabinet minister, puts through a customs tariff in France |
| 1892 | | Élie Metchnikoff discovers the relative values of red and white corpuscles |
| 1893 | | Financial panic in the United States; Gladstone introduces the second Home Rule Bill for Ireland; an independent labor party is established in England; Tschaikowsky composes his *Symphonie Pathétique;* Chicago World's Fair |
| 1894 | | The Dreyfus Affair begins in France; Gordon massacred at Khartoum |
| 1895 | | Jameson raid into the Transvaal leads toward the Boer War; Wilhelm Conrad Röntgen discovers X-rays |

1894

1899

| | |
|---|---|
| 1896 | Lenin publishes *Development of Capitalism* in Russia; Kitchener leads the Sudan Expedition to avenge General Gordon; the Italians are defeated in Ethiopia |
| 1897 | Rudolf Diesel patents the diesel engine; Cézanne paints *Lake of Annecy;* gold rush to the Klondike in Alaska begins; Queen Victoria's Diamond Jubilee is celebrated; Marconi perfects the wireless |
| 1898 | Radium is discovered by the Curies; the United States annexes Hawaii; the Spanish-American War begins; Theodore Roosevelt at San Juan Hill; Admiral Dewey's victory at Manila Bay |
| 1899 | Hague Peace Conference called by the czar of Russia; the Boer War begins; Cape to Cairo railway completed north to Rhodesia; the Boxer Rebellion breaks out in China and is repressed by the European powers, Japan, and the United States; Freud makes public his controversial treatise *Interpretation of Dreams* |
| 1900 | Italy's King Humbert is assassinated and succeeded by Victor Emmanuel; Max Planck presents his quantum theory; Paris Exhibition opens |

---

**EDWARDIAN**
**1901–1911**

| | |
|---|---|
| 1901 | Death of Queen Victoria and the accession of Edward VII; the first message is sent over Marconi's transatlantic wireless; Thomas Mann writes *Buddenbrooks* |
| 1902 | End of the Boer War; eruption of Mt. Pelée in Martinique |
| 1903 | Wright brothers fly the first successful airplane at Kitty Hawk, North Carolina; the Russian socialist groups, the Bolsheviks and Mensheviks, split over doctrine; regular wireless communication between England and America |

1905

1909

| 1904 | Great fire in Baltimore; the St. Louis Exhibition; the United States occupies the Panama Canal Zone; the Russo-Japanese War begins; the Trans-Siberian Railway is completed by the Russians |
| 1905 | Einstein presents his theory of relativity; revolution breaks out in Russia |
| 1906 | San Francisco earthquake; the Labor Party gains a foothold in Parliament by winning a major victory in the election of 1906 |
| 1907 | The Triple Entente is created; Bergson publishes *Creative Evolution;* Picasso paints *Demoiselles d'Avignon* |
| 1908 | The Congo Free State becomes the Belgian Congo; Georges Sorel writes *Reflections on Violence;* the Young Turks' Revolt seeks to rejuvenate the Ottoman Empire |
| 1909 | Blériot makes the first airplane flight across the English Channel; Admiral Peary discovers the North Pole; the Irish Question and Home Rule again become an issue in England |
| 1910 | The Los Angeles *Times* is dynamited; Portugal's monarchy is overthrown; Russell and Whitehead write *Principia Mathematica;* the Union of South Africa is formed; Stravinsky's *Firebird* is performed |
| 1911 | The United States orders the Standard Oil combine dissolved; the Agadir Crisis takes place in Morocco; Ernest Rutherford creates a nuclear model of the atom; Italy begins its conquest of Tripoli; Richard Strauss composes *Der Rosenkavalier;* death of Edward VII and the accession of George V |

# BACKGROUND

By the last decade of the nineteenth century, a kind of cultural malaise began to set in throughout Western European culture. The traditions of tight, sentimental, detailed, realistic Romanticism had begun to seem more dated and outworn than they had when Realism first appeared on the scene, and Realism seemed to many artists and intellectuals a mere reportage of facts, too narrow and mundane to be considered a major cultural style. Thus artists and intellectuals toward the close of the century wanted a true culturally based style to replace the tasteless, heavy-handed eclecticism that had been the substitute for style for almost a century. The direction of stylistic experiment during these years was always in the direction of probing below the surface of life and society to expose the subterranean wellsprings of human action and feeling. It is certainly no coincidence that this came at exactly the same time that Freud and his contemporaries in medicine were developing the whole new field of psychiatry and psychology.

The most influential of these new artists and writers were the symbolists. Following many of the suggestions of the poet Baudelaire, they were searching for a compositional form that would turn intuitive, irrational, and subliminal feelings into a carefully planned artistic product. Art was seen as a movement, a shape to be imposed on feeling—a self-conscious attempt to impose a personal style onto the intangible moods and feelings that lay below the surface of reality. Finally, following the symbolist and impressionistic experiments in painting and poetry in the late 1870s and 1880s, a new mass artistic style did develop in the early 1890s based on mood, feeling, and abstract form that would dominate Western European and American culture until World War I. *Art nouveau,* as it was called, was the precursor to modernism in all the arts and the first Europeanwide artistic movement since the Rococo. Its effects could be seen in furniture, architecture, book illustration, painting, posters, tablewear, ornamentation, and clothing.

Simultaneously in Paris, London, Brussels, Vienna, and New York, interiors and furniture began to take on the abstract growth lines and sinuous curves of the new style. An excellent example of an art nouveau interior may be seen in the entry to the Hotel von Eetvelde, designed by Victor Horta in 1895 (Fig. 22-1). Abstract growth lines of nature were organized to give an organic feeling of "style" that projects Oscar Wilde's idea that nature imitates art. These stylized growth lines flow over and beyond the natural structural boundaries of the room to establish a mood or a state of mind rather than just a room. An impression of growth and movement replaces the traditional concept of architecture as rational construction, and the result is a space that seems in the process of "becoming" a room. The furniture was also developed so that lines of structural support are obscured by the flowing, organic growth lines of the new style.

Many young artists and intellectuals at the close of the nineteenth century felt that civilization had reached a climax, and they were bored and disenchanted with the imperial expansion and industrial progress. The 1890s have even been described as a decade of malaise, a decade that showed the symptoms of overcivilized decadence—*mal de siècle*. Aubrey Beardsley's illustrations for Oscar Wilde's *Salome* sum up the outlook as does Wilde's *The Picture of Dorian Gray*. This attitude was gradually replaced in the early years of the twentieth century by a movement of rebellion against the perceived traditionalism of the status quo. There was the expanding drive for women's suffrage, the demand for labor and its new unions to be recognized, the push to curb the power of trusts and monopolies, a new participation by the United States in international affairs, and early questions about the morality of European and American imperialism.

In England the people were celebrating Victoria's Diamond Jubilee, feeling virtuous about imperial expansion and their moral duty to shoulder "the white man's burden." But with the coming of the Boer War, men began to question British imperial methods abroad, even though imperialism as an ideal remained intact until World War I. With the death of the

(a)
simple art nouveau
dining room chair
French
1905

(b)
Tiffany
art
nouveau
goblet
1900

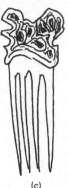

(c)
art nouveau
comb

(d)
glass cabinet
door
1902

(e)
fire
screen
1900

(f)
English chair
1900

Victor Horta, Entry to the Hotel von Eetvelde, Brussels; 1895.
Note that the weapon used here against the historical eclecticism
of the earlier nineteenth century is ornament that is not historical
but abstracted from the dynamic growth lines of nature to create a
world of fantasy, artificiality, and style. Photo courtesy of the
Museum of Modern Art.

**FIGURE 22-1**

388

queen in 1901, England entered the *Edwardian Age* during which the new king Edward VII, his wife Alexandra, and the court set a high example of taste and sophistication in upper-class circles. The period from 1890 to 1910 was also a high point in English theatrical art, with the stylish comedies of Shaw, Wilde, and Pinero as the most typical examples. There were also many thesis dramas, namely those by Galsworthy, Shaw, and Granville-Barker.

In America the frontier finally disappeared, and new challenges arose in the guise of labor trouble, big business monopolies, and mass immigration. Famous World Fairs were held in 1893 in Chicago and 1904 in St. Louis; as the United States moved into the new century, the country was dominated by the inventive "know-how" that was the major element displayed in these international exhibitions. There was the new horseless carriage, refinements in the bicycle, and soon after the thrill of the airplane. There was also an upsurge, after the passing of the frontier, of more physical outlets like tennis, swimming, bicycle riding, and many other forms of physical activity. Also after the Spanish-American War, the United States began to operate as a major power on the international scene under President Theodore Roosevelt, at the same time that it became even more dominant in the Western Hemisphere with the purchase of the Canal Zone and the building of the Panama Canal.

In France the period of the 1890s was dominated by the furies released through the Dreyfus Affair which set liberals against conservatives and brought out the worst anti-Semitic feelings. It was also a period in which Paris dominated, as at many moments in the past, the world of art and fashion, as well as an age in which the great French actress Sarah Bernhardt came to personify the theatrical star throughout Europe and America. In the early 1900s Paris became the center of ferment in the arts with the Fauvist exhibition, the opening of the art nouveau subway entrances by Hector Guimard, and the experiments in cubism led by Picasso and Braque. In women's fashions all new ideas flowed from the great designers and dress houses of Paris.

In Germany Kaiser Wilhelm II became a master showman, forever demonstrating on the European scene the military might of the German Empire. It was also a period in which German universities created a model for higher education that was even emulated in the United States, as well as a period in which German drama and theater, through the efforts of Brahm, Hauptmann, Wedekind, and Reinhardt, reached a high level of development.

Finally, this was also a period of renewal in theater, art, and literature in Russia, Italy, and Ireland. The first produced Chekhov, Stanislavsky, Bakst, and the Russian Ballet; the second produced the actress Duse, the playwright D'Annunzio, and the new futurist movement in art; while the last produced Yeats and his supporters and followers in the Abbey Theater.

## THE BASIC COSTUME SILHOUETTE

Although at first glance the clothing of this period may seem as rigid and restrictive as it had been in the preceding 40 years, this period actually marked a lightening in line and texture, particularly for women. Under the influence of impressionism in art, female fashion, with the help of layers or accents of lace, came to have a frothy, indefinite, full-blown look quite different from the restrictive lines of the bustle period that had preceded it.

Male fashions changed only slightly during this period, primarily in the area of casual and sport clothing. The fashionable ideal was the subtly tailored, elegantly fitted suit of clothes worn by the dandy or "dude" of the times. Most men were clean shaven, even though mustaches and occasional beards were still seen. Hair was much shorter and frequently parted in the middle. Hats included soft Homburgs and fedoras, straw boaters, and even caps, while the standard top hats and bowlers were more and more reserved for formal occasions. High, stiff collars were still the rule, whether winged or standing, but soft, turn-down collars were now equally fashionable. Ties consisted of the formal scarf ascot, the four-in-hand, and the bow tie; shirts, although most had separate collars and cuffs, occasionally had these items made as part of the garment. Starched fronts were still a must with tuxedos and tails and the formal use of frock and morning coats. These latter coats were reserved more for formal occasions, and business suits, blazers, Norfolk jackets, and contrasting sports jackets were now worn in situations other than sporting events. There was a great variety of double- and single-breasted waistcoats, often contrasting in their color and pattern with the trousers and jacket. Trousers were quite slim and by the end of the 1890s were being pressed with a crease in the front and the back. By 1905 cuffs began to make their appearance on trousers. Knee trousers or knickers were worn by young boys and for sports, usually with thick, woolen stockings, while shoes now gradually shifted from high-button laced or elastic-sided designs to the low-laced oxford. Spats to cover the shoe were very fashionable with the upper classes. For outerwear there were heavy or light overcoats, the plain Inverness with its shoulder cape, caped opera coats, and heavy, fur-trimmed and lined overcoats for the ostentatious and affluent. An example of upper-class casual wear for men may be seen in John Singer Sargent's *Interior in Venice* and the standard evening dress for men in Jean Béraud's *Jardin de Paris, The Night Beauties* (Figs. 22–2,3).

In female dress the first major sign of change was the disappearance of the bustle, leaving a much softer silhouette with only a certain amount of residual pleated fullness at the rear of the skirt. By the mid-1890s the skirt became a smooth, many-gored, funnel-shaped skirt, flaring out sharply from waist to floor with extra fullness at the back. The fitted bodice had large leg-o-mutton sleeves and a tiny waist that brought back a slight memory of the hourglass lines of the early nineteenth century. Dresses were still high necked and long sleeved for daytime, with short sleeves and décolletage reserved for evening. The tailored suit for women in the 1890s was a step beyond the fitted

jackets, vestees, and skirts of the bustle period and were worn with a quite masculine shirt-blouse and bow or ribbon tie—even though the usual daytime blouse was a frothy smother of lace, frills, and braid.

In the first years of the new century a new corset line appeared that pushed the bust forward and the hips back to create a sway-backed stance with an S-curved art nouveau line reminiscent of the curves in the furniture and interiors of the time. Hair, which in the 1890s had been drawn closely to the top of the head, became fuller, softer, and thicker—surrounding the temples, ears, and forehead in a massive halo of upswept waves that finished in a knot, roll, or bun at the back of the head. Flowered and beribboned hats, which previously had had relatively small brims, expanded to broad-brimmed creations saturated with plumes, ribbons, and birds. Then by 1908 the silhouette became slimmer, the bust higher and more prominent, and the hips narrower and tightly constricted by the corset. The Edwardian Period ended with a high-waisted revival of the Empire silhouette with a fairly prominent bust line and a slim, relatively cylindrical silhouette below the high waist.

To see both the similarities and the differences between the female line and look of the 1890s and that of the early 1900s, one might compare Sargent's *Interior in Venice* with Béraud's *Jardin de Paris, The Night Beauties* (Figs. 22–2,3). In each case the female costume seems layered and complexly cut with a stress on soft, lacy trim that gives the female costume a certain impressionistic frothiness. The idea in each painting is that the woman is still a "princess" or a "queen" set off from modern life, swathed in laces and layers of fabric that fall to the floor, the face framed by a fullness of hair and a spreading hat brim. The mood, which is reinforced by the way each painting is presented, is that of romantic illusion and impressionistic unreality. This is particularly true of the *Night Beauties* in which one is struck by the languor and sophistication that characterized the Edwardian era. The "ladies of the night" in their layers of semitransparent material seem to embody an impression of the male fantasy of the

(a)
gray felt
Homburg
1890

(b)
dress overcoat
1904

Second
Queen's
Regiment
1895
English

(c)

(d)
striped
shirt with
white collar and
cuffs, elastic braces
late 1890s

(e)
evening
tie,
waistcoat,
and
stiff bosom shirt
1898

(f)
black derby
1900

(g)
scarf tie
1890

(h)
ascot scarf with
pin
1899

(i)
cutaway morning
coat without
waist seam
1907

John Singer Sargent, *Interior in Venice;* Royal
Academy of Arts; London; 1899. Illustrates
the lighter, softer, somewhat more relaxed
lines in fashion at the turn into the twentieth
century. Note the light suit that has replaced
a dress on the lady at the left and the light
vest and trousers on her escort. Photo
courtesy of the Royal Academy, London.

(j)
Norfolk jacket,
knickerbockers,
ribbed hose, and
high shoes
1901

English
walking
suit
1907

(k)

Norfolk jacket
and
knickerbockers—
sport
1890s

(l)

striped
bathing
suit
1890s

(m)

**FIGURE 22-2**

corset with garters 1905 (a)

patent leather button shoe 1903 (b)

cycling blouse and bloomers with gaiters 1900 (c)

(d) back of a dolman wrap 1908

laced shoe 1905 (e)

evening pump 1905

(f) 1893

(i) 1894

walking coat 1905 (g)

combination corset cover and petticoat 1903 (j)

(h) straw sailor hat 1904

cloth redingote 1894 (k)

first kimonodress style 1910 (l)

(o) 1909

(n) 1899

(m) 1901 coiffure

(p) marcel wave 1907

Jean Béraud, *Jardin de Paris, The Night Beauties;* Musée Carnavalet; 1905. An image of languid sophistication created by the poses and the soft, feathery, layered, semitransparent fashions worn by the ladies. They express the male fantasy of this time—windblown birds of plumage or froths of meringue drifting among the black and white uniforms of male society. Photo courtesy of Giraudon, Paris.

**FIGURE 22-3**

female ideal of the day. It was the last stand of nineteenth-century romanticism in women's dress before the revolution in female clothing was brought about by women's suffrage and the arrival of the Japanese patterns and shapes that had influenced art nouveau illustrations and posters.

# LATE VICTORIAN COSTUME

**Masculine Dress** The sack suit of the 1890s with its broadened lapels and collar resembled a modern suit, but it buttoned much higher than those today. The frock coat and the morning coat (Fig. 22–2i) remained staple items that gave a more formal appearance; waistcoats were still double- and single-breasted and often contrasted with coats and trousers; and shirts retained the starched, separate collar and cuffs of the past (Fig. 22–2d). Shirt collars included those that were stiff and high standing, those with bent wing tips, and the popular turnover variety. The four-in-hand tie became the most popular neckwear, followed by the bow tie and the more formal, folded ascot (Fig. 22–2a,d,e,f,g,h). Trousers became a bit more comfortable in their fuller proportions and began to appear with front and back creases. The story goes that Edward (still prince of Wales at the time) tried on a pair of trousers at his tailor's that had been folded for some time and creases had been created, front and back. He liked the look, and soon the style spread to become a staple of fashion.

A summary of the elegance that was demanded by the very fashionable gentleman about town just before the opening of the Edwardian Age may be seen in Boldini's *Portrait of Count Robert de Montesquieu* (Fig. 22–4). Here we have an elegant tan grey frock coat, waistcoat, and trousers, with a high winged collar, loosely tied scarf tie, elegant gloves, and a bone-handled cane. The image is one of absolute sophistication and impractical elegance, an image that was almost completely swept away by World War I.

Outerwear was as in the past divided among the furlined and trimmed overcoat, the lighter covert wool topcoats, and the caped Inverness and opera coats (Fig. 22–2b). Hats were divided among the derby or bowler, the top hat, the fedora or the Homburg, and various caps

**FIG. 22–4** Giovanni Boldini, *Portrait of Count Robert de Montesquieu;* Museum of Modern Art, Paris; c. 1897. Illustrates the perfect gentleman at the close of the nineteenth century in his absolute sophistication, perfect tailoring, and subtle elegance. Photo courtesy of the French Musées Nationaux.

and straws for outings (Fig. 22–2a,f,k). For sports the Norfolk jacket worn with knickers, stockings, gaiters, and a cap was the most popular (Fig. 22–2j,l), although there were also Tyrolean hiking pants, knee-length tennis pants worn with stockings, and other variations in jackets and trousers for boating, polo, hockey, bicycling, and even bathing (Fig. 22–2m). The latter consisted of striped knit pullovers and pants with underwear and socks included.

One may take two sets of fashion drawings for 1899 as typical of the times and as images for male dress throughout the first decade of the new century (Fig. 22-5). One shows the fashionable cycling outfit, complete with Norfolk jacket, knickers, and cap; another gives the holiday-outing lounge suit with boater. The second set presents the formal costume for men about town consisting of frock coat and top hat with matching trousers in one case and a light, double-breasted vest and striped trousers in the other.

By the end of the 1890s the clean-shaven look finally outstripped beards and mustaches, and haircuts became quite short. Shoes were usually low oxfords with high shoes now reserved mostly for hiking or certain sporting events.

**Feminine Dress** In the decade of the 1890s female fashion, although in many ways continuing the corseted complexities of the preceding four decades, began to lighten and expand. The focus of attention shifted from the rear of the skirt to the sleeves, and many romantic touches from the early seventeenth and nineteenth centuries returned, particularly spreading lace collars and slashed puffed sleeves (Fig. 22-6). The smooth corseted bodice with its tiny waist remained but with more stress on its hourglass lines, while skirts by 1894 spread out in a smooth expansion of conical lines over the hips and downward and outward to the floor (Fig. 22-3k). The only extra fullness was in the center back. Collars for daywear increased in height and were stiffened with boning and crinoline, so there was an even greater emphasis on the regal swan neck than ever before. But it was the sleeves that made the revolutionary change in shape that gave this period its distinctive look. By 1892 the top of the sleeve was already gathered in to create a rising fullness above the armseye, and by 1894 the sleeves reached excessive proportions, held out by three or four layers of interlining. Usually in long-sleeved dresses there was a fitted undersleeve of light silk or the fabric of the garment, and over this was mounted a puffed sleeve held out by a flexible crinoline. These huge puffed

**FIG. 22-5** Male fashion designs for cycling, walking, and formal afternoon calls; 1899. Illustrates the very precise categories of clothing for each specialized occasion. Note the Norfolk jacket, cap, and knickerbockers for cycling; the straw boater for summer walking; and the frock coat, top hat, and high collar for formal calling. From a photo in the collection of the author.

FIG. 22-6 Female fashion design for attendance at the races; 1894. Illustrates the extreme size of the balloon sleeves, the expanding width of the hat brim, the narrowness of the waist, and the full flair of the triangular skirt of the mid-1890s. From a photo in the collection of the author.

ming. A tennis dress for the mid-1890s usually had a sailor blouse and collar, a firm belt at the waist, and a flared skirt with simple lines from waist to ankle or floor. But what came to be the most popular sporting style may be seen in Sargent's *Portrait of Mr. and Mrs. Newton Phelps Stokes*, (Fig. 22-7). Mrs. Stokes is seen in a pleated-front shirtwaist, a very plain, flaring

FIG. 22-7 John Singer Sargent, *Portrait of Mr. and Mrs. Newton Phelps Stokes;* Metropolitan Museum of Art; 1897. Illustrates the new sporting clothes for men and women that would become fashionable in the early twentieth century. Note the tailored jacket, mannish shirtwaist, plain skirt, bow tie, and straw boater worn by Mrs. Stokes in imitation of male fashion. Photo courtesy of the Metropolitan Museum of Art, Bequest of Edith Mintum Stokes, 1938.

sleeves were also used for evening but without a tight, lower undersleeve. As the sleeves expanded, so did the skirts, and these were shaped by using inside tapes to control gathers and pleats, horsehair and interlinings of taffeta and cambric to give stiffness and expansion out from the body, and weights to give the appropriate line to a train. (Fig. 22-6).

By 1897 the pendulum began to swing back, and the great puffed sleeves disappeared, as did the excessive width at the bottom of the skirt. A slim sleeve with a skirt that flared only moderately at the bottom became the fashion, and the female form had a taller, slimmer look (Fig. 22-2).

The major new area of female fashion during this period was in sportswear. There was a determined attempt to develop special costumes for tennis, cycling, boating, and swim-

skirt, a tailored jacket with slightly padded shoulders, and a straw boater that is exactly like a man's hat. This is the style that we associate with the Gibson Girl, developed by Charles Dana Gibson as an idealized symbol of the best in American womanhood during the last years of the nineteenth century. Bathing suits now had shorter sleeves and skirt but were still worn with stockings and rubber shoes.

Wraps of this period alternated between short capes and full coats—the latter tailored to fit over the great leg-o-mutton sleeves of the mid-1890s (Fig. 22–3k). Capes usually had high, flaring collars that framed the face and were of finger-tip length, although there were full mantles with trains for evening done in heavy lace over silk, in brocades, and in embroidered and beaded patterning. Coats were anywhere from finger tip to floor length, with long velvet and satin coats trimmed in ostrich and fur for evening.

Underwear became more important with its delicate laces and embroidery and was now openly advertised in mail-order catalogues. There were dainty silk or batiste camisoles edged in lace, elaborately decorated drawers,

and beautifully edged petticoats finished at the bottom with pleated *frou-frou*. The preferred fabric for the outer petticoat was still taffeta since it made such a delightful noise in movement. The ideal of silk shirts that rustled in movement did not disappear until World War I.

The hairdressing of this period, known as the *pompadour* (since it was loosely based on the hairdress of that famous courtesan), consisted of the hair drawn and brushed upward from neck and forehead and then knotted at the back of the crown. Tall hats and bonnets were now swept away, and the standard hat had a moderately wide brim and a low crown decorated with ruffles, bows, feathers, plumes, and flowers. Most were worn at a rakish angle and held in place with hatpins (Fig. 22–3f,h,i).

Footwear now had pointed toes and medium heels, and most daytime shoes were buttoned or laced high tops, with silk-covered, heeled slippers for evening and afternoon receptions. Carriage boots and winter walking boots were frequently lined in padded satin and trimmed in fur (Fig. 22–3,e).

## EDWARDIAN COSTUME

*Masculine Dress*  With the death of Queen Victoria and the accession of Edward VII, the elegant Edwardian Age began. Hair was kept relatively short and often parted in the middle, while the few mustaches that were worn were trim and small. Top hats and bowlers continued, but fashion interest lay in the many soft felt fedoras, felt slouch hats, and Homburgs that came into common use. Caps, tam-o'-shanters, and *fore and aft,* or deerstalker caps, were also popular along with the perennial straw boater and the newer Panama straw. High collars remained the rule with turnovers coming in a close second. Ties were divided among the ascot, bow, and four-in-hand, with the latter the most popular. With the new tuxedo it now became an iron rule that one wore a black bow tie. Formal shirts still usually opened up the back with the fronts heavily starched to give the "boiled front," though some daring

men wore finely pleated dress shirts instead of the stiff fronts. Business and sporting shirts were only lightly starched, and working-class shirts were usually worn without collars and with no starch. As the decade progressed, shirt cuffs were more often made as part of the shirt.

Knitted cardigans and pullover sweaters were popular for students and as at-home wear, while blazers were the most popular form of sporting jackets. In shaping the regular sack suits of the period, tailors stressed a square-shouldered look that demanded more and more padding. By 1910 the shoulder shape was almost grotesque. All coats including frock coats and cutaways were looser in fit, especially in the waist, than in the 1890s and with a longer line to the waist (Fig. 22–2k). Vests for business suits usually matched the coat and trousers and were cut somewhat lower than in the past to match the lower buttoning of the coat. Silk or lighter cotton vests were used with frock coats and cutaways, while very low-cut, white vests in satin or self-toned brocade were used with tails (Fig. 22–2e,i). Black faille or satin vests were used with the tuxedo.

Trousers were now pressed to have creases front and back, and many informal styles now had cuffs. Summer trousers were in cotton, linen, or cream flannel, sometimes with a small stripe, while winter trousers were in darker stripes, tweeds, or checks. At the end of the decade there was a flurry of interest in peg-top trousers with much fullness at the top. Knickers were still very evident on boys and for outings and sports.

Winter shoes were often ankle high and laced (some still buttoned), while summer ones were low oxfords, sometimes two-toned in white and black or brown. Spats were still used as a shoe covering by the fashionable for formal and semiformal occasions, and low, patent leather black pumps with bows were standard for full evening dress.

There were all manner of sweaters during this decade from turtlenecks through pullovers to cardigans, while overcoats were divided between the heavy woolen Chesterfields with velvet collars and the lighter linen driving coats or dusters often with a checked pattern (Fig. 22–8). With evening dress some men still wore the black opera coat with caped sleeves.

The military uniform of this period began to change from the romantic colors and tailored lines that had been in existence since the Napoleonic Wars to olive- or khaki-colored tunics and trousers with leggings or boots and simple brimmed or billed hats. The move was away from uniforms for parade and show and toward uniforms that were more practical and which blended more into the landscape. With the entry into the twentieth century, most of the romantic glamour faded from uniforms, except for very special occasions (Fig. 22–2c).

**Feminine Dress** Fashion from 1900 to 1910 favored the large, commanding, large-busted women with a certain cool dignity. This image was supported by a change in the corset line from the straight downward line that gave unhealthy pressure over the abdomen to an

**FIG. 22–8** Fashion design for a male motoring costume, 1904. Illustrates the continued proliferation of specialized garments for special occasions. Here the plaid driving coat or duster completely protects the suit from the dust of motoring and is usually worn with a matching cap and goggles. From a photo in the collection of the author.

S-curved line that threw the bust forward and the hips back (Fig. 22–3a). The skirt was smooth over the hips and with a minimum of fullness to the knees, then flared outward in a flourish of pleating, lace, or ruffles into a bell shape onto the floor (Fig. 22–3j). There was also a cascade of ruffles or lace on the bodice, particularly from the bust to the lowered line of the waist in front. In fact, lace seemed to be the passion of the time and appropriately conjured up a sweeping impression of frothy grandeur— an image that was a direct but unconscious outgrowth of impressionism in art, with its stress on a layered mistiness of detail (Fig.

22–3). To complement this rage for lace was an equal craving for feathers on hats and in boas about the neck—a demand that severely threatened wildlife in areas such as the Florida Everglades.

Heads from about 1900 to 1908 carried a soft, full, bulging pompadour that waved up in a curve away from the face, with curls or waves at the temples and a twist, knot, or bun at the top of the back (Fig. 22–3m). From about 1907 hair was frequently parted, with the hair at the sides waved and brushed upward from the face and secured by combs (Fig. 22–3p), but the back was still coiled or twisted into a bun. One other contribution to hairdressing during the period came with the addition of the permanent wave, invented in 1906 by Charles Nestlé, a fashionable hairdresser in London. Another hairdresser, Marcel, had invented a waving process with irons in the 1890s, but the new system of curling with electric heating machines gave curls or waves that lasted for months. With all the hairdressing, ornament was standard whether it was simple combs for domestic wear or jewels, bows, and flowers for formal afternoon or evening functions.

As for hats the only one that carried over from the 1890s was the straw boater, worn straight on the head with a dip forward. Other hats began to be larger and more elaborate (Fig. 22–3o). At first brims were not too wide and were turned up or down on the sides to frame and set off the great swirl of hair. All crowns were very shallow, and all hats were excessively trimmed in bows, feathers, and flowers. Brims began increasing in width, and by 1907 the female figure was dominated by excessively large hats, known as *Merry Widow* hats after the heroine of the Lehar operetta. The lady at the right center of Béraud's *Jardin de Paris, The Night Beauties* wears such a hat with a great frothy scarf under the chin (Fig. 22–3). Even more excessive hats may be seen in an illustration from *Album des Blouses Nouvelles* (Fig. 22–9). Note the size of the wrapped taffeta crown on the lady seated center and the width of the fur-trimmed brim at the right. Thus one can see that by 1910 high crowns were possible as well as brims that sloped down all the way around. Another hat making its appearance about 1910

**FIG. 22–9** Fashion designs from the *Album des Blouses Nouvelles*, 1910. Illustrates the slightly higher waist, narrower hips, large hats, and top-heavy silhouette that came to dominate female fashion between 1908 and 1911. Note particularly the excessive width and extravagance of the hats. Photo courtesy of the Bertarelli Collection, Milan.

was the famous *beehive,* worn by the lady seated right. A much smaller version of this was the *toque,* used with evening wear, that looked much like a soft turban. Along with most of these great milliners' creations veils were worn, sometimes covering the face, sometimes loosely to tie the hat to the head, sometimes framing the face like a curtain.

Necks or collars throughout this period were very high for street dresses, and only informal reception gowns and sporting wear ever displayed the neck to the base of the throat. Yet evening gowns were as low-cut as ever. Until about 1905 the high collars were the same height all around and often of the dress material and interlined. After that date collars were often of transparent lace or pleated silk, boned to stand up around the neck and dipping down in the front under the chin while rising to an even greater height under the ears and at the back of the neck than in the past (Fig. 22-3p). The top was frequently finished in a tiny lace ruffle. The same changes took place in the turnover collars for shirtwaists. Until 1905 they were relatively low, while after that they were much higher. These were worn with bow ties, a four-in-hand tie, or a scarf-stock tied in a bow in the front and based on the stock used for riding outfits (Fig. 22-3c). Many of the high lace collars also had a frothy jabot down the front of the dress or blouse, and many, if not most, such high collars with lace jabots were also finished with a pin or brooch at the base of the neck. As for evening necklines up to 1905 many gowns had dropped shoulder lines with narrow shoulder straps to keep up the gown, but after that date most necklines were square or rounded.

The corset line gave the distinctive shape to the body during the Edwardian Age. At first it was shaped to flatten the abdomen, lower the bustline, and give a thrust outward at the back of the hips. Less well-endowed women resorted to padding in both the bust and hip areas to gain the appropriate swaybacked S-curved line. Then about 1908 the new sheath corset came in that stressed a full bust and a hipless, slim figure all the way to the floor. Underwear, besides the corset, consisted of tubular, lace-edged drawers to below the knees, a knitted vest or light camisole under the corset, a muslin or flannel corset cover, and a short petticoat of muslin or flannel. After 1905 there was usually a chemise instead of the corset cover, and after 1908 drawers fitted smoothly over the hips and then flared out into a ruffled bloused line at the knees.

Blouses or shirtwaists, often pleated or tucked down the front, were invariably tucked in and not allowed to create a basque, or peplum, effect over the skirt. The waistline had a slightly dipped, rounded line until 1903, stressed a much larger dip in the front from 1903 to 1908, and after 1908 was straight around the waist or a little above it. Belts or shirred girdles were a standard way to accent and finish off the waist. Blouses or shirtwaists were in all manner of transparent fabrics— lace, china silks, muslins, and light linen—and were usually buttoned either up the front or back. From 1900 to 1906 they always were blousy all the way to the low front waistline, while after 1908 the fitted high-waisted blouse or shirtwaist began to dominate.

In jackets the stress was on a fairly severe tailored line that followed the shape of the corseted figure, some only bolero length, some fitted well down over the hips (Fig. 22-10). After

**FIG. 22-10** Fashion design from *The Ladies' Tailor* for 1907. Illustrates the dropped line of the bosom from bust to waist, the lift to the hips at the back, the pleated skirt with expanding fullness at the bottom, and the general swaybacked or S-curved corset and body line of the first seven years of the new century. From a photo in the collection of the author.

1908 they were frequently cut longer in back than in the front, often with a kind of "morning coat" curve down to the back. Usually they had lapels, a collar, and sometimes cuffs, and these could range from a very masculine look to a frilly, feminine effect with braid and ruffles.

The sleeves of blouses, dresses, and jackets were usually straight until 1903, after which there was apt to be a little fullness above the elbow and into the armseye, although some, known as *bishop sleeves,* were quite straight and puffed a little into the cuff at the bottom. The long, narrow sleeve returned from 1908 to 1911. For afternoon reception dresses and informal summer gowns, three-quarter sleeves were popular, and for evening the short cap sleeve or no sleeves with white gloves was standard.

Until at least 1910 women wore at least one petticoat, often of taffeta with spreading tiers of ruffles from the knees down (Fig. 22–3j). If ruffled muslin petticoats were substituted, at least two were worn. The skirt that fitted over these fit smoothly over the corset and then flared to the ground with slightly larger gores to the back than in the front, although there were also box-pleated skirts with pleats open from the hips down. Most gowns were floor length and for evening or afternoon receptions had a train, but some walking dresses were only ankle length. After 1908 many dresses did not touch the floor, and the shape changed to a fairly straight-line silhouette with pleating or braided trim at the sides.

In the winter high shoes were still standard, although after 1908 women were more apt to

**FIG. 22–11**  Jean Béraud, *The Cycling Hut in the Bois de Boulogne;* Musée de l'Ile de France, Sceaux; ca. 1910. Illustrates the somewhat humorous but fascinating fashions designed for women cyclists during the first decade of the new century. Note the use of straw boaters, cinched-in waists, and full bloomers. Photo courtesy of Bulloz, Paris.

wear spats over pumps or oxfords (Fig. 22–3b). Heels ranged from fairly low for walking to quite high for dressy suits (Fig. 22–3e). Such high shoes were either buttoned or laced and sometimes with uppers in a different tone from lowers. Summer shoes were either low pumps or oxfords; rubber-soled, white canvas shoes were used for tennis. Evening slippers were in satin or brocade to match the gown and were quite high-heeled. Silk stockings went all the way from plain, opaque, dark tones for daytime streetwear to embroidered, clocked whites and pastels for evening. Rubber overshoes were possible for inclement weather, and quilted satin carriage boots were worn over dance slippers to and from balls and receptions.

Outergarments consisted of both full-length coats and short, box coats with very special attention paid to the great enveloping duster from neck to floor for motoring (Fig. 22–3g). Evening wraps, from coats to spreading mantles, were made in rich silks, satins, or brocades and were often trimmed in ostrich, maribou, or fur. There were also many short walking capes, and a new dolman jacket with sleeves cut in one with the body (Fig. 22–3d). Also the sweaters that had originally been only for men began to materialize as a casual sporting outergarment for women.

Two other sporting outfits for women were the bathing suit and the cycling costume—each with a distinctive cut and based on the use of bloused bloomers. The former usually consisted of a sleeved, striped top with a ruffled or collared neck and sometimes a peplum skirt. This was worn over a pair of striped bloomers to the knee with a pair of rubber bathing shoes and a ribboned dust cap. Cycling costumes usually consisted of a mannish shirtwaist, flowing bow tie, tight belt, and very full bloomers to the knee with long stockings and laced shoes. Also worn with this was a light straw hat or a copy of the male straw boater (Fig. 22–11).

## FABRICS

The only change in fabrics for men was in the increase of tweeds and homespuns for sack suits and sporting jackets. Serge and broadcloth continued as major conservative woolens, while summer suits were of cream wool, light flannel, linen cotton duck, pongee, or seersucker.

All gowns required a great amount of fabric—the average was eight to ten yards of double width, with four to five yards of 54-inch fabric for skirts alone. Women's fabrics ranged from firm woolens to silks to crisp, semitransparent fabrics. Woolens included those worn by men as well as mohair, goats hair, cheviot, challis, merino, and various silk and wool mixtures. Silks ranged through satins, taffetas, silk-backed and changeable velvets, India silk, China silk, silk gauze, chiffon, raw silk and newer materials like georgette, crepe, and *meteor,* a newer crepe.

Among the cottons were gingham, organdy, various muslins, batiste, and piqué. Linen was used natural and colored for summer suits and in a natural tan for the motoring dusters of the time. But undoubtedly the most characteristic fabric accent of the time was lace, with some blouses made completely of lace or openwork embroidery.

Finally there were furs. During this period the short-haired furs were somewhat replaced by fox, lynx, and marten, although squirrel, Persian lamb, mink, chinchilla, sable, and ermine were still seen for hats, collars, cuffs, and even winter coat linings.

## ARTS AND ARTIFACTS

Although there was still much interest in revival-style interiors with a stress on the Rococo Period, the newer interior look was based first on the simplicities of the craftsman style and shortly thereafter on the emerging art nouveau look. The most fashionable rooms were soon outfitted with twining vinelike lines in paneling and furniture supports with much use of stained glass in selected windows and skylights. On a slightly more sober plane, there were heavy but simple walnut wood paneling, beamed ceilings, and large, solid, blocklike furniture covered in leather. Art nouveau furnishings also made their appearance with a stress on smooth, curving lines and semi-abstract shapes. Often it was the small articles in a room that gave it its distinctive new look—such as Tiffany lamps and vases, art nouveau statuettes, vinelike lighting fixtures, and touches of stained glass (Fig. 22–1a, b,c,d,e,f).

Accessories for men included pince-nez glasses, gloves, monocles, canes, and watches. Evening gloves were still white kid; daytime gloves were grey, tan, or brown. Pipes were very popular among young college men, and cigarettes also began to be important.

For women the major item was the purse or handbag, the most common known as the *chatelaine bag*. Beaded and silk purses were used for evening, large leather bags for daytime. In the bag one always carried an ornamental metal card case to hold the all-important calling cards. Gloves were long with short-sleeved dresses, shorter for long sleeves. Summer ones were light and washable. Fans were much in style for evening and followed eighteenth-century lines. Umbrellas were long-handled and of black silk, but parasols were light colored and often carried printed patterns, lace edgings, ribbons, and ruffles. Belts were now a major accessory with shirtwaists and with many women's suits.

Jewelry for men was still limited to tie pins, cuff links, signet rings, and the watch case, although the collegiate atmosphere of the first years of the new century made the fraternity pin a much-sought-after item. For women there were pin-on watches, breastpins and brooches (particularly the pins that went at the base of the neck on so many shirtwaists), small bracelets, and lockets. There were also the standard necklaces, earrings, and finger rings, and much stress on jeweled combs for the hair.

## VISUAL SOURCES

Artists who are excellent artistic resources for costume are John Singer Sargent; Jean Béraud, H. D. Etcheverry, H. Gervex, J. Veber, J. Lavery, V. Corcos, G. Boldini, and J. Cayron. Also of excellent value are the cartoons or illustrations of Charles Dana Gibson. There are many fashion journals, but the best are *The London Album, La Mode de Style, Le Moniteur de la Mode, Vogue, Godey's Lady's Book,* and *Harper's Bazaar.* Other sources are the *Sears, Roebuck Catalogs,* and magazines such as *The London Illustrated News, l'Illustration, Harper's Weekly, The Delineator, Burlington Magazine,* and the *Ladies' Home Journal.* Institutional resources that are most useful are the Metropolitan Museum of Art, the New York Public Library, the Brooklyn Museum, the Musée Carnavalet, the Collection Union Francaise des Arts du Costume, and the Bibliothèque Nationale. Useful books are H. C. Brown's *The Golden Nineties,* Hibbert's *Daily Life in Victorian England,* Peter Selz and Mildred Constantine's *Art Nouveau: Art and Design at the Turn of the Century,* and *This Fabulous Century: Prelude 1870–1900* and *This Fabulous Century: 1900–1910.*

## SUMMARY

This was a period when the arts and clothing gradually began the move into the modern technological age. Clothes which for over half a century had been an anachronism in a world of trains, industrial plants, and streetcars at last began to loosen up and move beyond the rigid prescriptions of the Victorian Age. This was also a period when art nouveau designs swept away the eclectic excesses of the past in favor of abstract organic growth lines in interiors, furniture, and artifacts and, to a lesser extent, in pattern motifs for female gowns. Thus with the death of Queen Victoria and the accession of Edward VII, the last decade of elegance and gentility began with a loosening of costume lines, a lightening of colors, a breaking down of prescribed uniforms for function, and an acceptance in society of many of the sporting and business clothes that had been on the periphery of fashion for several decades.

# chapter XXIII

# World War I and the Twenties:

# Early Art Deco

## Chronology

### (1911–1929)

BEFORE AND AFTER
WORLD WAR I
1911–1920

1912

| | | |
|---|---|---|
| 1911 | Ernest Rutherford creates a model of the atom; the Agadir Crisis in Morocco; the United States orders the Standard Oil combine dissolved |
| 1912 | The Titanic sinks; C. P. Rodgers makes the first transcontinental flight from New York to Pasadena; the Balkan Wars are a prelude to World War I |
| 1913 | Parcel post established, leading to the mail-order business; D. H. Lawrence writes *Sons and Lovers;* Woodrow Wilson inaugurated as president of the United States; Proust publishes Volume I of *A la Recherche du temps perdu* |
| 1914 | Archduke Franz Ferdinand is assassinated at Sarajevo; World War I begins; Matisse paints *Les Poussins Rouges* |
| 1915 | Major naval battles between Germany and England; Lusitania sunk; Edith Cavell, English nurse, executed by Germans; Panama-Pacific Exposition in San Francisco |

1914

1917

| 1916 | Preparedness Day bombing in San Francisco sends Tom Mooney to prison; the Battle of Verdun; Sir Roger Casement hanged in Ireland for treason; Naval Battle of Jutland; the Battle of the Somme; involvement of the U.S. on the Mexican border; Rasputin killed in St. Petersburg |
| 1917 | The Bolsheviks under Lenin seize power in Russia; the U.S. enters the war on the side of the Allies; the Battle of Cambrai; Jerusalem captured; the Eighteenth Amendment to the Constitution passed |
| 1918 | Battle of the Aisne and the Argonne Forest; Armistice, November 11; Czar Nicholas and his family executed |
| 1919 | Peace Conference is convened; the Black and Tans in Ireland; a Coalition government is installed in England; Boston police strike is settled by Calvin Coolidge; the Industrial Workers of the World (I.W.W.) gains ground; women's suffrage is achieved; the flight of the NC-4 across the Atlantic |

---

**THE TWENTIES
1920–1929**

1920

| 1920 | The League of Nations is formed; the Sacco-Vanzetti case |
| 1922 | Irish Free State established; The Teapot Dome scandal; radio first introduced in the home; Tutankhamen's tomb discovered in Egypt; Mussolini seizes control of Italy; Soviet Union formed |
| 1923 | The age of the flapper and of flaming youth begins; Turkey becomes a republic; surrealism in art reaches early maturity |
| 1924 | The Leopold-Loeb case tried; diphtheria serum taken to Alaska by dog sled to avert death; prince of Wales' American tour |

world war I and the twenties: early art deco   405

1922

1926

| 1925 | Scopes' anti-evolution trial in Tennessee; Locarno Pact ratified |
| 1926 | Great general strike in England |
| 1927 | Mississippi floods; Dirigible Shenandoah crashes; Lindbergh flies the Atlantic; high point of racketeers involved in bootlegging; first talking film |
| 1929 | Admiral Byrd makes his trip to Antarctica; stock market crashes after Black Tuesday, October 29 |

1928

# BACKGROUND

As we move into the period of World War I and its aftermath, we gradually leave behind the worn-out forms and traditions related to nineteenth-century Romanticism and the culture of the Victorian and Edwardian Ages. Romanticism with its stress on emotion and escape into the past had dominated art since the opening of the nineteenth century, and by World War I there still was a major division between the arts and technology. Even the realists and the impressionists, who originally painted and wrote scientifically to deepen the human insight into nature and the human condition, drifted into misty moodiness and subjective images. Thus what was needed by the artists and intellectuals in the opening years of the new century was a return to intellectual ideas and rationality in form and structure. In architecture, public and private buildings were still being constructed throughout western Europe before and after World War I in the *beaux-arts* tradition of the Paris Opera House (see Fig. 20-1). But with the experiments in cubism, futurism, and the construction of the first geometric glass-and-steel skyscrapers, a new era gradually dawned in which the abstract structure of a work of art was its own decoration and reason for being. Artists and intellectuals began to probe below the surface of reality to discover its structural components as well as to investigate the many realities that clustered together in a single moment or around a single object. The Age of Relativity had dawned by the early 1920s, and avante-garde writers such as James Joyce, André Gide, Gertrude Stein, and Luigi Pirandello were dissecting words and reality on many levels, just as scientists such as Albert Einstein and others were dissecting Newtonian physics and discovering relativity in the natural world.

In the world of popular culture the cinema was the great new experimental toy that allowed the concept of relativity to make an impact on the common people. Just as the box camera had been invented at the time when the nineteenth century became enamored with realism, so the moving picture camera seems to have come just at that moment when artists, scientists, and intellectuals came to view reality as a series of shifting, changing, multiple relationships. The most obvious effect of this concept was in the so-called *montage* in which many cinematic images were seen simultaneously instead of sequentially.

Also in the popular arts the period of World War I saw a slow transition from the lush, curvilinear abstractions of art nouveau decoration to the more mechanized, smooth, geometric forms of *art deco*. By the time of the famous Paris Exhibition of 1925, this cool, mechanized, decorative look dominated the interiors on display. A good example from a later 1929 exhibition is Saarinen's model design for a dining room (Fig. 23-1). The emphasis is on smooth, hard surfaces; simple, rather tight geometric decoration; and a created space that is a machine for living.

Politically and culturally, the end of the Edwardian Age and the beginning of World War I saw the demise of the age of gentility. The new world of revolutions, wars, mass displacements of people, dictatorships, and domination of Western life by technology successfully brought an end to the old ways of culture. The acceleration of events and communication, the fragmentation of vision, the further rise of the specialist, and tremendous increases in knowledge succeeded, along with all the political upheavals, in paving the way for the alienated person in the lonely crowd. Buffeted by events and deluged with information, people had a sense of discontinuity rather than continuity, a multifaceted sense of reality rather than an individual and personal perception of self inside society.

In England World War I brought a terrible awakening from the romantic dream of war as a great adventure. After the war there was a dedicated attempt to put aside the past and to return to a way of life that would make it seem as if the war had not occurred. It was a period of continued anguish and conflict in Ireland, with an uneasy conclusion in the founding of the Irish Republic. It was a period in which Edward, the prince of Wales, represented the Crown in society far more than George V and his wife Mary, and it was a period when the

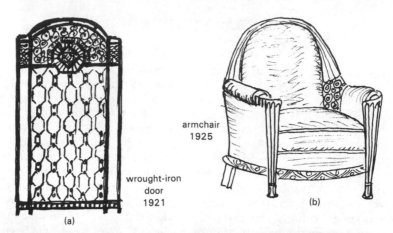

wrought-iron
door
1921

(a)

armchair
1925

(b)

Eliel Saarinen, Dining Room designed for
the Metropolitan Museum of Art 1929 Exhibition on the Architect and the Industrial
Arts. Illustrates the new, smooth, geometric
lines and machine-crafted look that came to
dominate interior decoration during the rise
of the art deco style in the 1920s and 1930s.
Photo courtesy of the Metropolitan Museum of Art.

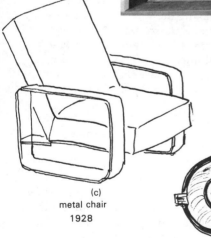

(c)
metal chair
1928

(d)
cigarette cases

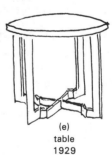

(e)
table
1929

**FIGURE 23-1**

Labor Party in England became strong enough to gain control of the government for a time. It was also a period when women finally achieved the right to vote and when the youth movement and the so-called Jazz Age dominated society news.

In France the war and its aftermath had an even more terrible effect in that the male elite among the youth of France were dead and the country weakened and unstable. Every attempt was made to return Paris to center stage as a mecca for artists and writers and a cultural center for the Western world, but the country's heart was heavy beneath the facade of gaiety.

In Italy the fierceness of the war in northern Italy and the demise of bordering monarchies caused government instability that led to the rise of dictatorship in 1923 under Benito Mussolini, nominally prime minister to the king, but in reality in complete control of the country.

Germany, which had entered the war with hope high and flags waving, came out exhausted, bitter, and defeated; the same instability reigned during the Weimar Republic as was evident in Italy before the rise of Mussolini. Thus the 1920s produced a society of decadence, insecurity, and instability in Germany that barely resisted the threats to its existence—such as castastrophic inflation and attempted fascist coups.

In the United States, which had finally been pushed into world affairs by its entry into the war, the aftermath brought a return to conservatism, "business-as-usual" capitalism, and a default on the commitments that President Wilson had made to the League of Nations. The explosive party atmosphere of the youth movement and the Jazz Age was complicated by the Prohibition Amendment which was violated by almost everyone and led to bootlegging, racketeers, and a great increase in lawlessness. But this age of "flaming youths and reckless maids" with its wild parties, bathtub gin, sex magazines, lipstick, rolled stockings, and Freudian analysis came to an abrupt end with the stock market crash of 1929, which brought on a depression that would last for years.

## THE BASIC COSTUME SILHOUETTE

Although art nouveau illustration, decoration, and furnishings dominated the world of upper-class Western culture by 1900, it was not until 1911 that a major and abrupt change toward art nouveau lines came in fashion, or more specifically in female fashion. Partly this was due to the rising interest in the women's suffrage movement, partly to the great rage for the Russian Ballet that was sweeping Paris at the time, and partly because the rush of modern ideas in all the arts was reaching a peak of hot experimentation at this moment. Suffice it to say that in 1910, the female image was still that of the "princess" or "queen" set apart from modern life in corset, layered fabric and lace, floor-length gown, and great picture hat. Then in 1912 a tremendous change occurred. The shimmering vision of the "queen" or "princess" gave way to the *femme fatale,* or vamp, in an evening gown that often had no sleeves, few seams, little shaping, and almost no underpin-

ning—all calculated to allow free, sensuous, relaxed movement. Take, for example, an evening gown design for the new dance craze, the tango, that swept Europe just before World War I (Fig. 23-2). In this fashion drawing for 1914, both the costume and the rendering technique have moved sharply into the modern world with a look bordering between the established art nouveau ideals and the coming ideals of art deco. Here there is no escape into an illusion or a removed-from-reality feminine ideal. This fashion drawing stresses the active attributes of the female body and stresses a lithe slimness instead of rounded fullness of form. The halo of hair of the 1900s has given way to a turban and short hair; the lines of decoration are bold, flat stripes; all trim except for an osprey plume has been put aside; and we have a strong, clear, flat-pattern silhouette that stresses a tall, cylindrical form and lithe movement. Thus as early as 1912 the basic body line

(a)
Windsor cap
1920s

(b)
round collar, silk cravat
1913

(c)
soft buttoned-down
collar attached
to shirt
1929

informal
evening
wear or
tuxedo with
satin shawl
collar
1912

(d)

raccoon
coat
1928

(e)

(f)
heavy
double-breasted
overcoat
1912

(g)
double-breasted
day vest
1920

(i)
elastic-sided
shoe
1912

(k)
gaiters
or
spats
1911–1925

(h)
stiff shirt and
collar, white silk
evening vest
1912

"plus fours"
or
Oxford
bags
with
patterned
golf
hose
1927

(j)

Fashion designs by C. Barbier for the *Journal des Dames et des Modes,* January 1, 1914. Illustrates the dramatic revolution in female dress that took place between 1911 and 1914. Note the sheathlike simplicity of the tunic dress to the left and the turban with osprey plumes; in the center note the lampshade top skirt over the tight hobble skirt with a turban and a feather for the close-cropped head. Photo courtesy of the Bertarelli Collection, Milan.

formal
evening
dress
with
black
patent
leather
pumps

(o)

(p)
World War I
soldier

(l)
snap brim felt
1924

(m)
Panama
straw
1911

(n)
smart battered
felt—collegiate
1925

**FIGURE 23–2**

(a) brassiere and girdle 1913

(b) dolman wrap 1912

(c) Empire revival evening dress 1911

(d) brocade and velvet shoe 1919

patent leather and kid 1912

(e) at-home evening negligee trimmed with maribou 1923

(f) foundation garment 1929

(g) hobble skirt 1912

(h) shingle cut 1923

(i) lampshade skirt 1914

(j) monkey fur cape 1920

(k) riding habit 1925

(l) straw cloche 1923

(m) wrapped coiffure 1914

(n) tennis dress 1928

(o) evening 1916

Fashion plate entitled *At the Theatre,* 1924. Note the emphasis in both male and female fashions and hairdressing on a sleek, cylindrical, machine-made, mannequin look. Note the boyish, no-waist look of the woman with the tall willowy pose and the sleek fit of the men's suits. From an advertisement in the collection of the author.

**FIGURE 23–3**

and dress shape was established that would prevail through the 1920s, despite the many yearly fashion changes decreed by the fashion houses of Paris.

For men there was less change, merely a gradual removal of the formalities remaining from the Victorian and Edwardian Periods. Gradually wing collars disappeared except for full morning or evening dress; the frock coat diminished in use and then disappeared; and the top hat was finally reserved for formal evening and morning dress, and the business suit became the standard daytime wear for all and changed only minimally during these years.

A few other changes included the emergence of the rounded or angular-tipped, turnover collar in place of the standing collar, the triumph of the *slouch* or *fedora hat* over the bowler, the almost complete disappearance of spats and high buttoned shoes in favor of the standard oxfords, and the slimming of the silhouette (Fig. 23–3). There was also a continued increase in the variety of sporting clothes available, particularly in the *plusfours* or *Oxford bags* for golfing, the simpler and more practical swimsuits, the beginning development of ski clothing, and the relaxed shirts and slacks for tennis.

The year 1912 was roughly the watershed in female fashion as functionalism began to triumph over complexity of line and excess of decoration. With the introduction of the kimono, draped dresses and coats fell loosely about the body. Daytime skirts became shorter in order to facilitate movement and decrease cleaning problems. By the time that women's suffrage became a fact in the United States, one could directly see the change toward efficiency in female fashion. After World War I straight lines, short hair, and boyish shapes became the feminine ideal, and by 1923 feminine fashions had developed a short, absolutely straight dress hanging from the shoulders, often without sleeves and with a waist dropped to the hips. The curves of the body were ignored, and the female form was treated as a tube without bust, hips or waist. The hair was cut short in an *Eton crop* or bobbed, and the *cloche* hat fitted down tightly over the ears and almost covered the eyebrows. A very revealing image is presented by the fashion drawing *At the Theatre* (Fig. 23–3). The smooth, machine-made look to the sketch itself gives a clue to the new fashion ideal—men and women seen as smooth cylinders with only a few undulating curves, their hair shiny and plastic looking, their bodies conceived of as smoothly oiled, functional artifacts in a geometrically smooth and abstract art deco room.

# WORLD WAR I AND THE TWENTIES: EARLY ART DECO COSTUME

**Masculine Dress**  About 1910 men's suits had rather broad shoulders and trousers cut rather wide at the top to create the peg-top look with fairly wide cuffs at the bottom. The dashing younger men often wore striped shirts with white collars and cuffs, and sometimes striped socks were even worn to tie in with the shirt. The more conservative still wore white shirt and collar (Fig. 23–2b). The lapels of the coat were longer than in the past and had a medium width.

During the war years the coats remained fairly long but were more snugly fitted, with shoulders still padded to a square outline. The conservative shirt continued to be plain (white or tinted with color) with attached collar and cuffs. The looser, less-fitted box coat was often worn as a less formal coat than the business suit jacket, and the tuxedo or dinner jacket often replaced tails for semiformal and formal evening wear (Fig. 23–2d).

With the war many male traditions were broken. The shorter length of the khaki tunics worn by soldiers led to the shorter suit and sports jackets for men (Fig. 23–2j). Also the soldiers' use of khaki shirts with collar and cuffs as part of the shirt led to a much greater acceptance of attached shirts and collars for everything but formal evening dress (Fig. 23–2c). Evening dress shirts were less stiffly starched and sometimes had a pleated front rather than a cardboard-stiff front inset (Fig. 23–2h). Belted jackets somewhat like the older Norfolk jacket became popular, and the sport jacket or blazer in which the trousers did not match the jacket were frequently seen. In the summer, jackets were usually unlined and made of cotton, linen, or alpaca; if worn with a vest, the latter was usually of piqué. White piqué or ribbed silk vests were the standard with tails for evening.

In the 1920s the male suit was much slimmer and sleeker in cut and usually of only medium length with medium-width lapels tapered to a fairly deep V in front. Sleeves were set smoothly in the armseye without fullness, and belted backs were popular. For a time silk shirts, pale or striped, were in vogue, but by 1925 cotton shirts had returned, usually with attached collars and cuffs and lightly starched (Fig. 23–2c). By the end of the decade many of these shirt collars had bone or celluloid stays to keep the collar points stiffly in position. Very conservative men often preferred the rounded, turnover collar. The four-in-hand tie was done in a small, single knot and held in place by a tie clip, although small bow ties were also popular. Colors throughout this period were generally conservative, with dark blue and brown predominating. Pin stripes and salt-and-pepper tweeds were also popular. The prince of Wales, quite a style-setter in the early 1920s (Fig. 23–4a,b,c,d), popularized the short-waisted, double-breasted waistcoat (Fig. 23–2g), often figured to match a diamond-patterned dress shirt. This was worn with either a winged or turn-down collar and a stiffly starched bow tie.

Trousers throughout the period usually matched the coat, except in summer wear, sporting outfits, and with blazers. The latter, in dark blue or grey, was often worn with plain trousers in cream or white, or striped trousers in grey flannel or serge. Trousers, after the brief vogue of the peg-top line from 1910 to 1912, returned to a straight line with moderately wide cuffs. A slightly slimmer trouser line prevailed during the 1920s, except at the very beginning of the decade when the prince of Wales popularized wide trousers pleated at the waist to go with his double-breasted waistcoats.

In 1924 the very wide sporting trousers, known as *Oxford bags,* appeared (Fig. 23–2j), sometimes measuring 26 inches at the knee and about 24 inches around the cuffs (Fig. 23–4a). Bell-bottomed, slimhipped Argentine *gaucho pants* came into brief vogue in the early 1920s, due to the films of Rudolph Valentino.

As for outercoats the loose, box overcoat was the most popular in either a tweed or some woolen mixture, while a black overcoat was standard for dress wear (Fig. 23–2f). Some of the more youthful overcoats had raglan sleeves and were often belted. Especially after the war the belted overcoat was popular for awhile as a reflection of the belted trench coat. About 1928 the oilskin coat and Cape Cod hat worn by fishermen were suddenly adopted by the young for rainy weather, and the raccoon coat became popular with young men for football games and riding in open cars (Fig. 23–2e).

In footwear, stockings for the more daring were often in bright colors, striped, dotted, or with clocked designs. Plain stockings in silk or lisle were used by the more conservative, and the standard conservative color was black (black was always used for evening). Oxford shoes were now the standard, although for a brief time about 1910 the bulldog shoe with thick soles and high rounded heels was popular with the young. Throughout the war years white canvas or buckskins were used for summer, while high laced or elastic-sided shoes were used among the conservative in winter (Fig. 23–2i). Spats all but disappeared by 1914, except for the very dapper (Fig. 23–2k).

Haircuts were quite short, and a side part was favored, although the pompadour effect was also seen. Trimmed mustaches were seen on older men, but the young were now completely clean shaven. Beards were completely gone except for a few grandfathers. During the 1920s the center part for men returned, and great stress was placed on the hair looking like a shiny, plastic cap in the way it was pomaded to the head. This was partially due to the great influence of Rudolph Valentino, whose black hair was plastered slickly to his head in all of his films.

In hats the felt slouch hat or fedora led all

**FIG. 23–4 a b c d**  Four photos of the Prince of Wales; late 1920s. Note the use of *plus fours,* the new knee-length baggy pants for golf (a); the slim lines to the suit (b); the riding pants flared at the thigh (c); and the aviator goggles and overcoat for flying (d). Photos courtesy of The Culver Picture Service.

others in popularity (Fig. 23–21,n), while the bowler was seen only on the very conservative or effete. The straw boater or Panama was worn in the summer (Fig. 23–2m), and collapsible silk top hats were worn with evening dress (Fig. 23–2o). Rudolph Valentino also had an influence on men's headgear by wearing the broad-brimmed, black Argentine gaucho hat, especially for the tango. Thus modified versions of this hat appeared for dashing young men, and even businessmen tilted their fedoras to approximate the line of the Valentino gaucho hat.

World War I brought a tremendous change in the nature of the military uniform. Khaki-colored wool was now standard for the Allied armies, while the Germans wore a dark grey (*feldgrau*). The reason for the change from more colorful uniforms was the need for low visibility in the new trench-style warfare. The standard pieces were the high-necked tunic with or without belt; riding pants with wrapped *puttees,* leggings, or boots; and a visored cap or flat, two-pieced trench cap. Only officers wore belts and pistols and for dress occasions a sword (Fig. 23–2p).

***Feminine Dress*** In the nine years that covered the rise to war and the making of the peace, the major item of dress was probably the skirt. In 1910 and 1911 the princess or empire line was very popular with a long, unbroken line from a slightly-higher-than-normal waist to the knee, which tended to increase the size of the waist and to decrease the size of the hips (Fig. 23–3c). Front panels in skirts also tended to emphasize this slim line, as did draping low at the back of the figure and gathering to a band at the bottom of the skirt. Then in 1911 and 1912 draping became even more important with one-half of the front crossed over a lightly draped other side, sometimes with a skirt gathered up in tiers above the knee in a *lampshade,* or modified panier, effect (Fig. 23–3i). All of the variations stressed narrowness at the bottom of the skirt or dress and thus gave rise to the so-called *hobble* look, which made women move with very small steps (Fig. 23–3g). By 1912 the kimono look arrived in earnest, and for a moment the dress, cut all in one including

sleeves, superseded the blouse and skirt ensemble. The fashion design for the evening dress of 1914 for dancing the tango is unique in its straight lines, simple cut, and bold, flat pattern (Fig. 23–2).

Much the same willowy lines in a daytime suit may be seen in a fashion design for 1914 (Fig. 23–5). It is surprisingly modern and seems impossible as a fashion line as early as the beginning of World War I. It proves that at the outbreak of the war, certain far-reaching

**FIG. 23–5** Fashion illustration from the *Journal des Dames et des Modes,* 1914. Note the remarkable change in female fashion lines already apparent by 1914. The line is sleek, tubular, soft, with a dropped waist and little sense of underpinning—all this a decade before the styles of the 1920s. Photo courtesy of the Bertarelli Collection, Milan.

changes had already been achieved in female dress that were not to be consolidated until well into the 1920s. Here the loose tunic top to the suit, the low sash at the hips, and the slim, pencil line to the skirt—as well as the casual look of hair, hat, shoes, and pose—present us with the modern woman.

Although this image was simple and appealing, at the very same time there were many effects that were more exaggerated and quite ridiculous. For example, two designs presented by Le Louvre Department Store in Paris for 1914 are a case in point (Fig. 23-6). The one at the left wears a lampshade skirt that flares out just above the knee to frame a slim underskirt below, while the other wears a fitted jacket that is reminiscent of the French Revolution over a hobble skirt that narrows sharply at the ankle. Both are in bold, bright colors with a use of checks and stripes as accent.

During the war the line became boxier, and skirts began to rise to the ankle or above. Many effects were borrowed from the uniforms of the period, particularly belts, pockets, collars for jackets, and some blouses. There were still some skirts with tiered ruffles and a spreading line from waist to mid-calf, but the general line was square and boxy. By 1919 the dropped waistline, briefly seen in the suit for 1914, definitely arrived as a major accent. The general line was now rather tubular, with a stress on soft draping and almost no stress on the bust, which was now obscured or even flattened (Fig. 23-7).

But we must go back for a moment and look at bodices and shirtwaists during this period. At the beginning of the period the shirtwaist or jacket followed a *bolero,* or Eton jacket, look with cut-in-one kimono sleeves with much pleating, draping, and soft folds. For daytime wear a surplice, cross-over style was often seen with a deep V in front and back that was filled in with ruffles, with more ruffles on the sleeves; this remained until about 1916. With the coming of the war the waist was cut in plain, boxy lines with cross straps, berthas, or pleated ruffles to give decoration. The waistline itself, which had started high in 1911 and was slightly raised until 1914, was rather blousy by 1916 and lower than normal after the war. Specific

FIG. 23-6  Fashions for Le Louvre Department Store, 1914. Illustrates some of the *hobble skirt* and *lampshade skirt* effects that were high fashion just before the outbreak of the war. Note the use of stripes, the willowy poses, and the contrast between the laced sandal shoes and the older, button variety. Photo courtesy of the Musée Carnavalet, Paris.

blouses that showed a relationship to the war were the *Russian style* and the *middy sailor blouse.*

Sleeves throughout this period were often cut in the kimono line and were shorter in the daytime than in the past, usually just above or below elbow length—although quite short and full-length sleeves were also seen. Evening gowns were usually completely without sleeves.

The coats followed much the same lines as the dresses, with great stress placed on lozenge-shaped coats with sleeves as part of the body of the coat (Fig. 23-3b). The cuffs were usually of fur as was the high turnover collar. In such coats the fullness was always held to the front of the figure by a single button at the waist. After the opening of the war most women's coats

**FIG. 23-7** Day dresses for 1919. Illustrates the so-called *barrel line* that came into vogue just after the war. Note that the bustline is gone, and women at this time began to wear bust flatteners; also note that the waist is now lowered to the hips. From a photo in the collection of the author.

were cut on a boxy, trench-coat line with deep pockets. Muffs were also used to tie into the fur on coats or to act as an accent with a dress (Fig. 23-5).

Silk stockings were now a necessity since skirts showed the bottom of the leg. Black was the standard color, although there were also dark blue and brown silk stockings. Black or white lace was frequent for evening stockings. Low oxfords and pumps now superseded the high-button shoe, and a Cuban heel height was favored except for evening (Fig. 23-3d).

Hair during the years before the war was usually full and swept around the head, finishing in a knot at the top back (Fig. 23-3m). Frequently the hair was confined by a ribbon or band (Fig. 23-3o). After 1914 the fullness flattened, any padding or ratting disappeared, and the hair was arranged snugly to the head with a puff or two pulled forward over the ears. Bobbed hair also made its appearance and became the standard style by the opening of the 1920s.

In 1911 hats were still large with plumes and feathers but were quickly superseded by the beehive or mushroom hats that completely enveloped the head and hair. Various toques without brims or with small turned-up brims were seen during the years from 1912 to 1919,

and for evening there was a great rage for tight caps and turbans (Fig. 23-2). Most hats were still decorated with small plumes and feathers, but the great age of plumage excess had passed.

The nine years before the stock market crash of 1929 was the period of the one-piece dress, with little use of the shirtwaist and skirt combination that had been so popular earlier. The underpinning for this one-piece, shapeless dress was a kind of elasticized corset which began below the normal waistline and ended above the knees (Fig. 23-3f). Garters attached to silk stockings held this cylindrical, body-shaping arrangement in control, and the young often would not wear such corsets, or *foundations,* or would slip out of them at dances for freer movement. Usually a vest and elastic-topped panties were worn under the foundation, and a slim petticoat was worn over it. The vest was cut straight across at the top with thin straps over the shoulder to keep the vest up. If the bust was medium to large, a bust confiner, or *brassiere,* was worn under the vest to make the bust line all but invisible. Thus the line of the 1920s, in general, was tubular with a slight accent at the hips—a reflection of the new freedom for women, a turn away from the historical hourglass figure, and a sign of the new love of machine shapes and efficiency.

The top or waist part of the 1920's dress began the decade with a rounded or square neckline, long open-cuffed sleeves that were often cut kimono fashion into the dress, and a bodice section that was either a fold-over surplice effect or a straight fall to a blouse at the hips (Fig. 23–3e). Good examples of this tubular, boxy line with abstract decoration geometrically applied may be seen in designs by Doucet for 1922 (Fig. 23–8).

As the 1920s progressed, the waist kept slipping lower until in 1925 it was at the lowest point on the hips. Around 1925 a slight variation in the neckline was introduced with the open V-neck edged with a turnover collar. Still another variation was the use of a bertha effect over the shoulders as in the seventeenth century. From 1925 through 1929 the low waistline was often slanted on a diagonal, ending in a bow or flowers either at the top or bottom of the diagonal. Tunic blouses were also popular and often reached well below the hips with rectangular panels often used down the front to emphasize the narrow, boxy line. Sleeves after 1925 were either long and closefitting, bell shaped and open, or short and ending well above the elbows.

Evening dresses were cut with round or V-necks or slightly draped at the shoulder and were often held up by the narrowest of shoulder straps. Sometimes they were caught at the hip with a flower, ribbon, bow, or other ornament, but often the dress fell straight from the shoulder to the calf. Many of these latter evening dresses were heavily covered with beading that was the major decorative accent and also gave the dress great weight. An excellent example of a sophisticated and somewhat decadent evening ensemble may be seen in the famous portrait of *Mme. Jasmy Alvin* (Fig. 23–9).

Although the skirt was usually part of a dress and not a separate item during most of this period, it may help to look at it separately, especially as to length. The length varied greatly

**FIG. 23-8**  Designs by Doucet; illustration from *La Gazette du Bon Ton,* 1922. Illustrates the new short, *bobbed* hair styles, the long cylindrical line without a waist or with the waist on the hips, the lack of a defined bustline, the use of the *cloche* hat, and the pointed toe and rounded instep with strap of the typical 1920s shoe. Photo courtesy of the Bertarelli Collection, Milan.

tle pleating, but for evening there was much emphasis on an uneven hem, diagonal draping, layering, and scalloped edges. Finally in 1928 and 1929 the skirts became a little longer, and the waistline moved slightly upward (Fig. 23-10).

Coats of the 1920s followed the same lines as the dresses—that is, they were short, cut without fullness, with high collars and deep revers. Sometimes the coat matched the dress

**FIG. 23-9** Kees van Dongen, *Portrait of Madame Jasmy Alvin;* Museum of Modern Art, Paris; 1925. The portrait has a hard, decadent, masculine quality that subordinates the beaded ornamentation to the straight, functional lines of the gown. The image created combines the unnatural, abstract effects found in the Egyptian bust of Nefertiti with a dehumanized, functional androgyny. Photo courtesy of the French Musées Nationaux.

during these nine years as did width of cut, although the effect was always short and shapeless by comparison with the past. In 1920 it was still fairly full with ruffles or draping about the lowered waist; scallops and pointed edges were used on light silk skirts. By 1921 to 1922 the side panel or cascade of fabric at the side of the figure was introduced, extending below the edge of the skirt. Then followed tiers of ruffles, side pleats, and diagonal layers. By 1925 the skirt was tight and narrow but just barely below the knee, and then in 1927 the skirt length went above the knee. For daytime, skirts were rather plain, relatively narrow, and possibly had a lit-

**FIG. 23-10** Photo of Madame Lucien Lelong; 1929. This evening dress and wrap of 1929 illustrates the lengthening of the skirt through insets, side pieces, and uneven hemlines. Note the hanging sleeve borrowed from the medieval past and the changing coiffure with a side part and longer waves over the ears. Photo courtesy of the BBC Hulton Picture Library.

and was cut like a long tunic open down the front with a single button at the low waistline. These two-piece ensembles—tunic coat over tunic dress—were often in satin or silk, and the coat was frequently trimmed with fur on collars and cuffs. One very unique coat of the period was the shaggy monkey fur coat, usually made of imitation monkey fur (Fig. 23–3j).

Silk stockings were a must during this period, although now there were silk substitutes. A flesh color in silk stockings was in great vogue among the young around 1924. Conservative women still preferred brown, grey, or even black silk stockings. In shoes, oxfords with a Cuban heel were used for everyday, while dress shoes had more pointed toes and a strap across the ankle. By 1925 many dress pumps were even more pointed and often had a French heel (Fig. 23–3d).

At the opening of the 1920s the hair was arranged in soft waves about the face, but soon the advocates of short, bobbed hair began to dominate the fashion scene. The very short, Eton crop that made the female head look exactly like that of a young schoolboy became fashionable (Fig. 23–3h), and the most fashionable was to have the ends of the bob curve up over the cheek. By 1928 bobbed hair had a bit more fullness with waves across the forehead, and this was rivaled by the so-called *windblown* bob.

Hats had deep crowns and a rolled brim pulled low over the eyes, and all hats were worn so low on the head that all of the forehead and ears were covered (Fig. 23–3l). There were a few wide-brimmed, transparent, wired hats for spring and summer garden parties, but the standard was the cloche hat plucked close around the ears. In 1925 hats were smaller and tighter, flaring open around the face and extending to the base of the neck in back to hide the clipped base of the hair.

As for sports, tennis dresses usually had a boxy top with thin shoulder straps and an accordion-pleated skirt to just above the knees (Fig. 23–3n). Bathing suits consisted of a knitted, tight-fitting jersey tunic with a skirt covering the hips and tight, knitted jersey mid-thigh shorts underneath. In 1922 the world of fashion was given the beach pajama suit which by the end of the decade was even found in the drawing room. Most innovative of all were ski outfits, which consisted of knitted cloth tunics to just above the knee with knitted trousers that fitted into ankle-high ski boots, and riding habits which resembled those worn by men (Fig. 23–3k).

## FABRICS

Materials during the period from 1911 to 1929 were the standard choices from the past including various silks, satin, velvet, taffeta, brocade, chiffon, faille, jersey, organdy, crepe, and stiffeners like buckram, crinoline, and tarlatan. The new items that made at least a peripheral impact were the synthetic items such as rayon or cellophane or combinations like silkolite or silkaline. There was more use of metal in fabric, and thus lamé became a major item for evening dresses and coats as did allover beaded decoration. Cottons were most prevalent for daytime wear, particularly in spring and summer, as well as linens for summer and the standard range of woolens for winter.

## ARTS AND ARTIFACTS

The furniture and interiors that had developed toward the end of the first decade of the twentieth century had stressed either the new sophisticated growth line of art nouveau or the heavy, natural, wooden forms of the mission or crafts- man style. Thus in the years before World War I, there continued to be a stress on natural woods, leather upholstery, and simple, flat patterns in wallpaper and furniture upholstery that mirrored in their motifs the gradual shift from art nouveau to art deco. During the 1920s natural surfaces were somewhat replaced by smooth plastic, metal, or artificial wood or stone surfaces. The stress was on machine-made smoothness with great weight on cylindrical, cubed, and rectangular forms. Even when past periods in furniture and ornamental interior accessories were copied, they were simplified, mechanized, and smoothed to a hard, reflective finish (Fig. 23-1a,b,c,d,e). The only past period style that commanded great respect among the conservatives of the 1920s without much adaptation was the Tudor style; whole houses were paneled and furnished in copies of Tudor interiors.

Personal ornaments and accessories for men during this period included the new wristwatches that gradually replaced the pocket watch, handkerchiefs worn in the upper left pocket of the suit jacket, pigskin or chamois gloves for driving, leather pocketbooks, small canes with gold knobs or crook handle tops, the jeweled pin that held the four-in-hand tie, and the standard gold or jeweled studs and cuff links. The beret was sometimes donned for motoring, and sweaters were in great favor, with pullovers for the younger men and but-toned cardigans for older men to wear about the house. The war brought greater use of the scarf or muffler as a decorative accent as well as for cold weather and greater use of cigarettes and the cigarette case.

For women during this period the major accessory was the vanity box, the forerunner of the compact which held powder, a powder puff, and a mirror. This was often carried in the purse or handbag (which was usually rectangular and carried by leather handles). Women also, after the model of nurses and Red Cross workers during the war, began to wear wristwatches. After the war berets also became fashionable for motoring—having been copied from the dashing headpieces worn by Alpine troops. Cigarettes had been a staple item for the soldier, and these, too, began to be fashionable for upper-class women after the war, as did the cigarette case. The neck scarf became a major decorative accent about 1925, and in the mid-1920s artificial flowers, long dangling earrings, locket necklaces, and large pocketbooks also became important. For evening a major decorative accent was the jeweled headband, or *bandeaux,* for the hair (Fig. 23-3e).

## VISUAL SOURCES

The best visual sources for this period are photographs and fashion illustrations, although there are a few artists who are helpful. Among the latter are van Dongen, Bonnard, Vuillard, Chagall, Grosz, Kirchner, Schmidt-Rottluff, Maxfield Parrish, and Dufy. The best magazines are *Harper's, Vogue, Life, Illustrated London News, International Studio, Connoisseur, Studio Esquire, Ladies' Home Journal, Good Housekeeping,* and *Sears, Roebuck Catalog.* The best institutional sources are the Metropolitan Museum of Art, the Bibliothèque Nationale, the Bertarelli Collection, the Collection Union Francaise des Arts du Costume, Collection Sirot, and the New York Public Library. Useful written references are Martin Battersby's *The Decorative Twenties,* Joel Colton's *Twentieth Century,* and Time-Life's *This Fabulous Century, 1910–1920* and *1920–1930.*

## SUMMARY

This was a period during which fashion, particularly for women, moved sharply into the modern world. In 1911 the remainders of the "grand dame" image still remained with many of the decorative effects that had been in existence since the Victorian Age. By the end of the 1920s women had made an immense shift toward Woman as an active, boyish, "streamlined" figure who reflected the new age of speed, efficiency, and worship of the machine.

Because of the Great War the old, upper-class, slow-paced, genteel way of life was replaced by a sleek, action-oriented, superficial sophistication. The old culture which had been interested in mood, impression, and a larger-than-life romantic ideal disappeared in favor of a new culture in which smooth efficiency, speed, and machine imagery were dominant—an age in which the human figure was both freed from the strictures of the past and subordinated to the textures and forms of the new machine age.

# chapter *XXIV*

# *The Thirties and World War II:*

# *Late Art Deco*

*Chronology*

(1929–1945)

| | | |
|---|---|---|
| THE THIRTIES 1929–1939 | 1929 | Papal State recreated; Tacna-Arica Treaty |
| | 1930 | Le Corbusier completes the Savoye House |
| | 1931 | Japan invades Manchuria; Spain becomes a republic |
| | 1932 | Lindbergh baby is kidnapped; Gandhi fasts and passively resists the British control in India; Roosevelt elected president of the United States |
| | 1933 | Bank "holidays"; gold retired from circulation; Long Beach earthquake; epidemic of gangsterism in the U.S.; capture of Dillinger and other public enemies; Hitler made chancellor with dictatorial powers in Germany |

1934        King Albert of Belgium killed in a mountain accident; New Deal begins to blossom in the U.S.; Philippine independence is granted; longshoremen's strike in U.S.; Dionne quintuplets born in Canada

1931

1935        Will Rogers is killed in an Alaskan air crash; Italian-Ethiopian War begins

1936        George V dies and is succeeded by Edward VIII; army mutiny in Japan; German troops occupy the Rhineland; "sit-down" strikes in France and elsewhere; soldier's bonus granted in the U.S.; great floods in the Ohio and Mississippi valleys; Bruno Hauptmann electrocuted for the Lindbergh baby murder; President Roosevelt on a trip to South America; the Spanish Civil War begins; abdication of Edward VIII and accession of George VI in England

1937        Coronation of George VI, May 12; the Duke of Windsor marries Wallis Warfield Simpson, June 3; Ramsay MacDonald dies; industrial "sit-down" strikes in U.S.; C.I.O. agitation; controversy over the reorganization of the Supreme Court of the U.S.; Amelia Earhart is lost; quarrel between the C.I.O. and the A.F.L.; U.S. gunboat *Panay* is bombed and three Americans are killed by the Japanese; Marconi dies; John D. Rockefeller, Sr. dies; Mussolini visits Hitler; Japanese enter Peking

1937

1938        Austria annexed by Hitler; continuing struggle of China against Japan

WORLD WAR II
1939–1945

1939

1942

| | |
|---|---|
| 1939 | Danzig annexed by Hitler; September 1, World War II begins with the invasion of Poland; earlier in the year Czechoslovakia annexed by Hitler; nonaggression pact signed with Russia |
| 1940 | Denmark, Norway, Belgium, the Netherlands, and northern France are subdued by Hitler; the *Luftwaffe* bombs London, Coventry, and other key cities in the Battle of Britain; Lend-Lease is established from the U.S. to Allies; the U.S. institutes Selective Service |
| 1941 | Japan makes a sneak attack on Pearl Harbor; U.S. enters the war on the side of the Allies; the U.S. institutes rationing and an immense program of military and industrial development; Germany invades Russia |
| 1942 | Atomic fission demonstrated on a laboratory scale; terrible air, sea, and beach battles in the South Pacific; Battle of Stalingrad; high point of Hitler's conquests; battles in North Africa |
| 1943 | Conquest of North Africa and Italy by the Allies with American help brings Italy's surrender in September; victory at Stalingrad; penicillin becomes major new medicine of the war |
| 1944 | Invasion of Brittany and Normandy by the Allies on June 6; late in the year Belgium and the Netherlands liberated; computers developed |
| 1945 | First large-scale atomic explosions at Los Alamos; Allies cross the Rhine, and on May 8 the war in Europe ends; in August atomic bombs are dropped on Japan; Japanese surrender September 2; United Nations founded in San Francisco |

# BACKGROUND

The 1930s were born prematurely and disastrously in October, 1929, with the crash of the New York stock market, and the events of that day were to affect millions of people throughout the Western world for a decade. In the days and months that succeeded that fateful date in October, the bubble of hectic gaiety and the delusion of prosperity for all was completely exploded, and a decade of hardship and depression followed. The arts survived under the patronage of government and wealthy citizens but made few forward strides. In most cases the ideals of the postwar period were consolidated and expanded, while the popular arts under the label of *art deco* spread and increased the image of interiors, furnishings, clothing, and artifacts as extensions of a slick, polished, "streamlined" machine world. This progress of art deco led from a period of austerity and simplicity in the early part of the decade to a moment of fantasy and romanticism just before the outbreak of World War II. Paris was still the center of the art deco movement through its great decorative expositions and the dominance of its fashion houses, but London and New York were not far behind. Also, because the one entertainment that everyone during the depression could afford was the cinema, Hollywood became a major source of style ideas in clothing, interiors, and artifacts.

With the outbreak of World War II and the occupation of France, there was a complete break in style. During the war years most ideas in clothing and the decorative arts were inspired by the military or the great military-industrial complex that developed in the United States. The war drained all inspiration away from the arts to the mammoth undertaking of winning a war that stretched over every major area of the globe for almost six years. When it ended in 1945 with the atomic bombing of Hiroshima and Nagasaki, the world was both exhausted and shocked to the core of its being by the terrible physical power that had been unleashed on Japan. The impact of the bomb on the soul of humankind was far greater than the actual physical impact of the atomic bomb itself.

If one were to choose an interior from this period to suggest the "streamlined," functional, machinelike background for living that was the ideal for the artistic avante-garde, the famed Tugendhat House in Brno, Czechoslovakia, designed by Miës van der Rohe, one of the most admired architects in the new international style, would be an excellent example (Fig. 24–1). Here in the dining room we can see the influence of the famed Bauhaus style based on a "machine aesthetic" in which all decoration or ornament-as-frosting has been eschewed. What we have is beauty through form and function alone, with the house conceived as a machine for living. Living spaces are not divided by solid walls but by panels or screens that allow space to flow in and around the objects and people in the room. The organization of the room is intended to facilitate the normal functioning of human movement inside the room, so that it can be thought of as a "machine for living." Even the furniture has a smooth, cold, geometric, abstract, machinelike quality that makes it look efficient even though it does not always seem to be designed for the contours of the human body or to please the natural human interest in warm textures and human emotions. The human being is here subordinated to abstract ideals of efficiency, organization, maximum output for energy expended, and other industrial considerations.

Politically the decade of the 1930s was very unstable and filled with revolutions, invasions, dictatorships, and the final weakening of the already weak and impotent League of Nations. Early in the decade there was the Japanese invasion of Manchuria and later China, and the overthrow of the monarchy in Spain. Then in 1933, at the height of the depression in the U.S. and Great Britain, Hitler was made chancellor of Germany by the aged President Hindenburg and proceeded to turn Germany into a powerful military dictatorship. Mussolini had already been a dictatorial leader in Italy for a decade under a puppet king, and when the Spanish Civil War broke out in 1936, both Mussolini and Hitler assisted the insurgent leader, Francisco Franco, with military and air power in

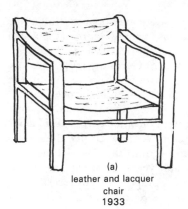

(a)
leather and lacquer
chair
1933

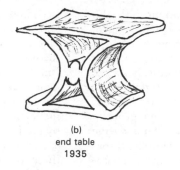

(b)
end table
1935

(c)
lamp
1935

(d)
carpet
pattern

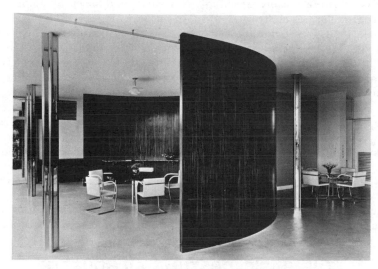

(e)
carpet
pattern

Miës van der Rohe; Dining Room of the Tugendhat House, Brno, Czechoslovakia; 1930. Illustrates
the architectural preoccupation with simple, cool,
abstract, geometric space blocks, enhanced by textures like chrome, marble, onyx, and ebony, that
marked progressive house design during the 1930s.
Photo courtesy of the Museum of Modern Art, New
York.

(f)
vase
with
curved
handles
1932

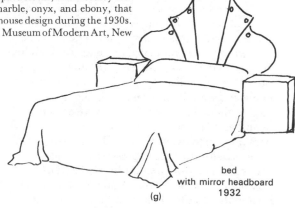

(g)

bed
with mirror headboard
1932

**FIGURE 24–1**

427

order to test their new military might. Italy also invaded Ethiopia in Africa, and the League of Nations displayed its powerlessness when it tried to halt the invasions. In the Soviet Union Stalin, who had been the Russian leader since the death of Lenin, consolidated his power and extended it through ruthless purges that were to cause shock waves throughout the growing communist parties of the world. Thus by the mid-1930s Europe and Asia were in the throes of military aggression, dictatorship, and ruthless repression. To escape from the bad news from abroad and the depression at home, Americans and Western Europeans turned to the cinema, and particularly to Hollywood, for an escape; the late 1930s, just before the outbreak of World War II, became a lush period for film production. While Hitler was establishing concentration camps, developing military plans, and rounding up Jews, the common people in Western Europe and in America were focusing on the lavish musical spectacles produced by Hollywood. While the terrible purges in Russia developed and the troops of General Franco wiped out, with German and Italian support, the last vestiges of the Spanish Republic, Hollywood produced some of the most costly escapist spectacles of all time.

With the invasion of Poland the world began to change, and it was soon apparent that a war had begun that was to engulf more of the world and last longer than World War I. Soon with the military power of Germany (supported by Italy) sweeping through Europe, even the Americans began to awaken to the need to support England and the various Allied governments in exile; with the attack on Pearl Harbor by the Japanese in 1941, the United States was catapulted abruptly into the war. In the next three and one-half years there was an all-out mobilization of manpower, resources, and military-industrial strength to defeat the Axis powers, and the entire globe was consumed in one fiery battle after another until the invasion of Normany and the defeat of the Germans brought the end in sight. During this period little thought was given to arts and culture or the normal details of politics—all effort was devoted to winning the war. Even films, novels, and fashions were either devoted to supporting the war or strongly influenced by military ideals. Then it all came to a horrifying conclusion, not completely recognized at the time due to the euphoria caused by the war's end, with the unleashing of the new atom bomb on Japan. The atomic bombing of Hiroshima and Nagasaki set off a psychological explosion in the mind of humankind that is still present today.

## THE BASIC COSTUME SILHOUETTE

With the coming of the depression, the saucy, boyish flair in women's clothing and the sleek look in men's dress came to an end. Fashion, particularly for women, seemed to be saying that the mad, flapper party was over and that a somewhat more conservative image, although still within the sleek, efficient, streamlined contours of the machine age, had been reinstated. The waist went back to normal, skirts lengthened to the ankle, long sleeves were seen once again, and the sexy, erogenous zone shifted from the legs to the bare back. Thus during the economic slump of the depression and the political repressions of the rise of Hitler, fashion took a slightly more sober course than it had during the 1920s. For men it meant a less smooth, sleek line with more stress on square-

ness, bulk, and padding, giving the male silhouette a boxy rather than a tubular look. In fact, except for the very fashionable figures in upper-class society, the average silhouette for this period was basically rather uninteresting—as may be seen in the clothes worn by a group of big city mayors and movie tycoons in the mid-1930s (Fig. 24–2).

By the end of the decade the boxy look had even come to women's clothing with padded shoulders and shorter skirts. With the arrival of World War II the influence of military and industrial uniforms had a major influence on dress. The boxy line of the military tunics, an emphasis on buttons, and a stress on straight lines were particularly apparent in women's clothes during the war, while men's civilian

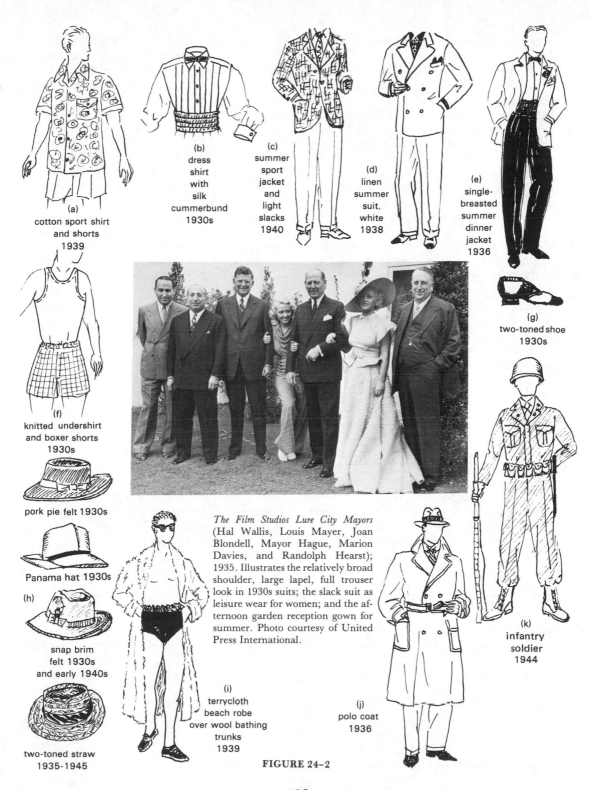

(a)
cotton sport shirt
and shorts
1939

(b)
dress
shirt
with
silk
cummerbund
1930s

(c)
summer
sport
jacket
and
light
slacks
1940

(d)
linen
summer
suit,
white
1938

(e)
single-
breasted
summer
dinner
jacket
1936

(g)
two-toned shoe
1930s

(f)
knitted undershirt
and boxer shorts
1930s

pork pie felt 1930s

Panama hat 1930s

(h)

snap brim
felt 1930s
and early 1940s

two-toned straw
1935-1945

*The Film Studios Lure City Mayors*
(Hal Wallis, Louis Mayer, Joan
Blondell, Mayor Hague, Marion
Davies, and Randolph Hearst);
1935. Illustrates the relatively broad
shoulder, large lapel, full trouser
look in 1930s suits; the slack suit as
leisure wear for women; and the afternoon garden reception gown for
summer. Photo courtesy of United
Press International.

(i)
terrycloth
beach robe
over wool bathing
trunks
1939

(j)
polo coat
1936

(k)
infantry
soldier
1944

**FIGURE 24-2**

429

clothes often followed the general shapes of the military uniforms.

In general, men's clothes during the 1930s and the years of World War II changed only slightly from the styles of the 1920s. The major change was in bulk and squareness. Suit shoulders were padded, there was much more use of the double-breasted coat, pants were wide with deep pleats at the top and large cuffs at the bottom, while fedora hats had very wide brims. The major additions during the depression were in sports clothing and evening dress. In the latter the white dinner jacket for summer was introduced, usually with a *cummerbund* to replace the earlier tuxedo vest, and with all tuxedos the wing collar gave way to the slightly starched turnover. For sports there were now *Bermuda shorts;* open-necked, short-sleeved shirts with or without light scarfs; casual slacks; many varieties of cardigan and pullover sweaters; checked and plain sports jackets; and the new swimming trunks without tops. The new outercoats were the *trench coat,* which had been adapted from the World War I officer's raincoat, and the *polo coat* of camel's hair that had derived from the coat thrown over the shoulders of players after a polo match.

In women's clothing the coming of the crash of 1929 brought an end to the insistent boyishness in dress and a return to slightly more traditional feminine lines—although within the sleek contours of the art deco decorative image. About 1930 evening gowns became much longer again, first at the back and then all the way around; and they were frequently cut on the bias so that they would shape themselves over the bust, hips, and thighs in a clinging series of subtle curves. But the newest form of body emphasis was the backlessness in many evening gowns, a style probably related to the backlessness of new bathing suits. For daytime wear the waist was normal once again, but like the new broad line for the shoulders of men's suits, the women's daytime fashions emphasized broad shoulders and slender hips. Toward the close of the 1930s, skirts began to rise to knee length; hats were either felts with tiny brims, pillboxes, or turbans; and hair was generally parted in the middle and waved and rolled up and to the back. There was also great experimentation in wide slacks, playsuits, tennis dresses, bathing suits, ski costumes, low and platform sandals, and shirtwaist frocks.

With the coming of the war in 1939, the new synthetic fabrics began to make major inroads in fashion, as sources for silk were closed and the utility and convenience of the new synthetics were recognized for their practicality in both civilian and military situations. The all-out effort to mobilize for war also made itself felt in what was left of the world of couturier fashion, and designers such as Mainbocher even turned to creating military uniforms for women that were both practical and yet retained a fashionable line. Women factory workers now found freedom in zippered coveralls, *Levis,* and practical slacks, and women at home shortened their skirts, eliminated metal accessories, and accepted substitutes for all those dress items that were now either scarce or needed in the war effort.

# THE THIRTIES AND WORLD WAR II: LATE ART DECO COSTUME

***Masculine Dress*** The major influence in men's styles in the 1930s came from sports clothing, and thus there was a move away from very dark blue or black suits to the browns, tans, plaids, and stripes in men's suits that had originally been seen only in sport jackets. More suit coats were given side vents rather than one in the center back, sleeves were medium large, lapels quite deep and pointed, pockets were large, and shoulders were padded (Fig. 24–3).

A good example of the general line may be seen in the suits worn by the duke of Gloucester and friends in 1936 (Fig. 24–4). Many more suits were now double-breasted than single-breasted, and for a time in the middle and late 1930s the single-breasted coat was almost exclusively limited to the sports jacket, which came in two- and three-button models with either slit or flap pockets (Fig. 24–2c). Materials used were worsteds, coverts, cheviots,

(a)
classic
evening
gown
1940

(b)
halter
and culottes
1933

(c)
knit and
elastic
foundation
1934

quilted
robe
1937

(d)

Spanish-style
evening
dress
1934

(e)

shirtwaist
dress
1930s

(g)

hat and
scarf
1940
(f)

knitted
cap
1932

(h)

beret
early
1930s

sandals
1936

(i)

platform
sandals
1940

gold
sandals
1935

Six London office workers wearing straw boaters in the rain; 1931. The *straw boater* made a return in the early 1930s only to be replaced later by the *Panama straw*. Note that the number of double-breasted suits is greater than in the 1920s and that trousers are fuller and have larger cuffs. Photo courtesy of the BBC Hulton Picture Library.

bulky
look
in
fur
coats
1939

(j)

(l)
velvet cap
late
1930s

Persian
lamb
cape
and
cap
1935

(k)

**FIGURE 24–3**

431

FIG. 24-4 Duke of Gloucester and automobile dealers at the Standard Motor Company Convention, Coventry; 1936. Note the variety in hats and overcoats. The two hats to the left are moderately wide, snap-brimmed *fedoras,* the center hat is a stiff *Homburg,* and the one to the right is a *bowler.* Both overcoats are double-breasted, and the four-in-hand ties are tied with a single knot. Photo courtesy of the BBC Hulton Picture Library.

flannels, and gabardines. Summer suits were of crash, alpaca, Congo and Palm Beach cloth (Fig. 24–2d) and were often single-breasted, unlined, and with less padding to give added coolness.

Trousers throughout the period were wide with one or two pleats at the waist and with moderate to wide cuffs at the bottom. Sometimes belts were sewn directly to the trousers, and the front fly began to have a zipper instead of buttons after Edward, prince of Wales, popularized the idea in the mid-1930s.

During the war there were many restrictions imposed on male clothing, both in fabric and in cut. Cuffs were often eliminated, along with vests for double-breasted suits. Wool was used primarily for the military, and many wartime suits were a mixture of wool, cotton, and rayon and were sharply rationed.

For evening wear tuxedos were still standard throughout the period but were now often in midnight blue and sometimes in maroon rather than black and were frequently double-breasted. White dinner jackets also appeared as well as the short mess jacket; with such jackets a black or colored sash or cummerbund was worn instead of a vest (Fig. 24–2e). In general, dress

clothes until 1941 had broad shoulders, a full chest, and a fairly slender waist. Tailcoats had the same lines with hip-hugging tails that fell to below the knee. Trousers invariably had a wide satin or grosgrain stripe down the side, and the white silk shirts were usually pleated in front, with one or two studs and a turn-down collar (the wing collar remained with tails) (Fig. 24–2b). A black or colored bow tie was worn with the dinner jacket, and a white lawn bow tie was worn with tails. Patent leather oxfords accompanied the dinner jacket, while patent leather pumps were worn with full dress. During the war evening clothes all but disappeared from the wardrobe, but those that remained showed little change.

Shirts generally had soft turn-down collars and for dress were usually white, grey, blue, tan, or lightly striped. The preferred fabric was preshrunk cotton broadcloth. During this period most cuffs were finished with buttons, and French cuffs with cuff links all but disappeared except for evening.

Ties were narrow, tied in small knots, and were about 48 inches long. Materials included foulard, satin, taffeta, madras, and after 1936 wool worsted and knits. Colors included all shades from pastel to brilliant primaries; designs included plaids, stripes, florals, and abstract patterns, with the hand-painted tie popular in the late 1930s. The bow tie was also popular throughout the 1930s, and it was repopularized by singer Frank Sinatra during the war.

Shoes were usually a conservative black or brown oxford, although white shoes and even sandals were acceptable for sportswear. Two-toned oxfords were also popular (shoes, in this style, were white with the toes and heels in black or brown) (Fig. 24–2g). By 1937 *loafers,* which were developed from Norwegian moccasins, were available, and by 1940 *saddle shoes* of white buckskin with brown saddle stripes were eagerly accepted by the young. Thick, crepe soles and even rope soles were possible on sports shoes by 1940, but for evening, patent leather oxfords with tuxedos and patent leather pumps with full dress continued.

Socks were usually dark, even with light shoes, and at the beginning of the 1930s usually were worn without garters, although some men still preferred them. Later men gradually adopted elastic-ribbed ankle socks. Socks were of rayon, cotton, or wool, with silk reserved for evening. Most popular among the young were diamond-patterned *Argyles* in bright colors. Men often wore knee socks in loud plaids or with heavy ribbing with shorts.

The felt slouch hat with a wide brim was standard during the period with the center creased. Homburgs still were used by the conservative. There were also Tyrolean hats, pork pie hats, yachting caps, velours, and Borsalinos—all usually fairly soft. There were still hard-brimmed straws, but the softer Panama was more popular (Fig. 24–2h). During the war the Montgomery beret was sometimes copied by civilians.

Overcoats throughout the period were full-cut and boxy for the most part, with large pockets, padded shoulders, and frequently belted (Fig. 24–2j). One newer style was the reversible topcoat that was gabardine and rain-resistant on one side and cloth on the other. Some topcoats had raglan sleeves, others were double-breasted, and were usually of tweed, worsteds, and wool gabardine or camel's hair.

For evening the topcoat was of black worsted with concealed buttons under a front fly. There were also short raincoats and car coats and longer raincoats with sheepskin or flannel linings that could be zippered in and out for various temperatures. Although there were also occasional fur coats and fur-collared coats, these were the exception during the 1930s. There were also the standard trench coats of the 1920s.

But the innovative area for men was sportswear. Here there was still the standard cardigan and pullover sweaters, but they were rivaled by a great variety of long- and short-sleeved *sports shirts* in whites, pastels, bright colors, and even in South Sea floral patterns (Fig. 24–2a). There were also heavier sports shirts that could be worn either "in or out"—that is, tucked into the pants or worn hanging loosely on the outside. They were made in knits, twills, broadcloths, rayons, and later nylons. If they were to be worn out, they often had patch pockets at the waist.

For skiing there were *loden jackets* with standing military collars and *windbreaker jackets* with tightly woven gabardine trousers fastened at the ankle. For golf there were coats and coat sweaters that were belted in the back. For hunting there were heavy plaid woolen shirts as well as zippered canvas jackets. For the beach there were white, colored, or striped T-shirts. For sailing there were denim dinghy shirts and turtlenecked knit sweaters. For strolling at the beach there were a variety of terry cloth shirts to be worn with white cotton slacks. For western riding there were yoked western shirts outlined in piping, tight riding trousers with piping on the slanted pockets, large Stetson hats with six-inch crowns, and hand-stitched cowboy boots with high heels and pointed toes. Connected with the western scene were Levi denim pants and jackets that faded and shrank after washing and wearing. Originally designed for miners and cowboys, they were adopted by the young as a form of casual wear during the later 1930s and early 1940s.

Bathing suits began in the 1930s with a tank top or undershirt above the waist, but by the end of the decade nothing remained but the trunks. Terry cloth beach coats or robes were frequently donned over the trunks for lounging on the beach or by the swimming pool (Fig. 24-2i).

In underwear some men still wore complete knitted union suits for winter, but the average man wore a lithe-ribbed, knitted top with a scoop neck and narrow shoulder straps and boxy shorts of broadcloth or ribbed knit (Fig. 24-2f). Pajamas were boxy in gay colors and stripes in cotton broadcloth, rayon, or silk. Lounging robes with a shawl collar and deep patch pockets were of cotton, silk, rayon, or wool and were frequently richly patterned or done in stripes and plaids.

In dressing the hair the side part was favored, with hair trimmed short on the sides and in the back. A few men still wore the hair brushed straight back, and some then left it a little fuller on the sides, but the standard was a very close haircut around the ears. A few thin mustaches were seen, but beards were almost never in evidence.

Military uniforms remained in essence what they had been in World War I until the end of the 1930s when America and Europe began to prepare for the eventualities of a new conflict. By the time the U.S. entered the war, the khaki dress tunic had civilian lapels and was worn over a khaki-colored shirt with tie. At first the tunic was skirted, but it later bloused slightly and ended at the waist and was then called the *Eisenhower jacket.* There were still billed caps for officers, but the standard headgear was a foldable, overseas cap. Long trousers with high shoes were worn for dress, but combat trousers were tucked into combat boots that came up over the ankle and strapped and buckled over the bottoms of the pants. Heavy woolen overcoats were worn in winter, and shorter, fatigue jackets were worn informally. In summer all parts of the uniform changed from wool khaki to tan twill (Fig. 24-2k).

In the navy the colors were navy blue and white—the former for winter, the latter for summer. Officers wore tunic jackets, shirts, ties, and straight trousers. Enlisted men wore pullover jumpers with sailor collar and tie, bell-bottomed pants with flap-buttoned fly at the top, and a bowl-crowned cap with turned-up, flaring brim worn at a rakish angle.

***Feminine Dress*** With the coming of the depression women's fashions suddenly became much more conservative. The waist dropped to an almost normal position, the skirt length dropped to within ten inches of the floor in 1930, and colors became much more subdued. Although there was no full return to boned corsets, there was a marked upswing in the use of soft, elastic-webbed corsets.

As for the year-by-year changes in fashion, the first change was the return to the normal waistline with a much longer skirt in 1930. Skirts were usually conservatively narrow with pleats or a slight flare at the bottom. The bertha neckline was in favor, with a deep dip in the back, and for evening, the skirt might be very long in back and higher in front. The evening skirt of tiered ruffles gathered to a yoke was also

**FIG. 24-5** Marcel Bochas design for fashionable beach pants, 1930. Here the first trousers for women, other than indoor negligee items, are soft and full cut at the bottom like the afternoon and evening skirts of the day. Note the knit skirt bodices and the loose jackets that go with them. Photo courtesy of the Bertarelli Collection, Milan.

popular (Fig. 24–3e). A major innovation for sportswear, popularized by actress Marlene Dietrich, was the new slacks with flared bottoms for sport and the beach. These were usually worn with short-sleeved knit tops and sleeved or sleeveless jackets (Fig. 24–5).

In 1931 skirts were tailored with pleats or a slight flare, and coats were cut straight—usually of hip length and with large pockets. Suits also returned to favor as did three-piece coat ensembles composed of blouse, three-quarter-length coat, and straight skirt. Evening dresses were cut backless, and evening skirts were now floor length, flaring at the very bottom and finished with a low bertha added over the shoulder. Neck scarfs were much in evidence during the day.

In 1932 the longer, straight lines with a normal waist continued, and sleeveless dresses were much in evidence. For informal wear lounging pajamas were a part of the well-stocked wardrobe as were shorts and slacks. A new style consisted of a high V-shape at the front of the dress top with a peplum extending down from it over the hips. The skirt worn under this was frequently shirred on each hip, and sleeves could be either long or short. Suits continued popular, especially knitted ones, and suit jackets were usually hip length and buttoned only at the waist. Evening dresses were usually sleeveless, clinging, low under the arm and in the back, with a relatively high waistline if one was indicated (Fig. 24–6).

In 1933 there a was return to a modified leg-o-mutton sleeve and the introduction of a square-cut masculine line. Only soft scarves at the neck softened the line. For the most part skirts were conservative in length and cut, but with silk dresses more flare was possible through the use of pleating and gathers. For outerwear, capes and caped coats were very popular.

In 1934 the draped collar line was popular, along with pleated or flared skirts of a moderate length and with a little more flair in cut. Separate, belted, hip-length blouses were popular, and evening dresses sometimes had long sleeves, occasionally a train, deep V-cuts at the back, and a bias cut of the fabric to make it cling to the torso, hips, and thighs (Fig. 24–7).

FIG. 24–6  An evening gown of the early 1930s. Note particularly the cutaway back to the gown, the bias cut of the fabric to make it cling to the body, and the light-reflective sheen to the satin crepe that reminds one of the chrome accents in the Tugendhat House. Photo courtesy of the BBC Hulton Picture Library.

Suits became even more popular in 1935, worn over blouses with plain or frilly white collars and cuffs. In evening gowns the same lines continued, but often with a pseudo-Greek draped neckline and the introduction of richer fabrics like soft gold, silver, and brocaded lamé that clung to the body (Fig. 24–3a). There were also flared evening jackets in metallic brocade.

Sporting clothing was the big influence in 1936, due probably to the Olympic Games. The shirtmaker dress was the standard for daytime with its simple, conservative lines, shorter skirt, and open collar (Fig. 24–3g). In fact, all skirts were much shorter by 1936, usually mid-calf or above. For evening sheath-

**FIG. 24–7** Victor Steibel informal evening fashions, 1933. Note the return of the waist, the clinging fit at the hips, the insistent geometric pattern of the fabric, and the new coiffure waved back over the ears from a side part. Photo courtesy of the BBC Hulton Picture Library.

like gowns were still standard, some with a top cut like a shirtwaist and fastened with jeweled buttons from neck to waist. For summer at the beach slacks, shorts, and sunsuits were the keys to a fashionable wardrobe.

In 1937 clothes for everyday remained simple with rich or textured fabrics reserved for evening. Colors became lighter and brighter, and skirts were now much shorter, usually just below the knee. For dress wear the neck was usually cut in a V, rounded, or worn with a

shawl collar. The bolero dress was fashionable with its printed blouse and sash under a plain bolero jacket and worn with a plain, matching skirt. Sometimes a circular, somewhat longer skirt was worn with the bolero.

In 1938 a new neckline appeared, consisting of a soft, standing band that could be tied in a bow in front. For the shirtmaker dress the action sleeve appeared, and for dressier models a criss-cross short sleeve was introduced. The hostess gown of this season was usually cut on princess lines with a zipper opening down the back or front. The housecoat worn with skirt or pajamas was also a popular new item, and between afternoon and evening there was the new so-called *cocktail dress* consisting of a rich jacket over a moderate length skirt. Skirts at this time were somewhat fuller with kick, swing, knife, or umbrella pleats, and a somewhat more circular cut. Jackets were square and boxy (Figs. 24–8,9).

The war years brought shorter, tighter skirts and short-sleeved dresses and blouses. The draping in blouses, and even skirts, was ingenious in making up for scantiness of cut. A high, rounded neckline usually finished with a turnover collar and fastened at the back was the most popular, while middy blouses returned along with the yoked shirtwaist. Skirts were cut with bell-shaped gores, center-front gathers or pleats, or set to a circular-styled yoke. In suits the square look of 1938 remained, with plain gabardines vying with plaids, and often skirts contrasting with jackets (Fig. 24–10). Most suit skirts had inverted box pleats in back or regular box pleats in front.

In underwear throughout the period there was the contrast between the lace and net areas of the corset or girdle and the elastic fabric used for the key insets and gores. By the end of the 1930s most women used an elastic girdle from the upper thighs to the waist and a reinforced brassiere, or *bra,* that molded or extended the bust (Fig. 24–3c). For evening a strapless bra was invented. Over the girdle were worn lace, silk, or rayon *panties* (often in black for dressy occasions), and then a *slip* of silk or rayon—cut on the bias with adjustable shoulder straps and an almost Empire waistline. Nightgowns of flannel, silk, or lace could be very short, knee

**FIG. 24–8** Stripes, checks, ribs, and plaid for 1938. Illustrates the simple, straight, tailored lines; small linear and geometric patterns; small hats related to the beret; and the man's *fedora* that gave a trim but very restrained look to fashions at the close of the 1930s. Photo courtesy of *Vogue*. Copyright © 1938 (renewed 1966) by the Condé Nast Publications, Inc.

length, or ankle length, and pajamas were usually loosely cut of silk or satin. The housecoat was three-quarter or floor length to be worn over pajamas or a nightgown in the morning around the house (Fig. 24–3d).

In silk and rayon stockings the trend was to natural beiges, tans, and browns. By 1935 there were those that had garters built into the tops, although most were still fastened by strap garters to the girdle. Ankle socks were very popular for sports and school girls.

In shoes plain pumps gave way to complex strapped sandals, gold and silver strapped evening sandals, platform sandals, or two-toned oxfords. Even evening slippers followed the sandal motif, and by 1935 daytime pumps gave way to sandals and the open-toed shoe. The key year for the platform shoe was 1938 when the firm of Ferragamo of Florence created the cothurnos-style sandal with cork, leather, or rope soles. This was followed by clogs, wedgies, and other platform shoes. During the war and with the onset of shoe rationing, more sober varieties like saddle shoes, loafers, and simple oxfords prevailed (Fig. 24–3i).

During the early 1930s outercoats followed the lines of the clothes beneath and tended to straight, long lines. Mannish collars, lapels,

and button fastenings were prominent in the mid-1930s, and fur coats were much in demand in fox, mink, opossum, beaver, Persian lamb, and leopard (Fig. 24–3j,k). Capes with padded shoulders and slits for arms were fashionable after 1937, and evening coats were usually of velvet or satin with fur collars. For sportswear there were swagger and car coats in plaid or tweed that reached to the lower thigh area or to the knees. During the war coats were trimly cut and often reflected the lines of military overcoats and trenchcoats.

Although the short bobbed hair had become standard, it was superseded after 1930 by many other waved arrangements in which the hair was worn in longer lengths. Usually moderately cut hair with waves set close to the head were the most popular in the early 1930s. The waves were set with a wave lotion, the curling

iron, or sometimes with patented curlers. The windblown bob remained popular with the younger set. In 1937 the hair was brushed and curled close to the head with an upswing at the back which was sometimes brushed to one side. By 1939 the upswing also included the sides so that there was an upswept roll all around the head, except in the front. During the war curls and waves gave way to smoothly brushed hair styles, sometimes with a neat bun at the back of the neck. The three-inch *shingle*, smoothly molded to the head, was briefly popular in 1943, and there were some women whose shoulder length hair was braided into buns or rolls. There was also use of the *page boy*, and for evening, curls were massed on top of the head.

In 1930 hats were very small, usually in velvet or felt, and set forward on the head (Fig. 24–3h). In 1932 the Eugénie hat made its reap-

FIG. 24-10 Boxy utility fashions used by women during World War II; 1943. Note the continued broad-shouldered look that remained from just before the war, the simplicity of cut, the lack of trim, the boxy lines, the knee length, and the prewar coiffure in which the hair was rolled up from the face and ears and then caught in a carefully controlled roll at the back of the head. Photo courtesy of the BBC Hulton Picture Library.

pearance with a peak in front and feather along the side. In the same year berets also appeared, while little dish hats with a narrow brim now perched jauntily on top of the head at a rakish angle. From 1932 to 1936 there were many variations of small hats that were worn at various angles atop a relatively short coiffure, while by 1936 there were some broader-brimmed hats. In 1937 a series of vertical hats with pointed, conical, and cylindrical crowns and moderate brims turned up on three sides, often draped with veils, were introduced (Fig. 24-3f). There were also varieties of pillboxes, toques, and berets (Fig. 24-3l). Then in 1938 came a flat pancake hat (that sat forward on the head) as well as a great variety of turbans. As the war began, millinery styles seemed to freeze; pillboxes, berets, turbans, and various low-crowned felts with moderate turned-up brims continued with little variation until 1945.

From 1929 to 1945 makeup for women became very important, and different colors and textures were developed for different faces and skin textures. Powder came in many shades and colors, lipstick came in hues from purple to light rose, fingernail polish alternated from translucent white to deep red, and even toenails in open-toed shoes had to have exactly the right color. There was much shaping, plucking, and dyeing of eyebrows and outlining of eyes, much use of false eyelashes, mascara, mud masks, and skin creams. The standard makeup of the 1930s followed the contours set by actress Joan Crawford—arched eyebrows widened at the inside and curved outward to a thinner line and widened lips, made up in a deep, rich red.

By 1937 the one-piece bathing suit of elastic knit with a V or rounded neck was standard, and the following year the separate bra with tight shorts was introduced. A rubber bathing cap that completely covered the hair was worn when actually swimming, not sun bathing. A group of bathing beauties for 1935–1936 as pictured in *Vogue Magazine* for England shows a variety of one- and two-piece bathing and sun suits with straw sun hats (Fig. 24–11).

**FIG. 24-11**  An exhibition of bathing fashions for June, 1936. Note that the standard cut was a body-hugging knit suit with a halter neck, cut-out back, and top-of-thigh length. Note also the relatively blunt toes on shoes and sandals and the relatively thick high heels. Photo courtesy of the BBC Hulton Picture Library.

# FABRICS

Aside from the standard silks, cottons, and woolens, the new items among materials were the synthetics. First, there was the continued improvement of rayon so that it no longer had a harsh sheen but could be woven into all fabrics that formerly had been of silk. There was also the introduction of processes that preshrunk and made fabrics wrinkle proof, but the most momentous introduction was that of nylon. This new synthetic was spurred forward in its introduction to the market by the war, during which many things including parachutes were made of nylon; by 1945 it was a major new fabric. Woolens still were the staple fabric for men, with gabardine and flannel the most popular lighter weaves. Wool jersey was popular with women, as well as silk, jersey, moiré, sharkskin, faille, and various metallic combinations. Among cottons, duvetyn and desert cloth were much in demand.

# ARTS AND ARTIFACTS

The furniture and interiors of this period continued the art deco image until the outbreak of the war. The major models for the latest interior decoration were the great movie palaces of the period with their mixture of streamlined forms, chrome trim, and flat, floral patterns. Furniture ran to tubular metal arms and legs. Polished and lacquered wooden tables, desks, and cabinets were usually shaped on very smooth, geometric lines (Fig. 24-1a,b,d,e,g). Lamps and chandeliers were often shaped from interlocked geometric circles and squares with a few abstracted and flattened decorative floral patterns as ornamentation (Fig. 24–1c,f). There was also a great use of glass and mirrors to reflect and enhance this smooth, polished, machine-oriented, decorative world.

In personal ornaments and accessories the innovations were also from the world of machine technology—transparent plastic raincoats, hats, and umbrellas; zippered fastening for all manner of clothes and accessories; and rubberized-elastic swim suits.

For men the accessory items were minor and made few changes from the past. There were still the "old-fashioned" pocket watches, but the wristwatch was now the accepted timepiece. There were still cuff links for those who preferred French cuffed shirts and studs for the full dress shirt. Men carried leather billfolds and wallets, key cases, cigarette cases, umbrellas, and occasionally a cane.

For women the handbag was the major accessory. These were usually flat with handles or (during the war) shoulder straps, and were made of plastic, suede, rubberized fabric, or leather. After 1938 most purses had a zippered closing, and some bags had several covers of different colors and materials to go with various outfits. For evening the bag was small, usually of silk, satin, beaded, or metallic material. Billfolds to match the bag were often seen; frequently the shoes, belt, gloves, and bag were all matched. The pouch shoulder bag came in during the war since it was the style worn by the WACS and WAVES. Purses also carried vanity boxes or compacts that contained rouge, powder, eyebrow pencil, and lipstick. The fully made-up face was often complemented by tinted fingernails, false eyelashes, and eye shadow.

Gloves were still very popular for evening, sports, and work, and evening gloves were usually long and made of cotton or silk jersey. Daytime gloves could be wrist length or longer and made from suede, doeskin, calfskin, or pigskin. Sporting or work gloves were usually of thicker, coarser suede or leather, while during the war knitted mittens appeared for warmth. Zippers were added to gloves in the early 1940s.

Costume jewelry replaced the real thing during the 1930s, and there were many matching sets that included earrings, clips, and a necklace. In the 1930s initial pins were very popular, in 1940 animal pins were in vogue, and during the war charm bracelets were popular. During the war costume jewelry became quite large and bulky with colored plastics worked into various decorative shapes.

Belts of silver and gold leather, natural leather, or suede leather were worn as well as the new plastic belts. Scarfs were also very popular, particularly long stole scarfs and peasant scarfs that tied under the chin *babushka-style*. Veils were an important accessory to the hat from 1939 on.

The major innovation in glasses was the variety of sun glasses in all shapes and sizes and the introduction of novelty frames for regular glasses. Handkerchiefs remained an important accessory for both men and women, although for the latter they were usually colored, floral, and often lace-edged.

## VISUAL SOURCES

The major sources for visual information during this period come from fashion magazines, particularly the British and American editions of *Vogue*. There are also *Harper's Bazaar, Good Housekeeping, Ladies' Home Journal, Life, McCall's, Woman's Home Companion, The London Illustrated News,* and *l'Illustration.* An excellent source for the general life of the times and the clothing of the common people (as well as the upper classes) is the Life/Time series, *This Fabulous Century, 1930–1940* and *1940–1950.* Two other invaluable sources are the *Sears, Roebuck Catalog* and Martin Battersby's *The Decorative Thirties.* Institutional sources include the New York Public Library, the Metropolitan Museum of Art, the Brooklyn Museum, and the Collection Union Francaise des Arts du Costume.

# SUMMARY

This was a period that continued the artistic ideals of art deco with its popularization of the decorative effects based on the new machine image. It was a period when some of the excesses of the 1920s were toned down by the Great Depression and when the new male and female ideals in manners and clothing came from the stars of the great silver screen—the one escapist pleasure that depressed America could still afford. The most memorable silhouettes for women were the long, straight lines of the early 1930s, the slinky, clinging, tubular evening creations of the mid-1930s, the boxy, square, padded look of the late 1930s, and the military look during the war. For men it was the boxy, padded, tweedy look of the 1930s with the broad, snap-brimmed hat. It was also a period of great repression and upheaval that culminated in six terrible years of world war.

# chapter *XXV*

# *The Cold War*

### *Chronology*

#### (1945–1963)

**THE COLD WAR
1945–1963**

**1948**

**1946**   MacArthur's reorganization of Japan; G.I. bill sends thousands of veterans back to college; housing shortages; terrible winter in Europe; Fourth Republic is founded in France

**1947**   Marshall Plan to aid European recovery; British rule ends in India; Jewish nation is founded in Palestine

**1948**   Tito breaks with Stalin; Israel becomes an independent nation; international war crimes trials continue in Nuremberg; Prince Charles born as heir apparent to the British throne; Juliana becomes queen of the Netherlands

**1949**   North Atlantic Treaty Organization is founded; West Germany becomes a Federal Republic; the communists under Mao Tse-tung take over China; Russia claims the secret of the atom bomb; commercial development of TV

**1950**   The Korean War begins; Le Corbusier begins work on Notre Dame du Haut, Ronchamp; U.S. develops the hydrogen bomb

**1951**

**1955**

**1958**

| | |
|---|---|
| 1951 | Japan and the United States sign a treaty of peace; Churchill and the Conservatives return to power in England |
| 1952 | Eisenhower elected president of the U.S.; outbreaks of Mau Mau terrorism in Kenya |
| 1953 | Death of Stalin; Beria expelled from his post as head of the Soviet secret police |
| 1954 | U.S. Supreme Court outlaws racial segregation in the public schools; the British evacuate the Suez Canal Zone; Senator Joseph McCarthy is censored by the Senate for his misguided investigative activities |
| 1955 | Eisenhower has a heart attack but recovers; Geneva Conference of the Big Four powers; peace treaty between Russia and the Austrians; Khrushchev becomes the dominant leader in Russia; Warsaw Pact signed |
| 1956 | Hungarian Revolution ruthlessly suppressed by the Russians; Khrushchev denounces Stalin; Egypt seizes the Suez Canal |
| 1957 | Anthony Eden, because of health and the Suez Crisis, steps down as prime minister of England; Common Market established in Europe; Gromyko becomes foreign minister of the Soviet Union; the Soviet Union orbits the first satellite |
| 1958 | Fifth Republic under General deGaulle in France; U.S. troops ordered to Lebanon |
| 1959 | Christian Herter replaces John Foster Dulles as Secretary of State; Eisenhower flies to Europe to confer with the leaders of France, Britain, and West Germany; Khrushchev visits the United States |

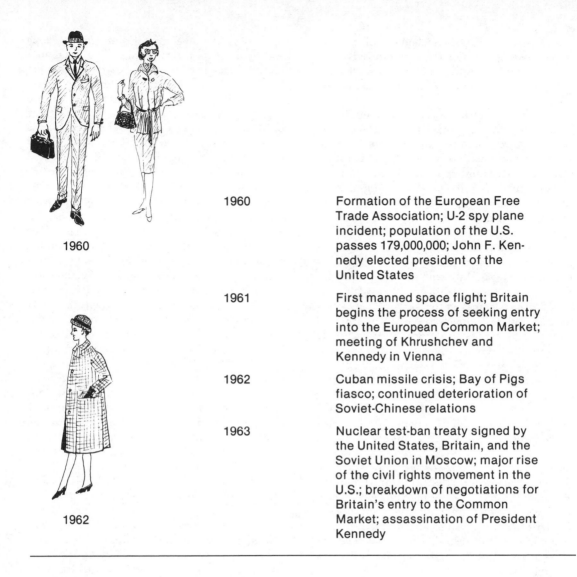

| 1960 | Formation of the European Free Trade Association; U-2 spy plane incident; population of the U.S. passes 179,000,000; John F. Kennedy elected president of the United States |
| 1961 | First manned space flight; Britain begins the process of seeking entry into the European Common Market; meeting of Khrushchev and Kennedy in Vienna |
| 1962 | Cuban missile crisis; Bay of Pigs fiasco; continued deterioration of Soviet-Chinese relations |
| 1963 | Nuclear test-ban treaty signed by the United States, Britain, and the Soviet Union in Moscow; major rise of the civil rights movement in the U.S.; breakdown of negotiations for Britain's entry to the Common Market; assassination of President Kennedy |

1960

1962

## BACKGROUND

The atomic bombing of Hiroshima and Nagasaki set off an explosion in the psychic mind of the world from which it may never recover, and the disturbance in the social, political, and psychological outlook of humanity continues to color all major decisions in the world today. The cultures of Western Europe and the United States turned to the rebuilding of a war-torn world and to a deadly military, psychological, and propaganda competition with the great new world power to the east, the Soviet Union. The period of the 1950s saw a conservative materialism at home and a psychological and military duel abroad, known as the *Cold War,* between the United States and its allies and the Soviet Union and its satellites. It was a period of massive scientific and technological activity as the two great superpowers poured time, money, and personnel into the great worldwide competition for military, scientific, and psychological superiority.

The horrors of the war, brought about the artists' retreat from the real world and from natural objects, culminating in the mid-1950s in action painting and abstract expressionism. Painters such as Jackson Pollock totally left the world of subjects and objects and entered into a physical relationship with their paintings as they spattered and dribbled pigment onto floor-spread canvases. Thus for a time the art world made no comment on the problems of the outside world but retreated to an inner world of personal relationship with process. The exhausted conclusion to this concern with pure relationships came in the early 1960s, when humor and real objects began to be inserted into paintings concerned primarily with field relationships. Gradually shapes, figures, and textures from the real world came back into art as important accents in a field of relationships, and early experiments began that were to lead to the explosion of pop art in the mid-1960s.

Even in the literature of the 1950s there was more stress on form, on the interweaving of structure on angles of vision, than there was on large-scale commentary on the problems of the present and future. Until the mid-1960s the denial of the complexities in cultural problems was so strong that the majority of authors did not try to comment on or interpret the cultural scene but merely recorded facts and relationships as fascinating, sad, humorous, or decorative effects.

In architecture and interior decoration the ideals sponsored by the twentieth-century love of science and machine technology continued in new ways. The great skyscrapers of the new international style were almost all based on the concept of a great, oblong box of glass and steel placed on end and reaching upward, pure and shimmering, into the sky. In home architecture, particularly in the western United States, the concept of the outside world penetrating the inside continued to develop. Walls became glass sliding doors, windows became glass walls, and the solid structure of the home seemed to dissolve into the outside gardens and pools of its surroundings. The Tremaine House, designed by the Austrian architect Neutra in Santa Barbara, California, is a case in point (Fig. 25–1). The inside is part of the outside, and the outside penetrates the interior until all normal divisions have been erased, as anyone can testify who has walked into a closed sliding glass door that looked to be open.

Politically and socially the years directly following the end of the war were devoted to rebuilding Europe and developing a solid front against Soviet communist expansion. By the early 1950s the United States was embarked on a wave of anticommunism in all forms, building a military response to Soviet might, and renewing the values of daily life disrupted by the war. Once it was known that Russia had detonated an atom bomb of its own, the arms race was on, first with the invention of the hydrogen bomb and later, after Russia's launching of *Sputnik,* with a race for space. Militarily there was the U.S. confrontation with communist aggression in Korea when the North Koreans invaded South Korea and were later supported by the Chinese communists. Some felt more secure to have a former Supreme Commander of the Allied Armies in Washington and so elected Eisenhower president in 1952, but crises continued. There was a brief hot war at the Suez Canal in 1956 as well as a violent outbreak of revolution in Hungary the same year. There was continuous tension between the new state of Israel and its Arab neighbors and silent warfare in Indochina. Although the United States was not directly involved in any of the hot wars, it was continuously involved in the Cold War duel with Russia, which increased following the election of Kennedy as president in 1960, first in the President's Berlin speech of 1961 and later in the famous Cuban Missile Crisis of 1962. Thus the entire period from the close of World War II until the assassination of President Kennedy was dominated by the Cold War, the arms and space race, and the continuous world tension caused by the many unsolved problems left from World War II.

Socially the 1950s were a period of retrenchment and a return to the values of family,

(a)

(b)

fiberglass and spun aluminum table, chair
1956

Richard Neutra, the Tremaine House; Santa Barbara, California; 1952. Typical of the domestic architecture in the southwestern United States in the 1950s. Note that the space surrounding the structure appears to penetrate directly into the home's interior. From a photo in the collection of the author.

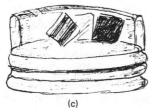

(c)
beige upholstered
couch with
pillows
1955

(d)
white plastic table
top with black
iron legs
1950s

(e)
record jacket
1950s

**FIGURE 25–1**

447

home, and business that had been disrupted by World War II. In a world of tension, instant communication, and massive increases in destructive technology, Americans and Western Europeans attempted to return to the normal world of capitalist competition and expansion; on the surface it was an age of conventionality, efficiency, and a tense normalcy. Although under the surface the volatile forces of human individuality (that were to explode in the following decade) were kept in check, it was the individualists and rebels of the time who captured public attention and punctuated the grey-flannel-suit facade of everyday reality that passed for the cultural norm.

## THE BASIC COSTUME SILHOUETTE

The overall image that we have of clothing in the period from the end of World War II to the death of President Kennedy is that of the man in the grey flannel suit and the woman in the simple, efficient, black cocktail sheath with a string of pearls. If one were to ask for a single photograph to sum up the average daily clothing image of the 1950s, the choice would probably fall on a photo of commuters returning from the business world at the close of the day (Fig. 25–2). The faceless dullness and greyness of this massed grouping of humanity came to be the cliché image of the middle-class man, deprecatingly referred to as the "Man in the Grey Flannel Suit."

The first stylistic changes in male clothing following the close of the war were generally backward-looking attempts to recreate the past. Particularly in London there was a flurry of Edwardian styles at the close of the 1940s with tight Eton jackets, tight trousers, bowler hats, and Edwardian overcoats. There were also *teddy boy* ensembles borrowed from the Edwardian, but with a broad-shouldered, tough-guy look as opposed to the smooth, tailored lines of the other neo-Edwardian styles.

But by the mid-1950s these slightly exotic, backward-looking fads were replaced by the true style of the Cold War years—the narrow-shouldered, narrow-lapeled suit worn with a narrow tie and a narrow-brimmed hat that gave the wearer a somewhat tight but very efficient look. (During this period the double-breasted suit almost completely disappeared.) It was this Madison Avenue look that was the target for all rebellions against Eisenhower dullness, mechanized man, middle-class mediocrity, and grey-flannel-suit seriousness. Thus the interesting men's clothes of the 1950s came from the varieties of sportswear available, particularly from those items sold for many years after the war in government surplus stores. There were toggle-fastened *duffle coats, fatigue jackets, Eisenhower jackets, windbreakers, flight jackets,* and many more fascinating items. Thus it was to be from casual and sports clothing that the new fashions for men developed, particularly with the individualistic-romantic explosion in fashion that occurred during the late 1960s. In fact, since the beginning of the modern industrial world in the late eighteenth century, it has always been from the items of sporting dress that the male formal styles of later generations have developed. For example, the most formal evening coat that we have is the black-tailed evening coat, and yet it began life in the very late eighteenth century as a riding coat with coat skirts missing in the front and on the sides for ease in riding.

One other great postwar change in male dress was effected by the introduction of many new chemical-plastic fibers that went into so-called wash-and-wear fabrics that changed the nature of clothing maintenance. Creaseless and stainless materials and long-wearing synthetic and natural fabric mixtures made male clothing more efficient and practical. One aspect of shirts almost completely disappeared and that was the use of starch to gain stiffness in collars and cuffs. Except for a few very formal dress shirts, the time-consuming process of starching shirts became a thing of the past.

In women's fashions there had been some innovations during the war in the introduction of military lines and accessories into female clothing, but it was not until 1947 that a sharp

(a) duffle jacket without hood 1950

(b) hood used with jacket

(c) backless waist coat in pearl gray daytime-formal

(d) slip-on town shoe 1957

(e) country tweed hat 1953

(f) 1953 Madras jacket and Bermuda shorts

(g) knitted cotton shirt 1956

(h) hunting cap

(i) fur-lined winter cap

(j) car coat 1950

(k) hard straw 1956

(l) cotton sport jacket 1956

(m) sheepskin winter coat, fleece inside

(n) formal evening 1953

(o) zoot suit 1945

(p) zip-out lining topcoat 1957

Photograph of commuters; Part Forest, Illinois; 1958. Illustrates the bland, grey-flannel look of the 1950s. Note that men's hat brims are a trifle narrower than in the 1930s, that the three ladies wear straight *A-line* cloth coats, and that the men's overcoats are all single-breasted. Photo courtesy of Sandra Weiner, New York.

**FIGURE 25–2**

449

break came in the square, short-skirted, padded-shoulder look that had dominated fashion since the late 1930s. The "New Look," established by Christian Dior in Paris, stressed narrow shoulders, a smooth bust, a normal waistline, moderate hips, and a long, almost ankle-length skirt with a wide hem. The image seemed to be a nostalgic glimpse back at a slightly more feminine look for women after the rough, efficient, and unflattering clothing worn during the war. Thus for a time women's fashion moved back from emancipation and active freedom to a more ladylike image adapted from the past. However, this movement did not last, and by the mid-1950s Dior launched his *H-line* look which was an efficient, short-skirted, tubular dress with a relatively low waist. This was accompanied by the *A-line* silhouette in which there was no defined waist and the dress spread youthfully from the neck in a triangular line to just above the knee. In the late 1950s Coco Chanel popularized the simple suit with boxy jacket and skirt that became the complement of the businessman's grey flannel

suit (Fig. 25–3). These simple, geometrically shaped basics for women dramatized the concept of nonemotional efficiency as the key to upper-middle-class clothing, at the very moment that the "beat generation" was challenging this whole way of life and dress. To these rebels, who savored individuality, variety, and the sensuous values in life, the simple, straight sheath, sack, and chemise dresses of plain fabric worn with simple pearls seemed an obvious symbol of the mechanized efficiency that was prized by "establishment" society in place of an individualized humanism. The same was true of their attack on the new plastic fabrics and wash-and-wear clothing which all seemed to place practicality and efficiency above interesting, varied textures and natural, organic fibers. "Establishment" clothing seemed a perfect extension of the glass and chrome boxes in which the middle-class suburbanite lived and worked, and it marked the high point in the simplification and mechanization that was to be fully attacked and overthrown in the mid-1960s.

## COLD WAR COSTUME

***Masculine Dress*** The first wild aberration in male clothing at the close of the war was a brief but highly publicized fad centered in southern California that was known as the *zoot suit* craze. Here the thigh-length, double-breasted coat had large lapels, and peg-topped trousers were worn with suspenders well above the normal waistline. They were extremely full at the top and tapered to a cuff so narrow that it was difficult to get the foot through the opening. Zoot suits were made in garish colors and outsize patterns and were always finished off by a large bow tie and a huge key chain that hung almost to the floor (Fig. 25–2o). This brief but wild postwar explosion in male dress might be compared to the exaggerations in cut and accessories that marked the clothing of the "Incroyables" at the close of the French Revolution—a manic release from the tensions of war.

In England another direction of release from the war was taken by the initiation of a return to Edwardian clothing. The male style-setters in

London in a nostalgic attempt to escape to a more settled time revived the narrow trousers and closefitting Eton jackets of the first decade of the century, accompanied by the use of bowler hats and fitted overcoats with velvet collars (Fig. 25–4). By 1950 men about Mayfair were wearing fitted, single-breasted coats with velvet collars; tight, drainpipe pants; narrow, horizontally striped shirts with stiff white collars; and rich patterned waistcoats; and were carrying a slim umbrella. From this nostalgic return to a very fashionable past came a new variation at the opening of the 1950s, the so-called teddy boys, who turned these Edwardian styles into aggressive images of a "tough-guy" style. They wore plain white shirts with the collar turned up or a string tie, a chain around the neck and wrist, tattoos on forearm and fingers, a thick, draped suit with padded shoulders, and crepe-soled shoes. Their hair was worn long and styled into greasy sideburns and slicked down in back. Although the style did not last for

(A-line)
broad hat
and
fur-trimmed
cloth coat
1948

(a)

1948

(b) 1956

1950

1957

1953

(c)
turban
1948

(d)
1956

(e)
beach
playsuit
1953

(f)
mid-1950s

(g)
bikini
1948

(h)
strapless
bra and waist
cincher
1947

(i)
black suede
1948

(j)
paisley
carry-all purse
1954

(k)
stiff net
crinoline
with
feather
boning
1951

H-line
dress
1954

(r)

(m)
black
leather
lucite
straps
1952

(l)
leather sport jacket
with wool sleeves
1952

sacque
dress
fitted
front
and
loose
back
1957

(n)

(o)
suede
and
leather
1953

(p)
figured
cardigan
sweater
1956

(q)
evening
sweater
trimmed
in beads
and braid
1950

Coco Chanel and a model; 1955. Illustrates the simple, practical suits
with boxy jackets and shirts popularized by this famous Parisian fashion designer that symbolized the
unemotional efficiency in women's
clothing in the 1950s. Photo courtesy
of *Paris Match.*

**FIGURE 25–3**

**FIG. 25–4** Teddy boy styles; 1954. Illustrates the attempt on the part of certain young men in England after the war to return to certain Edwardian accessories like velvet collars, longer coats, patterned vests, and striped ties. Photo courtesy of the BBC Hulton Picture Library.

many years, it had full publicity and a wide influence.

But in the mainstream of male clothing in the 1950s, the image was basically efficiency-oriented and dull. By the late 1950s waistcoats all but disappeared, and the typical Madison Avenue suit was a two-piece, single-breasted outfit with narrow shoulders and lapels, slim pants without cuffs, and usually made of grey flannel. Hats had much narrower brims than in the early 1940s (Fig. 25–2).

The major shift in shirts was the dress shirt with smaller collars, often buttoned down and without long points. These *Ivy League* shirts were made of a wide variety of fabrics from madras to drip-dry acetates and polyesters and were styled with either long or short sleeves. French or button cuffs were possible, but the lack of speed and efficiency in fastening French cuffs made the quick button cuff the most popular. Casual shirts had large collars, were made in bright colors and a variety of patterns, were buttoned down the front, and had either long or short sleeves (Fig. 25–2g). There were also a variety of knit polo, turtleneck, and golf shirts and also a wide array of striped and colored T-shirts. Sport shirts were worn with the neck open, although the very stylish sometimes tucked a scarf into the open neck. The ties of the 1950s became much slimmer than those of the late 1930s and early 1940s; bow ties were also quite narrow and often clipped on instead of being hand tied. One new variation as a casual tie or neck closing was the thong (*bolo*) tie with a polished stone or carved metal sliding guide to tighten it.

During the 1950s the sports jacket, which in the 1930s had been worn primarily on country weekends or outings, became an acceptable jacket for street wear, and it captured much of the interest in variety that was missing from the business suit. Although the cut of these sports jackets usually followed the small changes in the cut of the business suit jacket, the materials and patterns were much more exciting, ranging from tweeds, herringbones, and checks to stripes and plaids (Fig. 25–2f,l). The sports slacks that went with these jackets were usually gabardine and now lacked the large pleats at the waist and the fullness down the leg. They were usually quite slim and worn with a slim belt and could be with or without cuffs, although most men's pants by the late 1950s were without cuffs.

Formal clothing changed little during this period. The tails on a formal evening coat were slim and long, lapels were small to moderate, and wing collars were quite small and unobtrusive (Fig. 25–2n). Tuxedo or dinner jackets were made in a variety of rich, dark fabrics with lapels faced in taffeta or brocade of the same color. Sometimes tuxedo jackets also had thin cuffs and wide cummerbunds that matched the lapels, and some shirts were once again modestly ruffled. White dinner jackets were standard for summer, and backless pearl grey vests were used with a black jacket and grey striped trousers for daytime formal wear (Fig. 25–2c).

More active sporting clothes included the standard boxer-short swim trunks or the tight-fitting abbreviated variety in gay patterns and colors; *Bermuda shorts* (Fig. 25–2f) with or without knee-length socks for walking in warm climates; one-piece cotton jumpsuits for true comfort; the nylon pants and jackets devised for the ski slopes; and the slim-fitting, shrinkable, and faded blue denim Levi jeans and jackets adopted (particularly by students) from nineteenth- and twentieth-century cowboy wear. There were also the many items that were available in army surplus stores—like Eisenhower jackets, combat boots, duffle coats (Fig. 25–2a), nylon windbreakers, leather flight jackets, army raincoats, and fatigue jackets. All of these leftovers from the war gave a kind of lift to the fashion scene and took the edge off the relative dullness and uniformity of clothing during the period.

The overcoats of the 1950s were usually straight in line with either a calf or knee length and occasionally raglan sleeves. Often these coats had zip-in linings (Fig. 25–2p). They had simple, flat collars and were single-breasted. The most popular new coat was the *car coat* that was thigh length and sometimes had a hood (Fig. 25–2b,j). They were also sometimes fleece-lined and occasionally had very heavy zippers or metal hook devices instead of buttons (Fig. 25–2m). Formal overcoats included the Chesterfield with a velvet collar, and for the wealthy there were fur coats of various kinds.

Hats were generally the felt fedora or Homburg but with much smaller brims and shallower crowns than in the previous period (Fig. 25–2e). The straw boater (Fig. 25–2k) was replaced by a higher-crowned, narrow-brimmed straw shaped like a fedora, and for winter there were Russian fur caps, billed caps with ear-coverings, and knit stocking caps. (Fig.

25–2h,i). Young men either didn't wear hats or sported a flat-crowned pork pie hat.

Shoes changed very little, the laced oxford still holding center stage. There were also moccasin-type loafers (Fig. 25–2d), laced boots for hiking, and buckled engineer boots for loggers, bikers, and antiestablishment types. Toes of shoes were less rounded than in the early 1940s and somewhat more pointed; formal shoes were still patent leather pumps with flat bows over the instep; crepe and rubber soles began to challenge leather for everyday; and leather heels almost disappeared in favor of rubber.

Hair styles remained short for the most part. Some younger men went in for the very close crew cut, but the majority wore the regulation side-parted, Madison Avenue style with minimal sideburns.

Military wear remained basically the same as at the close of World War II.

**Feminine Dress**  When the war was over, there was an air of expectation as women waited for the new postwar styles, and magazines like *Vogue* spoke to servicewomen about the chance-of-a-lifetime to buy a completely new wardrobe. Moscow in the latter part of 1945 had a Soviet State Fashion Show in which 300 dresses were picked for mass production; in Paris there was a "Theatre de la Mode" at the Musée des Arts Decoratifs in which all the leading Parisian fashion stylists took part; and in London in 1946 there was an exhibition entitled "Britain Can Make It" which had a fashion hall divided into dresses that were inexpensive, moderate, or couture. Unfortunately there were no bold changes in these first postwar showings, just somewhat lower hems, nipped-in waists, and some new boned corsets. There was, therefore, an air of indecision and expectant waiting.

Then on February 12, 1947, the women present at the first showing of Christian Dior felt that now the war must be truly over as they viewed the fashions that were to establish the "New Look." Dior had decided to capitalize on a nostalgia for the past when the padded shoulder, tubular, boxy line, and short skirt (that had been around since before the war and was identified with uniforms) did not exist. The new silhouette had narrow shoulders, a natural but slightly pinched waist, an emphasis on the bust, and a quite long skirt with a wide hem (Fig. 25-5). The governments of the time were not pleased with this use of more fabric at a time of rationed necessities, but the New Look won the day. By 1949 women all over Europe and America were wearing various versions of the new style. The so-called New Puritanism that some said was contained in the New Look was not a matter of morality but of nostalgia for a time when women had not been in the military

FIG. 25-5 A Hardy Amies model displays the "New Look"; 1949. Illustrates the narrow shoulder, fitted bodice, natural waist, longer skirt, and wide hem that developed in 1949 from Christian Dior's New Look of 1947-1948. Note, however, that the modern sleek look has not disappeared. Photo courtesy of the BBC Hulton Picture Library.

service and the industrial war plants. It represented a desire to return to a more settled and agreeable past (Fig. 25-3a).

In 1948 and 1949 there were, of course, fashion variations on the New Look. Dior introduced his *envoi* line in which he superimposed an angle of fullness on an arrow-thin sheath, and his jackets jutted out sharply over tubular skirts and dresses. Some of these long tubular skirts were so tight that they had to be split for walking and had outer flying panels gathered at the waist for both evening and afternoon dresses. Most evening dresses were strapless, with very full, spreading skirts to the upper ankle or floor; the most fashionable outercoats of these last years of the 1940s were great triangles or pyramids of wool or faille (Fig. 25-3a).

In 1950 and 1951 various Parisian designers attempted a number of breaks with the New Look. There was Balenciaga's sculptured rounded forms for evening, done out of paper-stiff taffeta blown out and then rolled under to look like a pumpkin; there were rich sheath dresses swathed and draped with fabric on top for evening; there was Dior's new princess dress worn with a boxy, flaring jacket; and there was Jacques Fath's youthful suit with a matador jacket, a cummerbund at the waist, and a full skirt over petticoats. But with all the variations, the skirts remained relatively long, and the waist, when it showed, stayed in its normal position.

A typical three-quarter-length redingote of soft wool with large collar and pockets for the season of 1951-1952 may be seen in a design for *Vogue*. It is worn with a grosgrain beret and keeps the full, straight waistline and semi-tubular line that followed the New Look (Fig. 25-7). An evening dress by Hardy Amies for 1953 also retains the strapless lines, normal fitted waist, and flared skirt to the floor that was first introduced by Dior in 1947 (Fig. 25-8).

As fashion moved into the mid-1950s, there was much more influence, at least in sport clothes, from the teenage world. There were bulky sweaters (Fig. 25-3p), a striped or flowered blouse worn with a sash and knee-length *capri pants* or *pirate jeans,* straight drainpipe pants (Fig. 25-6), and full-circle felt skirts

**FIG. 25-6** Loose blouses, capri pants, and shorts for beach wear; 1958. Illustrates the popularity of *drainpipes* or *capri pants* that were body-hugging to the calf, loose blouses, and boxer shorts that all were popular for resort and beach wear in the late 1950s. Photo courtesy of *Vogue*. Copyright © 1958 by the Condé Nast Publications, Inc.

**FIG. 25-7** Cloth coats for 1952. Illustrates that coats by 1952 had lost the flaring line of the New Look in favor of the efficient-looking tubular line. Note the simplicity of the line and the use of tiny beret hats. Photo courtesy of *Vogue*. Copyright © 1952 (renewed 1980) by the Condé Nast Publications, Inc.

**FIG. 25-8** A Hardy Amies ball gown for 1953. Illustrates a frothy escapist fantasy during a period of sleek efficiency. It is made of white tulle with a draped satin bodice worn under a gathered tulle stole finished with pale orchid pink roses. Photo courtesy of the BBC Hulton Picture Library.

in bright colors for evening. From the couture houses of Paris the one new line that was almost universal was the dropped armhole, with loose collars and necks rolling back off the body like an oversized sweater (Fig. 25-3n). Dior captured attention by shortening skirts to 16 inches off the floor, and with this, the era of the longer skirt gradually began to come to an end. In 1954 Chanel reopened her house of fashion and began to revive the boxy look she had made famous in the 1930s. In many ways her designs were more practical and modern for the busy women than those of Dior, as can be seen in the simple, boxy lines of the suits that she put forth in 1955 (Fig. 25-3). At about this time there was a battle in Paris between those designers who presented fashions with a strong shape that was not geared to the wearer versus those who designed clothes that had no existence separate

from the movement of the wearer. Thus Dior introduced a triangular A-line that went from a small head and shoulders to a full pleated or stiffened hem, while Chanel and Balenciaga presented simple shapes in soft fabric.

The New Look suit was designed with a long, flaring skirt, a short, fitted jacket, and straight sleeves. In the early 1950s the A-line silhouette was retained but was gradually modified to a more slender outline with a slightly shorter skirt. By the mid-to-late 1950s suits had square, waist-length jackets and skirts just above the knees. The formal gowns that came with the New Look often stressed sleeveless bodices with either very thin shoulder straps or none at all. There were also beaded evening sweaters, to be worn with long skirts for less formal occasions (Fig. 25-3p). Waists were normal and tightly fitted, and skirts flared out over crinolines to the floor or to a ballerina length just above the ankle (Fig. 25-3k). Sometimes the hemlines were cut to reveal the feet in front but dipped into a train in the back. In the later 1950s the strapless top with fitted waist continued, but skirts (often of chiffon over satin or taffeta) fell with only a minimum of fullness straight to the floor. In sports clothing there was an ever-increasing development in casual styles with *pedal pushers,* calf-length, tightly fitted capri pants, stretch pants tightly fitted to the ankle, long pants with straps under the instep made of bonded knit fabric, and Bermuda shorts adapted from those worn by men. Swim and play suits were often made of cotton and cut like short-skirted dresses, with a fitted, sleeveless, and backless top held up by neck ties, or the more daring *bikini* with its breastband and miniscule, handkerchief-sized panties (Fig. 25-3e,g). There were also swim suits with halter tops and trunk bottoms and the one-piece knitted tank suit that fit the body like the skin. Slacks increased in importance and came in a variety of lines from very snug to quite loose, with all manner of trim and decoration. The blouses worn with slacks and shorts ranged from tailored shirts to frilly lace and eyelet creations. Ski costumes changed only minimally from the 1940s and were severely tailored, with a jacket and matching pants in bonded stretch knit. Car coats with attached hoods were also much in demand as an overgarment for winter outings, and there were leather jackets with woolen sleeves for casual outings (Fig. 25–2l).

By 1947 the short, boxy, hip-length jackets with three-quarter sleeves were being replaced by the long, full-backed coats of the New Look with its modestly puffed, bell or straight sleeves and fold-back cuffs. This basically A-line coat with narrow sloping shoulders (Fig. 25–3a) remained the norm for at least five years before the straighter, tubular lines of the mid-1950s became more fashionable. In raincoats there were the reversibles with wool on one side and chemically treated gabardine on the other, and in the late 1950s the glistening vinyl-coated raincoat made its appearance. There were also the very practical, clear plastic garments that could be folded up in a handbag. In fur wraps there were shoulder or cloth capes and stoles as well as the knee-length and calf-length fur coats. Mink was the most popular, but sable, leopard, and fox were also worn. There were also cloth coats with a variety of fur collars. Among formal wraps in the late 1940s and early 1950s great tiered capes of wide, horizontally arranged ruffles to the floor were popular as were see-through synthetic fabrics in bouffant puffs over an A-line silhouette. More tailored and severe were the straight-line coats to the floor in velvet or brocade, with standing collar and side slits.

The most typical hats of the New Look were flat with a moderately broad brim, while the hats of the early 1950s had brims that were asymmetrical, tilted up on one side, hugging the face on the other, and were made of velour trimmed in veils and feathers. Hats were usually set straight on the head, but by the mid-1950s most hats had no brim and were based on pillbox, dish, beret, or bag shapes (Fig. 25–3c,d,e,f).

Shoes gradually became more pointed with very high, slender heels and tops that were very shallow. Boots made their appearance, tentatively, in the first few years of the 1960s but were not to come into their own until the mid-1960s (Fig. 25–3i,o). For summer there were many forms of the sandal—from Japanese and thong styles to Grecian laced sandals.

Underwear remained relatively constant with a few innovations like the half slip and refinements in the shaping and padding of the brassiere. Hose were almost uniformly of nylon in beige or light brown without seams. Hose were usually fastened by garters to a garter belt that went around the waist or to a girdle. Girdles were still worn to control the figure and were usually made of elasticized fabric in short, panty-length or in longer, thigh-length styles. For the New Look waist the Merry Widow corset was introduced to sharply cinch in the waistline (Fig. 25–3h).

In hair styles the shape that was most approved with the New Look was a feather cut which was a gently curled cut that followed the shape of the head. There was also the *poodle clip* inspired by Mary Martin in *South Pacific* and then the *bouffant* hairdos that made their appearance in the mid-1950s. Next came the *beehive* coiffure which rose in a great swirl above the head by much backbrushing and lacquering. The *bubble* hair style was similar but without waves or curls. In the late 1950s there was the closely cropped cut, combed from the crown over gently teased hair at the back with forehead-concealing bangs and sideburn locks in front of the ears. There was also long, straight hair over the cheeks with long bangs on the forehead. Wigs began to make their appearance in the very late 1950s, and dyed hair began to be more prevalent. In all the new hair styles of the period, the use of shears and comb were as important as the setting and shape. All of the styles had a controlled and self-consciously set and manipulated look that was to be put aside when the natural look of the 1960s began (Fig. 25–3b).

In 1957 Christian Dior died, and his mantle was taken over by the young Yves St. Laurent. Skirts rose slightly along with the waists. The latter effect was heightened by the innovation of the stiff, four-inch-wide *waspie belt* that both raised the waist and exaggerated the hips, and became one of the most copied accessories for a number of years.

With the St. Laurent collection of 1958 the newest line was the *trapeze,* flaring gently from the shoulders to a shorter and wider hemline just covering the knees (Fig. 25–9). In 1959 St. Laurent tried to raise the skirt to the knees and

Within the figure (partial magazine text, largely illegible):

LLECTIONS
VES
:inate

FIG. 25-9 The St. Laurent trapeze dress for 1958. Illustrates the new flaring line of the *trapeze* or *A-line* dress that came to the fore in fashion about ten years after the introduction of the New Look. Note the lack of definition at the waist and bust and the flaring line of the hat to match the flare of the skirt. Photo courtesy of *Vogue*. Copyright © 1958 by the Condé Nast Publications, Inc.

there was a great outcry. He also belted all his sheath-sack dresses, and the headlines proclaimed that the waist was back to stay (Fig. 25-3r). But it was Chanel who established a practical, efficient line of clothes that did not change with each new season.

In 1960 some of the "beat generation" clothing characteristics began to spread into high fashion. Organic textures like leather made a big impact, and the resort clothes worn by Brigitte Bardot and Françoise Sagan at St. Tropez were picked up for beaches around the world the season after they first were seen in southern France. Thus it was youth more than sophisticated chic that began to be the major influence in fashion. Opposed to this were the standard efficiency fashions of Chanel with emphasis on tweed suits, knits, cardigans, and

edgings in navy braid. A suit that shows the conservative lines and yet is made from soft knit may be seen in a design for *Vogue* (Fig. 25-10). It should be noted that the large handbag carried by the model was now a major new accessory.

As fashion moved into the early 1960s, the established efficiency, simplicity, and geometry of the old order began to be breached by the political and social pressures of the new decade. By 1962 the new, youthful dance known as the "twist" arrived from Paris, and Truffaut's film *Jules et Jim* established the new "gamin" look for the young, with sleeveless pullovers, cardigans, knickerbockers, tweed caps, and long mufflers. The cult of youth was beginning to make itself felt, but it did not truly begin to dominate fashion until 1963–1964. Thus

What we see...

(far left), white with black braid margins, ... country living; becomes a look with the ... tailor handling that's more than middling ... fabric tweed-and-alpaca flecks. About ... Fifth Avenue. Coat: Julius Garfinckel... matter, is brisk unruffled chic, one ... and tweed coat (left). To see besides, the ... gloves, a tall fez, a catlskin satchel with ... ckerman. Hat: Christian Dior New York, ... also at Wanamaker's, Phila. Lucille bag, ... t's the pitch behind the soft black-and- ... fashion it's anything but meet with the ... handbag (above). Nettie Rosenstein suit ... n Teller. Suit bag; Hattie's, Harofield's.

FIG. 25-10 Soft checked suit with belted jacket; 1960. Illustrates a soft, relaxed version of the boxy suits championed by Chanel in the late 1950s. The overall look is relaxed, casual, youthful, simple, and efficient. Photo courtesy of *Vogue.* Copyright © 1960 by the Condé Nast Publications, Inc.

fashion-setters like Jacqueline Kennedy still retained the boxy lines championed by Chanel, and the designer Marc Bohan in his collection for 1962 still presented for the House of Dior a black and white tweed matched box coat with a bowl straw hat that had all the geometric, boxy simplicity that had reigned in the late 1950s (Fig. 25-11).

Thus the 18 years from the end of World War II to the death of President Kennedy, despite the many attempts at new fashion lines, was predominantly a period of smooth textures, strong silhouettes, and geometric lines—an era later maligned for its intellectual games played with clothing and for its plastic efficiency.

## FABRICS

From the basic silks, woolens, and cottons available early in the century, there were dozens of alternatives by the 1950s, with properties such as crease resistance, shrinkage control, glazed surfaces, permanent pleating, moth resistance, and perfect washability. Synthetics had begun to appear in the fashions of the late 1930s, but it was not until after the war that nylon transformed the wardrobe. Petticoats could now stand up by themselves, stockings could be almost invisible, laces could be given tremendous strength, nightdresses

FIG. 25–11 The youthful matchbox coat of 1962. Illustrates that as late as 1962 the prevailing image was boxy simplicity with a very youthful look. Note particularly the youthful line of the collar and the rounded unity of the mitrelike hat. Photo courtesy of *Vogue*. Copyright © 1962 by the Condé Nast Publications, Inc.

could be permanently pleated, and knitted fabrics could have a much longer life. The 1954 glossary of synthetic fibers included Dynel, Fibrolane, Orlon, Terylene, and soon after, Dacron. Washable, drip-dry clothes became the norm, making ironing unnecessary, and the nylon fibers in girdles made possible the new two-way stretch. Even when the traditional fibers were used in clothes, they were mixed with synthetics for better wear and washability.

## ARTS AND ARTIFACTS

Furniture and interiors during this period generally continued the international style pioneered before the war. Furniture shapes were smooth and polished, and the lines were geometrical and tubular; vinyls were used in place of leather, and solid-colored upholstery in nubby synthetics were more popular than patterns or floral prints. Sliding glass doors; smooth, polished wooden or synthetic material wall surfaces; plain or geometric patterned rugs; vinyl floors; and plastic accessories were the avant-garde norm (Fig. 25–1a,b,c,d,e).

In personal accessories for men there were the standard items like the wristwatch, a wedding or family heirloom finger ring, cuff links (often monogrammed) for shirts with French cuffs, the precious stone or metal tie clasp, and occasional oddities like identification bracelets or Phi Beta Kappa chains. For women costume jewelry was the accepted mode of adornment rather than precious stones; bracelets, necklaces, and earrings were changed from season to season. By 1960 plastic was used extensively for jewelry, and the most popular form·of bracelet with the young was the charm bracelet, with the charms of gold rather than the silver that had been used when the style first developed in the 1940s. Women's watches were much smaller than men's and fastened with tiny expandable chains around the wrist. As individualized variations one also saw pins, rings, and pendant watches, but these were considered a little odd. For the wealthy and for formal evening wear, jewelry of diamonds and precious stones were still worn, often designed in styles reminiscent of the French Empire Period. Among hand-held accessories the primary item was the purse or handbag which ranged from soft and moderately proportioned cloth styles to the large, envelope shapes and huge shoulder bags that made their appearance about 1960 (Fig. 25–3j). Another hand-held accessory was the umbrella which was considered both functional and decorative. They were made of plain or patterned waterproof fabrics as well as transparent plastic with long or short handles that sometimes folded or telescoped for easier handling. Often umbrellas were not carried as protection against the rain but as a fashion accessory to be used like a walking stick.

## VISUAL SOURCES

For this period the best sources are periodicals; the fullest and most complete source is *Vogue* magazine, both the U.S. and British editions, as well as the book *In Vogue: Sixty Years of Celebrities and Fashion from British Vogue.* Other periodicals are *Femina, Harper's Bazaar, Horizon, Time, Town and Country, Women's Wear Daily, Life,* and *The New York Times.* The *Time/Life* volumes *This Fabulous Century 1940–1950* and *1950–1960* are also very useful. Institutional sources are the Smithsonian Institute Costume Collection, the Metropolitan Museum of Art, the Collection Union Francaise des Arts du Costume, the Brooklyn Museum, and the Bertarelli Collection of Milan. Photos from famous couturier costume houses are also a good source of visual material as are various mail-order catalogs.

## SUMMARY

This was a period of retrenchment and consolidation after the war and in the face of the anxieties of an atomic age and a world with a Cold War mentality. It was a period much like that following World War I with its attempted return to normalcy. Interiors, furnishings, and clothing continued in variations of machine imagery and mechanized efficiency with a great stress on the use of plastics and synthetics. There was still a great admiration for the simple, clean, geometric lines that one found in industrialized technology and a great preference for smooth, polished surfaces and hard, flat, or light-reflective textures. It was the era of the man in the grey flannel suit and the woman in the boxy suit jacket and skirt or the black A-line or H-line cocktail dress accented with pearls.

# chapter *XXVI*

# *Contemporary*

## *Chronology*

### (1963–1980)

CONTEMPORARY
1963–1980

1965

| | | |
|---|---|---|
| 1964 | Free speech movement at the campus of the University of California at Berkeley; beginning of the civil rights movement in the South; Harold Wilson becomes prime minister of Great Britain; President Johnson's War on Poverty; Gulf of Tonkin incident escalates the U.S. involvement in Vietnam |
| 1965 | President Johnson, after reelection, proclaims the Great Society; Department of Housing and Urban Development added to the Cabinet; the Soviet Union abolishes regional economic councils to restore centralized authority; Rhodesia proclaims its independence of Britain |
| 1966 | Changes in the Soviet governmental system causes the ruling presidium to revert to the title of *politburo;* Wilson reaffirms his position as prime minister of Great Britain in a general election; wage and price freeze begins in England; President Johnson tours Asia; the hippie movement continues to grow; the Beatles are the most popular music group in Britain and the United States |

1967       Eugene McCarthy announces he will run for the presidency; the Haight-Ashbury in San Francisco becomes the hippie-flower children mecca; the high point of psychedelic-rock music experiences; *Hair,* the most famous musical of the late 1960s, opens in New York; Britain's application to the European Economic Community is rejected; black violence in American cities; brief war between Egypt and Israel

1968       Britain begins restrictions on immigration; violent demonstrations accompany the Chicago Democratic Convention; Martin Luther King is assassinated; Robert Kennedy is assassinated; funky clothes for youth are the rage; Richard Nixon is elected president of the U.S.; Paris erupts in a near revolution against the de Gaulle government; the Vietnam War intensifies; the Tet offensive

1969       The Living Theater produces *Paradise Now;* the Performance Group produces *Dionysus in '69;* Nixon announces the withdrawal of 25,000 troops from Vietnam; American astronauts land on the moon; Ted Kennedy is involved in the Chappaquiddick incident; Yasser Arafat elected chairman of the Palestine Liberation Organization

1970       Increasing tensions in Israel with its surrounding neighbors; U.S.S.R. and West Germany sign a trade agreement; the U.S. incursion into Cambodia; four students killed by National Guardsmen at Kent State; increase in skyjacking; the Chicago conspiracy trial; Salvador Allende elected president of Chile

1968

1971       Cooling off between Israel and Egypt; U.S. government lifts restrictions on travel to China; U.S.-North Vietnamese peace talks in Paris; conference in Brussels on the problems of Soviet Jewry; 7,000 arrests made in an antiwar protest in Washington; new reform government in Portugal; Attica prison riot

1972

1972       Renewed and increasing violence in Northern Ireland; two "Soledad Brothers" acquitted; devaluation of the American dollar; "Harrisburg 7" trial fails to reach a verdict; Watergate break-in; the twentieth Olympiad opens in Munich; last U.S. combat troops leave Vietnam; President Nixon is reelected

1973       Great Britain enters the Common Market; Former President Johnson dies; a "peace treaty" is signed with Vietnam; members of the Watergate break-in group are convicted; Black September terrorists occupy the Saudi Arabian Embassy at Khartoum; siege at Wounded Knee caused by militant American Indians; mistrial in the case of Daniel Ellsberg and the Pentagon Papers; General Franco resigns as premier of Spain; Watergate scandal spreads

1974       President Nixon resigns; U.S.S.R. deports Solzhenitsyn; the U.S. and Egypt resume diplomatic relations; Labour government takes over in Britain; French president Pompidou dies; coup d'etat in Portugal; India explodes a nuclear device; Houses of Parliament bombed by IRA; Ford becomes president and Rockefeller, vice president, of U.S.; Premier Karamanlis victorious in Greece; gold legal for sale in U.S. after 41 years

1975

| 1975 | Jury convicts the Watergate four; IRA ceasefire expires; Conservatives elect Margaret Thatcher as leader of their party; Alaskan pipeline construction begins; Chiang Kai-shek dies; North Sea oil flow begins; Haile Selassie of Ethiopia dies at 83; woman shoots at President Ford; Sakharov wins Nobel Peace Prize; Prince Juan Carlos to rule Spain |
|---|---|
| 1976 | Moynihan resigns as ambassador to U.N.; Princess Margaret and her husband separate; earthquake in northern Italy; Queen Elizabeth visits the U.S.; Olympic Games open in Montreal; Legionnaires' disease strikes in Pennsylvania; Prince Bernhard of The Netherlands in disgrace; Mao Tse-tung dies; Socialist government in Sweden defeated; Carter wins presidency of U.S. |
| 1977 | Czechoslovak intellectuals issue a manifesto on human rights; Carter becomes U.S. president; U.S. and Vietnam open talks in Paris; "Orient Express" makes its final run; Begin takes office in Israel; Alaskan oil finally reaches Valdez; disastrous blackout in New York; Laker Airways begins cheap flights between London and New York; Anwar Sadat goes to Israel |
| 1978 | President Tito of Yugoslavia visits the U.S.; Aldo Moro kidnapped in Rome; Palace of Versailles bombed; Indira Gandhi ousted from Congress Party in India; Shcharansky sentenced in the U.S.S.R.; first test tube baby in England; Pope Paul VI dies; Camp David Meeting; Pope John Paul II elected; crisis in Iran; Spaniards approve a new constitution |

1979

| 1979 | Shah driven from power in Iran; rising inflation along with rising oil prices in U.S.; Vietnam takes over most of Cambodia; Three Mile Island nuclear accident; Chrysler Corporation near bankruptcy; tragedy of the boat people of Vietnam; Ted Kennedy enters presidential race against Carter; Somoza of Nicaragua driven from power; Andew Young leaves his position at the U.N.; Lord Mountbatten assassinated; John Wayne dies; Godunov defects from Bolshoi Ballet |
| --- | --- |

# BACKGROUND

The tired and complacent culture of the United States in the 1950s with its images of the man in the grey flannel suit, suburban tract living, Cold War politics, Eisenhower conservatism, and narrowness and smugness of thought began to change in the early 1960s under the energetic and idealistic leadership of John F. Kennedy. Suddenly there arose a new feeling of commitment to human concerns in such diverse places as college campuses, black southern churches, and executive board rooms. From men at the bottom of the economic pyramid to others at the top there was a stirring of interest in human problems above and beyond the old Cold War mentality. This was reflected in the founding of the Peace Corps, the opening of the civil rights movement, and the commitment of the nation to the defense of freedom in the world. Throughout the United States and later in Western Europe there was an excitement and ferment that stressed human values above the organizational and analytical—people above societal structure. There was also a new concept brought about by the increasing interconnectedness of all the peoples of the globe—that the world was entering a new era as a totally interdependent global village. With the gradual dawning of the great space age,

philosophers and intellectuals saw how small and finite the earth really was and stressed that its resources must be conserved carefully for future generations. Economists such as John Galbraith commented on this growing interdependence through the rise of multinational corporations and the erosion of the national capitalism in favor of international business. Although often resisted by politicians and world leaders, there was a slow but sure trend in the developed world toward international concerns.

Even after the shock of the assassination of President Kennedy and the escalation of the war in Vietnam, which was violently opposed by the young as a war fostered by the "old" thinking, there was not a retreat from idealism but a more violent and militant support of the new ways of thinking. In the Berkeley free speech movement, the civil rights movement, the antiwar movement, and the human potential movement, there was a strong support for change. Out of the variety of new causes came an implied threat to the "old order" and a militant determination to bring about a new way of life. Lapel buttons of the 1960s carried such phrases as "We Shall Overcome," "Legalize Spiritual Discovery," "Turn On, Tune In,

Drop Out,'' ''Suppose We Gave a War and Nobody Came,'' ''I Am a Human Being: Do Not Fold, Spindle or Mutilate.'' The essence of all of this ferment was that for a brief time people became aware that the cold, mechanized, corporate, organizational approach to life had deadened feeling and dulled moral individual and human values in favor of abstract social concerns.

By the summer of 1967 the so-called hippies, who were romantic and naive children seduced by the marijuana euphoria of the ''new times,'' fled to gathering places like San Francisco's Haight-Ashbury, New England's woods, New York's East Village, the hills outside Los Angeles, and Boston Common for great gatherings. The climax of these gatherings took place near Woodstock, New York, in 1969, and flaunted the ideals of the new movement in a gigantic mass festival. For the first time in U.S. history the Protestant work ethic, the ideals of competitive capitalism, and the values of materialism were ignored. An entire generation plus all those who copied their clothing, hair styles, sexual freedom, rock music, and general outlook thought that they had turned against the plastic world of the ''establishment.''

But the new movement had a violent side, as the militant activists organized to oppose the war, and the black ghettos erupted to demand more equality. By the late 1960s the phenomenon was not just American but dominated much of Western Europe and Japan. In 1968 there was a pitched battle at the Democratic Convention in Chicago, a violent upheaval in Paris that almost overturned the government, and a number of vicious demonstrations in Tokyo. Violence also plagued college campuses throughout the world until the Vietnamese War began to wind down in the early 1970s. With financial recession, energy shortages, and the final disengagement in Vietnam, confrontation and revolt receded, and young people began to turn to private goals and a concern for self. Although there remained basic support for human over organizational values in the anger at Watergate, support for Amnesty International, concern for the Third World people, and interest in the human potential movement, there was a retrenchment into

the self and a quiet distillation of the explosive ideals of the 1960s. Like the somewhat repressive Romanticism that followed the explosive Romantic revolutions of 1830, the 1970s were a period of nostalgia and escapism.

In this period films like the heart-grabbing *Rocky* or the parable of good triumphant in *Star Wars* were runaway successes; tea dances, Viennese balls, and all manner of nostalgia crazes were characteristic. The interest in the occult demonstrated the romantic, irrational escapism that was a reaction to the explosive 1960s. The media were filled with stories about psychokinetics, ESP, biorhythm calculators, postdeath experiences, conversations with plants, and tales of ancient astronauts.

In interior decoration there was a sharp dualistic split in the late 1960s and 1970s between corporate existence and private living. In the former one still found smooth metal and vinyl-covered furniture, cold white corridors, technologial ornament, and a machine-made look, but in the latter rich and varied textures returned, with a new interest in antiques and a ''Third-World'' eclecticism that emphasized a new emotional interest in handicrafts from exotic places throughout the world. This movement originated in the ''hippie pads'' of the 1960s in which collected memorabilia, craft items, interesting castoffs from society, and items collected from everyday experience created a womblike refuge for the romantic and insecure that was similar in feeling to the respectable yet cluttered interiors of repressed Romanticism in the late nineteenth century. The new ''romantic'' rooms had the same personal and sentiment-producing qualities as in the Victorian Age except that the artifacts were now antisocial and anticultural. But when the upheavals of the late 1960s receded, the ''establishment'' gradually adopted many of these same ideas. Middle-class rooms also began to be filled with personally chosen antiques that appealed to the senses; rich woods, thick upholsteries, floral patterns, textured walls, gaily patterned rugs, and sensuous draperies returned to interior decoration. The stress was once again on sensuous human, rather than coldly intellectual, values. A good example is a room from *House and Home*

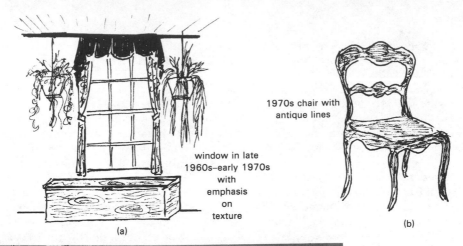

window in late
1960s–early 1970s
with
emphasis
on
texture

(a)

1970s chair with
antique lines

(b)

Michael Rose, house interior, Chevy Chase, Maryland; 1976. Illustrates the new interest in wooden furniture, antiques, worm-eaten paneling, stone fireplaces, and textured floors that appeal to the tactile, textural, sensuous interests of the inhabitants. Photo courtesy of Michael Rose. Photograph by J. Alexander.

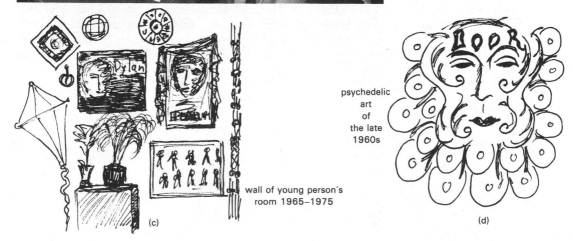

wall of young person's
room 1965–1975

(c)

psychedelic
art
of
the late
1960s

(d)

**FIGURE 26–1**

*Magazine* for January, 1977 (Fig. 26–1). Just as the conservative and traditionally-oriented Victorians of the 1840s tightened up the flamboyant Romanticism of the 1830s while still incorporating many of its basic premises in a more conservative way, so the 1970s did the same with the ideals of the 1960s.

## THE BASIC COSTUME SILHOUETTE

The youthful rebellion of the 1960s was strongly represented by dress, and clothes became an important weapon in the struggle against the "establishment" with its cliché images of the man in the grey flannel suit and the woman in the black cocktail sheath. The chic rebels of the late 1960s were barefoot, ragged, and primitive one day and the next decked out in colorful boots, leathers, blouses, and scarfs representing Gypsy attire. Hair was allowed to grow long and full, facial hair came back for men, and variety and personal choice, no matter how bizarre, were the key to youthful fashions. For the first time the style-setters were not an exclusive few designers and the elegant women who wore their clothes. Fashion now came from the street, and designers like Rudy Gernreich and Mary Quant watched what the young were wearing and then came out with their own adaptations.

For the male the key to fashion during this period was the growth of personal, individual choice in clothes at the expense of what was left of the century-and-a-half-old concept of gentility and the gentleman. Although in the 1970s the three-piece suit made a dramatic return, a major number of men, both young and old, no longer thought it necessary to wear the traditional capitalist uniform and wore instead a variety of garments including leather jackets, tight trousers, open-necked shirts, turtlenecks, and boots (Fig. 26–2). The explosion of the sensuous and the physical in the youthful styles of the late 1960s was reminiscent of the physical look admired in the 1490s (see Fig. 11–3) when the Renaissance had broken with the Gothic past and had not yet been corrupted by the repressions of the sixteenth century. Although the later 1970s saw a return to a more nostalgic, romantic conservatism in men's clothing, there was tremendous eclectic variety, even at formal functions. Leather and fashionable blue jean jackets were seen at the the theater, and at cocktail parties along with three-piece suits. After 1963 many fashions were derived from outdoor pastimes like motorcycling, riding, hiking, mountain climbing, and skiing. This made the art of tailoring for many less important, and the new male boutiques did not stress subtleties of cut and drape but texture, sexiness, variety, and romantic eroticism. The erotic principle that was missing from male attire in favor of dressing for position returned, and there was a feeling that the male should dress to please himself, be sexually attractive, and wear clothes that were physically and tactilely pleasing to him in his daily work.

An interesting example of what happened in this new era when style came from the bottom up may be seen in the fortunes of the Levi Strauss Company of San Francisco. The firm in the nineteenth century made heavy, blue denim jeans and jackets for miners and later cowboys, and these remained a specific lower-class uniform throughout the first half of the twentieth century with a faint aura of romanticisim connected with the open prairies and the nonurban freedom of the past. Then with the youthful revolt of the 1960s, boys and girls used faded and worn blue jeans and jackets as a symbol of romantic protest against "establishment" regimentation. Blue jeans and jackets were solidly proletarian and extremely physical. They faded so that the wearer looked as if he or she had weathered the clothes in the world of nature, and the pants shrank to show off the physical contours of the body. For a more undressed and primitive look, sleeves and legs were frequently raggedly cut off to give more exposure to the body, and at other times the faded denims were embroidered, patched, and inset with brightly colored fabrics. By the 1970s these practices had become institutionalized, and there were yearly contests for the best

(a) turtleneck shirt and sack suit 1968

(b) fringed suede vest, patterned short, blotch-bleached pants, beads— funky fads 1968

(c) psychedelic shirt and wide paisley tie 1967–1973

boots 1960s and 1970s

(d)

(e) Bowie tie worn with sport shirt 1960s and 1970s

brocade coat, velvet pants, ruffled shirt 1968

(f)

(g) blue jeans jacket and pants (levis), illustrated T-shirt, boots, mid-1960s and after

(h) 1960s wide belt

leather car coat 1960s, 1970s

(m)

beard and mustache 1973

(l)

hair and mustache late 1960s—early 1970s

(i) Nehru jacket, early to mid-1960s

(j) suit 1973

Male fashions of the mid-1970s. Illustrates a business suit and casual wear that include a leather jacket and boots on one model and a youthful three-piece business suit topped off with a short raincoat and a scarf on the other. Photo courtesy of the Emporium, San Francisco and the Sabina and Grimmé model agencies. Permission also granted by male models Jack Mice and Eddie Donlin.

(k) leather hat early 1970s

**FIGURE 26–2**

470

(a)
pants
suit
mid 1960s

(b)
leather
outfit
1964

(c)
lace
stockings
and white
kid zipper
boots
1964

(d)
1979

bootees
1978

1979

jersey
blouse
with sleeve
tied in leather
thongs, suede
pants open
at sides and
laced with
thongs
1968

(e)

satin dress
tied with
gold cord—
escapist
romantic
1968

(f)
sassoon
hairdo
1966

(g)
mini dress
1964

(h)
suit
1979

(i)
knitted
skirt and
cardigan
1973

(k)

maxicoat
and boots
1969

(j)

Embroidered blue denims, late 1960s and early
1970s. Illustrates the mystique attached to blue
denim clothes by the young in the late 1960s. The
jackets and jeans molded to the contours of the
body, gave a weathered, lower-class image, and
were exotically decorated to give a primitive, hand-
crafted look. Photo courtesy of Levi Strauss of San
Francisco. Photograph by Baron Wolman.

**FIGURE 26-3**

hand-crafted decorations and embroideries (Fig. 26–3). Flared bottoms were the fashion industry's answer to the flared effect created when the "hippies" inserted colored fabric in the bottom side seams of blue jeans to gain a floppy, colorful improvement on the straight legs of the standard Levis. Other mannered and artificial effects that were created include machine-stitched compartments to give surface interest, mechanized photographic reproduction of patches on jackets and pants, and designers' jeans with the designer's name or monogram prominently displayed. Thus the fashion industry created machine-made answers to hand-crafted embroidery and decoration, but the results were frequently mannered and artificial in the way that sixteenth-century clothing was often a mannered and artificial perversion of the open, natural, and human styles of the final decade of the fifteenth century.

Although the clothing for this period was remarkably similar for men and women, there was an even greater variety in the shapes and kinds of feminine dress. Certainly the most important political and social movement behind many changes in female fashion was the women's movement, and yet the first break with the styles of the 1950s came with the miniskirt which was even shorter than the skirts of the 1920s and was more a challenge to prudery and the status quo than it was a statement of women's lib. With the beginning of the youth revolt, there was a greater narrowing of the difference between men's and women's attire than ever before, particularly in the matter of long hair. Among the young, one could seldom tell boys from girls unless the boy wore a beard.

By the early 1970s and with the increasing importance of the women's movement, pants suits, slacks, and tight jeans with flared bottoms had become as important, if not more important, for the female wardrobe than dresses and skirts. Prominent women secretaries and executives as well as fashionable women about town wore pants suits on all but the most formal occasions. Skirts and dresses were often reserved primarily for balls and parties in which a woman could change from her sense of comfort, efficiency, and newfound position in society to indulge her taste in the romantic and exotic of past times and faraway places. In fact, the predominant fashion image of the decade, aside from the interest in trousers and male-inspired attire, was nostalgia for rich, natural textures and romantic images from the past or other cultures. There were romantic borrowings from the Russian, the Indian, the African, the Gypsy, and the Oriental—often in the same costume—all of which was a far cry from the uniform of the black cocktail dress of the late 1950s. Furs, leathers, rough knits, colorful woolens, and exotic silks in blouses, capes, shawls, jackets, and scarfs created a textural display that coincided with the male interest in self-pleasure and physical-sexual attractiveness. One of the strongest innovations of the period for both men and women, but particularly for women, was the varied and constant use of leather boots which gave a great boost to the physical-romantic image. Although the Chinese pioneered the regimented uniform for both men and women and designers tried to introduce the space suit look from time to time, the fashions of the Western world in the 1960s and 1970s were predominantly romantic, exotic, physical, individualistic, and unstructured (Fig. 26–4).

## CONTEMPORARY COSTUME

**Masculine Dress**   In the period between 1963 and 1980, men's clothing made some dramatic shifts: from the gentlemanly to the often frankly erotic, from the conventional to the individual, from a rather limited view of acceptable "establishment" dress to a tremendous variety. This variety was not just in color, cut, fabric, and kinds of garments but in reasons for wearing clothes and the sources from which these clothes were derived. Men now bought exclusively cut, three-piece suits at expensive tailors but also bought leathers, tight pants, exotic accoutrements derived from Third World cultures from a variety of bou-

**FIG. 26-4** Female fashions of the mid-1970s. Illustrates a group of separates in soft Dacron knit that gave a natural look. The idea was to mix casual and practical garments that connected women's new place in society with a romantic feminism. Photo courtesy of the Emporium, San Francisco, and the Sabina and Grimmé model agencies. Permission also granted by models Karen Mirner and Beverly Leftwich.

tiques, specialty shops, and craft fairs. In short, the greatest revolution of the period was in the variety and sources of male clothing.

In suits the early 1960s saw the slender trouser line that bespoke an Edwardian or Italian cut under a suit coat that had slim lines, relatively narrow lapels, and little shoulder padding. At this time the double-breasted suit

disappeared, and vests became less popular. With the explosion of individualism in men's clothing in the mid-to-late 1960s, there were a number of minor but rather dramatic shifts in the cut of suits. Flared cuffs or slightly bell-bottomed, cuffless trousers made their appearance, suit coats were often longer than in the past, the Nehru jacket suit with a small, standing collar and no lapels was briefly popular (Fig. 26-2i), and for the young, suits often began to appear in exotic fabrics (Fig. 26-2f) like velour and brocade (Fig. 26-5). Thus the romantic in clothing, particularly for the young, came with a great rush and with attempts to suggest the age of the maharajahs of India, the England of Jane Austen, and the Romany never-never land of the Gypsies, with hair styles that reminded one of Prince Valiant and King Arthur's court. Particularly strong inspiration came from the dress of the Beatles with their mixture of colorful styles loosely derived from the Edwardian. Even double-breasted suit jackets returned, often with belt loops at the waist for a wide, leather belt and wider lapels than had been seen in years. Such suits were often worn with open-neck, brilliantly colored and patterned shirts (Fig. 26-2c) or with lightweight turtleneck sweaters (Fig. 26-2a). Waistcoats returned and were as decorative as those of the early nineteenth century, with double- or single-breasted fronts and with or without lapels in all manner of rich fabrics and exotic colors. Even among slightly older men color came back into suits as may be seen in the fashionable double-knit synthetic fabrics of the late 1960s and early 1970s. One could see quite sedate businessmen and salesmen in bright greens, reds, or blues. The trousers that went with all these new suit changes were worn low on the hips with very wide belts and decorative buckles (Fig. 26-2h), were very tight-fitting over the buttocks, and flared into a wide, cuffless bottom that broke over the shoe and almost touched the floor at the back (Fig. 26-2j).

There were brief experiments with a one-piece jumpsuit, with a sleeveless sack suit for air travel, and many other fashion proposals that came and went before a certain new conservatism began to settle into business clothing

**FIG. 26–5** Exotic, rich, escapist romantic fantasies in clothing for the young at the close of the 1960s. Note the rich fabrics in the men's jackets, the oriental bolero jacket on one of the girls, and the Juliet dress on the other. The colors were rich and exotic blues, purples, and mauves. Photo courtesy of Richard Davis.

toward the middle of the 1970s. Colors and fabrics became subtler, there was less exaggeration in cut, more emphasis placed on fine tailoring, and less attention paid to richness and ostentation (Fig. 26-2). There was a great return to organic fabrics, a diminished use of all synthetics, and even the leathers that had made such an impact on the 1960s were cut with a new sense of form and subtle elegance. The most fashionable youthful suits had double vents in back; snug, high-waisted jackets with long skirts; and body-fitting pants to the thighs with a subtler flare at the bottom edge than in the past (Fig. 26-2j). The general effect was still romantic, physical, and even slightly erotic but in a much more restrained and subtle manner.

In casual and sporting clothes during these years there was such a variety of styles that one cannot mention them all, but the great contribution of the 1960s was the upgrading of Levi's and faded blue denim to a major element in fashion, along with all manner of suedes and leathers (Fig. 26-2g). Again it all began with the young, and when it moved from the ''hippie'' world into the lower levels of fashion, it was known as the *funky* look. It resulted from putting together things that didn't seem to go together and yet made an interesting combination pleasing to the individual wearing it (Fig. 26-2b). It involved fringed suede vests, beads, wraparound blouses and shorts from a second-hand store, brocades, blue jeans or duck pants, chains and decorative girdles for the hips, and

scores of other possible permutations (Fig. 26-6). In the world of Levi jackets and jeans it meant cutting, embroidering, beading, and decorating (with colored fabrics) what had been the proletarian garments of the cowboy (Fig. 26-3). In the slightly more middle-class world of the sports coat and trousers, the lines of cut were similar to that in suits, but there was much greater experimentation in color and pattern.

During this period the button-down-collared *Ivy League* shirt of the opening of the 1960s gave way to great experimentation, particularly among the young after the great success of the Beatles with their ruffled, patterned, and excessively colorful shirt-blouses. There were also Russian, Indian, and Gypsy shirts as well as the more restrained turtleneck knit shirt. The latter became very popular with even quite conservative types as an alternative to shirt and tie. Ties blossomed in size and in their colorful floral and abstract patterns (Fig. 26-2c), and even bow ties became very large. There were also neck scarfs and the bolo tie for western types (Fig. 26-2e). Only in the mid-1970s did these all begin to tone down in size and pattern to more subtly pleasing geometric patterns of relatively small size in subdued colors.

Formal wear changed less than most other things, even though during the late 1960s there were many more varieties of ruffled shirts and rich, colorful textures in dinner jackets, vests, and trousers. Men's formal stores displayed tails and morning coats in beige, pale blue, or

**FIG. 26-6** Funky youthful male fashions of the late 1960s. *Funky* meant putting things together that were exciting and interesting but wouldn't normally seem to work with each other. Here we have tie-dyed pants with a print shirt, many chains and girdles, and clean white pants with a fringed leather vest and beads. Photo courtesy of Raymundo de Larrain.

brown, trimmed in darker braid or velvet in the same color with matching top hat.

Swim suits did not change radically in this period except to be very brief, physical, and in a variety of colors and textures. Ski clothes were equally bright with many interlined jackets and trousers in water-repellent synthetics with a stripe down the sleeve and trouser sides. Jogging suits that made a splash in the late 1970s were of soft, cotton knits with loose-fitting trousers and hooded jackets, again with a stripe down the sleeve and trouser sides.

Outerwraps exploded in the mid-1960s with fur and fur-collared coats, a great variety of leather and suede car and overcoats (Fig. 26-2m), and even occasional capes for men. Standard wraps remained the water-repellent trench coat, the plastic raincoat, and overcoats and topcoats of plain and tweed woolens. Hats almost disappeared during this period except for the ultra-conservative; when headgear was worn, it was usually a cap, leather hat (Fig. 26-2k), or some kind of hood. The great innovation in footwear during this period was in the addition of boots to men's wear—from the heavy, work boots of the harness racer and cowboy to the smooth-fitting, elegant, calf-high cuts of the young men about town (Fig. 26-2d). Some were pull-on, many were zippered, and during the late 1960s moccasinlike "hippie" boots were popular with the young. There was also a great use of hand-crafted sandals, raised heels, and rounded, square, or pointed toes.

Hair became much longer in the late 1960s, beards and mustaches were more common than at any time since the late nineteenth century, and there was a great variety in hair length and in facial hair, if it was worn (Fig. 26-2).

The military uniforms of the Vietnamese War were similar to those at the close of World War II, with more stress on off-duty uniforms and the use of civilian dress when not on duty.

**Feminine Dress** As with men there was an explosion of romanticism and a variety of individual choices during the late 1960s for women. Again the sources for style were the imaginations of the young and the "street people" transformed into high fashion. In general, the styles were chosen to underline the physical agility of the female body with great stress placed on the hips and crotch as the key erogenous zone for emphasis and focus—all part of the sexual revolution of the 1960s. As with men variety was a key factor, and this variety was tied to individual choice rather than to establishment, ceremonial, or institutional demands. In the 1960s the image was that of rebellion, flamboyance, richness, and color, while later the general emphasis was on softness, casualness, and practical comfort, with a gradual return to the classic styles of the 1930s and 1940s as inflation rose and clothes had to be worn for more than one season.

In 1963 the change toward the later styles of the 1960s was ushered in by the early manifestations of the miniskirt, revealing the knees and the full leg, and the great explosion in boots for women. Some of the fashion boots reached to the thighs and disappeared under the skirt (Fig. 26–3b), while others had cuffs, laces, straps, or buckles. Except for the new short skirt line, dresses still leaned toward the sheath line, and suits were still rather boxy and geometric. The new haircut was the thick, chopped bob introduced by Vidal Sassoon to support the bone structure of the face (Fig. 26–3f). The newest shaped hat was the fur, knit, or leather helmet with or without bill or chin strap. Mary Quant put out a collection of cheap, simple, geometrically shaped clothes to be collected piece by piece and then put together in many variations, and St. Laurent made a splash with his black and white geometric shifts that caught the attention of many imitators.

In 1964 the miniskirt was at its peak (Fig. 26–3g), and pants suits (Fig. 26–3a) had single- and double-breasted fingertip jackets and slim trousers curved up over the ankle in front and dipped down in back (Fig. 26–7). There were evening pants suits of sequins and lamé and daytime suits with pants or skirts of a boxy cut that reflected many of the high fashion attempts to create space-age imagery through the use of white in geometric shapes (Fig. 26–7). Boots were still very important, and many legs were covered in lace ribbed or patterned stockings under miniskirts with the bottom of the leg zipped into leather or plastic boots (Fig. 26–3c).

In 1965 the British styles were "in," and many fashion ideas came from London and Carnaby Street. Jean Shrimpton, the model, shocked fashion audiences with skirts four inches above the knee. There was also the daring see-through dress with a net midriff of allover white crochet and the introduction of Rudy Gernreich's "no bra" bra. A very erotic and exotic note was struck by leather jumpsuits

FIG. 26–7  Courrèges fashions for 1964 that relate to space exploration and the so-called *moon girl* look. Note the knee-length camel coat over a white gabardine dress and a trouser suit of white cotton, both worn with "space helmets" and white kid boots. Photo courtesy of *British Vogue.* Copyright © 1964 by Condé Nast Publications, Inc.

lined in silk and worn with a hooded jersey sweater and leather helmet (Fig. 26–8).

1966 still saw more stress on the space look than on the funky look. There were crazy textures like plastic chain mail, plastic silver leatherette, plastic disc earrings, and silver stockings, and there was a craze for false hair and wigs as well as for excessive makeup. As an alternative style there was the growing interest in romantic lines and interesting textures that were present in St. Laurent's Gypsy shifts, shirts, and skirts and in the introduction of the Moroccan caftan, which soon be a major item of female fashion.

In 1967 and 1968 the new romantic look hit with a vengeance. Particularly for the young

**FIG. 26–8** Bonnie Cashin leather track suit lined in silk; 1965. The arrival of leather as a very organic, physical, sensuous texture is here linked with the image of the space suit, marking the transition from the efficient and mechanized look to the sensuous, physical, and romantic. Photo courtesy of *British Vogue.* Copyright © 1965 by the Condé Nast Publications, Inc.

there were fashions inspired by Marco Polo and the Orient, India with its draped saris, Regency and Empire dresses from the beginning of the nineteenth century, and jackets and accessories inspired by the Arabian Nights—often all blended within the same fashion grouping (Fig. 26-5). In practice the word *romantic* now covered three kinds of dress: the "flower children" with their Levis, Indian leather fringing, headband of patterned scarfs, beads, tassels, and long straight hair (Fig. 26-3e); the wealthier version of this "funky" look with Gypsy dresses, Oriental pants, Afghan coats of sheepskin, and exotic accessories and jewelry from all over the globe; and finally, the "ruffle and ringlet look" with velvet knee breeches, ruffled shirts, velour jackets, ruffled dresses in fragile fabrics with milkmaid sleeves, and hair worn in ringlets or tied in ribbon bunches (Fig. 26-3k). Thus this was the time when the pop

and space fashions were finally pushed aside by exotic and romantic Third World or minority images.

By 1969 the high tide of revolution had passed, and there was a sense that fashion was now individual and could range over the whole world for its choices of line and accessories. For example, skirts could now be mini, knee length, calf length or maxi, and everything was possible if it was right for the individual wearer. Dior introduced the "beat" look with pale zombie faces, leather suits and coats, knit caps, high turtlenecks, and an excessive use of black. There were also caped highwayman coats (Fig. 26-3j) and a return to the Russian ballet and its art deco inheritance in some of the patterned panné velvet evening gowns of the season. The antique clothes market became a thriving industry.

As the 1970s began, women's clothing

became more interested in decoration than silhouette, with colored hair, painted patterns on dresses, heavy use of cosmetics, and all manner of scarfs, jewelry, painted boots, and layered haircuts. In the summer there was an attempted return to the maxi skirt for everyone, but individuality was now entrenched and only a minority of women bought the longer skirts. There seemed to be no rules anymore, and the variety of styles in fashion magazines was immense. There was a return to the 1930s and 1940s for ideas (Fig. 26–9), and pants suits became more and more popular for young and

FIG. 26–10   Pants suits with a tweedy look; 1971. The pants suits of the early 1970s marked the renewed efforts of the women's rights movement, coupled with a strong interest in pattern, particularly plaids, tweeds, and pattern knits. Photo courtesy of *British Vogue.* Copyright © 1971 by the Condé Nast Publications, Inc.

FIG. 26–9   Saint Laurent printed shirt, printed wool skirt, and patchwork sweater vest; 1971. Illustrates the borrowings from the 1930s and 1940s that gave the romantic patterns and textures of the early 1970s a gentler, more nostalgic look than the exotic fashions of the late 1960s. Photo courtesy of *British Vogue.* Copyright © 1971 by the Condé Nast Publications, Inc.

old, particularly tweedy styles with bold, plaid patterns (Fig. 26–10).

In 1972 there was a great interest in sweater, trouser, and shoe combinations with the layered look of a patterned pullover worn over a turtleneck. Trousers were wider, some even pleated at the waist, there was a new interest in windbreaker jackets gathered into wide elastic bands at cuffs and waist, and sailor suits were in for summer. Shoes were preposterously high with thick platforms adding height to already tall heels; St. Laurent featured rope-soled espadrilles in primary colors laced over bright tights. As the wilder aspects of fashion continued to recede, hair also shifted from the long, straight styles of the late 1960s to the shorter, bobbed, and layered lines that continued through the mid-1970s.

By 1973 fashions came to be still more simple, with a return to some of the classic jacket and dress lines of the past, but with the difference that they were always cut to look uncontrived, soft, and easy (Fig. 26–3i). Cardigans, blouses, skirts, and suits were chosen as if each was a separate purchase with a variety of combination possibilities. With the young, jeans, T-shirts with photographed pictures and captions, long cotton skirts, full-sleeved shirts, and antique fur coats were popular.

By 1974 and 1975 clothes were not smart but easy and appropriate for wearer and occasion with stress on the simple, the wrapped, and the layered. Basically the wearer designed the clothes by changing combinations and accessories. As inflation grew, clothes were bought for more than a season, and the classic trench coats, suits, blouses, skirts, slacks, and sweaters became the standard items. One distinctive coat was the maxi (Fig. 26–3j) that was both warm and rather romantic, and when worn with a beret and large muffler was very appealing (Fig. 26–11). In dresses there were often groupings of social separates in very soft lines that gave a very natural look and might include a tank top, long skirt, pants, and a sheer peasant-poncho blouse. The idea was to mix casual and practical garments that reflected women's new place in society with a romantic feminism (Fig. 26–4).

Thus by the late 1970s there was a great variety of styles from the romantic boots, jeans, and Gypsy prints of the late 1960s to the newer woolen and knit classics that often harked back to the late 1930s and early 1940s for inspiration (particularly in extended shoulders), with the difference that the new versions were always softer and somewhat more casual and natural. In many ways the period saw little innovation

**FIG. 26–11** Maxi coat for 1974–1975. These great coats were warm and loose-fitting, could be wrapped about the body in varying ways, and with the help of a large scarf as accent were a whole winter's wardrobe. They stressed not fit or chic but the personality of the owner by the way they were worn. Photo courtesy of *British Vogue.* Copyright © by the Condé Nast Publications, Inc.

in fashion and only a nostalgic look to the past for a kind of escapist sense of security that was missing in the present (Fig. 26–3h). Nostalgia in fashion took many forms—from the junk market clothes that presented a mixture of past styles to the revival of the classics of the past that made oldtimers stop and look at the fashion models in a window a second time, certain that what they saw was directly lifted from 1939 or 1941.

# FABRICS

Fabrics during this period ran the gamut of possibilities. In the 1960s there seemed to be a battle between the synthetic materials worn by the "establishment" and the natural fibers preferred by the young. Among the former there were all manner of combinations of natural and polyester fibers; and among the young, aside from the faded blue denim fabric brought on by the craze for Levis, there were leather, panné velvet, printed cottons, muslin and other natural cottons from India, textured and knit woolens, fur, Third World brocades and prints, and hand-painted silks. By the end of the 1960s all these exotic fabrics were also being worn by the truly fashionable, although the synthetics were much too practical to be put aside. In the early 1970s there was a craze for polyester double-knits in men's jackets and slacks and in women's pants suits; by the mid-1970s a great emphasis was placed on soft Dacrons and Quianas for women's blouses and dresses. Then there was a gradual move away from synthetics to organic fibers and a great upsurge in pure wool jackets and suits, real silks for blouses and scarfs, and 100 percent cotton for summer wear, blouses, and skirts. Leather was probably the most innovative garment and boot material throughout the entire period.

# ARTS AND ARTIFACTS

In interiors and furnishings this period saw a return to organic materials and rich textures with a stress on leather rather than vinyl-covered couches and chairs, a complete break with tubular metallic furniture, a return to antiques and carving, and a new interest in antique copies and reproductions in fine woods. There was also a great new interest in exotic items of furnishings and decoration from all over the world, particularly from Third World countries. From the cluttered, chaotic, but personal, apartment or "pad" of the 1960s emerged the personalized and individualized interior of the 1970s in which personal preferences in carved paneling, imported rugs, or antique furnishings replaced the architect-designer look of the past (Fig. 26–1).

In accessories for men during this period one is always struck by the way items increased in size and interest in the later 1960s. There were wide wristwatch bands, identification bracelets, neck beads, pendants on leather thongs or chains, peace symbols, ethnic religious symbols, wide belts with complex, tooled metal buckles, exotic finger rings, and occasional use of the small, single earring. All of these continued in the 1970s but with less ostentation. Belts thinned down, buckles became simple and classic, wristwatch bands became smaller, and necklaces were less often seen, while the classic accessories of cuff links, studs, and tie clasps returned.

For women costume jewelry increased in size and richness with much use of handcrafted rings, bracelets, and necklaces in silver set with polished stones. There was a great interest in rings all the way from exotic antique items to the handcrafted, abstract, organic ones. Band bracelets in groups made of plastic, silver, or gold were popular and were worn not only on the wrist but sometimes on the upper arm. There was also body jewelry like rich girdles, silver and gold bras, and large collars. Shell necklaces and earrings were also very popular with the young, and watches were made with large faces, big numerals, and wide wristbands. Then with the coming of the 1970s came a more conservative bent in accessories and a return to the past for shapes and decorative ideas. When jewelry was worn, it was derived from elegant past periods particularly the French Empire, but in general, jewelry and accessories were far less important and less visible in this decade than in the preceding one.

Purses ranged from the great leather shoulder strap satchels for the young—tooled and fringed for rich effect—to the simple, beaded, clutch purses for evening, with plastic and straw medium-sized bags for everyday use. Umbrellas were less important as a fashion accessory than in the past, but one new style had a bowl rather than a plate shape to it, and many were made of transparent plastic rather than fabric.

## VISUAL SOURCES

*Vogue* magazine is still a most important visual source, in both its English and American editions, and the book *In Vogue: Sixty Years of Celebrities and Fashion From British Vogue* is an excellent source up to 1975. Other periodicals are *Harper's Bazaar, Time, Life, Town and Country, Women's Wear Daily,* the *New York Times* and the French magazine, *Elle.* Institutional sources are the Metropolitan Museum of Art, the Collection Union Francaise des Arts du Costume, and the Smithsonian Institution Costume Collection. Again the famous dress houses are an excellent source of photographs as are mail-order catalogs.

## SUMMARY

This period saw almost a lifetime of change—from the excitement of the civil rights movement through the "hippie" explosion to the violent peak of the antiwar movement and the explosion of romanticism and physicality as a protest against the plastic "establishment." Then with the tide of rebellion and revolution on the wane, a new conservatism set in, and the exotic, personalized, decorative, organically-based fashions of the late 1960s gave way to "establishment" versions of those fashions with machine-quilted denims, pre-faded Levi's and toned-down romanticism. As inflation, in-security, and recession gripped the Western world, fashion withdrew to a more classic, relaxed, comfortable line with fewer bizarre eruptions of style. By the late 1970s when the unpleasant present brought a backward-looking nostalgia, there was one fashion revival after another with the center of interest focused on the 1930s and 1940s. Just as the Revolution of 1830 gave way to the Victorian conservatism of the 1840s, fashion in the 1970s continued to use many of the fashion ideas of the 1960s in a more controlled and restricted manner.

# *Postcript*

It is a long journey from the rough skins of prehistoric times to the varied, complex, and changing fashions of the present, and in the great panorama of clothing presented by Western history, it has been fascinating to see in what ways each era has reflected humanity's relationship to the world and its morals, culture, and art through dress. It has been a very internal and personalized relationship for the most part—a study that is as interesting to the psychologist as it is to the æsthetician. Western clothing has demonstrated a tremendous facility for adaptation, change, and assimilation compared to the fashions of other cultures, and this seems to be directly related to the use of clothing for personalized self-expression as well as for the maintenance of traditional cultural and social values. Only in Western development would a man's headdress have derived from wearing a hood sideways (the *chaperon*) or a woman's headdress have come from a lady holding her hair up with a garter (the *Fontanges*). In other cultures clothing items and accessories usually derived from images that symbolized the gods or from the deliberate choices of a godlike monarch, but in the West, fashions came from a great range and variety of personal and social sources.

The greatest revolution in dress since the Neolithic revolution came with the Industrial Revolution of the nineteenth century which completely changed the natural levels of fashion as related to social level by revolutionizing the creation and marketing of clothing. Since the end of the nineteenth century, Western dress has forced all other ethnic fashions into the background or into the museum, and today all urban dwellers on the face of the globe look much alike. That this trend will change in the future seems very unlikely. As to the direction of fashion in the third millennium, one can only speculate. One thing is certain, it will always reflect in a very subliminal way the personal and public values of the times.

# Glossary

## Chapter I: Prehistoric

**kaunakes:**   A skirt or kilt of fur used in Sumer (an area near the mouth of the Tigris-Euphrates rivers) before the year 3000 B.C.

**Mesolithic:**   The scientific name for the transitional age between the Old Stone Age and the New.

**Neolithic:**   The scientific name for the New Stone Age in which humans settled down in tribes, cultivated the land, and raised domestic animals for meat and skins.

**Paleolithic:**   The scientific name for the Old Stone Age when man was a nomadic hunter.

**plastron:**   The name given to a leather, metal, or ornamental piece laced to the front of a woman's tunic or bodice.

**sagum:**   Coarse woolen cloak worn by the celts in Britain.

## Chapter II: Egyptian

**ankh:**   Decorative piece symbolizing Life, in the shape of a cross set on a circular handle and appearing on the crown or carried in the hand.

**as:**   Prince's Lock, hung down one side of the head.

**atef:**   See Mitre of Osiris.

**crook and flail:**   Symbols of the pharaoh were a crook (originally the boomerang), a flail with three lashes, and a tall, animal-headed staff.

**henna:**   Hand and nail dye, from a shrub or tree whose leaves gave a red-orange dye.

**Horus lock:**   A braid of false hair worn behind the right ear by fashionable women.

**kalasiris:**   A tightly molded, body-fitting sheath, which stops underneath the bosom, mainly worn by women.

**kilt:**   Pleated wraparound skirt worn by men.

**king's apron:**   A colored, triangular apron worn by the pharaoh; usually carefully decorated.

**klaft:**   A kerchief which wrapped around the front of the head and fastened at the back of the neck, usually striped horizontally. Later it was cut away so that it fit over the shoulders and was decorated heavily with beads, etc.

**kohl:**   A black cosmetic substance used in Egyptian makeup for eyes and eyebrows.

**menyet:**   A necklace composed of a hank of green beads, balanced by a gold plaque of equal weight at the other end, which could also be carried and waved during religious ceremonies.

**Mitre of Osiris:**   The white crown of the South, or upper Egypt. Also called *atef*.

**pectoral:**   A trapezoidal-shaped piece of metal jewelry worn about the neck by nobility.

**postiche:**   False beard, made of leather, felt, metal. Reserved for royalty.

**pschent:**   The red crown of lower Egypt, worn on the white crown when the two kingdoms of Egypt united.

**sacred uraeus:**   Crowns were often decorated with the uraeus, a rearing viper (asp), the symbol of royalty.

**schenti:**   A loincloth; a rectangular piece tied in front in a knot and made of linen.

**stibium:**   A mixture used for staining eyelids and eyebrows.

**vulture headdress:**   A headdress reserved for royalty, symbol of Maati, Goddess of Truth.

**Was and Tsam:**   Two staffs, or scepters, carried by dignitaries to signify support of heaven. Was—straight; Tsam—wavy.

## Chapter III: Mesopotamian

**aba:** A robe resembling Egyptian or Persian garments, still worn in Palestine today. Folded rectangle, left unseamed at the sides and held in place by cords under each arm; also a garment of virtually the same shape, seamed at the sides and open up the front, put on like a coat.

**abnet:** A long scarf or sash worn by a Jewish high priest and usually made of fine linen or embroidered wool.

**breastplate of judgment:** A 9″ rectangle, doubled over to form a $4\frac{1}{2}$″ pocket, ornamented with four rows of jewels, three in a row, which stood for the 12 tribes of Israel. Worn by Jewish High Priests.

**caftan:** A wide-sleeved, long-skirted tunic, trimmed with fringe or tassels on the edges.

**candys (kandis):** A long, flowing, cloth gown, looped over a belt at the sides; with or without voluminous sleeves, widening from shoulder to cuff, as the garment itself widened from shoulder to hem.

**catogan:** Male or female hair, arranged in a ball at the nape of the neck, sometimes decorated with pins and bands. The hair was often looped or braided.

**ephod:** A kind of Jewish scapular (two rectangles about 30″ by 10″, fastened together by shoulder straps about 10″ long), worn on top of the priestly robe. Attached to it was a girdle like that of the Levites, wrapped around the waist and tied in front.

**kaunakes:** A long, shaggy skirt, probably closed in front. It was made of hanks of wool fastened in horizontal lines like coarse fringe on cloth, or perhaps twisted locks of wool, still fastened to the hide. Sometimes it covered the left shoulder.

**kidaris:** Ribbed tiara or embroidered fez-shaped headdress, worn by a king.

**kilt:** A wraparound short skirt, made of strings or grass; worn by fishermen for protection.

**kyrbasia:** A hat similar to the Phrygian bonnet, worn in the Persian Empire. It also included Median caps with a soft, high crown which fell forward; usually there were flaps at the neck and at either side which could be fastened under the chin.

**petasos:** A brimmed sun hat or traveling hat.

**Phrygian bonnet:** A segmented, conical casque or hat worn by heavily armed Parthian and Sarmatian cavalry.

**phylacteries:** Narrow bands of parchment, with sacred passages written on them, bound about the foreheads and wrists of devout Hebrew men.

**tiara:** A king's headdress—a truncated, conical shape of white felt with a spiked top; purple infulae, two narrow tabs hanging almost to the waist in back.

**Tyrian purple:** Purple dye, made from a sea creature, the murex; very rare and very expensive, originally manufactured in the Phoenician city of Tyre. Color most probably blue red, rich plum, or garnet.

## Chapter IV: Greek

**aegis:** Animal skin worn with a slit for the head, with the head of the animal, usually a goat, on the breast.

**ampyz:** A diadem, female headdress.

**apodesme:** Bands of leather used as a brassiere.

**boss:** Point on shields and knees (armor).

**buskins:** Skin or cloth used to bind or swathe the feet or legs of common men.

**carabitine:** A sandal with a large toe, worn by peasants.

**catogan:** See *Mesopotamian.*

**causia:** A Thessalonian traveling hat for men or women, worn also by actors to indicate an arduous journey.

**ceryphalos:** A bandage-shaped fillet which fitted snugly about the head.

**chlamydon:** Short wrap, pleated over a band, which ran from the right shoulder under the left arm. Mainly for women.

**chlamys:** A smaller woolen rectangle than the himation, of Macedonian or Italian origin; sometimes bordered, pinned at right shoulder or front; worn with short chiton or alone by younger, more active men.

**chloene:** Like the chlamys, of coarse wool, worn hooked on one shoulder, running below the other breast; often folded over before fastening; originated in Macedonia or Thessaly.

**diplax:** The female equivalent of the chloene.

**Doric peplos** or **chiton:** A garment worn by all Greek women to the sixth century. It was of wool dyed indigo, madder, or saffron, frequently patterned, especially at the turn of the fifth century. Its upper edge was folded over to hang down on the breast; it was folded around the body, caught together on each shoulder by pins, leaving the arms uncovered, and though open down the right side, was held in place by the girdle, over which it bloused. In Corinth and Attica, it was sewn together down the side below the waistline. With time, the garment grew wider and was known as the Doric chiton, and the overfold deepened so that it was included in the girdling or hung over and concealed the girdle. When not girded, the overfold could be raised over the head in back as a shawl.

**exomia:** An intermediate form of sleeveless chiton, caught on one shoulder, worn by athletes and workers; often of sheepskin or leather.

**fibula:** Pin or brooch of ancient Greece and Rome which resembled in form the modern safety pin. Often richly decorated.

**fillet:** Piece of fabric bound around the head, as a sweatband.

**himation:** A rectangle of wool with weighted corners, slung over the left shoulder, leaving the right arm free; or worn, by married women, with the corner over the head like a shawl. Dorian men wore it as their only garment (as did the Athenians in their return to an earlier simplicity, in the third to second centuries B.C.). A man wearing the himation alone was always adequately dressed. It served also as a blanket. The colors were natural wool colors: white, natural, browns, and black; or dyed scarlet, crimson, or purple. The garment sometimes had woven patterns, selvages, and embroidery.

**Ionic chiton:** Of Phoenician origin. It was worn first by men, later by women also. It was made of thin woolens, probably crepelike, similar to materials still woven in Greece; also of linen, or the gauzy materials from Cos in Asia Minor, patterned in murex (Tyrian) purple. It was cut with ample width from two pieces, then sewn together, frequently pleated, and long, sometimes trailing. It was often sewn or caught together all the way down the arm, into the equivalent of sleeves, and sewed up the right side, with the left side open. It was worn in many ways by both men and women, and particularly by musicians and charioteers. The chiton was often worn with a short wrap, the chlamydon.

**kolobium** or **colobus:** Another form of chiton, which came into use about the beginning of the fourth century B.C. In shape it was two pieces of fabric, cut square and sewn together on the shoulders, leaving an opening in the middle for the head, and sewn down the sides with sufficient space left at the top for the arms to pass through. When the colobus was girded at the waist, it had very much the same appearance as the chiton, the difference being that the arms emerged at the top edge of the chiton and at the side edge of the colobus.

**kolpos:** The bloused part of the chiton, made by pulling up the chiton over the girdle to make it the proper length from the ground.

**nimbus:** A linen headband embroidered with gold.

**peplos:** The Archaic name for the Doric chiton.

**petasos:** Wide-brimmed traveling hat, worn also by peasants and shepherds.

**pharos:** Linen equivalent of the peplos, worn only by noblewomen upon special occasions.

**Phrygian bonnet:** Refer to *Mesopotamian.* Shows Scythian, Persian influence.

**pilos:** Cap worn by workers, shepherds, sailors.

**saccus:** A completely enveloping form of hair binding.

**soccus:** Comic actor's boot.

**sphendone:** A felt, leather, or metal sling, holding up the hair.

**stephanie:** Tiaralike crown worn as a headdress by women.

**strophium:** A type of corset made of linen, wool, or soft skin, consisting of shoulder straps and three supporting bands, one for the bust, one for the waist, and one for the hips.

**tellex:** Hair binding for athletes, refers to segmented windings around the hair, which was clubbed at the neck.

**tribon:** A small, oblong cloak of Balkan origin, worn by Spartan males over 12 years old as the only garment.

## Chapter V: Roman

**abolla:** A Roman military cloak similar to the Greek *chlamys.*

**balteus:** A form of baldric or sash that went over one shoulder and down to the waist on the opposite side.

**bracchae (braies):** Northern English breeches, tied with strings, worn by Roman provincial soldiers.

**bulla:** Medallion put around a male child's neck to ward off evil until he became an adult.

**byrrus** or **birrus:** A heavy woolen cloak with a cowl.

**calcaeus:** Strapped, cut-out, and laced sandals, varying in height from ankle to well up the calf. Those of senators were black; patricians and magistrates wore purple.

**caligula:** Heavy, often hobnail, military boot, rising well on the leg.

**chlamys:** Semicircular cape, hung over the left arm and fastened by a *fibula,* or clasp, at the right shoulder. It continued for many centuries as the outer garment for the upper classes of western Europe.

**clavi:** Purple bands on the *tunica,* indicating the wearer's rank. With time the clavus lost distinction, and by the first century it was worn by everyone. The clavi then became more elaborately decorative in character, broke into spots of decoration, and amalgamated with borders at the hem of the garment. *Augustus clavus* (pl. *clavi*): For equestrian knights; a narrow band running up over each shoulder and down to hem on tunic or ungirded *dalmatica. Latus clavus:* Single, wide clavus worn by senators.

**collobium:** The Greek *kolobus.* It is like the tunica, although sleeveless. When more than one tunica was worn, the under ones were called the tunica interior, or *subucula.*

**crepida:** Half-shoes, soles to which a piece of leather or fabric was attached enclosing the heel and sides of the foot. Fastened across the instep by straps or bands laced through eyelet holes set in the sides.

**cuculla:** An overgarment with hood, practically an oblong piece of cloth with a hole in the middle for the head. Used by all classes as a protection from weather and when traveling. Later prescribed for monks of the Benedictine order. (About A.D. 1500, given the name of *scapular* as an ecclesiastical garment.)

**dalmatica:** An outer garment, originally for males. Introduced c. A.D. 190 from Dalmatia. Prominent in Rome by third century A.D., it was cut like a tunic, but wider, and with wide sleeves to the forearm. It went on over the head, was worn without girdle, and was characteristically decorated by the clavus.

**feminalia:** Knee-length breeches for men.

**fibula:** See *Greek.*

**flammeum:** Veil of the Roman matron.

**lacerna:** Cloak similar to the *chlamys,* but light and short, which was worn by everyone in the last century of the Republic. Even senators wore it, in place of the toga, although this was frowned on.

**lorica:** This was a cuirass of brass or bronze, molded to the shape of the body with perfect fit and following the line of the abdomen. Frequently enriched with reliefs and ornaments in metal work.

**mappa:** Napkin used at table for wiping the mouth and hands, after washing before and after a meal, in a basin brought by a slave.

**orarium:** Large napkin, carried by servants and slaves over the left shoulder and used for cleaning vessels of all sorts.

**paenula:** A hooded, bell-shaped, weatherproof garment of leather or wool. It was already in use by the Etruscans in the fourth century B.C. It was worn by everyone, civil and military, particularly by centurions.

**pallium:** (*palla*–female). The Roman outdoor garment, which could also be used as a bedcovering. It was originally Greek, and in Rome it was draped like a Greek *himation,* held by a fibula, not hooked as in Greece. It was a rectangle as wide as from the wearer's shoulder to the floor and about three times as long, and was worn by men, women, and children, civil and military. Women wore the palla outdoors, often draped over the head but always in conjunction with a veil or cap. The *pallium* was the characteristic sole garment of the scholar and philosopher; (it was also the conventional mantle of Christ).

**paludamentum:** A purely military mantle, used as the official military mantle of the general in command, or the emperor while in the field. Used particularly in the earlier years, before the first century A.D. In cut, it resembled the *chlamys* or *lacerna* with two corners truncated to form an elongated, primitive semicircle.

**sagum:** Gallic in origin. Became the military wrap of the Roman army, used also as a blanket. Generals also wore it in red and purple. "Putting on the sagum" was the equivalent of declaring war. Square in shape, of thick, heavy, tightly woven wool.

**sapparum:** A shawl for women.

**solea:** Strapped slippers, like sandals.

**stola:** Woman's garment. Worn over the *tunica intima* (which was of similar cut, might or might not have sleeves, and which served as a housedress). The stola had sleeves like the men's *tunica,* or was pinned along the shoulder line and down the arms. It was girded once under the breast and often girdled again at the hips.

**sublagaculum:** Small garment or piece of cloth, worn bound around the hips as a loincloth. This was worn under the *toga,* or frequently without any other covering. It was a fashion copied from the Greeks, who themselves derived it from the Egyptians and Assyrians.

**sudarium:** Small piece of fine linen, often embroidered with silk or gold and equivalent to the modern handkerchief.

**tebenna:** The cloak of the ancient Etruscan man which was sometimes rectangular, but more often semicircular, and therefore the basis for the later Roman *toga*.

**toga (general):** Outergarment, which was the badge of the Roman citizen, rich or poor. Originally the rectangular Greek pallium made into an ellipse, the draping of which developed infinite complications. Of wool, it was characteristically in bleached white.

**toga candida:** It was worn plain by candidates for public office.

**toga picta:** Purple, embroidered official robe of the emperor, worn over the *tunica palmata;* in the second century A.D. it became part of the official garb of Roman consuls. Essentially a ceremonial dress, it constituted the correct costume of the Court during the whole of the Empire Period, until the center of government was transferred to Constantinople, where it was superseded by the paludamentum. From the *toga picta* all imperial and regal robes have descended.

**toga praetexta:** Had a purple hem, worn by senators, certain officials, priests.

**toga pulla:** Black, worn as a mourning robe or for sacrifices; of darker-colored wools, worn draped over the head.

**toga pura:** Actually natural-colored wool, not a bleached white; worn by the Roman citizen.

**toga trabea:** Worn by the equestrian knights, small toga striped in scarlet; basically white for soldiers.

**toga umbo,** or **contabulatum:** The ordinary toga, with a red or purple band, worn so that a pouch was formed at the waist. Came into fashion among high dignitaries toward the end of the second century A.D.

**toga virilis:** An all-white toga, worn by young males, 14 to 16 years of age.

**tunica:** Wide, shirtlike undergarment, the indoor dress of the Roman; worn outdoors without the toga only by working people. It was not, like the toga, distinctly Roman. Originally sleeveless and woolen, usually white, it acquired sleeves and was later made of linen and cotton as well. The tunic was girded with meticulous care to the exact length considered correct for the rank and sex of the wearer.

**tunica interior** or **subucula:** Woolen undertunic worn beneath the regular tunic.

**tunica palmata:** Part of the official garb of emperors. With the *toga picta,* it constituted part of the *Ornamenta tunica triumphalia.* Decorated richly and elaborately with gold embroideries of conventional foliage. It was also usual to have the *tunica* embroidered all over with the same design as that used on the *toga picta,* in circular, square, and lozenge-shaped motifs, with a border at the neck, wrists, and bottom.

**tunica talaris:** Fell to the feet and had long, loose sleeves; it was the marriage dress for men, but was looked down upon by the citizens of Rome and did not compete with the short tunic until the fourth century A.D.

**tutulus:** A stiff, pointed Eutruscan female headdress with a tiara-like brim.

## Chapter VI: Byzantine

**alb:** A liturgical vestment of the Catholic Church; derived from the *tunica alba* which passed out of Roman civil use in the sixth century. It is of white linen, narrow-sleeved, slit for the head to pass through, and girdled to clear the ground. It is worn over the cassock and under other liturgical garments.

**amice:** The first liturgical vestment to be assumed by the priest vesting himself for mass. Developed out of the Roman neckcloth, it is a strip of linen laid hoodlike over the head, dropped to the shoulders, and tied in position around the upper body with tapes sewed to two corners, forming a collar.

**bracchae** or **braies:** Semi-closefitting leg-covering, sometimes worn over hose; used with or without cross-gartering.

**camisa** or **chemise:** An undergarment with long sleeves that showed beneath the sleeves of the outer garment for women.

**cassock:** Originally derived from the Hebrew *casack* and the Roman-Gaulish *caracalla,* it became the daily wear of the dignified and elderly. It was retained by the Church after the change in lay fashions in the seventh and eighth centuries. It is now the ordinary dress of the Roman Catholic and, to a more limited extent, the Church of England clergy, upon which eucharistic and processional vestments and monastic habit are superimposed. Its color—black, purple, red, black with red pipings, or white—indicates rank—priest, bishop, cardinal, pope. Monks' cassocks are the color of the habit of the order.

**chasuble:** Outermost, and one of the most important liturgical, garments of the Catholic Church. Its shape has varied by period and country, but it is essentially a cape of silk or metallic cloth (never linen or cotton), with a hole for the head, shortened at the sides to the shoulder to leave the arms uncovered, and falling down the front and back. Derived from the Roman *paenula* or *casula,* it was also a barbaric garment to ward off bad weather.

**collobium:** A garment similar to the Greek *kolobus;* made of linen or wool and sewn on sides and at shoulder, if not woven all in one piece.

**cope:** A liturgical vestment of the Catholic Church and a choir vestment of some Anglican churches, it is a semicircular cape that is embroidered or brocaded and fastened across the chest by a wide ornamental band. This is sewn to one edge and hooked or pinned by a jeweled *morse* to the other. It has a vestigial hood or embroidered flap hanging down the back. It usually substitutes for the chasuble in all ceremonies outside the mass.

**dalmatic:** A knee-length, wide-sleeved ecclesiastical gown slit up the sides, it derives from the Roman *dalmatica* and is decorated with two vertical stripes over the shoulder to the hem taken from the *augusta clavi* of Roman dress. The dalmatic of a bishop is fringed on both sides and sleeves, and that of a deacon is fringed on the left side and sleeve only. Since the fourth century the dalmatic has been a vestment worn as a festal garment during mass, benedictions, and processions. It can be worn under the chasuble, never under the cope.

**dalmatica:** One of the most important garments of the Byzantine Empire, it had the same general wide-sleeved shape as in Roman times but with far more embroidery and decoration.

**hosa:** A closefitting covering for the leg.

**lorum:** A long, narrow, embroidered shawl with a hole for the head originating from the *pallium* and worn with Byzantine court costume from the eighth to twelfth centuries.

**maniple:** A narrow strip of silk three feet long, decorated with three crosses, hung or fastened over the left forearm. It is one of four distinctly Roman contributions to liturgical costume, originally a linen handkerchief or cloth derived from the folded consular *mappula* or napkin used to give signals at chariot races. It is part of the liturgical vestments of all orders above subdeacon.

**mitre:** A liturgical headdress of the Catholic Church, specifically worn by bishops but occasionally worn by abbots and other church dignitaries. It is a high hat composed of two identical stiffened pieces which fold flat against one another when not spread hornlike by the head. From the back hang two narrow, fringed strips. It sems to have developed out of the cone-shaped caps of the early popes, which in turn may relate back to the mitres of the Hebrews.

**orb:** A celestial sphere usually topped with a cross, carried by the emperor and empress.

**orphreys** or **apparels:** embroidered squares and bands used on the ecclesiastical alb, dalmatic, and chasuble.

**pallium:** A vestment worn by Catholic archbishops, it is a woven band of white lamb's wool "three fingers broad," worn over the chasuble. Derived from the Roman *pallium,* it was originally a longer strip draped over both shoulders and pinned to the left one; now it is a strip, decorated with four crosses, made into a circle, which is dropped on the shoulders and pinned front and back.

**paludamentum:** Originally a Roman general's cloak, now a half-circular imperial Byzantine mantle of rich material, often of purple silk embroidered in gold or gold and jewels.

**pastoral staff:** A five-foot staff that is the insignia for cardinals, bishops, and abbots of the Church. Heads were originally of four kinds: shepherd's crook, the knobbed crook, the bent crook, and the cross or crozier top. Today either the crozier or the pastoral shepherd's crook is seen.

**pedule:** Short hose, usually turned down at the knee.

**sarcenet:** A fine, thin silk cloth originating in the Orient and named from the Saracen.

**segmentae:** An embroidered circular decoration worn on the sleeve of a tunica or dalmatica.

**stole:** A liturgical vestment of the Catholic Church for mass, never for processional use. It is a long strip of material, usually silk, now decorated by three crosses at the ends and middle, and frayed at the hem. It is worn over the shoulder in different ways and is characteristic of deacon, priest, or bishop. It probably descended from the *orarium* given by the Emperor Aurelian in the third century to be waved in applause at games.

**sudarium:** A handkerchief, often embroidered with silver or gold.

**superhumeral:** A jeweled collar, usually worn by the empress or ladies of the Byzantine court.

**surplice:** Originally, as the Latin name shows, it was worn over fur-lined garments. Made of white linen, like the *alb,* it was originally long, becoming much shorter after the thirteenth century. It was usually trimmed in lace or embroidery.

**tablion:** The very elaborate, oblong decoration embroidered in red and gold on the back and front of the imperial Byzantine mantle. For other high officials and courtiers it varied in color.

**tunicle:** A smaller tunic peculiar to deacons at mass; bishops wear it under the dalmatic, but always under the chasuble, never under the cope. It is basically a plainer, narrower-sleeved dalmatic without clavi and usually fringed.

## Chapter VII: Romanesque

**almuce:** A hood with a small cape worn by monks and the nobility.

**barbe** or **barbette:** A piece of linen often pleated and worn under the chin, especially by a widow or a person in mourning.

**beguin (biggon, biggin):** A headcovering for both men and women as well as children from the twelfth century on into the Renaissance. It was worn in Byzantium and later by the Beguines, women of religious orders, and the name remained. It was a three-piece cap made of fine linen for aristocrats, of coarse wool for commoners, and of leather for under helmets. It was worn by clergy, and under the hats and crowns of the nobility. In the fifteenth century the linen was often replaced by felt or velvet, and in the eighteenth century it was often worn under a wig. A more common name for this cap was a *coif.*

**bliaut:** A garment worn by men and women, it originated about 1130 in the East and was brought to Europe at the end of the First Crusade. As worn by the upper classes at the end of the twelfth century, it consisted of a snug-fitting torso, often wide embroidered sleeves, a low skirt pulled into elegant pleats across the hips, and snug lacing up the back or under each arm. It was one of the first garments to depend on fit as well as cut.

**broigne:** A metal cuirass from Charlemagne's time.

**cagoule:** A semicircular cape of cloth or fur, with a hood; usually worn by peasants.

**cainsil** or **chainsil:** A very fine, lightweight or heavyweight flax cloth of simple weave; it is often used as a term to refer to fine linen.

**capuchon:** A hood usually attached to a cape, often with a long tail later known as a *liripipe.*

**caul:** Close-fitting gold hairnet worn by ladies of the aristocracy.

**chainse:** A body garment for men and women that later developed into the shirt or chemise. It was made of hemp, linen, wool, and sometimes silk with the fabric varying according to the wearer's level in society.

**corse:** A tight-fitting, sleeveless jacket of leather or metal discs laced up the front and worn under a male tunic or bliaut, forerunner of the term "corset."

**cote:** A long tunic with the sleeve cut in one piece with the garment. The length varied from the calf to the instep.

**couvrechief:** A woman's veil of the period.

**crispine** or **crispinette:** A headdress of gold net and pearls.

**diaper:** Silk, linen, or cotton cloth of one color woven in a sprinkled ornamental pattern.

**fibula:** The heavy metal or jewel-encrusted brooch used to fasten the mantle at the shoulder.

**girdle:** A type of waistband or belt that encircled the hips.

**gorget:** A wimple or *couvrechief* worn under the chin and tucked under the neckline of the gown.

**gown:** A "gunna" (from the Anglo-Saxon) was a tunic for women somewhat like the Roman and Byzantine stola.

**guimpe:** A chemisette worn with a low-cut dress.

**gypsire:** A pouch or bag worn at the hip from which alms were given.

**hauberk:** A coat of chain or linked mail used as body armor.

**headrail:** A colorful rectangular veil draped over the head and shoulder from left to right, passed around the neck and tied under the chin.

**heaume:** Military helmet of Charlemagne's time.

**jube** or **jupe:** An undergarment or shirt, sometimes furlined; worn by both men and women.

**kirtle:** Anglo-Saxon for tunic.

**liripipe:** The long, pointed tail on a hood.

**rheno:** A mantle without a hood.

**sherte:** A straight, knee-length garment with slits at front, back, and sides, resembling a modern shirt.

**smock:** Innermost garment of fine linen worn by women.

**surcote** or **surcoat:** A loose, lightweight garment originally worn by the Crusader over his armor as a protection against the sun. It soon became an overtunic worn over the *cote,* sometimes unseamed, sometimes sleeveless, sometimes with wide-open sleeves like a dalmatic. It could be belted or unbelted, and the length varied from the knee to the ankle.

**torque:** A neck or arm band, usually of gold or bronze, worn by the ancient Gauls, Britons, and Germans. It was a spirally twisted bar of gold bent into a hoop with an opening at the ends which were crafted into knobs or serpents' heads. When taken as spoils by the Romans, these torques were awarded to soldiers as a symbol of their valor during the campaigns.

## Chapter VIII: Early Gothic

**aglet, aiglet, point,** or **poynt:** A metal tag or point used to fasten pieces of plate armor or various parts of other garments like sleeves, hose, and *paltock*.

**aumônière:** A small bag carried in the Middle Ages by men and women. Originally of fabric or leather with a draw string, it hung from the belt or girdle and was treated as a hanging pocket. Finally during the Renaissance when pockets were added to garments, it gradually disappeared, although it continued for women and eventually became the purse or *reticule*.

**bateau neckline:** A boat-shaped neckline.

**baudequin:** A tissue of silk and gold threads that originated in Baghdad and was later made in Cypress and Palermo. It was brought back by the Crusaders and was used by the royalty and nobility of Europe for draping furniture and for court robes from the late twelfth through the sixteenth centuries.

**button:** A solid, dome-shaped top, with an eye at the base, used as trimming at the beginning of the Middle Ages; used as a fastening with buttonholes from the middle of the thirteenth century on.

**camail:** A chain-mail hood with a buckled fastening under the chin; worn by English soldiers of the thirteenth century over an iron skull cap.

**capuchon:** See *Romanesque*.

**castellated, dagged,** or **foliated:** Deep-cut scallops at the hem or other edges of a garment shaped in triangles, half-circles, squares, or leaflike foliations.

**coif:** A closefitting baby cap tied under the chin.

**cointise** or **quintise:** Cut-out decoration of the *cyclas;* also refers to a garment so decorated.

**coronet:** An ornamental circlet worn about the head.

**cotehardie:** A shaped garment, tight-fitting around the shoulder, waist, and hips. When worn by a woman it had a circular skirt; when worn by a man it usually ended at the hips or slightly below, often with dagged or scalloped edges. It could be hooked or laced up either the front or the back.

**cyclas:** An overgarment cut from a single piece of cloth, with a hole in the center for the head and partially seamed at the sides; sometimes lined with fur or silk.

**emblem** or **badge:** The distinguishing symbol worn by the Crusader which developed into the system of heraldry.

**ganache** or **garnache:** A *surcote* or robe with short, caped sleeves worn for extra warmth.

**gardecorp:** A *surcote* or robe with hanging sleeves slit to allow the arms to pass through.

**gorget:** See *Romanesque*.

**gueules:** A small, fur-lined shoulder cape with lower corners of the cape turned back in front; it was usually attached to the peliçon.

**herlot** or **lachet:** A string used to tie the hose to the *paltock* or the sleeve to the armhole of the *paltock*.

**paltock:** A short jacket to which undersleeves and hose were attached, later called *pourpoint*.

**particolored** or **pied:** A two-colored garment, often with one side embroidered.

**passemente:** Gold, silver, or colored braid.

**peliçon:** Any fur-lined garment of robe length.

**plastron:** A type of garment which later became the *stomacher*. It was most frequently of fur and was worn as a decorative front to a female costume.

**rocket** or **roquet:** This was a short, smocklike, woolen garment worn from the late twelfth century into the Renaissance. In the fifteenth century it was worn by commoners and pages with a hooded shoulder cape. In the eighteenth century it was worn by lower-class men and women in Europe and the Colonies as a kind of smock. It is related to the *rochet* or *rochette* found in ecclesiastical vestments.

**wimple:** A shaped kerchief for the head.

## Chapter IX: Middle Gothic

**bacinet** or **basinet:** A light helmet made of a single piece of steel with a conical shape. It is usually worn over a chain-mail hood.

**barbute:** A helmet of fourteenth-century Italian origin that first had a high pointed crown and later a round one. The face was almost completely covered with large cheek pieces.

**bellows** or **bagpipe sleeve:** A gathered sleeve having a cuff and a long vertical slit through which the hand could pass.

**braconnière:** The part of late-fourteenth- and fifteenth-century armor covering the hips. It was formed of overlapping hoop-shaped plates hinged on one side and fastened leather straps and buckles on the other. It gradually shortened and disappeared altogether by the seventeenth century.

**castellated:** Square or rectangular *dagges* or cuts in the hem or edge of a garment; named after the wall tops of castles.

**caul** (also **crepine, crestine, crespinette, tressure, tressour**): A woman's medieval headdress in which the hair was concealed in two silken, half-spherical cases on either side of the head covered with heavy net of reticulated gold or silver cord interspersed with pearls and beads.

**chaperon:** A caped hood with long tail, or *liripipe,* worn with the face opening around the head and the *liripipe* wound about the head and then draped under the chin.

**corset:** A fitted garment worn over the chemise with skirt attached and usually laced up the front.

**courtepy** or **jacquette:** A very short overgarment, or *cotehardie,* often particolored or embroidered with gems. It usually had a high collar.

**crackow** or **poulaine:** A long-tipped hose and shoe introduced during the reign of Richard II and named after the city of Crackow in Poland; later the length of the toe became so long that it had to be tied to the knee.

**doublet** or **doblet:** A short jacket or variety of *pourpoint,* sleeved or sleeveless, worn under a closefitting *pourpoint.* When used as an outergarment it was padded and had a short skirt.

**galoche:** A wooden platform with an ornamental strap fastening the base beneath the heel and ball of the foot; elevated to varying heights.

**hennin** or **cornet:** A truncated cone or steeple headdress with veil completely covering the female hairdo.

**houppelande:** A loose and comfortable gown of great size introduced during the reign of Charles VI in France which became very fashionable during the reign of Richard II in England. One style worn by men had long, flowing, bell-shaped sleeves, a long, fitted waist, and floor-length or longer skirt slit to the knees; another style, known as the *bastard houppelande,* was only knee to calf length. A high-standing collar was usually a part of this flamboyant costume. The woman's version of this robe had a soft, open collar, a short waist, a full skirt, and long, flowing sleeves.

**journade:** A short, circular garment which at first had large, full sleeves and later long, slit sleeves. It was often worn for riding.

**jupe:** A form of shirt or undertunic, sometimes fur-lined; worn by both men and women.

**jupon:** Overgarment having armorial blazonry, worn over armor in the fourteenth century; sometimes also referred to as a petticoat.

**paltock:** A jacket worn by pages in the fourteenth and fifteenth centuries. A short, fitted jacket of cloth or silk buttoned or laced like a waistcoat to which hose were fastened by laces.

**particolored:** A two- (or three-) colored garment based on the colors and emblems in a coat of arms.

**patten:** Iron support worn under a shoe.

**plastron:** A *stomacher*-shaped appendage, usually of fur or embroidered fabric, worn at the front of the *sideless gown* as both support and decoration.

**pomander:** A ball or hollow ornament often made of filigree, containing a sponge of perfume, suspended from a necklace or girdle.

**pourpoint:** A short jacket with tight sleeves buttoned from elbow to wrist, worn under the *cotehardie;* formerly known as a *paltock.*

**reticulation:** Decorative metal cages which confined the hair at the side of a woman's head.

**roundel** or **roundlet:** A headdress made of a thick roll of material with a scarf or *liripipe* hanging down one side and draped over the shoulder.

**sideless gown:** A woman's overgown cut away at the sides from under the arms to the hips to show the *cotehardie* or *kirtle* underneath; it was usually worn with a *plastron* at the front of the figure.

**tippet:** A band sewn around the elbow of the *cotehardie* sleeve with the end hanging as a streamer.

**tussoire:** A chain and clasp which hung from the girdle and held up one side of a long skirt.

## Chapter X: Late Gothic

**bag cap:** A cloth or velvet brimless cap with fur band and ornament. Resembled a turban.

**bevor** or **beaver:** A movable face piece of armor attached to helmets in the fifteenth and sixteenth centuries. When lowered it protected the face from swords and lances.

**biliment:** An elaborate female headdress of the late fifteenth and early sixteenth century of gold-threaded lace worked with beads, jewels, ribbons, gauze, and sometimes a feather. Usually seen in Italy.

**biretta:** A stiff, square cap with three or four points projecting from the crown. It was worn by the clergy as well as by academics. Today birettas are worn in purple by bishops, red by cardinals, and black by priests on nonformal occasions.

**brigandine:** A sleeveless, armored jacket of overlapping metal plates or scales sewn to linen, leather, or canvas, fitting to the waist with a short peplum below the waist.

**butterfly headdress:** Semitransparent linen, draped and wired to resemble a butterfly, worn over a tall hennin.

**crackow** or **poulaine:** See *Middle Gothic.*

**escarelle:** A pouch or purse attached to the waist on a hip belt into which a knife was frequently inserted.

**escoffion:** A tall, richly brocaded headdress, sometimes shaped like two horns, sometimes like a narrow, tall turban; usually had a veil of fine lawn about a yard wide.

**hennin:** See *Middle Gothic.*

**journade:** See *Middle Gothic.*

**liripipe:** Still retained from the chaperon as a tail of material coming from the donut shape of the *roundlet* and draping under the chin and over one shoulder.

**pointe:** See *High Renaissance.*

**pourpoint:** The name usually given to the short jacket with a pleated skirt of this period. Sleeves were either full at the top and tapering to the wrists, open and hanging behind a tight undersleeve, or slashed to allow the arm to come through.

**roundlet:** The donut-shaped, turbanlike headdress worn by most men of fashion until the later part of the fifteenth century.

**sallet** or **salade:** A simple metal helmet (with or without a visor) that extended over the back of the neck.

**sideless gown:** This gown, cut away under the arms to the hips, was usually covered with armorial bearings and remained as the ceremonial dress for women during this period.

## Chapter XI: High Renaissance

**barret:** A flat Spanish cap of gorgeous material which was slashed, puffed, and embroidered. (Related to the *beret* and the *biretta.*)

**bases:** Sixteenth-century pleated skirts for men, worn separate from the doublet; cartridge-pleated; often associated with Henry VIII.

**breeches** or **hosen:** Legcoverings, either cut from fabric or knitted, all in one piece.

**burgonet (burganet, bourquinotte):** A bonnetlike helmet or casque with cheek pieces and sometimes a nosepiece. Its distinctive feature was a browpiece to shade the eyes. It was first worn by the Burgundians in the late fifteenth century, and it lasted until the late seventeenth.

**calotte:** A skull cap, usually of expensive material, over which the *barret* was worn.

**caul:** Developed from the *crespinette;* a single meshwork covering for the hair, sometimes edged with jewels in a border.

**clog, chopine,** or **patten:** Wooden-soled platform attached to shoe, worn as a protection from mud and to gain height.

**codpiece:** A pouchlike appendage made from the same fabric as the *jerkin* or upper stocks and fastened by ties or buckles; a decorated covering for the opening in the front of breeches; forerunner of the fly.

**coif:** See *calotte.*

**jerkin:** A short velvet or leather jacket, usually sleeveless.

**kirtle:** A dress which evolved from the *cotehardie* about 1480. It was closefitting at shoulder, waist, and hips and had a full skirt.

**little hennin:** A headdress shaped like a truncated cone.

**mancheron:** A false, hanging sleeve.

**pantoffle:** A mule or slipper with a cork sole, worn as a protection for the shoe.

**points:** Metal-tipped ribbons or lacings sewed in corresponding pairs to sleeves and armseyes, or to doublet and hose.

**simarre:** A robe for men, derived from *chimer* or *chimere,* an ecclesiastical garment very much like it in shape. The neck part was somewhat on a double-breasted line, with no collar in back, but with wide revers turned back from the front edge of the robe. The robe was worn either ungirded or confined at the waist by a narrow silk scarf, knotted with one loop and two ends.

**slashing** (*puffs and slashes*): Vertical, horizontal, or diagonal slits in the fabric of the garment, through which appeared a different fabric. Often the shirt was the garment which puffed through.

**solleret:** A shoe with a rounded toe.

**upper stocks:** See *Early Mannerist Renaissance, trunkhose.*

## Chapter XII: Early Mannerist Renaissance

**barbe** or **barbette:** Pleated neck and shoulder covering worn with a hood (or *beguin*) by widows until the time of Catherine de Medici, when it was replaced by a wired-out hood, dipping low over the forehead or carried out into a beak. For a white mourning of a young queen, a veiled hood over a wired cap and a pleated barbe under the chin, such as we associate with Mary of Scotland, was worn.

**basquine:** Restraining fitted underbodices of heavy material from which the term *basque* comes. Used in the late sixteenth century.

**Beefeater's hat:** A black beaver hat with red, black, and white ribbon bows around the crown worn by British Yeomen of the Guard and the Wardens of the Tower of London in the sixteenth century.

**bombast:** Stuffing of wool, flax, or hair.

**bongrace:** A short headdress of silk, velvet, or chiffon which hung free in back but dipped over the forehead in a peak in the front. It was often finished on the forehead with a single pearl or other jewel. Also known as an *attifet* headdress.

**braguette:** The French word for *codpiece*.

**buckram:** A coarse open weave of linen or cotton sized with glue and used as early as the sixteenth century as a stiffening for parts of dress. The name comes from the floor coverings used under fine rugs in Bukhara.

**busk:** A rigid piece of wood set in the fake front or *stomacher,* which gave a straight-line effect.

**cale:** Bag of black velvet to conceal the hair; for the gable headdress or the French hood.

**cappa magna:** The long, trailing, luxurious cloak-vestment worn by ecclesiastics on ceremonial occasions. Usually of watered silk, hooded in ermine; worn in red by cardinals, violet by bishops.

**chain** or **order:** A heavy chain worn by a man across the chest and neckline as decoration; often denoted an order or organization to which he belonged.

**chamarre:** Large, square piece of fabric, slit up the front vertically and into a T-shape to leave a neck opening; with a collar attached to the top of the T-shaped slit and the sides folded back into revers. worn as a coat. Principally a French style.

**codpiece:** See *High Renaissance.*

**cordelière:** A long chain, usually of gold, which hung from the girdle.

**duckbilled** or **splayfooted shoes:** Very wide, square-toed, slipperlike shoes, usually decorated with jewels, puffs, or slashes.

**fall:** Like the *cale,* for the gable headdress, of black silk or velvet.

**farthingale:** Hoops of graduated size inserted in a petticoat. Of several types—see *Elizabethan.*

**fraise:** A small ruff which edged the standing collar. It is said Henry II adopted the neckline to hide a scar.

**gable headdress (kennel** or **pedimental):** Resembles in outline the pediment of a Greek temple. Its essentials were the piece that goes over the front part of the head and covers the ears and the veil or bag cap covering the rest of the head. With the formal styles of this headdress, no hair was visible, that at the forehead being covered with rolls or folds of cloth. There were, however, linen coifs shaped in the same outline which left the parted hair visible on the forehead. The front roll was of diagonally striped material or velvet. The *kennel* consisted of a stiff plane covered with rich material, pieces of which extended down the sides and might be pinned back on themselves. The cap at the back, joining the *kennel,* was like a bag with a square bottom. One side was turned back and pinned to the other at the back of the head. The bag was generally of black velvet.

**lower stocks** or **bas-de-chausses:** Silk or cloth stockings showing beneath *upper stocks* or trunk hose.

**Mary Stuart cap:** A heart-shaped cap worn by the Scottish queen.

**Medici collar:** The lace-edged ruff which opened into a standing fan-shaped frill, high in the back with low décolletage. Accompanied by matching cuffs.

**morion:** Brimmed helmet. English or Spanish.

**panes:** Loose, vertical bands used on sleeves, doublets, and trunk hose.

**partlet:** See *Late Mannerist Renaissance.*

**pomander:** A small apple-shaped ball of gold or silver filigree which held ambergris, musk, or other perfumes. It was usually worn suspended by a chain from a lady's girdle, although sometimes it was worn around the neck. Men sometimes carried it in the hand often hidden in a hollowed-out orange. The pomander was particularly used at outbreaks of the Plague to ward off infection.

**shakefold:** A stiffened pad on a wire frame, an early form of *farthingale.* The name was given to this part of the garment since it swayed back and forth as the wearer moved.

**simarre** or **simarra:** A man's long, sumptuous robe of rich brocade which originated in Venice in the early sixteenth century. It flared from neck to floor with wide Dalmatian sleeves and was sometimes worn by ladies of fashion with a long train.

**solleret** or **bear's paw:** Italian footwear of the sixteenth century that resembled the long-toed *poulaine* of the fifteenth century. Gradually the point disappeared, and It changed to the square toe with padding that became the standard male shoe shape from 1520 to 1550. The name *bear paw* was given to the shoes worn by the German mercenary soldiers (Landsknechte) of the period, whereas in England they were called *duckbilled* shoes.

**stomacher:** False front or ornamental covering on front of bodice.

**trunk hose, mellon hose,** or **haut-de-chausses:** Upper hose or full trunks that extended from upper thighs to waist.

## Chapter XIII: Late Mannerist Renaissance

**aglet, aiglet, point,** or **poynt:** A metal tag or point used to fasten armor or various parts of other garments including sleeves and hose to a *paltock* or underdoublet.

**attifet coiffure:** A heart-shaped style with a point dipping over the forehead often supporting a cap of heart shape stiffened by a wire frame. The style was first favored by Catherine de Medici and Mary Queen of Scots and was popular throughout the remainder of the sixteenth century.

**baize:** A coarse woolen cloth used for servants' clothes. During the reign of Queen Elizabeth it was made at Colchester, England, but was originally from Baza, Spain.

**baldric:** Any kind of band, ribbon, or leather, usually to hold a sword; used for several centuries. Here, a shoulder sash of satin, the fashion for both men and women, white being only for the king.

**basquine:** A boned bodice resembling a corset.

**bavolet:** A woman's headdress worn by the European middle class and peasants during the sixteenth century. It was a towellike piece of white linen about 2 yards long and about 18 yards wide with fringed ends, folded and pinned to a cap. Later the deep back ruffle on any bonnet was called by this name.

**bombast:** Padding for shaped breeches, composed of flock, rags, or any other serviceable material. Also used to stuff *peascod belly.*

**busk:** A rigid piece of wood set in a fake front or *stomacher* to give a straight-line effect.

**canions** or **upper stocks:** Tight knee breeches. The lower edges were covered by the *nether stocks* or stockings, usually rolled above the knee and secured by garters.

**cartwheel verdingale** or **farthingale:** The circular wheel support worn under the full drumshaped hoop skirt, also with underskirt.

**chopines:** High clogs, worn by Venetian women, serving both to increase their stature and to lift them well above the surfaces of dusty roads. These were made usually of cork, covered with leather or velvet. The vogue for them came to Europe from the Middle East by way of Venice.

**codpiece:** The stuffed and slashed appendage at the front opening of the male hose.

**cross-gartering:** Crisscrossed bands, ribbons, or cords tied below the knee.

**falling band:** Wide, flat collar, known as the Louis XIII collar, of sheer white fabric, with or without lace edge. Bands diminished in size from about 1640.

**fers:** Metal buttons used by a woman of rank, worn as decoration on costume.

**galligaskins:** Loose knee trousers that remained wide and open at the knee.

**gauntlets:** Elbow-length gloves of velvet or satin, silk- or gold-fringed, with backs embroidered or sewn with jewels. For courtier wear.

**golilla:** The starched, dishlike neckband introduced by Philip IV of Spain. It remained in favor for some 15 years after his pragmatic of 1623 against the large ruff (gran gola). It was worn usually in conjunction with plain turn-back wristbands.

**jerkin:** An outergarment, often of leather, which had a shoulder puff or wing, sometimes hanging sleeves or tied-in sleeves; worn over the doublet.

**kirtle:** Basic woman's garment of the period, often composed of two separate parts—the bodice and the skirt. For most of this period these two elements had emphatically contrasting forms, the bodice tapering to a sharp point at or below the waistline, while the skirt was in the shape of an upright cone, bell, or drum. The skirt derived its form from the shape of the *farthingale.*

**mahoîtres:** A high, standing, padded sleeve or shoulder puff worn during the late sixteenth century.

**mandilion:** A type of tabard. Worn by common folk in inclement weather since the early Gothic period, but in the later sixteenth century transformed into a straight-hanging, hip-length garment with open hanging sleeves. Worn as servants' livery or as a loose jacket by heralds and soldiers. Also often worn as a kind of cape thrown over the shoulders and fastened with one button or tied across the chest.

**marlotte:** A loose-bodied dress robe that many

European women wore with slight variations during the late sixteenth century. It was cut in a full funnel shape from neck to floor in rich brocade with a small standing collar and short puffed sleeves. It usually fastened only at the neck and flared out over the extended *farthingale* shape of the undergown.

**Medici collar:** This was shaped like the male falling band but pleated and wired rising from a low décolletage and standing high at the back of the head. It originated in Italy and was most popularized by Queen Marie de Medici of France, 1573–1642.

**morion:** A helmet which appeared in Europe about the middle of the sixteenth century; it was introduced by the Spaniards who had copied it from the Moors. It was worn by foot soldiers and had a crown shaped like two halves of a shell that met to form a crescent crest at the top. The brim was also in a crescent shape with a great curve like the line of a ship, and articulated earpieces covered the ears.

**mules:** Slippers without heels or heel counters worn in the sixteenth century by men and women, often as a second slip-on covering over other footwear in wet weather.

**neck whisk:** A standing, fan-shaped, wired collar.

**pantoffles:** Shoes or pumps of crimson, red, or violet velvet. Cut in the shape of a lobster tail.

**partlet:** a fine linen or lawn inset placed inside a square or round neckline that was then gathered into a neckband or drawn closed by a cord.

**peascod belly:** A padded doublet with a front shaped like a *peascod,* or pea pod.

**piccadil:** The tabbed finish on the edge of a garment; also a collar support underprop of tabs.

**plunderhose:** Huge German hose bloused to below the knee.

**ruff:** A starched figure-eight pleated collar for the neck.

**shoe roses:** Large ribbon ties in the form of rosettes for men's shoes. Worn at the buckle, with heeled shoes, during the reign of James I.

**shoulder wings** or **crescents:** Decorative pieces extending outward at the shoulder of the doublet.

**slops:** Unpadded trunk hose, termed *Spanish slops.* Very full breeches bagging at the knees were termed *full slops. Pansid slops* were a mere role at the waist.

**underproper** or **rebato:** A frame to hold up ornate, starched-lace collars.

**venetians:** Full, loose breeches without codpieces, fastening below the knee.

## Chapter XIV: Early Baroque (Cavalier)

**balagnie cloak:** An elegant cloak of the early seventeenth century from the reign of Louis XIII with a deep collar, usually draped over only one shoulder and held in place by cords attached under the collar.

**balandrana** or **supertotus:** A traveler's raincoat of the seventeenth century which had a hood and enveloping sleeves buttoned back on the arm.

**baldric, bandoleer,** or **bandolier:** A wide silk sash or leather belt, often richly decorated, worn over the right shoulder and fastened on the left hip to carry a sword.

**basquine** or **vasquine:** A fitted, boned, hip-length garment with a petticoat, in which a bolster tied around the waist over the petticoat and under the outerskirt created the drum-shaped silhouette seen in many of the Spanish court ladies painted by Velásquez. The male *basquine* was a fitted, padded doublet fastened tightly down the center front.

**batts:** A popular woman's shoe of the early seventeenth century that resembled the men's, with a medium heel and latchets tied over the tongue. These are the shoes we associate with many women's outfits in early New England.

**beaver hat:** A fur hat which was fashionable for both men and women in the seventeenth century. It was a costly item with a thick nap and usually broad-brimmed.

**boot hose:** Hose of sheer white linen with wide lace frills at the top worn to protect the gentleman's costly silk hose when worn with boots. The lace top was usually allowed to fall down over the leather cuff of the boot.

**bows à la échelle:** See *Late Baroque, echelon.*

**bucket-top boot:** Wide-topped boot, sometimes turned in a large cuff.

**buffcoat:** The military coat of the seventeenth century originally made of buffalo hide and worn with buff gauntlets. It had a body formed of four pieces with deep skirts and was often thong-laced up the front. Those worn by officers were often richly decorated with braid, loops, buttons, and lace.

**cadanette:** Love-lock, a long curl or strand over one shoulder, tied with a ribbon or a string with a rosette; used by the cavalier.

**canons:** A lace flounce attached just below the knee to the same stocking which was drawn up over the breeches.

**casaque** or **cassock:** A loose greatcoat, with big

sleeves, usually three-quarter in length, with turned-back cuff.

**falling band:**   A collar of fine white lawn edged with lace, later developed into the pleated *rabat*. It is the wide collar spreading out over the shoulders that is seen in the later portraits by Anthony Van Dyck, and in this width is sometimes known as a *rabatine*.

**galant:**   Ties or loops of ribbons used on sleeve, bodice, or skirt.

**la modeste, la friponne, le secret:**   The modish woman of the period wore a chemise, a corset, then several petticoats over the *verdingale,* or hoop. The hoop had grown smaller but continued to be worn until 1630. Over that was the gown, consisting of skirt and bodice or *stomacher,* with sleeves of light-colored satin or other fabric. Over that, a robe or sort of *redingote* of darker or contrasting colored material, opened the full length in front. The robe usually had slashed sleeves showing the undersleeves. This robe was invariably worn until 1645. The outer robe was called *la modeste;* when there were two skirts the outer one was called *la friponne* (*hussy* in English), the under one *le secret.*

**love-lock:**   Plait or curl of hair near left ear and tied with a ribbon; worn by both men and women.

**pantoffle:**   Type of soft slipper.

**pinners:**   In women's dresses, aprons of exquisite workmanship, matching lingerie accessories, such as sheer lingerie cuffs and collar (English term).

**points:**   See *aglet* under *Late Mannerist Renaissance.*

**quatre-foil spur leathers:**   Worn by early-seventeenth-century cavaliers on the instep of their boots to hide the fastenings of the spurs. The shape was that of a broad quatre-foil, or four-leafed petal.

## Chapter XV: Late Baroque (Restoration)

**à la Maintenon:**   A coiffure with hair parted in the center, trimmed in graduated lengths, curled and fluffed; designed by Mme. Martin, hairdresser to Mme. de Maintenon.

**apron:**   A length of cloth hemmed and usually ornamented, gathered into a waistband having long, ornamental strings; worn at the front of a full court gown.

**Brandenberg greatcoat:**   An overcoat adapted from the coats of Prussian soldiers.

**busk:**   See *Late Mannerist Renaissance.*

**canons** or **cannons:**   Bunches of ribbon loops affixed at the knee, worn between 1660 and 1670.

**cassock:**   Between 1650 and 1670 the *doublet* of

Charles I's reign was sometimes lengthened almost to the knee. Like its predecessor it could be worn either belted or beltless, but following the new trend it had a lower waistline; its skirts flared slightly. Except for length, it was essentially like the modern clerical cassock.

**cravat:**   Any type of neck dressing other than a collar. Of various types through several periods. Here the *rabat,* or lace *falling band,* with round corners became broad and long, and the *jabot,* or frill on the shirt front, frequently appeared with it. By the end of the 1670s the ends of the cravat became full lace tabs, tied under the chin with a *cravat string* of ribbon or lace.

**culotte:**   Breeches tied below the knee and trimmed in braid.

**echelon:**   Bowknots of graduated size on the *stomacher*. The bodice often laced in back, but when fastened in front it had jeweled clasps, buttons, or many bowknots with which to fasten it.

**falbalas:**   Heavy ruffles (anglicized name was furbelows) when gathered up the center were used as decoration on women's garments, particularly at the end of elbow-length sleeves.

**Fontanges:**   In 1680 the duchesse de Fontanges, having her hat blown off at a royal hunting party, tied her curls in place with her garter, arranging a bow with ends in front. From that incident a new fashion evolved—a cap of tier upon tier of upstanding wired and pleated ruffles of lawn, lace, and ribbons. The hair dressed in that fashion was called *coiffure à la Fontanges,* and the cap with its narrow rising front was known as *le bonnet à la Fontanges.* The cap often had two floating pieces of ribbon or lace in back, and over the whole arrangement was often worn a black silk hood or kerchief. In 1691 the headdress was reduced to two tiers of pleats and became known as the *commode.*

**galants** or **favors:**   Bunches of ribbon loops of variegated colors. Extravagant ornamentation in a braid of gold or silver, laces, and ribbons became the standard decoration for women's dress.

**habit à la française:**   Adhering to the three fundamentals of coat, vest, and breeches, the style began in the reign of Louis XIV, was perfected in design during the Regency, and then became the formal attire of European gentlemen for a century. The coat retained its name *habit à la française* to the end of the eighteenth century with very little change in cut.

**hurluberlu:**   Short curls worn over the entire head; introduced by Mme. de Maintenon, 1670.

**jackboot:**   A knee-high boot of heavy black leather

with broad heel worn by cavalrymen during the seventeenth century.

**justaucorps:** A long, fitted coat with full skirt, buttoned down the front with sleeves usually turned back in large cuffs; replaced the cassock about 1675–1680. It was slashed up the center back to the waist, originally necessary for riding. The sleeves, usually split partway up the back, were straight with wide cuffs. The skirt of the coat, reaching to the knees, was reinforced with linen, buckram, or whalebone and cut to flare when buttoned at the waist.

**lavallière:** A necklace with a pendant. Style introduced by Louise de La Vallière, first mistress of Louis XIV.

**mante:** A short scarflike cape, edged with ruffles or lace. This popular wrap for women and the *manteau* were probably made of Mantua silk imported from Italy. *Mantes,* or broad scarfs of gold or silver tissue, were worn only by women of high rank at court.

**manteau:** The formal female gown of the period of Louis XIV. The overskirt was looped back and held by ribbon bows. The looped-up folds were often bunched in back over an underskirt of taffeta; the looped-up outerskirt of brocaded silk ended in a train, the length of which was determined by the lady's social position. The train was carried over the left arm, except in the presence of royalty, when it trailed on the floor.

**Monmouth cockade:** A cocked hat of beaver with feather fringe made popular by the duke of Monmouth about 1670.

**montero:** A round fur cap with a turned-up brim.

**mouches:** This French word for *flies* was used to denote beauty patches of black silk court plaster cut in diamond, crescent, star, or other shapes and applied to the face, often to cover unsightly pockmarks.

**palatine:** A small shoulder cape introduced in 1671 by the Princess Palatine to avoid exposing her shoulders.

**passecaille:** The ribbon on which a muff was hung.

**pelerine:** A short shoulder cape, usually with long ends hanging down in front.

**periwig** or **peruque:** Wig that gained favor during the period of Louis XIV; hair at this time was worn shoulder length and in flowing curls. The head was then regularly shaved, the wig taking the place of the man's own hair. At first it was made to look like natural hair, but eventually an artificial effect was

cultivated. Masses of ringlets fell over the shoulders and down the back. By 1660 wig-making in France reached such a stage of perfection that the French periwig was in demand all over Europe.

**petticoat breeches** or **rhinegrave breeches:** Full breeches, ending in deep ruffles or *canons*. There were two styles of petticoat breeches—one which resembled a kilt, the other a divided skirt. By about 1660 the breeches were so wide that it is not always easy to distinguish between *Rhinegrave* breeches and a short skirt. Sometimes the legs of these garments attained a width of six feet.

**pretintailles:** Cut-out motifs of lace or gold embroidery, appliquéd or gummed to the bottoms of skirts, making elaborate ornamentation.

**rabat:** Type of cravat, with a vertically pleated front fall (see *falling band* under *Early Baroque*).

**ramillies wig:** Of English origin, named in honor of the Battle of Ramillies, won by the duke of Marlborough. The wig had one or two hanging braids, tied top and bottom with black ribbon. Later the end of the braid was often looped under and tied.

**spatterdashes:** High leather leggings, introduced about 1700. The joining of legging and shoe was covered by spur leathers.

**steinkirk:** A scarf of lace or lawn, loosely tied with the ends casually twisted into the vest or shirt front or drawn through a buttonhole or ring. Black silk steinkirks were introduced in the 1690s and were named after the Battle of Steinkirk, where the hurriedly garbed French, unable to tie their cravats, twisted the ends through buttonholes in their coats.

**taure:** A hairdress resembling a bull's head, introduced in 1673.

## Chapter XVI: Rococo

**bag wig** or **crapaud:** A wig having a bag in the back which held loose ends of the hair, tied at nape of neck with a bow.

**bagnolette:** Hood wired away from the face.

**bandore:** The widow's black-veiled headdress of the eighteenth century.

**banyan:** Men's eighteenth-century dressing gown, same cut as the coat.

**bombazine:** A stiff silk made in France and Milan in the eighteenth century.

**cadogan** or **catogan wig:** Style having the back hair looped under and tied with a concealed string or solitaire. Named after the first earl of Cadogan.

**calash:** Eighteenth-century hat, attached to capes,

to cover women's high wigs, folds back like a baby-buggy cover.

**festoons:**   Decorative elements on women's gowns; pieces of sheer fabric or flowers.

**frills:**   Decorative ornamentation—fabric gathered on one side, in contrast to *furbelows,* which were fabric strips gathered down the center.

**furbelows:**   See *falbalas* in *Late Baroque.* Decorative ornamentation for gowns.

**jabot:**   Developed from the military style of tying the ends of the large, flat collar in front by means of a band. A falling lace ruffle, which filled in the opening of the shirt.

**jupe:**   Richly decorated petticoat.

**leghorn:**   Large, straw picture hat.

**mantle:**   The long winter mante. Fully-lined throughout and buttoned down the length of the front.

**modestie:**   A *stomacher* ornamented with graduated ribbon loops or lacings of narrow ribbon, finished with gauze or lace. Often worn when the front neckline was low cut on a woman's dress. In English called the *modesty bit.*

**montero:**   Skull cap, often fur-trimmed, worn with *banyan.*

**paniers:**   These baskets to hold out the skirt returned in 1717 by way of England to France, where they had already been in fashion for six or seven years under the name of *hoop skirt,* but did not become really popular in France until 1730. The hoops were of reed or whalebone, held together with ribbons, basketlike (*panier* means *basket* in French). The framework was covered with a taffeta or brocade hoop. The hoop was first funnel-shaped, but from the 1730s to 1740s grew very broad at the sides and flat front and back.

**parapluie:**   Rain umbrella, made with a folding frame.

**perspective:**   A single eyeglass lens carried by men. The women's version, the *lorgnette,* had two lenses.

**polonaise:**   An overgown for women, with fitted back and front and a draped skirt, worn from 1767 to 1787. Its special feature was three *paniers,* one back and two side sections, which rounded away in front. The *paniers* of the *polonaise* were drawn up on cords and could also be let down to form a *flying gown.* The cords were run through slots and were finished with tassels and rosettes, although later the *paniers* were sewn in position with the cords being simply ornamental.

**quizzing glass:**   *Perspective* mounted on a stick.

**robe à la française:**   The 1730s version of the *Watteau gown.* By 1770 this loose gown was the formal dress for court functions, having six box pleats stitched flat to the back and ending in a train. Under the bodice was an attached, fitted lining which was laced in back.

**robe volante** or **flying gown:**   A variation of the gown with the Watteau pleat. The soft pleats flowed from shoulder to hem, both back and front. Usually ankle length, worn over a wide hoop which created an undulating movement when the wearer walked.

**roquelaure** or **roquelo:**   Knee-length cloak, first worn in the eighteenth century by the duke of Roquelaure, made of heavy woolen cloth in bright colors with a hood and buttoned down the front.

**skimmer:**   A wide, soft-brimmed, leghorn straw hat faced with silk, worn over a white lawn cap and tied under the chin with velvet ribbons. It developed in England about 1750.

**solitaire:**   A concealing string of black taffeta, satin, or velvet which tied the back hair of the *cadogan wig.* The ribbon, probably the forerunner of the black tie, was tied to the wig in a bow at the back, with the ends brought around under the white *cravat* and then tied in a bow under the chin. Sometimes the solitaire was held in front by a diamond pin or a barrette.

**tricorne:**   The standard three-cornered hat worn by gentlemen of the period.

**Watteau gown** or **sacque:**   The principal style of the Regency, named after Watteau the painter. The original Watteau gown was a loose sack or dress, worn over a tight bodice and very full underskirt. The loose folds falling from the shoulders in back became part of the skirt. The front of the gown varied in design, either hanging loose or fitted at the waist, worn closed or open, and, if open, revealing a bodice and underskirt. The elbow-length sleeves had vertical pleats and soft, wide cuffs. In the 1740s a pagoda-shaped sleeve developed, tight from shoulder to elbow where it spread into flaring ruffles headed by ribbon bows.

## Chapter XVII: Neoclassic and Revolution

**bicorne:**   Man's hat having a front and back flap with the highest point or corner in center front, caused by a pinching of the front flap, thereby resembling a *tricorne.* Developed from a variation of the Swiss military hat.

**bowknot:**   A flat black ribbon which secured the

*cadogan* coiffure worn by men in the later eighteenth century.

**cabriolet:**  A bonnet shaped like a cabriolet carriage top and tied under the chin. It was similar to the *calash* and could also be collapsed at will.

**cadogan hairdo:**  See *Rococo.*

**calash:**  A cage covering huge hairdos and therefore very large. Had reed or whalebone hoops which could be raised or lowered by a ribbon like the hood of a carriage. See *Rococo.*

**caraco gown:**  A gown with long *basque,* finished with a peplum ruffle and often a train called a *Figaro,* which was attached under the peplum.

**carmagnole:**  A short jacket worn by French Revolutionists. Originally worn by workers in Piedmont who came from Carmagnole, Italy; deputies from Marseilles introduced it to Paris in the early 1790s. It buttoned down the front, had revers, and a high turned-down collar.

**circassienne gown:**  A variation of the *polonaise,* it also had three *paniers* run on cords, but was very short and of even length. The gown had double sleeves—that is, the outerbodice had short cap sleeves worn over the longer sleeves of the underbodice.

**cockade:**  A rosette or similar ornament worn on the side of the hat.

**dormeuse bonnet** or **sleeping bonnet:**  So named because it was also worn at night, it hugged the head tightly covering the cheeks, and was threaded with a ribbon tied into a bow on top of the head. For daytime wear it was worn higher on the head, revealing the ears and back of the head.

**fichu:**  Piece of lightweight, almost transparent fabric, worn like a shoulder scarf with the different styles of gowns. It was bunched above the small, tight waist, giving a pouter-pigeon look to the figure.

**Gainsborough hat:**  A type of wide-brimmed hat, decorated with ribbons or ostrich plumes, that appeared in Gainsborough's paintings.

**hedgehog hairdo:**  A woman's hairdo that appeared in 1778. Resembled a short male hairdo, cut fairly short in front, frizzed to the ends, and brushed up high off the face with long, loose curls or the cadogan in back.

**Hessian boots:**  Worn by the Hessian mercenaries hired to fight the American colonists, this boot came to a heart-shaped curve at the top and finished with a tassel that hung from the dip in the top of the boot.

**Kevenhüller** or **androsmane:**  A Swiss military hat that was more a bicorne than a tricorne. Named

after a famous Austrian field marshal. It was built high in front and back with a gentle crease in front. When used by generals in the Continental army it was known as the *continental hat.*

**le gilet:**  Copy of the English sleeveless waistcoat, with a laced back of lining material, which fitted the figure.

**levite gown:**  A type of *redingote* with train. Its creation was inspired by the Englishman's *redingote,* or riding coat, of the same period. There was also a definite *redingote gown,* which had a double-breasted jacket with wide lapels and an overskirt with a train behind. This costume was considered very mannish.

**liars, menteurs,** or **trompeurs:**  Wires which supported the *fichu.*

**macaroni:**  Member of a London club who dressed in extreme fashions. The costume consisted of a bobtailed coat and a foot-high wig topped by a small *tricorne* hat.

**mobcap:**  Large cap with soft, full crown and wide brim which almost hid the face; usually trimmed with ribbon bands and loops; known in England and therefore not restricted to use in the French Revolution.

**nivernois:**  A diminutive *tricorne* worn by the English fops known as *Macaronies* on top of their high *cadogan* wigs in the 1770s. Named for the duke of Nivernois, Louis-Jules Mancin Mazarani.

**pelisse:**  A woman's fur-trimmed, capelike wrap, with armholes and broad collar.

**polonaise:**  See *Rococo.*

**pouf:**  Huge headdress with ornaments which were attached to a framework of gauze.

**redingote:**  A man's double-breasted, long coat with turned-down collar and two or three shoulder capes; of English origin.

**robe à la française:**  See *Rococo.*

**Robespierre collar:**  A high, turned-down collar worn with a frilly jabot and stock tied in a bow in front. Made popular by the famous French statesman about 1790.

**sans culottes:**  Name given to the French Revolutionists or Jacobins to distinguish them from the aristocrats who wore knee breeches. Since they wore the long trousers that had been used by only the lowliest of peasants in centuries past, they were literally without culottes or breeches.

**stock:**  A neckcloth or *cravat.*

**thérèse:**  A huge cage of fine gauze worn over a

high-dressed coiffure and kept in shape by fine wire. Popular in France in the 1780s.

**tricorne:** see *Rococo*.

## Chapter XVIII: Directoire and Empire

**a la titus** or **à la victime:** Type of coiffure resembling a condemned person's locks before execution; worn with a red shawl and red necklace.

**Austrian knots:** Heavy black silk braid ornamentation on military uniforms appliquéd in looped designs. It originally decorated Austrian uniforms and was then copied by Napoleonic armies as well as other countries'.

**barouche coat:** Tight-fitting, three-quarter-length coat having full sleeves, fastened down front with gold, barrel-shaped snaps and confined at the waist with elastic girdle and buckle.

**Blücher:** A half-boot or shoe invented by Field Marshall von Blücher, commander of the Prussian forces at Waterloo. A laced shoe in which the quarters reach to the front over the instep and are laced together over the tongue.

**Bonaparte helmet:** A gathered white silk bonnet with a forehead band of black velvet embroidered with gold laurel leaves and mounted with a panache of white ostrich.

**carrick greatcoat** or **capote:** Overcoat of the period, with several capes over the long-skirted *redingote*. It had originally been a coachman's coat.

**chemise à l'anglaise:** The soft, full lingerie gown with crushed satin sash; it was worn both summer and winter, and it originated in England.

**cherusse:** The name given to the starched lace collars or ruffs of Empire court costume.

**circassian wrapper:** A dress similar to a night chemise, with very low-laced bodice and with sleeves of lace and muslin in alternate stripes.

**clawhammer tails:** Any male coat with stepped-back front below the waist and very long tails at the rear.

**coal scuttle bonnet:** A bonnet with a huge, shovellike lip in front, worn during the Directoire Period.

**courrobe:** Sleeveless court outergown.

**curricle cloak:** A half- or three-quarter-length shaped cloak with sloping sides, edged with fur or lace. Worn 1801 to 1816.

**escarpins:** Pumps of soft leather with pointed toes, worn with silk stockings, either plain white or striped on white.

**hussar breeches:** Skintight breeches, often in canary yellow and bottle green, and usually worn with a frock coat.

**Incroyables:** A group of young dandies who went to extremes in their dress, right after the French Revolution. Their coats, which sloped away in front from the waist when buttoned, had a high, turned-down collar and very wide lapels and were usually worn open. Sometimes the coat had bulky pleats across the back, giving the ugly effect of a hump. The Incroyables strove for a careless, wrinkled appearance. With this coat was worn a waistcoat of contrasting colored satin and a very full, sheer white cambric cravat. The *cravat* or neckcloth was loosely wound around the neck several times, often over padded cushions so that it rose up over the chin with ends tied in front.

**Merveilleuses:** The feminine counterpart of the Incroyables. They wore diaphanous gowns with very low-cut, short, tight bodices. A sheer lingerie muffler resembling the masculine neckcloth was often added and worn in the same fashion. The women either went bareheaded or wore a bonnet with a very large brim at the front rising high off the forehead—an exaggerated version of the English jockey hat.

**mameluke sleeve:** A long, woman's sleeve done in a series of puffs down the arm. Named after a squadron of Mamelukes created by Napoleon.

**muscadine:** A pastille scented with musk. The name was applied to effeminate men who overdressed and used quantities of this scent. The muscadine carried a short or long stick, weighted with lead.

**pantalettes:** A separate legcovering of lace and ruffles that extended below the hem of the dress.

**pelisse:** Fur-lined outercoat for women.

**phrygian bonnet:** Red liberty cap of the Revolution.

**redingote:** The long cloth or velvet coat which became a fashion for women about 1812. It was high-waisted, at first knee length, and later dropped to 9 or 10 inches above the hem of the dress. By the end of the decade, the coat was full length and edged with wide bands of fur.

**reticule:** A small drawstring purse, used in lieu of pockets since none existed.

**roguelo dress:** A morning dress with a loose back and bias front.

**rotonde:** Short cape of the same material as the dress.

**sans culottes:** See *Neoclassic and Revolution*.

**shako:** A military headdress with a high stiff crown

finished in front with a brush or plume. It was of Hungarian origin and was much the same in most European and American armies during the Napoleonic period. The tall, black, polished felt with a leather pompon on the left side was prescribed by the U.S. Congress in 1810.

**spencer:** A very short-waisted jacket, worn by women with the Empire dress. Named after Lord Spencer.

**talma:** A man's cloak, sometimes hooded, named after the French tragedian François Joseph Talma.

**Wellington mantle:** Garment which resembled a Spanish cloak of merino lined with sarcenet.

**witzchoura:** A feminine *redingote* of about 1808 in a long Empire line and usually fur-lined. It was probably of Russian origin.

**yeoman hat:** A triangular hat turned up in front and ornamented at the top with button and tasseled cord.

## Chapter XIX: Romantic

**angoulême bonnet:** Bonnet with a high crown and tied at the side.

**banditti:** A small panache of feathers on a feminine bonnet in the early 1800s.

**basque belt:** A waist-pinching girdle.

**bateau neck:** A boat-shaped straight neckline reaching from shoulder to shoulder and equally high in front and back.

**beehive bonnet:** A lady's simple straw cottage bonnet of the early nineteenth century made in the shape of a beehive and trimmed with a ribbon tied under the chin.

**beret sleeve:** After 1813 the sleeves of evening gowns were short, puffed, and stiffened and called the *beret,* or *pancake sleeve.*

**bertha:** Wide collar on women's gowns of the period, which accentuated the dropped-shoulder look.

**bishop sleeve:** A wide, long sleeve gathered at the cuff.

**bottine** or **jemima:** A lady's gored boot of beige fabric with black leather tip and elastic inserts. It was first designed for Queen Victoria in 1836, since the first cloth or webbing made with stretchable rubber was invented in England shortly before this. The shoe was designed by J. Sparkes Hall, bootmaker to the queen. It usually had leather or cloth uppers with the elastic gussets set in at the sides. *Jemima* was the British term for the style, and it was soon worn by both men and women.

**Byron collar:** An unstarched collar left open at the throat and held together by a silk scarf carelessly tied.

**canezou:** The *Canezou Spencer* was a short, separate, transparent jacket with sleeves, its two scarflike ends held in place by the dress belt. Usually of sheer muslin with embroidery, it was worn over the bodice. The *false canezou* was a deep lace or ruffled shoulder cape falling over the short puffed sleeves of a bodice or blouse.

**crinoline:** A petticoat, corded and lined with horsehair and finished with a braid of straw at the hem (*crin* being the French word for horsehair). First appeared in the early 1840s.

**Donna Maria:** A full sleeve puffed to below the elbow and then tighter to the wrist.

**D'Orsay pump:** A gentleman's shoe with cut-away sides and a low broad heel introduced by Count D'Orsay, a society dandy who began his fashion reign in Paris but came to have most influence in London in the 1830s. The masculine evening pump of the twentieth century is an outgrowth of the style.

**frock coat:** A double-breasted coat having long skirts of equal length in front and back.

**frog fastening:** Ornamental fastening with cord loops and suspended buttons.

**Hessian boot:** A rather tight-fitting high boot.

**leg-o-mutton sleeve:** See *Donna Maria.*

**Macfarlane cloak:** A cloth topcoat with separate sleeve capes and side slits to permit the hands to reach inner pockets. About 1846.

**mackintosh:** A cloak of rubber-coated, waterproof fabric invented by Charles Mackintosh.

**mantelette:** Shaped scarf. Covered the back almost like a jacket and descended to the knees in front, being sloped off and narrow from the shoulders down.

**montespan:** A sleeve with the upper part full, a band at the elbow, and a ruffle extending over the forearm.

**nankeen trousers:** A strong, buff-colored, cotton trouser named after the Chinese city of Nanking. It was introduced in America from Sicily in 1828 and became especially popular for summer wear.

**opera cloak:** A man's knee-length cloak of velvet or fine woolen with a standing collar fastened by tasseled silk cords. It was worn by men with formal evening wear in lieu of an overcoat to give a dashing effect.

**pantalettes** or **drawers:** Leg coverings of lace and ruffles that extended below the knees. They were sometimes false, being ruffles held at the knees with tapes.

**pelerine:** A short, separate cape deriving its name from the shoulder cape of the medieval pilgrim; often of fur.

**pelisse:** A fur-lined or fur-trimmed cloth coat, used in France, although the English applied the name to any long outercoat.

**quizzing** or **perspective glass:** A single round lens carried on a black silk cord or ribbon, on a chain around the neck, or on a long handle of gold, tortoise shell, or ivory. It became fashionable among male dandies in the 1830s and women often set the lens into their painted fans.

**robe d'interieur:** At-home wear for men; robe of brilliantly figured silk or velvet. Also worn were lounging clothes or smoking suits with a velvet cap.

**sautoir:** A silver or gold chain upon which women carried a watch.

**stocks:** During the 1840s a fashionable, wide neck covering. As before, it was often neatly shaped to the neck, whaleboned at the sides, and secured by a strap and buckled in back. Often was plain across the front or had a piece brought around the back and fastened in a knot or bow.

**studs:** Jeweled shirt fasteners for formal and semiformal wear in gold, pearls, or cut stones. They were used to fasten collars and shirts and first appeared in the 1840s.

**taglioni overcoat:** A short, braid-bound overcoat used in the 1840s. Named after the Italian dancer Taglioni.

**tam-o-'shanter:** A jaunty bonnet-cap named after a poem by Robert Burns. It was usually of heavy brushed wool and varied colors, the number being varied according to a man's status. It became popular as a sporting cap during the Romantic Period and has remained a popular style until today.

**Zouave jacket:** A bolero jacket with round corners in deep blue Arabian cloth without collar or buttons but ornamented with braid and worn with full red pantaloons. It was the uniform of the Zouave regiment formed by the French in Algiers in the early 1830s which in 1838 became a unit in the French army.

## Chapter XX: Victorian and Second Empire

**antimacassar:** An ornamental, washable covering used to protect chair backs from the oil (*macassar*) used on men's hair.

**Armenian cloak:** A fashionable gentleman's cloak of the 1850s and 1860s. It was cut in one piece without inserted sleeves, but side seams formed loose armcoverings. Had a deep velvet collar.

**balmacaan:** A loose, flaring coat of Scottish origin with flaring sleeves, usually of tweed, gabardine, or raincoat fabric with a military standing collar and slashed pockets.

**balmoral:** A laced-up shoe or half-boot with closed throat introduced by Prince Albert in 1853. Everything new and smart at the time was named *Balmoral* after the royal castle in Aberdeenshire, built by the prince and Queen Victoria.

**basque:** The outer part of a dress sewn onto a boned bodice.

**bavolet:** A flounce sewn at the back of a bonnet.

**bertha:** A capelike collar of cloth or lace.

**bloomers:** Loose oriental trousers gathered at the knee; popularized by Amelia Bloomer in 1851.

**bolero:** A small jacket with rounded corners in front.

**bournouse** or **burnous:** A fringed, knee-length, Arabian-style mantle with hood worn in the 1850s.

**bowler** or **derby hat:** A stiff felt hat with a low, round crown and narrow brim; the *bowler,* which is the British term for *derby,* has a slightly wider brim and roll at the sides.

**braces:** Suspender straps extending from the waist belt in the front over the shoulder to support trousers.

**cage américaine:** Another term for the whale-bone, metal crinoline, or hoop skirt.

**canezou:** *See Romantic.*

**capote:** Elaborate mid-Victorian bonnet with ribbon bows tied at the side or front.

**cardigan:** Originally a short military jacket of knit worsted designed and worn by the earl of Cardigan, a British general during the Crimean War. Trimmed in fur, braid, and buttons. Later the name for a knit sweater jacket of hip length.

**chignon:** A heavy twist or knot of real or false hair worn high or low at the back of the head.

**chimneypot** or **stovepipe hat:** A tall, cylindrical hat with very little brim; worn by men.

**crinoline:** A stiff or unpliable material used to stiffen a costume, but at this time was the name also given to the spring steel hoops set into a petticoat or onto cloth strips to hold the petticoats and skirts away from the body in a bell shape.

**dundrearies, Dundreary whiskers,** or **Piccadilly**

**weepers:** Long side whiskers worn by Lord Dundreary in *Our American Cousin* by Tom Taylor, 1858.

**Empire jupon:** A petticoat with gores and two or three steel frames at the bottom.

**Empress Eugénie hat:** A flat-crowned straw with a rolled brim and ribbons falling down the back, used by the Empress Eugénie for riding and traveling.

**Figaro jacket:** A closefitting short jacket with epaulets on the shoulder and cut away at the side in a bolero style.

**forage cap** or **képi:** In the mid-1800s replaced the military *shako*. A cap with a hard front brim and a soft, low crown often raised a bit at the back. It was first adopted by the French in 1857 and by the American forces during the Civil War.

**frock coat:** A double-breasted coat having long skirts of equal length in front and back; the skirts had less flare than in the Romantic Period.

**four-in-hand tie:** See *Later Victorian*.

**Garibaldi jacket:** A shirt of bright scarlet merino wool, decorated on the front with black braid and buttons. Named after the popular Italian hero.

**Gladstone collar:** A comfortable standing collar with flaring points worn with a silk scarf in a bowknot. Worn in the 1850s by William Ewart Gladstone who later became prime minister of Great Britain.

**imperial:** A small, tufted beard on the chin, usually worn with a waxed mustache; named after the style worn by the Emperor Napoleon III.

**Inverness cape:** A full, sleeveless cape which fitted closely around the neck; from Inverness in Scotland.

**morning coat:** The swallowtail or curved, cutback, skirted coat worn by gentlemen for formal morning wear.

**mutton chops:** Heavy sideburns.

**New York surtout:** A man's fashionable, short, black overcoat with straight-cut skirts and a wide collar to the waistline finished with black silk braid. Popular in the 1850s.

**pagoda sleeve:** A sleeve shaped like a funnel, tight above and gradually widening at the bottom, often finishing in several ruffles over a soft lawn undersleeve.

**paisley shawl:** A copy of an Indian shawl made in Paisley, Scotland.

**paletot:** A capelike outdoor garment hanging in stiff pleats from shoulder to flounce of dress, with a flap over the armhole and a number of still shorter shoulder capes.

**pea jacket:** A heavy, short coat worn by sailors from 1850 on. Made of heavy, tightly woven cloth in dark blue. Sometimes used as a model in lighter fabric for young boys' coats.

**peignoir:** A dress with a boneless bodice and bishop sleeve.

**pork pie hat:** A hat worn with a dish-shaped fold in the crown.

**Prince Albert:** Another name for the double-breasted frock coat with satin lapels, named after the consort of Queen Victoria who favored the style.

**princess gown:** A full-length gown cut in one from shoulder to waist with a number of gores and full enough in the skirt to go over a hoop. Usually it buttoned up the front.

**raglan coat:** A coat with sleeves cut to fit into the shoulders all the way to the neckline of the garment. Named after Lord Raglan.

**Russian jacket:** A sleeveless short coat.

**Russian vest:** A loose blouse resembling the Garibaldi jacket.

**sack suit:** A loose-fitting combination of vest, coat, and trousers of the same material, with the coat ending at the finger tips and having high, short lapels. It was used in commerce and in sports.

**shirtwaist:** A masculine style of bodice that looked like a male shirt with high collar and cuffs.

**Victoria mantle:** A knee-length mantle with collar and wide, hanging sleeves; usually with a deep-colored border.

**waistcoat:** The forerunner of the present-day vest.

**waterproof coat:** An outdoor garment with or without a cape, worn as a protection from the rain.

**zouave jacket:** see *Romantic*.

## Chapter XXI: Later Victorian: The Gilded Age

**ascot tie:** A scarf tied in a knot with horizontal ends, then crossed diagonally. The whole usually held in place with a jeweled stickpin.

**balayeuse, dust ruffle,** or **street sweeper:** A ruffle on the inner side of the hem of a skirt or petticoat to protect it from the ground.

**basque:** A short, skirt-like termination of an upper garment (originally on the male doublet) which was adopted by women in the 1870s. The style is said to have developed when the princess of Wales wore a fisherman's jersey pulled tightly over her rigidly corseted figure.

**blazer:**   A lightweight sport jacket.

**boater:**   A man's hard straw hat coated with shellac from India that became popular for summer outings and sporting events in the 1870s. The English wore it boating (hence the name). Standard summer wear in America from June to September.

**braces:**   See *Victorian* and *Second Empire.*

**bustle:**   Whalebone or steel strips placed in the top back of the petticoat or in a separate panier puff in order to hold out the elaborate draping at the back of the overskirt.

**camargo:**   A jacket with a built-in panier.

**camisole:**   The light cloth cover worn over the corset.

**cardigan:**   A collarless sweater with a front opening.

**Chesterfield overcoat:**   A fitted dress overcoat with hidden buttons and a velvet collar, worn in the late nineteenth century.

**dolman:**   A three-quarter-length outerwrap made of brocade, silk, or woolen fabric with sleeves cut in one with the body.

**Eton jacket:**   A short jacket with side lapels first worn by the students at Eton College in England.

**fedora:**   A velour hat with a fairly high, tapering crown that was usually creased in the middle.

**fore and aft cap** or **deerstalker:**   A cap having a visor front and back, worn with an Inverness cape.

**four-in-hand:**   A type of necktie originally used by coachmen that is tied in a slip knot.

**frou-frou dress:**   A dress with a low corsage and a light pink underskirt covered with many small flounces.

**homburg:**   A carefully blocked, stiff felt hat with a medium tapering crown creased in the middle and a brim that was rolled up on the sides and finished in grosgrain ribbon.

**Hussar jacket:**   A jacket with braiding and frog fastenings; worn with a waistcoat. Heavily influenced by uniforms of English troops in Egypt.

**jersey sweater:**   A slipover sweater, fairly closefitting. Copied from a fisherman's sweater.

**knickerbockers:**   Full, knee-length breeches gathered in at the knee; named after Father Knickerbocker, who came to New Amsterdam in 1674.

**Langtry bonnet:**   A small, closefitting bonnet.

**monocle:**   A single glass with a ribbon, fitted into the eye socket to help the wearer improve the vision of one eye as well as to look aristocratic.

**mousquetaire glove:**   A heavy leather glove with wrist extensions fringed in silk from the seventeenth century was adapted in the 1870s into the long forearm evening glove with a tiny wrist opening (fastened with small pearl buttons) by Sarah Bernhardt. It soon became *de rigueur* for formal evening dress.

**Norfolk jacket:**   A jacket with box pleats or straps of the same material passing over the belt and extending from shoulder to hem in front and back; usually worn for sport occasions.

**polonaise:**   See *Rococo:*

**pompadour:**   Hair style formed by drawing the hair straight up and back from the forehead.

**reefer:**   A double-breasted, closefitting jacket.

**rubbers:**   Low overshoes of rubber worn to protect regular shoes from wet weather. The style developed for men during the 1870s.

**Russian bonnet:**   A type of bonnet with a large bow tied under the chin with steel embroidered crown and a lace brim.

**spats:**   Short coverings for the ankles and instep, usually made of felt and buttoned on the outside.

**swallowtail coat:**   Formerly a riding coat with skirts buttoned back, it now had the skirts cut back in a gentle curve to behind the knees.

**tam-o'-shanter:**   A round, flat cap with a tight-fitting headband. See *Victorian and Second Empire.*

**toque:**   A small, closefitting female hat without a brim.

**tucker:**   Fabric used to cover the neck above a very low bodice.

**tuxedo:**   An informal dinner jacket introduced from England, but the name is of American origin.

**ulster:**   A fitted, double-breasted coat having several capes; at first made of frieze, a coarse woolen cloth with shaggy mat on one side made in Ulster, Ireland.

**Windsor tie:**   A large, flowing tie.

**wing collar:**   A high, stiff collar with turned-back corners.

## Chapter XXII: Late Victorian and Edwardian: Art Nouveau

**aigrette:**   A feather or plume from the egret, which is a kind of heron.

**alpaca:** The long hair of the Peruvian llama that was woven into woolen cloth for men's and women's suits during the last years of the nineteenth century and the first years of the twentieth. Thus one often reads references to ''my alpaca jacket or coat'' in literature of the time.

**American shoulders:** Known in France as *épaules américaines* because of the broad shoulders worn by American male tourists about 1905. This style was popular for men's fashions from 1905 to 1909 and again in the later 1930s.

**balaclava:** A heavy woolen helmet crocheted or knitted for British soldiers as a winter cap in the years before World War I. Its name came from the seaport village in the Crimea that was the site of the Charge of the Light Brigade in 1854.

**Balkan blouse:** A low-waisted bodice with a belt girding the hips.

**bateau neck:** A wide, curved, fairly low neckline.

**beau-catcher:** The coquettish curl in the middle of a woman's forehead that was popular as a coiffure accent at the turn into the twentieth century.

**beehive hat:** A large hat shaped like an extended beehive that came down well over the head and was fashionable from 1910 to 1914.

**bertha:** A capelike collar of varying length and usually of lace which was popular in the early years of the twentieth century for women and recalled the Palatine capes of the seventeenth century.

**bishop sleeves:** See *Romantic.*

**bloomers:** Loose underdrawers usually gathered at the knee.

**boa:** A long or short cylindrical neck scarf of fur or feathers.

**boater:** See *Later Victorian: The Gilded Age.*

**brassiere:** A band worn around the bust, usually as a support.

**bulldog toe:** The high, rounded, blunt toe of a shoe.

**bungalow apron:** A simple, straight-line dress.

**bust improver:** A device used to make the bust appear larger.

**Buster Brown collar:** A wide, starched collar worn with a Windsor tie and identified with the character, Buster Brown, in the comic strip of the period.

**chatelaine bag:** A pouch bag of pin-seal with silver mountings attached to a belt.

**chemisette:** An underbodice of lawn and lace with short or long sleeves. It was often worn to supply sleeves and cover the cutaway neck of a jumper dress. The style was popular for ladies and girls from about 1890 to 1910.

**deerstalker cap:** See *Later Victorian.*

**diadem:** A form of tiara or small jeweled crown for evening.

**dog collar:** A closefitting necklace that hugs the throat; also known as a *choker.*

**duster:** A coat of panama, pongee, alpaca, or natural linen used for driving and motoring.

**fascinator:** A lacy woolen square or triangular headcovering.

**friendship bracelet:** It consisted of similar links given by various friends and later put together to form a bracelet.

**Gainsborough hat:** A velvet, beaver, or straw hat having a low crown and a broad brim, trimmed with feathers.

**Gibson girl blouse:** A blouse with a single pleat which extended over each shoulder front and back, hiding the armseye of the shirtwaist.

**gigot sleeve:** A full sleeve with more fullness at the elbow than at the shoulder or wrist.

**godet pleats:** Fluting insets in a skirt held in place by a fine steel in the hem; used at the back and sides.

**harem skirt:** A divided skirt.

**knickers:** Full breeches gathered or pleated into kneebands and buckled at the knee; based upon the *knickerbockers* of the preceding period.

**la pliant:** An invention of 1896 consisting of pieces of steel, enclosed in cotton or silk ribbon tapes, which held out the stiff and heavy skirt in the back and was much lighter than the use of numerous petticoats. It was possible to transfer the steels to different skirts.

**leggings:** Fitted coverings for the legs, usually fastened with a strap under the shoe and extending above the knee or to the waist.

**leg-o-mutton sleeves:** A sleeve that was extremely wide at the top and tapered to the wrist.

**Lillian Russell dress:** The fashion identified with the American actress (1861–1922) who had a buxom figure and loved form-fitting gowns with a train. Her marcel-waved pompadour was topped by a large black velvet hat of Gainsborough style with ostrich plumes.

**mackintosh:** A waterproof coat bearing the name of the originator of rubberized cloth garments. See *Romantic.*

**marabou:**   Trimming made from the feathers of a certain species of stork; also a kind of raw silk or fabric made from it.

**marcel waves:**   A type of artificial waving of the hair devised by Marcel of France in 1907.

**Merry Widow hat:**   An extremely large hat named from the musical comedy of the same name.

**mesh bag:**   A bag made of interwoven metal links.

**morning-glory** or **serpentine skirt:**   A skirt which fitted snugly at the hip and flared bell-like at the hem.

**Mother Hubbard:**   A loose-fitting housedress worn for comfort when doing housework.

**mushroom-style hat:**   A large female hat suggesting the shape of a mushroom; worn between 1908 and 1913.

**Napoleon costume:**   A woman's dress of 1905 having a straight, standing collar with deep turnover, wide revers, and braid trimming.

**opera hat:**   A tall, silk hat that folded flat.

**orby cutaway:**   An American-designed man's single-breasted walking cutaway that eliminated the waistline seam. The seam down the center back ended at the waistline.

**oxford:**   A low shoe for men, women, and children laced or tied over the instep. The first oxford was a half-boot of heavy black leather dating from seventeenth-century England. These finally developed into a lightweight dress shoe at the beginning of the twentieth century. There were also button oxfords with a leather piece over the instep that buttoned to one side.

**Panama hat:**   A hand-woven hat of fine straw from Ecuador and Colombia, South America.

**peek-a-boo waist:**   A very thin blouse.

**peg-top trousers:**   Trousers that were wide and pleated at the top and very narrow at the ankles. The name *peg-top* originally applied to a boy's cone-shaped spinning top.

**permanent wave:**   The vogue of the marcel wave in the 1890s and early 1900s led to the invention of the permanent wave in 1906 by Charles Nestlé, a fashionable coiffeur in London. The wave was first applied by an electric heat machine, but a later method used lotions instead of heat and was called a *cold wave.* This was much faster than the heated machine method.

**Peter Pan collar:**   A small, soft, turnover collar, named from the costume worn by Maude Adams in *Peter Pan* by James M. Barrie.

**pettibockers:**   Like bloomers, these were ankle-length, silk jersey pantaloons worn by women.

**pompadour:**   The full halo of hair brushed up off the face and neck and waved over a stuffed circlet of cotton or horsehair known as a *rat.* The original pompadour style of the eighteenth century, named after the famous mistress of Louis XV, had been much tighter and closer to the head, while the style that developed in the late 1890s, popularized by the Gibson girl, was much fuller and looser.

**Prince Rupert:**   A velvet or plush smoking jacket worn open at the front and resembling a Louis XV coat.

**rainy daisy:**   The nickname given to a woman who belonged to the Rainy Day Club and who wore a *rainy daisy,* or walking skirt, two to three inches off the ground in rainy weather.

**rat:**   Padding worn to make the hair extend outward from the head.

**Rough Rider shirt:**   A khaki shirt similar to that worn by Theodore Roosevelt and his cavalry in Cuba in 1898.

**street sweepers:**   Ruffles worn under the hem of a skirt to protect it from dust and dirt.

**sun-ray skirt:**   A skirt with accordion pleating.

**switch:**   A separate tress of real or artificial hair bound at one end.

**ulster:**   A heavy overcoat originally worn by men and women in Ulster, Ireland. In the early 1900s it was a loose-fitting overcoat, usually double-breasted with a full or half belt. The coat was originally made of Ulster frieze (a stout woolen cloth with a shaggy pile).

**umbrella skirt:**   A full, bell-shaped skirt.

**wrapper:**   An unshapely housedress of about 1905.

**yoke skirt:**   A skirt which had a shaped piece in front and two side pieces which extended around the hips and joined in the back. The lower part of the skirt was attached to this yoke.

## Chapter XXIII: World War I and the Twenties: Early Art Deco

**Algerian purse:**   A purse made of Algerian leather, usually tooled and embossed in colors or in gold.

**apron tunic:**   A tunic having an overskirt, cut away in the back and forming an apron in front.

**arctics** or **galoshes:**   A rubberized overshoe worn as a protection against rain and snow.

**babushka:** A scarf worn around the head and tied under the chin. Russian word for *grandmother*.

**Balkan blouse:** A blouse with full, loose sleeves gathered into a wide band around the waist. Came into fashion after the Balkan Wars.

**balmacaan:** A type of loose-fitting, flaring overcoat with raglan sleeves.

**bandeau:** A band worn around the head to hold the hair tightly to the head.

**bed jacket:** A short jacket worn while resting in bed.

**beer jacket:** A simple, straight jacket of flannel, cotton, or linen which male students wore to beer parties in the 1920s and 1930s.

**black tie:** A popular term given to men's semiformal evening wear, which consisted of tuxedo dinner jacket, black waistcoat or cummerbund, and a black bow tie worn with a soft white shirt. The term is often used in opposition to *white tie* which refers to formal evening wear.

**blazer:** A bright-colored sport jacket, originally striped vertically.

**bobbed hair:** The style had originally been for boys wearing a Dutch hair cut with bangs and straight hanging hair to the top of the neck, but in the 1920s the designer Paul Poiret adopted a coiffure for his mannequins in which the hair was swept back from the face and lightly waved to the bottom of the ears and upper part of the neck. Later even shorter bobbed hair developed to complement the head-hugging cloche hat. After that came the boyish bob or shingle, which was almost like a male cut except for the curved points of hair that came forward from the ears, and the tousled bob cut.

**boutonnière:** A real flower or an artificial nosegay worn in the buttonhole of the left lapel.

**box coat:** A loose, short, fingertip-length coat of a boxy cut.

**bush jacket:** A belted, hip-length jacket with tailored collar and two sets of pockets, worn by a hunter in the African jungle.

**camisole neckline:** An evening dress with a neckline resembling that of a camisole-top slip, which was straight above the bustline with a strap over each shoulder.

**cardigan:** A knitted sweater-jacket that opened up the front.

**chemise dress:** A one-piece dress which was slipped over the head. It had short sleeves, long waist, and narrow belt and became the basic style for all dresses in the 1920s. It was also called the *tube* or *pillowslip* dress.

**cloche:** A closefitting, bell-shaped hat.

**compact:** A small ornamental box containing powder and rouge.

**cowl neckline:** The loose neckline of a dress falling in graceful curves across the chest with the draping of the fabric resembling the soft folds of a monk's cowl.

**crew-neck sweater:** A sweater with a flat, close, round neckline.

**dolman wrap:** A coat with sleeves cut in one with the body and the whole tapering toward the ankles.

**fedora:** See *Late Victorian: The Gilded Age*.

**ferris-waist:** The trade name given to a fitted waist which had buttons on tabs to hold the supporters. It was worn mainly by young girls.

**foulard:** A thin, soft material of silk, or silk and cotton.

**harlequin hat:** A hat with wide, turned-up brim and oblique at the sides.

**helmet:** A closefitting cap worn toward the back of the head and with sides extending over the ears.

**hobble skirt:** A very narrow skirt that inhibited walking and was very popular from about 1912 to 1914.

**Hoover apron:** A wraparound, coverall apron with sleeves. It originated in World War I when Herbert Hoover was Food Administrator.

**Irene Castle bob:** A haircut, loosely waved and combed back from the forehead. It was introduced by the dancer Irene Castle.

**jodhpurs:** Breeches used for riding; designed with fullness above the knee, closefitting below, cuff at ankle, and often with a strap under the instep.

**Kiki skirt:** An extremely tight, knee-length skirt which appeared after it was worn by Leonore Ulric in the play *Kiki*.

**kimono:** A loose Japanese robe or gown of silk tied with a sash and with sleeves cut in one with the body that was used as a dressing gown or negligee robe in the 1920s.

**kimono dress:** A loose gown with sleeve and body cut in one piece that was popular about 1910 when there was a great interest in Japanese art.

**lampshade dress:** A two-tiered skirt with the top tier flared out in the shape of a lampshade. The style was popular just before World War I.

**Lindbergh jacket:**   A heavy, warm, woolen or leather jacket with large pockets and elastic, fitted waist and wrist bands. It was worn by Charles Lindbergh on his 1927 flight over the Atlantic.

**middy blouse:**   A young girl's straight blouse with a braid-trimmed sailor collar, bearing the nickname of the English midshipman; the three stripes on the collar represent the three great naval victories of Lord Nelson.

**monastic silhouette:**   A dress resembling a monk's robe, hanging loosely from the shoulder, with fullness held in place by a belt at the hips.

**monkey fur coat:**   A woman's outercoat actually made of monkey fur or to imitate monkey fur.

**off-the-face** or **halo hat:**   A hat worn to the back of the head with the brim framing the face.

**Oxford bags** or **plus fours:**   These loose knee trousers were an exaggeration of the earlier knickers and were usually reserved for golf.

**pajamas:**   Loose trousers and jacket, usually of silk, used for sleeping by both men and women during the 1920s.

**patch pocket:**   A pocket sewn on the outside of a garment and made of the same material.

**peg-top:**   A skirt with a fullness of draping around the hip and very narrow at the hem that was popular in the years just before World War I.

**Peter Pan hat:**   Small hat with a feather at the side, similar to that worn in the play of the same name by Maude Adams.

**pinch-back coat:**   A coat with inverted pleats at the back which were stitched into a belt.

**planter's punch:**   A firm straw hat, shaped like a fedora, which originated in Jamaica about 1923; it had a creased crown and a wide, pleated ornamental band.

**pocket cascade:**   A pocket formed in the fold and draped section at the side of the skirt.

**polo coat:**   A light-colored, soft-surfaced topcoat for informal wear and sports.

**polo shirt:**   A sport shirt, usually knitted, with an open collar and short sleeves.

**profile hat:**   A hat worn on one side of the head, forming a background for the profile of the wearer.

**raccoon coat:**   A very bulky outercoat or overcoat of raccoon fur, worn for display as well as for warmth at sporting events, particularly at football games.

**saddle shoe:**   A two-toned oxford with an ornamental strip of leather across the instep.

**shawl collar:**   An attached collar having a rounded, unbroken outline, often extending to the waistline.

**shingle bob:**   A mode of cutting the hair very close to the head in the back to show the natural contour of the head.

**skimmer sailor:**   A flat-crowned sailor hat with a heavy and wide straight brim.

**tonneau silhouette:**   A skirt that was similar to the peg-top style in shape that developed briefly about 1914.

**trench coat:**   A tan-colored topcoat with a belt, a double yoke at the shoulder that was loose at the bottom, and epaulet straps at the shoulder; resembled a military coat and was used as a protection in bad weather.

**T-shirt:**   A short term for tennis or sports shirt of knitted lightweight cotton (or wool) with a crew or V-neck and usually white. It was usually sleeveless but could have long sleeves and sometimes a mock turtleneck. The style developed in the 1920s.

**turtleneck sweater:**   A slip-on, knit sweater with a high turnover collar.

**tyrolean hat:**   A hat with a feather usually of soft, fuzzy felt similar to those worn in the highlands of Bavaria and Austria.

## Chapter XXIV: The Thirties and World War II: Late Art Deco

**aloha shirt:**   A brilliantly colored printed silk shirt which was a copy of the Hawaiian man's shirt or tunic which hung down over his trousers. Its breezy comfort made it a style that appealed to men on vacation from the 1930s until today.

**argyles:**   a multicolored diamond pattern in woolen socks and sweaters. Argyll is the name of the clan whose tartan is imitated by this pattern.

**beanie (beany)** or **calotte:**   This skullcap was originally Greek and worn by all classes, but particularly the lower classes, and the fabric varied according to the position of the wearer. Later as a small round skullcap it was worn under a priest's hood to cover his *tonsure,* and gradually in varying colors it came to denote ecclesiastic rank among churchmen. In the 1930s under the name *beanie* instead of *calotte* it became a popular female fashion as well as a cap for young boys.

**Bermuda shorts:**   Knee-length shorts for summer sportswear.

**borselino:**   An Italian-made felt hat in which the

fibers are aged for several years and the detailing is done by hand; supposedly the finest of men's hats.

**crew cut:** A haircut developed during World War II and often favored by young men in the late 1940s and early 1950s. The hair was cropped very close to the head except on top where it made a bristly stand of less than an inch. Although also known as the *G.I. haircut,* it was really a collegiate style which originated among varsity rowing crews to differentiate them from other undergraduates. When the top was slightly longer and tousled, it became a *feather crew* or *Ivy League cut.*

**culottes:** A trouserlike garment that has the fullness to make it look like a full skirt when the wearer is not in motion. It was originally the name given to aristocratic knee breeches in the eighteenth century, but in the 1930s came to be used specifically to describe divided skirts.

**congo** and **palm beach suits:** Originally summer suits of white cotton and mohair, later applied to all white summer suits.

**cummerbund:** A wide cloth band worn around the waist to imitate the same item worn by Spanish and Latin American men as a first waist sash. The term comes from the Hindu word *kamarband*—a wide, soft sash worn around the waist with little pockets for carrying small possessions. In the hot summer of 1893 it was adopted by Europeans to replace the waistcoat, and by the 1930s it had become a standard replacement (in black silk or faille) for the black waistcoat usually worn with a tuxedo dinner jacket.

**Eisenhower jacket:** A waist-length military tunic in khaki worn by General Eisenhower during World War II and adapted for civilian use after the war.

**halter:** A more or less triangular piece of sturdy material made to tie at the back of the neck and at the back of the waist. In the 1930s for beach wear it was often the only garment above the waist, leaving the arms and back bare for tanning.

**halter neckline:** A neckline new in the 1930s which was high in the neck at the center front, leaving the shoulders and the back completely bare. It was first designed for beachwear, but a version for afternoon and evening soon followed.

**handkerchief tunic:** A tunic made from a square of material, the center of which was cut out for a waistline, the corners falling in graceful folds at the sides of the skirt.

**Hollywood top slip:** A fitted slip with a single or a double V top.

**Levis:** See *Contemporary*

**loafer:** Heelless Norwegian slipper shoe introduced in 1940.

**lodencoat:** A coat made of waterproof green tyrolean woolen fabric with wooden toggles and loops instead of buttons. See *toggle coat* under *The Cold War.*

**Montgomery beret:** A dashing military beret associated with the British general Montgomery.

**polo coat:** See *World War I and the Twenties.*

**polo shirt:** See *World War I and the Twenties.*

**saddle shoe:** See *World War I and the Twenties.*

**sash blouse:** A blouse with wide pieces that crossed in front like a surplice with attached ends forming a sash or girdle, which was tied or fastened in the back.

**sequin calotte:** A small beanielike cap covered in sequins—a style fashionable in the 1930s.

**shirtwaist dress:** A one-piece belted and tailored dress having a tucked shirtwaist.

**slacks:** Loose trousers worn for informal wear.

**snap brim:** A soft felt hat having a medium crown and brim pulled down in front in a jaunty manner.

**snood:** Originally a ribbon or *fillet* worn by unmarried Scottish maidens. Later it signified the coarse hairnet or fabric which was attached to the back of a Victorian hat to hold the hair—a style which had its origins in the use of the medieval *caul* or hairnet of gold thread. The snood returned to fashion in the 1930s, sometimes with a tiny hat attached.

**swagger coat:** A coat having a very loose skirt, or flare from shoulder to hem.

**swing skirt:** A circular skirt with gores that gave a swinging motion when the wearer was walking. The shirt was also popular in the 1930s when swing music was popular.

**tab collar shirt:** A collar with a long point on each side extending down the front.

**teddies:** A straight garment, combining a shapeless brassiere and a straight skirt with a wide strap separating the garment into two separate parts or legs.

**windbreaker:** A lined leather or closely woven cloth jacket with a zipper that was used as a protection against the weather in place of a longer or a heavier coat when a sport shirt and slacks were worn.

## Chapter XXV: The Cold War

**A-line:** A triangular or A-shaped dress, either belted or unbelted and usually sleeveless.

**American blade:** A coat with a broad shoulder and with fullness at the upper arm and back to prevent strain.

**ballerina skirt:** A very full, usually ankle-length, gored or flare skirt, sometimes made of three or four tiers of ruffles, resembling the type worn by a Spanish dancer.

**ballet slipper:** A flat, low slipper laced around the ankle and worn for casual or evening wear.

**beach coat:** A short, loose coat of terry cloth, plain cotton, or synthetic fiber used for beach wear.

**Blücher:** A shoe with a long vamp and a strap across the instep, derived from the style of boot worn by General Blücher during the Battle of Waterloo.

**blue jeans:** Trousers made of denim, a heavy, twilled cotton cloth; formerly worn by cowboys and workmen, they had become the standard day-to-day wear of many young people and students by the early 1960s.

**boy coat:** A short jacket with collar and cuffs that resembled the jackets worn by small boys.

**butcher linen:** A strong, heavy cloth made of long-fiber flax and used for the aprons worn by butchers; when it was white it was used for dresses and suitings. Made of either rayon or rayon and cotton.

**cabin boy breeches:** Short, tight-fitting knee pants laced at the knee.

**cache-chignon:** A velvet bow used to catch loose ends of hair.

**capri** or **pirate pants:** Similar to pedal pushers but loose and tapered, ending at midcalf.

**car coat:** A fingertip-length coat with patch pockets and a turn-up collar used for traveling in an open sports car.

**chukka boot:** A two-eyelet, ankle-high shoe of suede or smooth leather with rubber or leather soles. Related to the *jodhpur boot* which fastened with a strap. The name *chukka* is of East Indian origin and is the name for a period of play in polo.

**cinch belt:** A tight, wide, elastic belt.

**cocktail dress:** A party dress appropriate for wear in the late afternoon; often longer than a daytime dress.

**cobbler's apron:** A sleeveless, hip-length, belted apron with huge pockets across the front, worn for dress or for utility.

**convertible jumper:** A sleeveless dress worn with a sweater for sportswear, with a dressy blouse for daytime, and without a blouse for evening.

**cowichan** or **Siwash sweater:** A sweater with a striking Indian pattern in black on white or grey background, made by the Siwash Indians of Vancouver Island, B.C.

**desert cloth:** a relatively stiff and medium-coarse weave cotton in bright colors that was used for sportskirts in the 1950s.

**Directory suit:** A suit with high midriff and very short cutaway jacket; in general followed the silhouette of the French Directoire.

**dirndl:** A very full, gathered skirt resembling the skirt of Tyrolean peasants.

**duffle coat:** A warm woolen coat of fingertip length with hood attached, having frogs of wood and rope. It came into use on the ski lift after World War II when surplus English Navy coats were made available to civilians. Worn by men and women and children, they are frequently of Tyrolean cloth with wooden toggles and hemp loops. See *loden coat* under *The Thirties and World War II.*

**duvetyn:** A type of cotton suede cloth with a soft, fuzzy right side and a hard underside; used for skirts during the 1940s and 1950s.

**flyaway collar:** A collar with points that flare to the side in the manner of a winged collar.

**flyaway jacket:** A very short jacket with a very full back.

**gaucho pants:** Calf-length pants, wrapped across the front, with trouser leg tapered below the knee; resembling pants worn by the cowboys of Argentina.

**halter-top:** A blouse with bare back, having the neckline continued around the back of the neck.

**harem-hem skirt:** A soft hem, draped to give a bloomer effect.

**hippies:** (slang) A cult of young people of the 1960's devoted to a primitive look through the use of old or worn clothes and accessories; they are usually associated with long hair, mysticism, beards, bare feet, and alienation from conventional society.

**huarache:** A sandal woven of leather or raffia strips; used by the Mexican Indians.

**lumber jacket:** Short, heavy, plaid woolen jacket, belted and with patch pockets.

**mandarin jacket:** A loose-fitting jacket resembling a Chinese tunic-coat.

**martingale belt:** A half-belt in back of a jacket or coat. The word has been long applied to a leather strap extending from the bit of reins in a horse's bridle to the girdle.

**mixed-match separates:** A jacket and skirt of unlike but harmonizing fabrics that can be worn interchangeably with other garments.

**moat collar:** A narrow standing collar worn around a high, broad neckline.

**monk shoe:** A low shoe, plain across the instep and fastened with a buckle.

**New Bold Look:** An organized program of manufacturers and retailers to assist men to coordinate an ensemble and to create a demand for new male styles.

**New Look:** Styles for women introduced in 1947 by Christian Dior.

**pageboy hairdo:** A medieval hair style adopted by women in the 1940s. It involves shoulder-length hair with the ends turned under.

**paratrooper boot:** A Blücher-style boot of stout, oiled, brown leather, water resistant and laced with leather thongs over hooks on either side of the front opening. Later in World War II because of the dangerous hooks, they were replaced by the eyelets used on the *chukka boot.*

**parka, anorak,** or **amout:** A hip-length hooded garment of sealskin worn by Eskimos. The name comes from the Aleutian Islands. The modern parka used in Europe and the U.S. developed in Scandinavia. It was made of lightweight cotton or silk, was very wind resistant and water repellent, and had allowance for ventilation when used for sports such as skiing or sailing.

**pedal pushers:** Closefitting pants extending below the knee, made in various colors, frequently of blue denim, and with or without a cuff.

**poodle cloth:** A woolen material with a surface of thickly woven loops, popular in 1952.

**poodle haircut:** A woman's hairdress in which the hair was cut uniformly to about one-and-a-half inches and loosely curled.

**puggree:** Wide, soft band arranged in a fold around a hat.

**reefer:** A single- or double-breasted tailored coat.

**sack dress:** A straight dress with no shape, cut from shoulder to hem like a bag or sack.

**sarong:** A short, wraparound skirt of colorful fabric, usually with Polynesian designs.

**sheath dress:** A tight-fitting dress.

**shift:** Another straight dress without shape that was worn without a belt at the waist and which rode on shoulders and hips.

**shrug jacket:** A very short jacket or sweater with sleeves cut in one with the body.

**sleeveless blazer:** A short, sleeveless jacket with pockets, knitted or made of fabric.

**sleeveless look:** A dress or a blouse without sleeves or decorations at the armhole.

**sling neckline:** A pointed neckline that extended diagonally and joined the side opening of a dress.

**Sloppy Joe:** A costume including a man's shirt, usually several sizes too large and worn on the outside over blue jeans carelessly rolled up at the knee; also the name given to a loose, baggy sweater, also worn too large.

**square dance dress:** A dress with a full blouse, sleeveless or puff sleeve, and a full skirt.

**stocking bodice:** A knitted woolen tube, to be pulled over the head and fastened with a drawstring or shirred on elastic, worn with shorts, skirts, or dinner dress.

**sundress** or **sunback dress:** A cotton dress with the back cut out.

**teddy boy:** Exaggerated outfits worn after the war in England by those young boys who were trying to attract attention by their exaggerated dress and gang behavior.

**tent dress:** First launched in 1951 by Balenciaga in a wonderfully simple, black, woolen coat flaring widely from a low standing collar. It was followed in the early 1960s by Yves St. Laurent's *A-line silhouette.*

**toggle coat:** A coat that fastened with wooden blocks and loops instead of buttons and buttonholes. The toggle of smooth wood about an inch long and the thickness of a wide pencil was secured to the coat by a cord around a groove in the middle and was then pushed through a loop on the opposite side for fastening.

**toreador pants:** Short, tight-fitting pants buttoned at the knee, resembling those worn by the Spanish toreador.

**trapeze line:** In 1958 Yves St. Laurent, the protégé and successor of Christian Dior, was acclaimed for his *trapeze* line which later evolved into the *A-line.*

**Tremont hat:** A man's hat with a tapered crown, center crease, and a fairly narrow brim worn up or down; sometimes with a pinched crown and a snap brim.

**trumpet coat dress** or **trumpet skirt:** Garments that were fairly tight over the hips with pleating or fullness from just above the knee.

**TV lounging jacket:** A loose-fitting jacket for watching television.

**TV sets:** Lounging separates worn while watching TV programs.

**vicuña:** A wild animal of the Andes mountains that lives in herds in Ecuador and Bolivia. Its soft wool and fur was made into the softest, most expensive woolen overcoats (often with fur collars) sold in Europe and America; also used in suitings and fine sweaters. Became famous in the 1960s as the political gift which brought scandal to the Eisenhower Administration and the resignation of Sherman Adams.

**waspie belt:** A very wide, shiny, imitation leather belt that both raised the waist and lowered the belt line in the period from 1957 to 1959.

**wedgie:** A shoe having a very thick sole and a wedge-shaped heel.

**weskit:** A waist-length, tight-fitting, sleeveless jacket.

## Chapter XXVI: Contemporary

**Afro hairdo:** A frizzed-out halo of hair that surrounded the head in a great bush of hair. First worn by American blacks in the 1960s to establish connection with their roots in Africa; later adopted by both male and female whites to give an antiestablishment look. The style was achieved by a heavy backcombing of the hair.

**braless look:** During the revolution in styles that erupted among young people in the 1960s with its stress on natural, sensuous bodies there was a movement to throw out the *brassiere* as a symbol of establishment repression. The braless look was sometimes literally due to not wearing a brassiere; at other times it was simulated as much as possible by the thinness and flexibility of a barely existent bra.

**caftan:** Originally a long, coatlike garment worn by both sexes in the Levant and adopted as a robe by members of the Mohammedan priesthood. The variation introduced in the 1960s, more like the Egyptian robe, consisted of a great square of material front and back reaching from wrist to wrist and sewn on the shoulders and sides to make a great flowing gown to be worn belted or unbelted by women wishing to give a luxuriant, sensual, exotic, Eastern flavor to their dress.

**flower children:** A name given to the antiestablishment young in the late 1960s who left their homes to congregate in places like the Haight-Ashbury in San Francisco. They were so called because they often adorned their deliberately shabby jeans and T-shirts with flowers.

**hot pants:** A style intermittently seen in the late 1960s and early 1970s in which very tight-fitting short shorts were worn by women with tights and boots or even with just the bare leg showing from boot tops (often vinyl) to the crotch.

**Levis:** A tight-fitting blue denim trouser with a U-shaped crotch, worn by boys and younger men (there are also levi waist-length jackets); originally part of a western cowboy outfit, the trousers were and still are manufactured by Levi Strauss of San Francisco. During the 1960s they became a symbol of the natural, outdoor, shabby look of the "hippies" and "flower children" who often cut, fringed, and remade the jackets and pants as well as insetting them with colored fabric and embroidering them with colored thread and yarn.

**maxi coat:** Huge, blanketlike overcoats in tightly woven wool that reached to the ankles and were worn with mufflers, knit caps, and boots in winter. Often worn over the *mini skirt*.

**maxi skirt:** Very full, long, gypsy skirts worn with boots in the late 1960s and early 1970s. The length was ankle or floor length.

**micro skirt:** The shortest of the *mini skirts,* this one came to just a little below the crotch and was usually worn with tights and boots in the 1960s.

**midi skirt:** A brief and erratic reaction to the *mini skirt* in which designers (fairly unsuccessfully) attempted in the late 1960s to lower skirts to the mid-calf and below. They were usually intended to be worn with boots.

**mini skirt:** A very short skirt that ended well above the knees. Popular between 1963 and the early 1970s.

**mod clothing:** A contraction of "modern" clothing used to apply to the exaggerated, smartly cut clothes for young people that came out of Carnaby Street, London, since 1963.

**moon girl style:** In 1963 and 1964 Courrèges in Paris introduced this style as a reflection of the great interest in the space program that was supposed to reach the moon by the end of the decade. Representative styles, always in whites or silvers, were made of silver sequin pants, white jackets, and white vinyl boots.

**Nehru jacket:** A Mohammedan, fitted tunic with a low standing collar instead of lapels worn by East Indian men of the Punjab and Kashmir. Introduced into London and Paris styles for men in the 1960s and made of all manner of fabrics from velvet to brocade, from wool and cotton to silk. The name comes from Prime Minister Nehru of India who popularized the style in the 1950s.

**Nouveau Classique:** A style introduced in 1963 by Emmanuelle Khanh that revived the classic architectural lines of Chanel but with many carefully planned curves instead of angles. The jackets had a drooped, "no-shoulder look," and the outfits were usually worn with a Sassoon haircut.

**Op Art:** Designs based on optical illusions created through playing with simple geometric forms in primary colors. Often used in dress design in the 1960s.

**palazzo pajamas:** Evening outfits with soft jackets, tunics, and trousers that were introduced for evening wear in the early 1960s. An updated version of the at-home silk pajama outfits developed in the 1920s.

**pants suits:** By the late 1960s and early 1970s trouser suits for women coincided with the rise of interest in the women's liberation movement and the support for the Equal Rights Act. Such suits had fitted jackets that were tailored much like the male suit with matching or contrasting vest and matching trousers. The style waned in the later 1970s.

**poncho:** A large square or rectangular piece of material, often in gay colors, with a hole cut out of the middle for the head. Originally worn by Mexican peasants, the style became very popular in the U.S. as a rain garment or a colorful outerwrap in soft hand-woven woolens in the 1960s and early 1970s.

**pop art:** Paintings and designs based on photographs or cartoons or on the advertising art of the day. Designs based on such Pop Art were often incorporated in fashions of the 1960s.

**punk:** Name given to excessive makeup, clothing, haircoloring, and attitudes that were meant to violate every expected social norm. The name comes from Punk Rock music and the styles were worn by nihilistic followers of the Punk Rock bands in the 1970s and 1980s.

**Sassoon cut:** A hair style named after Vidal Sassoon, who became the most fashionable hairdresser in London in the 1960s. In his hands the permanent wave straightened into a *fall* which stood high over the forehead with the long ends on the shoulders. Often he curtained the forehead with a deep fringe of straight hair.

**tent shape:** This full spreading line for women first introduced by Balenciaga in 1951 as the *A-line* came back in full force in 1967 in the tent-silhouetted evening gowns of Madame Grès.

**trouser suits:** Another name for the pants suits of the late 1960s and early 1970s. *Trouser suit* was the name more frequently used during the mid-1970s.

**turtleneck:** Originally a masculine or feminine knitted or jersey sweater with a long, straight, tubelike collar which was rolled down to the height desired. In the 1960s such pullovers in very soft jersey came into fashion for men with suits and sports jackets and have continued in popularity as a replacement for a shirt and tie.

**velcro:** The trade name of a nonmetallic overlapping fastener of two strips of fabric faced with tiny nylon hooks which when pressed together hold fast. To undo the strips they are simply pulled apart. The closing was invented by Georges de Mestral of Switzerland and was first used in the early 1960s.

**vinyl:** A trademarked American-made couture fabric introduced about 1965. Originally used for waterproof umbrellas and raincoats, it was soon seen in boots, jackets, belts, and even drapes. It takes dye and prints in bright colors and is often seen in simple geometric patterns as well as in its original semi-transparent form.

# Bibliography

## GENERAL

Barton, Lucy. *Historic Costume for the Stage.* Boston: W. H. Baker, 1935. A standard costume history text that has remained in full use for over 40 years. It covers the history of Western dress from Egypt to World War I with small, clear line drawings.

Batterberry, Michael & Ariane. *Mirror Mirror: A Social History of Fashion.* New York: Holt, Rinehart & Winston, 1977. A coffee-table survey in large format with excellent photographic coverage of primary sources from primitive man to the present.

Blum, Andre. *Histoire de Costume: Les Modes au XIXième Siècle.* Paris: Hachette, 1931. A good standard source in France, now somewhat dated.

Boucher, François. *20,000 Years of Fashion.* New York: Harry Abrams, 1967. One of the finest general histories, fully illustrated from original sources in full color. In general the picture coverage is excellent, while the text is a little heavy and too tightly compartmentalized.

Brooke, Iris. *Western European Costume.* Vol. 1, London: Harrap, 1939; Vol. 2, London: Theatre Arts, 1964. A two-volume set similar to the series on the history of English dress by the author, again with line drawings that must be used with caution.

———. *A History of English Costume.* New York: Theatre Arts, 1968. A compendium of the information and sketches in a series of earlier books on the various periods of English history, again with line drawings by the author.

Contini, Mila. *Fashion.* New York: Odyssey Press, 1965. A coffee-table volume that is somewhat superficial in its writing but excellent in its color photographs and gives a quick overall survey of Western dress.

Davenport, Millia. *The Book of Costume.* New York: Crown, 1948. The most comprehensive compilation of photos from original sources ever put together in one volume on the history of dress. Unfortunately many of the photos are very dark, and the writing, although interesting, is fragmented and anecdotal. Still one of the most important sources for study.

Fletcher, Sir Bannister. *A History of Architecture on the Comparative Method.* 17th ed. New York: Scribner's, 1965. Still after many years the drawings in this volume are some of the best in depicting all aspects of architectural decoration and structure from Egypt and Mesopotamia to the nineteenth century.

Ghorsline, Douglas. *What People Wore.* New York: Viking, 1952. A popular survey with rather unstylish line drawings.

Janson, H. S. *History of Art.* Englewood Cliffs, N.J.: Prentice-Hall, 1969. An excellent history of art that is simply and clearly written to introduce the student to the mainstream of artistic development in the Western world.

Kohler, Carl. *A History of Costume.* New York: Dover, 1963. This standard costume history from the early twentieth century is here reprinted in paperback and is still a useful reference.

Laver, James. *Style in Costume.* New York: Oxford University Press, 1949. A very interesting discussion of the changing style in fashion and its relation to the overall style of a culture.

———. *The Concise History of Costume and Fashion.* New York: Scribner's, 1969. A useful and easy-to-read survey on the history of dress in the Western world from primitive times to the present with a small but select group of illustrations.

PAYNE, BLANCHE. *History of Costume.* New York: Harper & Row, 1965. A very excellent standard costume history that has been widely used as a text in costume-history classes for the past 15 years.

PRAZ, MARIO. *An Illustrated History of Furnishing from the Renaissance to the Twentieth Century.* New York: Braziller, 1964. A useful survey of interiors and furniture since the Renaissance that is particularly useful to students of costume since many of the illustrations include people in period dress.

SPELTZ, ALEXANDER. *Styles of Ornament* (trans. and rev. by David O'Connor). New York: Grosset and Dunlap, n.d. Although mainly of interest to interior decorators and architects, the drawings in this book also give good information on the style of ornament used in costume down through the ages to the middle of the nineteenth century.

SQUIRE, GEOFFREY. *Dress and Society,* 1560–1970. New York: Viking Press, 1974. An excellent study of the relationship between the visual arts and cultural ideals of a period and their involvement in the development of fashion.

TILKE, MAX. *A Pictorial History of Costume.* London: A. Zwemmer Ltd., 1955. A very useful series of watercolor plates depicting costume from the earliest times to the end of the nineteenth century, with special emphasis on Africa, the Orient, and peasant costume.

WILCOX, RUTH TURNER. *The Mode in Furs.* New York: Scribner's, 1951. A very useful survey of the use of furs in clothing from Egypt to the 1950s, with very clear line drawings that also give an excellent idea of the variety of clothing styles within each period.

———. *The Mode in Costume.* New York: Scribners, 1957. Still a useful source of reference on the history of Western dress through the many excellent line drawings that extend from Egypt to the end of the Cold War period. The text is of limited value.

———. *Five Centuries of American Costume.* New York: Scribner's, 1963. Another useful survey with clear line drawings covering military and civil dress in America since 1500.

WILDEBLOOD, JOAN. *The Polite World.* London: Davis-Poynter, 1973. A very useful survey on manners, movement, and deportment in England from the medieval period to the years following World War I.

## CHAPTER I. PRIMITIVE

BOAS, FRANZ. *Primitive Art.* New ed. New York: Dover, 1955. An excellent and easy-to-follow survey on how art developed as a magical tool for ancient man to use in hunting and later in primitive religion.

POWELL, T. G. *Prehistoric Art.* New York: Praeger, 1966. A finely illustrated volume on the nature of primitive art before the rise of Egypt and Mesopotamia.

STROMMENGER, EVA, & HIRMER, MAX. *5000 Years of the Art of Mesopotamia.* New York: Abrams, 1964. A richly illustrated book on the art of the ancient Near East from its beginnings until Roman times.

## CHAPTER II. EGYPT

CASSON, LIONEL. *Daily Life in Ancient Egypt.* A Horizon Book. New York: American Heritage, 1975. A fascinating and useful book, with excellent illustrations on all aspects of living in ancient Egypt.

GARBINI, GIOVANNI. *The Ancient World.* Landmarks of the World's Art Series. New York: McGraw-Hill, 1966. An excellent and beautifully illustrated survey with many color plates on the development of art in ancient Egypt and Mesopotamia. The text is secondary to the plates.

HOUSTON, MARY G. *Ancient Egyptian, Mesopotamian and Persian Costume.* London: A. & C. Black. An excellent technical explanation of the cut and drape of Egyptian, Mesopotamian, and Persian costume with a few color plates and over 250 line drawings.

## CHAPTER III. MESOPOTAMIA

FRANKFORT, HENRI. *The Art and Architecture of the Ancient Orient.* Pelican History of Art Series. Baltimore: Penguin Books, 1955. A comprehensive survey of the development and growth of art in Mesopotamia and the surrounding areas from primitive times until the Greek conquest.

GARBINI, GIOVANNI. *The Ancient World.* Landmarks of the World's Art Series. New York: McGraw-Hill, 1966. An excellent and beautifully illustrated survey with many color plates on the development of art in ancient Egypt and Mesopotamia. The text is secondary to the plates.

HOUSTON, MARY G. *Ancient Egyptian, Mesopotamian and Persian Costume.* London: A. & C. Black. An excellent technical explanation of the cut and drape of Egyptian, Mesopotamian, and Persian costume with a few color plates and over 250 line drawings.

LLOYD, SETON. *The Art of the Ancient Near East.* New York: Praeger, 1961. A beautifully illustrated survey of the arts of the Tigris-Euphrates Valley and the surrounding areas from primitive times to the Greek conquest.

STROMMENGER, EVA, & HIRMER, MAX. *5000 Years of the Art of Mesopotamia.* New York: Abrams, 1964. A richly illustrated book on the art of the ancient Near East from its beginnings until Roman times.

TISSOT, JAMES. *The Life of Our Savior, Jesus Christ* (trans. with notes and drawings by Mrs. Arthur Bell). New York: Doubleday-McClure, 1899. Although very ancient, this work, illustrated with paintings by Tissot, is an excellent and accurate source for Biblical costume during the life of Christ.

———. *Old Testament Selections.* Paris: M. de Brunoff, 1904. Again Tissot, after extensive research in Palestine, rendered a series of paintings illustrating the Old Testament that are accurate statements of Biblical dress.

## CHAPTER IV. GREEK

BOWRA, C. M. *Classical Greece.* The Great Ages of Man Series. New York: Time-Life Books, 1965. A concise text covering the major artistic, cultural, and intellectual developments from Archaic through Hellenistic Greek times; beautifully illustrated with extensive color photography.

BROOKE IRIS. *Costume in Greek Classical Drama.* New York: Theatre Arts, 1961. A very useful book with clear line drawings of costumes used in the Greek theatre.

HILDEBRAND, ALICE, ed. *Greek Culture.* The Cultures of Mankind Series. New York: Braziller, 1966. An excellent compilation of writings from original Greek sources on the nature of the Greek cultural outlook.

HOUSTON, MARY G. *Ancient Greek, Roman and Byzantine Costume and Decoration.* 2nd ed. London: A. & C. Black, 1959. An excellent technical explanation of the cut and drape of Greek, Roman, and Byzantine dress with a few color plates and over 250 line drawings.

NORRIS, HERBERT. *Costume and Fashion: The Evolution of European Dress through the Earlier Ages.* London: J. W. Dent & Sons, Ltd., 1947. A very useful book, with some color plates and many line drawings by the author, tracing the development of clothing and ornament from Greek to early medieval times. It is especially helpful on early Christian and Byzantine dress.

RICHTER, GISELA. *A Handbook of Greek Art.* 2nd rev. ed. London: Phaiden, 1960. A useful reference that shows much about Greek clothing styles through a study of the statuary of the time.

STRONG, DONALD. *The Classical World.* Landmarks of the World's Art Series. New York: McGraw-Hill, 1965. Deals with Greek and Roman art from the early Minoan period to the fall of Rome, beautifully illustrated with many color plates.

## CHAPTER V. ROME

CASSON, LIONEL. *Daily Life in Ancient Rome.* A Horizon Book. New York: American Heritage and McGraw-Hill, 1975. An excellent introductory book with telling illustrations of the social and cultural life of Rome.

HADAS, MOSES. *Imperial Rome.* The Great Ages of Man Series. New York: Time-Life Books, 1965. Written for the average reader, this beautifully illustrated book with extension color plates covers the intellectual, artistic, and cultural developments in ancient Rome.

HOUSTON, MARY G. *Ancient Greek, Roman and Byzantine Costume and Decoration.* 2nd ed. London: A. & C. Black, 1959. An excellent technical explanation of the cut and drape of Greek, Roman, and Byzantine dress with a few color plates and over 250 line drawings.

KAHLER, HEINZ. *The Art of Rome and her Empire* (translated by J. R. Foster). New York: Crown, 1963. A good survey of Roman art that covers the far reaches of the Empire as well as Rome itself.

NORRIS, HERBERT. *Costume and Fashion: The Evolution of European Dress through the Earlier Ages.* London: J. W. Dent & Sons, Ltd., 1947. A very useful book, with some color plates and many line drawings by the author, tracing the development of clothing and ornament from Greek to early medieval times. It is especially helpful on early Christian and Byzantine dress.

STRONG, DONALD. *The Classical World.* Landmarks of the World's Art Series. New York: McGraw-Hill, 1965. Covers Greek and Roman art from the early Minoan period to the fall of Rome; beautifully illustrated with many color plates.

WILLS, GARRY, ed. *Roman Culture.* The Cultures of Mankind Series. New York: Braziller, 1966. An excellent and useful compilation of writings from original Roman sources on the Roman view of life and the nature of Roman culture.

WILSON, LILIAN MAY. *The Clothing of the Ancient Romans.* Baltimore: Johns Hopkins University Press, 1938. A standard source on the clothing of ancient Rome that is still a useful reference.

## CHAPTER VI. BYZANTINE

HOUSTON, MARY G. *Ancient Greek, Roman and Byzantine Costume and Decoration.* 2nd ed. London: A.

& C. Black, 1959. An excellent technical explanation of the cut and drape of Greek, Roman, and Byzantine dress with a few color plates and over 250 line drawings.

LASSUS, JEAN. *The Early Christian and Byzantine World.* Landmarks of the World's Art Series. New York: McGraw-Hill, 1967. Covers all aspects of eastern Mediterranean art in the thousand years following the acceptance of Christianity in Rome. Excellent illustrations with many color plates.

NORRIS, HERBERT. *Costume and Fashion: The Evolution of European Dress through the Earlier Ages.* London: J. W. Dent & Sons, Ltd., 1947. A very useful book, with some color plates and many line drawings by the author, tracing the development of clothing and ornament from Greek to early medieval times. It is especially helpful on early Christian and Byzantine dress.

RICE, DAVID TALBOT. *Art of the Byzantine Era.* New York: Praeger, 1963. An excellent and beautifully illustrated survey on the visual arts of Byzantium.

SHERRARD, PHILIP. *Byzantium.* The Great Ages of Man Series. New York: Time-Life Books, 1966. Intended for the average reader, this beautifully illustrated book, with extensive color photography, covers the major cultural, intellectual, and artistic developments in the Byzantine Empire.

## CHAPTER VII. ROMANESQUE

BRANTL, RUTH, ed. *Medieval Culture.* The Culture of Mankind Series. New York: Braziller, 1966. An excellent compilation of writings from original sources on early and later medieval culture.

BROOKE, IRIS. *English Costume of the Early Middle Ages.* London: A. & C. Black, 1936. A useful coverage of the costume in England from 900 to 1300 with line drawings by the author. These must be used with a certain caution in conjunction with original sources.

CUNNINGTON, C. WILLET, & CUNNINGTON, PHILLIS. *Handbook of English Medieval Costume.* Philadelphia: Dufour, 1952. Another standard research volume in a series on English dress by two of England's foremost authorities on costume.

FREEMANTLE, ANNE. *Age of Faith.* The Great Ages of Man Series. New York: Time-Life Books, 1965. Covers the intellectual, artistic, and cultural developments in Europe from the Romanesque through the Gothic periods.

HARTLEY, DOROTHY, & ELLIOT, MARGARET M. *Life and Work of the People of England from the Eleventh to the Thirteenth Century.* New York: Putnam, 1931. Still a very useful book from which to obtain a picture of medieval life in England during the early middle ages.

HOUSTON, MARY G. *Medieval Costume in England and France.* London: A. & C. Black, 1939. An excellent technical explanation of the cut and drape of medieval clothing in northern Europe with a few color plates and over 250 line drawings.

KIDSON, PETER. *The Medieval World.* Landmarks of the World's Art Series. New York: McGraw-Hill, 1967. Covers the art of the medieval period from pre-Romanesque times through the Gothic period.

NORRIS, HERBERT. *Costume and Fashion: From Senlac to Bosworth.* London: J. W. Dent & Sons, Ltd., 1927. A very useful book, with some color plates and many excellent line drawings, diagrams, and patterns by the author that trace the development of clothing (primarily in England) from William the Conqueror to Richard III.

————. *Costume and Fashion: The Evolution of European Dress through the Earlier Ages.* London: J. W. Dent & Sons, Ltd., 1947. A very useful book, with some color plates and many line drawings by the author, tracing the development of clothing and ornament from Greek to early medieval times. It is especially helpful on early Christian and Byzantine dress.

## CHAPTER VIII. EARLY GOTHIC

BOEHN, MAX VON. *Die Mode: Menschen und Moden im Mittelalter.* Munich: Brückmann, 1909. One volume of an early twentieth-century standard work that is still useful today as a source for the Middle Ages.

BRANTL, RUTH, ed. *Medieval Culture.* The Culture of Mankind Series. New York: Braziller, 1966. An excellent compilation of writings from original sources on early and later medieval culture.

BROOKE, IRIS. *English Costume of the Early Middle Ages.* London: A. & C. Black, 1936. A useful coverage of the costume in England from 900 to 1300 with line drawings by the author. These must be used with a certain caution in conjunction with original sources.

CUNNINGTON, C. WILLETT, & CUNNINGTON, PHILLIS. *Handbook of English Medieval Costume.* Philadelphia: Dufour, 1952. Another standard research volume in a series on English dress by two of England's foremost authorities on costume.

FREEMANTLE, ANNE. *Age of Faith.* The Great Ages of Man Series. New York: Time-Life Books, 1965. Covers the intellectual, artistic, and cultural developments in Europe from the Romanesque through the Gothic periods.

HARTLEY, DOROTHY, & ELLIOT, MARGARET M. *Life and Work of the People of England from the Eleventh to the Thirteenth Century.* New York: Putnam, 1931. Still a very useful book from which to obtain a picture of medieval life in England during the early Middle Ages.

HOUSTON, MARY G. *Medieval Costume in England and France.* London: A. & C. Black, 1939. An excellent technical explanation of the cut and drape of medieval clothing in northern Europe with a few color plates and over 250 line drawings.

KIDSON, PETER. *The Medieval World.* Landmarks of the World's Art Series. New York: McGraw-Hill, 1967. Covers the art of the medieval period from pre-Romanesque times through the Gothic period.

NORRIS, HERBERT. *Costume and Fashion: From Senlac to Bosworth.* London: J. W. Dent & Sons, Ltd., 1927. A very useful book, with some color plates and many excellent line drawings, diagrams, and patterns by the author that trace the development of clothing (primarily in England) from William the Conqueror to Richard III.

WINSTON, CLARA & RICHARD. *Daily Life in the Middle Ages.* A Horizon Book. New York: American Heritage and McGraw-Hill, 1975. Gives interesting insights into medieval life and contains excellent and infrequently published illustrations.

## CHAPTER IX. MIDDLE GOTHIC

BOEHN, MAX VON. *Die Mode: Menschen und Moden im Mittelalter.* Munich: Brückmann, 1909. One volume of an early twentieth-century standard work that is still useful today as a source for the Middle Ages.

BRANTL, RUTH, ed. *Medieval Culture.* The Culture of Mankind Series. New York: Braziller, 1966. An excellent compilation of writings from original sources on early and later medieval culture.

BROOKE, IRIS. *Medieval Theatre Costume.* New York: Theatre Arts, 1967. A useful volume illustrated with line drawings on the costumes for the medieval theatre.

CUNNINGTON, C. WILLETT, & CUNNINGTON, PHILLIS. *Handbook of English Medieval Costume.* Philadelphia: Dufour, 1952. Another standard research volume in a series on English dress by two of England's foremost authorities on costume.

FREEMANTLE, ANNE. *Age of Faith.* The Great Ages of Man Series. New York: Time-Life Books, 1965.

Covers the intellectual, artistic, and cultural developments in Europe from the Romanesque through the Gothic periods.

HOUSTON, MARY G. *Medieval Costume in England and France.* London: A. & C. Black, 1939. An excellent technical explanation of the cut and drape of medieval clothing in northern Europe with a few color plates and over 250 line drawings.

KIDSON, PETER. *The Medieval World.* Landmarks of the World's Art Series. New York: McGraw-Hill, 1967. Covers the art of the medieval period from pre-Romanesque times through the Gothic period.

NORRIS, HERBERT. *Costume and Fashion: From Senlac to Bosworth.* London: J. W. Dent & Sons, Ltd., 1927. A very useful book, with some color plates and many excellent line drawings, diagrams, and patterns by the author that trace the development of clothing (primarily in England) from William the Conqueror to Richard III.

WINSTON, CLARA & RICHARD. *Daily Life in the Middle Ages.* A Horizon Book. New York: American Heritage and McGraw-Hill, 1975. Gives interesting insights into medieval life and contains excellent and infrequently published illustrations.

## CHAPTER X. LATE GOTHIC

BRANTL, RUTH, ed. *Medieval Culture.* The Culture of Mankind Series. New York: Braziller, 1966. An excellent compilation of writings from original sources on early and later medieval culture.

BROOKE, IRIS. *English Costume of the Later Middle Ages.* London: A. & C. Black, 1935. A useful coverage of English costume from 1300 to 1500 with line drawings by the author. These must be used with caution in conjunction with original sources.

———. *Medieval Theatre Costume.* New York: Theatre Arts, 1967. A useful volume illustrated with line drawings on the costumes for the medieval theatre.

CUNNINGTON, C. WILLETT, & CUNNINGTON, PHILLIS. *Handbook of English Medieval Costume.* Philadelphia: Dufour, 1952. Another standard research volume in a series on English dress by two of England's foremost authorities on costume.

FREEMANTLE, ANNE. *Age of Faith.* The Great Ages of Man Series. New York: Time-Life Books, 1965. Covers the intellectual, artistic, and cultural developments in Europe from the Romanesque through the Gothic period.

HALE, JOHN R. *Renaissance.* The Great Ages of Man Series. New York: Time-Life Books, 1965. A beautifully illustrated book with extensive color photography, covering the major cultural, intellectual, and artistic developments of the Renaissance.

KIDSON, PETER. *The Medieval World.* Landmarks of the World's Art Series. New York: McGraw-Hill, 1967. Covers the art of the medieval period from pre-Romanesque times through the Gothic period.

MARTINDALE, ANDREW. *Man and the Renaissance.* Landmarks of the World's Art Series. New York: McGraw-Hill, 1966. This volume is beautifully illustrated in color and black and white and covers European artistic development during the fifteenth and sixteenth centuries.

MATES, JULIAN, & CANTELUPE, EUGENE, eds. *Renaissance Culture.* The Cultures of Mankind Series. New York: Braziller, 1966. An excellent compilation of writings from original sources on the Renaissance view of life and culture.

NORRIS, HERBERT. *Costume and Fashion: From Senlac to Bosworth.* London: J. W. Dent & Sons, Ltd., 1927. A very useful book, with some color plates and many excellent line drawings, diagrams, and patterns by the author that trace the development of clothing (primarily in England) from William the Conqueror to Richard III.

WINSTON, CLARA & RICHARD. *Daily Life in the Middle Ages.* A Horizon Book. New York: American Heritage and McGraw-Hill, 1975. Gives interesting insights into medieval life and contains excellent and infrequently published illustrations.

## CHAPTER XI. HIGH RENAISSANCE

HALE, JOHN R. *Renaissance.* The Great Ages of Man Series. New York: Time-Life Books, 1965. A beautifully illustrated book with extensive color photography, covering the major cultural, intellectual, and artistic developments of the Renaissance.

MARTINDALE, ANDREW. *Man and the Renaissance.* Landmarks of the World's Art Series. New York: McGraw-Hill, 1966. This volume is beautifully illustrated in color and black and white and covers European artistic development during the fifteenth and sixteenth centuries.

MATES, JULIAN, & CANTELUPE, EUGENE, eds. *Renaissance Culture.* The Cultures of Mankind Series. New York: Braziller, 1966. An excellent compilation of writings from original sources on the Renaissance view of life and culture.

MEE, CHARLES L., JR. *Daily Life in Renaissance Italy.* A Horizon Book. New York: American Heritage and McGraw-Hill, 1975. A fascinating and

useful book concerning all aspects of daily life in the Italian Renaissance with excellent illustrations.

NORRIS, HERBERT. *Costume and Fashion: The Tudors, Book I.* London: J. W. Dent & Sons, Ltd., 1938. A very useful book, with some color plates and many excellent line drawings, diagrams, and patterns by the author that trace the development of clothing (primarily in England) during the reigns of Henry VII and Henry VIII.

## CHAPTER XII. MANNERIST

BOEHN, MAX VON. *Die Mode: Menschen und Moden im Sechzehnten Jahrhundert.* Munich: Brückmann, 1923. One volume of an early twentieth-century standard work that is still useful today as a source for the sixteenth century.

BROOKE, IRIS. *English Costume in the Age of Elizabeth.* London: A. & C. Black, 1933. A helpful coverage of the sixteenth century in England by ten-year periods with line drawings by the author. The drawings must be used with caution along with original sources.

CUNNINGTON, C. WILLETT, & CUNNINGTON, PHILLIS. *Handbook of English Costume in the Sixteenth Century.* London: Faber, 1954. Another standard research volume in a series on English dress by two of England's foremost authorities on costume.

HALE, JOHN R. *Renaissance.* The Great Ages of Man Series. New York: Time-Life Books, 1965. A beautifully illustrated book with extensive color photography, covering the major cultural, intellectual, and artistic developments of the Renaissance.

LAVER, JAMES, ed. *Costume of the Western World.* New York: Harper & Row, 1951. This was the first volume in a comprehensive series that was to be a complete coverage of the history of dress. This volume on the sixteenth century was the only one completed, but it remains a very useful source.

MARTINDALE, ANDREW. *Man and the Renaissance.* Landmarks of the World's Art Series. New York: McGraw-Hill, 1966. This volume is beautifully illustrated in color and black and white and covers European artistic development during the fifteenth and sixteenth centuries.

MATES, JULIAN, & CANTELUPE, EUGENE, eds. *Renaissance Culture.* The Cultures of Mankind Series. New York: Braziller, 1966. An excellent compilation of writings from original sources on the Renaissance view of life and culture.

NORRIS, HERBERT. *Costume and Fashion: The Tudors, Book I.* London: J. W. Dent & Sons, Ltd., 1938. A very useful book, with some color plates and many excellent line drawings, diagrams, and patterns by the author that trace the development of clothing (primarily in England) during the reigns of Henry VII and Henry VIII.

WATERHOUSE, E. K. *Painting in Britain 1530-1790.* Pelican History of Art Series. Baltimore: Penguin Books, 1966. This volume relates British painting in the seventeenth century to that of the sixteenth and eighteenth. It gives some excellent coverage of dress through portraiture.

WÜRTEMBERGER, FRANSZEPP. *Mannerism: The European Style of the Sixteenth Century* (translated by Michael Heron). New York: Holt, Rinehart & Winston, 1963. An excellent and fascinating study of mannerism in Europe during the century preceding Shakespeare.

## CHAPTER XIII. ELIZABETHAN

BOEHN, MAX VON. *Die Mode: Menschen und Moden in Sechzehnten Jahrhundert.* Munich: Brückmann, 1923. One volume of an early twentieth-century standard work that is still useful as a source for the sixteenth century.

BROOKE, IRIS. *English Costume in the Age of Elizabeth.* London: A. & C. Black, 1933. A helpful coverage of the sixteenth century in England by ten-year periods with line drawings by the author. The drawings must be used with caution along with original sources.

CUNNINGTON, C. WILLETT, & CUNNINGTON, PHILLIS. *Handbook of English Costume in the Sixteenth Century.* London: Faber, 1954. Another standard research volume in a series on English dress by two of England's foremost authorities on costume.

HALE, JOHN R. *Renaissance.* The Great Ages of Man Series. New York: Time-Life Books, 1965. A beautifully illustrated book with extensive color photography, covering the major cultural, intellectual, and artistic developments of the Renaissance.

LAVER, JAMES, ed. *Costume of the Western World.* New York: Harper & Row, 1951. This was the first volume in a comprehensive series that was to be a complete coverage of the history of dress. This volume on the sixteenth century was the only one completed, but it remains a very useful source.

MARTINDALE, ANDREW. *Man and the Renaissance.* Landmarks of the World's Art Series. New York: McGraw-Hill, 1966. This volume is beautifully illustrated in color and black and white and covers European artistic development during the fifteenth and sixteenth centuries.

MATES, JULIAN, & CANTELUPE, EUGENE, eds. *Renaissance Culture.* The Cultures of Mankind Series. New York: Braziller, 1966. An excellent compilation of writings from original sources on the Renaissance view of life and culture.

MORSE, HARRIET K. *Elizabethan Pageantry.* London: Studio, 1934. This book has been out almost 50 years and yet it is still an excellent visual look at the Elizabethan period.

NORRIS, HERBERT. *Costume and Fashion: The Tudors, Book II.* London, J.W. Dent & Sons, Ltd., 1938. A very useful book, with some color plates and many excellent line drawings, diagrams, and patterns by the author that trace the development in clothing in both Europe and England during the reigns of Edward VI, Mary I, and Elizabeth I.

VECELLIO, CESARE. *Habiti Antichi et Moderni.* Venice, 1598. The first of the great books on clothing and fashion is still a useful source of information on the late sixteenth century.

WATERHOUSE, E. K. *Painting in Britain 1530-1790.* Pelican History of Art Series. Baltimore: Penguin Books, 1966. This volume relates British painting in the seventeenth century to that of the sixteenth and eighteenth. It gives some excellent coverage of dress through portraiture.

WÜRTEMBERGER, FRANSZEPP. *Mannerism: The European Style of the Sixteenth Century* (translated by Michael Heron). New York: Holt, Rinehart & Winston, 1963. An excellent and fascinating study of mannerism in Europe during the century preceding Shakespeare.

## CHAPTER XIV. CAVALIER-BAROQUE

BLITZER, CHARLES. *Age of Kings.* The Great Ages of Man Series. New York: Time-Life Books, 1967. Intended for the average reader, this beautifully illustrated book is a concise and useful text on the major artistic, intellectual, and cultural developments in Europe during the seventeenth century.

BROOKE, IRIS. *English Costume of the Seventeenth Century.* London: A. & C. Black, 1934. A useful coverage of English costume of the seventeenth century with line drawings by the author. These must be used with a certain caution in conjunction with original sources.

CUNNINGTON, C. WILLETT, & CUNNINGTON, PHILLIS. *Handbook of English Costume in the Seventeenth Century.* London: Faber, 1955. Another standard volume in a series on English dress by two of England's foremost authorities on costume.

KITSON, MICHAEL. *The Age of the Baroque.* Landmarks of the World's Art Series. New York: McGraw-Hill, 1966. This beautifully illustrated book with many color plates deals with the art of Europe from the beginning of the seventeenth century to the middle of the eighteenth.

TAPIÉ, VICTOR L. *The Age of Grandeur.* New York: Praeger, 1960. Although published 20 years ago, this is still an excellent and complete introduction to the Baroque style in Europe in the seventeenth century with excellent supporting illustrations.

WATERHOUSE, E. K. *Painting in Britain 1530–1790.* Pelican History of Art Series. Baltimore: Penguin Books, 1966. This volume relates British painting in the seventeenth century to that of the sixteenth and eighteenth. It gives some excellent coverage of dress through portraiture.

WEINSTEIN, LEO, ed. *The Age of Reason.* The Cultures of Mankind Series. New York: Braziller, 1965. An excellent compilation of writings from original sources on the Baroque view of life and culture.

## CHAPTER XV. LATE BAROQUE

BLITZER, CHARLES. *Age of Kings.* The Great Ages of Man Series. New York: Time-Life Books, 1967. Intended for the average reader, this beautifully illustrated book is a concise and useful text on the major artistic, intellectual, and cultural developments in Europe during the seventeenth century.

BOEHN, MAX VON. *Die Mode: Menschen und Moden im Siebzehnten Jahrhundert.* Munich: Brückmann, 1913. One volume of an early twentieth-century standard work that is still useful today as a source for the seventeenth century.

BROOKE, IRIS. *English Costume of the Seventeenth Century.* London: A. & C. Black, 1934. A useful coverage of English costume of the seventeenth century with line drawings by the author. These must be used with a certain caution in conjunction with original sources.

KITSON, MICHAEL. *The Age of the Baroque.* Landmarks of the World's Art Series. New York: McGraw-Hill, 1966. This volume is beautifully illustrated in color and black and white and covers European artistic developments in the seventeenth and eighteenth centuries.

PEPYS, SAMUEL. *Diary and Correspondence of Samuel Pepys.* 10 vols. New York: Dodd, Mead, 1885. Pepys is an invaluable literary source of information on fashion during the Restoration period in England.

TAPIÉ, VICTOR L. *The Age of Grandeur.* New York: Praeger, 1960. Although published 20 years ago, this is still an excellent and complete introduction to the Baroque style in Europe in the seventeenth century with excellent supporting illustrations.

WATERHOUSE, E. K. *Painting in Britain 1530–1790.* Pelican History of Art Series. Baltimore: Penguin Books, 1966. This volume relates British painting in the seventeenth century to that of the sixteenth and eighteenth. It gives some excellent coverage of dress through portraiture.

WEINSTEIN, LEO, ed. *The Age of Reason.* The Cultures of Mankind Series. New York: Braziller, 1965. An excellent compilation of writings from original sources on the Baroque view of life and culture.

## CHAPTER XVI. ROCOCO

BOEHN, MAX VON. *Die Mode: Menschen und Moden im Achtzehnten Jahrhundert.* Munich: Brückmann, 1909. One volume of an early twentieth-century standard work, which is still a very usable source for the eighteenth century.

BROOKE, IRIS. *English Costume of the Eighteenth Century.* London: A. & C. Black, 1931. A useful coverage of English costume during the eighteenth century with line drawings by the author. These must be used with caution along with original sources.

CUNNINGTON, C. WILLETT, & CUNNINGTON, PHILLIS. *Handbook of English Costume in the Eighteenth Century.* London: Faber, 1957. Another standard volume in a series on English dress by two of England's foremost authorities on costume.

FANIEL, STÉPHANE, ed. *French Art of the Eighteenth Century.* New York: Simon & Schuster, 1957. An invaluable work in full color on all aspects of French art of the eighteenth century, including furnishings, decorative and minor arts, and interior decoration as well as painting and sculpture.

GAY, PETER. *Age of Enlightenment.* The Great Ages of Man Series. New York: McGraw-Hill, 1965. Beautifully illustrated with extensive color photography, this concise text for the nonacademic reader covers the main intellectual, cultural, and artistic developments of the eighteenth century.

GREEN, FREDERICK C. *Eighteenth Century in France.* New York: Frederick Ungar, 1965. An excellent historical and cultural survey on France during the eighteenth century.

HARTLEY, DOROTHY, & ELLIOT, MARGARET M. *Life and Work of the People of England in the Eighteenth*

*Century*. New York: Putnam, 1931. Still a useful book from which to obtain a picture of social life in England in the eighteenth century.

KIMBALL, SIDNEY FISKE. *The Creation of the Rococo.* Philadelphia: Philadelphia Museum of Art, 1943. A famous standard work on the development of the Rococo style in early eighteenth-century France and its spread to the rest of Europe after 1740.

KITSON, MICHAEL, *The Age of the Baroque.* Landmarks of the World's Art Series. New York: McGraw-Hill, 1966. This volume is beautifully illustrated in color and black and white and covers European artistic developments in the seventeenth and eighteenth centuries.

SCHNEIDER, ISADOR, ed. *The Enlightenment.* The Cultures of Mankind Series. New York: Braziller, 1965. An excellent compilation of original sources on life and culture during the Enlightenment.

SOEHNER, HALLDOR, & SCHÖNBERGER, ARNO. *The Rococo Age.* New York: McGraw-Hill, 1960. Another excellent volume that gives a rounded picture of the Rococo style in art, from which much valuable information about clothing may be obtained.

WATERHOUSE, E. K. *Painting in Britain 1530-1790.* Pelican History of Art Series. Baltimore: Penguin Books, 1966. This volume relates British painting in the seventeenth century to that of the sixteenth and eighteenth. It gives some excellent coverage of dress through portraiture.

## CHAPTER XVII. NEOCLASSIC

BOEHN, MAX VON. *Die Mode: Menschen und Moden im Achtzehnten Jahrhundert.* Munich: Brückmann, 1909. One volume of an early twentieth-century standard work, which is still a very usable source for the eighteenth century.

BRION, MARCEL. *Art of the Romantic Era: Romanticism, Classicism, Realism.* New York: Praeger, 1966. An excellent survey of art during the Romantic age.

BROOKE, IRIS. *English Costume of the Eighteenth Century.* London: A. & C. Black, 1931. A useful coverage of English costume during the eighteenth century with line drawings by the author. These must be used with caution along with original sources.

CUNNINGTON, C. WILLETT, & CUNNINGTON, PHILLIS. *Handbook of English Costume in the Eighteenth Century.* London: Faber, 1957. Another standard volume in a series on English dress by two of England's foremost authorities on costume.

CANADAY, JOHN. *Mainstreams of Modern Art.* New York: Holt, Rinehart & Winston, 1959. Covering European and American art from the American Revolution to the middle of the twentieth century, this book gives much valuable information on culture, clothing, and artistic styles.

FANIEL, STÉPHANE, ed. *French Art of the Eighteenth Century.* New York: Simon & Schuster, 1957. An invaluable work in full color on all aspects of French art of the eighteenth century, including furnishings, decorative and minor arts, and interior decoration as well as painting and sculpture.

*La Galerie des Modes.* Paris: Jacques Esnauts & Michel Rapilly, 1778-1787. A very useful fashion plate source for the neoclassic period.

*The Gallery of Fashion.* London: Nicolaus Wilhelm von Heideloff, 1794-1803. A useful source for fashion plates of the French Revolution and after in both England and France.

GAY, PETER. *Age of Enlightenment.* The Great Ages of Man Series. New York: McGraw-Hill, 1965. Beautifully illustrated with extensive color photography, this concise text for the nonacademic reader covers the main intellectual, cultural, and artistic developments of the eighteenth century.

GREEN, FREDERICK C. *Eighteenth Century in France.* New York: Frederick Ungar, 1965. An excellent historical and cultural survey of France during the eighteenth century.

HARTLEY, DOROTHY, & ELLIOT, MARGARET M. *Life and Work of the People of England in the Eighteenth Century.* New York: Putnam, 1931. Still a useful book from which to obtain a picture of social life in England in the eighteenth century.

KITSON, MICHAEL. *The Age of the Baroque.* Landmarks of the World's Art Series. New York: McGraw-Hill, 1966. This volume is beautifully illustrated in color and black and white and covers European artistic developments in the seventeenth and eighteenth centuries.

LYNTON, NORBERT. *The Modern World.* Landmarks of the World's Art Series. New York: McGraw-Hill, 1965. Beautifully illustrated with many color plates, this book discusses European art from the American Revolution to the middle of the twentieth century.

SCHNEIDER, ISADOR, ed. *The Enlightenment.* The Cultures of Mankind Series. New York: Braziller, 1965. An excellent compilation of original sources on life and culture during the Enlightenment.

WATERHOUSE, E. K. *Painting in Britain 1530-1790.* Pelican History of Art Series. Baltimore: Penguin Books, 1966. This volume relates British painting in the seventeenth century to that of the sixteenth and eighteenth. It gives some excellent coverage of dress through portraiture.

## CHAPTER XVIII. EMPIRE

BOEHN, MAX VON. *Die Mode: Menschen und Moden im Neuzehnten Jahrhundert.* Munich: Brückmann, 1909. One volume of an early twentieth-century standard work that is still usable today as a source for the nineteenth century.

BROOKE, IRIS. *English Costume of the Nineteenth Century.* London: A. & C. Black, 1929. A useful coverage of English costume of the nineteenth century with line drawings by the author. These must be used with caution in conjunction with original sources.

CANADAY, JOHN. *Mainstreams of Modern Art.* New York: Holt, Rinehart & Winston, 1959. Covering European and American art from the American Revolution to the middle of the twentieth century, this book gives much valuable information on culture, clothing, and artistic styles.

*The Gallery of Fashion.* London: Nicolaus Wilhelm von Heideloff, 1794–1803. A useful source for fashion plates of the French Revolution and after in both England and France.

GONZALEZ-PALACIOS, ALVAR. *The French Empire Style.* London: The Hamlyn Publishing Group, Ltd., 1970. A beautifully illustrated reference to the style in painting, sculpture, architecture, porcelain, textiles, furniture, and objets d'art of the period from 1800 to 1815.

*Journal des Dames et des Modes* (Costumes Parisiens). Paris: de Carpentier-Mericourt, 1797–1839. A very useful source for fashion plates of the Empire and Romantic periods.

LYNTON, NORBERT. *The Modern World.* Landmarks of the World's Art Series. New York: McGraw-Hill, 1965. Beautifully illustrated with many color plates, this book discusses European art from the American Revolution to the middle of the twentieth century.

## CHAPTER XIX. ROMANTIC

BOEHN, MAX VON. *Die Mode: Menschen und Moden im Neuzehnten Jahrhundert.* Munich: Brückmann, 1909. One volume of an early twentieth-century standard work that is still usable as a source for the nineteenth century.

BROOKE, IRIS. *English Costume of the Nineteenth Century.* London: A. & C. Black, 1929. A useful coverage of English costume of the nineteenth century with line drawings by the author. These must be used with caution in conjunction with original sources.

CANADAY, JOHN. *Mainstreams of Modern Art.* New York: Holt, Rinehart & Winston, 1959. Covering European and American art from the American Revolution to the middle of the twentieth century, this book gives much valuable information on culture, clothing, and artistic styles.

COURTHION, PIERRE. *Romanticism* (translated by Stuart Gilbert). New York: Skira, 1961. Another excellent and well-illustrated volume on Romanticism during the early nineteenth century.

CUNNINGTON, C. WILLETT. *English Women's Clothing in the Nineteenth Century.* London: Faber, 1937. A standard work by one of England's foremost authorities on the history of dress.

*Illustrated London News* (1842– ) London. Very useful as a source of information on manners, fashions, customs, and styles during the later nineteenth century.

*L'Illustration* (1843– ). Paris. A useful source of information on manners, fashions, customs, and styles during the late nineteenth and early twentieth centuries.

*Journal des Dames et des Modes* (Costumes Parisiens). Paris: de Carpentier-Mericourt, 1797–1839. A very useful source for fashion plates of the Empire and Romantic periods.

LYNTON, NORBERT. *The Modern World.* Landmarks of the World's Art Series. New York: McGraw-Hill, 1965. Beautifully illustrated with many color plates, this book discusses European art from the American Revolution to the middle of the twentieth century.

*Les Modes Parisiennes.* Paris: 1843–1875. A useful source for fashion plates during the late Romantic period and the Second Empire.

NEWTON, ERIC. *The Romantic Rebellion.* New York: St. Martin's Press, 1966. A very popular and readable look at the cultural, social, and artistic rebellion that we now label Romanticism.

*Petit Courrier des Dames.* Paris: 1822–1865. A useful source for fashion plates during the Romantic period and the Second Empire.

## CHAPTER XX. VICTORIAN AND SECOND EMPIRE

BROOKE, IRIS. *English Costume of the Nineteenth Century.* London: A. & C. Black, 1929. A useful coverage of English costume of the nineteenth century with line drawings by the author. These must be used with caution in conjunction with original sources.

BURCHELL, S. C. *Age of Progress.* Great Ages of

Man Series. New York: Time-Life Books, 1966. A beautifully illustrated book, with extensive color photographs, that covers the major intellectual, artistic, and cultural developments in the late nineteenth century.

CANADAY, JOHN. *Mainstreams of Modern Art.* New York: Holt, Rinehart & Winston, 1959. Covering European and American art from the American Revolution to the middle of the twentieth century, this book gives much valuable information on culture, clothing, and artistic styles.

CRANKSHAW, EDWARD. *The Hapsburgs: Portrait of a Dynasty.* New York: Viking, 1971. A very useful picture of aristocratic life in Vienna and throughout the Empire, particularly from 1848 to 1914.

CUNNINGTON, C. WILLETT. *English Women's Clothing in the Nineteenth Century.* London: Faber, 1937. A standard work by one of England's foremost authorities on the history of dress.

GERNSHEIM, HELMET. *The History of Photography from the Earliest Use of the Camera Obscura in the Eleventh Century up to 1914.* London: Oxford University Press, 1969. Very useful as a source of costume information for the period from 1850 to World War I.

*Harper's Monthly Magazine* (1850–   ). New York. A very useful source for costume information during the late nineteenth century.

*Harper's Weekly* (1857–1916). New York. A useful source of information, particularly in the line drawings that filled each issue, on the styles, fashions, manners, and customs from before the Civil War to World War I.

HIBBERT, CHRISTOPHER. *Daily Life in Victorian England.* A Horizon Book. New York: American Heritage and McGraw-Hill, 1975. This beautifully illustrated book gives particularly interesting insights into Victorian life.

*Illustrated London News* (1842–   ). London. Very useful as a source of information on manners, fashions, customs, and styles during the later nineteenth century.

*L'Illustration* (1843–   ). Paris. A useful source of information on manners, fashions, customs, and styles during the late nineteenth and early twentieth centuries.

LARKIN, OLIVER. *Art and Life in America.* New York: Holt, Rinehart & Winston, 1949. A study of art in America in the late nineteenth century and its relation to culture.

LYNTON, NORBERT. *The Modern World.* Landmarks of the World's Art Series. New York: McGraw-Hill, 1965. Beautifully illustrated with many color plates, this book discusses European art from the American Revolution to the middle of the twentieth century.

*Les Modes Parisiennes.* Paris: 1843–1875. A useful source for fashion plates during the late Romantic period and the Second Empire.

*Peterson's Magazine* (1846–1898). Philadelphia. A useful source of fashion information and fashion plates for clothing style in the United States during the Victorian Age.

*Petit Courrier des Dames.* Paris: 1822–1865. A useful source for fashion plates during the Romantic period and the Second Empire.

REYNOLDS, GRAHAM. *Victorian Painting.* London: Studio Vista, 1966. A very useful look at the themes, subjects, and outlooks of the artists painting in and around London in the late nineteenth century. Some very good portraiture is included.

WORTH, J. P. *A Century of Fashion.* Boston: Little, Brown, 1928. An interesting book by the last member of the Worth family documenting the contribution of the House of Worth to the development of fashion from the period of the Second Empire until after World War I.

## CHAPTER XXI. LATER VICTORIAN: THE GILDED AGE

BROOKE, IRIS. *English Costume of the Nineteenth Century.* London: A. & C. Black, 1929. A useful coverage of English costume of the nineteenth century with line drawings by the author. These must be used with caution in conjunction with original sources.

BROWN, H. C. *New York in the Elegant Eighties.* New York: Valentine, 1927. A very useful volume, now difficult to find, on the social scene in New York in the last years of the bustle in a period known as the Gilded Age.

BURCHELL, S. C. *Age of Progress.* Great Ages of Man Series. New York: Time-Life Books, 1966. A beautifully illustrated book with extensive color photographs that cover the major intellectual, artistic, and cultural developments in the late nineteenth century.

CANADAY, JOHN. *Mainstreams of Modern Art.* New York: Holt, Rinehart & Winston, 1959. Covering European and American art from the American Revolution to the middle of the twentieth century, this book gives much valuable information on culture, clothing, and artistic styles.

CRANKSHAW, EDWARD. *The Hapsburgs: Portrait of a Dynasty.* New York: Viking, 1971. A very useful picture of aristocratic life in Vienna and throughout the Empire, particularly from 1848 to 1914.

CUNNINGTON, C. WILLETT. *English Women's Clothing in the Nineteenth Century.* London: Faber, 1937. A standard work by one of England's foremost authorities on the history of dress.

GERNSHEIM, HELMET. *The History of Photography from the Earliest Use of the Camera Obscura in the Eleventh Century up to 1914.* London: Oxford University Press, 1969. Very useful as a source of costume information for the period from 1850 to World War I.

*Harper's Weekly* (1857–1916). New York. A useful source of information, particularly in the line drawings that filled each issue, on the styles, fashions, manners, and customs from before the Civil War to World War I.

HIBBERT, CHRISTOPHER. *Daily Life in Victorian England.* A Horizon Book. New York: American Heritage and McGraw-Hill, 1975. This beautifully illustrated book gives particularly interesting insights into Victorian life.

*Illustrated London News* (1842–    ). London. Very useful as a source of information on manners, fashions, customs, and styles during the later nineteenth century.

*L'Illustration* (1843–    ). Paris. A useful source of information on manners, fashions, customs, and styles during the late nineteenth and early twentieth centuries.

LARKIN, OLIVER. *Art and Life in America.* New York: Holt, Rinehart & Winston, 1949. A study of art in America in the late nineteenth century and its relation to the culture.

LYNTON, NORBERT. *The Modern World.* Landmarks of the World's Art Series. New York: McGraw-Hill, 1965. Beautifully illustrated with many color plates, this book discusses European art from the American Revolution to the middle of the twentieth century.

*Peterson's Magazine* (1846–1898). Philadelphia. A useful source of fashion information and fashion plates for clothing style in the United States during the Victorian Age.

REYNOLDS, GRAHAM. *Victorian Painting.* London: Studio Vista, 1966. A very useful look at the themes, subjects, and outlooks of the artists painting in and around London in the late nineteenth century. Some very good portraiture is included.

*This Fabulous Century: Prelude 1870–1900.* New York: Time-Life Books, 1970. First volume in a wonderful series by the editors of Time-Life in which a bird's-eye view of the last century (1870–1970) is covered in photos and essays on such things as entertainment, education, occupations, sports, law, and fashion.

## CHAPTER XXII. LATE VICTORIAN AND EDWARDIAN: ART NOUVEAU

BROOKE, IRIS. *English Costume of the Nineteenth Century.* London: A. & C. Black, 1929. A useful coverage of English costume of the nineteenth century, with line drawings by the author. These must be used with caution in conjunction with original sources.

BROWN, H. C. *The Golden Nineties.* New York: Valentine, 1928. A very useful volume, now difficult to find, that gives a social picture of New York in the last decade of the nineteenth century. Good pictures.

BURCHELL, S. C. *Age of Progress.* Great Ages of Man Series. New York: Time-Life Books, 1966. A beautifully illustrated book, with extensive color photographs, that covers the major intellectual, artistic, and cultural developments in the late nineteenth century.

COLTON, JOEL. *Twentieth Century.* The Great Ages of Man Series. New York: Time-Life Books, 1968. Beautifully illustrated with extensive color, this concise and easy-to-read text covers the major artistic, cultural, and intellectual developments up to the early 1960s.

CRANKSHAW, EDWARD. *The Hapsburgs: Portrait of a Dynasty.* New York: Viking, 1971. A very useful picture of aristocratic life in Vienna and throughout the Empire, particularly from 1848 to 1914.

CUNNINGTON, C. WILLETT. *English Women's Clothing in the Nineteenth Century.* London: Faber, 1937. A standard work by one of England's foremost authorities on the history of dress.

GERNSHEIM, HELMET. *The History of Photography from the Earliest Use of the Camera Obscura in the Eleventh Century up to 1914.* London: Oxford University Press, 1969. Very useful as a source of costume information for the period from 1850 to World War I.

*Good Housekeeping* (1885–    ). New York. A useful source of information on styles, fashions, manners, and customs from the Gilded Age to the present.

GREENBERG, CLEMENT. *Art and Culture: Critical Essays.* Gloucester, Mass.: Peter Smith, n.d. An interesting collection of essays relating artistic and cultural developments in the early twentieth century.

HAMILTON, GEORGE HEARD. *Painting and Sculpture in Europe,* 1880–1940. The Pelican History of Art Series. Baltimore: Penguin Books, 1967. An excellent survey that documents the arrival of relativism in the arts, with some excellent portraiture.

*Harper's Bazaar* (1867–    ). New York. A useful source of information on styles, fashions, manners, and customs, particularly from the beginning of this century to the present.

*Harper's Monthly Magazine* (1850–    ). New York. A very useful source for costume information during the late nineteenth century.

*Harper's Weekly* (1857–1916). New York. A useful source of information, particularly in the line drawings that filled each issue, on the styles, fashions, manners, and customs from before the Civil War to World War I.

HIBBERT, CHRISTOPHER. *Daily Life in Victorian England.* A Horizon Book. New York: American Heritage and McGraw-Hill, 1975. This beautifully illustrated book gives particularly interesting insights into Victorian life.

*Illustrated London News* (1842–    ). London. Very useful as a source of information on manners, fashions, customs, and styles during the later nineteenth century.

*Ladies' Home Journal* (1883–    ). Philadelphia. A periodical that has many useful insights into fashions and manners since it began publishing in the late nineteenth century. It can be consulted both for visual and written information.

LARKIN, OLIVER. *Art and Life in America.* New York: Holt, Rinehart & Winston, 1949. A study of art in America in the late nineteenth century and its relation to the culture.

LYNTON, NORBERT. *The Modern World.* Landmarks of the World's Art Series. New York: McGraw-Hill, 1965. Beautifully illustrated with many color plates, this book discusses European art from the American Revolution to the middle of the twentieth century.

*Peterson's Magazine* (1846–1898). Philadelphia. A useful source of fashion information and fashion plates for clothing style in the United States during the Victorian Age.

REYNOLDS, GRAHAM. *Victorian Painting.* London: Studio Vista, 1966. A very useful look at the themes, subjects, and outlooks of the artists painting in and around London in the late nineteenth century. Some very good portraiture is included.

*Sears, Roebuck Catalog, The* (1894–    ). Chicago. These illustrated catalogs are an invaluable source of information about fashion for the twentieth century,

particularly details like blouses, ties, shoes, cuff links, collars, and purses.

SELZ, PETER, & CONSTANTINE, MILDRED, eds. *Art Nouveau: Art and Design at the Turn of the Century.* New York: Museum of Modern Art and Doubleday, 1960. An excellent pictorial survey of art nouveau design at the turn of the century with great application as to how it was used in dress.

*This Fabulous Century: 1900–1910.* New York: Time-Life Books, 1969. A volume in a series by the editors of Time-Life that gives an incisive bird's-eye view of the first decade of the twentieth century, with pictures and essays on women, sports, the rich, entertainment, immigrants, and so on.

*This Fabulous Century: Prelude 1870–1900.* New York: Time-Life Books, 1970. First volume in a wonderful series by the editors of Time-Life in which a bird's-eye view of the last century (1870–1970) is covered in photos and essays on such things as entertainment, education, occupations, sports, law, and fashion.

*Vogue Magazine* (1892–    ). New York. This periodical, devoted primarily to female fashion, is one of the best sources of clothing information since the close of the nineteenth century.

## CHAPTER XXIII. WORLD WAR I AND THE TWENTIES: EARLY ART DECO

BATTERSBY, MARTIN. *The Decorative Twenties.* New York: Walker & Co., 1971. A useful and well-illustrated book on the nature of the artistic and cultural outlook of the 1920s with a section on fashion.

CANADAY, JOHN. *Mainstreams of Modern Art.* New York: Holt, Rinehart & Winston, 1959. Covering European and American art from the American Revolution to the middle of the twentieth century, this book gives much valuable information on culture, clothing, and artistic styles.

COLTON, JOEL. *Twentieth Century.* The Great Ages of Man Series. New York: Time-Life Books, 1968. Beautifully illustrated with extensive color, this concise and easy-to-read text covers the major artistic, cultural, and intellectual developments up to the early 1960s.

*Good Housekeeping* (1885–    ). New York. A useful source of information on styles, fashions, manners, and customs from the Gilded Age to the present.

GREENBERG, CLEMENT. *Art and Culture: Critical Essays.* Gloucester, Mass.: Peter Smith, n.d. An interesting collection of essays relating artistic and cultural developments in the early twentieth century.

HAMILTON, GEORGE HEARD. *Painting and Sculpture in Europe, 1880–1940*. The Pelican History of Art Series. Baltimore: Penguin Books, 1967. An excellent survey that documents the arrival of relativism in the arts, with some excellent portraiture.

*Harper's Bazaar* (1867–      ). New York. A useful source of information on styles, fashions, manners, and customs, particularly from the beginning of this century to the present.

*L'Illustration* (1843–      ). Paris. A useful source of information on manners, fashions, customs, and styles during the late nineteenth and early twentieth centuries.

*Ladies' Home Journal* (1883–      ). Philadelphia. A periodical that has many useful insights into fashions and manners since it began publishing in the late nineteenth century. It can be consulted both for visual and written information.

LYNTON, NORBERT. *The Modern World*. Landmarks of the World's Art Series. New York: McGraw-Hill, 1965. Beautifully illustrated with many color plates, this book discusses European art from the American Revolution to the middle of the twentieth century.

*Sears, Roebuck Catalog, The* (1894–      ). Chicago. These illustrated catalogs are an invaluable source of information about fashion for the twentieth century, particularly details like blouses, ties, shoes, cuff links, collars, and purses.

*This Fabulous Century: 1910–1920*. New York: Time-Life Books, 1969. One volume in a series covering the hundred years from 1870–1970, published by the editors of Time-Life. It gives a wonderful bird's-eye view of the United States before, during, and after World War I, with pictures and essays on such things as movies, the new woman, the automobile, culture, games, Broadway, and the war.

*This Fabulous Century: 1920–1930*. New York: Time-Life Books, 1969. One volume in a series covering the United States in the hundred years from 1870 to 1970, published by the editors of Time-Life. Gives an excellent picture of life in the United States in the twenties through photographs and essays on such topics as aviation, jazz, sports stars, the press, prohibition, notables, fads, travel, and flaming youth.

*Vogue Magazine* (1892–      ). New York. This periodical, devoted primarily to female fashion, is one of the best sources of clothing information since the close of the nineteenth century.

## CHAPTER XXIV. THE THIRTIES AND WORLD WAR II: LATE ART DECO

BATTERSBY, MARTIN. *The Decorative Thirties*. New York: Walker & Co., 1971. A very useful and well-illustrated book on the nature of the artistic and cultural outlook of the 1930s with a section on fashion.

CANADAY, JOHN. *Mainstreams of Modern Art*. New York: Holt, Rinehart & Winston, 1959. Covering European and American art from the American Revolution to the middle of the twentieth century, this book gives much valuable information on culture, clothing, and artistic styles.

COLTON, JOEL. *Twentieth Century*. The Great Ages of Man Series. New York: Time-Life Books, 1968. Beautifully illustrated with extensive color, this concise and easy-to-read text covers the major artistic, cultural, and intellectual developments up to the early 1960s.

*Esquire Magazine* (1937–      ). New York. A useful source of information on style, manners, and cultural outlook during the past half century.

*Good Housekeeping* (1885–      ). New York. A useful source of information on styles, fashions, manners, and customs from the Gilded Age to the present.

GREENBERG, CLEMENT. *Art and Culture: Critical Essays*. Gloucester, Mass.: Peter Smith, n.d. An interesting collection of essays relating artistic and cultural developments in the early twentieth century.

HAMILTON, GEORGE HEARD. *Painting and Sculpture in Europe, 1880–1940*. The Pelican History of Art Series. Baltimore: Penguin Books, 1967. An excellent survey that documents the arrival of relativism in the arts, with some excellent portraiture.

*Harper's Bazaar* (1867–      ). New York. A useful source of information on styles, fashions, manners, and customs, particularly from the beginning of this century to the present.

*Ladies' Home Journal* (1883–      ). Philadelphia. A periodical that has many useful insights into fashions and manners since it began publishing in the late nineteenth century. It can be consulted both for visual and written information.

*Sears, Roebuck Catalog, The* (1894–      ). Chicago.

These illustrated catalogs are an invaluable source of information about fashion for the twentieth century, particularly details like blouses, ties, shoes, cuff links, collars, and purses.

*This Fabulous Century: 1930–1940.* New York: Time-Life Books, 1969. A volume in a series covering life in the United States from 1870 to 1970, published by the editors of Time-Life. Gives an excellent picture of the thirties through photographs and essays on such topics as radio, the Great Depression, gangsters, F.D.R., cafe society, movies, politics, and swing.

*This Fabulous Century: 1940–1950.* New York: Time-Life Books, 1969. A volume in a series covering life in the United States during and after World War II, published by the editors of Time-Life. Gives an excellent picture of the times through photographs and essays on teenagers, the war, the home front, fashion, theater, and sports.

*Vogue Magazine* (1892–    ). New York. This periodical devoted primarily to female fashion is one of the best sources of clothing information since the close of the nineteenth century.

## CHAPTER XXV. THE COLD WAR

CANADAY, JOHN. *Mainstreams of Modern Art.* New York: Holt, Rinehart & Winston, 1959. Covering European and American art from the American Revolution to the middle of the twentieth century, this book gives much valuable information on culture, clothing, and artistic styles.

COLTON, JOEL. *Twentieth Century.* The Great Ages of Man Series. New York: Time-Life Books, 1968. Beautifully illustrated with extensive color, this concise and easy-to-read text covers the major artistic, cultural, and intellectual developments up to the early 1960s.

*Esquire Magazine* (1937–    ). New York. A useful source of information on style, manners, and cultural outlook during the past half century.

*Good Housekeeping* (1885–    ). New York. A useful source of information on styles, fashions, manners, and customs from the Gilded Age to the present.

GREENBERG, CLEMENT. *Art and Culture: Critical Essays.* Gloucester, Mass.: Peter Smith, n.d. An interesting collection of essays relating artistic and cultural developments in the early twentieth century.

*Harper's Bazaar* (1867–    ). New York. A useful source of information on styles, fashions, manners,

and customs, particularly from the beginning of this century to the present.

*Harper's Monthly Magazine* (1850–    ). New York. A very useful source for costume information during the late nineteenth century.

*In Vogue: Sixty years of celebrities and fashion from British Vogue.* London: Penguin Books, 1978. An excellent source for pictures and year-by-year fashion details from 1916 to 1975.

*Ladies' Home Journal* (1883–    ). Philadelphia. A periodical that has many useful insights into fashions and manners since it began publishing in the late nineteenth century. It can be consulted both for visual and written information.

LYNTON, ROBERT. *The Modern World.* Landmarks of the World's Art Series. New York: McGraw-Hill, 1965. Beautifully illustrated with many color plates, this book discusses European art from the American Revolution to the middle of the twentieth century.

*Sears, Roebuck Catalog, The* (1894–    ). Chicago. These illustrated catalogs are an invaluable source of information about fashion for the twentieth century, particularly details like blouses, ties, shoes, cuff links, collars, and purses.

*This Fabulous Century: 1940–1950.* New York: Time-Life Books, 1969. A volume in a series covering life in the United States during and after World War II, published by the editors of Time-Life. Gives an excellent picture of the times through photographs and essays on teenagers, the war, the home front, fashion, theater, and sports.

*This Fabulous Century: 1950–1960.* New York: Time-Life Books, 1969. A volume in a series covering life in the United States from 1870 to 1970, published by the editors of Time-Life. Gives an excellent picture of the times through photographs and essays on fads, personalities, beatniks, politics, music, suburbia, culture, rebels, and television.

*Vingt Ans* (1947–    ). Paris. A useful periodical that illustrates youthful female fashions since the end of World War II and the rise of the New Look.

*Vogue Magazine* (1892–    ). New York. This periodical, devoted primarily to female fashion, is one of the best sources of clothing information since the close of the nineteenth century.

## CHAPTER XXVI. CONTEMPORARY

COLTON, JOEL. *Twentieth Century.* The Great Ages of Man Series. New York: Time-Life Books, 1968. Beautifully illustrated with extensive color, this concise and easy-to-read text covers the major artistic, cultural, and intellectual developments up to the early 1960s.

*Esquire Magazine* (1937–    ). New York. A useful source of information on styles, manners, and cultural outlook during the past half century.

*Good Housekeeping* (1885–    ). New York. A useful source of information on styles, fashions, manners, and customs from the Gilded Age to the present.

*Harper's Bazaar* (1867–    ). New York. A useful source of information on styles, fashions, manners, and customs, particularly from the beginning of this century to the present.

*In Vogue: Sixty years of celebrities and fashion from British Vogue.* London: Penguin Books, 1978. An excellent source for pictures and year-by-year fashion details from 1916 to 1975.

*Ladies' Home Journal* (1883–    ). Philadelphia. A periodical that has many useful insights into fashions and manners since it began publishing in the late nineteenth century. It can be consulted both for visual and written information.

*Sears, Roebuck Catalog, The* (1894–    ). Chicago. These illustrated catalogs are an invaluable source of information about fashion for the twentieth century, particularly details like blouses, ties, shoes, cuff links, collars, and purses.

*This Fabulous Century: 1960–1970.* New York: Time-Life Books, 1970. A volume in a series covering life in the United States from 1870 to 1970, published by the editors of Time-Life. Gives an excellent picture of the times through photographs and essays on "Camelot," youth trips, fashions, the media, black culture, science, singles, and the Vietnam War.

*Vingt Ans* (1947–    ). Paris. A useful periodical that illustrates youthful female fashions since the end of World War II and the rise of the New Look.

*Vogue Magazine* (1892–    ). New York. This periodical, devoted primarily to female fashion, is one of the best sources of clothing information since the close of the nineteenth century.

# Index

536

542